Study Guide Plus

for

Henslin
Sociology
A Down-to-Earth Approach

Fifth Edition

Prepared by

Gwendolyn E. Nyden
Oakton Community College

Allyn and Bacon
Boston London Toronto Sydney Tokyo Singapore

TABLE OF CONTENTS

SUCCESSFUL STUDY STRATEGIES

Welcome to Sociology! You are about to embark on a fascinating journey in which you will discover all sorts of new and interesting information about yourself and the world around you. This study guide has been prepared to accompany the textbook *Sociology: A Down-to-Earth Approach* by James M. Henslin. This introductory chapter presents you with some strategies for developing good study habits and maximizing your learning in order to achieve academic success. You will learn about some preliminary steps to take, strategies for success, and hints for taking different kinds of tests.

☞BECOMING A BETTER STUDENT

Whether you are a seasoned college student or just starting out, there are some preliminary steps you can take that will make you a better student.

Becoming Familiar with Campus Resources

One key to student success is becoming more familiar with resources available on your college campus and using those resources to your advantage. Here are just a few that may be open to you:

- **Student services:** Many colleges have student services centers; here you are likely to find counselors who provide academic, personal and career counseling, seminars and workshops on topics such as health and wellness or learning how to achieve a balanced lifestyle, and information on wide range of issues of special concern to you.
- **Services for special populations:** If you are a student who is returning to college after many years, a student with physical or learning disabilities, a minority student, or a student from another country, there may be a center to assist you in meeting your specific academic goals.
- **Instructional support services:** You may also discover that your college offers instructional support services, sometimes through a learning lab or a tutoring center. These are set up to assist you in developing study, reading, and writing skills which are all essential if you want to succeed not only in this sociology course but in every course you take over your college career.

Working Out Your Own Strengths and Weaknesses

You will also want to think about your strengths and weaknesses as a student. Begin by assessing what kind of learner you are. Do you remember material best when you've heard it or when you've read it for yourself? Do you learn best when you cover all the material in one large unit or when you break the material up into smaller units? A counselor in a student services office or an on-campus learning center may be able to help you determine your personal learning style.

Besides understanding how you learn, you should also evaluate your current study habits. Do you study better when you're alone or in a group? Do you study best when your study periods have a definite beginning and ending time and tasks are clearly outlined? Do other commitments -- work, family, or friends -- interfere with your study time? Do you find it hard to identify which information in the course is important? Do you get anxious when it comes to taking tests? Do essay tests intimidate you?

Managing Your Time Efficiently

Another important step towards college success is learning to manage your time better. Beyond the time spent sleeping and eating, you have some flexibility in allocating the remaining hours. Take a few minutes and jot down what a "typical" day looks like--noting tasks that must be accomplished and the time each involves.

WEEKLY SCHEDULE FOR FALL SEMESTER							
	Sunday	Monday	Tuesday	Wednesday	Thursday	Friday	Saturday
7:00 am		wake up	wake up	wake up	wake up	wake up	
8:00		breakfast/ school	breakfast/ school	breakfast/ school	breakfast/ school	breakfast/ school	
9:00		class--SOC	class--BIO	class--SOC	class--BIO	class--SOC	wake up
10:00	wake up	class--ART	class--LIT	class--ART	BIO lab	class--ART	
11:00							
12:00 pm		lunch		lunch		lunch	work
1:00	volunteer-- ecology ctr.	class--HIS	lunch	class--HIS	lunch--HIS	class	
2:00		work	work	work	work	work	
3:00							
4:00							
5:00	work-out	work-out	work-out	work-out	work-out	work-out	work-out
6:00	dinner	dinner	dinner	dinner	dinner	dinner	dinner
7:00	study	study	study	study	study	party with friends	party with friends
8:00							
9:00	study break	study break	study break	study break	study break		
10:00	study	study	study	study	study		
11:00	bed	bed	bed	bed	bed		
12:00 am						bed	bed

Figure 1: AN EXAMPLE OF A TYPICAL SEMESTER SCHEDULE

From this you can develop a schedule for the entire semester. Figure 1 provides an example of a weekly schedule. The days of the week are listed across the top and the hours in the day run down the side. Activities that are done regularly--sleep, meals, job, classes, exercise, and volunteer commitments--are noted within the appropriate boxes. The blank boxes represent "free time." What happens during these times changes from week to week, depending upon what comes up. By mapping fixed commitments out at the beginning of the semester, you will be able to maximize your use of the resulting discretionary time.

It would also be helpful for you to have a schedule of all of your assignments for the entire semester. Figure 2 illustrates this schedule; to make one of your own, you will want to list the courses

ASSIGNMENT SCHEDULE--FALL SEMESTER					
	Sociology	Art	History	Biology	Literature
WK 1					
WK 2	essay on culture	charcoal project due	proposal on research topic	quiz--Ch 1-2 lab assign. 1	
WK 3				quiz--Ch 3-4	review Pride & Prejudice
WK 4	observation at day care ctr.			quiz--Ch 5-6 lab assign. 2	
WK 5		watercolor project due	preliminary bibliography	quiz--Ch 7-8	
WK 6	evaluation of trip to county jail			quiz--Ch 9-11 lab assign. 3	review Emma
WK 7	MID TERM				
	tst--Ch 1-8	NO MID-TERM	tst--Ch 1-10	tst--Ch 1-11	
WK 8	review of major sociology bk		Outline of research paper	quiz--Ch 12 lab assign. 4	
WK 9		pastels project due		quiz--Ch 13-14	
WK 10	family history due			quiz--Ch 15-16; lab assign. 5	review Sense & Sensibility
WK 11		acrylic project due	annotated bibliography due	quiz--Ch 17-18	
WK 12	observation of political rally			quiz--Ch 19; lab assign. 6	
WK 13		oil painting due		quiz--Ch 20	review Persuasion
WK 14			research paper due	quiz--Ch 21; lab assign. 7	Final paper on Austen
FINALS WK	tst--Ch 9-15	Final project due	tst--Ch 11-18	tst-Ch 12-21	NO FINAL

Figure 2: AN EXAMPLE OF A TYPICAL ASSIGNMENT SCHEDULE

across the top and the weeks of the semester down the side. Within the boxes list tasks that must be completed for each class in a specific week. You can note tests, paper assignments, as well as other course work that has a deadline. This will help you in planning how you will divide your time among each of your courses over the semester.

In addition to these semester-based schedules, that can be posted in a highly visible location like a bulletin board above your desk or inside your assignment book, get into the habit of using a daily schedule. This is a list of the day's tasks and the time frame in which you plan to accomplish each. A good time to make up this daily schedule is the evening before; spend a few minutes thinking about and then writing down all the things that you need to do the next day. Not only will this free your mind of thinking about what lies ahead so that you will sleep more easily, but when you get up in the morning you will be prepared to begin the day and not have to waste time organizing at the last minute. Although this daily schedule reflects all the tasks that need to be done during the course of the day, some things are more important than others; get into the habit of prioritizing your list so that the most important are at the top and are guaranteed to get done first.

While making and using schedules is important to your success in college, so is learning to take advantage of spare moments in the day that are otherwise wasted; once you become aware of them you can begin to use them for impromptu study periods. Here are some ideas to consider:

- Most of us spend some time each day just waiting -- for a bus or train, for an appointment with a doctor or professor, or for service in a bank or store. Bring something along to occupy yourself while you wait. It could be a book or article you've been assigned to read, a notebook with notes, or flash cards with formulas or vocabulary on them.
- While you're driving in the car, exercising, or cleaning house, listen to recorded tapes of important vocabulary, passages from text, or series of questions and answers on course material.
- Use the time immediately before class begins to recall main points from the previous class lecture, think about questions you have on the material that was covered in the last class or that will be covered in this class, or glance through notes.
- Keep a small notebook of ideas, questions, or thoughts you have about course material; whenever one of these comes into your mind you can write it down and think about the answers later.

Finally, don't forget to devote some time each day to study breaks; these are rewards for hard work. Schedule them into your day and then stick to them. They are not only something to look forward to as you are studying hard, but they actually enhance your overall learning. After taking a jog or walk, having coffee with friends, watching a TV show, or reading the newspaper you will return to the task of studying with a mind that is once again ready to tackle important course material.

Developing better concentration

Concentration is a skill that you need to develop if you are going to get the most out of your study periods. When you concentrate you are focusing all of your attention on the task in front of you. If you are able to eliminate distractions you will find this easier to do. But how do you go about doing this? Begin by finding a space that is suitable for studying, one that you associate first and foremost with that activity and not some other. For instance, trying to study on your bed or in the snack bar of the student union is not a good idea, because those areas are not associated primarily with studying.

Many students choose to study in their college library. There are a number of advantages to using the library: it is unlikely that you could find any quieter space in which to concentrate on your school work, the lighting in the library is designed for study, and you can usually claim adequate space in which to spread out your materials. It is also easier at the library to eliminate visual and auditory distractions, as well as telephone and social interruptions. Finally, many libraries have lounges for students to use for periodic breaks. Remember, while we can never completely eliminate all distractions in our world, finding a quiet place away from the hustle and bustle of our everyday lives will help enormously when it comes to studying.

Because concentration is enhanced when we are able to eliminate distractions, here are some additional measures you can take to achieve better concentration:

Use lists. One list is a reminder of what you have to do during the study period; as you accomplish a task, check it off and move on to the next. A second list is for things you have to do later. Many times you find yourself preoccupied with some problem in your life and your mind continues to return to this problem time and time again. While you are trying to study, your concentration is broken by these other thoughts that pop randomly into your mind; if you keep a second list, you can write these interruptions down on it, promising yourself that you will return to the list after you finish studying.

Take regular breaks. Use a timer to keep track of your study time; when the alarm goes off, get up and take a break. This way, you will not be tempted to look at your watch every fifteen minutes, wondering how long you've studied and when your next break time is due.

Set a goal for each study session -- so many pages read or vocabulary words mastered, etc. When you've reached the session goal, close your books and notes until the next time.

DEVELOPING SUCCESSFUL LEARNING STRATEGIES

Using campus resources, assessing your strengths and weaknesses, managing your time, and learning to concentrate better are the first steps to college success. In addition, there are some strategies for acquiring course-specific skills and knowledge. Begin by figuring out what's important and what's not and learning how to make the most of the course materials, and then work on achieving mastery over the course contents.

Figuring out what's important in the course

The first place to look for information about what's important in any course is the course syllabus that the professor hands out on the first day, or first few days, of class. This document should provide you with an outline of the topics that will be covered over the semester and information on the course work expected of you as a student: how many tests and quizzes there are, the nature of these tests and quizzes and when they are scheduled throughout the semester, as well as deadlines and due dates for written assignments and other class projects. You can use this information when organizing your different time schedules. The syllabus should also include information on how the professor calculates your final grade; you should be able to determine which course work he or she places the most emphasis on by looking at how much each component in the course counts towards that final grade.

Making the most of course materials

You will be expected to purchase the required text or texts for the course; often the professor also includes some recommended reading--it's up to you whether or not you read these additional texts. Increasingly in courses such as the one you're taking in sociology there are study guides like this one that accompany the text. This particular study guide includes the following:

- a **Chapter Summary** that summarizes the main ideas found in the chapter.
- a set of **Learning Objectives** that provides statements concerning the main ideas of the chapter. If you want to check your responses, refer back to the page numbers listed with each question.
- a **Glossary of Difficult-to-Understand Words** that includes some of the words that may be unfamiliar, along with their meanings. It is designed to be a resource for you to use as you read the textbook. If there are words that you don't know that are not included in this glossary, be sure to look them up in a dictionary.
- a listing of **Key Terms** that contains the concepts that are introduced within the chapter.
- a listing of **Key People** that includes some of the major sociologists whose work is discussed within the chapter. In some cases, these are early sociologists who contributed theoretical understanding and research insights to the discipline; in other cases, they are contemporary sociologists who are doing research and developing theory on the subject.
- a **Self-Test** that provides you with an opportunity to see how much of the information you have retained. Each self-test includes multiple choice, true-false, fill-in, matching and essay questions.
- a section entitled **Down-to-Earth Sociology** that asks questions about the material you have read so that you can relate it to your own life and the world with which you are familiar. Remember there is not necessarily a right and wrong answer for these; rather, they are designed to get your opinion, based on your understanding of the facts you have read.
- an **Answer Key** that provides answers for all of the questions in the Self-Test. Check your answers against this; if you got the question wrong, refer to the pages in the textbook and read those again.

The study guide is intended to be used together with the text to maximize your mastery of the material. Here are some suggestions for making the best use of the resources in the text and study guide:

- Before reading each chapter, **refer to the Chapter Summary and Learning Objectives** that are found in the Study Guide. The Summary will provide you with a capsule statement of what the chapter is about, and the Learning Objectives will tell you how you should be focusing your attention. Then read the textbook.
- Rather than plunging headlong into the chapter, **take a few minutes and orient yourself**. Start with the chapter title. This tells you what broad area of sociology will be discussed. Keep the title in mind as you read through the chapter and try to create a mental picture of how the various parts of the chapter fit together within this broad area.
- **Approach each chapter one section at time.** Use the section headings to pose questions that you can ask yourself when you finish reading the section. As you finish a section, go back to the Learning Objectives in the Study Guide and try to answer the statement(s) that apply. If you can provide an answer, then proceed to the next section; if you can't, go back to the textbook and review the section you've just read.
- **Remember to read the boxed text**; these pertain to the material in the body of the textbook and are included to give you insights into U.S. society as well as societies around the world. They are designed to bring sociology alive for you.

Achieving mastery over the material

In general, mastery is facilitated by good organization. Students who succeed are generally those who are able to stay on top of the course because they have developed a system for keeping track of all the materials. One suggestion is to purchase a loose-leaf notebook for each course, with the syllabus, handouts, assignments, and notes from your readings and lectures in separate tabbed sections.

Students often think sociology will not require much new learning; after all, they are part of society and thus intimately familiar with it. This is their first mistake; sociology, like every other discipline, has its own vocabulary that students must learn in order to be successful. Here are some ideas to help you :

- **Identify the concepts.** As you are reading the text pay attention to the concepts that are in bold-face type. The definition is provided for you; refer back to that definition as you read.
- **Think of examples.** Try to think of some examples of your own; if you can relate the material to the world with which you are most familiar, you are more likely to remember it.
- **Make up flash cards.** Many times it helps to make up flash cards, with the word on one side and the definition and an example on the other side. Keep these with you and review them while you're waiting in line or stopped at a red light.

All of these strategies will guarantee that you will incorporate new and unfamiliar concepts into your framework and will remember them when the time comes for a test.

Achieving mastery over the material requires more than just learning key concepts. As a general rule, it is best to read the assigned material <u>prior</u> to class. As you read, get into the habit of taking notes. These should include summaries of the main points of the section you've read, connections between what you're reading now and what you read earlier in the semester, and examples to illustrate these ideas, as well as any questions that were raised in your mind in connection with the reading.

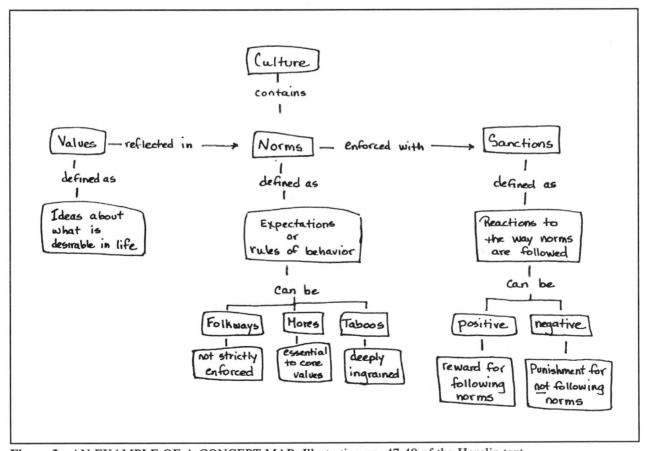

Figure 3: AN EXAMPLE OF A CONCEPT MAP, Illustrating pp. 47-49 of the Henslin text

Sometimes students find it easier to master new and unfamiliar material by drawing a concept map, which presents relationships between ideas and concepts in a visual format. Figure 3 provides an illustration of such a concept map. Concept maps can be drawn for separate sections or topics found within a chapter and then combined into a map for each chapter. The key to mapping successfully is to be able to identify the key concepts that relate to the section or topic and then linking other concepts or ideas to each of these key concepts. Concept maps are helpful because they create a "picture" of the material that summarizes what must be mastered, showing the links between ideas.

If you have taken the time to read the material in advance, when you go to class you should be prepared for what the professor is going to cover. If you have questions from the reading, now is the time to raise them. Before class begins, divide the pages of your notebook vertically into two columns-- a narrower one to the left, representing about one-third the width of the page, and a wider one on the right representing the remaining two-thirds of the page. As you take notes, use the wider column to record what the professor says. Later, as you review what you've written down, use the narrower column in the same way that you would use the margins of your text--for making connections, writing down main ideas, and noting any questions you might have. You can also use this space to make reference to textbook pages that correspond to what the professor has said; this will come in handy when you are studying for exams.

Remember, if you miss a class for any reason, it is still your responsibility to find out what was covered. If you know in advance that you will be absent, make arrangements with another student to pick up any handouts that are distributed; you should also make sure that you can get the class notes from the student. It is also a good idea to talk with the professor about making up any class assignments. If the absence is unexpected, you should make a point of getting the notes from another student and talk with the professor about any missed work; don't wait until the end of the semester to do this, do it as soon as you return to school.

Once you feel you have achieved some familiarity with the material, go back to the study guide and follow these steps:

Check the list of Key Terms. Review the definition for each word and think of an example. If you need help thinking of an example, refer back to the textbook chapter.
Check the list of Key People. See how many you know and whether or not you can identify their contribution to sociology. If you can't, go back to the textbook and locate them within the chapter. (A quick way to do this is to refer to the Index at the back of the textbook, and then go directly to the page listed.)
Take the Self-Test. Mark those questions that you got wrong, and go back to the text to find the correct answer. Then a few days later try them again to see if you've now mastered the material. Use the Self-Test to review the material just before a test.

All of these aid in your review of the information You might also want to once again review the chapter outline. This provides you with a broad understanding of the ideas that were covered in the chapter. If there is information in the outline that is still unfamiliar to you, go back to the textbook and reread that section. The outline and the self-test can also be used when you are reviewing the material just before a test.

SCORING HIGH MARKS ON TESTS

If you have made good use of the suggestions and strategies in the preceding pages, you should be well prepared when it comes time to take tests. Some students also find it helpful to organize study groups prior to major tests. Whether or not this is a help or a hindrance depends on your own personal study style, as well as the character of the group; you will need to assess both before making a decision about getting involved with such an activity. Whatever your decision, keeping up with the reading assignments, learning how to organize your time and your notes, having a place to study that is quiet and free of distractions are all important for mastering the material and demonstrating to the professor that you have learned your lessons by doing well on the test. In addition, there are some specific ideas for approaching tests, including understanding the different types of tests and developing strategies for taking different types of tests.

Strategies for taking objective tests

Most of you reading this guide are quite familiar with objective tests--multiple choice, true/false, matching, and fill-in-the blank questions. In fact, the self-tests contained in the chapters that follow include questions of this nature. These types of questions focus on more detailed information and on your ability to recognize the correct answer. In general, when studying for objective tests you will want to focus on details--definitions of key concepts, accomplishments of key figures, specific facts, etc. Here are some strategies that will help you do well on tests of this nature:

Read instructions carefully. Many students, anxious to begin the test, do not take enough time to read the instructions carefully. Consequently, they often end up making mistakes when it comes to selecting and recording the correct answers.

Take time to read each question. Likewise, students read questions and answers too quickly, often missing important clues that would help them to select the correct answer.

Pace yourself. Perhaps students rush because they are afraid they will not have enough time to complete the exam. If you want to avoid this problem and improve your chances of getting high marks, start by finding out in advance how many questions will be on the test and use this information to calculate about how much time per item you will have. Then, during the test you can pace yourself so that you don't run out of time and rush at the end.

Learn to recognize qualifiers. In writing the questions, the professor will use qualifying words to change the meaning of seemingly straightforward statements; *all, always, only,* most, usually, some, sometimes, *none,* and *never* are frequently used in this way. You will notice that these range along a continuum from positive to negative--those italicized words on each end set up a qualification that applies 100 percent of the time, while the ones in the middle mean that sometimes the condition exists and sometimes it doesn't. If you see an absolute qualifier and you know that condition occurs only sometimes, then you can eliminate that choice; likewise, you can rule out statements that contain variable qualifiers if you are certain that the condition occurs all of the time.

For instance, the following multiple choice question makes use of qualifiers:

- Sanctions:
  - a.   are *always* material.
  - b.   can be positive or negative.
  - c.   have *very little* impact on *most* people today.
  - d.   All of the above.

In approaching the question, you would begin by asking yourself whether or not there are sanctions that are non-material. Since there are non-material sanctions--a smile, a frown, a compliment or a reprimand--then "a" is incorrect. Likewise, since sanctions do have an impact on most people, then "c" is incorrect. The correct answer is "b."

- **Watch for negatives.** In addition to qualifiers, you must learn to notice negatives. Obvious negatives are words like *not, no*, and *never*; negatives can also be created by adding prefixes like "un-" to words like "important." When students read a question too quickly they may overlook these negatives and end up answering incorrectly.

Another common use of the negative is to ask students to identify which of the following is not, as is illustrated by the following question:

- All of the following are ways of neutralizing deviance, except:
  - a.   appeal to higher loyalties.
  - b.   denial of responsibility.
  - c.   denial of deviant labels.
  - d.   denial of injury and of a victim.

In answering this question, you need to identify which *are* ways of neutralizing deviance; three of the four are. The correct answer would be "c;" "denial of deviant labels" is not one of the ways in which people neutralize deviance.

Besides these general guidelines, here are some hints about each type of question that is likely to be found on the typical objective test:

- **Multiple Choice questions:** Begin by reading all the answer choices and ruling out those options that you know are incorrect. You may discover that only one option is left. If more than one option remains, and you have been instructed to choose only one, then you need to give some further thought to the answers. Are there any qualifiers that you need to consider? Are there grammatical clues--subject/verb agreement issues, correct fit between the stem and the answer, etc? Is there an option "all of the above" or "A and C;" it may very well be that there is more than one correct answer, but unless you have been given such an option, you need to rule out all but one choice.
- **True/False questions:** Remember you have a 50-50 chance of being correct regardless of what you choose on this type of question. It is easier to write a true statement than a false one, and most professors want to make sure that students leave the course remembering what is true rather than being confused about what is false. Therefore, you are very likely to find more true statements than false ones. For this reason, when you really don't know the answer, it is better to choose "true" than "false." Again, pay attention to the use of qualifying words and negatives.

- **Matching questions:** One of the biggest problems with matching questions, especially if there is a long list to match, is becoming confused about which options you've already chosen and which you haven't. If you're recording your answers on a separate answer sheet, ask the professor if it is okay to mark on the test; if the answer is affirmative, get into the habit of marking which ones you've chosen as you go along. Match those that are most familiar first; by the process of elimination you will end up only with those you don't know and you can then make the best possible guess among what is left.

- **Fill-in-the-Blank questions:** Perhaps these are the most difficult--and dreaded--questions on objective tests because the answers are usually not provided. Sometimes the question is worded in such a way that it is unclear to you what type of answer is being sought; if you run across such questions, ask the professor for some clarification. Sometimes a sentence will contain one blank, other times more than one blank; don't automatically assume that a single blank means the professor is looking for a single word, because he or she may use a single blank but want you to supply a string of words or a complete name. If you see only one blank, but suspect the answer may encompass more than one word, as the professor for clarification.

Here are two examples that illustrate the preceding discussion:

- *One blank--only one word expected:*
  A _____ system is a form of social stratification in which individual status is determined by birth and is lifelong. [The correct term to use here is *caste*.]

- *One blank-two (or more) words expected:*
  _____ is a particular form of violence directed exclusively against women. [The sentence is making reference to *female circumcision*.]

Sometimes you may find more than one blank in a statement, indicating that the professor wants you to provide more than one response. If this is the case, think about concepts or ideas that are linked together in some way and see if they'll fit.

Here are two examples of multiple blanks:

- *More than one blank in a sequence:*
  According to Max Weber, the three dimensions of social class are: (1)_____; (2)_____; and (3)_____. [To complete this sentence, you need to think of three concepts that are linked together in Weber's work; the correct answers are: *wealth, power,* and *prestige*.]

- *More than one blank separated in the sentence:*
  A _____ allows its owners to purchase goods but to be billed later while a _____ allows its owner to charge purchases against his or her bank account. [The first statement is referring to a *credit card*, while the second is talking about a *debit card*.]

Strategies for taking essay tests

While the previous tips may help you get through the objective test, they are not suited to essay tests, which are written to maximize your recall of the material and your ability to synthesize and summarize what you have learned. When studying for essay tests you will want to review more global information--trends, theories, and perspectives.

Just as there are strategies for managing the objective test, so too there are ways of managing an essay test in order to maximize your results.

- Once again **read the directions carefully.** Ascertain how many essay questions you are expected to answer and whether they are to be drawn from separate parts of the test--for instance, the professor may want you to answer two from section A and one from section B or one each from sections A, B, and C.
- Once you have gone over the directions, **plan how you will divide the allotted time** among the questions; you want to be able to have enough time to answer all the questions fully. Ask the professor if it makes any difference what order you answer the questions. If it doesn't matter, then decide for yourself the sequence in which to answer them; many students find that getting the easiest question(s) out of the way first allows them to spend more time on those that are more difficult.
- Make sure you **understand what the question is asking** you to do. Essay questions may ask you to compare (show similarities); contrast, differentiate, or distinguish (discuss differences); discuss, evaluate, or criticize (present strengths and weaknesses); demonstrate, justify, prove, show, or support (give evidence that supports an idea or statement); list, identify, enumerate, or state (list with or without a brief discussion or example). As you can see, each is asking you to do something different and you need to understand exactly what the professor wants you to do before you begin.
- In answering an essay question **start with a rough outline**, jotting down ideas that you want to cover. Include both the main ideas and the supporting evidence in your quick outline. By taking a few minutes in the beginning to do this you are assured that your information will be organized carefully and completely.
- In your response **get right to the point**; your introduction should contain a statement of what position you will be taking in trying to answer the question. The paragraphs that follow should provide supporting statements linked to theories, research and key concepts that you have learned in the course of the semester.
- **Avoid using personal opinions in your essays,** unless otherwise asked to. Remember even when asked to take a position, you should be prepared to support your position with facts, not personal opinions. Your concluding paragraph should summarize what you have stated, perhaps connecting your argument with some body of knowledge within the particular discipline.
- In general, **stay focused on the subject** and avoid bringing in irrelevant facts simply to pad your essay. Likewise, don't try to stretch a short essay by restating the same thesis several times. A professor will conclude that you really don't have anything to say and will give you the same grade he or she would have if you had written the thesis only once in a briefer essay.
- You should also take care to **write neatly** so the professor can read what you've written. By the time you get to college you are well aware of whether or not your handwriting is legible. If it is not, try printing your response. An essay that is illegible, regardless of how good the ideas and organization are, will most likely not be read or graded by the professor.

Overcoming test anxiety

For many students, taking a test is guaranteed to generate a high level of anxiety. No matter how much preparation you do, when the time for the test rolls around, you are consumed with anxiety. If you're one of those students, check out student services or the learning lab to see if your school offers workshops on overcoming such fears. At the same time, here are a few things you can try for yourself to see if any help to reduce these feelings:

- **Learn to relax.** When you're relaxed you can think more clearly about the task ahead. One way to relax is to learn to do slow, deep breathing--inhaling through your nose and drawing the air up into your lungs and then exhaling through your mouth; yoga is sometimes recommended as an excellent way to become more relaxed.
- **Give yourself pep talks**. Counter negative thoughts that pop into your head with positive ones. You'll feel more confident when your head is filled with positive thoughts than negative ones, and that confidence could make a difference.
- **Visualize**. Try to picture yourself being successful at taking the test. While there is no guarantee that this will produce a successful outcome, it's another strategy for boosting your confidence. This may be all you need to do a great job when the test rolls around.
- **Take control.** Most importantly, you need to feel in control of the situation. When you feel powerless to do anything, the result is often to panic; on the other hand, if you feel powerful, you will be able to master whatever task confronts you.

I hope you have found the preceding tips useful. If you begin to incorporate some of them into your regular study routines, attend class regularly, take good notes on material covered in class, read each chapter (ideally before the material is presented in class and then review the chapter as you are going over the material in class), and use the resources in the Study Guide you should finish the semester with good grades and a better understanding not only of sociology, but of yourself and your social world. I hope that you will enjoy your adventure and find that this subject opens new vistas of understanding to you. Good Luck!

Gwen Nyden, Ph.D.
Oakton Community College
Des Plaines, Illinois

Sources:

Jalongo, Mary Ranck, Twiest, Megan Mahoney, and Gail J. Gerlach. *The College Learner: How to Survive and Thrive in an Academic Environment.* Englewood Cliffs, NJ: Prentice-Hall, 1996.

Lenier, Minnette, and Janet Maker. *Keys to College Success*, 4th edition. Upper Saddle River, NJ: Prentice-Hall, 1998.

Pauk, Walter. *How to Study in College*, 6th edition. Boston: Houghton Mifflin Company, 1997.

CHAPTER 1
THE SOCIOLOGICAL PERSPECTIVE

☞CHAPTER SUMMARY

- Sociology offers a perspective--a view of the world--which stresses that people's social experiences underlie their behavior. For C. Wright Mills, this is the interaction of biography and history.
- Sociology is the scientific study of society and human behavior and, as such, is one of the social sciences, which study human behavior, in contrast to the natural sciences, which focus on nature.
- Sociology emerged during the upheavals of the Industrial Revolution. Early sociologists such as Auguste Comte, Herbert Spencer, Karl Marx, Emile Durkheim, Max Weber, and Harriet Martineau focused on how the sweeping social changes brought about by the Industrial Revolution affected human behavior.
- Sociologists agree that sociological research should be value free, but disagree concerning the proper purposes and uses of social research. Some believe its purpose should be only to advance understanding of human behavior; others, that its goal should be to reform harmful social arrangements.
- Weber believed that sociologists must try to see the world from another's perspective in order to understand their behavior (*Verstehen*); Durkheim stressed the importance of uncovering the objective social conditions that influence behavior (social facts).
- In the early years of sociology, only a few wealthy women received an advanced education. Harriet Martineau was an Englishwoman who wrote about social life in Great Britain and the United States and published a book entitled *Society in America*.
- In North America, departments of sociology began to be established at the end of the nineteenth century. In the early years, the contributions of women and minorities were largely ignored.
- Pure sociology is research whose only purpose is to make discoveries, while applied sociology is the use of sociology to solve social problems in settings ranging from the work place to the family.
- A theory is a general statement about how sets of facts are related to one another. Because no one theory encompasses all of reality, sociologists use three primary theoretical frameworks: (1) symbolic interactionism, concentrating on how people use symbols to develop and share their views of the world, usually focuses on the micro level; (2) functional analysis, stressing that society is made up of various parts which, when working properly, contribute to the stability of society, focuses on the macro level; and (3) conflict theory, emphasizing that social life is based on a competitive struggle to gain control over scarce resources, also focuses on the macro level.
- Sociology today is coming closer to its roots of applying sociological knowledge to social change. Two major trends are applied sociology and globalization. This latter trend is likely to broaden the scope of sociological inquiry beyond its traditional concentration on U.S. society.

☞LEARNING OBJECTIVES

As you read Chapter 1, use these learning objectives to organize your notes. After completing your reading, briefly state an answer to each of the objectives, and review the text pages in parentheses.

1. Explain the sociological perspective, discussing how ideas like social location, the connection between biography and history, and increased globalization contribute to our understanding of human behavior. (4-5)

2.   Distinguish between the natural and social sciences and identify the goals of scientific inquiry. Define sociology and compare it with the other social sciences. (6-9)

3.   Discuss how and why sociology emerged as a science in the middle of the nineteenth century in Europe, explaining each of the following sociologists' contributions to the development of sociology: Auguste Comte, Herbert Spencer, Karl Marx, Emile Durkheim, and Max Weber. (9-14)

4.   State the key issues in the debate about the proper role of values in sociology. (14-15)

5.   Explain what Max Weber meant by *Verstehen* and Emile Durkheim by social facts and how these two can fit together. (16-17)

6.   Explain the absence of women in the early years of sociology. (17)

7.   Trace the development of sociology in the United States from its origins in the late 19th century to its present-day perspectives, identifying the contributions that each of the following made to the development of sociology in North America: Albion Small, Jane Addams, W.E.B. Du Bois, Talcott Parsons, C. Wright Mills. (17-22)

8.   Explain the chief differences in three major theoretical perspectives: symbolic interactionism, functional analysis, and conflict theory. (22-31)

9.   Compare micro-level and macro-level analysis and state which level of analysis is utilized by each of the major theoretical perspectives. (31-32)

10.   Describe the three phases of sociology in the United States and identify the trends now shaping the future of sociology in the United States. (32-33)

☞ CHAPTER OUTLINE

I.   **The Sociological Perspective**
   A.   This perspective is important because it provides a different way of looking at familiar worlds. It allows us to gain a new vision of social life.
   B.   This perspective stresses the broader social context of behavior by looking at individuals' social location--employment, income, education, gender, age, and race--and by considering external influences--people's experiences--which are internalized and become part of a person's thinking and motivations. We are able to see the links between what people do and the social settings that shape their behavior.
   C.   This perspective enables us to analyze and understand both the forces that contribute to the emergence and growth of the global village and our unique experiences in our own smaller corners of this village.

II.   **Sociology and The Other Sciences**
   A.   Science is the systematic methods used to obtain knowledge and the knowledge obtained by those methods. It can be divided into the natural sciences and the social sciences. Sociology is defined as "the scientific study of society and human behavior."
   B.   The natural sciences attempt to comprehend, explain, and predict events in our natural environment.
   C.   Social sciences attempt to objectively study the social world. Like the natural sciences, the social sciences are divided into specialized fields based on their subject matter.
      1.   Political science focuses on politics or government.
      2.   Economics analyzes the production, distribution, and allocation of the material goods and services of a society.
      3.   Anthropology attempts to understand culture (a people's total way of life) by

focusing primarily on preliterate people.

    4.   Psychology concentrates on processes that occur within the individual.

    5.   Sociology is similar to the other social sciences in some ways but it is distinct because it looks at all social institutions, focuses on industrialized societies, and looks at external factors which influence people.

D.   All sciences have certain goals.

    1.   The first goal is to explain *why* something happens.

    2.   The second goal is to make generalizations by looking for patterns.

    3.   The third goal is to predict what will happen in the future, given current knowledge.

E.   To achieve these goals, scientists must move beyond common sense and rely on conclusions based on systematic study.

III.   The Origins of Sociology

A.   Sociology developed in the middle of the 19th century when European social observers began to use scientific methods to test their ideas. Four factors led to its development:

    1.   the social upheaval in Europe as a result of the Industrial Revolution and led to changes in the way people lived their lives;

    2.   the political revolutions in America and France, which encouraged people to rethink their ideas about social life;

    3.   the development of imperialism--as the Europeans conquered other nations, they came in contact with different cultures and began to ask why cultures varied; and

    4.   the success of the natural sciences, which created a desire to apply scientific methods in order to find answers for the questions being raised about the social world as well.

B.   Auguste Comte coined the term "sociology" and suggested the use of positivism--applying the scientific approach to the social world--but he did not utilize this approach himself. Comte did believe that this new science should not only discover sociological principles, but should then apply those principles to social reform.

C.   Herbert Spencer viewed societies as evolutionary, coined the term "the survival of the fittest," and became known for social Darwinism. Spencer was convinced that no one should intervene in the evolution of society and that attempts at social reform were wrong.

D.   Karl Marx, whose ideas about social classes and class struggle between the bourgeoisie and the proletariat was the foundation of the conflict perspective, believed that class conflict was the key to human history. Marx argued that people should take active steps to change society.

E.   Emile Durkheim played an important role in the development of sociology.

    1.   One of his primary goals was to get sociology recognized as a separate academic discipline.

    2.   He was interested in understanding the social factors that influence individual behavior; he studied suicide rates among different groups and concluded that social integration, the degree to which people are tied to their social group, was a key social factor in suicide.

    3.   Durkheim's third concern was that social research be practical; sociologists should not only diagnose the causes of social problems but should also develop solutions for them.

F.   Max Weber was one of the most influential of all sociologists, raising issues that remain controversial even today. Disagreeing with Karl Marx, Weber defined religion as a central force in social change (i.e. Protestantism encourages greater economic development and was the central factor in the rise of capitalism in some countries).

1. The Protestant belief system encouraged its members to embrace change.

2. Protestants sought "signs" that they were in God's will; financial success became a major sign. The more money they made, the more secure they were about their religious standing.

3. Weber called this behavior the *Protestant ethic*; he called their readiness to invest capital in order to make more money the *spirit of capitalism*.

IV. **The Role of Values in Social Research**

A. Weber advocated that sociological research should be value free--personal values or biases should not influence social research--and objective--totally neutral. Sociologists agree that objectivity is a proper goal but acknowledge that no one can escape values entirely. Replication--repeating a study to see if the same results are found--is one means to avoid the distortions that values can cause.

B. While sociologists may agree that research should be objective, the proper purposes and uses of sociology are argued among sociologists, with some taking the position that the proper role of sociology is to advance understanding of social life, while others believe that it is the responsibility of sociologists to explore harmful social arrangements of society.

C. On the one side are those who say that understanding social behavior is sociology's proper goal and that the knowledge gained through research belongs to the scientific community and can be used by anyone for any purpose. On the other side are those who say the goal of sociological research should be to investigate harmful social conditions and that sociologists should lead the way in reforming society.

V. *Verstehen* **and Social Facts**

A. Weber argued that sociologists should use *Verstehen* ("to grasp by insight") in order to see beyond the social facts to the subjective meanings that people attach to their own behavior.

B. Durkheim believed that social facts, patterns of behavior that characterize a social group, reflect underlying conditions of society and should be used to interpret other social facts.

C. Social facts and *Verstehen* fit together because they reinforce each other; sociologists use *Verstehen* in order to interpret social facts.

VI. **Sexism in Early Sociology**

A. In the early years of sociology, the field was dominated by men because rigidly defined social roles prevented most women from pursuing an education.

1. Women were supposed to devote themselves to the four K's--*Kirche, Küchen, Kinder, und Kleider* (church, cooking, children, and clothes).

2. At the same time, a few women from wealthy families managed to get an education; a few even studied sociology although the sexism in the universities stopped them from earning advanced degrees, becoming professors, or having their research recognized.

B. Harriet Martineau studied social life in both Great Britain and the United States, publishing *Society in America* decades before Durkheim and Weber were even born. While her original research has been largely ignored by the discipline, she is known for her translations of Comte's ideas into English.

VII. **Sociology in North America**

A. The first departments of sociology in the U.S. were at the University of Kansas (1889) and the University of Chicago (1892); the first in Canada was at McGill University (1922).

1.   Albion Small, founder of the department of sociology at the University of Chicago, also established the *American Journal of Sociology*.
2.   The department of sociology at the University of Chicago dominated North American sociology; other early sociologists from the University of Chicago were Robert E. Park, Ernest Burgess, and George Herbert Mead.

B.   The situation of women in North America was similar to that of European women and their contributions to sociology met a similar fate. Denied a role in the universities, many turned to social activism, working with the poor and regarded as social workers.
1.   Jane Addams is an example; she founded Hull House, a settlement house for the poor, and worked to bridge the gap between the powerful and the powerless.
2.   Sociologists from nearby University of Chicago visteed Hull House frequently.
3.   She is the only sociologist to have won the Nobel Peace Prize, being awarded this in 1931.

C.   African American professionals also faced problems.
1.   W.E.B. DuBois was the first African American to earn a Ph.D. from Harvard. He conducted extensive research on race relations in the U.S., publishing a book a year on this subject between 1896 and 1914.
2.   Despite his accomplishments he encountered prejudice and discrimination in his professional and personal life. Frustrated at the lack of improvements in race relations, he turned to social action, helping to found the National Association for the Advancement of Colored People (NAACP) along with Jane Addams, Florence Kelley and others from Hull House.
3.   Until recently, his contributions to sociology were overlooked.

D.   Many early North American sociologists combined the role of sociologist with that of social reformer. For example, University of Chicago sociologists Park and Burgess, studied many urban problems and offered suggestions on how to alleviate them. By the 1940s, as sociologists became more concerned with establishing sociology as an academic discipline, the emphasis shifted from social reform to social theory.
1.   Talcott Parsons developed abstract models of society to show how the parts of society harmoniously work together.
2.   Countering this development was C. Wright Mills, who urged sociologists to get back to social reform. He saw the emergency of the *power elite* as an imminent threat to freedom.

E.   The debate over what should be the proper goals of sociological analysis--analyzing society vs. reforming society--continues today.
1.   Applied sociology exists between these two extremes. One of the first attempts at applied sociology was the founding of the NAACP.
2.   Today, applied sociologists work in a variety of settings, from business and hi-tech to government and not-for-profit agencies.
3.   Applied sociology is the application of sociological knowledge in some specific setting, rather than an attempt to rebuild society.

VIII. Theoretical Perspectives in Sociology
A.   Theory is a general statement about how some parts of the world fit together and how they work; it is an explanation of how two or more facts are related to one another. Sociologists use three different theoretical perspectives to understand social behavior.
B.   Symbolic interactionism views symbols, things to which we attach meaning, as the basis of social life.

1.   Through the use of symbols people are able to define relationships to others, to coordinate actions with others thereby making social life possible, and to develop a sense of themselves.

2.   A symbolic interactionist studying divorce would focus on how the changing meanings of marriage, family and divorce have all contributed to the increase in the rate of divorce in U.S. society.

C.   The central idea of functional analysis is that society is a whole unit, made up of interrelated parts that work together.

1.   To understand society, we must look at both structure, how the parts of society fit together to make up the whole, and function, how each part contributes to society.

2.   Robert Merton used the term function to refer to the beneficial consequences of people's actions to keep society stable and dysfunction to refer to consequences that undermine stability. Functions can be either manifest (actions that are intended) or latent (unintended consequences).

3.   In trying to explain divorce, a functionalist would look at how industrialization and urbanization both contributed to the changing function of marriage and the family.

D.   According to conflict theory, society is viewed as composed of groups competing for scarce resources.

1.   Karl Marx focused on struggles between the bourgeoisie, the small group of capitalists who own the means of production, and the proletariat, the masses of workers exploited by the capitalists.

2.   Contemporary conflict theorists have expanded this perspective to include conflict in all relations of power and authority.

3.   Divorce is seen as the outcome of the shifting balance of power within a family; as women have gained power and try to address inequalities in their relationships, men resist.

E.   The perspectives differ in their level of analysis. Functionalists and conflict theorists provide macro-level analysis because they examine the large-scale patterns of society. Symbolic interactionists carry out micro-level analysis because they focus on the small-scale patterns of social life.

F.   Each perspective provides a different and often sharply contrasting picture of the world. However, sociologists often use all three perspectives because no one theory or level of analysis encompasses all of reality.

IX.   **Trends Shaping the Future of Sociology**

A.   To understand the tension between social reform and social analysis, sociologists have found it useful to divide sociology into three phases.

1.   In the first phase the primary concern of sociologists was making the world a better place.

2.   During the second phase sociologists sought to establish sociology as a respected field of knowledge, emphasizing basic, or pure, sociology.

3.   In the third (current) phase there has been an attempt to merge sociological knowledge and practical work with the development of applied sociology. This trend has gained momentum in recent years.

4.   Despite being able to identify three phases, each of which has been characterized by a different position on reform vs. analysis, there has never been complete consensus on which approach is better.

B.   Globalization is a second major trend destined to leave its mark on sociology.

1.   Globalization is the breaking down of national boundaries because of advances in communications, trade and travel.
2.   Globalization is likely to broaden the scope of sociological analysis as sociologists look beyond the boundaries of the United States in considering global issues.

C.   Globalization is one of the most significant events in world history. This book stresses the impact of globalization on our lives today.

☞ KEY TERMS

After reading the chapter, review the definitions for each of the key terms listed below.

anomie: Durkheim's term for a condition of society in which people become detached, cut loose from the norms that usually guide their behavior

applied sociology: the use of sociology to solve social problems--from the micro level of family relationships to the macro level of crime and pollution

authority: power that people consider legitimate

bourgeoisie: Karl Marx's term for capitalists. those who own the means to produce wealth

class conflict: Marx's term for the struggle between the proletariat and the bourgeoisie

common sense: those things that "everyone knows" are true

conflict theory: a theoretical framework in which society is viewed as composed of groups competing for scarce resources

functional analysis: a theoretical framework in which society is viewed as composed of various parts, each with a function that, when fulfilled, contributes to society's equilibrium; also known as functionalism and structural functionalism

generalization: a statement that goes beyond the individual case and is applied to a broader group or situation

Globalization: the extensive interconnections among nations due to the expansion of capitalism

Globalization of capitalism: capitalism (investing to make profits within a rational system) becoming the globe's dominant economic system

macro-level analysis: an examination of large-scale patterns of society

micro-level analysis: an examination of small-scale patterns of society

natural sciences: the intellectual and academic disciplines designed to comprehend, explain, and predict events in our natural environment

nonverbal interaction: communication without words through gestures, space, silence, and so on

objectivity: total neutrality

patterns: recurring characteristics or events

positivism: the application of the scientific approach to the social world

proletariat: Marx's term for the exploited class, the mass of workers who do not own the means of production

pure or basic sociology: sociological research whose only purpose is to make discoveries about life in human groups, not to make changes in those groups

replication: repeating a study in order to check the findings of a previous study

science: the application of systematic methods to obtain knowledge and the knowledge obtained by those methods

scientific method: the use of objective, systematic observations to test theories

social facts: Durkheim's term for the patterns of behavior that characterize a social group

social integration: the degree to which people feel a part of social groups

social interaction: what people do when they are in one another's presence

social location: the group memberships that people have because of their location in history and society

social sciences: the intellectual and academic disciplines designed to understand the social world objectively by means of controlled and repeated observations

society: a term used by sociologists to refer to a group of people who share a culture and a territory

sociological perspective: an approach to understanding human behavior by placing it within its broader social context

sociology: the scientific study of society and human behavior

subjective meanings: the meanings that people give to their own behavior

symbolic interaction: a theoretical perspective in which society is viewed as composed of symbols that people use to establish meaning, develop their views of the world, and communicate with one another

theory: a general statement about how some parts of the world fit together and how they work; an explanation of how two or more facts are related to one another

value free: the view that a sociologist's personal values or biases should not influence social research

values: ideas about what is good or worthwhile in life; attitudes about the way the world ought to be

Verstehen: a German word used by Weber that is perhaps best understood as "to have insight into someone's situation"

☞ KEY PEOPLE

The following are key people in the development of sociology.

Jane Addams: Addams was the founder of Hull House--a settlement house in the immigrant community of Chicago. She invited sociologists from nearby University of Chicago to visit. In 1931 she was a winner of the Nobel Peace Prize.

Auguste Comte: Comte is often credited with being the founder of sociology, because he was the first to suggest that the scientific method be applied to the study of the social world.

Lewis Coser: Coser pointed out that conflict is likely to develop among people in close relationships because they are connected by a network of responsibilities, power and rewards.

Ralf Dahrendorf: Dahrendorf's work is associated with the conflict perspective; he suggested that conflict is inherent in all relations that have authority.

W.E.B. Du Bois: Du Bois was the first African American to earn a doctorate at Harvard University. For most of his career he taught sociology at Atlanta University. He was concerned about social injustice, wrote about race relations, and was one of the founders of the National Association for the Advancement of Colored People.

Emile Durkheim: Durkheim was responsible for getting sociology recognized as a separate discipline. He was interested in studying how individual behavior is shaped by social forces and in finding remedies for social ills. He stressed that sociologists should use social facts--patterns of behavior that reflect some underlying condition of society.

Harriet Martineau: An Englishwoman who studied British and U.S. social life and published *Society in America* decades before either Durkheim or Weber were born.

Karl Marx: Marx believed that social development grew out of conflict between social classes; under capitalism, this conflict was between the *bourgeoisie*--those who own the means to produce wealth--and the *proletariat*--the mass of workers. His work is associated with the conflict perspective.

George Herbert Mead: Mead was one of the founders of symbolic interactionism, a major theoretical perspective in sociology.

Robert Merton: Merton contributed the terms *manifest and latent functions* and *dysfunctions* to the functionalist perspective.

C. Wright Mills: Mills suggested that external influences--or a person's experiences--become part of his or her thinking and motivations and explain social behavior.   As the emphasis in sociology shifted from social reform to social theory, Mills urged sociologists to get back to their roots.   He saw the emergency of the power elite--composed of top leaders of business, politics and the military--as an imminent threat to freedom.

Talcott Parsons: Parsons' work dominated sociology in the 1940s-1950s.   He developed abstract models of how the parts of society harmoniously work together.

Albion Small: Small was the founder of the sociology department at the University of Chicago and the *American Journal of Sociology*.

Herbert Spencer: Another early sociologist, Spencer believed that societies evolve from barbarian to civilized forms.   The first to use the expression "the survival of the fittest" to reflect his belief that social evolution depended on the survival of the most capable and intelligent and the extinction of the less capable.   His views became known as *social darwinism*.

Max Weber: Weber's most important contribution to sociology was his study of the relationship between the emergence of Protestant belief system and the rise of capitalism.   He believed that sociologists should not allow their personal values affect their social research; objectivity should become the hallmark of sociology.   He argued that sociologists should use *Verstehen*--those subjective meanings that people give to their behavior.

☞ "DOWN-TO-EARTH SOCIOLOGY"

This is your opportunity to apply the sociological perspective to the world around you.   The questions in this section refer to material introduced in this chapter of your text.   Many ask you to think about ideas and information presented in the various special "boxes" that are located throughout this chapter.

1.   What is the morale of the "Elephant Story" on page 8?   What does it suggest about the role of the different social sciences in explaining human behavior?

2.   Were you surprised to learn that all of the common sense notions in the quiz on pages 9-10 were not true?   Can you think of other common sense ideas that may or may not be true?

3.   In the debate over the purposes and uses of sociological research (pp. 14-15), what is your position?   Do you think sociologists should only advance our understanding of social life or is it their responsibility to explore harmful social arrangements and try to alleviate human suffering?

4.   After reading an excerpt from one of W.E.B. Du Bois's books on page 20, what conclusions can you draw about the position of African Americans in U.S. society at the end of the 19th century?   How does this picture of race relations from the past compare with one drawn today?

5.   Reflecting on the introduction to sociological perspectives that was presented in this chapter, does your think view on social life fit most closely with the symbolic interactionist, functionalist, or conflict perspective?   Why?

6.   Now that you have a basic understanding of sociology, why might a background in sociology be useful in helping to solve social problems?   You might reflect on some of the real examples of people you read about in this chapter who are applying their sociological knowledge to real situations.

☞ SELF-TEST

After completing this self-test, check your answers against the Answer Key beginning on page 337 of this Study Guide and against the text on the page(s) indicated in parentheses.

MULTIPLE CHOICE QUESTIONS

1.   An approach to understanding human behavior by placing it within its broader social context is known as: (4)
        a.   social location.
        b.   the sociological perspective.
        c.   common sense.
        d.   generalization.

2.   Going beyond individual cases and making statements that apply to broader groups or situations is called: (7)
        a.   objectivity
        b.   *Verstehen*
        c.   generalization
        d.   social facts

3.   Which of the following was <u>not</u> important to the development of sociology? (9-10)
        a.   the Industrial Revolution
        b.   the British revolution
        c.   imperialism
        d.   the development of the scientific method

4.   The application of the scientific approach to the social world is known as: (11)
        a.   ethnomethodology.
        b.   sociobiology.
        c.   natural science.
        d.   positivism.

5.   The principle of "the survival of the fittest" was first stated by: (11)
        a.   Herbert Spencer.
        b.   Charles Darwin.
        c.   Auguste Comte.
        d.   Karl Marx.

6.   According to Karl Marx, capitalists, who own the means of production, exploit the: (12)
        a.   bourgeoisie.
        b.   proletariat.
        c.   masses.
        d.   peasants.

7. According to Emile Durkheim, suicide rates can be explained by: (13)
   a. social factors.
   b. common sense.
   c. the oppression of the proletariat by the bourgeoisie.
   d. the survival of the fittest.

8. What did Durkheim identify as the key to explaining patterns of suicide? (13)
   a. the individual mental state of the person committing suicide
   b. the degree to which individuals are integrated into their social groups and feel a sense of attachment
   c. the strength of religious beliefs regarding the importance of life
   d. the influence of seasonal factors like the amount of sunlight or the temperature

9. Max Weber's research on the rise of capitalism identified _____ as the key. (14)
   a. ownership of property
   b. political reforms
   c. religious beliefs
   d. slavery

10. Replication: (15)
   a. helps researchers overcome distortions that values can cause.
   b. makes it possible to see how results compare when a study is repeated.
   c. involves the repetition of a study by other researchers.
   d. All of the above.

11. Social facts and *Verstehen*: (16)
   a. have no relationship to each other.
   b. have been disproved.
   c. go hand-in-hand.
   d. were both concepts developed by Durkheim.

12. In the 19th century, it was unlikely that women would study sociology because: (17)
   a. they were more interested in fields of study like English and foreign languages.
   b. sex roles were rigidly defined and it was not considered appropriate or necessary for women to get an education.
   c. they had no training in scientific methods.
   d. they were not interested in social inquiry or social reform.

13. Which of the following North American sociologists wrote extensively on race relations, experienced prejudice and discrimination personally and professionally, and helped to found the NAACP? (18-19)
   a. C. Wright Mills
   b. Talcott Parsons
   c. W.E.B. Du Bois
   d. Jane Addams

14.   Sociologists who research social problems for government commissions or agencies are: (22)
    a.   politically correct.
    b.   basic sociologists.
    c.   applied sociologists.
    d.   pure sociologists.

15.   The theoretical perspective which views society as composed of symbols that we use to establish meaning, develop our views of the world, and communicate with one another is: (24)
    a.   functionalism.
    b.   symbolic interactionism.
    c.   dramaturgical theory.
    d.   conflict theory.

16.   In explaining the high U.S. divorce rate, the _____ perspective would focus on explanations such as emotional satisfaction, the meaning of children, and the meaning of parenthood. (25)
    a.   conflict
    b.   functional
    c.   symbolic interaction
    d.   exchange

17.   According to Robert Merton, an action intended to help maintain a system's equilibrium is a: (27)
    a.   manifest function.
    b.   latent function.
    c.   dysfunction.
    d.   latent dysfunction.

18.   Industrialization and urbanization have undermined the traditional purposes of the family, according to theorists using _____ analysis. (28)
    a.   conflict
    b.   exchange
    c.   symbolic interaction
    d.   functional

19.   The idea that conflict is inherent in all relations that have authority was first asserted by: (30)
    a.   Karl Marx.
    b.   Emile Durkheim.
    c.   Ralph Dahrendorf.
    d.   Auguste Comte.

20.   Conflict theorists might explain the high rate of divorce by looking at: (31)
    a.   the changing meanings associated with marriage and divorce.
    b.   society's basic inequalities between males and females.
    c.   changes which have weakened the family unit.
    d.   the loss of family functions which held a husband and wife together.

21.	According to your text, which theoretical perspective is best for studying human behavior? (32)
	a.	the functionalist perspective.
	b.	the symbolic interactionist perspective.
	c.	the conflict perspective.
	d.	A combination of all of the above.

22.	The first phase of sociology in the United States was characterized by: (32)
	a.	a concern with establishing sociology as a social science.
	b.	a focus on establishing sociology as a respectable field of knowledge.
	c.	an interest in using sociological knowledge to improve social life and change society.
	d.	a broad acceptance of women and racial minorities within the discipline.

23.	Research which makes discoveries about life human groups rather than make changes in those groups is: (32)
	a.	pure or basic sociology.
	b.	applied sociology.
	c.	clinical sociology.
	d.	None of the above.

24.	According to the text, in recent years sociologists have once again emphasized: (33)
	a.	pure research.
	b.	clinical sociology.
	c.	applied sociology.
	d.	grantsmanship.

25.	What trend does the author of your text suggest is likely to transform the scope and focus of U.S. sociology in the future? (33)
	a.	race, class, and gender inequalities
	b.	cultural diversity
	c.	technology
	d.	globalization

TRUE-FALSE QUESTIONS

T F	1.	The sociological perspective helps us to understand that people's social experiences underlie what they feel and what they do. (4)

T F	2.	Social location is where people are located in history and society. (4)

T F	3.	Political scientists study the ways in which people govern themselves. (6)

T F	4.	Sociologists believe that internal mechanisms are very important in explaining an individual's thinking and motivations. (7)

T F	5.	Anthropology focuses on preliterate peoples. (7)

T F	6.	Sociology has few similarities to other social sciences. (7)

T F	7.	Historically, the success of the natural sciences led to the search for answers to the social world as well. (11)

T F	8.	Herbert Spencer believed that human societies evolve like those of animal species. (11)

T F	9.	Karl Marx thought that a classless society eventually would exist. (12)

T F 10. According to Durkheim, social integration is the degree to which people feel that they are a part of a social group. (13)

T F 11. The ideas of Max Weber and Karl Marx are almost identical. (14)

T F 12. According to Weber, subjective meanings are important in understanding human behavior. (16)

T F 13. To Durkheim, social facts are patterns of behavior that characterize a social group. (16)

T F 14. Harriet Martineau was widely recognized for her pioneering studies of social life in Great Britain and the United States. (17)

T F 15. There are three major theoretical perspectives within the discipline of sociology. (22)

T F 16. Symbolic interactionists primarily analyze how our definitions of ourselves and others underlie our behaviors. (23-24)

T F 17. According to functionalists, the family has lost all of its traditional purposes. (27)

T F 18. All conflict theorists focus on conflict between the bourgeoisie and the proletariat. (30)

T F 19. Micro-level analysis focuses on social interaction. (31)

T F 20. Currently, most sociologists do not feel that sociology should be used to solve social problems. (32)

FILL-IN QUESTIONS

1. People's group memberships because of their location in history and society is known as _____. (4)

2. The _____ are the intellectual and academic disciplines designed to comprehend, explain, and predict the events in our natural environment. On the other hand, the _____ examine human relationships. (6)

3. The use of objective systematic observation to test theories is _____. (11)

4. _____ was Karl Marx's term for the struggle between the proletariat and the bourgeoisie. (12)

5. Durkheim used the term _____ to refer to the degree to which people feel a part of social groups. (13)

6. _____ is the view that a sociologist's personal values or biases should not influence social research, while _____ is total neutrality. (14-15)

7. The meanings that people attach to their own behavior is called _____. (16)

8. Durkheim used the term _____ to refer to patterns of behavior that characterize a social group. (16)

9. A _____ is a general statement about how some parts of the world fit together and how they work. (22)

10. The theoretical perspective in which society is viewed as composed of symbols that people use to establish meaning, develop their views of the world, and communicate with one another is _____. (23)

11. _____ analysis is a theoretical framework in which society is viewed as composed of various parts, each with a function that contributes to society's equilibrium. (27)

12. _____ stresses that women have traditionally been regarded as property and passed by one male, the father, to another, the husband. (31)

13. _____ analysis examines large-scale patterns of society, while _____ analysis examines small-scale patterns of society. (31)

14. _____ sociology makes discoveries about life in human groups, not to make changes in those groups; _____ sociology is the use of sociology to solve problems. (32-33)

15. _____ is the process by which national boundaries are broken down because of advances in communication, trade, and travel. (33)

MATCH THESE SOCIAL SCIENTISTS WITH THEIR CONTRIBUTIONS

___1. Auguste Comte
___2. Herbert Spencer
___3. Karl Marx
___4. C. Wright Mills
___5. Emile Durkheim
___6. Harriet Martineau
___7. Robert Merton
___8. W.E.B. Du Bois
___9. Max Weber

a. *coined the phrase "survival of the fittest"*
b. *was an early African American sociologist*
c. *proposed the use of positivism*
d. *stressed social facts*
e. *believed religion was a central force in social change*
f. *believed the key to human history was class struggle*
g. *encouraged the use of the sociological perspective*
h. *published Society in America and translated Comte's work into English*
i. *distinguished between functions and dysfunctions*

ESSAY QUESTIONS

1. Explain what the sociological perspective encompasses and then, using that perspective, discuss the forces that shaped the discipline of sociology.

2. The textbook notes that *Verstehen* and social facts go hand in hand; explain how this is so. Assume that you have been asked to carry out research to find out more about why growing numbers of women and children are homeless and what particular problems they face. Discuss how you could you use both *Verstehen* and social facts in your study.

3. Explain each of the theoretical perspectives that are used in sociology and describe how a sociologist affiliated with one of another of the perspectives might undertake a study of gangs. Discuss how all three can be used in research.

CHAPTER 2
CULTURE

☞ CHAPTER SUMMARY

- Culture is universal; all human groups create a design for living that includes both material and nonmaterial culture. Ideal culture, a group's ideal norms and values, exists alongside its real culture, the actual behavior which often falls short of the cultural ideals.

- All people perceive and evaluate the world through the lens of their own culture. People are naturally ethnocentric, that is, they use their own culture as a standard against which to judge other cultures. In comparison, cultural relativism tries to understand other peoples within the framework of their own culture.

- The central component of nonmaterial culture is symbols; these include gestures, language, values, norms, sanctions, folkways and mores. Language is essential for culture because it allows us to move beyond the present, sharing with others our past experiences and our future plans. According to the Sapir-Whorf hypothesis, language not only expresses our thinking and perceptions but actually shapes them.

- All groups have values and norms and use positive and negative sanctions to show approval or disapproval of those who do or don't follow the norms.

- A subculture is a group whose values and behaviors set it apart from the general culture; a counterculture holds values that stand in opposition to the dominant culture.

- Although the U.S. is a pluralistic society made up of many groups, each with its own set of values, certain core values dominate. Some values cluster together to form a larger whole. Core values that contradict one another indicate areas of social tension and are likely points of social change.

- Cultural universals are values, norms or other cultural traits that are found in all cultures.

- To the extent that some animals teach their young certain behavior, animals also have culture; however, no animals have language in the sociological sense of the term.

- Cultural lag refers to a condition in which a group's nonmaterial culture lags behind its changing technology. Today the technology in travel and communication makes cultural diffusion occur more rapidly around the globe than in the past, resulting in some degree of cultural leveling, a process by which cultures become similar to one another.

☞ LEARNING OBJECTIVES

As you read Chapter 2, use these learning objectives to organize your notes. After completing your reading, briefly state an answer to each of the objectives, and review the text pages in parentheses.

1. Define culture and explain its material and nonmaterial components. (38-39)
2. Explain why ethnocentrism is a natural tendency and why this orientation towards your own and other cultures can lead to culture shock. (39-40)
3. State what cultural relativism is and discuss why it is a worthwhile goal even though it presents challenges to us. (40-41)
4. Identify the components of symbolic culture. (42)
5. Explain the importance of gestures for communications, and discuss how gestures relate to culture. (42-43)
6. Discuss the different ways in which language makes human life possible. (43-47)

31

7.   Define the following terms: values, norms, sanctions, folkways, mores, and taboos. (47-49)
8.   Compare and contrast dominant culture, subcultures, and countercultures. (49-50)
9.   List the core values in U.S. society as identified by Robin Williams and James Henslin. (50-51)
10. Explain what is meant by value contradictions and value clusters. (51-53)
11. Discuss why core values do not change without meeting strong resistance. (54)
12. Explain what the author of your text means when he says values can act as blinders. (54)
13. Explain the difference between "ideal" and "real" cultures. (54-55)
14. Define cultural universals and state whether, in actuality, they exist or not. (55)
15. Answer the question, "Do animals have culture?" (56-57)
16. State what technology is and explain its sociological significance. (57-58)
17. Define cultural lag and explain its role in relationship to cultural change. (58)
18. Discuss the link between technology, cultural diffusion, and cultural leveling. (58-59)

☞ CHAPTER OUTLINE

I.   **What is Culture?**
   A.   Culture is defined as the language, beliefs, values, norms, behaviors, and even material objects passed from one generation to the next.
      1.   Material culture is things such as jewelry, art, buildings, weapons, machines, clothing, hairstyles, etc.
      2.   Nonmaterial culture is a group's ways of thinking (beliefs, values, and assumptions) and common patterns of behavior (language, gestures, and other forms of interaction).
   B.   Culture provides a taken-for-granted orientation to life.
      1.   We assume that our own culture is normal or natural; in fact, it is not natural, but rather is learned. It penetrates our lives so deeply that it is taken for granted and provides the lens through which we evaluate things.
      2.   It provides implicit instructions that tell us what we ought to do and a moral imperative that defines what we think is right and wrong.
      3.   Coming into contact with a radically different culture produces "culture shock," challenging our basic assumptions.
      4.   A consequence of internalizing culture is ethnocentrism, using our own culture (and assuming it to be good, right, and superior) to judge other cultures. It is functional when it creates in-group solidarity, but can be dysfunctional if it leads to harmful discrimination.
   C.   Cultural relativism consists of trying to appreciate other groups' ways of life in the context in which they exist, without judging them as superior or inferior to our own.
      1.   This view helps us to appreciate other ways of life.
      2.   Robert Edgerton argues that those cultural practices that result in exploitation *should* be judged morally inferior to those that enhance people's lives.
II. **Components of Symbolic Culture**
   A.   Sociologists sometimes refer to nonmaterial culture as symbolic culture.
      1.   A central component of culture is the symbols--something to which people attach meaning--that people use to communicate.
      2.   Symbols include gestures, language, values, norms, sanctions, folkways, and mores.

B. Gestures, using one's body to communicate with others, are shorthand means of communication.
    1.   Gestures are used by people in every culture, although the gestures and the meanings differ; confusion or offense can result because of misunderstandings over the meaning of a gesture or misuse of a gesture.
    2.   There is disagreement over whether there are any universal gestures.

C. Language consists of a system of symbols that can be put together in an infinite number of ways in order to communicate abstract thought. Each word is a symbol to which a culture attaches a particular meaning. It is important because it is the primary means of communication between people.
    1.   It allows human experiences to be cumulative; each generation builds on the body of significant experiences that is passed on to it by the previous generation, thus freeing people to move beyond immediate experiences.
    2.   It allows shared perspectives or understandings of the past and the future.
    3.   It allows humans to exchange perspectives, i.e. ideas about events and experiences.
    4.   It allows people to engage in complex, shared, goal-directed behavior.
    5.   The Sapir-Whorf hypothesis states that our thinking and perception not only are expressed by language but actually are shaped by language because we are taught not only words but also a particular way of thinking and perceiving. Rather than objects and events forcing themselves onto our consciousness, our very language determines our consciousness.

D. Culture includes values, norms, and sanctions.
    1.   Values are the standards by which people define good and bad, beautiful and ugly. Every group develops both values and expectations regarding the right way to reflect them.
    2.   Norms are the expectations, or rules of behavior, that develop out of a group's values.
    3.   Sanctions are the positive or negative reactions to the way in which people follow norms. Positive sanctions (a money reward, a prize, a smile, or even a handshake) are expressions of approval; negative sanctions (a fine, a frown, or harsh words) denote disapproval for breaking a norm.

E. Norms vary in terms of their importance to a culture.
    1.   Folkways are norms that are not strictly enforced, such as passing on the left side of the sidewalk. They may result in a person getting a dirty look.
    2.   Mores are norms that are believed to be essential to core values and we insist on conformity. A person who steals, rapes, and kills has violated some of society's most important mores.
    3.   Norms that one group considers to be folkways another group may view as mores. A male walking down the street with the upper half of his body uncovered may be violating a folkway; a female doing the same thing may be violating mores.
    4.   Taboos are norms so strongly ingrained that even the thought of them is greeted with revulsion. Eating human flesh and having sex with one's parents are examples of such behavior.

F. Subcultures and countercultures are often found within a broader culture.
    1.   Subcultures are groups whose values and related behaviors are so distinct that they set their members off from the dominant culture. Each subculture is a world within

the larger world of the dominant culture, and has a distinctive way of looking at life, but remains compatible with the dominant culture.

    2.   Countercultures are groups whose values set their members in opposition to the dominant culture. While usually associated with negative behavior, some countercultures are not. Countercultures are often perceived as a threat by the dominant culture because they challenge the culture's values; for this reason the dominant culture will move against a particular counterculture in order to affirm its own core values.

III. Values in U.S. Society

    A.   Identifying core values in U.S. society is difficult because it is a pluralistic society with many different religious, racial, ethnic, and special interest groups.

        1.   Sociologist Robin Williams identified twelve core values: achievement and success (especially, doing better than others); individualism (success due to individual effort); activity and work; efficiency and practicality; science and technology (using science to control nature); progress; material comfort; humanitarianism (helpfulness, personal kindness, philanthropy); freedom; democracy; equality (especially of opportunity); and racism and group superiority.

        2.   Henslin updated Williams's list by adding education; religiosity (belief in a Supreme Being and following some set of matching precepts); and romantic love and monogamy.

    B.   Some values conflict with each other. There cannot be full expressions of democracy, equality, racism, and sexism at the same time. These are value contradictions and as society changes some values are challenged and undergo modification.

    C.   Values are not independent units; value clusters are made up of related core values that come together to form a larger whole. In the value cluster surrounding success, for example, we find hard work, education, efficiency, material comfort, and individualism all bound together. A cluster that is emerging within U.S. society--in response to fundamental changes in U.S. society--is one made up of the values of leisure, self-fulfillment, physical fitness, and youngness.

    D.   Core values do not change without meeting strong resistance.

    E.   Values and their supporting beliefs may blind people to other social circumstances. Success stories blind many people in the United States to the dire consequences of family poverty, lack of education, and dead-end jobs.

    F.   Ideal culture refers to the ideal values and norms of a people. What people actually do usually falls short of this ideal, and sociologists refer to the norms and values that people actually follow as real culture.

IV. Cultural Universals

    A.   Although there are universal human activities, there is no universally accepted way of doing any of them.

        1.   Anthropologist George Murdock concluded that all human groups have certain cultural universals: customs about courtship, cooking, marriage, funerals, games, laws, music, myths, incest taboos, and toilet training are present in all cultures.

        2.   Even so, the specific customs differ from one group to another: by way of example, there is no universal form of the family, no universal way of disposing of the dead, and even the methods of toilet training differ from one culture to another.

B. Animals do not have the vocal apparatus necessary to utter the complex sounds that make up language. Research with different animal species indicates that animals are capable of learning language and using that language to communicate.
1. Jane Goodall's research with chimps in the wild demonstrates that they use hand signals to communicate.
2. Psychologists Allen and Beatrice Gardner taught American Sign Language to Washoe, a female chimp. She learned the signs and then began to apply them to many different situations. She eventually learned 160 signs and could put signs together in the equivalent of simple sentences.
3. Irene Pepperberg has taught Alex, an African Gray parrot, the names of objects and how to tell how many objects there were.
4. Despite this evidence, it is still too soon to say whether animals have the capacity for language.

V. **Technology in the Global Village**
A. In its simplest sense, technology can be equated with tools. In its broadest sense, technology also includes the skills or procedures necessary to make and to use those tools.
1. The emerging technologies of an era, that make a major impact on human life, are referred to as new technologies. The printing press and the computer are both examples of new technologies.
2. The sociological significance of technology is that it sets the framework for the nonmaterial culture, influencing the way people think and how they relate to one another.
B. Not all parts of culture change at the same pace; cultural lag was William Ogburn's term for situations where the material culture changes first and the nonmaterial culture lags behind.
C. Although for most of human history, cultures had little contact with one another, there has always been some contact with other groups, resulting in groups learning from one another.
1. This transmission of cultural characteristics is cultural diffusion; it is more like to produce changes in material culture than the nonmaterial culture.
2. Cultural diffusion occurs more rapidly today, given the technology.
3. Travel and communication unite the world to such an extent that there almost is no "other side of the world." For example, Japan, no longer a purely Eastern culture, has adapted Western economic production, forms of dress, music, and so on. This leads to cultural leveling--cultures become similar to one another.

☞ KEY TERMS

After studying the chapter, review the definition for each of the following terms.

counterculture: a group whose values, beliefs, and related behaviors place its members in opposition to the values of the broader culture

cultural diffusion: the spread of cultural characteristics from one group to another

cultural lag: William Ogburn's term for a situation in which nonmaterial culture lags behind changes in the material culture

cultural leveling: the process by which cultures become similar to one another, and especially by which Western industrial culture is imported and diffused into industrializing nations

cultural relativism: understanding a people in the framework of its own culture

cultural universal: a value, norm, or other cultural trait that is found in every group

culture: the language, beliefs, values, norms, behaviors, and even material objects that are passed from one generation to the next

culture shock: the disorientation that people experience when they come in contact with a fundamentally different culture and can no longer depend on their taken-for-granted assumptions about life

ethnocentrism: the use of one's own culture as a yardstick for judging the ways of other individuals or societies, generally leading to a negative evaluation of their values, norms, and behaviors

folkways: norms that are not strictly enforced

gestures: the ways in which people use their bodies to communicate with one another

ideal culture: the ideal values and norms of a people, the goals held out for them

language: a system of symbols that can be combined in an infinite number of ways and can represent not only objects but also abstract thought

material culture: the material objects that distinguish a group of people, such as their art, buildings, weapons, utensils, machines, hairstyles, clothing, and jewelry

mores: norms that are strictly enforced because they are thought essential to core values

negative sanction: an expression of disapproval for breaking a norm, ranging from a mild, informal reaction such as a frown to a formal prison sentence or an execution

new technology: the emerging technologies of an era that have a significant impact on social life

nonmaterial culture: a group's ways of thinking (including its beliefs, values, and other assumptions about the world) and doing (its common patterns of behavior, including language and other forms of interaction)

norms: the expectations, or rules of behavior, that develop out of values

pluralistic society: a society made up of many different groups

positive sanction: a reward given for following norms, ranging from a smile to a prize

real culture: the norms and values that people actually follow

sanctions: expressions of approval or disapproval given to people for upholding or violating norms

Sapir-Whorf hypothesis: Edward Sapir and Benjamin Whorf's hypothesis that language itself creates ways of thinking and perceiving

sociobiology: a framework of thought that views human behavior as the result of natural selection and considers biological characteristics to be the fundamental cause of human behavior

subculture: the values and related behaviors of a group that distinguish its members from the larger culture; a world within a world

symbol: something to which people attach meaning and then use to communicate with others

symbolic culture: another term for nonmaterial culture

taboo: a norm so strong that it brings revulsion if it is violated

technology: in its narrow sense, tools: its broader sense includes the skills or procedures necessary to make and use those tools

value clusters: a series of interrelated values that together form a larger whole

value contradictions: values that conflict with one another; to follow the one means to come into conflict with the other

values: the standards by which people define what is desirable or undesirable, good or bad, beautiful or ugly

☞ KEY PEOPLE

Review the major theoretical contributions or findings of these people.

Charles Darwin: Darwin studied the principles upon which natural selection occurred.

Robert Edgerton: Edgerton attacks the concept of cultural relativism, suggesting that because some cultures endanger their people's health, happiness, or survival, there should be a scale to evaluate cultures on their "quality of life."

Allen & Beatrice Gardner: These psychologists taught American Sign Language to a young female chimpanzee, who not only learned the signs but put them together in simple sentences.

Douglas Massey: This sociologist has studied the impact that immigration is having on Miami, predicting that the city will become the first "truly bilingual" city.

George Murdock: Murdock was an anthropologist who sought to determine cultural values, norms, or traits -- if any -- were found universally across the globe.

William Ogburn: Ogburn coined the term "cultural lag."

Irene Pepperberg: This researcher has taught Alex, an African Gray parrot, to name 80 objects and to tell how many objects there are in groups up to six.

Edward Sapir and Benjamin Whorf: These two anthropologists argued that language not only reflects thoughts and perceptions, but that it actually shapes the way a people think and perceive the world.

JoEllen Shively: This sociologist's research demonstrated that Native American's identification with cowboys in Westerns was based on the symbolism of the West as a free, natural way of life. She discovered that they think of themselves as the real cowboys.

William Sumner: Sumner developed the concept of ethnocentrism.

Robin Williams: He identified twelve core U.S. values.

Edward Wilson: Wilson is an insect specialist who claims that human behavior is also the result of natural selection.

☞ "DOWN-TO-EARTH SOCIOLOGY"

This is your opportunity to apply the sociological perspective to the world around you. The questions in this section refer to material introduced in this chapter of your text. Many ask you to think about ideas and information presented in the various special "boxes" that are located throughout this chapter.

1.   Do you use the Internet to "talk" with your friends? Do you every use some of the "new shorthand" strategies outlined on page 45 to convey your emotions, gestures, and facial expressions? To what extent do these enrich our on-line conversations?

2.   Try applying the Sapir-Whorf hypothesis to the discussion of racial labels (p. 46). How do the terms we use help to shape our consciousness and perceptions of differences? Do you think our views would change if we just eliminated the labels?

3.   In what ways does the presence of two sizeable language groups in Miami create problems ("Cultural Diversity in U.S. Society," p. 48)? Do you think it is important for Americans to learn another language or should others learn English in order to communicate with us?

4.   Were you surprised to learn that Native Americans like Westerns (p. 52)? Given the findings of Shively's research, what would happen if Native Americans were suddenly to be portrayed with the same traits as those associated with cowboys in movies and books about the West?

5.   What is your evaluation of the sociobiology argument (pp. 55-56)? Do you think you were "programmed" from birth to be a certain person and to do specific things in your life? Do you

think people are prisoners of their genes?

6.   Is culture, as we know it, possible among intelligent computers? Why or why not? After reading the "Sociology and New Technology" box on page 60, do you think we will allow ourselves to be replaced by computers? Why or why not?

☞ SELF-TEST

After completing this self-test, check your answers against the Answer Key beginning on page 341 of this Study Guide and against the text on page(s) indicated in parentheses.

MULTIPLE CHOICE QUESTIONS

1.   Which of the following would you use to describe a group's ways of thinking and doing, including language and other forms of interaction? (38)
        a.   material culture.
        b.   nonmaterial culture.
        c.   ideological culture.
        d.   values.

2.   Which of the following is not part of material culture? (38)
        a.   weapons and machines
        b.   eating utensils
        c.   jewelry, hairstyles, and clothing
        d.   language

3.   Which of these statements regarding culture is not true? (39)
        a.   People generally are aware of the effects of their own culture.
        b.   Culture touches almost every aspect of who and what a person is.
        c.   At birth, people do not possess culture.
        d.   Culture is the lens through which we perceive and evaluate what is going on around us.

4.   In the textbook the author describes his reaction to life in Morocco. Which of the following best describes what he was feeling? (39)
        a.   cultural diffusion
        b.   cultural leveling
        c.   cultural relativism
        d.   cultural shock

5.   An American thinks citizens of another country are barbarians if they like to attend bullfights. Which of the following concepts best describes his reaction? (39)
        a.   cultural shock
        b.   cultural relativism
        c.   ethnocentrism
        d.   ethnomethodology

6. Which of the following statements about cultural relativism is <u>incorrect</u>? (40-41)
   a. Cultural relativism does presents a challenge to our ordinary thinking.
   b. None of us can be entirely successful at practicing cultural relativism.
   c. Robert Edgerton argues that we should accept other cultures according to their customs and values.
   d. Cultural relativism is an attempt to appreciate other ways of life.

7. Which of the following statements about gestures is <u>correct</u>? (42-43)
   a. Gestures are studied by anthropologists but not sociologists.
   b. Gestures are universal.
   c. Gestures always facilitate communication between people.
   d. Gestures can lead to misunderstandings and embarrassment.

8. Which of the following makes it possible for human experience to be cumulative and for people to share memories? (43-46)
   a. language
   b. cultural universals
   c. gestures
   d. computers

9. As Eskimo children learn their language they learn distinctions between types of snowfalls in a way that is not apparent to non-Eskimo children. Which of the following perspectives is reflected in this example? (45-46)
   a. sociobiology
   b. the Davis-Moore theory
   c. the Sapir-Whorf hypothesis
   d. the Linguistic perspective

10. Moral holidays are: (47)
    a. times when people can break the norms and not be sanctioned.
    b. often center around people getting drunk and being rowdy.
    c. celebrations like Mardi Gras.
    d. all of the above

11. As you rush from one class to the next, you absentmindedly forget to hold the door open for the person coming through behind you. The consequence is that the door slams in his face. Which of the following cultural components has been violated as a result of your behavior? (48)
    a. taboos
    b. mores
    c. values
    d. folkways

12. Which of the following statements about mores is <u>correct</u>? (48)
    a. Mores are essential to our core values and require conformity.
    b. Mores are norms that are not strictly enforced.
    c. Mores state that a person should not try to pass you on the left side of the sidewalk.
    d. Mores are less important in contemporary societies.

13.   Subcultures: (49)
        a.   are a world within a world.
        b.   have values and related behaviors that set its members apart from the dominant culture.
        c.   include occupational groups.
        d.   All of the above.

14.   Heavy metal adherents who glorify Satanism, cruelty, and sexism would be an example of: (50)
        a.   ethnocentrists.
        b.   perverted people.
        c.   countercultures.
        d.   subcultures.

15.   U.S. society is made up of many different groups. Which of the following terms would a sociologist use to describe this type of society? (50)
        a.   a melting pot
        b.   a pluralist society
        c.   a conflicted society
        d.   a counterculture

16.   Which of the following statements concerning core values is not correct? (50-54)
        a.   They are shared by the many groups that make up U.S. society.
        b.   They include achievement and success, individualism, and progress.
        c.   They change over time.
        d.   They rarely create much conflict as they change.

17.   Which of the following reflects conditions under which value contradictions can occur? (51)
        a.   A value, such as the one that stresses group superiority, comes into direct conflict with other values, such as democracy and equality.
        b.   Societies have very little social change.
        c.   A series of interrelated values bind together to form a larger whole.
        d.   Values blind people to many social circumstances.

18.   According to the author of your text, a new value cluster is emerging in the United States. Which of the following combination of core values make up this new value cluster? (53)
        a.   achievement and success, activity and work, material comfort
        b.   individualism, freedom, democracy, equality
        c.   leisure, self-fulfillment, physical fitness, youngness
        d.   youngness, self-fulfillment, romantic love, material comfort

19.   Which of the following statements about ideal culture is correct? (54-55)
        a.   Ideal culture is a value, norm, or other cultural trait that is found in every group.
        b.   Ideal culture reflects the values and norms which people in a culture attempt to hold.
        c.   Ideal culture is the norms people follow when they know they are being watched.
        d.   Ideal culture is not a sociological concept.

20. Who identified a list of cultural universals? (55)
    a.   Robert Edgerton
    b.   Charles Darwin
    c.   George Murdock
    d.   William Ogburn

21. What is the perspective that views human behavior as the result of natural selection and considers biological characteristics to be the fundamental cause of human behavior? (55)
    a.   natural science
    b.   social science
    c.   anthropology
    d.   sociobiology

22. What would the printing press or the computer be considered? (57)
    a.   revolutionary technologies
    b.   diffused technologies
    c.   examples of cultural leveling
    d.   new technologies

23. There are computer tests that outperform physicians in diagnosing and prescribing treatment, yet most of us still visit doctors and rely on their judgement. What does this situation reflect? (58)
    a.   resistance to new technologies
    b.   cultural diffusion
    c.   the social construction of technology
    d.   cultural lag

24. Today bagels, woks, and hammocks are all a part of U.S. culture. The adoption of these objects illustrates which of the following processes or concepts? (59)
    a.   cultural leveling
    b.   nonmaterial culture
    c.   cultural diffusion
    d.   cultural universals

25. Exporting the Golden Arches of McDonald's around the globe has led to: (59)
    a.   a more diversified menu at McDonald's.
    b.   cultural leveling.
    c.   enrichment of local cultures through contact with U.S. material culture.
    d.   culture shock.

TRUE-FALSE QUESTIONS

T F 1.   Speech, gestures, beliefs and customs usually are taken for granted by people (39)
T F 2.   Culture has little to do with people's ideas of right and wrong. (39-40)
T F 3.   No one can be entirely successful at practicing cultural relativism. (40)
T F 4.   Robert Edgerton is a strong critic of cultural relativism, arguing that cultures should be rated on the basis of their "quality of life." (40)
T F 5.   The gesture of nodding the head up and down to indicate "yes" is universal. (43)

T F   6.   Without language, humans could still successfully plan future events. (44)

T F   7.   Sanctions are positive or negative reactions to the ways people follow norms. (47)

T F   8.   While folkways may change across cultures, mores are universally the same. (48)

T F   9.   Motorcycle enthusiasts who emphasize personal freedom and speed, while maintaining values of success, form part of a counterculture. (48)

T F   10.   Racism and group superiority are core values in U.S. society. (51)

T F   11.   It is not uncommon for some values to conflict with one another. (51)

T F   12.   In her research, JoEllen Shively found that while both Anglos and Native Americans identified with cowboys, the ways in which they identified were quite different. (52)

T F   13.   Concern for the environment has always been a core value in U.S. society. (53)

T F   14.   Core values do not change without meeting strong resistance. (54)

T F   15.   Although certain activities are present in all cultures, the specific customs differ from one group to another. (55)

T F   16.   Most sociologists do not agree with sociobiology. (55-56)

T F   17.   Research by Allen and Beatrice Gardner provides evidence that animals are capable of acquiring language. (57)

T F   18.   While new technologies may affect material culture, including the way things are done in a society, they have only minimal impact on nonmaterial culture, including the way people think and what they value. (57-58)

T F   19.   According to William Ogburn, a group's nonmaterial culture usually changes first, with the material culture lagging behind. (58)

T F   20.   As a result of contacts between different cultural groups, changes occur in the groups' technology or material culture. (58-59)

FILL-IN QUESTIONS

1.   Objects such as art, buildings, weapons, utensils, machines, hairstyles, clothing, and jewelry that distinguish a group of people are known as _____; their ways of thinking and doing are _____. (38)

2.   A _____ is something to which people attach meaning and then use to communicate with others. (42)

3.   _____ is a system of symbols that can be combined in an infinite number of ways and can represent not only objects but also abstract thought. (43)

4.   _____ are ideas of what is desirable in life. (47)

5.   The expectations or rules of behavior that develop out of values are referred to as _____. (47)

6.   A _____ is a norm so strongly ingrained that even the thought of its violation is greeted with revulsion. (49)

7.   The term that describes a world within the larger world of the dominant culture is _____. (49)

8.   _____ are a series of interrelated values that together form a larger whole. (53)

9.   Sociologists call the norms and values that people actually follow _____. (55)

10.   _____ may not exist because even though there are universal human activities, there is no universally accepted way of doing any of them. (55)

11.   In its broader sense, _____ includes the skills or procedures necessary to make and use tools. (57)

12.   Both the printing press and the computer represent _____ because they had a

significant impact on society following their introduction. (57)

13.   William Ogburn used the term _____ to reflect the condition in which not all parts of a culture change at the same pace. (58)

14.   The spread of cultural characteristics from one group to another is _____. (59)

15.   When Western industrial culture is imported and diffused into developing nations, the process is called _____. (59)

MATCH THESE SOCIAL SCIENTISTS WITH THEIR CONTRIBUTIONS

___1. Edward Sapir and Benjamin Whorf   a. *taught language to a parrot*
___2. Robin Williams   b. *introduced the concept of cultural lag*
___3. George Murdock   c. *looked for cultural universals*
___4. Irene Pepperberg   d. *taught chimps a gestural language*
___5. Robert Edgerton   e. *studied Native Americans' identification with Westerns*
___6. Edward Wilson   f. *stated that language shapes perceptions of reality*
___7. William Sumner   g. *believed natural selection produces human behavior*
___8. Allen and Beatrice Gardner   h. *criticized aspects of cultural relativism*
___9. William Ogburn   i. *noted core values of U.S. society*
__10. JoEllen Shively   j. *developed the concept of ethnocentrism*

ESSAY QUESTIONS

1.   Explain cultural relativism and discuss both the advantages and disadvantages of practicing it.

2.   Consider the degree to which the real culture of the United States falls short of the ideal culture. Provide concrete examples to support your essay.

3.   Evaluate what is gained and what is lost as technology advances in society.

CHAPTER 3
SOCIALIZATION

☞ CHAPTER SUMMARY

- Scientists have attempted to determine how much of people's characteristics come from heredity and how much from the social environment. Observations of feral, isolated, and institutionalized children help to answer this question. These studies have concluded that language and intimate interaction are essential to the development of human characteristics.

- Charles H. Cooley, George H. Mead, Jean Piaget, Lawrence Kohlberg, Carol Gilligan and Sigmund Freud provide insights into the social development of human beings. The work of Cooley and Mead demonstrates that the self is created through our interactions with others. Piaget identified four stages in the development of our ability to reason: (1) sensorimotor; (2) pre-operational; (3) concrete operational; and (4) formal operational. Kohlberg and Gilligan focused on the development of morality. Freud defined the personality in terms of the id, ego, and superego; personality developed as the inborn desires (id) clashed with social constraints (superego); the ego develops to balance the id and the superego.

- Socialization influences not only *how* we express our emotions, but *what* emotions we feel.

- Gender socialization is a primary means of controlling human behavior, and a society's ideals of sex-linked behaviors are reinforced by its social institutions.

- The main agents of socialization--family, religion, day care, school, peer groups, the mass media, sports, and the workplace--together contribute to our socialization, enabling us to become full-fledged members of society.

- Resocialization is the process of learning new norms, values, attitudes and behaviors. Intense resocialization takes place in total institutions. Most resocialization is voluntary, but some is involuntary.

- Socialization, which begins at birth, continues throughout the life course; at each stage the individual must adjust to a new set of social expectations.

- Although socialization lays down the basic self and is modified by our social location, humans are not robots but rational beings who consider options and make choices.

☞ LEARNING OBJECTIVES

As you read Chapter 3, use these learning objectives to organize your notes. After completing your reading, briefly state an answer to each of the objectives, and review the text pages in parentheses.

1. Discuss major studies of feral, isolated, and institutionalized children, as well as studies of deprived animals, and state what they demonstrate about the importance of early contact with other humans for the social development of children. (64-68)

2. Define socialization. (68)

3. Distinguish between the theories of human development offered by Charles H. Cooley, George H. Mead, Jean Piaget, Lawrence Kohlberg and Carol Gilligan and consider the limits of applying these individuals' work to cultures around the globe. (68-72)

4. Review Freud's theory of personality development, noting what sociologists appreciate about this theory as well as their criticisms of it. (72-73)

5.   Summarize the research on the universal nature of emotions, the role of socialization in the expression of emotions, and the relationship between socialization into emotions and social control. (73-76)

6.   Describe ways in which gender socialization by the family channels human behavior. (76)

7.   Identify the ways in which cultural stereotypes of the sexes are perpetuated in the mass media and how peer groups use media images to construct ideas about gender appropriate behavior. (76-79)

8.   List and describe the influence of each agent of socialization on individuals. (79-84)

9.   Define the term resocialization and discuss the process of resocialization that takes place within total institutions. (84-86)

10.   Discuss socialization through the life course by summarizing each of the stages. (86-91)

11.   Explain why human beings are not prisoners of socialization. (91)

☞ CHAPTER OUTLINE

I.   **What Is Human Nature?**
   A.   For centuries, people have tried to find an answer to the question of what is human about human nature.
   B.   In trying to find out how much of our behavior is inherited and how much is a result of our social environment, identical twins and children who have been raised with minimal human contact have been studied.

II.   **Feral Children**
   A.   Feral (wild) children, supposedly abandoned or lost by their parents at a very early age and then raised by animals, act like wild animals. Most social scientists believe that they were raised by their parents as infants but then abandoned because of mental retardation.
   B.   Isolated children show what humans might be like if secluded from society at an early age. Isabelle is a case in point. Although initially believed to be retarded, a surprising thing happened when she was given intensive language training. She began to acquire language and in only two years she had reached the normal intellectual level for her age.
   C.   Institutionalized children show that traits such as intelligence, cooperative behavior, and friendliness are the result of early close relations with other humans. Research with children raised in orphanages and cases like Genie, the 13 ½-year-old who had been kept locked in a small room for years, demonstrate the importance of early interaction for human development.
   D.   Studies of monkeys raised in isolation have reached similar results. The longer and more severe the isolation, the more difficult adjustment becomes.
   E.   Babies do not "naturally" develop into human adults; although their bodies grow, human interaction is required for them to acquire the traits we consider normal for human beings.

III.   **Socialization into Self, Mind, and Emotions**
   A.   Socialization is the process by which we learn the ways of our society.
   B.   Charles H. Cooley (1864-1929) concluded that human development is socially created--that our sense of self develops from interaction with others. He coined the term "looking-glass self" to describe this process.
      1.   According to Cooley, this process contains three steps: (1) we imagine how we look to others; (2) we interpret others' reactions (how they evaluate us); and (3) we develop a self-concept.
      2.   A favorable reflection in the "social mirror" leads to a positive self-concept, while

a negative reflection leads to a negative self-concept.

   3. Even if we misjudge others' reactions, the misjudgments become part of our self-concept.

   4. This development process is an ongoing, lifelong process.

C. George H. Mead (1863-1931) agreed with Cooley, but added that play is critical to the development of a self. In play, we learn to take the role of others: to understand and anticipate how others feel and think.

   1. Mead concluded that children are first able to take only the role of significant others (parents or siblings, for example); as the self develops, children internalize the expectations of other people, and eventually the entire group. Mead referred to the norms, values, attitudes and expectations of people "in general" as the generalized other.

   2. According to Mead, the development of the self goes through stages: (1) imitation (children initially can only mimic the gestures and words of others); (2) play (beginning at age three, children play the roles of specific people, such as a firefighter or the Lone Ranger); and (3) games (in the first years of school, children become involved in organized team games and must learn the role of each member of the team).

   3. He distinguished the "I" from the "me" in development of the self: the "I" component is the subjective, active, spontaneous, creative part of the social self (for instance, "I shoved him"), while the "me" component is the objective part--attitudes internalized from interactions with others (for instance, "He shoved me").

   4. Mead concluded that not only the self but also the mind is a social product. We cannot think without symbols--and it is our society that gives us our symbols by giving us our language.

D. After years of research, Jean Piaget (1896-1980) concluded that there are four stages in the development of cognitive skills.

   1. The sensorimotor stage (0-2): Understanding is limited to direct contact with the environment (touching, listening, seeing).

   2. The preoperational stage (2-7): Children develop the ability to use symbols (especially language) which allow them to experience things without direct contact.

   3. The concrete operational stage (7-12): Reasoning abilities become much more developed. Children now can understand numbers, causation, and speed, but have difficulty with abstract concepts such as truth.

   4. The formal operational stage (12+): Children become capable of abstract thinking, and can use rules to solve abstract problems ("If X is true, why doesn't Y follow?").

E. Psychologist Lawrence Kohlberg concluded that humans go through a sequence of stages in the development of morality.

   1. The amoral stage is when the child does not distinguish between right and wrong.

   2. The preconventional stage is when the child follows the rules in order to stay out of trouble.

   3. The conventional stage is when the child follows the norms and values of society.

   4. The post-coventional stage is when the child reflects on abstract principles of right and wrong, using these principles to judge behavior.

F. Carol Gilligan studied differences between males and females in how they view morality.

       1.   She found that females tend to evaluate morality in terms of personal relationships and how actions will affect others.

       2.   Males think in terms of abstract principles of right and wrong.

       3.   Other researchers tested Gilligan's conclusions and found no gender differences. Based on this subsequent work, Gilligan no longer supports her original position.

G.   While it appears that the looking glass self, role taking and the social mind are universal phenomenon, there is not consensus about the universality of Piaget's four stages of cognitive development.

       1.   Some adults never appear to reach the fourth stage, whether due to particular social experiences or to biology.

       2.   The content of what we learn varies from one culture to another; with very different experiences and the thinking processes that revolve around these experiences, we can not assume that the developmental sequences will be the same for everyone.

H.   Sigmund Freud (1856-1939) believed that personality consists of three elements--the id, ego, and superego.

       1.   The id, inherited drives for self-gratification, demands fulfillment of basic needs such as attention, safety, food, and sex.

       2.   The ego balances between the needs of the id and the demands of society.

       3.   The superego, the social conscience we have internalized from social groups, gives us feelings of guilt or shame when we break rules, and feelings of pride and self-satisfaction when we follow them.

       4.   Sociologists object to Freud's view that inborn and unconscious motivations are the primary reasons for human behavior, for this view denies the central tenet of sociology: that social factors shape people's behaviors.

I.   Emotions are not simply the result of biology; they also depend on socialization within a particular society.

       1.   Anthropologist Paul Ekman concluded that everyone experiences six basic emotions: anger, disgust, fear, happiness, sadness, and surprise.

       2.   The expression of emotions varies according to gender, social class and culture.

       3.   Socialization not only leads to different ways of expressing emotions, but even to what we feel.

J.   Most socialization is meant to turn us into conforming members of society. We do some things and not others as a result of socialization. When we contemplate an action, we know the emotion (good or bad) that would result; thus, society sets up controls on our behavior.

IV.   Socialization Into Gender

A.   By expecting different behaviors from people because they are male or female, society nudges boys and girls in separate directions from an early age, and this foundation carries over into adulthood.

B.   Parents begin the process; researchers have concluded that in our society mothers unconsciously reward their female children for being passive and dependent and their male children for being active and independent.

C.   The mass media reinforce society's expectations of gender in many ways:

       1.   Ads perpetuate stereotypes by portraying males as dominant and rugged and females as sexy and submissive.

       2.   On TV, male characters outnumber females two to one and are more likely to be portrayed in higher-status positions.

3. Males are much more likely than females to play video games; we have no studies of how these games affect their players' ideas of gender.

4. Sociologist Melissa Milkie concluded that males use media images to discover who they were and what was expected of them as males.

V. **Agents of Socialization**

A. Our experiences in the family have a life-long impact on us, laying down a basic sense of self, motivation, values, and beliefs.

1. Parents--often unaware of what they are doing--send subtle messages to their children about society's expectations for them as males or females.

2. Research by Melvin Kohn suggests that there are social class and occupational differences in child-rearing. The main concern of working-class parents often is their children's outward conformity while middle-class parents show greater concern for the motivations for their children's behavior. The type of job held by the parent is also a factor: the more closely supervised the job is, the more likely the parent is to insist on outward conformity.

B. The neighborhood has an impact on children's development. Some neighborhoods are better for children to grow up in than other neighborhoods.

C. Religion plays a major role in the socialization of most Americans, even if they are not raised in a religious family. Religion especially influences morality, but also ideas about the dress, speech, and manners that are appropriate.

D. With more mothers today working for wages, day care is now a significant agent of socialization.

1. Researchers have found that the effects of day care depend on the child's background and the quality of the care provided.

2. Overall, the research findings suggest that children living in poverty and from dysfunctional families benefit from day care.

3. Children in better quality day care interact better with children and have fewer behavioral problems.

4. One national study of young children found that the more hours per week that children were in day care, the weaker the bond between mother and child and the more negative their interactions. While the findings of this study are indisputable, the explanation for them is another matter.

E. Schools serve many manifest (intended) functions for society, including teaching skills and values thought to be appropriate. Schools also have several latent (unintended) functions.

1. At school children are placed outside the direct control of friends/relatives and exposed to new values and ways of looking at the world. They learn universality, or that the same rules apply to everyone.

2. Schools also have a hidden curriculum: values not explicitly taught but inherent in school activities. For example, the wording of stories may carry messages about patriotism and democracy; by teaching that our economic system is just, schools may teach children to believe problems such as poverty are never caused by oppression and exploitation.

F. One of the most significant aspects of education is that it exposes children to peer groups. A peer group is a group of people of roughly the same age who share common interests. Next to the family, peer groups are the most powerful socializing force in society.

1. Research by Patricia and Peter Adler document how peer groups enable children to resist the efforts of parents and schools to socialize them their way.

2.   It is almost impossible to go against a peer group, whose cardinal rule is to conform or be rejected. As a result, the standards of peer groups tend to dominate our lives.

G.   Sports are also powerful socializing agents; children are taught not only physical skills but also values.

H.   The workplace is a major agent of socialization for adults; from jobs, we learn not only skills but also matching attitudes and values. We may engage in anticipatory socialization, learning to play a role before actually entering it, and enabling us to gradually identify with the role.

VI.   Resocialization

A.   Resocialization refers to the process of learning new norms, values, attitudes and behaviors. Resocialization in its most common form occurs each time we learn something contrary to our previous experiences, such as going to work in a new job. It can be an intense experience, although it does not have to be.

B.   Erving Goffman used the term total institution to refer to places--such as boot camps, prisons, concentration camps, or some mental hospitals, religious cults, and boarding schools--where people are cut off from the rest of society and are under almost total control of agents of the institution.

1.   A person entering the institution is greeted with a degradation ceremony which may include fingerprinting, shaving the head, banning personal items, and being forced to strip and wear a uniform. In this way his current identity is stripped away and a new identity is created.

2.   Total institutions are quite effective as a result of isolating people from outside influences and information; supervising their activities; suppressing previous roles, statuses, and norms, and replacing them with new rules and values; and controlling rewards and punishments.

VII.   Socialization Through the Life Course

A.   Socialization occurs throughout a person's entire lifetime and can be broken up into different stages.

B.   Childhood (birth to 12): In earlier times, children were seen as miniature adults, who served an apprenticeship. To keep them in line, they were beaten and subjected to psychological torture. Industrialization changed the way we see children. The current view is that children are tender and innocent, and parents should guide the physical, emotional, and social development of their children, while providing them with care, comfort, and protection.

C.   Adolescence (13-17): Economic changes resulting from the Industrial Revolution brought about material surpluses that allowed millions of teenagers to remain outside the labor force, while at the same time the demand for education increased. Biologically equipped for both work and marriage but denied both, adolescents suffer inner turmoil and develop their own standards of clothing, hairstyles, language, music, and other claims to separate identities.

D.   Young Adulthood (18-29): Adult responsibilities are postponed through extended education. During this period the self becomes more stable, and the period usually is one of high optimism.

E.   The Middle Years (30-65): This can be separated into two periods.

1.   Early Middle Years (30-49): People are surer of themselves and their goals in life than before, but severe jolts, such as divorce or being fired, can occur. For U.S.

women, it can be a trying period as they try to "have it all"--job, family, and everything.

2.   Later Middle Years (50-65): A different view of life--trying to evaluate the past and coming to terms with what lies ahead--emerges. Individuals may feel they are not likely to get much farther in life, while health and mortality become concerns. However, for most people it is the most comfortable period in their entire lives.

F.   Older years (66 and beyond): This can also be separated into two periods.

1.   The Early Older Years: Improvements in nutrition, public health, and medical care delay the onset of old age. For many, this period is an extension of middle years. Those who still work or are socially active are unlikely to see themselves as old.

2.   The Later Older Years: This period is marked by growing frailty and illness, and eventually death.

G.   The social significance of the life course is how it is shaped by social factors--the time period in which the person is born and lives his or her life as well as social location, the individual's social class, gender and race.

VIII.   Are We Prisoners of Socialization?

A.   Sociologists do not think of people as little robots who simply are the result of their exposure to socializing agents. Although socialization is powerful, and profoundly affects us all, we have a self, and the self is dynamic. Each of us uses his or her own mind to reason and make choices.

B.   In this way, each of us is actively involved even in the social construction of the Self. Our experiences have an impact on us, but we are not doomed to keep our orientations if we do not like them.

☞ KEY TERMS

After studying the chapter, review the definition for each of the following terms.

agents of socialization: people or groups that affect our self-concept, attitudes or other orientations towards life

anticipatory socialization: because one anticipates a future role, one learns part of it now

degradation ceremony: a term coined by Harold Garfinkel to describe an attempt to remake the self by stripping away an individual's self-identity and stamping a new identity in its place

ego: Freud's term for a balancing force between the id and the demands of society

feral children: children assumed to have been raised by animals, in the wilderness isolated from other humans

gender role: the behaviors and attitudes considered appropriate because one is male or female

gender socialization: the ways in which society sets children onto different courses in life because they are male or female

generalized other: the norms, values, attitudes, and expectations of people "in general;" the child's ability to take the role of the generalized other is a significant step in the development of a self

id: Freud's term for our inborn basic drives

latent function: the unintended consequences of people's actions that help to keep a social system in equilibrium

life course: the stages of our life as we go from birth to death

looking-glass self: a term coined by Charles Horton Cooley to refer to the process by which our self develops through internalizing others' reactions to us

manifest function: the intended consequences of people's actions designed to help some part of the social system

mass media: forms of communication, such as radio, newspapers, and television, that are directed to mass audiences

peer group: a group of individuals roughly the same age linked by common interests

personal identity kit: items people use to decorate their bodies

resocialization: process of learning new norms, values, attitudes, and behaviors

self: the unique human capacity of being able to see ourselves "from the outside;" the picture we gain of how others see us

significant other: an individual who significantly influences someone else's life

social environment: the entire human environment, including direct contact with others

social inequality: a social condition in which privileges and obligations are given to some but denied to others

socialization: the process by which people learn the characteristics of their group--the attitudes, values, and actions thought appropriate for them

superego: Freud's term for the conscience, the internalized norms and values of our social groups

taking the role of the other: putting oneself in someone else's shoes; understanding how someone else feels and thinks and thus anticipating how that person will act

total institution: a place in which people are cut off from the rest of society and are almost totally controlled by the officials who run the place

☞ KEY PEOPLE

Review the major theoretical contributions or findings of these people.

Patricia and Peter Adler: These sociologists have documented how peer groups socialize children into gender-appropriate behavior.

Charles H. Cooley: Cooley studied the development of the self, coining the term "the looking-glass self."

Paul Ekman: This anthropologist studied emotions in several countries and concluded that people everywhere experience six basic emotions--anger, disgust, fear, happiness, sadness, and surprise.

Sigmund Freud: Freud developed a theory of personality development that took into consideration inborn drives (id), the internalized norms and values of one's society (superego), and the individual's ability to balance the two competing forces (ego).

Carol Gilligan: Gilligan was uncomfortable with Kohlberg's conclusions regarding the development of morality because they did not match her own experiences. She studied gender differences in morality, concluding that men and women use different criteria in evaluating morality.

Erving Goffman: Goffman studied the process of resocialization within total institutions.

Susan Goldberg and Michael Lewis: Two psychologists studied how parents' unconscious expectations about gender behavior are communicated to their young children.

Harry and Margaret Harlow: These psychologists studied the behavior of monkeys raised in isolation and found that the length of time they were isolated affected their ability to overcome its effects.

Lawrence Kohlberg: This psychologist studied the development of morality, concluding that individuals go through a sequence of developmental stages.

Melvin Kohn: Kohn has done extensive research on the social class differences in child-rearing patterns.

George Herbert Mead: Mead emphasized the importance of play in the development of the self, noting that children learn to take on the role of the other and eventually learn to perceive themselves as others do.

Michael Messner: Messner interviewed former male professional athletes and other men for whom sports provided a central identity during adolescence in order to determine what role sports plays in male socialization.

Melissa Milkie: This sociologist studied how adolescent boys use media images to discover who they are as males.

Jean Piaget: Piaget studied the development of reasoning skills in children.

H.M. Skeels and H.B. Dye: These two psychologists studied the impact that close social interaction had on the social and intellectual development of institutionalized children.

☞ "DOWN-TO-EARTH SOCIOLOGY"

This is your opportunity to apply the sociological perspective to the world around you. The questions in this section refer to material introduced in this chapter of your text. Many ask you to think about ideas and information presented in the various special "boxes" that are located throughout this chapter.

1.   What do studies of identical twins tell us about heredity and environment (p. 65)? Do you know any identical twins? How are they similar? How are they different?
2.   Think about learning the emotions that are appropriate for you because of your age, race or ethnicity, gender, and social class background. How were you socialized into emotions; for example, "little boys don't cry" and "little girls don't fight!"?
3.   After reading about the Ik on page 75, do you think that money is becoming more important than values in our own society? What are the social conditions that have contributed to our obsession with achievement and material goods? Do you think that eventually we will lose the ability to perceive truth, beauty, and goodness?
4.   Have you ever played video games? Have you ever thought about the images of gender that these games convey? Would you agree with the author when he suggests that the gender change is mostly one-way, with females adopting traditional male characteristics (p. 78)?
5.   Why is it problematic to be caught between two worlds, like Richard Rodriguez was (p. 82)? Do you consider yourself to be caught between two worlds? What are those worlds?
6.   How would you characterize your own experiences with sports (p. 85)? For the males who are reading this: If you have played sports, what role have they played in your socialization? If you haven't, do you feel you missed out? For the females reading this: If you played a sport, were your experiences similar to those related by the researcher? Why or why not?
7.   What kinds of things did you do in anticipation of being in college? In your first few months in school, what kinds of things did you have to learn that were new or different?
8.   What are some of the ways in which boot camp resocializes recruits (p. 87)? What are some degradation ceremonies? What is the point of subjecting recruits to this experience?
9.   What are some of the challenges facing you at whatever stage in the life course you are at right now? How have changes in society contributed to these challenges?

☞ SELF-TEST

After completing this self-test, check your answers against the Answer Key beginning on page 344 of this Study Guide and against the text on page (s) indicated in parentheses.

MULTIPLE CHOICE QUESTIONS

1.   Which of the following statements best describes feral children? (64)
        a.   After their parents supposedly abandoned or lost them, they were raised by someone else.
        b.   They supposedly were abandoned or lost by their parents and then raised by animals.
        c.   Most social scientiest consider them significant for our understanding of human nature.
        d.   They quickly recovered from their experiences of deprivation once they were rescued.

2.   What conclusions can be drawn from the case of Isabelle? (64-65)
        a.   Humans have no natural language.
        b.   Isabelle was retarded.
        c.   A person who has been isolated cannot progress through normal learning stages.
        d.   All of the above.

3.   What conclusions can be made from Skeels and Dye's study of institutionalized children? (66-67)
        a.   Mental retardation was biological.
        b.   Early physical contact did little to change the intelligence levels of these children.
        c.   The absence of stimulating social interaction was the basic cause of low intelligence among these children, not some biological incapacity.
        d.   Children who are cared for by a mentally retarded adult will "learn" to be retarded, while those who are cared for by professional staff will not.

4.   What do studies of isolated rhesus monkeys demonstrate? (67-68)
        a.   The monkeys were able to adjust to monkey life after a time.
        b.   They instinctively knew how to enter into "monkey interaction" with other monkeys.
        c.   They knew how to engage in sexual intercourse.
        d.   The monkeys were not able to adjust fully to monkey life and did not know instinctively how to enter into interaction with other monkeys.

5.   Which of the following statements about the looking-glass self is incorrect? (68-69)
        a.   The development of self is an ongoing, lifelong process.
        b.   We move beyond the looking-glass self as we mature.
        c.   The process of the looking-glass self applies to old age.
        d.   The self is always in process.

6.   According to Mead's theory, at what stage do children pretend to take the roles of specific people such as the Lone Ranger, Supergirl, or Batman? (70)
        a.   imitation
        b.   game
        c.   play
        d.   generalized other

7.   To George Mead, what is the "I"? (70)
        a.   It is the self as subject.
        b.   It is the self as object.
        c.   It is the same as the id.
        d.   It represents the passive robot aspect of human behavior.

8.   According to Jean Piaget, at what stage do children develop the ability to use symbols? (71)
     a.   sensorimotor
     b.   preoperational
     c.   concrete operational
     d.   formal operational

9.   Larry is 8 years old. He tries very hard to be nice to his younger sister, because he knows that his mother gets very upset when the two of them fight and hit each other. According to Lawrence Kohlberg, which stage of moral development is reflected in Larry's behavior? (71-72)
     a.   amoral
     b.   preconventional
     c.   conventional
     d.   post-conventional

10. Gilligan's early research suggests that women evaluate morality in terms of: (72)
     a.   abstract principles.
     b.   a code of ethics.
     c.   personal relationships.
     d.   concrete values.

11. What is the term Freud used to describe the balancing force between the inborn drives for self-gratification and the demands of society? (73)
     a.   id
     b.   superego
     c.   ego
     d.   libido

12. Which of the following statements about emotions is correct? (73-74)
     a.   People around the world feel the same emotions and express them in the same way.
     b.   How we express emotions depends on our culture and our social location.
     c.   For the most part, emotions are the result of biology.
     d.   Socialization has little to do with emotions.

13. According to this chapter, what is one of the most effective ways in which society sets controls over our behavior? (74-75)
     a.   hiring police officers and other law enforcement officials
     b.   defining those who do not abide by the rules as "deviants"
     c.   socializing us into self and emotions
     d.   using the media effectively

14. What do we call the ways in which society sets children onto different courses for life purely because they are male or female? (76)
     a.   sex socialization
     b.   gender socialization
     c.   masculinization and feminization
     d.   brainwashing

15. What conclusions did psychologists Susan Goldberg and Michael Lewis reach after observing mothers with their six-month-old infants in a laboratory setting? (76)
   a. The mothers kept their male children closer to them.
   b. They kept their male and female children about the same distance from them.
   c. They touched and spoke more to their sons.
   d. They unconsciously rewarded daughters for being passive and dependent.

16. Which of the following statements reflects the findings of research by Melissa Milkie? (77)
   a. Young males actively used media images to help them understand what was expected of them as males in our society.
   b. Young males avoided talking about male images in television and movies because they wanted to avoid being labeled a "weenie."
   c. Young females are passive consumers of media images, rather than active ones.
   d. Young males were very similar to young females in how they used media images as role models for "cool" behavior.

17. What do middle-class parents try to develop in their children, according to Melvin Kohn? (79-80)
   a. outward conformity
   b. neatness and cleanliness
   c. curiosity, self-expression, and self-control
   d. obedience to rules

18. What is it that participation in religious services teaches us? (80)
   a. beliefs about the hereafter
   b. ideas about dress
   c. speech and manners appropriate for formal occasions
   d. All of the above

19. Which of the following statements summarizes the research findings on the impact that day care has on preschool children? (80-81)
   a. Regardless of the quality, day care benefits children.
   b. Children from poor and dysfunctional families do not benefit from day care, while children from stable families do.
   c. Children from stable families receive no clear benefits or harm from day care, but children from poor and dysfunctional families benefit from quality day care.
   d. It is not the quality of the day care, but the quality of home life that makes the difference.

20. What is it that teachers are doing when they teach young people to think that social problems, such as poverty and homelessness, have nothing to do with economic power, oppression and exploitation? (82)
   a. following the formal curriculum
   b. teaching the hidden curriculum
   c. fulfilling a manifest function of education
   d. satisfying a latent function of education

21. What conclusions can be drawn about peer groups and academic achievement from Adler and Adler's research? (83)
    a. Both boys and girls avoid doing well academically.
    b. Boys want to do well academically in order to boost their standing in the peer group, but girls avoid being labeled as smart, because it will hurt their image.
    c. Both boys and girls believe that good grades will translate into greater popularity among their respective peer groups.
    d. For boys, to do well academically is to lose popularity, while for girls, getting good grades increases social standing.

22. Under which of the following conditions is resocialization likely to occur ? (84)
    a. When we take a new job.
    b. If we were to join a cult.
    c. When we are sent to military boot camp.
    d. All of the above would involve resocialization.

23. Which of the following statements about total institutions is <u>incorrect</u>? (84-85)
    a. They suppress preexisting statuses, so that the inmates will learn that previous roles mean nothing and that the only thing that counts is their current role.
    b. They are not very effective in stripping away people's personal freedom.
    c. They are isolated, with barriers to keep inmates in and keep outsiders from interfering.
    d. They suppress the norms of the "outside world," replacing them with their own values, rules and interpretations.

24. What is it that historians have concluded about childhood? (86-87)
    a. It has always existed as a special time in a child's life.
    b. It was not as harsh in the past as it is today.
    c. It didn't exist in the past, as we know it; children were viewed miniature adults.
    d. It was longer in the past, because children stayed home until they were married.

25. For many people, which stage is likely to be the most comfortable period of their entire lives? (90)
    a. young adulthood
    b. early middle years
    c. later middle years
    d. early older years

TRUE-FALSE QUESTIONS

T F 1. Without language, there can be no culture. (66)

T F 2. Studies of institutionalized children demonstrate that some of the characteristics that we take for granted as being "human" traits result from our basic instincts. (66-67)

T F 3. Because monkeys and humans are so similar, it is possible to reach conclusions about human behavior from animal studies. (68)

T F 4. George H. Mead introduced the concept of the generalized other to sociology. (69)

T F 5. Despite research that demonstrates both men and women use personal relationships and abstract principles when they make moral judgments, Gilligan stands behind her original claims of gender differences. (72)

T F   6.   According to Freud, the ego is the balancing force between the id and the demands of society that suppress it. (73)

T F   7.   Since emotions are natural human responses, socialization has very little to do with how we feel. (73-74)

T F   8.   Much of our socialization is intended to turn us into conforming members of society. (74-75)

T F   9.   Parents may give their sons and daughters different toys to play with, but they do not have different expectations about how they will behave or the kind of play in which they engage. (76)

T F   10.   Advertisements continue to perpetuate gender stereotypes by portraying males as dominant and rugged and females as sexy and submissive. (77)

T F   11.   Researchers have found that video games have a profound impact on their players' ideas of gender. (77)

T F   12.   The benefits of day care depend on the child's background. (80-81)

T F   13.   A latent function of education is transmitting the skills and values appropriate for earning a living. (81)

T F   14.   Next to the family, the peer group is the most powerful socializing force in society. (83)

T F   15.   Resocialization always requires learning a radically different perspective. (84)

T F   16.   Total institutions are very effective in stripping away people's personal freedom. (86)

T F   17.   Adolescence is a social creation in industrialized societies. (88)

T F   18.   In the middle years, some U.S. women find that "having it all" may be somewhat a myth. (89)

T F   19.   Industrialization brought with it a delay in the onset of old age. (90)

T F   20.   Most sociologists view humans as little robots: the socialization goes in and the expected behavior comes out. (91)

FILL-IN QUESTIONS

1.   Sociologists are interested in studying how _____ influence the development of human characteristics. (64)

2.   _____ is the process by which people learn the characteristics of their group--the attitudes, values, and actions thought appropriate for them. (68)

3.   Charles H. Cooley coined the term _____ to describe the process by which a sense of self develops. (69)

4.   _____ is the term Mead used to describe someone, such as a parent and/or a sibling, who plays a major role in our social development. (69)

5.   According to George Herbert Mead, the development of the self through role-taking goes through three stages: (1) _____ ; (2) _____; and (3) _____. (70)

6.   The idea that personality consists of the id, ego, and superego was developed by _____. (72-73)

7.   We refer to the behaviors and attitudes which are considered appropriate for females and males as _____. (76)

8.   Television, music, and advertising are all types of _____ which reinforce society's expectations of gender. (76)

9.   _____ include the family, school, religion, peers, mass media, and workplace. (79)

10.   Reading, writing, and arithmetic are all part of the _____ of education. (81)

11.   The _____ refers to values that may not be taught explicitly, but nevertheless form an

inherent part of a school's "message." (82)

12. _____ are made up of individuals the same age linked by common interests. (83)
13. The mental rehearsal for some future activity, or learning to play a role before actually entering it, is referred to as _____ . (84)
14. Resocialization generally takes place in _____ such as boot camps, prisons, and concentration camps. (84)
15. _____ refers to the attempt to remake the self by stripping away an individual's self-identity and stamping a new identity in its place. (84)

MATCH THESE SOCIAL SCIENTISTS WITH THEIR CONTRIBUTIONS

___1. Melvin Kohn
___2. Erving Goffman
___3. George Herbert Mead
___4. Charles H. Cooley
___5. Jean Piaget
___6. Harry and Margaret Harlow
___7. Sigmund Freud
___8. Melissa Milkie

a. *coined the term "looking-glass self"*
b. *conducted studies of isolated rhesus monkeys*
c. *coined the term "generalized other"*
d. *studied total institutions*
e. *found social class differences in child rearing*
f. *asserted that human behavior is based on unconscious drives*
g. *discovered that there are four stages in cognitive development*
h. *studied the impact of media messages on adolescent males*

ESSAY QUESTIONS

1. Explain what is necessary in order for us to develop into full human beings.

2. Why do sociologists argue that socialization is a process and not a product?

3. How would you answer the question "Are We Prisoners of Socialization?"

CHAPTER 4
SOCIAL STRUCTURE AND SOCIAL INTERACTION

☞ CHAPTER SUMMARY

- There are two levels of sociological analysis; macrosociology investigates the large-scale features of social structure, while microsociology focuses on social interaction. Functional and conflict theorists tend to use a macrosociological approach while symbolic interactionists are more likely to use a macrosociological approach.

- The term social structure refers to a society's framework, which forms an envelop around us and sets limits on our behavior. The individual's location in the social structure affects his or her perceptions, attitudes, and behaviors. Culture, social class, social status, roles, groups, and institutions are the major components of the social structure.

- Social institutions are the organized and standard means that a society develops to meet its basic needs. Functionalists view social institutions as established ways of meeting universal group needs; however, conflict theorists see social institutions as the primary means by which the elite maintains its privileged position.

- Over time, social structure undergoes changes. Sometimes this change is very dramatic, as illustrated by Durkheim's concepts of mechanical and organic solidarity and Tönnies' constructs of *Gemeinschaft* and *Gesellschaft*.

- In contrast to functionalist and conflict theorists who, as macrosociologists, focus on the "big picture," symbolic interactionists tend to be microsociologists who look at social interaction in everyday life. They examine how people look at things and how that, in turn, affects their behavior.

- Stereotypes, assumptions we make about others based on their visible characteristics, guide our behavior toward them; they, in turn, are influenced to behave in ways that reinforce our stereotypes.

- Symbolic interactionists note that each of us is surrounded by a "personal bubble" that we carefully protect. The size of the bubble varies from one culture to another. Americans have four different "distance zones": intimate, personal, social, and public.

- The dramaturgical analysis provided by Erving Goffman analyzes everyday life in terms of the stage. At the core of this approach is the analysis of the impressions we attempt to make on others by using sign-vehicles (setting, appearance, and manner), teamwork, and face-saving behavior.

- Ethnomethodologists try to uncover our background assumptions which provide us with basic ideas about the way life is. The social construction of reality refers to how we each create a view, or understanding, of our world.

- Both macrosociology and microsociology are needed to understand human behavior because we must grasp both social structure and social interaction.

☞ LEARNING OBJECTIVES
As you read Chapter 4, use these learning objectives to organize your notes. After completing your reading, briefly state an answer to each of the objectives, and review the text pages in parentheses.

1. Differentiate between macrosociology and microsociology and indicate which are most likely to be used by functionalists, conflict theorists, and symbolic interactionists. (96-97)

2. Discuss social structure and explain how one's location in this structure affects that person's perceptions, attitudes, and behaviors. (97-98)

3. Define the following concepts: culture, social class, social status, roles, and groups. (98-102)

4. Explain what social institutions are and why they are sociologically significant, identify the social institutions common to industrialized and post-industrialized societies, and summarize the basic features of each. (102-104)

5. Compare and contrast functionalists' and conflict theorists' views of social institutions. (105-106)

6. Use Durkheim's concepts of mechanical and organic solidarity and Tönnies' typology of *Gemeinschaft* and *Gesellschaft* to explain what holds societies together, and discuss their continuing relevance. (106-108)

7. Using the microsociological perspective of symbolic interactionism, explain how stereotypes influence an individual's expectations and behavior, and how personal space, touching, and eye contact are used differently in different cultures. (108-112)

8. Outline the key components of the dramaturgical view of everyday life and discuss how we manage our impression using sign-vehicles, teamwork, and face-saving behavior. (113-117)

9. Discuss what background assumptions are, according to ethnomethodology. (117-118)

10. Explain what "the social construction of reality" means and how this is related to the Thomas theorem. (118-120)

11. Indicate why macrosociology and microsociology are both needed to understand social life. (121)

☞ CHAPTER OUTLINE

I. **Levels of Sociological Analysis**
    A. Macrosociology places the focus on large-scale features of social structure. It investigates large-scale social forces and the effects they have on entire societies and the groups within them. It is utilized by functionalist and conflict theorists.
    B. Microsociology places the emphasis on social interaction, or what people do when they come together. Symbolic interactionism is an example.
    C. Each yields distinctive perspectives, and both are needed to gain a more complete understanding of social life.

II. **The Macrosociological Perspective: Social Structure**
    A. Social structure is defined as the patterned relationships between people that persist over time. Behaviors and attitudes are determined by our location in the social structure. Components of social structure are culture, social class, social status, roles, groups, and institutions.
    B. Culture refers to a group's language, beliefs, values, behaviors, and gestures. It includes the material objects used by a group. It determines what kind of people we will become.
    C. Social class is based on income, education, and occupational prestige. Large numbers of people who have similar amounts of income and education and who work at jobs that are roughly comparable in prestige make up a social class.
    D. Social status refers to the positions that an individual occupies.
        1. Status set refers to all the statuses or positions that an individual occupies.
        2. Ascribed statuses are positions an individual either inherits at birth or receives involuntarily later in life. Achieved statuses are positions that are earned, accomplished, or involve at least some effort or activity on the individual's part.
        3. Status symbols are signs that identify a status.

4.   A master status--such as being male or female--cuts across the other statuses that an individual occupies. Status inconsistency is a contradiction or mismatch between statuses.

E.   Roles are the behaviors, obligations, and privileges attached to a status. The individual occupies a status, but plays a role. Roles are an essential component of culture because they lay out what is expected of people, and as individuals perform their roles, those roles mesh together to form the society.

F.   A group consists of people who regularly and consciously interact with one another and typically share similar values, norms, and expectations.

1.   Involuntary memberships or involuntary associations--such as one's family, or sexual, ethnic, and racial groupings--are groups to which people are assigned membership rather than choosing to join.

2.   Voluntary memberships or voluntary associations--such as professional associations or clubs--are groups to which people choose to belong.

III.   **Social Institutions**

A.   Social institutions are society's standard ways of meeting its basic needs.

1.   The family, religion, law, politics, economics, education, science, medicine, and the military all are social institutions.

2.   In industrialized societies, social institutions tend to be more formal, in non-literate societies more informal.

B.   Social institutions are sociologically significant because they set limits and provide guidelines for our behavior.

C.   The mass media is an emerging social institution; it influences our attitudes toward social issues, other people, and even our self-concept. Of interest is who controls the mass media. Functionalists would say that the mass media represent the varied interests of the many groups that make up the nation, while conflict theorists would see that the interests of the political elite are represented.

D.   The functionalists and conflict theorists differ in how they see social institutions.

1.   Functionalists view social institutions as established ways of meeting group needs, such as replacing members; socializing new members; producing and distributing goods and services; preserving order; and providing a sense of purpose.

2.   Conflict theorists look at social institutions as the primary means by which the elite maintains its privileged position.

E.   Changes in social structure occur as a result of changes in culture, globalization, shifts in social classes and racial and ethnic groups, and so forth.

F.   Many sociologists have tried to find an answer to the question of what holds society together.

1.   Emile Durkheim found the key to social cohesion, the degree to which members of a society feel united by shared values and other social bonds, in the concepts of mechanical solidarity and organic solidarity. Mechanical solidarity is a collective consciousness that people experience as a result of performing the same or similar tasks while organic solidarity is a collective consciousness based on the interdependence brought about by an increasingly specialized division of labor-- how people divide up tasks.

2.   Ferdinand Tönnies analyzed how intimate community *(Gemeinschaft)* was being replaced by impersonal associations *(Gesellschaft). Gemeinschaft* is a society in which life is intimate; a community in which everyone knows everyone else and

people share a sense of togetherness and *Gesellschaft* is a society dominated by impersonal relationships, individual accomplishments, and self interest.

3. These concepts are still relevant today, helping us to understand contemporary events such as the rise of Islamic fundamentalism.

IV. The Microsociological Perspective: Social Interaction in Everyday Life

A. The microsociological approach places emphasis on face-to-face social interaction, or what people do when they are in the presence of one another.

B. Symbolic interactionists are interested in the symbols that people use to define their worlds, how people look at things, and how that affects their behavior. Included within this perspective are studies of stereotypes, personal space and touching.

1. Stereotypes are used in everyday life. First impressions are shaped by the assumptions one person makes about another person's sex, race, age, and physical appearance. Such assumptions affect one's ideas about the person and how one acts toward that person. Stereotypes tend to be self-fulfilling; that is, they bring out the very kinds of behavior that fit the stereotype. They even have an impact on what we accomplish. People can also resist stereotypes and change outcomes.

2. Personal space refers to the physical space that surrounds us and that we claim as our own. The amount of personal space varies from one culture to another.

3. Anthropologist Edward Hall found that Americans use four different distance zones: (1) Intimate distance--about 18 inches from the body--for lovemaking, wrestling, comforting and protecting. (2) Personal distance--from 18 inches to 4 feet--for friends, acquaintances, and ordinary conversations. (3) Social distance--from 4 feet to 12 feet--for impersonal or formal relationships such as job interviews. (4) Public distance--beyond 12 feet--for even more formal relationships such as separating dignitaries and public speakers from the general public.

4. From our culture we learn rules about touching. Both the frequency and the meaning of touching vary from one culture to the next. Men and women react differently to being touched.

5. We protect our personal space by controlling eye contact.

C. Dramaturgy is an analysis of how we present ourselves in everyday life.

1. Dramaturgy is the name given to an approach pioneered by Erving Goffman analyzing social life in terms of drama or the stage.

2. According to Goffman, socialization prepares people for learning to perform on the stage of everyday life. Front stage is where performances are given (wherever lines are delivered). Back stage is where people rest from their performances, discuss their presentations, and plan future performances.

3. Role performance is the particular emphasis or interpretation that an individual gives a role, the person's "style". Role conflict occurs when the expectations attached to one role are incompatible with the expectations of another role--in other words, conflict between roles. Role strain refers to conflicts that someone feels within a role.

4. We tend to become the roles we play. Some roles become part of our self-concept.

5. Impression management is the person's efforts to manage the impressions that others receive of her or him.

6. Three types of sign-vehicles are used to communicate information about the self: (1) social setting--where the action unfolds, which includes scenery (furnishings used to communicate messages); (2) appearance--how a person looks when he or

she plays his or her role, and this includes props which decorate the person; and (3) manner--the attitudes demonstrated as an individual plays her or his roles.

      7.   Teamwork, when two or more players work together to make sure a performance goes off as planned, shows that we are adept players.

      8.   When a performance doesn't come off, we engage in face-saving behavior--ignoring flaws in someone's performance.

  D.   Ethnomethodology involves the discovery of rules concerning our views of the world and how people ought to act.

      1.   Ethnomethodologists try to undercover people's background assumptions, which form the basic core of one's reality, and provide basic rules concerning our view of the world and of how people ought to act.

      2.   Harold Garfinkel founded the ethnomethodological approach.

  E.   The social construction of reality refers to what people define as real because or their background assumptions and life experiences.

      1.   Symbolic interactionists believe that people define their own reality and then live within those definitions.

      2.   The Thomas theorem (by sociologist W. I. Thomas) states, "If people define situations as real, they are real in their consequences."

V.   The Need for Both Macrosociology and Microsociology

  A.   To understand human behavior, it is necessary to grasp both social structure (macrosociology) and social interaction (microsociology).

  B.   Both are necessary for us to understand social life fully because each in its own way adds to our knowledge of human experience.

☞ KEY TERMS

After studying the chapter, review the definitions of the following terms.

achieved statuses: positions that are earned, accomplished, or involve at least some effort or activity on the individual's part

appearance: how an individual looks when playing a role

ascribed statuses: positions an individual either inherits at birth or receives involuntarily later in life

back stage: where people rest from their performances, discuss their presentations, and plan future performances

background assumptions: deeply embedded common understandings, or basic rules, concerning our view of the world and how people ought to act

division of labor: the splitting of a group's or a society's tasks into specialties

dramaturgy: the name given to an approach, pioneered by Erving Goffman, analyzing social life in terms of drama or the stage; also called dramaturgical analysis

ethnomethodology: the study of how people use background assumptions to make sense of life

face-saving behavior: techniques used to salvage a performance that is going sour

front stage: where performances are given

functional requisites: the major tasks that a society must fulfill if it is to survive

Gemeinschaft: a type of society in which life is intimate; a community in which everyone knows everyone else and people share a sense of togetherness

Gesellschaft: a type of society dominated by impersonal relationships, individual accomplishments, and self-interests

group: people who regularly and consciously interact with one another

impression management: the term used by Erving Goffman to describe people's efforts to control the impressions that others receive of them

involuntary memberships (or involuntary associations): groups in which people are assigned membership rather than choosing to join

macrosociology: analysis of social life focusing on broad features or social structure, such as social class and the relationships of groups to one another; an approach usually used by functionalist and conflict theorists

manner: the attitudes that people show as they play their roles

master status: a status that cuts across the other statuses that an individual occupies

mechanical solidarity: a shared consciousness that people experience as a result of performing the same or similar tasks

microsociology: analysis of social life focusing on social interaction; an approach usually used by symbolic interactionist

organic solidarity: solidarity based on the interdependence brought about by the division of labor

role: the behaviors, obligations, and privileges attached to a status

role conflict: conflict that someone feels *between* roles because the expectations attached to one role are incompatible with the expectations of another role

role performance: the ways in which someone performs a role within the limits that the role provides; showing a particular "style" or "personality"

role strain: conflicts that someone feels *within* a role

sign-vehicles: the term used by Goffman to refer to how people use social setting, appearance, and manner to communicate information about the self

social class: a large number of people with similar amounts of income and education who work at jobs that are roughly comparable in prestige

social cohesion: the degree to which members of a group or society feel united by shared values and other social bonds

social construction of reality: the process by which people use their background assumptions and life experiences to define what is real for them

social institutions: the organized, usual, or standard ways by which society meets its basic needs

social interaction: what people do when they are in the presence of one another

social setting: the place where the action of everyday life unfolds

social structure: the framework that surrounds us, consisting of the relationship of people and groups to one another, which give direction to and set limits on behavior

status: the position that someone occupies in society or a social group

status symbols: items used to identify a status

status set: all of the statuses or positions that an individual occupies

status inconsistency (or discrepancy): a contradiction or mismatch between statuses

stereotype: assumptions of what people are like, based on previous associations with them or with people who have similar characteristics, or based on information, whether true or false

teamwork: the collaboration of two or more persons to manage impressions jointly

Thomas theorem: William I. Thomas's classic formulation of the definition of the situation: "If people define situations as real, they are real in their consequences."

voluntary memberships (or voluntary associations): groups that people choose to join

☞ KEY PEOPLE

Review the major theoretical contributions or findings of these people.

William Chambliss: Chambliss used macro and microsociology to study high school gangs and found that social structure and interaction explained the patterns of behavior in these groups.

Emile Durkheim: Durkheim identified mechanical and organic solidarity as the keys to social cohesion.

Harold Garfinkel: Garfinkel is the founder of ethnomethodology; he conducted experiments in order to uncover people's background assumptions.

Erving Goffman: Goffman developed dramaturgy, the perspective within symbolic interactionism that views social life as a drama on the stage.

Edward Hall: This anthropologist found that personal space varied from one culture to another and that North Americans use four different "distance zones."

Mark Snyder: Snyder carried out research in order to test whether or not stereotypes are self-fulfilling; he found that subjects were influenced to behave in a particular way based on their stereotypes.

W. I. Thomas: This sociologist was known for his statement, "If people define situations as real, they are real in their consequences."

Ferdinand Tönnies: Tönnies analyzed different types of societies that existed before and after industrialization. He used the terms *Gemeinschaft* and *Gesellschaft* to describe the two types of societies.

☞ "DOWN-TO-EARTH SOCIOLOGY"

This is your opportunity to apply the sociological perspective to the world around you. The questions in this section refer to material introduced in this chapter of your text. Many ask you to think about ideas and information presented in the various special "boxes" that are located throughout this chapter.

1.   After reading "College Football as Social Structure" on page 99, can you identify the social structure of some group to which you belong? What conclusions can you draw about the importance of social structure?

2.   Were you aware of the Amish before reading the piece on page 109 of this chapter? In what ways does their way of life reflect a *Gemeinschaft*? Why are they concerned about social change? If you were given the opportunity to go live in one of the Amish communities, would you be comfortable doing so? Why or why not?

3.   After reading about the mass media and the presentation of the body in everyday life on page 116, think about your own sense of your body. How do you see yourself? How do you think others see you? To what degree do you think that your views reflect cultural expectations? Do you think that our cultural standards concerning body image are tougher on women than men?

4.   After reading this chapter, try and analyze the statuses, roles, and so on in your own life. How does when and where you were born affect your life? What are your current status's and roles? What kinds of role conflict or role strain have you experienced in these roles?

☞ SELF-TEST

After completing this self-test, check your answers against the Answer Key beginning on page 348 of this Study Guide and against the text on page(s) indicated in parentheses.

MULTIPLE CHOICE QUESTIONS

1.   Which of the following statements applies to microsociology? (96)
        a.   It focuses on social interaction.
        b.   It investigates large-scale social forces.
        c.   It focuses on broad features of social structure.
        d.   It is used by functionalists and conflict theorists.

2.   Which level of analysis do sociologists use to study social class and group structure? (96)
        a.   dramaturgy
        b.   ethnomethodology
        c.   macrosociology
        d.   microsociology

3.   You want to study how homeless mothers care for their children. Which would you use? (96)
        a.   macrosociology
        b.   microsociology
        c.   functionalism
        d.   conflict perspective

4.   On what is social class is based? (98)
        a.   income.
        b.   education.
        c.   occupational prestige.
        d.   all of the above.

5.   Which of the following refers to the position that an individual holds in a social group? (98)
        a.   social class
        b.   social status
        c.   social role
        d.   social location

6.   A person is simultaneously a daughter, a wife, and a mother. All together, what are these? (98)
        a.   social status
        b.   social class
        c.   status position
        d.   status set

7.   Which of the following describe an individual's race, sex, and inherited social class? (99)
        a.   ascribed statuses
        b.   achieved statuses
        c.   status inconsistencies
        d.   status incongruities

8.   Wedding rings, military uniforms, and clerical collars are all examples of what? (100)
        a.   social stigma
        b.   social class
        c.   status symbols
        d.   achieved statuses

9.   Which of the following statements regarding status symbols is <u>incorrect</u>? (100)
        a.   Status symbols are signs that identify a status.
        b.   Status symbols often are used to show that people have "made it."
        c.   Status symbols are always positive signs or people would not wear them.
        d.   Status symbols are used by people to announce their statuses to others.

10.   What is a master status? (100)
        a.   It is always an ascribed status.
        b.   It is a status that cuts across the other statuses that a person holds.
        c.   It can be fairly easily changed.
        d.   It is a status that identifies high ranking members of a society.

11.   Under what conditions is status inconsistency most likely to occur? (100)
        a.   When a contradiction or mismatch between statuses exists.
        b.   When we know what to expect of other people.
        c.   When a person wears too many status symbols at once.
        d.   When a society has few clearly defined master statuses.

12.   What do we call the behaviors, obligations, and privileges attached to statuses? (101)
        a.   status sets
        b.   master statuses
        c.   status differentiations
        d.   roles

13.   Why are roles of sociological significance? (101)
        a.   Sociologists need something concrete to study.
        b.   Roles lay out what is expected of people.
        c.   Most deviant behavior occurs in roles.
        d.   So many people are engaged in performing roles every day.

14.   Of what are religion, politics, education, and the military all examples? (102)
        a.   involuntary groups
        b.   voluntary associations
        c.   social institutions
        d.   social fixtures

15.   The term for activities like the replacement of members or socialization of new members is: (105)
        a.   functional necessities
        b.   functional requisites
        c.   functional prerequisites
        d.   dysfunctional prerequisites

16. According to _____, social institutions are used by an elite for its own advantage? (105-106)
    a.   functionalists
    b.   conflict theorists
    c.   symbolic interactionists
    d.   dramaturgists

17. Which of the following would be found in a society characterized by organic solidarity? (106)
    a.   a highly specialized division of labor
    b.   members who are interdependent on one another
    c.   a high degree of impersonal relationships
    d.   All of the above

18. What type of society is it where everyone knows everyone else, they conform because they are sensitive to others' opinions and want to avoid gossip, and they are comforted by being part of an intimate group? (107)
    a.   *Gemeinschaft*
    b.   *Gesellschaft*
    c.   mechanical society
    d.   organic society

19. Personal space might be a research topic for a sociologist using which type of perspective? (108)
    a.   macrolevel analysis
    b.   functional analysis
    c.   symbolic interactionism
    d.   the conflict perspective

20. According to Goffman, where do we go when we want to be ourselves? (113)
    a.   front stage
    b.   back stage
    c.   inside the drama
    d.   outside the drama

21. Susan is a college student who takes classes in the evening after work. One day her boss asks her to move from working days to working evenings; he wants her to work the same hours as she is supposed to be in class. In this situation what is Susan experiencing? (114)
    a.   role strain
    b.   role performance
    c.   role demands
    d.   role conflict

22. The professor poses a question in class. You know the answer and want to raise your hand, but are afraid that if you do, you will show up the other students in the class. What are you experiencing in this situation? (114)
    a.   role strain
    b.   role conflict
    c.   role distance
    d.   role performance

23. Which of the following statements apply to social setting, appearance, and manner? (115)
    a. They are less important than role performance for impression management.
    b. They are sign-vehicles used by individuals for managing impressions.
    c. They are more important for females than males.
    d. They are techniques for saving face when a performance fails.

24. Which of the following reflects the views of ethnomethodologists? (118)
    a. Background assumptions are so deeply embedded in our consciousness that it is virtually impossible for sociologists to ever determine what they are.
    b. Background assumptions can be easily understood and change frequently.
    c. People use common sense understandings to make sense out of their lives.
    d. Background assumptions are fairly stable from one culture to another.

25. Within which sociological perspective would you place the Thomas theorem? (119)
    a. functionalism
    b. conflict theory
    c. symbolic interactionism
    d. exchange theory

TRUE-FALSE QUESTIONS

T F 1. Social structure has little impact on the typical individual. (97)
T F 2. A person's ideas, attitudes, and behaviors largely depend on his or her social class. (98)
T F 3. To sociologists, the terms "social class" and "social status" mean the same thing. (98)
T F 4. Being a student is an example of an achieved status. (99)
T F 5. The purpose of status symbols is to tell the world that you've made it to a particular place in society. (100)
T F 6. Being male or female is not considered a master status. (100)
T F 7. You occupy a status, but you play a role. (101)
T F 8. Groups generally don't have that much control over many aspects of our behavior. (102)
T F 9. Sociologists have identified five basic social institutions in contemporary societies. (102)
T F 10. There is agreement within sociology that the mass media is a social institution. (104)
T F 11. According to Emile Durkheim, as a society's division of labor becomes more complex, it becomes much more difficult to achieve social cohesion. (106)
T F 12. *Gemeinschaft* society is characterized by impersonal, short-term relationships. (107)
T F 13. We have a tendency to make assumptions about a person based on his or her visible features; these stereotypes may affect how we act toward that person. (108-110)
T F 14. The amount of personal space people prefer varies from one culture to another. (111)
T F 15. Researchers have found that lower-status individuals tend to touch more, because touching is a way of claiming more status. (112)
T F 16. According to Erving Goffman, back stages are where we can let our hair down. (113)
T F 17. The same setting will rarely serve as both a back and a front stage. (113)
T F 18. Role conflict is a conflict that someone feels within a role. (114)
T F 19. A face-saving technique in which people give the impression that they are unaware of a flaw in someone's performance is known as impression management. (116)
T F 20. Symbolic interactionists assume that reality has an independent existence, and people must deal with it. (119)

FILL-IN QUESTIONS

1. _____ investigates such things as social class and how groups are related to one another. (96)
2. The level of sociological analysis used by symbolic interactionists is _____ . (96)
3. _____ is all of the statuses or positions that an individual occupies. (98)
4. A social position that a person assumes voluntarily is _____ . (99)
5. _____ are signs used to identify a status. (100)
6. Groups in which people are assigned membership rather than choosing to join are _____ . (102)
7. The _____ perspective states that societies must replace their members, teach new members, produce and distribute goods and services, preserve order, and provide a sense of purpose. (105)
8. A society's basic needs, that are required in order to guarantee survival, are called _____ . (105)
9. Durkheim referred to a collective consciousness that people experience due to performing the same or similar tasks as _____ . (106)
10. The assumptions we make about what people are like, based on our previous associations with them or with people who have similar characteristics are _____ . (108)
11. Erving Goffman believed that in order to communicate information about the self, individuals use three types of _____ . (115)
12. Goffman called the sign-vehicle that refers to the attitudes that we demonstrate as we play our roles _____ . (115)
13. _____ are the ideas that we have about the way life is and the way things ought to work. (118)
14. What people define as real because of their background assumptions and life experiences is the _____ . (119)
15. The _____ states, "If people define situations as real, they are real in their consequences." (119)

MATCH THESE SOCIAL SCIENTISTS WITH THEIR CONTRIBUTIONS

___1. Emile Durkheim   a. *described* **Gemeinschaft** *and* **Gesellschaft** *societies*
___2. Ferdinand Tönnies b. *wrote about mechanical and organic solidarity*
___3. Edward Hall   c. *analyzed everyday life in terms of dramaturgy*
___4. Erving Goffman   d. *studied the concept of personal space*
___5. W. I. Thomas   e. *wrote a theorem about the nature of social reality*

ESSAY QUESTIONS

1. Choose a research topic and discuss how you approach this topic using both macrosociological and microsociological approaches.
2. Today we can see many examples of people wanting to re-create a simpler way of life. Using Tönnies' framework, analyze this tendency.
3. Assume that you have been asked to give a presentation to your sociology class on Goffman's dramaturgy approach. Describe what information you would want to include in such a presentation.

CHAPTER 5
HOW SOCIOLOGISTS DO RESEARCH

☞ CHAPTER SUMMARY

- Sociologists conduct research about almost every area of human behavior. The choice of research topics depends on the sociologist's interests, the availability of subjects, the appropriateness of methods, and ethical considerations.

- Sociological research is needed because common sense is highly limited and its insights often incorrect.

- Eight basic steps are included in scientific research: (1) selecting a topic, (2) defining the problem, (3) reviewing the literature, (4) formulating a hypothesis, (5) choosing a research method, (6) collecting the data, (7) analyzing the results, and (8) sharing the results.

- Sociologists use six research methods (or research designs) for gathering data: surveys, participant observations, secondary analysis, documents, unobtrusive measures, and experiments. The choice of a research method depends on the research questions to be answered, the researcher's access to potential subjects, the resources available, the researcher's training, and ethical considerations.

- Ethics are of concern to sociologists, who are committed to openness, honesty, truth, and protecting subjects.

- Research and theory must work together because without theory research is of little value, and if theory is unconnected to research it is unlikely to represent the way life really is. Real-life situations often force sociologists to conduct research in less than ideal circumstances, but even research conducted in an imperfect world stimulates the sociological theorizing by which sociology combines data and theory.

☞ LEARNING OBJECTIVES

As you read Chapter 5, use these learning objectives to organize your notes. After completing your reading, briefly state an answer to each of the objectives, and review the text pages in parentheses.

1. Describe what sociologists consider to be valid topics for their research. (126)
2. Explain why common sense is an inadequate source of knowledge behavior. (126)
3. Identify the eight steps in a research model. (126-129)
4. Define the following terms: hypothesis, variables, operational definition, research methods, validity, reliability, and replication. Explain the role each plays in the research process. (128-129)
5. Describe the six research methods, noting advantages and disadvantages of each. (129-139)
6. Define the following terms and discuss each one's place in the research process: population, sampling, interviewer bias, rapport, generalizability, and the Hawthorne effect. (129-139)
7. Identify the conditions that are necessary in order for the researcher to prove causation. (137)
8. Enumerate the four primary factors involved in a researcher's choice of method. (139)
9. Differentiate between quantitative techniques and qualitative techniques. (139)
10. Discuss the significance of gender in social research. (142)
11. Describe the major ethical issues involved in sociological research; demonstrate these issues by using the Brajuha and Humphreys research as examples. (142-144)
12. Discuss how research and theory work together. Note reasons why most research must be conducted under less than ideal circumstances. (144-145)

☞ CHAPTER OUTLINE

I.   **What is A Valid Sociological Topic?**
   A.   Sociologists research just about every area of human behavior.
   B.   No human behavior is ineligible for research, whether it is routine or unusual, respectable or reprehensible.

II. **Common Sense and the Need for Sociological Research**
   A.   Common sense cannot be relied on as a source of knowledge because it is highly limited and its insights often are incorrect.
   B.   To move beyond common sense and understand what is really going on, it is necessary to do sociological research.

III. **A Research Model**
   A.   Selecting a topic is guided by sociological curiosity, interest in a particular topic, research funding from governmental or private source, and pressing social issues.
   B.   Defining the problem involves specifying what the researcher wants to learn about the topic.
   C.   Reviewing the literature uncovers existing knowledge about the problem, helps to narrow down the problem, and provide ideas about what questions to ask.
   D.   Formulating a hypothesis involves stating the expected relationship between variables, based on a theory. Hypotheses need operational definitions--precise ways to measure the variables.
   E.   Choosing a research method is influenced by the research topic.
   F.   Collecting the data involves concerns over validity, the extent to which operational definitions measure what was intended, and reliability, the extent to which data produce consistent results. Inadequate operational definitions and sampling hurt reliability.
   G.   Analyzing the results involves the use of either qualitative or quantitative techniques to analyze data. Computers have become powerful tools in data analysis because they reduce large amounts of data to basic patterns, take the drudgery out of analyzing data, allow the researcher to use a variety of statistical tests, and give the researcher more time to interpret the results.
   H.   By writing up and publishing the results, the findings are available for replication.

IV. **Research Methods**
   A.   Surveys involve collecting data by having people answer a series of questions.
      1.   The first step is to determine a population, the target group to be studied, and selecting a sample, individuals from within the target population who are intended to represent the population to be studied.
      2.   In a random sample everyone in the target population has the same chance of being included in the study. A stratified random sample is a sample of specific subgroups (e.g. freshmen, sophomores, juniors) of the target population (a college or university) in which everyone in the subgroup has an equal chance of being included in the study.
      3.   The respondents (people who respond to a survey) must be allowed to express their own ideas so that the findings will not be biased.
      4.   The questionnaires can be administered either by asking respondents to complete the survey themselves (self-administered questionnaires) or by directly questioning respondents (interviews).

5.   In designing a questionnaire the research must consider the effects that interviewers have on respondents that lead to biased answers (interview bias) and whether to make the questions structured (closed-ended questions in which the answers are provided) or unstructured (open-ended questions which people answer in their own words).

6.   It is important to establish rapport--a feeling of trust between researchers and subjects.

B.   In participant observation, the researcher participates in a research setting while observing what is happening in that setting. Generalizability--the extent to which the findings from one group (or sample) can be generalized or applied to other groups (or populations)--is a problem in participant observation studies.

C.   Secondary analysis--analysis of data already collected by other researchers--is used when resources are limited and/or existing data may provide excellent sources of information. However, because the researcher did not directly carry out the research, he or she can not be sure that the data were systematically gathered, accurately recorded, and biases avoided.

D.   Documents--written sources--may be obtained from many sources, including books, newspapers, police reports, and records kept by various organizations.

E.   Unobtrusive measures involves observing social behavior of people who do not know they are being studied.

F.   Experiments are especially useful to determine causal relationships.

1.   Experiments involve independent (factors that cause a change in something) and dependent variables (factors that are changed).

2.   Experiments require an experimental group--the group of subjects exposed to the independent variable--and a control group--the group of subjects not exposed to the independent variable.

3.   There are always unknown third variables that complicate experiments. Randomly dividing subjects into experimental and control groups and replicating experiments with other groups of subjects are two ways to minimize the impact of these unknown variables.

4.   Experiments are seldom used in sociology because sociologists are interested in broad features of society or social behavior, or in the actual workings of some group in a natural setting, neither of which lends itself well to an experiment.

G.   Deciding which method to use involves four primary factors:

1.   resources; the researcher must consider both time and money available.

2.   access to subjects; the sample may be physically unaccessible to researcher, thereby influencing the choice of methods.

3.   purpose of the research; the researcher will choose the method that will be most suitable for obtaining answers to the questions posed.

4.   the researcher's background or training; those trained in use of quantitative research methods (emphasis is placed on precise measurement, the use of statistics and numbers) are likely to choose surveys, while those trained in use of qualitative research methods (emphasis is placed on describing and interpreting people's behavior) lean toward participant observation.

V.   Gender in Sociological Research

A.   Because gender can be a significant factor in social research, researchers take steps to prevent it from biasing their findings.

    B.   Gender can also be an obstacle to doing research, particularly when the gender of the researcher is different from that of the research subjects and the topic under investigation is a sensitive one.

    C.   There are also questions regarding the degree to which findings from a sample made up exclusively of one gender can be generalized to the other.

VI. Ethics In Sociological Research

    A.   Ethics are of fundamental concern to sociologists when it comes to doing research.

    B.   Ethical considerations include being open, honest, and truthful, not harming the subject in the course of conducting the research, protecting the anonymity of the research subjects, and not misrepresenting themselves to the research subjects.

    C.   The Brajuha research demonstrates the lengths sociologists will go to in order to protect the anonymity of research subjects, while the Humphreys research illustrates questionable research ethics.

VII. How Research and Theory Work Together

    A.   Sociologists combine research and theory in different ways. Theory is used to interpret data (i.e. functionalism, symbolic interaction and conflict theory provide frameworks for interpreting research findings) and to generate research. Research helps to generate theory.

    B.   Social researchers must operate under less than ideal circumstances because of real-life situations. Researchers must often settle for something that falls short of the ideal.

☞ KEY TERMS

After studying the chapter, review the definition for each of the following terms.

closed-ended questions: questions followed by a list of possible answers to be selected by the respondent

control group: the group of subjects not exposed to the independent variable in the study

dependent variable: a factor that is changed by an independent variable

documents: in its narrow sense, written sources that provide data; in its extended sense, archival material of any sort, including photographs, movies and so on

experiment: the use of control groups and experimental groups and dependent and independent variables to test causation

experimental group: the group of subjects exposed to the independent variable in a study

generalizability: the extent to which the findings from one group (or sample) can be generalized or applied to other groups (or populations)

hypothesis: a statement of the expected relationship between variables according to predictions from a theory

independent variable: a factor that causes a change in another variable, called the dependent variable

interview: direct questioning of respondents

interviewer bias: effects that interviewers have on respondents that lead to biased answers

open-ended questions: questions that a respondent is able to answer in his or her own words

operational definition: the way in which a variable in a hypothesis is measured

participant observation (or fieldwork): research in which the researcher *participates* in a research setting while *observing* what is happening in that setting

population: the target group to be studied

qualitative research method: research in which the emphasis is placed on observing, describing and interpreting people's behavior

quantitative research method: research in which the emphasis is placed on precise measurement, the use of statistics and numbers

questionnaires: a list of questions to be asked

random sample: a sample in which everyone in the target population has the same chance of being included in the study

rapport: a feeling of trust between researchers and subjects

reliability: the extent to which data produce consistent results

replication: repeating a study in order to test its findings

research method (or research design): one of six procedures sociologists used to collect data: surveys, participant observation, secondary analysis, documents, unobtrusive measures, and experiments

sample: the individuals intended to represent the population to be studied

secondary analysis: the analysis of data already collected by other researchers

self-administered questionnaire: questionnaires filled out by respondents

stratified random sample: a sample of specific subgroups of the target population in which everyone in the subgroups has an equal chance of being included in the study

structured interviews: interviews that use closed-ended questions

survey: the collection of data by having people answer a series of questions

unobtrusive measures: the various ways of observing people who do not know they are being studied

unstructured interviews: interview that use open-ended questions

validity: the extent to which an operational definition measures what was intended

variable: a factor or concept thought to be significant for human behavior, which varies from one case to another

☞ KEY PEOPLE

Review the major theoretical contributions or findings of these people.

Chloe Bird and Patricia Rieker: These sociologists caution against assuming that research findings that apply to one sex apply to the other. Because women's and men's lives differ significantly, research on only one-half of humanity is complete.

Mario Brajuha: During an investigation into a restaurant fire, officials subpoenaed notes taken by this sociologist in connection with his research on restaurant work. He was threatened with jail.

Laud Humphreys: This sociologist carried out doctoral research on homosexual activity, but ran into problems when he misrepresented himself to his research subjects. Although he earned his doctorate degree, he was fired from his position because of his questionable ethics.

Elton Mayo: Mayo is famous for his research at the Western Electric Company Hawthorne plant during the 1920s. He found that workers' productivity changed in directions that had not been originally hypothesized. He concluded that workers adjusted their productivity because they knew they were being observed. This phenomenon came to be known as the *Hawthorne effect*.

C. Wright Mills: Mills argued that research without theory is of little value, simply a collection of unrelated "facts", and theory that is unconnected to research is abstract and empty, unlikely to represent the way life really is.

Peter Rossi: Rossi produced a controversial piece of research related to counting of the homeless, which revealed that the average number of homeless on any given night was far less than homeless advocates had been stating.

Diana Scully and Joseph Marolla: These two sociologists interviewed convicted rapists in prison and found that rapists are not sick or overwhelmed by uncontrollable urges, but rather men who have learned to view rape as appropriate in various circumstances.

☞ "DOWN-TO-EARTH SOCIOLOGY"

This is your opportunity to apply the sociological perspective to the world around you. The questions in this section refer to material introduced in this chapter of your text. Many ask you to think about ideas and information presented in the various special "boxes" that are located throughout this chapter.

1.   If you became a sociologist, what topics would you find interesting? What methods would you use?
2.   Can you give examples similar to those in your text where researchers have loaded the dice (p. 132) to enhance the qualities of a product or a political candidate?
3.   Try explaining cause, effect, and spurious correlations to a friend after reading page 137.
4.   Have you ever changed your appearance or behavior because you knew you were being observed or studied? Was your change an example of the Hawthorne effect (p. 138)?
5.   After reading about how some sociologists use their training and knowledge to do marketing research (pp. 139-140), do you see this is as legitimate area of research for them? How does it relate to the ethical concerns of the profession? the need to be objective?
6.   Were you surprised by the findings on homelessness reported on pages 140-142? How did the reaction to the research reflect the political nature of the problem? Why do you think the homeless advocates were upset by the outcome of the research?
7.   The author provides examples of two different research projects that involved some ethical considerations. In both of these cases, did you agree or disagree with the position taken by the researcher? How would you have reacted in the same situation?
8.   Why do you think that sociologists like Scully and Marolla (pp. 145-146) pursue certain research topics even when it requires them to work under less than ideal conditions?

☞ **SELF-TEST**

After completing this self-test, check your answers against the Answer Key beginning on page 352 of this Study Guide and against the text on page(s) indicated in parentheses.

<u>MULTIPLE CHOICE QUESTIONS</u>

1.   A researcher interested in doing a macro level study would choose _____ as a topic. (126)
      a.   waiting in public places
      b.   race relations
      c.   interactions between people on street corners
      d.   meat packers at work

2.   Sociologists believe that research is necessary because: (126)
      a.   common sense ideas may or may not be true.
      b.   they want to move beyond guesswork.
      c.   researchers want to know what really is going on.
      d.   All of the above.

3.   _____ steps are involved in scientific research. (126-129)
      a.   Four
      b.   Six
      c.   Eight
      d.   Ten

4. Which of the following is <u>not</u> one of the reasons why researchers review the literature? (127)
    a. To help them to narrow down the problem by pinpointing particular areas to examine.
    b. To get ideas about how to do their own research.
    c. To find out whether or not the topic is controversial.
    d. To determine whether or not the problem has been answered already.

5. A relationship between or among variables is predicted: (128)
    a. by a hypothesis.
    b. by use of operational definitions.
    c. when the researcher selects the topic to be studied.
    d. when the researcher is analyzing the results.

6. Reliability refers to: (128)
    a. the extent to which operational definitions measure what they are intended to measure.
    b. the extent to which data produce consistent results from one study to the next.
    c. the integrity of the researcher.
    d. the ways in which the variables in a hypothesis are measured.

7. In analyzing data gathered by participant observation, a researcher is likely to choose: (129)
    a. computer analysis.
    b. quantitative analysis.
    c. qualitative analysis.
    d. statistical analysis.

8. Replication: (129)
    a. is the extent to which operational definitions measure what was intended.
    b. is the examination of a source to identify its themes.
    c. is the repetition of research by others in order to test its findings.
    d. is copying the work of some other researcher.

9. Based on Table 5.2 in your text, all of the following are ways to measure "average" <u>except:</u> (131)
    a. medial.
    b. mean.
    c. median.
    d. mode.

10. Which of the following is <u>not</u> a method for gathering data? (129-139)
    a. ethnomethodology.
    b. surveys.
    c. unobtrusive measures.
    d. secondary analysis.

11. A sample is defined as: (130)
    a. people available to be studied.
    b. a partial representation of the target group.
    c. the individuals intended to represent the population to be studied.
    d. specific subgroups of the population who have volunteered to participate.

12. You have decided to compare the experiences of freshmen and seniors. You identify students in the two classes you are interested in studying, and then you select a certain number from each group, making sure that each person has an equal chance of being selected. Which of the following sampling methods have you used? (131)
    a. target sampling
    b. random sampling
    c. stratified random sampling
    d. random subsampling

13. You have been hired to do a survey of a community's views on a proposed anti-crime program. With only a small budget, you need to contact at least 70 percent of the residents living in the affected areas within the next month. Which method are you most likely to choose? (133)
    a. participant observation
    b. self-administered questionnaires
    c. interviews
    d. structured interviews

14. Why might a researcher "load the dice" in designing a research project? (132)
    a. The researcher doesn't know any better.
    b. The researcher may have a vested interest in the outcome of the research.
    c. The researcher is short on time and money but wants to be sure he gets the desired results.
    d. All of the above.

15. The advantage of structured interviews is that: (133-134)
    a. a larger number of people can be sampled at a relatively low cost.
    b. they are faster to administer and make it easier for answers to be coded.
    c. they make it possible to test hypotheses about cause and effect relationships.
    d. None of the above.

16. Problems which must be dealt with in conducting participant observation include: (134-135)
    a. the researcher's personal characteristics.
    b. developing rapport with respondents.
    c. generalizability.
    d. All of the above.

17. The analysis of data already collected by other researchers is referred to as: (135)
    a. surveying the literature.
    b. use of documents.
    c. secondary analysis.
    d. replication.

18. Sources such as newspapers, diaries, bank records, police reports, household accounts and immigration files are all considered: (135-136)
    a. unreliable data sources.
    b. documents that provide useful information for investigating social life.
    c. useful for doing quantitative research, but not valid when doing qualitative analysis.
    d. of limited validity because it would be difficult to replicate the study.

19. To study patterns of alcohol consumption in different neighborhoods, you decide to go through the recycling bins and count the beer cans, wine and liquor bottles. You would be using: (136)
    a.   participant observation.
    b.   experimental methods.
    c.   unobtrusive methods.
    d.   qualitative methods.

20. When you analyze your data you find that men who abuse women are often drunk at the time the abuse takes place. How do sociologists refer to the simultaneous presence of both alcohol and abuse? (137)
    a.   simulation
    b.   correlation
    c.   association
    d.   intervening variable

21. Which method will a researcher use if he/she is interested in determining causal relationships? (136)
    a.   an experiment
    b.   survey research
    c.   participant observation
    d.   None of the above

22. In an experiment, the group not exposed to the independent variable in the study is: (136)
    a.   the guinea pig group.
    b.   the control group.
    c.   the experimental group.
    d.   the maintenance group.

23. The change in behavior that occurs when subjects know they are being studied is: (138)
    a.   the Hawthorne effect.
    b.   the Humphreys effect.
    c.   the unobtrusive effect.
    d.   the obtrusive effect.

24. Surveys are more likely to be used by researchers trained in: (139)
    a.   social psychology.
    b.   ethnomethodology.
    c.   quantitative research methods.
    d.   qualitative research methods.

25. Research ethics require: (142-143)
    a.   openness.
    b.   that a researcher not falsify results or plagiarize someone else's work.
    c.   that research subjects should not be harmed by the research.
    d.   All of the above.

TRUE-FALSE QUESTIONS

T F   1.   Date rape is an acceptable topic for sociological research. (126)
T F   2.   After selecting a topic, the next step in the research model is defining the problem. (126-127)
T F   3.   An operational definition refers to the precise ways in which researchers measure their variables. (128)
T F   4.   In general, researchers give higher priority to reliability than validity. (128)
T F   5.   Reliability is the extent to which data produce consistent results. (128)
T F   6.   Sharing the results is the final step in the research model. (129)
T F   7.   Computers are valuable to research sociologists because they can store a great deal of information very efficiently. (129)
T F   8.   One of the first steps in conducting survey research is to determine a population. (129)
T F   9.   In survey research, it is undesirable for respondents to express their own ideas. (132)
T F   10.   The wording of questionnaires can affect research results. (132-133)
T F   11.   Structured interviews always use closed-ended questions. (133)
T F   12.   Establishing rapport is extremely important in participant observation. (134)
T F   13.   Secondary analysis and use of documents mean the same thing in terms of research methods. (135)
T F   14.   It is always unethical to observe social behavior in people when they do not know they are being studied. (136)
T F   15.   The purpose of an experiment is to identify causal relationships. (136)
T F   16.   Before a researcher can conclude a cause-effect relationship exists, it is necessary to rule out possible spurious corrections. (137)
T F   17.   Quantitative research methods emphasize precise measurement, the use of statistics and numbers. (139)
T F   18.   Gender does not play a very large role in social research. (142)
T F   19.   Research conducted by sociologists must meet professional ethical criteria. (142-143)
T F   20.   The research by Scully and Marolla demonstrate that research must be done under ideal conditions in order for the findings to be valid. (145-146)

FILL-IN QUESTIONS

1.   A factor or concept thought to be significant for human behavior, which varies from one case to another is a(n) _____. (128)
2.   Hypotheses need _____, which are precise ways to measure variables. (128)
3.   _____ is the extent to which data produce consistent results. (128)
4.   The six research methods are: (1) _____, (2) _____, (3)_____, (4) _____, (5) _____, and (6)_____. (129-139)
5.   A(n) _____ is when the researcher asks the respondent questions directly, either face-to-face or by telephone. (133)
6.   Closed-ended questions are used in _____. Open-ended questions are used in _____. (133)
7.   _____ is a feeling of trust between researchers and subjects. (134)
8.   Generalizability is one of the major problems in _____. (135)
9.   In _____ a researcher analyzes data that was originally collected by someone else. (135)

10.   A research method that involves observing the behavior of people who do not know they are being studied is _____. (136)

11.   To conduct an experiment, the researcher has two groups: (1) _____ and (2)_____. (136)

12.   Research in which the emphasis is placed on precise measurement, the use of statistics and numbers is _____. (139)

13.   Research in which the emphasis is placed on describing and interpreting people's behavior is _____. (139)

14.   Research _____ require openness, honesty, and truth. (142)

15.   Research and _____ are interdependent, and sociologists combine them in their work. (144)

MATCH THESE CONCEPTS WITH THEIR DEFINITIONS

___1. Hawthorne effect
___2. population
___3. sample
___4. interview bias
___5. coding
___6. secondary analysis
___7. documents
___8. independent variable
___9. dependent variable
___10. unobtrusive measures

a. *the observations of people who are unaware of being watched*
b. *behavior change due to subject's awareness of being studied*
c. *the interviewer effect on respondents that leads to biased answers*
d. *a factor that is changed by an independent variable*
e. *written sources*
f. *the target group to be studied*
g. *the analysis of data already collected by other researchers*
h. *the individuals intended to represent the population to be studied*
i. *categorizing data*
j. *a factor that causes a change in another variable*

ESSAY QUESTIONS

1.   Choose a topic and explain how you would go through the different steps in the research model.

2.   Discuss some of the things that can go wrong in the process of doing research and provide suggestions on how to overcome such problems.

3.   Explain why ethical guidelines are necessary in social science research.

CHAPTER 6
SOCIETIES TO SOCIAL NETWORKS

☞ CHAPTER SUMMARY

- Groups are the essence of life in society. By standing between the individual and the larger society, groups help to prevent anomie. An essential feature of a group is that its members have something in common and that they believe what they have in common makes a difference. Society is the largest and most complex group that sociologists study.

- Five types of societies have existed: (1) hunting and gathering, (2) pastoral and horticultural, (3) agricultural, (4) industrial, and (5) postindustrial. Each type of society is characterized by a distinctive level and pattern of social inequality. The shift from one type of society to the next is accompanied by a social revolution linked to new technology; this transformation has continued into the current postindustrial society, which is based on information, services, and technology.

- The following types of groups exist within society: primary groups, secondary groups, in-groups and out-groups, reference groups, and social networks. Changed technology has given birth to a new type of group--the electronic community.

- Group dynamics concerns the ways in which individuals affect groups and the ways in which groups affect individuals. Group size is a significant aspect of group dynamics. Leaders can be either instrumental (task-oriented) or expressive (socioemotional); both are essential for the functioning of the group. Three main leadership styles are: authoritarian, democratic, and laissez-faire.

- The Asch experiment demonstrates the influence of peer groups over their members, while the Milgram experiment shows how powerfully people are influenced by authority. Groupthink, which occurs when political leaders become isolated, poses a serious threat to society's well-being.

☞ LEARNING OBJECTIVES
As you read Chapter 6, use these learning objectives to organize your notes. After completing your reading, briefly state an answer to each of the objectives, and review the text pages in parentheses.

1. Explain why groups are so important to individuals and to societies. (150)
2. Trace the transformation of societies through the five stages of development and identify the characteristics of each, including the degree of social inequality present in each stage. (150-155)
3. Distinguish between a group, an aggregate, and a category and describe primary groups and secondary groups, as well as in-groups and out-groups. (155-158)
4. Explain the important roles that reference groups and social networks play in our lives. (158-160)
5. Identify the changes that have contributed to the emergence of the electronic community and consider the consequences of this new type of group. (161-162)
6. Explain the concept of group dynamics and indicate how group size affects interaction. (161-165)
7. Describe the two types of leaders in groups, the three basic styles of leadership and why researchers have concluded that democratic leaders are more effective than authoritarian or laissez-faire ones. (165-166)
8. Discuss the impact of peer pressure on conformity by analyzing the Asch experiment. (167)
9. Explain the following about the Milgram experiment: purpose of study, how it was conducted, conclusions reached, and why the methodology was questioned. (167-169)

10.   Discuss groupthink, explain how it can be dangerous for a society, and identify how this can be prevented. (169-170)

☞ CHAPTER OUTLINE

I.   **Social Groups and Societies**
A.   Groups are the essence of life in society; the groups to which we belong help to determine our goals and values, how we feel about ourselves, and even how we feel about life itself.
B.   An essential element of a social group is that its members have something in common and that they believe what they have in common makes a difference.
C.   Society, which consists of people who share a culture and a territory, is the largest and most complex group that sociologists study.

II.   **The Transformation of Societies**
A.   The first societies were hunting and gathering societies.
1.   Their survival depended on hunting animals and gathering plants. Since an area could only support a limited number of people who obtained food this way, the groups were small in size and nomadic, moving elsewhere when the supply of food ran out.
2.   They had few social divisions beyond that based on sex; the family was the basic unit--distributing food, educating the children, nursing the sick, etc.
3.   Since what they gathered was perishable, they did not accumulate possessions. Of all societies, they were the most egalitarian.
B.   Hunting and gathering societies were transformed into pastoral (characterized by the pasturing of animals) and horticultural (characterized by the growing of plants) societies as a result of the domestication revolution.
1.   The domestication of plants and animals is called the first social revolution, although the process was extremely gradual.
2.   The resulting societies created food surpluses which allowed for increased population size and some specialized division of labor.
3.   Increased trade and interaction between groups developed, and people began to accumulate objects they considered valuable.
4.   As families or clans acquired more goods than others, feuds and wars erupted.
5.   Leaders began to accumulate more of these possessions than other people did, and to pass these advantages along to their descendants. As a result, simple equality began to give way to inequality.
C.   The agricultural revolution (the second social revolution) occurred with the invention of the plow about 5,000 to 6,000 years ago. Pastoral and horticultural societies were transformed into agricultural societies.
1.   Since plows pulled by animals were used instead of hoes and digging sticks, a much larger food surplus was produced. This allowed people to engage in activities other than farming.
2.   Sometimes referred to as the dawn of civilization, this period produced the wheel, writing, and numbers. Cities developed, and groups were distinguished by their greater or lesser possessions. An elite gained control of the surplus resources.
3.   Social inequalities became a fundamental feature of social life. Those with greater resources surrounded themselves with armed men to protect their possessions and

growing privileges. They began to levy taxes on their "subjects." This concentration of resources and power, along with the oppression of the powerless, was the forerunner of the state.

    4.   Females became subjugated to males; Elise Boulding suggests that this change occurred because men were in charge of plowing and the cows.

D.   The Industrial Revolution (the third social revolution) began in 1765, when the steam engine was first used to run machinery. Agricultural societies were transformed into industrial societies.

    1.   The industrial societies developed and harnessed many mechanical power sources, resulting in a dramatic shift from agriculture to manufacturing as the major sources of power, wealth, and prestige.

    2.   Initially social inequality increased greatly, as did the size of the population. The individuals who first utilized the new technology accumulated great wealth, controlling the means of production and dictating the conditions under which people could work for them. A huge surplus of labor developed, as masses of people were thrown off the land their ancestors had farmed.

    3.   Initially denied the right to unionize or strike, workers eventually won their demands for better living conditions. The consequence was that wealth spread to larger segments of society.

    4.   As industrialization continued, the pattern of growing inequality was reversed. Indicators of greater equality include better housing and a vast increase in consumer goods.

E.   Industrial societies are being transformed into postindustrial societies; these social changes are linked to the new technology of the microchip.

    1.   Postindustrial societies are moving away from production and manufacturing to service industries. The basic component of this new society is information.

    2.   The U.S. was the first country to have more than 50 percent of its work force employed in service industries. Australia, New Zealand, western Europe, and Japan soon followed.

    3.   Social analysts are suggesting that we are witnessing a fourth social revolution because our way of life has been radically transformed by the microchip.

III.   Groups Within Society

A.   Groups are viewed as a buffer between individuals and society.

    1.   Durkheim believed that small groups serve as a sort of lifeline that helps to prevent anomie.

    2.   Sociologists distinguish between aggregates, categories and groups. An aggregate is made up of individuals who temporarily share the same physical space but do not have a sense of belonging together; a category is a collection of people who have similar characteristics. Unlike groups, the individuals who make up aggregates or categories do not interact with one another or take one another into account.

B.   Sociologist Charles H. Cooley used the term "primary group" to refer to groups characterized by cooperative, intimate, long-term, face-to-face relationships.

    1.   The group becomes part of the individual's identity and the lens through which to view life.

    2.   It is essential to an individual's psychological well-being, since humans have an intense need for associations that promote feelings of self-esteem.

C.   Secondary groups are larger, relatively temporary, more anonymous, formal, and impersonal than primary groups, and are based on some interest or activity.
   1.   Members are likely to interact on the basis of specific roles, such as president, manager, worker, or student.
   2.   In industrial societies, secondary groups have multiplied and become essential to our welfare.
   3.   Secondary groups tend to break down into primary groups within the larger group, such as friendship cliques at school or work. The primary group serves as a buffer between the individual and the needs of the secondary group.

D.   Groups toward which individuals feel loyalty are called in-groups, while those toward which they feel antagonisms are called out-groups.
   1.   The division is significant sociologically because in-groups provide a sense of identification or belonging, which often produce rivalries between groups.
   2.   In-group membership leads to discrimination; given our loyalty, we favor members of our in-group. Sociologist Robert K. Merton identified a double standard produced by this: the behaviors by members of an in-group are seen as virtues, while the same behaviors by members of an out-group are viewed as vices.
   3.   Dividing the world into "we" and "them" can sometimes lead to acts directed against the out-groups.

E.   Reference groups are the groups we use as standards to evaluate ourselves, whether or not we actually belong to those groups.
   1.   They exert great influence over our behavior; people may change their clothing, hair style, speech, and other characteristics to match what the reference group would expect of them.
   2.   Having two reference groups that clearly conflict with each other can produce intense internal conflict.

F.   Social networks consist of people linked by various social ties.
   1.   Interaction takes place within social networks that connect us to the larger society.
   2.   Stanley Milgram did an experiment which demonstrated how small our social world really is; he found that social networks are so interrelated that almost everyone in the U.S. is connected by just five links.
   3.   The term "networking" refers to the conscious use or even cultivation of contacts that people think will be helpful to them, for instance by joining and belonging to clubs. Many networks are hard to break into; the "old boy" network, for instance, tends to keep the best positions available to men only, rather than women.

G.   In the 1990s, due to technology, an entirely new type of human group made its appearance--the electronic community.
   1.   Through the Internet, people around the world interact with one another in news groups.
   2.   While most news groups are an interesting, new way of communicating, some meet our definition of a group, because the people who use them have established relationships and think of themselves as belonging together.

IV.   **Group Dynamics**
   A.   How individuals affect groups and groups affect individuals is known as group dynamics.
      1.   The study of group dynamics focuses on group size, leadership, conformity and decision making.

2. Sociologists recognize a small group as one that is small enough for everyone in it to interact directly with all the other members.

B. As Georg Simmel (1858-1918) noted, the size of the group is significant for its dynamics.

    1. A dyad is a social group containing two members. It is the smallest and most fragile of all human groupings. Marriages and love affairs are examples: if one member loses interest, the dyad collapses.

    2. A triad is a group of three persons--a married couple with a first child, for example. Triads basically are stronger than dyads, but still are extremely unstable. It is not uncommon for the bonds between two members to seem stronger, with the third person feeling hurt and excluded.

    3. As more members are added to a group, intensity decreases and stability increases, for there are more linkages between more people within the group. The groups develop a more formal structure to accomplish their goals, for instance by having a president, treasurer, etc. This structure enables groups to survive over time.

    4. Research by Darley and Latané found that as groups grow larger, they tend to break into smaller groups, people are less willing to take individual responsibility (diffusion of responsibility), and they interact more formally towards one another.

C. A leader may be defined as someone who influences the behavior of others.

    1. There are two types of group leaders. Instrumental (task-oriented) leaders are those who try to keep the group moving toward its goals, reminding the members of what they are trying to accomplish. Expressive (socioemotional) leaders are those who are less likely to be recognized as leaders but help with the group's morale. These leaders may have to minimize the friction that instrumental leaders necessarily create.

    2. There are three types of leadership styles. Authoritarian leaders are those who give orders and frequently do not explain why they praise or condemn a person's work. Democratic leaders are those who try to gain a consensus by explaining proposed actions, suggesting alternative approaches, and giving "facts" as the basis for their evaluation of the members' work. Laissez-faire leaders are those who are very passive and give the group almost total freedom to do as it wishes.

    3. Psychologists Ronald Lippitt and Ralph White discovered that the leadership styles produced different results when used on small groups of young boys. Under authoritarian leaders the boys became either aggressive or apathetic; under democratic leaders they were more personal and friendly; and under laissez-faire leaders they asked more questions, made fewer decisions, and were notable for their lack of achievement.

    4. Different situations require different leadership styles.

    5. Sociologists would disagree that people are born to be leaders. Rather, they find that people with certain characteristics are more likely to become leaders--those who represent the group's values, are seen as capable of leading the group out of crisis, are more talkative, express determination and self-confidence, are taller or are judged better looking.

D. A study by Dr. Solomon Asch indicates that people are strongly influenced by peer pressure. Asch was interested in seeing whether individuals would resist the temptation to change a correct response to an incorrect response because of peer pressure.

    1. Asch held cards up in front of small groups of people and asked them which sets of cards matched; one at a time, they were supposed to respond aloud. All but one

of the group members was a confederate, having been told in advance by the researcher how to answer the question.

    2.   After two trials in which everyone answered correctly, the confederates intentionally answered incorrectly, as they had previously been instructed to do.

    3.   Of the fifty people tested, 33 percent ended up giving the incorrect answers at least half of the time, even though they knew the answers were wrong; only 25 percent always gave the right answer despite the peer pressure.

E.   Dr. Stanley Milgram sought to determine why otherwise "good people" apparently participated in the Nazis' slaughter of Jews and others.

    1.   He conducted experiments in which one person (the "teacher") was instructed to administer an electric shock to the other person (the "learner") for each wrong answer given to certain questions, and to increase the voltage of the shock after each wrong answer.

    2.   In fact, the "learner" was playing a role, intentionally giving wrong answers but only pretending to be receiving an electrical shock.

    3.   Since a person in apparent authority (scientist, white coat, university laboratory) continually stated that the experiment had to go on, most of the "teachers" gave in to that authority and continued to administer the "shocks" even when they appeared to produce extreme pain.

    4.   The scientific community was disturbed not only by Milgram's findings but also by his methods. Associations of social researchers accordingly adopted codes of ethics to require that subjects be informed of the nature and purpose of social research, and almost all deception was banned.

F.   Sociologist Irving Janis coined the word "groupthink" to refer to situations in which a group of people think alike and any suggestion of alternatives becomes a sign of disloyalty. Even moral judgments are put aside for the perceived welfare of the group.

    1.   The Asch and Milgram experiments demonstrate how groupthink can develop.

    2.   U.S. history provides examples of governmental groupthink: presidents and their inner circles have committed themselves to a single course of action (e.g., refusal to believe the Japanese might attack Pearl Harbor; continuing and expanding the war in Vietnam; and the Watergate scandal) even when objective evidence showed the course to be wrong. The leaders became cut off from information that did not coincide with their own opinions.

    3.   Groupthink can be prevented only by insuring that leaders regularly are exposed to individuals who have views conflicting with those of the inner circle.

☞ KEY TERMS

After studying the chapter, review the definition for each of the following terms.

aggregate: individuals who temporarily share the same physical space but do not see themselves as belonging together

agricultural revolution: the second social revolution, based on the invention of the plow, which led to agricultural society

agricultural society: a society based on large-scale agriculture, dependent on plows drawn by animals

authoritarian leader: a leader who leads by giving orders

category: people who have similar characteristics

clique: a cluster of people within a larger group who choose to interact with one another; an internal faction

coalition: the alignment of some members of a group against others

democratic leader: a leader who leads by trying to reach a consensus

domestication revolution: the first social revolution, based on the domestication of plants and animals, which led to pastoral and horticultural societies

dyad: the smallest possible group, consisting of two persons

electronic community: individuals who more or less regularly interact with one another on the Internet

"electronic primary group": individuals who regularly interact with one another on the Internet, who see themselves as a group. and who develop close ties with one another

expressive leader: an individual who increases harmony and minimizes conflict in a group; also known as a socioemotional leader

group: defined differently by various sociologists, but in a general sense, people who have something in common and who believe that what they have in common is significant; also called a social group

group dynamics: the ways in which individuals affect groups and the ways in which groups affect individuals

groupthink: Irving Janis's term for a narrowing of thought by a group of people, leading to the perception that there is only one correct answer, in which to even suggest alternatives becomes a sign of disloyalty

horticultural society: a society based on cultivating plants by the use of hand tools

hunting and gathering society: a human group dependent on hunting and gathering for its survival

Industrial Revolution: the third social revolution, occurring when machines powered by fuels replaced most animal and human power

industrial society: a society based on the harnessing of machines powered by fuels

in-groups: groups toward which one feels loyalty

instrumental leader: an individual who tries to keep the group moving toward its goals; also known as a task-oriented leader

laissez-faire leader: an individual who leads by being highly permissive

leader: someone who influences the behaviors of others

leadership styles: ways in which people express their leadership

networking: using one's social networks for some gain

out-groups: groups toward which one feels antagonisms

pastoral society: a society based on the pasturing of animals

postindustrial society: a society based on information, services, and high technology, rather than on raw materials and manufacturing

primary group: a group characterized by intimate, long-term, face-to-face association and cooperation

reference group: Herbert Hyman's term for the groups we use as standards to evaluate ourselves

secondary group: compared with a primary group, a larger, relatively temporary, more anonymous, formal, and impersonal group based on some interest or activity, whose members are likely to interact on the basis of specific roles

shaman: a priest (or an intermediary with the spirit world) in a tribal society

small group: a group small enough for everyone to interact directly with all the other members

social network: the social ties radiating outward from the self that link people together

society: people who share a culture and a territory

triad: a group of three persons

☞ KEY PEOPLE

Review the major theoretical contributions or findings of these people.

Solomon Asch: Asch is famous for his research on conformity to group pressure.

Elise Boulding: This sociologist hypothesized that women's status in agricultural societies declined sharply once men were put in charge of plowing and the cows.

Charles H. Cooley: It was Cooley who noted the central role of primary groups in the development of one's sense of self.

John Darley and Bibb Latané: These researchers investigated how group size affects members' attitudes and behaviors. They found that as the group grew, individuals' sense of responsibility diminished, their interactions became more formal, and the larger group tends to break down into small ones.

Emile Durkheim: Durkheim viewed the small group as a buffer between the individual and society, helping to prevent anomie.

Lloyd Howells and Selwyn Becker: These social psychologists found that factors such as location within a group underlie people's choices of leaders.

Irving Janis: Janis coined the term "groupthink" to refer to the tunnel vision that a group of people sometimes develop.

Ronald Lippitt and Ralph White: These social psychologists carried out a classic study on leadership styles and found that the style of leadership affected the behavior of group members.

Robert K. Merton: Merton observed that the traits of in-groups become viewed as virtues, while those same traits in out-groups are seen as vices.

Stanley Milgram: Milgram's research has contributed greatly to sociological knowledge of group life. He did research on social networks as well as individual conformity to group pressure.

Georg Simmel: This early sociologist was one of the first to note the significance of group size; he used the terms dyad and triad to describe small groups.

☞ "DOWN-TO-EARTH SOCIOLOGY"

This is your opportunity to apply the sociological perspective to the world around you. The questions in this section refer to material introduced in this chapter of your text. Many ask you to think about ideas and information presented in the various special "boxes" that are located throughout this chapter.

1. After reading about "How Our Social Networks Perpetuate Social Inequality" on page 160, think about your own in-groups, reference groups, and social networks. Do they reflect inequalities? Do you think they help to perpetuate inequalities? Given what you know about group structure and dynamics, is it possible to break this cycle? How would you go about doing this?

2. Are you a member of an electronic community like the ones described on page 162? If you are, how would you describe your relationships with others in your particular community? Do you find yourself in closer relationships with your electronic friends than those you see everyday? Why do you think that is? If you have never participated in an electronic community, why not?

3. After reading about the research that Darley and Latané conducted on page 162, have you ever witnessrd an accident or some other occurrence that demonstrated the diffusion of responsibility? Are you more likely to help another person if you are the only person around? Why or why not?

4. After reading about the Milgram experiments (pages 167-169), consider how you would have reacted if you had been selected to participate. Under what conditions would you have carried out the orders? Under what conditions would you have disobeyed? Did the fact that Milgram was able to discover an important aspect of human behavior justify the methods which he used?

☞ SELF-TEST

After completing this self-test, check your answers against the Answer Key beginning on page 355 of this Study Guide and against the text on page(s) indicated in parentheses.

MULTIPLE CHOICE QUESTIONS

1. What term is used to describe two or more people who have something in common and who believe that what they have in common is significant? (150)
    a. assembly
    b. aggregate
    c. category
    d. group

2. What is the largest and most complex group that sociologists study? (150)
    a. the global community
    b. a society
    c. a nation-state
    d. a secondary group

3. There is a society in which there are few social divisions and the major unit of organization is the family, which fulfills needed social functions. This is a small, nomadic society with high death rates due to unpredictable food sources. What type of society is this? (150-151)
    a. horticultural societies
    b. pastoral societies
    c. hunting and gathering societies
    d. primitive societies

4. Of all types of societies, which is the most egalitarian? (151)
    a. hunting and gathering societies
    b. horticultural societies
    c. agricultural societies
    d. industrial societies

5. On what are pastoral societies   based? (152)
    a. the cultivation of plants
    b. the pasturing of animals
    c. the invention of the plow
    d. large-scale agriculture

6. Which of the following was a consequence of the domestication revolution? (152)
    a. Human group became larger.
    b. A food surplus was created.
    c. The division of labor became more specialized.
    d. All of the above.

7.   The plow's invention ushered in a new type of society called: (152)
   a.   pastoral society
   b.   farming society
   c.   agricultural society
   d.   agrarian society

8.   In an industrial society, which of the following was an indicator of increasing equality? (154)
   a.   better housing
   b.   the abolition of slavery
   c.   a move toward more representative political systems
   d.   All of the above

9.   On what is postindustrial society based? (154)
   a.   information, services, and high technology.
   b.   emphasis on raw materials.
   c.   the production of new products.
   d.   All of the above.

10.   Which was the first to have more than 50 percent of its work force in the service sector? (154)
   a.   Japan
   b.   the United States
   c.   Australia
   d.   Great Britain

11.   Which of the following do we use to describe people who have similar characteristics? (155)
   a.   group
   b.   aggregate
   c.   category
   d.   society

12.   According to Emile Durkheim, what is the value of small groups? (155)
   a.   They promote diversity.
   b.   They generate change.
   c.   They prevent anomie.
   d.   They encourage conformity.

13.   According to Cooley, which are essential to an individual's psychological well-being? (156)
   a.   primary groups
   b.   secondary groups
   c.   therapy groups
   d.   interpersonal groups

14.   Secondary groups: (156-157)
   a.   have members who are likely to interact on the basis of specific roles.
   b.   are characteristic of industrial societies.
   c.   are essential to the functioning of contemporary societies.
   d.   All of the above.

15. How do sociologists refer to groups which provide a sense of identification or belonging? (157)
    a. personal groups
    b. in-groups
    c. my-group
    d. homeboys' groups

16. Attacks against immigrants, or a national anti-immigration policy, are examples of: (158)
    a. homophobia.
    b. arachnaphobia.
    c. agoraphobia.
    d. xenophobia.

17. Why are reference groups important? (159)
    a. They meet our intense need for face-to-face interaction.
    b. They are an efficient way in which to achieve goals or complete tasks.
    c. They provide us with standards we use to evaluate ourselves.
    d. They are groups towards which we feel an intense sense of loyalty.

18. What term describes the social ties radiating out from the self, linking people together? (159)
    a. social networks
    b. reference groups
    c. cliques
    d. inner-circles

19. While the implications for social relationships of cybercommunications are still tentative, the author of your text suggests that one development which some find disturbing is that: (162)
    a. the Internet fosters intense in-group loyalties.
    b. the Internet provides easy access to people in distant lands, but can separate us from people living close by.
    c. intimacy between people is significantly reduced because they are not interacting face-to-face.
    d. not everyone can participate in the on-line discussions.

20. Dyads: (161)
    a. are the most intense or intimate of human groups.
    b. require continuing active participation and commitment of both members.
    c. are the most unstable of social groups.
    d. All of the above.

21. An expressive leader: (165)
    a. tries to keep the group moving toward its goals.
    b. is also known as a task-oriented leader.
    c. increases harmony and minimizes conflict in a group.
    d. is the director of the drama club.

22.   According to Lippitt and White, which type of leader is *best* for most situations? (166)
    a.   authoritarian
    b.   democratic
    c.   laissez-faire
    d.   instrumental

23.   According to sociologists, leaders tend to have certain characteristics which may include: (166)
    a.   they are more outgoing.
    b.   they tend to be taller and are judged better-looking than others.
    c.   where they sit in a group.
    d.   All of the above.

24.   What did the Milgram experiment demonstrate? (167-168)
    a.   That people who know they are being studied will behave differently as a result.
    b.   That peer groups have an awesome influence over their members.
    c.   That people are strongly influenced by authority.
    d.   That political leaders can become isolated.

25.   According to the author of the text, what is the key to preventing groupthink? (170)
    a.   making sure that the membership of groups is constantly changing
    b.   having decisions made by the widest possible audience, rather than committees acting alone
    c.   making sure that the results of social science research and the information gathered by media reporters is widely circulated
    d.   making sure that committees represent a diversity of interests

TRUE-FALSE QUESTIONS

T F   1.   Society is the largest and most complex group that sociologists study. (150)

T F   2.   The domestication of animals and plants was the first social revolution. (152)

T F   3.   According to Elise Boulding, women's status in agricultural societies increased with the development of metals that were then attached to plows. (153)

T F   4.   Industrial societies were brought about by the invention of the plow. (153)

T F   5.   Social inequality increased during the first stage of industrialization, while social equality increased as industrialization progressed. (154)

T F   6.   Japan was the first country to have more than 50 percent of its work force employed in service industries. (154)

T F   7.   The basic component of the postindustrial society is information. (154)

T F   8.   Anomie is most likely to occur in the absence of ties to primary groups. (155)

T F   9.   Members of primary groups are likely to interact on the basis of specific roles. (156-157)

T F   10.   Robert Merton observed that traits of our in-groups tend to be viewed as virtues, while those same traits are seen as vices when found among members of out-groups. (158)

T F   11.   Reference groups are the groups we use as standards to evaluate ourselves. (159)

T F   12.   A person has to be a member of his or her reference groups. (159)

T F   13.   Research by Stanley Milgram demonstrates how small our social world really is. (159)

T F   14.   Networking refers to the conscious use or even cultivation of networks. (160)

T F   15.   Dyads are more intimate and stable than triads. (161-163)

T F 16. As a small group grows larger, its intensity decreases and its stability increases. (163)

T F 17. Researchers have demonstrated that group size is a factor in determining whether strangers will help one another when a problem arises. (164)

T F 18. Sociologically speaking, a leader is one who is officially appointed or elected to be the "leader." (165)

T F 19. The Asch experiment used fake shocks to demonstrate that people would do anything for authority figures. (167)

T F 20. The decision by President Kennedy to send troops to invade Cuba is an example of groupthink. (169)

FILL-IN QUESTIONS

1. The simplest societies are called _____ societies. (150)

2. The _____ revolution was brought about by the invention of the plow. (152)

3. A society based on information, services, and high technology is called the _____ society. (154)

4. The term _____ is used to describe individuals who temporarily share the same physical space but do not see themselves as belonging together. (155)

5. A _____ group is characterized by relatively temporary, more anonymous, formal, and impersonal relationships. (156-157)

6. _____ provide a sense of identification or belonging while producing feelings of antagonisms towards _____. (157-158)

7. The groups we use as standards to evaluate ourselves are _____. (159)

8. The social ties radiating outward from the self, that link people together are known as _____. (159)

9. Individuals who interact with one another on the Internet, whether on a regular basis or not, are known as a(n) _____. (161)

10. Individuals who regularly interact on the Internet and develop close ties with one another make up a(n) _____. (162)

11. The smallest possible group is a(n) _____. (161)

12. Someone who influences the behavior of others is a(n) _____. (165)

13. An individual who tries to keep the group moving toward its goals is a(n) _____ leader. An individual who increases harmony and minimizes conflict is a(n) _____ leader. (165)

14. A(n) _____ leader is one who gives orders; a(n) _____ leader is one who tries to gain consensus among group members; and a(n) _____ leader is one who is highly permissive. (165)

15. _____ is a narrowing of thought by a group of people, which results in overconfidence and tunnel vision. (169)

MATCH THESE SOCIAL SCIENTISTS WITH THEIR CONTRIBUTIONS

___1. Irving Janis
___2. Georg Simmel
___3. Emile Durkheim
___4. Stanley Milgram
___5. Solomon Asch
___6. Charles H. Cooley
___7. Robert K. Merton
___8. Ronald Lippitt & Ralph White

a. *primary groups*
b. *obedience to authority*
c. *dyads*
d. *classic study on leadership styles*
e. *small groups and anomie*
f. *groupthink*
g. *conformity to peer pressure*
h. *in-group prejudice leads to double standard*

ESSAY QUESTIONS

1.   After summarizing the fundamental social changes that resulted from each of the different social revolutions, evaluate the degree to which the new technology of the microchip is contributing to a similar level of fundamental change.

2.   Discuss the benefits and drawbacks to in-groups and out-groups.

3.   Explain the three different leadership styles and suggest reasons why the democratic leader is the best style of leader for most situations.

CHAPTER 7
BUREAUCRACY AND FORMAL ORGANIZATIONS

☞ CHAPTER SUMMARY

- The rationalization of society refers to a major transformation in the way people think--from a desire to protect time-honored ways to a concern with efficiency and practical results. Max Weber traced the rationalization of society to Protestantism, while Marx attributed it to capitalism.

- As a result of the emphasis on rationality, formal organizations--secondary groups designed to achieve explicit objectives--have proliferated. Their most common form is a bureaucracy which Weber characterized as having an hierarchy of authority, a division of labor, written rules, written communications, and impersonality. Weber's characteristics of bureaucracy are an "ideal type" which may not accurately describe any real organization.

- The dysfunctions of bureaucracies include alienation, red tape, lack of communication between units, goal displacement, and incompetence. In Weber's view, the impersonality of bureaucracies tends to produce alienation among workers. In Marx's view, workers experience alienation when they lose control of the work process and are cut off from the finished product of their labor.

- In the United States voluntary associations--groups made up of volunteers who organize on the basis of some mutual interest--also have proliferated. The iron law of oligarchy--the tendency of formal organizations to be dominated by a small, self-perpetuating elite--is a problem in voluntary associations.

- The concept of corporate culture refers to the organization's traditions, values, and norms. Much of this culture is invisible. It can affect its members, either negatively or positively, depending upon the members' available opportunities to achieve.

- Greater emphasis is now being placed on humanizing work settings to develop human potential. Among the characteristics of more humane bureaucracies are expanded opportunities on the basis of ability and contributions rather than personal characteristics, a more even distribution of power, less rigid rules, and more open decision making.

- The Japanese corporate model provides a contrast to the American corporate model, although the reality of life in the Japanese corporation is at variance with the model that is generally presented.

☞ LEARNING OBJECTIVES

As you read Chapter 7, use these learning objectives to organize your notes. After completing your reading, briefly state an answer to each of the objectives, and review the text pages in parentheses.

1. Explain what is meant by the "rationalization of society," and differentiate between the views of Max Weber and Karl Marx on this process. (174-176)
2. State the definition of formal organizations and list the characteristics of bureaucracies. (177-179)
3. Describe the difference in "ideal" versus "real" bureaucracy. (179)
4. Discuss the dysfunctions of bureaucracies and give examples of each type of problem. (180-182)
5. Explain the tendency of bureaucracies to become self-perpetuating. (182-183)
6. Consider the sociological significance of bureaucracies. (183-184)
7. Indicate the functions of voluntary associations, the different motivations for joining, and explain how the problem of oligarchy occurs in such organizations. (184-186)

8.　Identify the consequences of hidden values in the corporate culture, especially noting their impact on women and minority participants. (186-187)

9.　Explain what it means to humanize the corporate culture, discussing the contribution that quality circles, employee stock ownership, small work groups, and corporate day care can each make in moving towards this goal. (187-190)

10.　Discuss cooperatives as an alternative to corporate capitalism. (190)

11.　Explain the criticisms made by conflict theorists of the move to humanize the work place. (190-191)

12.　Describe how computer technology can be used to control workers. (191)

13.　Compare and contrast the Japanese and United States corporate organizational models. (191-193)

☞ CHAPTER OUTLINE

I.　**The Rationalization of Society**

　　A.　Rationality--the acceptance of rules, efficiency, and practical results as the right way to approach human affairs--is a characteristic of industrial societies.

　　B.　Historically, the traditional orientation to life is based on the idea that the past is the best guide for the present; however this orientation stands in the way of industrialization.

　　　　1.　Capitalism requires a shift in people's thinking -- away from the idea that "This is the way we've always done it," to "Let's find the most efficient way to do it."

　　　　2.　Personal relationships are replaced by impersonal, short-term contracts.

　　　　3.　The "bottom line" becomes the primary concern.

　　C.　Marx said that the development of capitalism caused people to change their way of thinking, not the other way around. Because capitalism was more efficient, and it produced the things that they wanted in greater abundance, people changed their ideas.

　　D.　Weber believed that religion held the key to understanding the development of capitalism.

　　　　1.　He noted that capitalism emerged first in predominantly Protestant countries.

　　　　2.　In *The Protestant Ethic and the Spirit of Capitalism* Weber proposed that a set of behaviors rooted in Protestantism led to the development of capitalist activity and the rationalization of society.

　　　　3.　Weber argued that because of the Calvinistic belief in predestination, people wanted to show they were among the chosen of God. Financial success in life became a sign of God's approval; however, money was not to be spent on oneself. Rather, the investment of profits became an outlet for their excess money, while the success of those investments became a further sign of God's approval.

　　　　4.　Because capitalism demanded rationalization (the careful calculation of practical results), traditional ways of doing things, if not efficient, must be replaced, for what counts are the results.

II.　**Formal Organizations and Bureaucracy**

　　A.　Formal organizations--secondary groups designed to achieve explicit objectives--have become a central feature of contemporary life.

　　B.　Early examples of formal organization were guilds and the army. With industrialization, secondary groups became more common. Formal organizations, especially as they increase in size, tend to develop into bureaucracies.

　　C.　The essential characteristics of bureaucracies are:

　　　　1.　a hierarchy where assignments flow downward and accountability flows upward;

2.   a division of labor;

3.   written rules;

4.   written communications and records; and

5.   impersonality.

D.   Weber's characteristics of bureaucracy describe an ideal type--a composite of characteristics based on many specific examples. The real nature of bureaucracy often differs from its ideal image.

E.   Weber's model only accounts for part of the characteristics of bureaucracies. Dysfunctions can also be identified.

1.   Red tape, or the strict adherence to rules, results in nothing getting accomplished.

2.   A lack of communication between units means that they are sometimes working at cross purposes; sometimes one unit "undoes" what another unit has accomplished because the two fail to inform one another what each is doing.

3.   Bureaucratic alienation, a feeling of powerlessness and normlessness, occurs when workers are assigned to repetitive tasks in order for the corporation to achieve efficient production, thereby cutting them off from the product of one's labor.

4.   To resist alienation, workers form primary groups within the larger secondary organization, relating to one another not just as workers, but as people who value one another.

5.   The alienated bureaucrat is one who feels trapped in the job, does not take initiative, will not do anything beyond what she or he is absolutely required to do, and uses rules to justify doing as little as possible.

6.   Bureaucratic incompetence is reflected in the Peter principle--members of an organization are promoted for good work until they reach their level of incompetence. In reality, bureaucracies are remarkably successful.

F.   Goal displacement occurs when an organization adopts new goals after the original goals have been achieved and there is no longer any reason for it to continue.

G.   To the sociologist, bureaucracies are significant because they represent a fundamental change in how people relate to one another. Prior to this rationalization, work focused on human needs--for instance, making sure than everyone had an opportunity to earn a living; with rationalization, the focus shifts to efficiency in performing tasks and improving the bottom line.

III.   **Voluntary Associations**

A.   Voluntary associations are groups made up of volunteers who have organized on the basis of some mutual interest.

B.   All voluntary associations have one or more of the following functions:

1.   to advance the particular interests they represent (e.g. youth in Scouting programs);

2.   to offer people an identity and, for some, a sense of purpose in life;

3.   to help govern the nation and maintain social order (e.g. Red Cross disaster aid);

4.   to mediate between the government and the individual;

5.   to train people in organizational skills so they can climb the occupational ladder;

6.   to help bring disadvantaged groups into the political mainstream; and

7.   to challenge society's definitions of what is "normal" and socially acceptable.

C.   Voluntary associations represent no single interest or purpose. The idea of mutual interest is characteristic of all voluntary associations; a shared interest in some view or activity is the tie that binds members together.

        1.   The motivation for joining a group differs widely among its members, from the expression of strong convictions to the cultivation of personal contacts.

        2.   Because of this, membership turnover tends to be high.

  D.   Within voluntary associations is an inner core of individuals who stand firmly behind the group's goals and are committed to maintaining the organization. Robert Michels used the term "iron law of oligarchy" to refer to the tendency of this inner core to dominate the organization by becoming a small, self-perpetuating elite.

        1.   Some are disturbed because, when an oligarchy develops, many people are subsequently excluded from leadership because they don't reflect the inner circle's values or background.

        2.   If the oligarchy gets too far out of line with the membership, it runs the risk of rebellion by the grassroots.

IV.   **Careers in Bureaucracies**

  A.   Rosabeth Moss Kanter's organizational research demonstrates that the corporate elite maintains hidden values. These function to keep members of the elite in power and also provide better access to information, networking, and "fast tracks" for workers like themselves, usually white and male.

        1.   Workers who fit in are given opportunities to advance; they outperform others and are more committed.

        2.   Those who are judged outsiders and experience few opportunities think poorly of themselves, are less committed, and work below their potential.

        3.   These hidden values create this self-fulfilling prophecy and contribute to the iron law of oligarchy.

  B.   The hidden values of the corporate culture contribute to the iron law of oligarchy.

        1.   The top leadership reproduces itself by favoring people who "look" like its members, i.e. white and male.

        2.   Because females and minorities do not match the stereotype of a corporate leader, they may by treated differently. They may experience "showcasing"--being put in highly visible positions with little power so that the company is in compliance with affirmative action. These positions are often "slow-track" positions--jobs where promotions are slow because accomplishments in these areas seldom come to the attention of top management.

  C.   Morale is influenced by the level one achieves in an organization; the higher people go, the higher their morale.

V.   **Humanizing the Corporate Culture**

  A.   Humanizing a work setting refers to efforts to organize the work place in such a way that it develops rather than impedes human potential. More humane work are ones in which:

        1.   access to opportunities is based on ability and contributions rather than personal characteristics;

        2.   power is more equally distributed; and

        3.   rules are less rigid and decision making more open.

  B.   Corporate attempts to make work organizations more humane include:

        1.   quality circles. These are small groups of workers and a manager or two who meet regularly to try to improve the quality of the work setting and the product.

        2.   employee stock ownership where employees own some stock. This does not mean that working conditions and employee-management relations are friction-free because profitability still is the key.

3.   small work groups. Within these groups workers are able to establish primary relationships with other workers so that their identities are tied up with their group; the group's success becomes the individual's success.

4.   corporate day care facilities at work. These ease the strain on parents, leading to reduced turnover, less absenteeism, and shorter maternity leaves.

C.   The cooperative represents an alternative to bureaucracy. These are collectives owned by members who collectively make decisions, determine goals, evaluate resources, set salaries, and assign work tasks. The economic results of cooperatives have been mixed-- some are more profitable than private organizations, some are less.

D.   Conflict theorists point out that the basic relationship between workers and owners is confrontational regardless of how the work organization is structured. Their basic interests are fundamentally opposed.

E.   While the computer has the capacity to improve the quality of people's lives, it also holds the potential of severe abuse.

1.   Computers allow managers to increase surveillance without face-to-face supervision.

2.   Computers can create the "maximum-security workplace," potentially keeping track of every movement a worker makes while on the job. Some worry that it is only a short step from this type of workplace to the "maximum-security society."

VI.   **Myths and Realities of The Japanese Corporate Model**

A.   William Ouchi lists five ways in which this model differs from the U.S. system:

1.   Hiring and promotion: The Japanese model features a team approach; a starting cohort of workers gets the same salary, is rotated through the organization, and develops intense loyalty to one another and to the organization. In the U.S. model, employees are hired on the basis of what the individual can contribute; the emphasis is on competition; and individual loyalty is to the individual himself or herself, not to the company.

2.   Lifetime security: The Japanese model takes lifetime security for granted; the company is loyal to the employee, and expects the employee to be loyal to the company. In the U.S. model, lifetime security is unusual; continued employment is based on good and/or bad economic conditions; and workers are expected to look out for themselves.

3.   Almost total involvement: Work is like a marriage in Japan in that the company and the employee are committed to each other. In the U.S., the work relationship is highly specific; fulfill your job obligations and the rest of your time is your private life, separated from the firm.

4.   Broad training: In Japan, workers move from one job to another within the corporation. In the U.S., employees are expected to perform one job well and then be promoted to a job with more responsibility.

5.   Decision-making by consensus: In Japan, decision-making occurs after lengthy deliberations in which each person to be affected by a decision is included in the process. In the U.S., the individual responsible for the unit does as much consulting as she or he thinks necessary and then makes the decision.

B.   Research on Japanese corporations suggests that the Japanese corporate model fails to adequately reflect the reality of Japanese corporate life.

☞ KEY TERMS

After studying the chapter, review the definition for each of the following terms.

alienation: Marx's term for the experience of being cut off from the product of one's labor that results in a sense of powerlessness and normlessness

bureaucracy: a formal organization with a hierarchy of authority; a clear division of labor; emphasis on written rules, communications, and records; and impersonality of positions

capitalism: the investment of capital with the goal of producing profits

formal organization: a secondary group designed to achieve explicit objectives

goal displacement: a goal displaced by another, in this context, the adoption of new goals by an organization; also known as *goal replacement*

humanizing a work setting: organizing a workplace in such a way that it develops rather than impedes human potential

ideal type: a composite of characteristics based on many specific examples ("ideal" in this case means a description of the abstract characteristics, not what one desires to exist)

the iron law of oligarchy: Robert Michels's phrase for the tendency of formal organizations to be dominated by a small, self-perpetuating elite

McDonaldization of society: the process by which ordinary aspects of life are rationalized and efficiency comes to rule such things as food production

Peter Principle: a bureaucratic "law," according to which the members of an organization are promoted for good work until they reach their level of incompetence, the level at which they can no longer do good work

rationality: the acceptance of rules, efficiency, and practical results as the right way to approach human affairs

rationalization of society: a widespread acceptance of rationality and a social organization built around this idea

traditional orientation: the idea, characteristic of tribal, peasant, and feudal societies, that the past is the best guide for the present

voluntary association: a group made up of volunteers who have organized on the basis of some mutual interest

☞ KEY PEOPLE

Review the major theoretical contributions or findings of these people.

Alexis de Tocqueville: This Frenchman traveled across the United States in the 1830s in order to observe the customs of the new nation. He commented on the tendency of Americans to join voluntary associations.

Peter Evans and James Rauch: These sociologists examined government bureaucracies in 35 developing nations and found that those with centralized bureaucracies in which workers are hired on the basis of merit were more prosperous than those that lacked such organization.

Elaine Fox and George Arquitt: These sociologists studied local posts of the VFW and found three types of members and evidence of the iron law of oligarchy.

Rosabeth Moss Kanter: Kanter studied the hidden corporate culture and found that for the most part it continually reproduces itself by promoting those workers who fit the elite's stereotypical views.

Gary Marx: Marx has written about the "maximum security" workplace, given the increased use of computers to control workers.

Karl Marx: Marx believed that the emergence of rationality was due to capitalism. Capitalism changed the way people thought about life, rather than people's orientation to life producing capitalism.

Robert Michels: Michels first used the term "the iron law of oligarchy" to describe the tendency for the leaders of an organization to become entrenched.

William Ouchi: Ouchi studied the Japanese corporation and identified its characteristics.

George Ritzer: Ritzer coined the term the "McDonaldization of society" to describe the increasing rationalization of modern social life.

Joyce Rothchild and Allen Whitt: These sociologists researched the history of cooperatives in the U.S.

David Sills: Sills identified four additional functions that some voluntary groups perform.

Max Weber: Weber studied the rationalization of society by investigating the link between Protestantism and capitalism and identifying the characteristics of bureaucracy.

Shoshana Zuboff: Zuboff has researched the degree to which computer technology increases managers' ability to carry out surveillance on workers without face-to-face interaction.

☞ "DOWN-TO-EARTH SOCIOLOGY"

This is your opportunity to apply the sociological perspective to the world around you. The questions in this section refer to material introduced in this chapter of your text. Many ask you to think about ideas and information presented in the various special "boxes" that are located throughout this chapter.

1. Acquire a copy of the organizational chart for your own school. Compare it with Figure 7.1 (p. 178) to determine ways in which the charts are similar and ways in which they differ. What are some of your own experiences with bureaucracies, especially bureaucratic dysfunctions?

2. What was your reaction to the "Down-to-Earth Sociology" box on page 180? Can you see evidence of McDonaldization in your own life? What do you see as the advantages of this trend? What do you see as the disadvantages? Is it possible to resist this trend? Why or why not?

3. What is the purpose -- or goal -- of corporate diversity training (p. 188)? Why are corporations offering these initiatives today? In what ways can such diversity training be beneficial? How could it create heightened tensions between workers?

4. Do you think employers should go after cyberslacking or should employees be protected against such actions (p. 192)? How would you feel if you were employed in a workplace where such surveillance was carried out? How might this new development contribute to alienation?

5. What has contributed to the "cracks" in the facade of the Japanese corporate model (p. 194)? In what ways do the recent experiences of both Japanese and U.S. corporations reflect the idea that today we live in a global marketplace for ideas as well as products?

☞ SELF-TEST

After completing this self-test, check your answers against the Answer Key beginning on page 359 of this Study Guide and against the text on page(s) indicated in parentheses.

MULTIPLE CHOICE QUESTIONS

1. What is rationality? (174)
   a. the idea that the past is the best guide for the present
   b. making excuses for bureaucratic incompetence
   c. accepting rules, efficiency, and practical results as the way to approach human affairs
   d. None of the above

2.   The idea that what the past is the best guide for the present is referred to as: (174)
      a.   traditional orientation.
      b.   modern orientation.
      c.   status quo.
      d.   rationalization.

3.   What was one of the major obstacles to industrialization? (174)
      a.   the medieval church
      b.   a traditional orientation
      c.   money lenders
      d.   the traditional family

4.   According to Max Weber, capitalism: (176)
      a.   is the investment of capital in the hopes of producing profits.
      b.   became an outlet for the excess money of Calvinists.
      c.   produced success for many that became a sign of God's approval.
      d.   All of the above.

5.   In reconciling Weber's and Marx's views on rationality, sociologists feel that: (176)
      a.   Weber was most correct.
      b.   Marx was most correct.
      c.   Weber and Marx were both incorrect.
      d.   no analyst has yet reconciled the opposing views to their satisfaction.

6.   A secondary group designed to achieve explicit objectives is the sociological definition of: (177)
      a.   a social institution.
      b.   a formal organization.
      c.   a rationalized system.
      d.   None of the above.

7.   All of the following are characteristics of bureaucracy, except: (177-179)
      a.   a division of labor.
      b.   a hierarchy with assignments flowing upward and accountability flowing downward.
      c.   written rules, communications and records.
      d.   impersonality.

8.   Ideal types: (179)
      a.   are composites of characteristics based on many specific examples.
      b.   are the model or perfect way to do something.
      c.   largely are not used in sociology because they are unrealistic.
      d.   All of the above.

9.   George Ritzer used the term "the McDonaldization of society" to refer to: (180)
      a.   the preference for McDonald's over Burger King.
      b.   the spread of McDonald's world-wide.
      c.   the increasing rationalization of daily living.
      d.   All of the above.

10. What is the force behind "the McDonaldization of society"? (180)
    a. the desire the control the marketplace with uniform products
    b. the increased efficiency which contributes to lower prices
    c. the security that comes from knowing the product
    d. corporate greed

11. Dysfunctions of bureaucracies include: (180-182)
    a. alienation.
    b. bureaucratic incompetence.
    c. red tape.
    d. All of the above.

12. As a worker in a large corporation, Linda is often unhappy. At work she feels that no one appreciates her and that the work she does is boring and repetitive. Which of the following best describes Linda's situation? (181)
    a. bureaucratic incompetence
    b. alienation
    c. goal displacement
    d. goal frustration

13. How do workers resist alienation? (181-182)
    a. by forming primary groups
    b. by praising each other and expressing sympathy when something goes wrong
    c. by putting pictures and personal items in their work areas
    d. All of the above

14. According to your text, what is the alienated bureaucrat likely to do? (182)
    a. quit his or her job once unhappiness and dissatisfaction sets in
    b. seek counseling to overcome the problem
    c. not do anything for the organization beyond what he or she is required to do
    d. return to school for further training in order to move up in the organization

15. The Peter Principle: (182)
    a. states that each employee of a bureaucracy is promoted to his or her level of competence.
    b. states that each employee of a bureaucracy is promoted to his or her level of incompetence.
    c. is generally true and explains why so many bureaucracies fail.
    d. was first stated by Max Weber.

16. When does goal displacement occurs? (182)
    a. When a bureaucrat has the inability to see the goals of the organization and to function as a cooperative, integrated part of the whole.
    b. When goals conflict with one another.
    c. When an organization adopts new goals.
    d. When members of an organization are promoted until they reach their level of incompetence.

17.   Voluntary associations: (184)
        a.   are groups made up of volunteers who organize on the basis of some mutual interest.
        b.   include political parties, unions, professional associations, and churches.
        c.   have been an important part of American life.
        d.   All of the above.

18.   Why do voluntary associations exist in the United States? (184)
        a.   They meet people's basic needs.
        b.   People are required to belong to these organizations.
        c.   People don't have anything to do other than work.
        d.   They take the place of government agencies.

19.   What is the term that describes the tendency for organizations to be dominated by a small, self-perpetuating elite? (185)
        a.   the Peter Principle
        b.   bureaucratic engorgement
        c.   the iron law of oligarchy
        d.   the corporate power struggle

20.   According to Rosabeth Moss Kanter, what is the nature of the corporate culture? (186-187)
        a.   The corporate culture determines an individual's corporate fate.
        b.   The people with the best qualifications typically will rise to the top of an organization.
        c.   The employees who work the hardest and are the most cooperative have the greatest likelihood of being promoted.
        d.   All of the above.

21.   What does it mean to humanize a work setting? (187)
        a.   Employees bring plants, pictures, and other personal items to the office.
        b.   Having a period of time in which workers visit with each other, tell jokes, and get to know each other more personally.
        c.   Purchasing furniture which is more comfortable for employees.
        d.   Organizing a workplace so that human potential is developed rather than impeded.

22.   Research on the costs and benefits of employer-financed day care demonstrated that: (187)
        a.   such a benefit is costly to the employer because of strict government regulations that must be met.
        b.   such a benefit cuts into stockholder's dividends by eating up profits.
        c.   few employees took advantage of the benefit.
        d.   such a benefit can save the employer money by reducing turnover and absenteeism.

23.   Which type of organization attempts to provide a high level of personal satisfaction for members as they work towards their goals? (190)
        a.   corporations
        b.   cooperatives
        c.   collectives
        d.   small businesses

24.   Which of the following reflects the views of conflict theorists? (190-191)
   a.   Quality circles, employee stock ownership, and small work groups are excellent ways to solve the problems encountered in bureaucracies
   b.   The interests of workers and owners both may be met by humanizing the work setting
   c.   The interests of workers and owners is fundamentally opposed and, in the final analysis, workers are always exploited
   d.   There is less conflict in the Japanese corporate model than in the U.S. model

25.   Computers in the workplace: (191)
   a.   have the potential of improving the quality of work life.
   b.   could lead to more surveillance of workers by managers.
   c.   may be the first step towards a society in which every move a citizen makes is recorded.
   d.   all of the above.

TRUE-FALSE QUESTIONS

T F   1.   Rationality involves the acceptance of rules, efficiency, and practical results as the right way to approach human affairs. (174)

T F   2.   Traditional orientation is based on the idea that the present is the best guide for the future. (174)

T F   3.   Marx argued that rationality was the result of economics. (175)

T F   5.   Max Weber believed that the growth of capitalism contributed to the rise of the Protestant ethic. (176)

T F   5.   Calvinists believed that thrift was a virtue and that money should not be spent on the luxuries of life. (176)

T F   6.   Either primary or secondary groups can be formal organizations. (177)

T F   7.   Weber identified five essential characteristics of bureaucracy. (177-179)

T F   8.   Most colleges and universities do not have written systems of accountability for faculty members. (177-178)

T F   9.   In a bureaucracy, each worker is a replaceable unit. (179)

T F   10.   The characteristics of bureaucracy identified by Max Weber are ideal types. (179)

T F   11.   Marx coined the term alienation to describe the feelings of workers that they are often treated more like objects than people. (181)

T F   12.   According to conflict theorists, workers can successfully resist becoming alienated if they work at it. (181-182)

T F   13.   The Peter Principle has been proven to be true. (182)

T F   14.   Voluntary associations are made up of volunteers who have organized on the basis of some mutual interest. (184)

T F   15.   Voluntary associations can be pave the way to social change. (185)

T F   16.   The iron law of oligarchy was defined by Robert Michels. (185)

T F   17.   Bureaucracies are likely to disappear as our dominant form of social organization in the near future. (187)

T F   18.   Quality circles, employee stock ownership, and small work groups are three ways companies have been attempting to modify their bureaucracies. (188-189)

T F   19.   Conflict theorists believe that bureaucracies exploit workers regardless of the way in which work is set up. (190)

T F   20.   The Japanese corporate model emphasizes teamwork and lifetime security. (191-192)

FILL-IN QUESTIONS

1. _____ is the acceptance of rules, efficiency, and practical results as the right way to approach human affairs. (174)
2. The idea that the past is the best guide for the present is known as _____. (174)
3. _____ was written by Max Weber and emphasizes that religion holds the key to understanding the development of certain types of economic systems. (176)
4. The investment of capital in the hope of producing profits is called _____. (176)
5. A secondary group designed to achieve explicit objectives is referred to as a(n) _____. (177)
6. A type of formal organization with a hierarchy of authority and a clear division of labor is a _____. (177)
7. A composite of characteristics that reflects many specific examples is a(n) _____. (179)
8. George Ritzer has coined the term _____ to refer to the increasing rationalization of life's routine tasks. (180)
9. _____ is a feeling of powerlessness and normlessness; the experience of being cut off from the product of one's labor. (181)
10. _____ occurs when new goals are adopted by an organization to replace previous goals which may have been fulfilled. (182)
11. A group made up of volunteers who have organized on the basis of some mutual interest is called a(n) _____. (184)
12. _____ refers to the tendency of formal organizations to be dominated by a small, self-perpetuating elite. (185)
13. _____ consist of perhaps a dozen workers and a manager or two who meet regularly to try to improve the quality of the work setting and of the company's products. (188)
14. Humanizing a work setting is just another attempt to manipulate workers into active cooperation in their own exploitation, according to _____ theorists. (190)
15. Almost total involvement, broad training, and decision making by consensus are characteristics of the _____ model. (191-193)

MATCH THESE SOCIAL SCIENTISTS WITH THEIR CONTRIBUTIONS

___1. Max Weber
___2. Robert Michels
___3. William Ouchi
___4. Karl Marx
___5. Rosabeth Mass Kanter
___6. George Ritzer

a. *the iron law of oligarchy*
b. *the McDonaldization of society*
c. *hidden values in the corporate culture*
d. *exploitation of workers by capitalists*
e. *rationalization of society*
f. *Japanese corporate model*

ESSAY QUESTIONS

1. Explain what an ideal type is and why such constructs are useful.
2. Define the iron law of oligarchy and discuss why this problem occurs in voluntary associations.
3. Evaluate whether or not the use of technology to control workers is an inevitable aspect of bureaucracy.

CHAPTER 8
DEVIANCE AND SOCIAL CONTROL

☞ CHAPTER SUMMARY

- Deviance, which refers to violations of social norms, is relative; what people consider deviant varies from one culture to another and from group to group within a society. It is not the act itself, but the reaction to the act, that makes something deviant. To explain deviance, biologists and psychologists look for reasons within people, such as genetic predispositions or personality disorders, while sociologists look for explanations in social relationships.

- Symbolic interactionists use differential association theory, control theory, and labeling theory to analyze how group membership influences people's behaviors and views of the world.

- Many people succeed in neutralizing the norms of society and are able to commit deviant acts while thinking of themselves as conformists. Primary, secondary, and tertiary deviance refer to stages in people's reactions to their own socially unacceptable behaviors. Although most people resist being labeled deviant, there are those who embrace deviance.

- Functionalists state that deviance is functional, using strain theory and illegitimate opportunity structures to argue that widespread socialization into norms of material success accounts for much of the crime committed by the poor.

- Conflict theorists argue that the group in power imposes its definitions on other groups--the ruling class directs the criminal justice system against the working class, which commits highly visible property crimes, while it diverts its own criminal activities out of the criminal justice system.

- Reactions to deviance include negative sanctions, degradation ceremonies, and imprisonment; imprisonment is motivated by the goals of retribution, deterrence, rehabilitation and incapacitation. The conclusions of both symbolic interactionists and conflict theorists cast doubts on the accuracy of official crime statistics.

- Society may deal with deviance by medicalizing it and calling it mental illness. Thomas Szasz disagrees, claiming that deviance is just problem behavior, not mental illness.

- With deviance inevitable, the larger issues are how to protect people from deviant behaviors that are harmful to their welfare, to tolerate those that are not, and to develop systems of fairer treatment for deviants.

☞ LEARNING OBJECTIVES

As you read Chapter 8, use these learning objectives to organize your notes. After completing your reading, briefly state an answer to each of the objectives, and review the text pages in parentheses.

1. Explain what sociologists mean when they say that deviance is relative. (198)
2. Compare and contrast the functionalist and the conflict views on social control. (199-200)
3. Explain the importance of norms and the need for a system of social control. (200-201)
4. Compare biological, psychological, and sociological explanations of deviance. (201-202)
5. State the key components of the symbolic interaction perspective on deviance and briefly explain differential association theory, control theory, and labeling theory. (202)
6. Distinguish between primary, secondary, and tertiary deviance. Give examples of each. (206)
7. Describe how the deviant label is not only powerful, but is sometimes even embraced by those on

whom it is applied. (207-208)

8. Discuss the major reasons why functionalists view deviance as functional for society. (208-209)

9. Describe Merton's strain theory, and list and briefly explain the four types of responses to anomie. (210-211)

10. Identify the relationship between social class and crime by using the illegitimate opportunity theory and perspectives on street crime and white-collar crime. (211-213)

11. Explain the conflict view of the relationship between class, crime, and the criminal justice system. (214-215)

12. State why there is a need to use more than one theory of deviance in trying to explain this behavior and discuss how the different theories can be combined. (216)

13. Describe the range of reactions to deviance, from sanctions to degradation ceremonies and imprisonment. (216-217)

14. Identify the problems with imprisonment, including the lack of agreement on why people should be put in prison. (219-220)

15. Discuss the purpose behind using the death penalty and indicate the ways in which it is biased in its use. (220)

16. State why official statistics may not accurately reflect the nature and extent of U.S. crime. (222)

17. Explain what is meant by the medicalization of deviance and discuss how social conditions like homelessness can contribute to mental illness, just as mental illness is seen as contributing to these same conditions. (222-223)

18. Explain why U.S. society needs to find a more humane approach to dealing with deviance. (224)

☞ CHAPTER OUTLINE

I. **Gaining a Sociological Perspective of Deviance**
    A. Sociologists use the term deviance to refer to a violation of norms.
        1. According to sociologist Howard S. Becker, it is not the act itself that makes an action deviant, but rather how society reacts to it.
        2. Because different groups have different norms, what is deviant to some is not deviant to others.
        3. Deviants are people who violate rules, whether the infraction is minor (jaywalking) or serious (murder). To sociologists, all people are deviants because everyone violates rules from time to time.
        4. Erving Goffman used "stigma" to refer to attributes that discredit one's claim to a "normal" identity; a stigma (e.g. physical deformities, skin color) defines a person's master status, superseding all other statuses the person occupies.
    B. In trying to answer the question of where definitions of deviance come from, functional and conflict perspectives agree that social groups develop norms, along with a system of social control with formal and informal means of enforcing them.
        1. In tribal societies, agreement on how life should be lived is relatively simple, because these societies are small with strong social bonds. In industrial societies, because there are many competing groups, techniques of social control are set up to enforce different groups' version of what is good.
        2. To functionalists, social control emerges as individuals and groups attempt to achieve a balance between competing interest groups. According to the pluralistic theory of social control, in societies like the U.S., the central government often plays a mediating role between groups.

3.   To conflict theorists, the purpose of social control is to maintain power for an elite group, primarily consisting of wealthy, white males who work behind the scenes to control government. Official deviance (the statistics on victims, lawbreakers, and the outcome of criminal investigations and sentencing) reflects the elite's concern with protecting its interests.

C.   Norms make social life possible by making behavior predictable. Without norms, social chaos would exist. The reason deviance is seen as threatening is because it undermines predictability. Thus, social control (the formal and informal means of enforcing norms) is necessary for social life.

D.   Comparing Biological, Psychological, and Sociological Explanations

1.   Psychologists and sociobiologists explain deviance by looking within individuals; sociologists look outside the individual.

2.   Biological explanations focus on genetic predisposition--factors such as intelligence, "XYY" theory (an extra Y chromosome in men leads to crime), or body type (squarish, muscular persons more likely to commit street crimes). Psychiatrist Dorothy Lewis found that when compared with non-delinquents, delinquents had suffered significantly more head injuries.

3.   Psychological explanations focus on personality disorders (e.g., "bad toilet training," "suffocating mothers," etc.). Yet these do not necessarily result in the presence or absence of specific forms of deviance in a person.

4.   Sociological explanations search outside the individual: crime is a violation of norms written into law, and each society has its own laws against certain types of behavior, but social influences--such as socialization, subcultural group memberships, or social class (people's relative standing in terms of education, occupation, income and wealth)--may "recruit" some people to break norms.

II.   **The Symbolic Interaction Perspective**

A.   Differential association is Edwin Sutherland's term to indicate that those who associate with groups oriented toward deviant activities learn an "excess of definitions" of deviance and, thus, are more likely to engage in deviant activities.

1.   The key to differential association is the learning of ideas and attitudes favorable to following the law or favorable to breaking it. Some groups teach members to violate norms (e.g. families involved in crime may set their children on a lawbreaking path; some friends and neighborhoods tend to encourage deviant behavior; even subcultures contain particular attitudes about deviance and conformity that are learned by their members).

2.   Symbolic interactionists stress that people are not mere pawns, because individuals help produce their own orientation to life and their choice of association helps to shape the self.

B.   Control Theory

1.   According to control theory everyone is propelled towards deviance, but two control systems work against these motivations to deviate.

2.   Inner controls are our capacity to withstand temptations toward deviance, and include internalized morality, integrity, fear of punishment, and desire to be good; outer controls involve groups (e.g. family, friends, the police) that influence us to stay away from crime.

3.   Travis Hirschi noted that strong bonds to society, based on attachments, commitments, involvements, and beliefs, lead to more effective inner controls.

C.   Labeling theory is the view that the labels people are given affect their own and others' perceptions of them, thus channeling their behavior either into deviance or into conformity.

    1.   Gresham Sykes and David Matza use the term "techniques of neutralization" to describe the strategies deviants employ to resist society's label. These are (1) denial of responsibility ("I didn't do it"); (2) denial of injury ("Who really got hurt?"); (3) denial of a victim ("She deserved it"); (4) condemnation of the condemners ("Who are you to talk?"); and (5) appeal to higher loyalty ("I had to help my friends").

    2.   Sometimes an individual's deviant acts begin casually, and he or she gradually slides into more serious deviance.

    3.   Edwin Lemert identified primary deviance as fleeting acts that are not absorbed into an individual's self-concept and secondary deviance as deviant acts that are absorbed into one's self-concept. As a consequence, the deviant individual often redefines deviant behavior as nondeviant; this is referred to as tertiary deviance.

    4.   Most people resist being labeled deviant, but some revel in a deviant identity (e.g., motorcycle gangs who are proud of getting in trouble, laughing at death, etc.).

    5.   William J. Chambliss's study of the Saints (troubled boys from respectable middle class families) and the Roughnecks (boys from working class families who hang out on the streets) provides an excellent illustration of labeling theory--labels given to people affect how others perceive them and how they perceive themselves, thus channeling their behavior into deviance or conformity. The study showed how labels open and close doors of opportunity for the individuals involved.

III. The Functionalist Perspective

A.   Emile Durkheim stated that deviance, including crime, is functional, for it contributes to social order.

    1.   Deviance clarifies moral boundaries (a group's ideas about how people should act and think) and affirms norms.

    2.   Deviance promotes social unity (by reacting to deviants, group members develop a "we" feeling and collectively affirm the rightness of their own ways).

    3.   Deviance promotes social change (if boundary violations gain enough support, they become new, acceptable behaviors).

B.   Robert Merton developed strain theory to analyze what happens when people are socialized to desire cultural goals but denied the institutionalized means to reach them.

    1.   Merton used "anomie" (Durkheim's term) to refer to the strain people experience when they are blocked in their attempts to achieve those goals.

    2.   The most common reaction to cultural goals and institutionalized means is conformity (using lawful means to seek goals society sets).

    3.   He identified four types of deviant responses to anomie: innovation (using illegitimate means to achieve them); ritualism (giving up on achieving cultural goals but clinging to conventional rules of conduct); retreatism (rejecting cultural goals, dropping out); and rebellion (seeking to replace society's goals).

    4.   According to strain theory, deviants are not pathogenic individuals but the products of society.

C.   Illegitimate Opportunity Theory

    1.   Social classes have distinct styles of crime due to differential access to institutionalized means.

2.   Illegitimate opportunity structures are opportunities for remunerative crime woven into the texture of life. According to sociologists Richard Cloward and Lloyd Ohlin, they may result when legitimate structures fail.

3.   For the urban poor, there are opportunities to make money through "hustles" -- robbery, burglary, drug dealing, prostitution, pimping, gambling, and other crimes. The "hustler" is a role model because he/she is one of the few who comes close to the cultural goals of success.

4.   White-collar crime (crimes that people of respectable and high social status commit in the course of their occupations) results from an illegitimate opportunity structure among higher classes. Such crimes exist in greater numbers than commonly perceived, and can be very costly--may total several hundred billion dollars a year. They can involve physical harm and sometimes death; for instance, unsafe working conditions kill about 100,000 Americans each year--about five times the number of people killed by street crime.

D.   There have been some recent changes in the nature of white-collar crime. A major change is the growing ranks of female offenders. As women have become more involved in the professions and the corporate world, they too have been enticed by illegitimate opportunities.

IV. The Conflict Perspective

A.   The state's machinery of social control represents the interests of the wealthy and powerful; this group determines the laws whose enforcement is essential for maintaining its power.

B.   The law is an instrument of repression, a tool designed to maintain the powerful in privileged positions and keep the powerless from rebelling and overthrowing the social order. When members of the working class get out of line, they are arrested, tried and imprisoned in the criminal justice system.

C.   The criminal justice system directs its energies against violations by the working class; while it tends to overlook the harm done by the owners of corporations, flagrant violations are prosecuted. The publicity given to this level of white collar crime helps to stabilize the system by providing evidence of fairness.

D.   Law enforcement is a cultural device through which capitalists carry out self-protective and repressive policies.

V. The Need for Multiple Theories

A.   All of the different theories have merit in helping to explain deviance. However, while each explains the social conditions that contribute to deviance, none alone explain why only a few of us who are exposed to opportunities to deviate actually do deviate.

B.   There is a need to use control theory in combination with the other theories. The author suggests that the likelihood of deviance is due to a combination of motivation, exposure to opportunities and individual self control.

VI. Reactions to Deviance

A.   Sanctions are either negative (punishments ranging from frowns and gossip to imprisonment, exile, and capital punishment) or positive (rewards for desired behavior, ranging from smiles to awards). Most negative sanctions are informal.

B.   Degradation ceremonies are rituals designed to mark an individual with the status of an outsider. Typically, an individual is called before a group and denounced; when pronounced guilty, steps are taken to strip the individual of his/her identity as a group member. Such proceedings signal that the individual is no longer a group member.

C. Imprisonment--which follows the degradation ceremony (public trial/pronouncement that the person is unfit to live among law-abiding people)--is an increasingly popular reaction to crime but fails to teach inmates to stay away from crime.
1. The recidivism rate (the proportion of persons who are rearrested) in the United States runs as high as 85-90 percent, and those given probation do no better.
2. There is disagreement within U.S. society as to why criminals should be imprisoned. Different reasons include retribution (righting a wrong by making the offender suffer, or making them pay back what they stole); deterrence (creating fear in people about the certainty of punishment so that they won't break the law); rehabilitation (resocializing offenders so that they can become conforming citizens); and incapacitation (removing offenders from circulation).
D. The death penalty is the most extreme and controversial measure the state can take.
1. Its purpose is a mixture of retribution, deterrence, and incapacitation.
2. Many argue that there are biases in the use of the death penalty. These reflect regional, gender, social class and racial/ethnic biases.
E. The definition of behavior as deviant varies across societies, groups and time periods. The emergence of hate crime legislation in the U.S. is an example of this.
F. Caution is needed in interpreting official crime statistics because the reactions of authorities are influenced by social class of the offender.
G. Medicalization of deviance is the view of deviance as a symptom of some underlying illness that needs to be treated by physicians.
1. Thomas Szasz argues that mental illness is simply problem behaviors: some forms of "mental" illnesses have organic causes (e.g. depression caused by a chemical imbalance in the brain); while others are responses to troubles with various coping devices.
2. Szasz's analysis suggests that social experiences, and not some illness of the mind, underlie bizarre behaviors.
3. Being mentally ill can sometimes lead to other problems like homelessness; but being homeless can lead to unusual and unacceptable ways of thinking that are defined by the wider society as mental illness.

VII. **The Need for a More Humane Approach**
A. With deviance inevitable, one measure of a society is how it treats its deviants.
B. The larger issues are how to protect people from deviant behaviors that are harmful to their welfare, to tolerate those that are not, and to develop systems of fairer treatment for deviants.

☞ KEY TERMS

After studying the chapter, review the definition for each of the following terms.

capital punishment: the death penalty
capitalist class: the wealthy who own the means of production and buy the labor of the working class
control theory: the idea that two control systems--inner controls and outer controls--work against our tendencies to deviate
crime: the violation of norms that are written into law
criminal justice system: the system of police, courts, and prisons set up to deal with people who are accused of having committed a crime
cultural goals: the legitimate objectives held out to the members of a society

degradation ceremonies: rituals designed to strip an individual of his or her identity as a group member; for example, a court martial or the defrocking of a priest

deterrence: creating fear so people will refrain from breaking the law

deviance: the violation of rules or norms

genetic predispositions: inborn tendencies, in this context, to commit deviant acts

hate crime: crimes to which more severe penalties are attached because they are motivated by hatred (dislike, animosity) of someone's race-ethnicity, religion, sexual orientation, or disability

illegitimate opportunity structures: opportunities for crimes woven into the texture of life

incapacitation: to take away someone's capacity to commit crimes, in this instance, by putting the offender in prison

institutionalized means: approved ways of reaching cultural goals

labeling theory: the view, developed by symbolic interactionists, that the labels people are given affect their own and others' perceptions of them, thus channeling their behavior either into deviance or into conformity

marginal working class: the most desperate members of the working class, who have few skills, little job security, and are often unemployed

medicalization of deviance: to make deviance a medical matter, a symptom of some underlying illness that needs to be treated by physicians

negative sanction: a punishment or negative reaction for disapproved behavior, for deviance

official deviance: a society's statistics on lawbreaking; its measures of crime, victims, lawbreakers, and the outcomes of criminal investigations and sentencing

personality disorders: the view that a personality disturbance of some sort causes an individual to violate social norms

pluralistic theory of social control: the view that society is made up of many competing groups, whose interests manage to become balanced

police discretion: the practice of the police, in the normal course of their duties, to arrest someone for an offense or to overlook the matter

positive sanction: reward or positive reaction for approved behavior, for conformity

primary deviance: Edwin Lemert's term for acts of deviance that have little effect on the self-concept

recidivism rate: the proportion of persons who are rearrested

rehabilitation: the resocialization of offenders so that they can become conforming citizens

retribution: the punishment of offenders in order to restore the moral balance upset by the offense

secondary deviance: Edwin Lemert's term for acts of deviance incorporated into the self-concept, around which an individual orients his or her behavior

social control: a group's formal and informal means of enforcing norms

social order: a group's usual and customary social arrangements, on which its members depend and on which they base their lives

stigma: "blemishes" that discredit a person's claim to a "normal" identity

strain theory: Robert Merton's term for the strain engendered when a society socializes large numbers of people to desire a cultural goal (such as success) but withholds from many the approved means to reach that goal; one adaptation to the strain is crime, the choice of an innovative means (one outside the approved system) to attain the cultural goal

street crime: crimes such as mugging, rape, and burglary

techniques of neutralization: ways of thinking or rationalizing that help people deflect society's norms

tertiary deviance: "normalizing" behavior considered deviant by mainstream society; relabeling behavior as nondeviant

white-collar crime: Edwin Sutherland's term for crimes committed by people of respectable and high social status in the course of their occupations; for example, bribery of public officials, securities violations, embezzlement, false advertising, and price fixing

working class: those who sell their labor to the capitalist class

☞ KEY PEOPLE

Review the major theoretical contributions or findings of these people.

Howard Becker: Becker observed that an act is not deviant in and of itself, but only when there is a reaction to it.

William Chambliss: Chambliss demonstrated the power of the label in his study of two youth gangs--the Saints and the Roughnecks.

Richard Cloward and Lloyd Ohlin: These sociologists identified the illegitimate opportunity structures that are woven into the texture of life in urban slums and provide an alternative set of opportunities for slum residents when legitimate ones are blocked.

Nanette Davis: Davis studied young girls in order to find out what led them to become prostitutes. She found that they had experienced a gradual slide from promiscuity to prostitution.

Emile Durkheim: Durkheim noted the functions that deviance has for social life.

Robert Edgerton: This anthropologist's studies document how different human groups react to similar behaviors, demonstrating that what is deviant in one context is not in another.

Harold Garfinkel: Garfinkel used the term degradation ceremonies to describe formal attempts to mark an individual with the status of an outsider.

Erving Goffman: Goffman wrote about the role of stigma in the definition of who and what is deviant.

Travis Hirschi: Hirschi studied the strength of the bonds an individual has to society in order to understand the effectiveness of inner controls.

Ruth Horowitz: This sociologist conducted participant observation in a Chicano neighborhood in Chicago. She found that attitudes about honor, which were common among residents, helped to propel young men into deviance.

Martin Sánchez Jankowski: Jankowski studied gangs and identified traits that characterize gang members and the function that gangs play in urban neighborhoods.

Edwin Lemert: Lemert distinguished between different types of deviance--primary, secondary, and tertiary deviance--in terms of the degree to which the deviant label has been incorporated into the individual's identity.

Robert Merton: Merton developed strain theory to explain patterns of deviance within a society.

Donald Partington: This lawyer examined executions for rape and attempted rape in Virginia between 1908 and 1963 and found that only black men were executed for these crimes during those years.

Walter Reckless: Reckless developed control theory, suggesting that our behavior is controlled by two different systems, one external (outer controls like the police, family and friends) and the other internal (inner controls like our conscience, religious principles, and ideas of right and wrong).

Edwin Sutherland: Sutherland not only developed differential association theory, but was the first to study and give a name to crimes that occur among the middle class in the course of their work--white collar crime.

Gresham Sykes and David Matza: These sociologists studied the different strategies delinquent boys use to deflect society's norms--techniques of neutralization.

Thomas Szasz: Szasz argued that mental illness represents the medicalization of deviance.

Mark Watson: Watson studied motorcycle gangs and found that these people actively embraced the deviant label.

☞ "DOWN-TO-EARTH SOCIOLOGY"

This is your opportunity to apply the sociological perspective to the world around you. The questions in this section refer to material introduced in this chapter of your text. Many ask you to think about ideas and information presented in the various special "boxes" that are located throughout this chapter.

1. What can we learn about deviance from a cross-cultural perspective (p. 199)? How would the typical American feel about driving a hunting knife through his elderly father's heart at the father's command? What would happen in the U.S. if a wife gathered her friends around her husband's bed to beat him because he had not satisfied her sexually? Can you think of some examples of covert norms that represent the real norms in our own society?

2. After reading "Is It Rape or Is It Marriage" (p. 203), think about what the reaction should be when cultures clash. Should the full force of the law be applied? Why or why not?

3. How do you feel about the rights of Internet users to access pornography (p. 209)? Do you agree with our government's actions to ban child pornography on the Internet? Where would you draw the line? Is there anything more that can be done to control this activity?

4. How did the findings of Jankowski's research on U.S. gangs (p. 212) fit with your own picture of gangs? Do you agree with the author when he says that gangs will always be part of the city? Why or why not? What does this suggest about proposals for fighting gangs?

5. How could you use the theories presented in this chapter to develop a sociological explanation for the increased rates of imprisonment and the patterns of imprisonment discussed on pages 217-218?

6. After reading about some of the unanticipated consequences of mandatory sentencing on page 219, what do you think should be done? Are there changes that could be made to address some of the issues that have arisen? How would each of the different sociological perspectives explain this development?

7. In thinking about contemporary U.S. society, what broader social changes have contributed to the passage of hate crime legislation (p. 221)? What are some problems associated with enforcement of these laws? Do you agree that we need such legislation? Why or why not?

☞ SELF-TEST

After completing this self-test, check your answers against the Answer Key beginning on page 362 of this Study Guide and against the text on page(s) indicated in parentheses.

MULTIPLE CHOICE QUESTIONS

1. In sociology, to what does the term deviance refer? (198)
    a. behavior that sociologists believe is bad enough to warrant being punished by society
    b. all violations of social rules
    c. the violation of serious rules
    d. crime

2. According to Erving Goffman, what is the function of stigma? (198)
    a. to punish the person because she/he violates the norms
    b. to reward society for conforming to the norms
    c. to identify the person who violates the norm as deviant
    d. to regulate behavior

3. The view that different groups mediate and balance competing interests in order to achieve social stability is the _____ theory of social control. (200)
    a.   conflict
    b.   equilibrium
    c.   mediation
    d.   pluralistic

4. According to conflict theorists, social control: (200)
    a.   is based on balancing tensions between competing groups in society.
    b.   represents the interests of the wealthy and powerful.
    c.   represents the interests of the general public.
    d.   is important for mediation in a pluralistic society.

5. Differential association theory is based on the: (202)
    a.   functionalist perspective.
    b.   conflict perspective.
    c.   symbolic interactionist perspective.
    d.   psychological perspective.

6. The idea that two control systems--inner controls and outer controls--work against our tendencies toward deviance is called: (205)
    a.   conflict theory.
    b.   differential association theory.
    c.   control theory.
    d.   strain theory.

7. Which of the following is not one of the ways of neutralizing deviance? (205-206)
    a.   appeal to higher loyalties.
    b.   denial of responsibility.
    c.   denial of deviant labels.
    d.   denial of injury and of a victim.

8. What is the term for acts of deviance that have little effect on the self-concept? (206)
    a.   primary deviance.
    b.   secondary deviance.
    c.   tertiary deviance.
    d.   None of the above.

9. How do we describe deviant behavior that is normalized by relabeling it as nondeviant? (206)
    a.   primary deviance
    b.   secondary deviance
    c.   tertiary deviance
    d.   normalized deviance

10. What does William Chambliss's study of the Saints and the Roughnecks suggest? (207-208)
    a. Labels are easy to cast off once a person gets away from the group doing the labeling.
    b. People often live up to the labels that a community gives them.
    c. People often rebel against the labels given them and lead a completely different life.
    d. Sociological research on labeling has produced few conclusions.

11. For Chambliss, what factors influence whether or not people are seen as deviant? (208)
    a. social class
    b. the visibility of offenders
    c. styles of interaction
    d. All of the above

12. Which perspectives stresses that deviance promotes social unity and social change? (208-209)
    a. functionalist
    b. conflict
    c. symbolic interactionist
    d. differential association

13. All of the following are responses to anomie as identified by Robert Merton, except: (210-211)
    a. ritualism.
    b. rebellion.
    c. retreatism.
    d. recidivism.

14. According to strain theory, who gives up pursuit of success by abusing alcohol or drugs? (211)
    a. rebels.
    b. retreatists.
    c. neurotics.
    d. ritualists.

15. The illegitimate opportunity structures theory is based on: (211)
    a. the conflict perspective.
    b. the symbolic interactionist perspective.
    c. the exchange perspective.
    d. the functionalist perspective.

16. What are crimes committed by high status people in the course of their occupations called? (211)
    a. upper-class crime.
    b. crimes of respectability.
    c. white-collar crime.
    d. tuxedo crime.

17. Who falls into the marginal working class? (215)
    a. people with few skills
    b. people with low-paying, part-time, seasonal jobs
    c. the most desperate members of the working class
    d. All of the above.

18.   Of what are frowns, gossip, and crossing people off guest lists all examples? (216)
      a.   retribution
      b.   degradation ceremonies
      c.   negative sanctions
      d.   institutionalized means to achieve goals

19.   A court martial where the guilty officer is publicly stripped of his rank is an example of: (216-217)
      a.   degradation ceremonies.
      b.   humiliation ceremonies.
      c.   stigmatization.
      d.   deinstitutionalization.

20.   What are halfway houses? (220)
      a.   are community support facilities where ex-prisoners supervise aspects of their own lives.
      b.   are examples of deterrence.
      c.   do not require residents to report to authorities.
      d.   All of the above.

21.   _____ focuses on resocializing criminals so that they become conforming citizens. (219-220)
      a.   Deterrence
      b.   Retribution
      c.   Rehabilitation
      d.   Incapacitation

22.   Which policy removes offenders from "normal" society, taking them "off the streets?" (220)
      a.   retribution
      b.   incapacitation
      c.   rehabilitation
      d.   deterrence

23.   According to statistics on hate crimes, which group is most likely to be victimized? (221)
      a.   African Americans
      b.   whites
      c.   Latinos
      d.   Asian Americans

24.   According to official statistics: (222)
      a.   middle-class boys and working-class boys are about equally prone toward delinquency.
      b.   working-class boys are more delinquent than middle-class boys.
      c.   middle-class boys are more delinquent than working-class boys.
      d.   None of the above.

25.   The medicalization of deviance refers to: (222)
      a.   the castration of sex offenders.
      b.   use of lethal injections for the death penalty.
      c.   viewing deviance as a medical matter.
      d.   All of the above.

TRUE-FALSE QUESTIONS

T F 1. Across all cultures, certain acts are considered to be deviant by everyone. (198)
T F 2. According to your text, a college student cheating on an exam and a mugger lurking on a dark street have nothing at all in common. (198)
T F 3. Social control includes both formal and informal means of enforcing norms. (200)
T F 4. Functionalists agree with the pluralistic theory of social control. (200)
T F 5. Conflict theorists maintain that an elite group of wealthy, white males maintains power by controlling the government. (200)
T F 6. Sociologists believe that while biological factors may influence deviant behavior, they are not the only source for deviance. (202)
T F 7. According to differential association theory, the source of deviant behavior may be found in a person's socialization, or social learning. (202)
T F 8. In secondary deviance, the deviance is normalized by relabeling it nondeviant. (206)
T F 9. No one embraces deviance or wants to be labeled with a deviant identity. (207)
T F 10. Outlaw bikers hold the conventional world in contempt and are proud of getting into trouble. (207)
T F 11. In the study by Chambliss, the Saints and the Roughnecks both turned out largely as their labels would have predicted. (208)
T F 12. The functionalist perspective states that deviance contributes to the social order. (208)
T F 13. According to strain theory, everyone has a chance to get ahead in society, but some people prefer to use illegal means to achieve their goals. (210)
T F 14. According to strain theory, some people experience greater pressures to deviate from society's norms because of their social location. (210)
T F 15. Illegitimate opportunity structures are readily available in urban slums. (211)
T F 16. White-collar crime is not as costly as street crime. (212)
T F 17. Both functionalists and conflict theorists agree that the criminal justice system functions for the well-being of all citizens. (214-215)
T F 18. Researchers have found that the U.S. recidivism rate is as high as 85 to 90 percent. (219)
T F 19. The purpose of retribution is to create fear so that others won't break the law. (219)
T F 20. Official statistics are accurate counts of the crimes committed in our society. (222)

FILL-IN QUESTIONS

1. _____ is the violation of rules or norms. (198)
2. Erving Goffman used the term _____ to refer to attributes that discredit people. (198)
3. Formal and informal means of enforcing norms constitute a system of _____. (200)
4. According to the _____ perspective, society is made up of competing groups, and the group that holds power uses social control to maintain its position of privilege. (200)
5. _____ make social life possible by making behavior predictable. (200)
6. _____ is a group's usual and customary social arrangements, on which its members depend and on which they base their lives. (201)
7. _____ theory is the idea that two control systems--inner controls and outer controls--work against our pushes and pulls toward deviance. (205)
8. Labeling theory is based on the _____ perspective. (205)
9. _____ occurs at the point when individuals incorporate a deviant identity into their self-concept. (206)

10. Strain theory is based on the idea that a large number of people are socialized into desiring _____ (the legitimate objects held out to everyone) but many do not have access to _____ in order to achieve those goals. (210)

11. Robert Merton used the term _____ to describe the sense of normlessness that some people are frustrated in their efforts to achieve success. (210)

12. Edwin Sutherland used the term _____ to refer to crimes that people of respectable and high social status commit in the course of their occupations. (211)

13. In combination the policy, courts, and prisons that deal with people who are accused of having committed crimes make up the _____. (214)

14. Steps to strip an individual of his or her identity as a group member occur during _____. (216)

15. The view that deviance, including crime, is the product of mental illness is referred to as _____. (222)

MATCH THESE SOCIAL SCIENTISTS WITH THEIR CONTRIBUTIONS

____1. Edwin Sutherland
____2. Robert Merton
____3. Erving Goffman
____4. Thomas Szasz
____5. Emile Durkheim
____6. William Chambliss
____7. Gresham Sykes & David Matza
____8. Walter Reckless
____9. Harold Garfinkel

a. *strain theory*
b. *control theory*
c. *degradation ceremonies*
d. *white-collar crime*
e. *functions of deviance*
f. *effects of labeling*
g. *importance of stigma*
h. *techniques of neutralization*
I. *myth of mental illness*

ESSAY QUESTIONS

1. Discuss how the different sociological perspectives could be combined in order to provide a more complete picture of deviance.

2. Explain how forms of deviance such as street gangs can be both functional and dysfunctional at the same time.

3. In light of the different explanations for deviance, evaluate the effectiveness of the various reactions to deviance.

CHAPTER 9
GLOBAL STRATIFICATION

☞ CHAPTER SUMMARY

- Social stratification is a system in which people are divided into layers according to their relative power, property, and prestige. The nations of the world, as well as people within a nation, are stratified into groups based on relative power, prestige, and property.

- Four major systems of social stratification include: (1) slavery--owning other people; (2) caste-lifelong status determined by birth; (3) estate--feudal society divided into nobility, clergy, and commoners; and (4) class--based on possession of money or material possessions. Class systems are characteristic of industrialized societies. Gender discrimination cuts across all forms of social stratification.

- Early sociologists disagreed about the meaning of social class in industrialized nations. Karl Marx argued that a person's relationship to the means of production was the only factor determining social class. Max Weber argued that three elements--property, prestige, and power--dictate an individual's standing in society.

- Various arguments have been developed to explain the universal presence of stratification. Kingsley Davis and Wilbert Moore argued that society must offer rewards in order to assure that important social positions are filled by the most competent people. Gaetano Mosca believed that leadership perpetuates inequality. Conflict theorists see that stratification is the consequence of group struggles for scarce resources. Gerhard Lenski combined different views to explain the historical evolution of stratification systems.

- To maintain stratification within a nation, the ruling class controls ideas and information, depends on social networks, and relies on force.

- In Britain, the most striking features of the class system are differences in speech and accent and differences in education. In the former Soviet Union, communism resulted in one set of social classes being replaced by another.

- The model of global stratification presented in this text divides nations into three groups: the "Most Industrialized," the "Industrializing," and the "Least Industrialized" Nations.

- Four theories explaining the origins of global stratification are colonialism, world system theory, dependency theory, and the culture of poverty. International stratification is maintained through neocolonialism, the ongoing dominance of the Least Industrialized Nations by the Most Industrialized Nations, and multinational corporations which operate across national boundaries. The new technology gives advantage to the world's Most Industrialized Nations.

☞ LEARNING OBJECTIVES

As you read Chapter 9, use these learning objectives to organize your notes. After completing your reading, briefly state an answer to each of the objectives, and review the text pages in parentheses.

1. Define social stratification. (228)
2. Describe the characteristics of slavery and note the uses of slavery in the New World. (229-231)
3. Identify the features of caste systems. Give examples of different ones. (231-234)
4. Describe an estate system. (234)

5. List the characteristics of a class system and contrast its features with those of other systems of stratification. (234-235)
6. State the relationship between gender and social stratification. (235)
7. Identify the basic assumptions of Karl Marx regarding what determines social class. (235-236)
8. Explain why Max Weber was critical of Marx's perspective, and summarize Weber's views regarding social class position. (236-237)
9. State the basic assumptions of functionalists like Davis and Moore, and present Tumin's criticisms of this viewpoint. (237-238)
10. Discuss Mosca's perspective on the universality of social stratification and explain why he is considered to be a forerunner of the conflict view. (238-239)
11. Compare Marx's early conflict-oriented perspective with that of later conflict theorists. (239)
12. Summarize the synthesis of functionalist and conflict views offered by Gerhard Lenski. (239)
13. Explain the mechanisms by which the elite maintains stratification. (240-241)
14. Compare and contrast social stratification in Great Britain and the former Soviet Union. (241-243)
15. Describe the major characteristics of the three worlds of development, name at least three countries which fit in each category, and summarize some of the problems presented by this classification. (243-248)
16. Outline the major theories of how the world's nations became stratified. (248-250)
17. Explain how global stratification has been maintained. (250-252)

☞ CHAPTER OUTLINE

I. **What is Social Stratification?**
    A. Social stratification is a system in which large groups of people are divided into layers according to their relative power, property, and prestige.
    B. Stratification exists within a society and between nations and affects our life chances and our orientations to life.

II. **Systems of Social Stratification**
    A. Slavery is a form of social stratification in which some people own other people.
        1. Initially, slavery was based on debt, punishment for violation of the law, or defeat in battle.
        2. Slavery could be temporary or permanent and was not necessarily passed on to one's children. Typically, slaves owned no property and had no power; however, this was not universally true.
        3. The first form of slavery in the New World was indentured service--a contractual system in which someone voluntarily sold his or her services for a specified period of time; at the end of that time the individual was freed.
        4. Given the shortage of indentured servants, American colonists first tried to enslave Indians and then turned to Africans, who were being brought to North and South America by the British, Dutch, English, Portuguese, and Spanish.
        5. When American slave owners found it was profitable to own slaves for life, they developed beliefs to justify what they wanted and to make slavery inheritable. The practice of slavery was written into law.
        6. There is some debate as to whether or not slavery is still practiced in certain parts of the world today. Although denied by their governments, accusations have been made that the slave trade has been revived in Sudan and Mauritania.

B.   In a caste system, status is determined by birth and is lifelong.

    1.   Ascribed status is the basis of a caste system. Caste societies try to make certain that boundaries between castes remain firm by practicing endogamy (marriage within their own group) and developing rules about ritual pollution--teaching that contact with inferior castes contaminates the superior caste.

    2.   Although abolished by the Indian government in 1949, the caste system remains part of everyday life in India, as it has for almost three thousand years. This system is based on religion and is made up of four main castes, or *varnas*, which are subdivided into thousands of specialized subcastes or *jati*. The lowest caste is considered to be "untouchable," and *ablution*--washing rituals--are required to restore purity for those contaminated by individuals from this group.

    3.   South Africa's caste system was called apartheid and based on the separation of the races. By law there were four different racial castes, and the law specified where people could live, work, and go to school. While this system has been dismantled by the government following decades of international protest, its legacy continues to haunt South Africa.

    4.   An American racial caste system developed in the United States when slavery ended. Even in the earlier parts of this century, all whites were considered higher than all African Americans and separate accommodations were maintained for the races in the South.

C.   The estate system that developed in Europe during the Middle Ages consisted of three groups, or estates.

    1.   The *first estate* was made up of the nobility who ruled the land.

    2.   The *second estate* consisted of the clergy, who not only owned vast tracts of land and collected taxes from commoners, but also set its seal of approval on rulers.

    3.   The *third estate* was made up of commoners. They were born into this estate and had few opportunities to move up.

    4.   Women belonged to the estate of their husbands.

D.   A class system is a form of social stratification based primarily on the possession of money or material possessions.

    1.   Initial social class position is based on that of one's parents (ascribed status).

    2.   With relatively fluid boundaries, a class system allows for social mobility--movement up or down the social class ladder--based on achieved status.

E.   No matter what system a society may use to divide people into different layers, gender is always an essential part of those distinctions within each layer. On the basis of gender, people are sorted into categories and given differential access to rewards. Social distinctions have always favored males.

III.   What Determines Social Class?

A.   According to Karl Marx, social class is determined by one's relationship to the means of production--the tools, factories, land, and investment capital used to produce wealth.

    1.   The bourgeoisie (capitalists) own the means of production; the proletariat (workers) are the people who work for those who own the means of production.

    2.   As capital becomes more concentrated, the two classes will become increasingly more hostile to one another.

    3.   Class consciousness--awareness of a common identity based on position in the means of production--will develop; it is the essential basis of the unity of workers, according to Marx.

4. Marx believed that the workers would revolt against the capitalists, take control of the means of production, and usher in a classless society. However, the workers' unity and revolution are held back by false consciousness--the mistaken identification of workers with the interests of capitalists.

B. Unlike Marx, Max Weber did not believe that property was the sole basis of a person's position in the stratification system, but rather that property, prestige, and power determine social class.

1. Property is an essential element; however, powerful people, like managers of corporations, control the means of production although they do not own them.

2. Prestige may be derived from ownership of property; however, it also may be based on other factors such as athletic skills.

3. Power is the ability to control others, even over their objections.

IV. **Why is Social Stratification Universal?**

A. According to the functionalist view expressed by Kingsley Davis and Wilbert Moore, stratification is inevitable.

1. Society must make certain that its important positions are filled; to guarantee that the more important positions are filled by the more qualified people, society must offer them greater rewards.

2. Davis and Moore argued that society offers greater rewards for its more responsible, demanding, and accountable positions.

B. Melvin Tumin was the first to present a number of criticisms to the Davis and Moore thesis.

1. He asked how the importance of a position is measured (e.g. "Is a surgeon really more important to society than a garbage collector?"). Rewards can not be used to measure the importance of a job; there must be some independent measure of importance.

2. He noted that if stratification worked as Davis and Moore describe it, society would be a meritocracy--a form of social stratification in which all positions are awarded on the basis of merit--but it does not work this way (e.g. the best predictor of college entrance is family income, not ability).

3. He also argued that money and fringe benefits are not the only reasons people take jobs.

4. Finally, he noted that stratification is dysfunctional to many people, thus not functional.

C. Gaetano Mosca argued that every society will be stratified by power. According to Mosca, stratification is inevitable; the ruling class is well organized and enjoys easy communication among its relatively few members; it is extremely difficult for the majority, whom they govern, to resist.

1. Society cannot exist unless it is organized, thus, there must be politics to get the work of society done.

2. Political organization results in inequalities of power because some people take leadership positions and others follow.

3. It is human nature to be self-centered, thus, people in positions of power use their positions to bring greater rewards to themselves.

D. Conflict theorists stress that conflict, not function, is the basis of social stratification.

1. Every society has only limited resources to go around, and in every society groups struggle with one another for those resources.

2. Whenever a group gains power, it uses that power to extract what it can from the groups beneath it. The dominant group takes control of the social institutions, using them to keep other groups weak and to preserve the best resources for itself. Ruling classes develop an ideology to justify people's relative positions.

3. Modern conflict theorists such as C. Wright Mills, Ralf Dahrendorf, and Randall Collins stress that conflict between capitalists and workers is not the only important conflict in contemporary society, but rather, that groups within the same class compete for scarce resources, resulting in conflict between many groups (e.g. young vs. old; women vs. men).

E. Gerhard Lenski offered a synthesis between functionalist and conflict theories.

1. Functionalists are right when it comes to societies that have only basic resources and do not accumulate wealth, such as hunting and gathering societies.

2. Conflict theorists are right when it comes to societies with a surplus. In such societies humans pursue self-interests and struggle to control those surpluses. This leads to the emergence of a small elite who then builds inequality into the society, resulting in a full-blown system of social stratification.

V. **How Do Elites Maintain Stratification?**

A. Social stratification is maintained within a nation by elites who control ideas and information, maintain social networks, and use force.

1. The control of ideas and information can be remarkably more effective than the use of brute force and is used by elites everywhere to maintain their positions of power--whether in dictatorships or in democracies.

2. Technology, especially monitoring devices, helps the elite maintain its position.

3. Social networks are also critical in maintaining social stratification because they supply valuable information and tend to perpetuate social inequality.

B. Underlying the maintenance of stratification is control of social institutions--the legal establishment, the police, and the military.

VI. **Comparative Social Stratification**

A. Great Britain's class system can be divided into upper, middle, and lower classes. A little over half of the population is in the lower or working class, close to half of the population is in the middle class, and only about 1 percent is in the upper class. Language and speech patterns are important class indicators. Education is the primary way the class system is perpetuated from one generation to the next.

B. The ideal of communism--a classless society--was never realized in the former Soviet Union. Before the Communist revolution the elite was based on inherited wealth; afterwards, it consisted of top party officials, a relatively small middle class, and a massive lower class of peasants and unskilled workers. How recent reforms will impact the stratification system is yet to be seen, but a class of newly-rich individuals is emerging. Some of these had political connections, others had the foresight and initiative to take advantage of the changes.

VII. **Global Stratification:**

A. Until the 1980s, a simple model was used, consisting of the First World (industrialized, capitalistic nations), Second World (communist nations), and Third World (any nations that didn't fit the other categories). A more neutral way of categorizing nations is to use terms related to a nation's level of industrialization: "Most Industrialized," "Industrializing," and "Least Industrialized."

B. The Most Industrialized Nations (U.S., Canada, Great Britain, France, Germany,

Switzerland, Japan, Australia, New Zealand), are capitalistic, although variations exist in economic systems.

    1.   These nations have only 16 percent of the world's population, but have 31 percent of the world's land.

    2.   The poor in these nations live better/longer than the average citizens of the least industrial Nations.

C.   The Industrializing Nations include the former Soviet Union, Poland, Czechoslovakia, Hungary.

    1.   These nations account for 16 percent of the world's population and 20 percent of the land.

    2.   The people of these nations have considerably lower income and a lower standard of living than people in the Most Industrialized Nations; while their access to electricity, indoor plumbing, and other material goods is more limited than those in the Most Industrialized Nations, it is higher than those in the Least Industrialized Nations.

D.   In the Least Industrialized Nations of the world most people live on farms or in villages with low standards of living.

    1.   These nations account for 49 percent of the earth's land and 68 percent of the world's population.

    2.   These nations are characterized by high birth rates and rapidly growing populations (placing even greater burdens on limited facilities).

    3.   Most people in these nations live on less than $1000 per year.

E.   Classifying the nations of the world into these three categories creates certain problems.

    1.   How much industrialization does a nation need in order to be classified as Most Industrialized or Industrializing?

    2.   Does the fact that some nations have become "postindustrial" mean that a separate classification needs to be created?

    3.   While the oil-rich nations of the world are immensely wealthy, they are not industrialized. How are they classified?

VIII. **How the World's Nations Become Stratified**

A.   The theory of colonialism focuses on how the nations that industrialized first got the jump on the rest of the world.

    1.   With profits generated by the Industrial Revolution, industrialized nations built powerful armaments and fast ships and then invaded weaker nations, making colonies of them and exploiting their labor/natural resources. European nations tended to focus on Africa, while the U.S. concentrated on Central and South America.

    2.   Colonalism shaped many of the Least Industrialized Nations. Often, the Most Industrialized Nations created states disregarding tribal or cultural considerations.

B.   According to world system theory as espoused by Immanuel Wallerstein, countries are politically and economically tied together.

    1.   There are four groups of interconnected nations: (1) core nations, where capitalism first developed; (2) semi-periphery (Mediterranean area), highly dependent on trade with core nations; (3) periphery (eastern Europe), mainly limited to selling cash crops to core nations, with limited economic development; (4) external area (most of Africa/Asia) left out of growth of capitalism, with few economic ties to core nations.

2.   A capitalist world economy (capitalist dominance) results from relentless expansion: even external area nations are drawn into commercial web.

3.   Globalization (the extensive interconnections among nations resulting from the expansion of capitalism) has been speeded up because of new forms of communication and transportation. The consequence is that no nation is able to live in isolation.

C.   Dependency theory attributes the Least Industrialized Nations' low economic development to dominance by the Most Industrialized Nations. The Most Industrialized Nations turned the Least Industrialized Nations into their plantations and mines, taking whatever they needed; many of the Least Industrialized Nations thus specialized in a single cash crop.

D.   John Kenneth Galbraith argued that some nations remained poor because they were crippled by a culture of poverty, a way of life based on traditional values and religious beliefs that perpetuated poverty from one generation to the next and kept some of the Least Industrialized Nations from developing.

E.   Most sociologists find colonialism, world system, and dependency theory explanations preferable to the culture of poverty theory because the last places the blame on the victim, but each theory only partially explains global stratification.

IX.   **Maintaining Global Stratification**

A.   Neocolonialism is the economic and political dominance of the Least Industrialized Nations by the Most Industrialized Nations. Michael Harrington asserts that the Most Industrialized Nations control the Least Industrialized Nations because they control markets, set prices, etc. The Most Industrialized Nations move hazardous industries to the Least Industrialized Nations. The Most Industrialized Nations sell weapons and manufactured goods to the Least Industrialized Nations on credit, turning these countries into eternal debtors. They use resources to pay off the debt thereby preventing them from developing their own industrial capacity.

B.   Multinational corporations contribute to exploitation of the Least Industrialized Nations.

1.   Some exploit the Least Industrialized Nations directly by controlling national and local politics, running them as a fiefdom.

2.   The Most Industrialized Nations are primary beneficiaries of profits made in the Least Industrialized Nations.

3.   They often work closely with the elite of the Least Industrialized Nations, many times in informal partnerships that are mutually beneficial.

4.   In some situations, multinational corporations may bring prosperity to the Least Industrialized Nations because new factories provide salaries and opportunities which otherwise would not exist for workers in those countries.

C.   The new technology favors the Most Industrialized Nations, enabling them to maintain their global domination.

1.   The profits of multinational corporations can be invested in developing and acquiring the latest technology, thereby generating even greater profits.

2.   Many of the Least Industrialized Nations do not have the resources to invest in new technology, creating an even greater gap between the levels of industrialization globally.

☞ KEY TERMS

After studying the chapter, review the definition for each of the following terms.

apartheid: the separation of races as was practiced in South Africa
bourgeoisie: Karl Marx's term for the people who own the means of production
capitalist world economy: the dominance of capitalism in the world along with the international interdependence that capitalism has created
caste system: a form of social stratification in which one's status is determined by birth and is lifelong
class consciousness: Karl Marx's term for awareness of a common identity based on one's position in the means of production
class system: a form of social stratification based primarily on the possession of money or material possessions
colonialism: the process by which one nation takes over another nation, usually for the purpose of exploiting its labor and natural resources
culture of poverty: a culture that perpetuates poverty from one generation to the next
dependency theory: the view that the Least Industrialized Nations have been unable to develop their economies because they grew dependent on the Most Industrialized Nations
divine right of kings: the idea that the king's authority comes directly from God
endogamy: marriage within one's own group
estate stratification system: the stratification system of medieval Europe, consisting of three groups or estates; the nobility, the clergy, and serfs (or peasants)
false consciousness: Karl Marx's term to refer to workers identifying with the interests of capitalists
globalization: the extensive interconnections among world nations due to the expansion of capitalism
ideology: beliefs about the way things ought to be that justify social arrangements
indentured service: a contractual system in which someone sells his or her body (services) for a specified period of time in an arrangement very close to slavery, except that it is voluntarily entered into
means of production: the tools, factories, land, and investment capital used to produce wealth
meritocracy: a form of social stratification in which all positions are awarded on the basis of merit
multinational corporations: companies that operate across many national boundaries; also called transnational corporations
neocolonialism: the economic and political dominance of the Least Industrialized Nations by the Most Industrialized Nations
proletariat: Karl Marx's term for the people who work for those who own the means of production
slavery: a form of social stratification in which some people own other people
social mobility: movement up or down the social class ladder
social stratification: the division of large numbers of people into layers according to their relative power, property, and prestige; applies to both nations and to people within a nation, society, or other group
world system: economic and political connections that tie the world's countries together

☞ KEY PEOPLE

Review the major theoretical contributions or findings of these people.

Kingsley Davis and Wilbert Moore: According to these functionalists inequality is universal because it motivates the most qualified members of society to strive for the most important social positions.

John Kenneth Galbraith: This economist argued that the Least Industrialized Nations remain poor because their own culture holds them back.

Michael Harrington: Harrington saw that colonialism has been replaced by neocolonialism.

Gerhard Lenski: Lenski offered a synthesis of functionalist and conflict views of stratification.

Gerda Lerner: This historian noted that women were usually the first enslaved by war and conquest.

Karl Marx: Marx concluded that social class depended exclusively on the means of production; an individual's social class was determined by whether or not he owned the means of production.

Gaetano Mosca: Mosca argued that every society is inevitably stratified by power.

Melvin Tumin: Tumin was the first to offer a criticism of the functionalist view on stratification.

Immanuel Wallerstein: This historian proposed a world system theory to explain global stratification.

Max Weber: Weber argued that social class was based on three components--class, status, and power.

☞ **"DOWN-TO-EARTH SOCIOLOGY"**

This is your opportunity to apply the sociological perspective to the world around you. The questions in this section refer to material introduced in this chapter of your text. Many ask you to think about ideas and information presented in the various special "boxes" that are located throughout this chapter.

1.   Were you surprised to learn that slavery persists today? In what ways are the conditions of slavery, as described in "What Price Freedom? Slavery Today" on page 232, similar to that which exists long ago? Should we support the purchase of slaves as a strategy for ending slavery? Why or why not? What do you think we could do to end this form of inhumanity?

2.   Look at the maps and tables on pages 244-245. Why do you think the income per person is so much higher in Most Industrialized Nations? Does money just "go a lot farther" in the Least Industrialized Nations or do people in these countries have much lower standards of living than people in Most Industrialized Nations? Could you live on $1,000 a year?

3.   What was your reaction after reading about poor children in the Least Industrialized Nations (pp. 246-247)? How does this image of slum life compare with your image of life in U.S. inner-city ghettos? Do you think the Most Industrialized Nations should do anything about this situation?

4.   Read "Sex Tourism and The Patriotic Prostitute" on page 251. What do you think would happen if the U.S. government encouraged prostitution as a service to one's country? What would happen if the President suggested that young women prostitute themselves to earn money and contribute their earnings to the country to cut this nation's debt? Why do women's groups protest the international sex trade such as that described in this article?

☞ **SELF-TEST**

After completing this self-test, check your answers against the Answer Key beginning on page 366 of this Study Guide and against the text on page(s) indicated in parentheses.

MULTIPLE CHOICE QUESTIONS

1.   What is the division of large numbers of people into layers according to their relative power, property, and prestige? (228)
   a.   social distinction
   b.   social stratification
   c.   social distance
   d.   social diversification

2.	What is a form of social stratification in which some people own other people? (229)
	a.	a caste system
	b.	slavery
	c.	a class system
	d.	apartheid

3.	Slavery in the United States: (230)
	a.	started as indentured service.
	b.	was based on the ideology of racism that justified importing slaves from Africa.
	c.	became inheritable.
	d.	All of the above.

4.	Where is the best example of a caste system found? (231)
	a.	the United States
	b.	South America
	c.	India
	d.	South Africa

5.	In which type of stratification system is the practice of endogamy is most likely to be found? (231)
	a.	class system
	b.	caste system
	c.	meritocracy
	d.	socialist system

6.	In the system that existed in Europe during the Middle Ages, who was in the *second estate*? (234)
	a.	nobility
	b.	military leaders
	c.	the clergy
	d.	commoners

7.	Which of the following characterizes class systems? (234-235)
	a.	social mobility
	b.	geographic mobility
	c.	distribution of social standings belonging to an extended network of relatives
	d.	fixed boundaries between layers of the stratification system

8.	According to Marx, on what does social class depend? (235)
	a.	wealth, power, and prestige.
	b.	the means of production.
	c.	where one is born in the social stratification system.
	d.	what a person achieves during his or her lifetime.

9.	According to Max Weber, what determines social class? (236)
	a.	one's property, prestige, and power
	b.	one's relationship to the means of production
	c.	one's tasks and how important they are to society
	d.	one's political power

10. Which of these statements is consistent with the functionalist view of stratification? (237)
    a. Stratification is dysfunctional for society.
    b. Stratification is the outcome of conflict between different social classes.
    c. Stratification will disappear in societies that are characterized by a meritocracy.
    d. Stratification is an inevitable feature of social organization.

11. Which of these is not one of Tumin's criticisms of the functionalist theory of stratification? (238)
    a. The importance of a social position cannot be measured by the rewards it carries.
    b. The functionalists ignore the impact of family background.
    c. Stratification is not functional for everyone.
    d. The functionalists focus too much on the status and power and not enough on income.

12. A form of social stratification in which positions are awarded based on merit is called a(n): (238)
    a. meritocratic system.
    b. egalitarian system.
    c. socialistic system.
    d. democratic system.

13. Gaetano Mosca argued that every society will be stratified by: (238)
    a. wealth.
    b. class.
    c. individuals' relation to the mean of production.
    d. power.

14. According to conflict theorists, the basis of social stratification is: (239)
    a. functional necessity in society.
    b. conflict over limited resources.
    c. ascribed statuses.
    d. the way in which individuals perceive their social class position.

15. The key to maintaining national stratification is: (240)
    a. having a strong police force and military to demand compliance.
    b. control of social institutions.
    c. control of information.
    d. All of the above.

16. The British perpetuate their class system from one generation to the next by: (242)
    a. emphasis on material possessions such as clothes and cars.
    b. religion.
    c. education.
    d. encouraging persons in all classes to marry others within their own class.

17. In the former Soviet Union, the system of stratification was based on: (242)
    a. occupation.
    b. trade union membership.
    c. Communist party membership.
    d. education.

18. Why is it difficult to know how to classify some nations into a global system of stratification? (246)
   a. It is difficult because the dividing line between levels--Most Industrialized, Industrializing, and Least Industrialized--are soft.
   b. Some nations have moved beyond industrialization, becoming "post-industrial" nations.
   c. Some nations have not yet industrialized but are still extremely wealthy.
   d. All of the above reflect problems with classifying nations into a global system.

19. The majority of the world's population lives in _____ Nations. (247)
   a. Most Industrialized
   b. Industrializing
   c. Least Industrialized
   d. old-rich

20. In what way did U.S. colonialism differ from that of European nations? (248)
   a. The U.S. restricted its invasions to Asian nations like the Philippines or Hawaii.
   b. The U.S. usually chose to plant corporate flags rather than national flags.
   c. Colonialism undertaken by the U.S. was on a much larger scale than that of other industrialized nations.
   d. The U.S. was always sensitive to the cultural and religious differences of its colonies.

21. According to world system theory, all of the following are groups of interconnected nations, except: (249)
   a. core nations.
   b. nations on the semiperiphery.
   c. nations on the periphery.
   d. nations on the internal area which have extensive connections with the core nations.

22. Which of the following theories about global stratification refers to "banana republics?" (249)
   a. world system theory
   b. dependency theory
   c. culture of poverty theory
   d. neocolonialism

23. The culture of poverty theory was used to analyze global stratification by: (249)
   a. Immanuel Wallerstein.
   b. Max Weber.
   c. John Kenneth Galbraith.
   d. Karl Marx.

24. Neocolonialism refers to: (250)
   a. recent efforts by the Most Industrialized Nations to colonize Least Industrialized Nations.
   b. the economic policies of the Most Industrialized Nations that are designed to control the markets of the Least Industrialized Nations.
   c. programs like the Peace Corps that attempt to teach residents of the Least Industrialized Nations the skills necessary to survive in an industrial society.
   d. the economic policy of the Least Industrialized Nations in which they hold the Most Industrialized Nations hostage by controlling access to national resources like oil.

25.   Multinational corporations: (250-251)
      a.   are companies that operate across many national boundaries.
      b.   always exploit the Least Industrialized Nations directly.
      c.   benefit the Least Industrialized Nations as much as the Most Industrialized Nations.
      d.   All of the above.

TRUE-FALSE QUESTIONS

T F   1.   Social stratification refers only to individuals. (228)
T F   2.   Throughout history, slavery has always been based on racism. (229)
T F   3.   The first form of slavery in the New World was indentured service. (230)
T F   4.   A caste system is a form of social stratification in which individual status is determined by birth and is lifelong. (231)
T F   5.   A class system is based primarily on money or material possessions. (235)
T F   6.   Gender discrimination cuts across all systems of social stratification. (235)
T F   7.   According to Karl Marx, the means of production is the only factor in determining social class. (235)
T F   8.   According to Max Weber, class standing is a combination of power, prestige, and property. (236)
T F   9.   J. Edgar Hoover's power derived from his position as the head of a powerful government agency, the F.B.I. (237)
T F   10.   Functionalists believe that people should be rewarded for their unique abilities and the type of position they hold in society is not important. (237)
T F   11.   Most people in the United States view meritocracy as bad for societies. (238)
T F   12.   According to conflict theorists, the oppressed often support laws even when the laws operate against their own interests. (239)
T F   13.   Gerhard Lenski said that the functionalist view of stratification was most appropriate when studying societies with a surplus of wealth. (239)
T F   14.   The idea of the divine right of kings is an example of how the ruling elite uses ideas to maintain stratification. (240)
T F   15.   In maintaining stratification, elites find that technology is not particularly useful, because everyone can access technology. (241)
T F   16.   Colonialism was an important force in shaping many of the Least Industrialized Nations. (248)
T F   17.   Most European nations rejected colonialism as a strategy for gaining access to cheap raw materials. (248)
T F   18.   The expansion of capitalism resulted in a capitalist world economy dominated by the core nations. (249)
T F   19.   The culture of poverty thesis is generally preferred by sociologists as an explanation of global stratification. (250)
T F   20.   Neocolonialism is the economic and political dominance of the Least Industrialized Nations by the Most Industrialized Nations. (250)

FILL-IN QUESTIONS

1.   _____ is a system in which people are divided into layers according to their relative power, property, and prestige. (228)

2.   A form of social stratification in which some people own other people is _____. (229)

3.   A(n) _____ system is a form of social stratification in which individual status is determined by birth and is lifelong. (231)

4.   The South African practice of racial separation that existed until recently is _____. (233)

5.   Sociologists refer to movement up or down the social class ladder as _____. (235)

6.   According to Marx, the tools, factories, land, and investment capital used to produce wealth is _____. (235)

7.   According to Marx, the awareness of a common identity based on one's position in the means of production is _____. (236)

8.   Karl Marx's term for the mistaken identification of workers with the interests of capitalists was _____. (236)

9.   A _____ is a form of social stratification in which all positions are awarded on the basis of merit. (238)

10.   The _____ is the idea that the king's authority comes directly from God. (240)

11.   _____ is the process in which one nation takes over another nation, usually for the purpose of exploiting its labor and natural resources. (248)

12.   _____ is the extensive interconnections among world nations resulting from the expansion of capitalism. (249)

13.   _____ is a way of life that perpetuates poverty from one generation to the next. (249)

14.   _____ refers to the economic and political dominance of the Least Industrialized Nations by the Most Industrialized Nations. (250)

15.   Companies that operate across many national boundaries are _____. (250)

MATCH THESE SOCIAL SCIENTISTS WITH THEIR CONTRIBUTIONS

____1. Karl Marx   a. *world system theory*
____2. Kingsley Davis & Wilbert Moore   b. *criticism of functional view of stratification*
____3. Gaetano Mosca   c. *stressed culture of poverty*
____4. Immanuel Wallerstein   d. *false consciousness*
____5. Michael Harrington   e. *stated functionalist view of stratification*
____6. John Kenneth Galbraith   f. *forerunner of conflict view of stratification*
____7. Max Weber   g. *neocolonialism*
____8. Melvin Tumin   h. *class based on property, prestige and power*

ESSAY QUESTIONS

1.   Compare Marx's theory of stratification with Weber's theory. Discuss why Weber's is more widely accepted by sociologists.

2.   Consider why ideology is a more effective way of maintaining stratification than brute force.

3.   In the 1960s most former colonies around the globe won their political independence. Since that time the position of these countries has remained largely unchanged within the global system of stratification. Provide some explanation as to why political independence alone was not enough to alter their status.

CHAPTER 10
SOCIAL CLASS IN THE UNITED STATES

☞ CHAPTER SUMMARY

- Most sociologists have adopted Weber's definition of social class as a large group of people who rank closely to one another in terms of wealth, power, and prestige. Wealth consists of property and income; power is defined as the ability to carry out one's will despite the resistance of others; and prestige is a measure of the regard or respect accorded an individual or social position. Most people are status consistent, meaning that they rank high or low on all three dimensions of social class. People who rank high on some dimensions and low on others are status inconsistent. The frustration of status inconsistency tends to produce political radicalism.
- Sociologists use two models to portray the social class structure. Erik Wright developed a four class model based on the ideas of Karl Marx. Dennis Gilbert and Joseph Kahl developed a six class model based on the ideas of Max Weber.
- Social class leaves no aspect of life untouched. Class membership affects child rearing, educational attainment, religious affiliation, political participation and contact with crime and the criminal justice system.
- In studying the mobility of individuals within society, sociologists look at intergenerational mobility, individual changes in social class from one generation to the next, exchange mobility, the movement of large numbers of people from one class to another, and structural mobility, the social and economic changes that affect the social class position of large numbers of people.
- Poverty is unequally distributed in the United States. Minorities, children, female-headed households, and the rural poor are more likely to be poor. Sociologists generally focus on structural factors, such as employment opportunities, in explaining poverty.
- The Horatio Alger myth encourages people to strive to get ahead, and blames failures on individual shortcomings.

☞ LEARNING OBJECTIVES

As you read Chapter 10, use these learning objectives to organize your notes. After completing your reading, briefly state an answer to each of the objectives, and review the text pages in parentheses.

1. Define social class and explain why sociologists do not agree on what the components of social class are. (256)
2. Outline and explain the three dimensions of social class. (256-262)
3. Define status inconsistency and discuss the consequences for individual behavior. (262)
4. Explain Erik Wright's updated model of Marx's class theory. (263)
5. Discuss Gilbert and Kahl's updated model of Weber's perspective. (263-266)
6. Examine the consequences of social class on physical and mental health, family life, education, religion, politics, the criminal justice system, and new technology. (267-270)
7. Distinguish between the different types of social mobility. (270-272)
8. Discuss the patterns of social mobility for both men and women within the United States. (272)
9. Note the role that technology has played in terms of mobility, both upward and downward. (272-273)

10.   Explain some of the costs of social mobility. (273)
11.   Indicate how the poverty line is drawn. State the major characteristics of the poor in the United States. (273-278)
12.   Relate the research findings on duration of poverty. (279)
13.   Assess individual versus structural explanations of poverty. (297)
14.   Explain what conflict theorists mean when they say that the welfare system is designed to maintain an army of reserve workers. (297-280)
15.   Identify the social functions of the Horatio Alger myth. (281)

☞ CHAPTER OUTLINE

I.   **What Is Social Class?**
   A.   Social class can be defined as a large group of people who rank close to each other in wealth, power, and prestige.
   B.   Wealth consists of property (what we own) and income (money we receive). Wealth and income are not always the same--a person may own much property yet have little income, or vice versa. Usually, however, wealth and income go together.
      1.   Ownership of property (real estate, stocks and bonds, etc.) is not distributed evenly: 10 percent of the U.S. population owns 68 percent of the wealth, and the wealthiest 1 percent of families are worth more than the entire bottom 90 percent of Americans.
      2.   Income is also distributed disproportionately: the top 20 percent of U.S. residents acquire 47 percent of the income; the bottom 20 percent receive less than 5 percent. Each fifth of the U.S. population receives approximately the same proportion of national income today as it did in 1945; those changes that have occurred reflect growing inequality.
      3.   Apart from the very rich, the most affluent group in U.S. society is the executive officers of the largest corporations. Their median income (excluding stock options) is $3.1 million a year.
   C.   Power is the ability to carry out your will despite resistance. Power is concentrated in the hands of a few--the "power elite"--who share the same ideologies and values, belong to the same clubs, and reinforce each other's world view. No major decision in U.S. government is made without their approval.
   D.   Prestige is the respect or regard people give to various occupations and accomplishments.
      1.   Occupations are the primary source of prestige, although some people gain prestige through inventions, feats, or doing good to others. Occupations with the highest prestige pay more, require more education, entail more abstract thought, and offer greater autonomy.
      2.   For prestige to be valuable, people must acknowledge it. The elite traditionally has made rules to emphasize their higher status.
      3.   Status symbols, which vary according to social class, are ways of displaying prestige. In the United States, they include designer label clothing, expensive cars, prestigious addresses, and attending particular schools.
   E.   Status inconsistency is the term used to describe the situation of people who have a mixture of high and low rankings in the three components of social class (wealth, power, and prestige).

      1.   Most people are status consistent--they rank at the same level in all three components. People who are status inconsistent want others to act toward them on the basis of their highest status, but others tend to judge them on the basis of their lowest status.

      2.   Sociologist Gerhard Lenski determined that people suffering the frustrations of status inconsistency are more likely to be radical and approve political action aimed against higher status groups.

II.   Sociological Models of Social Class

    A.   How many classes exist in industrial society is a matter of debate, but there are two main models, one that builds on Marx and the other on Weber.

    B.   Sociologist Erik Wright realized that not everyone falls into Marx's two broad classes (capitalists and workers, which were based upon a person's relationship to the means of productions). For instance, although executives, managers, and supervisors would fall into Marx's category of workers, they act more like capitalists.

      1.   Wright resolved this problem by regarding some people as simultaneously members of more than one class, which he called contradictory class locations.

      2.   Wright identified four classes: capitalists (owners of large enterprises); petty bourgeoisie (owners of small businesses); managers (employees who but have authority over others); and workers.

    C.   Using the model originally developed by Weber, sociologists Dennis Gilbert and Joseph Kahl created a model to describe class structure in the U.S. and other capitalist countries.

      1.   The capitalist class (1% of the population) is composed of investors, heirs, and a few executives; it is divided into "old" money and "new" money. The children of "new" money move into the old money class by attending the right schools and marrying "old" money.

      2.   The upper-middle class (15% of the population) is composed of professionals and upper managers, almost all of whom have attended college or university and frequently have postgraduate degrees.

      3.   The lower-middle class (32% of the population) is composed of lower managers, craftspeople and foremen. They have at least a high school education.

      4.   The working class (32% of the population) is composed of factory workers and low-paid white collar workers. Most have high school educations.

      5.   The working poor (16% of the population) is composed of relatively unskilled blue-collar and white-collar workers, and those with temporary and seasonal jobs. If they graduated from high school, they probably did not do well in school.

      6.   The underclass (4% of the population) is concentrated in the inner cities and has little connection with the job market. Welfare is their main support.

    D.   The homeless are so far down the class structure that their position must be considered even lower than the underclass. They are the "fallout" of industrialization, especially the post-industrial developments that have led to a decline in the demand for unskilled labor.

    E.   The automobile industry illustrates the social class ladder as described by Gilbert and Kahl.

      1.   The Ford family and Ford executives represent both the upper and lower levels of the capitalist class.

      2.   Owners of Ford dealerships are members of the upper middle class, while a salesperson in their employ is drawn from the lower middle class.

      3.   Mechanics who repair Ford automobiles are members of the working class. The working poor are presented by the "detail" workers.

4.   If the agency employs day laborers to mow the lawn or clean the lot, they would come from the underclass.

III.   **Consequences of Social Class**

A.   The lower a person's social class, the more likely that person is to die at an earlier age than people in higher classes; this is true at all ages. Since medical care is expensive, the higher classes receive better medical care, despite government aid to the poor; the result is a two-tiered system of medical care.

B.   Mental health is worse for the lower classes because of stresses associated with their class position. Those higher in the class system are better able to afford vacations, psychiatrists and counselors; their class position gives them greater control over their lives.

C.   Social class also plays a role in family life.

1.   Children of the capitalist class are under great pressure to select the right mate in order to assure the continuity of the family line. Parents in this social class play a large role in mate selection.

2.   Marriages are more likely to fail in the lower social classes; the children of the poor thus are more likely to live in single-parent households.

3.   Child rearing varies by class, with each class raising its children with attitudes and behaviors suited to the kinds of occupations they will eventually hold. Lower class families teach children to defer to authority, as is required in their jobs. Higher class families encourage freedom, creativity, and self-expression, as is found in their jobs.

D.   Education levels increase as one moves up the social class ladder. The change occurs not only in terms of the amount of education obtained, but also in terms of the type of education, with the capitalist class bypassing public schools in favor of exclusive private schools, where its children are trained to take a commanding role in society.

E.   All aspects of religious orientation follow class lines. Social classes tend to cluster around different denominations. Lower classes are attracted to spontaneous worship services and louder music, while higher classes prefer more restrained worship services.

F.   Political views and involvement are influenced by social class.

1.   The rich and the poor take divergent political paths, with people in lower social classes more likely to vote Democrat, while those in higher classes vote Republican; the parties are seen as promoting different class interests.

2.   People in working class are more likely to be liberal on economic issues (more government spending) and more conservative on social issues (opposition to abortion).

3.   Political participation is not equal: the higher classes are more likely to vote and get involved in politics than those in lower social classes.

G.   The criminal justice system is not blind to class: members of lower classes are more likely to be arrested, are more likely to be on probation, parole, or in jail, and more crimes occur in lower class neighborhoods.

H.   The new technology does not affect social classes in the same way.

1.   The higher one is on the social class ladder, the more likely they are to benefit from technology. For the capitalist class, the new technology is a means to extensive, worldwide profits.

2.   The upper-middle class also benefits because the new technology enables them to achieve in their chosen professions, and their education prepares them to take a leading role in managing in the new global system.

3.   Below these top two classes, technology creates much more uncertainty, with uncertainty increasing as you move down the ladder. Those at the bottom have few technological skills.

IV.   **Social Mobility**
A.   There are three basic types of social mobility: intergenerational, structural, and exchange.
1.   Intergenerational mobility is the change that family members make in their social class from one generation to the next. As a result of individual effort, a person can rise from one level to another; in the event of individual failure, the reverse can be true.
2.   Structural mobility involves social changes that affect large numbers of people. By way of example, when computers were invented, many opportunities opened up for people to switch from blue-collar to white-collar work. While individual effort played a role, the major reason for the change in position was structural.
3.   Exchange mobility is movement of people up and down the social class system, where, on balance, the system remains the same. The term refers to general, overall movement of large numbers of people that leaves the class system basically untouched.
B.   Women have been largely ignored in studies of occupational mobility. Studies of social mobility among men indicate that about one-half of sons have moved beyond their fathers; about one-third have stayed at the same level; and about one-sixth have fallen down the ladder.
1.   As structural changes in the U.S. economy have created opportunities for women to move up the social class ladder, studies of their mobility patterns have appeared.
2.   One study indicated that women who did move up were encouraged by their parents to postpone marriage and get an education.
C.   Technology is responsible for much of the uncertainty and downward mobility of U.S. workers. Computers and instantaneous communications enable companies to relocate production worldwide, locating in areas with lower paid, nonunionized work forces.
D.   The costs of social mobility include risking the loss of one's roots. One study found that among working class families in which the adult children had achieved upward social mobility because of parental sacrifices that enabled them to get an education, the parent-adult child relationship was marked by estrangement, lack of communication, and bitterness.

V.   **Poverty**
A.   The U.S. government classifies the poverty line as being families whose incomes are less than three times a low-cost food budget. Any modification of this measure instantly adds or subtracts millions of people, and thus has significant consequences.
B.   Certain social groups are disproportionately represented among the poor population.
1.   With the exception of California, the poor tend to be clustered in the south. The poverty rate for the rural poor is higher than the national average. While they show the same racial/ethnic characteristics as the nation as a whole, they are less likely to be on welfare or to be single parents, less skilled and less educated, and the jobs available to them pay less.
2.   Race is a major factor. Racial minorities are much more likely to be poor: 11 percent of whites, 27 percent of Latinos and African-Americans live in poverty.
3.   The chances of being poor decrease as the amount of education increases.

4.   The sex of the person who heads a family is another major predictor of whether or not a family is poor. Most poor families are headed by women. The major causes of this phenomenon, called the feminization of poverty, are divorce, births to unwed mothers, and the lower wages paid to women.

5.   Although the percentage of poor people over age 65 is practically the same as their overall percentage, elderly Hispanic Americans and African Americans are almost three times more likely to be poor than elderly white Americans.

C.   Children are more likely to live in poverty than are adults or the elderly. This holds true regardless of race, but poverty is much greater among minority children.

D.   In the 1960s Michael Harrington and Oscar Lewis suggested that the poor get trapped in a "culture of poverty" as a result of having values and behaviors that make them "fundamentally different" from other U.S. residents.

1.   National statistics indicate that most poverty is short, lasting one or less years. Only 12 percent of the poor live in poverty for five or more years.

2.   Since the number of people who live in poverty remains fairly constant, this means that as many people move into poverty as move out of it.

E.   In trying to explain poverty, the choice is between focusing on individual explanations or on social structural explanations.

1.   Sociologists look to such factors as inequalities in education, access to learning job skills, racial, ethnic, age, and gender discrimination, and large-scale economic change to explain the patterns of poverty in society.

2.   The other explanation is individualistic, focusing on the characteristics of individuals that are assumed to contribute to their poverty.

F.   In 1996, welfare reform was enacted. There are caps on welfare assistance and recipients are required to look for work.

1.   In the aftermath of this, welfare rolls dropped.

2.   Conflict theorists argue that the purpose of the welfare system is to maintain an army of reserve workers. In times of economic expansion, welfare requirements are tightened, forcing workers into the job market. When recession hits, welfare rules are relaxed.

G.   Because the poor don't see the future as different from the past, they find it difficult to defer gratification--give up things now for the sake of greater gains in the future.

H.   Because of real-life examples of people from humble origins who climbed far up the social ladder, most U.S. residents (including minorities and the working poor) believe that they have a chance of getting ahead.

1.   The Horatio Alger myth obviously is a statistical impossibility. Despite this, functionalists would stress that this belief is functional for society because it encourages people to compete for higher positions, while placing the blame for failure squarely on the individual.

2.   As Marx and Weber both noted, social class affects our ideas of life and our proper place in society. At the same time, the dominant ideology often blinds us to these effects in our own lives.

☞ KEY TERMS

After studying the chapter, review the definition for each of the following terms.

contradictory class location: Erik Wright's term for a position in the class structure that generates contradictory interests

culture of poverty: the assumption that the values and behaviors of the poor make them fundamentally different from other people, that these factors are largely responsible for their poverty, and that parents perpetuate poverty across generations by passing these characteristics on to their children

deferred gratification: forgoing something in the present in the hope of achieving greater gains in the future

downward social mobility: movement down the social class ladder

exchange mobility: about the same numbers of people moving up and down the social class ladder, such that, on balance, the social class system shows little change

feminization of poverty: a trend in U.S. poverty whereby most poor families are headed by women

Horatio Alger myth: the belief that due to limitless possibilities anyone can get ahead of he or she tries hard enough

intergenerational mobility: the change that family members make in social class from one generation to the next

poverty: lacking resources to meet your basic needs

poverty line: the official measure of poverty; calculated to include those whose incomes are less than three times a low-cost food budget

power: the ability to get your way in spite of the desires of other people

power elite: C. Wright Mills's term for the top people in U.S. corporations, military, and politics who make the nation's major decisions

prestige: respect or regard

social class: according to Weber, a large group of people who rank close to one another in wealth, power, and prestige; according to Marx, one of two groups: capitalists who own the means of production and workers who sell their labor

status: social ranking

status consistency: ranking high or low on all three dimensions of social class

status inconsistency (or status discrepancy): a condition in which a person ranks high on some dimensions of social class and low on others

structural mobility: movement up or down the social class ladder that is attributable to changes in the structure of society, not to individual efforts

underclass: a small group of people for whom poverty persists year after year and across generations

upward social mobility: movement up the social class ladder

wealth: property and income

☞ KEY PEOPLE

Review the major theoretical contributions or findings of these people.

William Domhoff: Drawing upon the work of C. Wright Mills, Domhoff analyzed the workings of the ruling class.

Dennis Gilbert and Joseph Kahl: These sociologists developed a more contemporary stratification model based on Max Weber's work.

Ray Gold: In research on status inconsistency, Gold studied tenant reactions to janitors who earned more than they did. He found that the tenants acted "snooty" to the janitors, and the janitors took pleasure in knowing the intimate details of the tenants lives.

Elizabeth Higgenbotham and Lynn Weber: These sociologists studied the mobility patterns for women. They found that those women who experienced upward mobility were most likely to have strong parental support to defer marriage and get an education.

Melvin Kohn: Kohn studied social class differences in child-rearing patterns.

Gerhard Lenski: Lenski noted the everyone wants to maximize their status, but that others often judge an individual on the basis of his lowest status despite the individual's efforts to be judged on the basis of his highest status.

C. Wright Mills: Mills used the term power elite to describe the top decision-makers in the nation.

Daniel Moynihan: Now a U.S. senator, back in the 1960s this sociologist attributed the high rate of childhood poverty in the African American community to the breakdown of the family.

Richard Sennett and Jonathan Cobb: Sennett and Cobb studied the impact that a child's upward mobility had on his relationship with his parents. They found that the parents' sacrifices in order to afford the educational costs for their children were rarely appreciated; with increased education the child grew distant from the parents' world.

Erik Wright: Wright proposed an updated version of Marx's theory of stratification.

☞ **"DOWN-TO-EARTH SOCIOLOGY"**

This is your opportunity to apply the sociological perspective to the world around you. The questions in this section refer to material introduced in this chapter of your text. Many ask you to think about ideas and information presented in the various special "boxes" that are located throughout this chapter.

1.   Study Figure 10.3 on page 259 and then explain the consistency of income distribution across the years to someone who is unfamiliar with U.S. society.

2.   After reading about "How the Rich Live" on page 260, think about how the really wealthy spend their money. What are some examples of status symbols? If you were as rich as John Castle, how would you spend your money?

3.   Can you find your future occupation listed in Table 10.2 (p. 261)? If it is ranked high on this table, was prestige a consideration in your decision to hold this occupation? If it is ranked lower on the scale, what other factors make it appealing to you?

4.   In the box on "Closing the Digital Divide" on page 271, the author suggests that one way for us to assure that every child has the opportunity to become computer literate is to use tax dollars to connect every American to the Internet and to buy a computer for every child. What do you think about this? How likely is this to happen? Do you think we have a responsibility to see that every child has equal access to computers?

5.   In what ways did David Croteau's personal account of upward mobility (p. 274) reflect the impact that social class has on our individual opportunities? In other words, how did the fact that his parents were working class affect his life chance? What was it that motivated him to go to college? How did his upward mobility change his life and his relationships with his family?

6.   Which myths about the poor that are listed on page 276 reflect your own ideas about poverty? Did the facts help you in understanding the realities of poverty?

7.   After reading "Children in Poverty" (p. 278), should childhood poverty be a concern only for the poor or is it everyone's concern? What should be done to relieve the problem?

8.   Do you often distinguish the deserving poor from the undeserving poor (pp. 279-280)? Why do

you think we do this? What are the social characteristics of both groups? What are the social conditions that contribute to their poverty? What can be done about it?

9.   Why do you think the author presents a brief glimpse into his own life (p. 282)? How do his own experiences fit with the sociological theories and research that were presented in this chapter?

10. Can you think of some contemporary Horatio Alger heros, people who have moved up the social class ladder from poverty to wealth? Why do you think it is so important to continually hold up such individuals for all of us to see? What function do they serve?

☞ SELF-TEST

After completing this self-test, check your answers against the Answer Key beginning on page 369 of this Study Guide and against the text on page(s) indicated in parentheses.

MULTIPLE CHOICE QUESTIONS

1.   According to your text, on what do most sociologists agree concerning social class? (256)
   a.   It has a clear-cut, accepted definition in sociology.
   b.   It is best defined by the two classes as set out by Marx.
   c.   It is best defined by Weber's dimensions of social class.
   d.   It has no clear-cut, accepted definition and, thus, is used differently by all sociologists.

2.   What percent of the nation's families own 68 percent of the wealth in the U.S.? (257)
   a.   1
   b.   5
   c.   10
   d.   20

3.   According to Paul Samuelson, if an income pyramid were made out of a child's blocks, where would most U.S. residents be? (257)
   a.   near the top of the pyramid.
   b.   near the middle of the pyramid.
   c.   near the bottom of the pyramid.
   d.   None of the above.

4.   Which of the following statements best describes changes in the distribution of U.S. income? (257)
   a.   The income distribution has remained virtually unchanged across time.
   b.   The percentage of income going to the richest 20 percent of U.S. families have declined while the percentage going to the poorest 20 percent has increased.
   c.   The percentage of income going to the middle income groups has increased at the expense of groups at both the top and bottom of the income scale.
   d.   The percentage of income going to the richest 20 percent of U.S. families have increased while the percentage going to the poorest 20 percent has decreased.

5.   What term did Mills use to refer to decision makers at the top of society? (259)
   a.   the decision elite
   b.   the power elite
   c.   the power corps
   d.   the power brokers

6. Which of the statements regarding the jobs that have the most prestige is <u>not</u> true? (260)
    a.   they pay more.
    b.   they require more education.
    c.   they require special talent or skills.
    d.   they offer greater autonomy.

7. Based on his research, what did Ray Gold discover about status inconsistency? (262)
    a.   College professors tend to be politically radical
    b.   Most people ignore their own inconsistent status while focuses on others.
    c.   Tenants related to the inconsistent status of the apartment building janitors by acting "snooty" towards them.
    d.   Status inconsistency is a very uncommon situation because most people try to be placed in approximately the same place in all three dimensions of stratification.

8. How did Erik Wright update Marx's class categories in response to criticisms that they were too broad? (263)
    a.   He divided each of the two classes into three sub-classes, making six classes in all.
    b.   He created an open scale in which people place themselves into classes.
    c.   He recommended listing people's different associations and then classifying them on the basis of their most important one.
    d.   He recognized that some people can be members of more than one class at the same time.

9. According to Gilbert & Kahl,, the members of which social class can attribute their location in the class system to having a college or post-graduate education? (265)
    a.   the capitalist class
    b.   the upper middle class
    c . the lower middle class
    d.   the working class

10. According to Gilbert and Kahl, all of the following are characteristics of the working class, <u>except</u>: (265)
    a.   most are employed in relatively unskilled blue-collar and white-collar jobs.
    b.   most have attended college for one or two years.
    c.   most hope to get ahead by achieving seniority on the job.
    d.   about thirty percent of the population belong to this class.

11. According to your text, the typical mechanic in a Ford dealership would be in the: (266)
    a.   upper-middle class.
    b.   lower-middle class.
    c.   working class.
    d.   underclass.

12. What factor or factors explain the social class difference in death rates? (267)
    a.   differential risk of dying from accidents
    b.   nutritional differences
    c.   unequal access to medical care
    d.   all of the above explain differences in death rates

13. Which of the following statements about social class differences in mental health is <u>correct</u>? (268)
    a. The rich have less control over their wealth, since it is invested in the stock market, so they worry more about becoming poor.
    b. The poor have less job security and lower wages than the non-poor, which contribute to higher levels of stress.
    c. The rich experience more divorce and alcoholism, which can undermine their mental health.
    d. The middle class is squeezed by higher and higher taxes, which produces feelings of discontent and poor mental health.

14. According to Melvin Kohn lower class parents are concerned that their children be: (269)
    a. creative.
    b. independent.
    c. conformists.
    d. all of the above.

15. Which class tends to bypass public schools entirely, in favor of exclusive private schools? (269)
    a. capitalist
    b. upper-middle
    c. middle
    d. All of the above.

16. Which class tends to be conservative on social issues but liberal on economic ones? (269)
    a. upper class
    b. middle class
    c. lower class
    d. working class

17. Members of the _____ class are more likely to be robbed, burglarized, or murdered. (270)
    a. upper
    b. middle
    c. lower
    d. None of the above.

18. Which class or classes benefit from technology? (270)
    a. working class and the working poor
    b. upper and lower middle classes
    c. lower middle and working classes
    d. capitalist and upper middle classes

19. A homeless person whose father was a physician has experienced: (271)
    a. exchange mobility.
    b. structural mobility.
    c. upward mobility.
    d. downward mobility.

20.   As compared with their fathers, most U.S. men: (272)
       a.   have a status higher than that of their fathers.
       b.   have the same status their fathers did.
       c.   have a status lower than that of their fathers.
       d.   The relative statuses of fathers and sons can't be compared because of structural mobility.

21.   Higgenbotham and Weber found that for career women from working class backgrounds: (272)
       a.   intergenerational mobility was greater for sons than for daughters.
       b.   upwardly mobile women achieved higher positions despite their parents reservations.
       c.   upwardly mobile women achieved higher class positions because of parental encouragement that began when they were just little girls.
       d.   any upward mobility was due entirely to structural changes in the economy rather than individual effort or parental influences.

22.   The measure of poverty that is based on a figure three times a low-cost food budget is the: (273)
       a.   adjusted income level.
       b.   the welfare distribution scale.
       c.   the poverty line.
       d.   the welfare line.

23.   In the U.S., which group has poverty rates that are lower than the national average? (277)
       a.   women
       b.   racial minorities
       c.   the elderly
       d.   children

24.   In trying to explain poverty, sociologists are most likely to stress: (279)
       a.   individual characteristics that are assumed to contribute to poverty.
       b.   features of the social structure that contribute to poverty.
       c.   decisions made by the poor that prevent them from ever moving out of poverty.
       d.   that poverty is intergenerational, so that most who are born poor will remain poor.

25.   The Horatio Alger myth: (281)
       a.   is beneficial for society, according to the functionalists.
       b.   reduces pressures on the social system.
       c.   motivates people to try harder to succeed because anything is possible.
       d.   all of the above.

TRUE-FALSE QUESTIONS

T F   1.   Within sociology there is a clear-cut, widely agreed-upon definition of social class. (256)
T F   2.   Wealth and income are the same thing. (256)
T F   3.   The richest one percent of U.S. families are worth more than the entire bottom 90 percent of Americans. (257)
T F   4.   Apart from the very rich, the most affluent group in U.S. society consists of the chief executive officers of the nation's largest corporations. (257)
T F   5.   Occupational prestige rankings vary widely across countries and over time. (261)

T F   6.   For many, prestige is a primary factor in deciding what college to attend. (262)
T F   7.   College professors typically are an example of status inconsistency. (262)
T F   8.   According to Gilbert and Kahl, the capitalist class has the ability to shape the consciousness of the nation. (264)
T F   9.   The distinctions between lower middle class and working class are more blurred than those between other classes. (265)
T F   10.   The underclass is concentrated in the inner city with few ties to the job market. (265-266)
T F   11.   The homeless are the "fallout" of industrialization, especially of post-industrial developments. (266)
T F   12.   Social class affects a person's chances of living and dying. (267)
T F   13.   Marriages of the poor are more likely to fail and their children to group up in broken homes. (269)
T F   14.   Members of the lower classes are more likely to be on probation, on parole, or in jail than members of the upper classes. (270)
T F   15.   Structural mobility refers to social and economic changes that affect the status of large numbers of people. (272)
T F   16.   Exchange mobility leaves the class system basically untouched. (272)
T F   17.   The rural poor do not differ significantly from the urban poor. (274)
T F   18.   Whites have higher rates of poverty than ethnic/racial minorities simply because there are so many more whites in the U.S. population. (275)
T F   19.   The majority of the poor live below the poverty line for long periods of time. (279)
T F   20.   Sociological explanations of poverty tend to focus on structural features of society more than on any particular characteristics of poor individuals. (279)

FILL-IN QUESTIONS

1.   According to Max Weber, the three dimensions of social class are: (1)_____; (2)_____; and (3)_____. (256)
2.   Property and income together make up an individual's _____. (256)
3.   According to C. Wright Mills, the _____ makes the big decisions in U.S. society. (259)
4.   A condition in which someone has a mixture of high and low ranks on the different dimensions of social class is referred to as _____. (262)
5.   Erik Wright referred to a position in the class structure that generates inconsistent interests as _____. (263)
6.   According to Gilbert and Kahl, the capitalist class can be divided into two groups: (1) _____ and (2) _____. (264)
7.   The _____ is a small group of people for whom poverty persists year after year and across generations. (265)
8.   _____ is movement up the social class ladder. (271)
9.   Movement up or down the social class ladder that is attributed to changes in the structure of society, not to individual efforts, is _____. (272)
10. The official measure of poverty is referred to as the _____; it is calculated to include those whose incomes are less than three times a low-income food budget. (272)
11. _____ is a trend whereby most poor families in the U.S. are headed by women. (273)
12. In the 1960s, social scientists like Michael Harrington and Oscar Lewis suggested that some of the poor get trapped in a _____. (279)

13.   The _____ are people who, in the public mind, are poor through no fault of their own, while the _____ are viewed as having brought on their own poverty. (279-280)

14.   Foregoing something in the present in hope of achieving greater gains in the future is _____ . (281)

15.   The belief that anyone can get ahead if they only try hard enough is referred to as the _____ . (281)

MATCH THESE SOCIAL SCIENTISTS WITH THEIR CONTRIBUTIONS

___1. Gerhard Lenski   a. *power elite*

___2. C. Wright Mills   b. *social class patterns of child rearing*

___3. Erik Wright   c. *hidden costs of mobility*

___4. Gilbert & Kahl   d. *status inconsistency*

___5. Daniel Moynihan   e. *updated Marx's model*

___6. Sennett & Cobb   f. *childhood poverty and the breakdown of the family*

___7. Melvin Kohn   g. *updated Weber's model*

___8. Higgenbotham & Weber   h. *women's patterns of social mobility*

ESSAY QUESTIONS

1.   Identify the three dimensions of social class and discuss some of the consequences of social class.

2.   Discuss why you think women have been largely ignored in studies of mobility.

3.   Describe which groups are a greatest risk of poverty and then suggest ways in which poverty can be reduced by targeting these populations.

CHAPTER 11
SEX AND GENDER

☞ CHAPTER SUMMARY

- Gender stratification refers to unequal access to power, property, and prestige on the basis of sex. Each society establishes a structure that, on the basis of sex and gender, opens and closes access to privileges. Sex refers to biological distinctions between males and females; gender refers to behaviors and attitudes thought to be socially acceptable for males and females. In the "nature versus nurture" debate, almost all sociologists take the side of nurture. In recent years the door to biology has opened somewhat.

- George Murdock found a pattern of sex-typed activities among premodern societies, with greater prestige given to those performed by males. Patriarchy, or male dominance, appears to be universal.

- The dominant theory to explain the status of women as a minority group focuses on the physical limitations imposed by childbirth.

- Although feminist movements in the United States have battled to eliminate some of the most blatant forms of gender discrimination, there are still many areas of inequality. More females than males now attend college, but both generally end up in gender-biased academic fields although there are some signs of change today. Two indicators of gender inequality in everyday life are the general devaluation of femininity and the male dominance of conversation.

- In the work place women's problems include discrimination in pay and sexual harassment.

- Traditional gender patterns still exist in regard to violent behavior. Female circumcision is a special case of violence against women.

- Women's traditional roles as homemakers and child care providers used to keep them out of politics, but today the trend is towards greater political equality.

- As females come to play a larger role in decision-making processes of U.S. social institutions, stereotypes and role models will be broken. It is possible that a new concept of the human personality--one that allows males and females to pursue their individual interests unfettered by gender--might occur.

☞ LEARNING OBJECTIVES

As you read Chapter 11, use these learning objectives to organize your notes. After completing your reading, briefly state an answer to each of the objectives, and review the text pages in parentheses.

1. Define gender stratification and differentiate between sex and gender. (285-286)
2. Discuss the continuing controversy regarding the biological and cultural factors which come into play in creating gender differences in societies. (286-289)
3. Summarize findings of research studies that suggest biology does play a role in gender behavior. (289-291)
4. Describe the global nature of gender inequality. (291-294)
5. Discuss the dominant theory about the origins of discrimination against women. (295-297)
6. Describe the major factors which contributed to the two "waves" of feminism in the United States and note how successful this movement has been up to this point in time. (297-298)

7. Describe how gender inequality is expressed in the U.S. educational system and in the everyday lives of Americans. (299-302)
8. Explain gender relations in the workplace, including the pay gap, the glass ceiling and glass escalator, the "mommy track," and sexual harassment. (302-309)
9. Explain what the author means when he says gender violence is a "one-way street." (309-311)
10. Explain why women historically have not taken over politics and transformed American life and identify the factors that point to a fundamental transformation in women's political participation today. (311-313)
11. Describe what the future looks like in terms of gender relations in the United States. (313)

☞ CHAPTER OUTLINE

I. **Issues of Sex and Gender**
    A. Gender stratification refers to men's and women's unequal access to power, prestige, and property.
    B. Sex and gender reflect different bases.
        1. Sex is biological characteristics distinguishing males and females--primary sex organs (organs related to reproduction) and secondary sex organs (physical distinctions not related to reproduction).
        2. Gender is a social characteristic which varies from one society to another and refers to what the group considers proper for its males and females. The sociological significance of gender is that it is the means by which society controls its members; it sorts us, on the basis of sex, into different life experiences.
    C. Some researchers argue that biological factors (two X chromosomes in females, one X and one Y in males) result in differences in conduct, with men being more aggressive and domineering and women being more comforting and nurturing.
    D. The dominant sociological position is that social factors explain why we do what we do. People in every society determine what the physical differences separating men and women mean to them.
        1. Children learn these contrasting explanations of life and then take the positions that society assigns to them on the basis of their sex.
        2. Sociologists argue that if biology was the primary factor in human behavior, then women the world over would all behave the same way, as would men. In fact, ideas of gender vary greatly from one culture to another.
    E. Alice Rossi suggested that women are better prepared biologically for "mothering" than are men: nature provides biological predispositions which are overlaid with culture.
    F. Real life cases provide support for the argument that men's and women's behavior is influenced by both culture and biology.
        1. A medical accident led to a young boy being reassigned to the female sex. Reared as a female, the child behaved like a girl; however, by adolescence she was unhappy and having a difficult time adjusting to being a female. In adolescence, the child underwent medical procedures to once again become a male.
        2. A study of Vietnam veterans found that the men who had higher levels of testosterone tended to be more aggressive and to have more problems.
II. **Gender Inequality in Global Perspective**
    A. Historian and feminist Gerda Lerner has concluded that women as a group have never held

decision-making power over men as a group. This was true even in the earliest known societies, in which there was much less gender discrimination.

B. George Murdock, who surveyed 324 premodern societies, found activities to be sex typed in all of them; activities considered female in one society may be male in another. There is nothing about anatomy that requires this.

C. Universally, greater prestige is given male activities regardless of what they are. If caring for cattle is men's work, it carries high prestige; if it is women's work, it has less prestige.

D. Globally, gender discrimination occurs in the areas of education, politics, paid employment, and violence against women.

III. How Females Became a Minority Group

A. Around the world, gender is *the* primary division between people. Because society sets up barriers to deny women equal access, they are referred to as a minority even though they outnumber men.

B. Although the origin of patriarchy (male dominance) is unknown, the dominant theory assumes that patriarchy is universal and that biology, along with social factors, plays a role in male dominance.

1. In early societies, life was short and many children needed to be born in order for the group to survive. Consequently, women were pregnant or nursing young children for much of their adult lives. As a result of these biologically-driven activities, women were limited in terms of alternatives and assumed tasks associated with the home and child care.

2. Men took over tasks requiring greater strength and longer absences, such as hunting animals. This enabled men to make contact with other tribes, trade with those other groups, and wage war and gain prestige by returning home with prisoners of war or with large animals to feed the tribe; little prestige was given to women's more routine tasks.

C. The answer as to the accuracy of this theory is buried in human history and there is no way of testing either this one or others suggested by Marvin Harris, Frederick Engels, or Gerda Lerner. Whatever the origin, male dominance continues into the present.

IV. Gender Inequality In the United States

A. A society's culture and institutions both justify and maintain its customary forms of gender inequality.

B. Until this century, U.S. women did not have the right to vote, hold property, make legal contracts, or serve on a jury.

1. Males did not willingly surrender their privileges; rather, greater political rights for women resulted from a prolonged and bitter struggle waged by a "first wave" of feminists in the 19th and early 20th centuries.

2. This movement was divided into radical and conservative branches. The radical branch wanted to reform all social institutions, while the conservative branch concentrated only on winning the vote for women. After 1920 and the achievement of suffrage for women, the movement dissolved.

3. A "second wave" of feminism began in the 1960s. As more women gained an education and began to work outside the home, they compared their wages and working conditions to those of men. As awareness of gender inequalities grew, protest and struggle emerged. The goals of this second wave of feminism are broad, from changing work roles to changing policies on violence against women.

4. The second wave of feminism was also characterized by two branches--one

conservative and the other liberal--each of which has had different goals and different tactics.

    5.   While women enjoy more rights today, gender inequality still exists.

C.   There is evidence of educational gains made by women--more females than males are enrolled in U.S. colleges and universities, females earn 56% of all bachelor's degrees, women complete bachelor's degrees faster than men, and the proportion of professional degrees earned by women has increased sharply. Despite these gains, some old practices and patterns persist.

    1.   Women's sports are still underfunded because they are not considered as important as men's sports.

    2.   There is still the matter of gender tracking. At college males and females are channeled into different fields; 85% of engineering degrees are awarded to males, while 86% of library science degrees are awarded to women.

    3.   In graduate school, the proportion of females enrolled in programs decreases with each passing year.

    4.   There is gender stratification in both the rank and pay within higher educational institutions. Women are less likely to be in the higher ranks of academia, and at all levels are paid less than their male counterparts.

D.   Patterns of gender discrimination continue to exist in everyday life.

    1.   Females' capacities, interests, attitudes, and contributions are not taken as seriously as those of males'. For example, the worst insult that can be thrown at a male is that he is a sissy, or that he does things like a girl.

    2.   Patterns of conversation reflect inequalities between men and women. Men are more likely than women to interrupt a conversation and to control a change in topics.

V.   **Gender Inequality in the Workplace**

A.   Although the number of women who work outside the home for wages continues to increase, men still earn more.

    1.   At all levels of educational achievement women earn less than men; women who work full-time average only 67 percent of what men are paid.

    2.   The gender gap in pay characterizes all industrialized countries, although only Japan has a larger gap than we do.

    3.   Research by Fuller and Schoenberger found that upon entry to a career, women averaged lower pay than men, even when they have more qualifications than their male counterparts; five years after graduation from college, the pay gap was even wider than it was upon entering the job market.

    4.   Not one of the CEOs of the 350 largest U.S. corporations is a woman.

B.   The "glass ceiling" describes an invisible barrier that women face in trying to reach the executive suites.

    1.   Researchers find that women are not in the positions like marketing, sales, and production--positions from which top executives are recruited. Rather they are in human resources and public relations; their work is not appreciated to the same degree because it does not bring in profits.

    2.   Much of the blame for this situation rests with the male corporate culture. Those in power look for potential leaders who have the same characteristics as themselves; they steer white males into the "pipeline" for promotions and women and minorities into other positions.

3.   Another explanation for the situation is that women lack mentors; male executives are reluctant to mentor them because they fear the gossip and sexual harassment charges if they get too close to female subordinates, or because they see women as weak.

4.   There are cracks in the glass ceiling as women learn to play by "men's rules" and develop a style with which men feel comfortable.

5.   Christine Williams found that men who go into nontraditional fields do not encounter a glass ceiling; rather they find a "glass escalator"--they move up more quickly than female co-workers.

C.   Since most wives spend more time and take greater responsibility in caring for the children, it has been suggested that corporations offer women a choice of two parallel career paths.

1.   The "fast track" (may require 60 or 70 hours of work per week, unexpected out-of-town meetings, etc.); or the "mommy track" (stresses both career and family).

2.   Critics suggest that the mommy track would encourage women to be satisfied with lower aspirations and fewer promotions, it would perpetuate or increase the executive pay gap, and it would confirm stereotypes about female executives.

3.   Felice Schwartz, who first proposed these alternatives, counters critics with the idea of a "zigzag" track, in which both men and women would slow down during the time that their children were small, picking up speed once again when the children are older.

4.   Critics suggest that a better way than the mommy track is for husbands to share responsibility at home and for firms to provide day care.

D.   Until the 1970s, women did not draw a connection between unwanted sexual advances on the job and their subordinate positions at work.

1.   As women began to discuss the problem, they named it (sexual harassment) and came to see such unwanted sexual advances by men in powerful positions as a structural problem. The change in perception resulted from reinterpreting women's experiences--giving them a name.

2.   The meaning of the term is vague; court cases are the basis for determining what is and what is not sexual harassment.

3.   Sexual harassment is an abuse of power that is structured into relationships of inequality in the workplace.

VI.   Gender and Violence

A.   Most victims of violence are females.

1.   Each year almost three in every 1,000 American women aged 12 and older is raped; the rapists are almost always young males.

2.   Date rape--sexual assault in which the assailant is acquainted with the victim--is not an isolated event and is most likely to occur between couples who have known each other for about a year.

3.   Males are more likely than females to commit murder and be the victim of murder.

4.   Other forms of violence against women include battering, spousal abuse, incest and female circumcision.

5.   Although women are less likely than men to kill, when they do judges are more likely to be lenient on them. We need more research to understand why this pattern exists.

B.   Feminists use symbolic interactionism to understand violence against women. They stress that U.S. culture promotes violence by males. It teaches men to associate power, dominance, strength, virility and superiority with masculinity. Men use violence to try and maintain a higher status.

C.   To solve violence we must first break the link between violence and masculinity.

VII. **The Changing Face of Politics**

A.   Despite the gains U.S. women have made in recent elections, they continue to be under-represented in political office, especially in higher office.

1.   Reasons for this include the fact that women have been underrepresented in law and business, the careers from which most politicians are drawn; they have not necessarily seen themselves as a voting bloc who need political action to overcome discrimination; they have generally found the roles of mother and politician incompatible; and men have rarely incorporated women into the centers of decision making or presented them as viable candidates.

2.   There are signs that this pattern is changing. More women are going into law and business; child care is now more likely to be seen as a mutual responsibility; and in some areas of the country, party leaders are searching for qualified candidates, who can win, regardless of their sex.

B.   Trends in the 1990s indicate that women will participate in political life in far greater numbers than in the past.

VIII. **Glimpsing the Future -- With Hope**

A.   As women play a fuller role in decision-making processes, further structural obstacles to women's participation in society will give way.

B.   As gender stereotypes are abandoned, both males and females will be free to feel and express their needs and emotions, something that present arrangements deny them.

☞ KEY TERMS

After studying the chapter, review the definition for each of the following terms.

feminism: the philosophy that men and women should be politically, economically, and socially equal, and organized activity on behalf of this principle

gender: the social characteristics that a society considers proper for its males and females; masculinity or femininity

gender stratification: males' and females' unequal access to power, prestige, and property on the basis of their sex

matriarchy: a society in which women dominate men

minority group: a group that is discriminated against on the basis of its members' physical or cultural characteristics

patriarchy: a society in which men dominate women

sex: biological characteristics that distinguish females and males, consisting of primary and secondary sex characteristics

sex typing: the association of behaviors with one sex or the other

sexual harassment: the abuse of one's position of authority to force unwanted sexual demands on someone

☞ KEY PEOPLE

Review the major theoretical contributions or findings of these people.

Janet Chafetz: Chafetz studied the second wave of feminism in the 1960s, noting that as large numbers of women began to work in the economy, they began to compare their working conditions with those of men.

Donna Eder: This sociologist discovered that junior high boys call one another "girl" when they don't hit each other hard enough during a football game.

Frederick Engels: Engels was a colleague of Karl Marx and wrote a book about the origins of the family in which he argued that male dominance developed with the origin of private property.

Cynthia Fuchs Epstein: Epstein is a proponent of the view that differences between males' and females' behavior is solely the result of social factors such as socialization and social control.

Douglas Foley: This sociologist's study of sports lends support to the view that things feminine are generally devalued.

Rex Fuller and Richard Schoenberger: These economists examined the starting salaries of business majors and found that women averaged 11 percent lower pay than men right out of college, and that the gap grew to 14 percent after five years in the workforce.

Steven Goldberg: This sociologist's view is that the differences between males and females are not due to environment but to inborn differences that direct the emotions and behaviors of the two genders.

Marvin Harris: This anthropologist suggested that male dominance grew out of the greater strength that men had which made them better suited for the hand-to-hand combat of tribal societies; women became the reward to entice men into battle.

Gerda Lerner: While acknowledging that in all societies women--as a group--have never had decision-making power over men, Lerner suggested that patriarchy may have had different origins in different places around the globe.

Catharine McKinnon: McKinnon is an activist lawyer who published a book identifying sexual harassment as a structural problem in work places.

George Murdock: This anthropologist surveyed 324 premodern societies around the world and found that in all of them activities were sex typed.

Alice Rossi: This feminist sociologist has suggested that women are better prepared biologically for "mothering" than are men.

Felice Schwartz: Schwartz is the founder of Catalyst, an organization that focuses on women's issues in the workplace. She is associated with the notion of dual career tracks -- one for women who want to combine work and motherhood (the Mommy track) and the other for women who want to devote their time and energies to a career (the fast track).

Jean Stockard and Miriam Johnson: These sociologists observed boys playing basketball and heard them exchange insults that reflect a disrespect and devaluation of women.

Samuel Stouffer: In his classic study of combat soldiers during World War II, Stouffer noted the general devaluation of things associated with women.

Christine Williams: Williams found that men in non-traditional careers and occupations often experience a glass escalator -- moving more quickly than women into desirable work assignments, higher-level positions, and larger salaries.

☞ **"DOWN-TO-EARTH SOCIOLOGY"**

This is your opportunity to apply the sociological perspective to the world around you. The questions in this section refer to material introduced in this chapter of your text. Many ask you to think about ideas and information presented in the various special "boxes" that are located throughout this chapter.

1.   Read "Thinking Critically About Social Controversy" on pages 288-289. Select one view or the other to adopt (at least temporarily) as your own and prepare a statement in which you justify your position. If you have taken the side of nurture, consider all of the forces that shape our behavior and attitudes as men or women. On the other hand, if you take the side of nature, consider whether or not this means that male dominance and discrimination against women is inevitable. After you have considered one side, try doing the same thing with the opposing side. Then come up with an argument that combines elements of both.

2.   What was your reaction to the "Perspectives" piece on female circumcision (page 294)? How is the purpose of this procedure fundamentally different from male circumcision? Do you think that international pressure should be applied to end this procedure? Should parents who immigrate to this country and continue to practice this ritual be prosecuted for child abuse? Why or why not?

3.   After reading about the experiences of women in China (p. 295), what do you see as some of the factors that make it difficult for women there to improve their status today? Which do you think is a more powerful force in shaping women's position in society--economics or politics? What lessons could Chinese women learn from the struggles of U.S. women for greater equality with men?

4.   Did you realize before reading "Making the Invisible Visible" on page 298 that physicians often do not take women's medical complaints as seriously as those of men? How can this type of problem be a matter of life or death? Do you think gender bias ever affects your own perceptions and behavior?

5.   What is your view on the recent incidents involving sexual harassment in the military (p. 308)? After reading this chapter, do you think that the problem is between individuals--young men with overactive sex drives--or social structural--related to society and the inequalities based on gender?

6.   Were you shocked as you read about the popular Japanese TV show *Super Jockey* on page 311? What about the author's discussion of how the U.S. media uses violence against women to draw viewers? Why are stories in which women are victimized so appealing? Using what you have learned about gender inequalities in this chapter, develop an explanation for this pattern.

☞ **SELF-TEST**

After completing this self-test, check your answers against the Answer Key beginning on page 373 of this Study Guide and against the text on page(s) indicated in parentheses.

MULTIPLE CHOICE QUESTIONS

1.   Which of the following statements about gender stratification is <u>incorrect</u>? (286)
       a.   It cuts across all aspects of social life.
       b.   It cuts across all social classes.
       c.   It refers to the unequal access to power, prestige, and property on the basis of sex.
       d.   Unlike class stratification, it is not a structured feature of society.

2. To what does the term "sex" refer? (286)
    a. the social characteristics that a society considers proper for its males and females
    b. the biological characteristics that distinguish females and males
    c. masculinity and femininity
    d. All of the above

3. If biology is the principal factor in human behavior, around the world what would we find? (288)
    a. Things to be just like they are.
    b. Men and women to be much more like each other than they currently are.
    c. Women to be one sort of person and men another.
    d. None of the above.

4. Patriarchy: (289)
    a. is a society in which men dominate women.
    b. has existed throughout history.
    c. is universal.
    d. All of the above.

5. What is the association of behaviors with one sex or the other called? (291)
    a. sex typing
    b. sex-association
    c. sex-discrimination
    d. sex-orientation

6. When anthropologist George Murdock surveyed 324 premodern societies, which of the following was <u>not</u> one of his findings? (291-292)
    a. Activities were sex typed in all of them.
    b. Every society associates activities with one sex or the other.
    c. Biological requirements were the basis for men and women being assigned different tasks.
    d. Activities considered "female" in one society may be considered "male" activities in another.

7. In regard to the prestige of work: (292)
    a. greater prestige is given to activities which are considered to be of great importance to a society, regardless of whether they are performed by females or males.
    b. greater prestige goes to female activities that males can't do, like pregnancy and lactation.
    c. greater prestige is given to male activities.
    d. None of the above.

8. Which statement concerning global discrimination is <u>incorrect</u>? (293)
    a. Of about 1 billion adults around the world who can't read, two-thirds are women.
    b. The U.S. leads the world in the number of women who hold public office.
    c. Around the globe, women average less pay than men.
    d. A global human rights issue has become violence against women.

9.   In which of the following countries do women still not have the right to vote? (293)
      a.   Kenya
      b.   Kuwait
      c.   Bosnia
      d.   Vietnam

10.   Which of the statements below applies to minority groups? (295)
      a.   A minority group is the politically-correct way of referring to those who feel that life has treated them unfairly.
      b.   A minority group is of little interest to sociologists, who study dominant groups instead of minority ones.
      c.   A minority group is a group that is discriminated against on the basis of its smaller size.
      d.   A minority group is a group that is discriminated against on the basis of its members' physical or cultural characteristics.

11.   Historically in the United States, women: (297)
      a.   did not have the right to vote until the 1950s.
      b.   were allowed to make legal contracts but had to be represented by an attorney because it was assumed that they were like children.
      c.   could not serve on juries or hold property in their own name.
      d.   could spend their own wages but had to tell their fathers how the money was spent.

12.   A "second wave" of protest and struggle against gender inequalities: (297-298)
      a.   occurred when women began to compare their working conditions with those of men.
      b.   began in the 1960s.
      c.   had as its goals everything from changing work roles to changing policies on violence against women.
      d.   all of the above.

13.   Gender inequality in education: (299-300)
      a.   has virtually disappeared today.
      b.   is allowed by law.
      c.   is perpetuated by the use of sex to sort students into different academic disciplines.
      d.   disappears by the time men and women enter graduate school.

14.   Researchers who have studied conversation patterns between men and women conclude that: (302)
      a.   women talk more and interrupt men more frequently than the other way around.
      b.   men and women are social equals when it comes to everyday conversation.
      c.   even in everyday conversation, the talk between a man and a woman reflects social inequality.
      d.   men interrupt more in conversations, but women control the topics that are discussed.

15.   The pay gap between men and women: (304)
      a.   is found primarily among those with less than a high school education.
      b.   is found primarily among those with college and graduate education.
      c.   is found at all educational levels.
      d.   largely has disappeared.

16.   The glass ceiling: (305-306)
      a.   keeps both men and women out of nontraditional occupations.
      b.   has largely been shattered by today's generation of business women.
      c.   refers to the invisible barrier that keeps women from reaching the executive suite.
      d.   All of the above.

17.   Which of the following is not a reason for women's absence from core corporate positions? (305-306)
      a.   The male corporate culture stereotypes potential leaders as people who look like themselves; women are seen as better at providing "support."
      b.   Women do not seek out opportunities for advancement and do not spend enough time networking with powerful executives.
      c.   Women lack mentors who take an interest in them and teach them the ropes.
      d.   Women are generally steered away from jobs that are stepping stones to top corporate office; instead they are recruited for jobs in human resources and public relations.

18.   Felice Schwartz suggested that corporations create two parallel career paths. These are: (307)
      a.   the college-bound and the vocational-technical.
      b.   the "partner-material" path and the "non-partner-material" path.
      c.   the "mommy track" and the "daddy track."
      d.   the "mommy track" and the "fast track."

19.   Which of the following statements about sexual harassment is incorrect? (307-308)
      a.   It is no longer exclusively a female problem.
      b.   It is rooted in the structure of the workplace rather than individual relationships.
      c.   It involves a person in authority using the position to force unwanted sex on subordinates.
      d.   Male victims of sexual harassment receive more sympathy than female victims.

20.   The pattern of date rape shows: (309)
      a.   that it is not an isolated event.
      b.   that it is more likely to happen with couples who have dated for a period of time.
      c.   it is difficult to prosecute.
      d.   all of the above.

21.   Which of the following is not among feminist explanations for gender violence? (310-311)
      a.   higher testosterone levels in males
      b.   males reassert their declining power and status
      c.   the association of strength and virility with violence
      d.   cultural traditions that are patriarchal

22.   Women have been underrepresented in politics because: (312)
      a.   they are not really interested in pursuing political careers.
      b.   they are not viewed as serious candidates by the voters.
      c.   their roles as mothers and wives are incompatible with political roles.
      d.   they lack the proper educational backgrounds.

23.   In many parts of the U.S. today, the primary concern of voters is: (313)
       a.   the gender of the candidate.
       b.   whether the candidate can win.
       c.   whether the candidate is the primary caretaker of young children.
       d.   how much money the candidate spends.

24.   What is it that keeps most males and females locked into fairly rigid gender roles? (313)
       a.   social structural obstacles
       b.   socialization
       c.   stereotypes
       d.   all of the above

25.   What is most likely to break the stereotypes locking us into traditional gender activities? (313)
       a.   stricter laws
       b.   equal pay
       c.   increased female participation in the decision-making processes of social institutions
       d.   increased male participation in nurturing activities

TRUE-FALSE QUESTIONS

T F   1.   The terms sex and gender basically mean the same thing to sociologists. (286)
T F   2.   The study of Vietnam veterans cited in the text supports the view that biology is destiny. (290-291)
T F   3.   Research by a number of social scientists has established that there was great variability in terms of the amount of prestige accorded to male and female activities. (292)
T F   4.   Around the globe, women are more likely than men to be illiterate. (293)
T F   5.   Although female circumcision was once common in parts of Africa and southeast Asia, it is quite rare today. (294)
T F   6.   According to the primary theory on the origins of patriarchy, the dominance of men in society grew out of a need to shelter women because of their capacity to give birth and nurse infants. (295-296)
T F   7.   In the U.S. women's political rights were gained only after a prolonged and bitter struggle. (297)
T F   8.   In the second wave of the U.S. women's movement, the liberal wing of the movement had a radical wing, while the conservative faction did not. (298)
T F   9.   In the past, some educators have claimed that women's wombs dominated their minds. (299)
T F   10.   Today women and men have equal levels of achievement in higher education. (301)
T F   11.   Women are less likely to hold the rank of full professor in colleges and universities, and if they do, they are likely to get paid less than male counterparts. (301)
T F   12.   In a study of World War II combat soldiers, Samuel Stouffer reported that officers used feminine terms as insults to motivate soldiers. (302)
T F   13.   Women are more likely to interrupt a conversation and to control changes in topics. (302)
T F   14.   Research by Fuller and Schoenberger found that women college graduates were able to close the income gap within five years of graduating. (304-305)
T F   15.   The "glass ceiling" and "mommy track" both have a more negative impact on women than on men in corporations and the professions. (305-307)

T F   16.   The "glass escalator" refers to the opportunities that women have to advance quickly in traditional male occupations. (306)

T F   17.   Once sexual harassment was defined as a problem, women saw some of their experiences in a different light. (307)

T F   18.   In the United States, males kill at about the same rate as that of females. (309)

T F   19.   Although women are less likely to kill, when they do kill judges are more likely to be lenient with them. (310)

T F   20.   The only reason there are not more women in public office is because men keep them out. (312)

FILL-IN QUESTIONS

1.   Males' and females' unequal access to power, prestige, and property on the basis of sex reflects _____. (286)

2.   _____ refers to biological characteristics that distinguish females and males, consisting of primary and secondary sex characteristics. (286)

3.   The social characteristics that a society considers proper for its males and females make up an individual's _____. (286)

4.   You inherit your _____, but you learn your _____ as you are socialized into specific behaviors and attitudes. (286)

5.   A society in which women dominate men is called a _____. (289)

6.   When activities become associated with one sex or the other they are said to be _____. (291)

7.   _____ is a particular form of violence directed exclusively against women. (294)

8.   A _____ is a group that is discriminated against on the basis of its members' physical characteristics. (295)

9.   _____ is the philosophy that men and women should be politically, economically, and socially equal. (297)

10.   The _____ prevents women from advancing to top executive positions. (305)

11.   One reason why women do not reach top corporate positions is because they lack _____, successful executives who take an interest in them and teach them the ropes. (306)

12.   Men who move into traditionally women's occupations are likely to climb onto a _____, moving very quickly into more desirable work assignments, higher level positions, and larger salaries. (306)

13.   The proposed _____ would address the stresses that many working women experience when they attempt to combine careers and families. (307)

14.   The abuse of one's position of authority to force unwanted sexual demands on someone is referred to as _____. (307)

15.   _____ most commonly occurs between couples who have known each other about a year. (309)

MATCH THESE SOCIAL SCIENTISTS WITH THEIR CONTRIBUTIONS

___1. Janet Chafetz
___2. Alice Rossi
___3. Felice Schwartz
___4. Christine Williams
___5. Gerda Lerner
___6. Catharine McKinnon
___7. George Murdock
___8. Samuel Stouffer
___9. Marvin Harris
__10. Steve Goldberg
__11. Frederick Engels
__12. Douglas Foley

a. *surveyed 324 societies and found evidence of sex-typed activities*

b. *men in nontraditional occupations often experience a glass escalator*

c. *male dominance grew out of the greater strength that men had*

d. *study supports the view that things feminine are generally devalued*

e. *associated with the notion of the mommy track and the fast track*

f. *differences between males and females are due to inborn differences*

g. *women are better prepared biologically for "mothering" than are men*

h. *identified sexual harassment as a structural problem in work places*

i. *patriarchy may have had different origins around the globe*

j. *male dominance developed with the origin of private property*

k. *noted the devaluation of things associated with women among soldiers*

l. *studied the second wave of feminism in the 1960s*

ESSAY QUESTIONS

1.   Summarize the sociobiology argument concerning behavioral differences between men and women. Explain which position most closely reflects your own--biological, sociological, or sociobiological.

2.   Compare and contrast the two waves of the feminist movement in this country by identifying the forces that contributed to both waves.

3.   Evaluate Felice's Schwartz's proposed "mommy track," stating both the strengths and weaknesses of this approach to the problem of gender inequality.

CHAPTER 12
RACE AND ETHNICITY

☞ CHAPTER SUMMARY

- Race is a complex and often misunderstood concept. Race is a reality in the sense that inherited physical characteristics distinguish one group from another. However, race is a myth in the sense of one race being superior to another and of there being pure races. The *idea* of race is powerful, shaping basic relationships between people. Race refers to inherited biological characteristics, ethnicity to cultural ones.

- A minority group is defined as one singled out for unequal treatment by members of the dominant group. Both race and ethnicity can be a basis for unequal treatment. The extent of ethnic identification depends upon the relative size of the group, its power, broad physical characteristics, and the amount of discrimination. Ethnic work is the process of constructing an ethnic identity.

- Prejudice refers to an attitude and discrimination to unfair treatment. Individual discrimination is the negative treatment of one person by another, while institutional discrimination is discrimination built into society's social institutions.

- Psychological theories explain the origin of prejudice in terms of stress frustration that gets directed towards scapegoats and in terms of the development of authoritarian personalities. Sociologists emphasize how different social environments affect levels of prejudice. They look at the benefits and costs of discrimination, the exploitation of racial-ethnic divisions by those in power, and the self-fulfilling prophecies that are the outcome of labeling.

- Dominant groups typically practice one of five policies toward minority groups: genocide, population transfer, internal colonialism, segregation, assimilation, or pluralism.

- The major ethnic groups in the United States--ranked from largest to smallest--are European Americans, African Americans, Latinos, Asian Americans, and Native Americans.

- Each minority group faces different issues. African Americans are increasingly divided into middle and lower classes, with very different experiences. Latinos are divided by country of origin. The well-being of Asian Americans varies by country of origin. For Native Americans, the issues are poverty, nationhood, and settling treaty obligations.

- The primary issues that dominate race-ethnic relations today are immigration, affirmative action, and how to develop a truly multicultural society.

☞ LEARNING OBJECTIVES

As you read Chapter 12, use these learning objectives to organize your notes. After completing your reading, briefly state an answer to each of the objectives, and review the text pages in parentheses.

1. Explain how race can be both a reality and a myth and distinguish between the concepts of race and ethnicity. (318-321)
2. Define the term "minority group," explain the process by which a group becomes a minority, and identify five characteristics shared by minority groups worldwide. (321-323)
3. Discuss the process of constructing an ethnic identity and engaging in ethnic work. (323-324)
4. Differentiate between prejudice and discrimination. (324-325)
5. Explain the extent of prejudice among racial and ethnic groups and relate how it can contribute to

self-segregation, as is seen today on some college campuses. (325)

6. Compare and contrast individual and institutional discrimination and give examples of each type of discrimination. (326-327)
7. Discuss the different psychological perspectives on prejudice. (328-329)
8. Outline the functionalist, conflict, and symbolic interactionist perspectives on prejudice. (329-331)
9. List and describe the six patterns of intergroup relations. (332-335)
10. Compare and contrast the experiences of White Europeans, African Americans, Latinos, Asian Americans, and Native Americans in the United States. (336-349)
11. Identify some of the issues tied to the current debates over immigration and affirmative action. (349-350)
12. Discuss the conditions which must be present in order for the United States to become a multicultural society. (350-351)

☞ CHAPTER OUTLINE

I. **Laying a Sociological Foundation**
    A. Race, a group with inherited physical characteristics that distinguish it from another group, is both a myth and a reality.
        1. It is a reality in the sense that humans come in different colors and shapes.
        2. It is a myth because there are no pure races; what we call "races" are social classifications, not biological categories. In addition, it is a myth that any one race is superior to another.
        3. The myth makes a difference for social life because people believe these ideas are real and they act on their beliefs.
    B. Race and ethnicity are often confused due to the cultural differences people see and the way they define race. Ethnicity and ethnic refers to cultural characteristics that distinguish a people.
    C. Minority groups are people singled out for unequal treatment and who regard themselves as objects of collective discrimination.
        1. They are not necessarily in the numerical minority. Sociologists refer to those who do the discriminating as the dominant group--they have greater power, more privileges, and higher social status. The dominant group attributes its privileged position to its superiority, not to discrimination.
        2. A group becomes a minority through expansion of political boundaries by another group. Another way for a group to become a minority is by migration into a territory, either voluntarily or involuntarily.
        3. Shared characteristics of minorities worldwide: (1) membership is ascribed involuntarily through birth; (2) the physical or cultural traits that distinguish them are held in low esteem by the dominant group; (3) they are unequally treated by the dominant group; (4) they tend to marry within their own group; and (5) they tend to feel strong group solidarity.
    D. Some people feel an intense sense of ethnic identity while others feel very little.
        1. An individual's sense of ethnic identity is influenced by the relative size and power of the ethnic group, its appearance, and the level of discrimination aimed at the group. If a group is relatively small, has little power, has a distinctive appearance, and is an object of discrimination, its members will have a heightened

sense of ethnic identity.

2. Ethnic work refers to how ethnicity is constructed and includes enhancing and maintaining a group's distinctiveness or attempting to recover ethnic heritage.

E. Prejudice and discrimination exist throughout the world in, for example, the United States, Northern Ireland, Israel, and Japan.

1. Discrimination is unfair treatment directed toward someone. When based on race, it is known as racism. It also can be based on features such as age, sex, sexual preference, religion, or politics.

2. Prejudice is prejudging of some sort, usually in a negative way.

3. Ethnocentrism is so common that each racial/ethnic group views other groups as inferior in at least some way. Studies confirm that there is less prejudice among the more educated and among younger people.

F. Sociologists distinguish between individual discrimination (negative treatment of one person by another) and institutional discrimination (negative treatment of a minority group that is built into society's institutions).

1. Race/ethnicity is a significant factor in getting a mortgage. Researchers found that even when two mortgage applicants were identical in terms of credit histories, African Americans and Latinos were 60 percent more likely than whites to be rejected.

2. Researchers compared the age, sex, race and income of heart patients and found that whites were 89 percent more likely than minorities to be given coronary bypass surgery.

II. **Theories of Prejudice**

A. Psychological Perspectives

1. According to John Dollard, prejudice results from frustration: people unable to strike out at the real source of their frustration find scapegoats to unfairly blame.

2. According to Theodor Adorno, highly prejudiced people are insecure, intolerant people who long for the firm boundaries established by strong authority; he called this complex of personality traits the authoritarian personality.

3. Subsequent studies have generally concluded that people who are older, less educated, less intelligent and from a lower social class are more likely to be authoritarian.

B. Sociological Perspectives

1. To functionalists, the social environment can be deliberately arranged to generate either positive or negative feelings about people. Prejudice is functional in that it creates in-group solidarity and out-group antagonism, but dysfunctional in that it destroys human relationships. Functionalists do not justify what they discover but simply identify functions and dysfunctions of human action.

2. To conflict theorists, the ruling class systematically pits group against group; by splitting workers along racial ethnic lines they benefit, because solidarity among the workers is weakened. The higher unemployment rates of minorities creates a reserve labor force from which owners can draw when they need to expand production temporarily. The existence of the reserve labor force is a constant threat to white workers, who modify their demands rather than lose their jobs to unemployment.

3. To symbolic interactionists, the labels we learn color our perceptions, leading us to see certain things and be blind to others. Racial and ethnic labels are especially

powerful because they are shorthand for emotionally laden stereotypes. Symbolic interactionists stress that we learn our prejudices in interactions with others. These stereotypes not only justify prejudice and discrimination, but they also lead to a self-fulfilling prophecy--stereotypical behavior in those who are stereotyped.

III. **Global Patterns of Intergroup Relations**

A. Genocide is the actual or attempted systematic annihilation of a race or ethnic group that is labeled as less than fully human. The Holocaust and the U.S. government's treatment of Native Americans are examples.

B. Population transfer is involuntary movement of a minority group. Indirect transfer involves making life so unbearable that members of a minority then leave; direct transfer involves forced expulsion. A combination of genocide and population transfer occurred in Bosnia, in former Yugoslavia, as Serbs engaged in the wholesale slaughter of Muslims and Croats, with survivors forced to flee the area.

C. Internal colonialism is a society's policy of exploiting a minority, by using social institutions to deny it access to full benefits. Slavery is an extreme example.

D. Segregation is the formal separation of groups that accompanies internal colonialism. Dominant groups maintain social distance from minorities yet still exploit their labor.

E. Assimilation is the process by which a minority is absorbed into the mainstream. Forced assimilation occurs when the dominant group prohibits the minority from using its own religion, language, customs. Permissive assimilation is when the minority adopts the dominant group's patterns in its own way and/or at its own speed.

F. Multiculturalism, also called pluralism, permits or encourages ethnic variation.

IV. **Race and Ethnic Relations in the United States**

A. White Anglo-Saxon Protestants (WASPs) established the basic social institutions in the U.S. when they settled the original colonies.

1. WASPs were very ethnocentric and viewed immigrants from other European countries as inferior. Subsequent immigrants were expected to speak English and adopt other Anglo-Saxon ways of life.

2. White ethnics are white immigrants to the United States whose culture differs from that of WASPs. They include the Irish, Germans, Poles, Jews, and Italians. They were initially discriminated against by WASPs who felt that something was wrong with people with different customs.

3. The institutional and cultural dominance of Western Europeans set the stage for current ethnic relations.

B. African Americans face a legacy of racism.

1. In 1955, African Americans in Montgomery, Alabama, using civil disobedience tactics advocated by Martin Luther King, Jr., protested laws believed to be unjust. This led to the civil rights movement, that challenged existing patterns of racial segregation throughout the South.

2. The 1964 Civil Rights Act and 1965 Voting Rights Act heightened expectations. Frustration over the pace of change led to urban riots and passage of the 1968 Civil Rights Act.

3. Since then, African Americans have made political and economic progress. For example, African Americans have quadrupled their membership in the U.S. House of Representatives in the past 25 years, and enrollment in colleges continues to increase. African Americans such as Jesse Jackson, Douglas Wilder, and Clarence Thomas have gained political prominence.

4. Despite these gains, however, African Americans continue to lag behind in politics, economics, and education. Currently no U.S. senator is African American; African Americans average 61% of whites' incomes; only 15% of African Americans have graduated from college; and African American males are more than seven times as likely to be homicide victims as are white males.

5. According to William Wilson social class (not race) is the major determinant of quality of life. The African American community today is composed of a middle-class who took advantage of the opportunities created by civil rights legislation and advanced economically--living in good housing, having well-paid jobs, and sending their children to good schools--and a large group of poorly educated and unskilled African Americans who were left behind as opportunities for unskilled labor declined--living in poverty, facing violent crime and dead-end jobs, and sending their children to terrible schools.

6. Others argue that discrimination on the basis of race persists, despite gains made by some African Americans.

7. Afrocentrism--an emphasis on uniquely African-American traditions and customs--has developed in response to ongoing discrimination.

C. Latinos are the second largest ethnic group in the United States, and include Mexicans and Mexican Americans, Puerto Ricans, Cuban Americans, and people from Central or South America. While most are legal residents, large numbers have entered the United States illegally and avoid contact with public officials. Concentrated in four states (California, Texas, New York, and Florida), they are causing major demographic shifts.

1. The Spanish language distinguishes them from other minorities; perhaps half are unable to speak English without difficulty. This is a major obstacle to getting well-paid jobs. Some Anglos perceive the growing use of Spanish as a threat and have initiated an "English only" movement and have succeeded in getting states to consider making English their official language.

2. Divisions of social class and country of national origin prevent political unity.

3. Compared with non-Latino whites, Latinos are worse off on all indicators of well-being. The country of origin is significant, with Cuban Americans scoring much higher on indicators of well being and Puerto Rican Americans scoring the lowest.

D. Asian Americans have long faced discrimination in the United States.

1. Today Asian Americans are the fastest growing minority in the U.S. They are a diverse group divided by separate cultures. Although there are variations in income among Asian American groups, on the average Asian Americans have been extremely successful. This success can be traced to three factors: (1) a close family life; (2) educational achievement; and (3) assimilation into the mainstream.

2. In the past, Chinese Americans frequently were victims of vigilante groups and anti-Chinese legislation. Largely excluded from Anglo life, they formed segregated communities called "Chinatowns." As discrimination lessened, the more affluent moved into integrated neighborhoods, and were replaced by new immigrants from China.

3. Filipino Americans are almost invisible in American society, despite the fact that there are about 2 million living here. They tend to maintain strong loyalty to their families, the Roman Catholic church, and their cultural community.

4. After the attack on Pearl Harbor in World War II, hostilities towards Japanese Americans increased; with many being imprisoned in "relocation camps." In the

years following World War II, prejudice and discrimination gradually diminished. Today, the intermarriage rate is so high that 2/3rds of all children born to Japanese Americans have a parent who is not Japanese American.

    5. Recent immigration has been from Vietnam. Despite initial problems of settlement, these immigrants have adjusted well.

E. Due to the influence of old movie westerns, many Americans tend to hold stereotypes of Native Americans as uncivilized savages, as a single group of people subdivided into separate bands.

    1. In reality, however, Native Americans represent a diverse group of people with a variety of cultures and languages. Although originally numbering between 5 and 10 million, their numbers were reduced to a low of 500,000 due to a lack of immunity to European diseases and warfare. Today there are about 2 million Native Americans.

    2. At first, relations between European settlers and the Native Americans were peaceful. However, as the number of settlers increased, tension increased. Because they stood in the way of expansion, many were slaughtered. Government policy shifted to population transfer, with Native Americans confined to reservations.

    3. Today, they are an invisible minority. Almost half live in three states: Oklahoma, California, and Arizona; most other Americans are hardly aware of them. They have the highest rates of poverty, unemployment, suicide, and alcoholism of any U. S. minority. These negative conditions are the result of Anglo domination.

    4. In the 1960's Native Americans won a series of legal victories that restored their control over the land and their right to determine economic policy. Many Native Americans have opened businesses on their land, ranging from industrial parks to casinos. Today many Native Americans are interested in recovering and honoring their own traditions.

    5. Pan-Indianism emphasizes elements that run through all Native American cultures in order to develop self-identification that goes beyond any particular tribe.

V. Looking Toward the Future

A. Central to this country's history, immigration and the fear of its consequences is once again an issue facing the United States as it moves into the next century. The concern has been that "too many" immigrants will alter the character of the United States, undermining basic institutions and contributing to the breakdown of society.

B. Another central concern is the role of affirmative action. Liberals argue that this policy is the most direct way in which to level the playing field of economic opportunity, while conservatives believe that such practices result in reverse discrimination.

C. In order for the United States to become a multicultural society, people must respect differences and be willing to work together without any one group dominating others.

☞ KEY TERMS

After studying the chapter, review the definition for each of the following terms.

Afrocentrism: an emphasis on African-American traditions and concerns

assimilation: the process of being absorbed into the mainstream culture

authoritarian personality: Theodor Adorno's term for people who are prejudiced and rank high on scales of conformity, intolerance, insecurity, respect for authority, and submissiveness to superiors

civil disobedience: the act of deliberately but peacefully disobeying laws considered unjust

compartmentalize: to separate acts from feelings or attitudes

discrimination: an act of unfair treatment directed against an individual or a group

dominant group: the group with the most power, greatest privileges, and highest social status

ethnic (and ethnicity): having distinctive cultural characteristics

ethnic cleansing: a policy of population elimination, including forcible expulsion and genocide. The term emerged in 1992 among the Serbians during their planned policy of expelling Croats and Muslims from territories claimed by them during the Yugoslav wars.

ethnic work: activities designed to discover, enhance, or maintain ethnic/racial identification.

genocide: the systematic annihilation or attempted annihilation of people based on their presumed race or ethnicity

individual discrimination: the negative treatment of one person by another on the basis of that person's perceived characteristics

institutional discrimination: negative treatment of a minority group that is built into a society's institutions; also called *systemic discrimination*

internal colonialism: the policy of economically exploiting a minority group

melting pot: the view that Americans of various backgrounds would blend into a sort of ethnic stew

minority group: people who are singled out for unequal treatment, and who regard themselves as objects of collective discrimination

multiculturalism (also called pluralism): a philosophy or political policy that permits or encourages ethnic variation

pan-Indianism: a movement that focuses on the common elements in Native American culture in order to develop a mutual self-identity and to work toward the welfare of all Native Americans

pluralism: a philosophy that permits or encourages ethnic variation

population transfer: involuntary movement of a minority group

prejudice: an *attitude* or prejudging, usually in a negative way

race: inherited physical characteristics that distinguish one group from another

racism: prejudice and discrimination on the basis of race

reserve labor force: the unemployed; unemployed workers who are thought of as being "in reserve" -- capitalists take them "out of reserve" (put them back to work) during times of high production and lay them off (put them back in reserve) when they are no longer needed

rising expectations: the sense that better conditions are soon to follow, which, if unfulfilled, creates mounting frustration

scapegoat: an individual or group unfairly blamed for someone else's troubles

segregation: the policy of keeping racial or ethnic groups apart

selective perception: seeing certain features of an object or situation but remaining blind to others

split-labor market: workers are split along racial, ethnic, gender, age or any other lines; this split is exploited by owners to weaken the bargaining power of workers

WASP: a white Anglo-Saxon Protestant; narrowly, an American of English descent; broadly, an American of western European ancestry

white ethnics: white immigrants to the United States whose culture differs from that of WASPs.

☞ KEY PEOPLE

Review the major theoretical contributions or findings of these people.

Theodor Adorno: Adorno identified the authoritarian personality type.

Lawrence Bobo and James Kluegel: These sociologists' research demonstrated that prejudice varied by age and educational level.

Emery Cowen, Judah Landes and Donald Schaet: In an experiment, these psychologists found that students directed frustrations onto people who had nothing to do with their problems.

Ashley Doane: Doane identified four factors that affect an individual's sense of ethnic identity.

John Dollard: This psychologist first suggested that prejudice is the result of frustration and scapegoats become the targets for their frustration.

Rapheal Ezekiel: This sociologist did participant observation of neo-Nazis and the Ku Klux Klan in order to examine racism from inside racist organizations.

Joe Feagin: This sociologist interviewed a sample of middle-class African Americans about their experiences and found that racism permeates the everyday lives of its victims.

Maria Krysan and Reynolds Farley: In a random sample of people in Detroit, these researchers found that both whites and African Americans judged Latinos as less intelligent than themselves.

Ashley Montagu: This physical anthropologist pointed out that some scientists have classified humans into only two races while others have identified as many as two thousand.

Donald Muir: Muir measured racial attitudes of white students who belonged to fraternities and sororities and compared them to nonmembers.

Alejandro Portes and Rueben Rumbaut: These sociologists looked at the impact that immigration has had on our country, pointing out that there has always been an anti-immigrant sentiment present.

Muzafer and Carolyn Sherif: The Sherifs researched the functions of prejudice and found that it builds in-group solidarity.

George Simpson and Milton Yinger: These men wrote about the nature of selective perception.

W.I. Thomas: Thomas observed that once people define a situation as real, it is real in its consequences.

Charles Wagley and Marvin Harris: These anthropologists identified the characteristics of minorities worldwide.

Mark Wenneker and Arnold Epstein: These physicians studied patients admitted to Massachusetts hospitals for circulatory disease or chest pain and found that whites were more likely than nonwhites to be given coronary by-pass surgery.

William Wilson: Wilson is known for his work on racial discrimination, in which he argues that class is a more important factor than race in explaining patterns of inequality.

Louis Wirth: Wirth offered a sociological definition of minority group.

☞ "DOWN-TO-EARTH SOCIOLOGY"

This is your opportunity to apply the sociological perspective to the world around you. The questions in this section refer to material introduced in this chapter of your text. Many ask you to think about ideas and information presented in the various special "boxes" that are located throughout this chapter.

1.	In what ways does Tiger Woods reflect race as both a myth and a reality (p. 320)? Does it matter what race he is? Do you think it is important for the government to know someone's race? Why or why not?

2.	Read "Self-Segregation: Help or Hindrance for Race Relations on Campus" (p. 326). What are the arguments in favor of self-segregation? What are the arguments in opposition? Which argument do you find more compelling? Why?

3.	Is hate speech dangerous? Read "Preaching Hatred: Crime or Inalienable Right?" on page 329, then answer the previously posed question. Should those whose views of other racial and ethnic groups reflect hatred be denied the right to speak? Where do we draw the line? What if one of these groups wanted to come on your campus to distribute its literature and establish a chapter?

How would you feel? What would you do?

4.   After reading about "The Racist Mind" on page 332, why do you think that hate groups have recently grown in number? What changes in our society have contributed to the emergence of such groups? How does Ezekiel's research findings fit with Adorno's concept of the authoritarian personality?

5.   After reading about the experiences of two young Haitians on page 335, what would you say are the costs of assimilation? What are the benefits? Why do you think the Haitians have had a particularly difficult time assimilating?

6.   Were you surprised by the experiences with racism of middle class African Americans (p. 341)? What toil does racism take on individuals? Why might it be more difficult to attack these expressions of racism than it was to fight in the past against segregation?

7.   Why are the arguments in support of expanding school curricula to include materials that present the history and experiences of diverse social groups (p. 351)?

☞ **SELF-TEST**

After completing this self-test, check your answers against the Answer Key beginning on page 377 of this Study Guide and against the text on page(s) indicated in parentheses.

MULTIPLE CHOICE QUESTIONS

1.   Race: (318)
      a.   means having distinctive cultural characteristics.
      b.   means having inherited physical characteristics that distinguish one group from another.
      c.   means people who are singled out for unequal treatment.
      d.   is relatively easy to determine.

2.   People often confuse race and ethnicity because: (321)
      a.   they dislike people who are different from themselves.
      b.   of the cultural differences people see and the way they define race.
      c.   they are unaware of the fact that race is cultural and ethnicity is biological.
      d.   All of the above.

3.   A minority group: (321)
      a.   is discriminated against because of physical or cultural differences.
      b.   is discriminated against because of personality factors.
      c.   does not always experience discrimination.
      d.   All of the above.

4.   To what does the dominant group in a society almost always consider its position to be due? (322)
      a.   its own innate superiority.
      b.   its ability to oppress minority group members.
      c.   its ability to control political power.
      d.   All of the above.

5.   Which of the following factors affects a group's sense of ethnic identity? (323)
     a.   the amount of power the group has
     b.   the size of the group
     c.   the degree to which the group's physical appearance differs from the mainstream
     d.   all of the above.

6.   Prejudice and discrimination: (324)
     a.   are less prevalent in the United States than in other societies.
     b.   are more prevalent in the United States than in other societies.
     c.   appear to characterize every society, regardless of size.
     d.   appear to characterize only large societies.

7.   Prejudice: (325)
     a.   is an attitude.
     b.   may be positive or negative.
     c.   often is the basis for discrimination.
     d.   All of the above.

8.   According to research by Lawrence Bobo and James Kluegel, which group of whites was more willing to have close, sustained interactions with other racial and ethnic groups? (325)
     a.   older and less educated whites
     b.   rural whites
     c.   urban whites
     d.   younger and more educated whites

9.   The negative treatment of one person by another on the basis of personal characteristics is: (326)
     a.   individual discrimination.
     b.   individual prejudice.
     c.   institutional discrimination.
     d.   institutional prejudice.

10. What do the findings of research on patterns of mortgage lending confirm? (327)
     a.   Discrimination is the result of individual bankers' decisions.
     b.   Decisions to reject loans reflect sound banking practices.
     c.   While African Americans and Latinos were rejected more often than whites, the rate was not significant.
     d.   Discrimination is built into the country's financial institutions.

11. Why do functionalists consider prejudice functional for some groups? (330)
     a.   It is a useful weapon in maintaining social divisions.
     b.   It contributes to the creation of scapegoats.
     c.   It helps to create solidarity within the group by fostering antagonisms directed against other groups.
     d.   It affects how members of one group perceive members of other groups.

12. According to conflict theorists, prejudice: (330-331)
    a. benefits capitalists by splitting workers along racial or ethnic lines.
    b. contributes to the exploitation of workers, thus producing a split-labor market.
    c. keeps workers from demanding higher wages and better working conditions.
    d. All of the above.

13. Symbolic interactionists stress that prejudiced people: (331)
    a. are born that way.
    b. have certain types of personalities.
    c. learn their prejudices in interaction with others.
    d. None of the above.

14. From his research on racist groups, Raphael Ezekiel concluded that the leaders of these movements: (332-333)
    a. are basically ignorant people who want to stir up problems.
    b. take advantage of the masses' anxieties concerning economic insecurity and of their tendency to see the "Establishment" as the cause of economic problems.
    c. are able to distinguish clearly the nuances of racial classification, but exploit the masses' perceptions that "black is black, and white is white."
    d. use race as a handy concept for recruiting followers, but that it is not really very useful in understanding why people are the way they are.

15. Genocide: (332)
    a. occurred when Hitler attempted to destroy all Jews.
    b. is the systematic annihilation of a race or ethnic group.
    c. often requires the cooperation of ordinary citizens.
    d. All of the above.

16. The process of expelling a minority from a country or a particular area is called: (334)
    a. population redistribution.
    b. direct population transfer.
    c. indirect population transfer.
    d. expelled population transfer.

17. A society's policy of exploiting a minority group, using social institutions to deny the minority access to the society's full benefits is referred to as: (334)
    a. segregation.
    b. pluralism.
    c. internal colonialism.
    d. genocide.

18. The process of being absorbed into the mainstream culture is: (334)
    a. pluralism.
    b. assimilation.
    c. cultural submersion.
    d. internal colonialism.

19. Which of the following statements about WASPs is <u>incorrect</u>? (337)
    a. They embraced whites from other European nations, helping them to assimilate.
    b. They took power and determined the national agenda, controlling the destiny of the nation.
    c. The term refers to White Anglo-Saxon Protestants whose ancestors came from England.
    d. They were highly ethnocentric and viewed other immigrants as inferior.

20. According to William Wilson, what was it that created new opportunities for middle-class African Americans to move up the social class ladder? (340)
    a. economic prosperity
    b. organized religion
    c. civil rights legislation
    d. technological advances

21. Afrocentrism: (342)
    a. is an emphasis on unique African American traditions and concerns.
    b. has encouraged the establishment of black studies courses and academic departments.
    c. is a modified version of black nationalism.
    d. All of the above.

22. According to your text, Latinos are distinguished from other ethnic minorities in the United States by: (342-343)
    a. the Spanish language.
    b. the fact that virtually all Latinos entered the United States illegally.
    c. the length of time Latinos have been in the United States.
    d. All of the above.

23. Which of the following statements about the experiences of Asian Americans is <u>incorrect</u>? (344-347)
    a. Much of the hostility directed towards Japanese Americans was due to Pearl Harbor.
    b. Asian Americans are today the fastest growing minority.
    c. The view that Asian Americans have been successful in this country is basically correct.
    d. Most Asian Americans grow up in tight-knit families.

24. Which of the following groups is often referred to as an "invisible minority?" (348)
    a. African Americans.
    b. Asian Americans.
    c. Latinos.
    d. Native Americans.

25. What is a difference between the earlier wave of immigration at the turn of the last century and the current wave? (349-350)
    a. The current wave is much smaller.
    b. The current wave is more global in content.
    c. The current wave is experiencing a more welcoming environment.
    d. All of the above.

TRUE-FALSE QUESTIONS

T F 1. Scientists generally agree on just how many races there are in the world. (319)
T F 2. Sociologists often use the terms race and ethnicity interchangeably. (321)
T F 3. Physical or cultural differences can be a basis of unequal treatment in societies. (321)
T F 4. A group must represent a numerical minority to be considered a minority group. (322)
T F 5. Certain characteristics are shared by minorities worldwide. (322-323)
T F 6. Minorities often have a shared sense of identity and of common destiny. (323)
T F 7. Ethnic work depends on the degree to which an individual has an ethnic identity. (323)
T F 8. Discrimination is unfair treatment based solely on racial characteristics. (324)
T F 9. Although prejudice can be either positive or negative, most prejudice is negative, involving a prejudging of other groups as inferior. (325)
T F 10. One recent study found that members of fraternities and sororities were no more likely than nonmembers to be prejudiced. (325)
T F 11. Sociologists believe that individual discrimination is an adequate explanation for discrimination in the U.S. (326)
T F 12. Research shows that African Americans and Latinos are 60 percent more likely than whites to be rejected for mortgages, all other factors being similar. (327)
T F 13. According to research, even mild levels of frustration can lead to higher levels of prejudice. (328)
T F 14. The Sherif study demonstrates that the social environment can be deliberately arranged to generate either positive or negative feelings about people. (330)
T F 15. Functionalists focus on the role of the capitalist class in exploiting racism and ethnic inequalities. (330)
T F 16. Symbolic interactionists stress that the labels we use encourage us to see things selectively. (331)
T F 17. Genocide often relies on labeling and compartmentalization. (332-334)
T F 18. Segregation allows the dominant group to exploit the labor of the minority while maintaining social distance. (334)
T F 19. Social class and national origin are major obstacles to Latino political unity. (343-344)
T F 20. It is accurate to describe the experiences of Native Americans as ranging from genocide to containment. (347-349)

FILL-IN QUESTIONS

1. The systematic annihilation or attempted annihilation of a race or ethnic group is _____. (318)
2. _____ is inherited physical characteristics that distinguish one group from another. (318)
3. Membership in a minority group is a(n) _____ status; that is, it is not voluntary, but comes through birth. (322)
4. _____ is discrimination on the basis of race. (324)
5. _____ discrimination is the negative treatment of a minority that is built into a society's institutions. (326)
6. Theodor Adorno's term for people who are prejudiced and rank high on scales of conformity, intolerance, insecurity, respect for authority, and submissiveness to superiors is _____. (328)
7. _____ theorists believe that prejudice can be both functional and dysfunctional. (330)

8. Split-labor market is used by _____ theorists to explain how racial and ethnic strife can be used to pit workers against one another. (330)
9. The term used to describe the unemployed who can be put to work during times of high production and then discarded when no longer needed is _____ . (330)
10. _____ is the ability to see certain points but remain blind to others. (331)
11. The types of population transfer are: (1) _____ and (2) _____ . (334)
12. The policy of forced expulsion and genocide is referred to as _____ . (334)
13. _____ is the process of being absorbed into the mainstream culture. (334)
14. _____ is a philosophy or political policy that permits or even encourages ethnic variation. (335)
15. Assimilation to a particular segment of a culture, rather than to the mainstream culture, is called _____ . (335)

MATCH THESE CONCEPTS WITH THEIR DEFINITIONS

____1. Theodor Adorno
____2. Ashley Doane
____3. John Dollard
____4. Raphael Ezekiel
____5. Louis Wirth
____6. Joe Feagin
____7. Donald Muir
____8. William Wilson
____9. Charles Willie
____10. W. I. Thomas

a. *measured racial attitudes of white students*
b. *argues that class is more important than race in explaining inequality*
c. *observed that defining a situation as real, makes it real in its consequences*
d. *identified the authoritarian personality type*
e. *argues that race is still an important criterion for discrimination*
f. *identified four factors that affect an individual's sense of ethnic identity*
g. *suggested that prejudice is the result of frustration*
h. *researched everyday racism*
i. *offered a sociological definition of minority group*
j. *studied racism in neo-Nazis and KKK organizations*

ESSAY QUESTIONS

1. Explain what the author means when he says that race is both a myth and a reality.

2. Using the experiences of different racial and ethnic groups in the U.S., identify and discuss the six patterns of intergroup relations.

3. Explore how both psychological and sociological theories can be used together to gain a deeper understanding of prejudice and discrimination.

CHAPTER 13
THE ELDERLY

☞ CHAPTER SUMMARY

- There are no universal attitudes, beliefs or policies regarding the aged; they range from exclusion and killing to integration and honor. Today there is a trend for people to live longer. In the United States, the rising proportion of older people in the population is referred to as the "graying of America." Because of this trend, the cost of health care for the elderly has become a social issue, and sentiment about the elderly seems to be shifting.

- The symbolic interaction perspective identifies four factors that influence when people label themselves as "old": biological changes, biographical events, gender age, and cultural timetables. Ageism is based on stereotypes which are influenced by the mass media.

- The functional perspective analyzes the withdrawal of the elderly from positions of responsibility. Disengagement and activity theories are two functional theories arising from research in this area.

- Conflict theorists study the competition for scarce resources by rival interest groups (e.g., how different age cohorts may be on a collision course regarding Social Security, Medicare, and Medicaid).

- Elderly women are most likely to be alone and to be poor. At any one time, about 4 percent of the elderly live in nursing homes. About one-third of elderly men and one-half of women will spend at least some time in nursing homes. Problems of dependency for the elderly include inadequate nursing homes, elder abuse, and poverty.

- Industrialization has changed the individual's experience with death. The process of dying involves denial, anger, negotiation, depression, and acceptance. Hospices, a recent cultural device, are intended to provide dignity in death, to reduce the emotional and physical burden on relatives, to reduce costs, and to make people comfortable during the living-dying interval. Suicide increases with age and shows sharply different patterns by sex and race.

☞ LEARNING OBJECTIVES

As you read Chapter 13, use these learning objectives to organize your notes. After completing your reading, briefly state an answer to each of the objectives, and review the text pages in parentheses.

1. Explain what the "social construction of aging" means and how industrialization affects the aged population. (356-358)
2. Examine what the term "graying of America" means and why different racial and ethnic groups have differing proportions of elderly within the population. (358-362)
3. Discuss the major conclusions drawn by symbolic interactionists regarding aging. (362-363)
4. Use cross-cultural comparisons to show how societies vary widely on their perceptions of what makes a person old, what it means to grow old, and how the elderly are viewed. (363-364)
5. Review how the meaning of old age has changed over time in the U.S. and consider some of the factors that contributed to this change. (364-366)
6. Discuss ways in which the mass media perpetuates these ideas. (366-367)
7. Summarize the functional perspective on aging and explain disengagement and activity theories. (367-369)

8.   Explain why conflict theorists see social life as a struggle between groups for scarce resources and note how this impacts different age cohorts. (369-375)
9.   State some of the problems of dependency, especially in regard to isolation, nursing homes, elder abuse, and poverty. (375-379)
10.   Examine the effects of industrialization and new technology on the process of death and dying. (380)
11.   Outline the stages people go through when they are told they have an incurable disease. (381)
12.   Explain the functions of hospices in modern societies. (381-382)
13.   Give reasons for the high rate of suicide among the elderly. (382-383)

☞ CHAPTER OUTLINE

I.   **Aging in Global Perspective**
      A.   Every society must deal with the problem of people growing old; as the proportion of the population that is old increases, those decisions become more complex and the tensions between the generations grow deeper.
      B.   Attitudes about aging are socially constructed--how a society views the aged--and the aging process depends on culture, not on biology.
            1.   The Abkhasians may be the longest-lived people in the world, with many claiming to live past 100.
            2.   The main factors that appear to account for their long lives are diet, lifelong physical activity, and a highly developed sense of community.
      C.   As a country industrializes, more of its people reach older ages.
            1.   This reflects the higher standard of living, better public health measures, and successes in fighting deadly diseases.
            2.   As the proportion of elderly increases, so does the bill that younger citizens must pay in order to provide for their needs. Among industrialized nations, this bill has become a major social issue.
      D.   In the United States, the "graying of America" refers to the proportion of older persons in the U.S. population.
            1.   Today almost 13% of the population has achieved age 65; there are almost 7 million more elderly Americans than teen-agers.
            2.   While life expectancy--the number of years an average newborn can expect to live--has increased, the life span--maximum length of life--has not.
            3.   Because the proportion of non-whites in the U.S. is growing, the number of minority elderly is also increasing; differences in cultural attitudes about aging, types of family relationships, work histories, and health practices will be important areas of sociological investigation in the coming years.
II.   **The Symbolic Interactionist Perspective**
      A.   There are several factors that push people to apply the label.
            1.   Biology changes how a person looks and feels; the person adopts the role of "old" (acts the way old people are thought to act) upon experiencing these changes.
            2.   Personal history (an injury that limits mobility) or biography (becoming a grandmother at an early age) may affect self-concept regarding age.
            3.   Gender age also plays a part. The relative values that culture places on men's ages is less than that of women's ages.

4.   When a particular society defines a person as "old," the person is likely to feel "old." These timetables are not fixed; groups sometimes adjust expectations about the onset of old age.

B.   Aging is relative; when it begins and what it means varies from culture to culture.
  1.   For the traditional Native American, the signal for old age is more often the inability to perform productive social roles rather than any particular birthday.
  2.   The Tiwi tribe is a gerontocracy (a society run by the elderly) where older men are so entrenched in power that they control all of the wealth and all of the women.
  3.   To grow old in traditional Eskimo society meant voluntary death. Eskimo society was so precarious that a person no longer able to pull his or her own weight was expected to simply go off and die.

C.   Robert Butler coined the term ageism to refer to prejudice, discrimination, and hostility directed at people because of their age.
  1.   With the coming of industrialization, the traditional bases of respect for the elderly eroded. The distinctiveness of age was lost and new ideas of morality made the opinions of the elderly outmoded. The meaning of old age was transformed--from usefulness to uselessness, from wisdom to foolishness, from an asset to a liability.
  2.   The meaning of old age is being transformed with the increasing wealth of the U.S. elderly and the coming of age of the Baby Boom generation. The Baby Boom generation, given their vast numbers and economic clout, are likely to positively affect our images of the elderly.

D.   The mass media communicates messages about the aged, influencing our ideas about the elderly.

III.   The Functionalist Perspective

A.   Functionalists examine age from the standpoint of how those persons who are retiring and those who will replace them in the work force make mutual adjustments.

B.   Elaine Cumming and William Henry developed disengagement theory to explain how society prevents disruption to society when the elderly retire.
  1.   The elderly are rewarded in some way (pensions) for giving up positions rather than waiting until they become incompetent or die; this allows for a smooth transition of positions.
  2.   For many, disengagement begins during middle age, long before retirement. While not immediately disengaging, the individual begins to assign priority to certain goals and tasks.
  3.   This theory is criticized because it assumes that the elderly disengage and then sink into oblivion.

C.   According to activity theory older people who maintain a high level of activity tend to be more satisfied with life than those who do not.
  1.   Most research findings support the hypothesis that more active people are more satisfied people.
  2.   Underlying people's activities are finances, health, and individual orientation.

IV.   The Conflict Perspective

A.   Conflict theorists examine social life as a struggle between groups for scarce resources. Social Security legislation is an example of that struggle.
  1.   In the 1920s-30s, two-thirds of all citizens over 65 had no savings and could not support themselves. Francis Townsend enrolled one-third of all Americans over

65 in clubs that sought a national sales tax to finance a monthly pension for all Americans over age 65. To avoid the plan without appearing to be opposed to old-age pensions, Social Security was enacted by Congress.

    2.   Conflict theorists state that Social Security was not a result of generosity, but rather of competition among interest groups.

B.   Since equilibrium is only a temporary balancing of social forces, some form of continuing conflict between the younger and the older appears inevitable.

    1.   The huge costs of Social Security have become a national concern. Conflict is inevitable, as proportionately fewer working people are forced to pay for the benefits received by an increasing number of senior citizens.

    2.   Some argue that the elderly and children are on a collision course. Data indicate that as the number of elderly poor decreased, children in poverty increased. It has been argued that the comparison is misleading because the money that went to the elderly did not come from money intended for the children. Framing the issue in this way is an attempt to divide the working class, and to force a choice between suffering children and suffering elderly.

C.   Empowering the elderly, some organizations today work to protect the hand-won gains of the elderly.

    1.   The Gray Panthers was organized in the 1960s to encourage persons of all ages to work for the welfare of both the elderly and the young. On the micro level, the goal is to develop positive self-concepts; on the macro level, the goal is to build a power base with which to challenge all institutions that oppress the poor, young or old alike.

    2.   To protect their gains, older Americans organized the American Association of Retired Persons, with 33 million members. This association monitors proposed federal and state legislation and mobilizes its members to act on issues affecting their welfare.

V.   **Problems of Dependency**

A.   While the elderly are not as isolated as stereotypes would lead us to believe, there are differences between men and women. Women are especially likely to be isolated. Because of differences in mortality, most older males (73%) are married and live with their wives, while most older women do not (only 41% live with husbands).

B.   About 4 percent of Americans over 65 are in nursing homes at any one time; each year about 13 percent of all U.S. citizens aged 65 and over are admitted to nursing homes. About one-half of elderly women and one-third of elderly men will spend some time in a nursing home.

    1.   Nursing home residents are likely to be quite ill, or over 80, or never to have married and thus have no family to take care of them.

    2.   The cost is high and even the better ones tend to strip away human dignity.

    3.   In 1987 the U.S. Congress passed the Nursing Home Reform Amendments, a bill of rights for nursing home residents. Residents have a right to be informed about their treatment and to refuse it, the right to privacy, and the right to complain without reprisal.

    4.   Computers and the Internet help some elderly overcome problems of isolation, depression and anomie.

C.   Elder abuse is a significant problem. Most abusers are members of the elderly person's family. Some researchers say the abuse occurs when an individual feels obligated to take care of a person who is highly dependent and demanding, which can be very stressful.

    D.   A major fear of the elderly is that their money may not last as long as their life does.

        1.   Women are twice as likely as men to be poor.

        2.   Elderly African Americans and Latinos are almost three times as likely as whites to be poor.

        3.   As a result of governmental programs, the elderly now are less likely than the average American to be poor.

VI.   The Sociology of Death and Dying

    A.   In preindustrial societies, the sick were cared for at home and died at home. With the coming of modern medicine, dying was transformed into an event to be managed by professionals; most people never have personally seen anyone die.

        1.   The process of dying has become strange to most people; we hide from the fact of death, we even construct a language of avoidance--a person is "gone" or "at peace now," rather than dead.

        2.   New technology has produced "technological lifespace." This is neither life nor death; the person is brain dead, but the body lives on.

    B.   Elisabeth Kübler-Ross identified the stages a person passes through when told that she or he has an incurable disease: (1) denial; (2) anger; (3) negotiation; (4) depression; and (5) acceptance. Kübler-Ross noted that not everyone experiences all of these stages and not everyone goes through them in order.

    C.   Elderly persons want to die with dignity in the comforting presence of friends and relatives. Due to advances in medical technology, most deaths in the U.S. occur after the age of 65.

        1.   Hospitals are awkward places to die, surrounded by strangers in hospital garb in an organization that puts routine ahead of individual needs. Patients experience what sociologists call "institutional death."

        2.   Hospices have emerged as a solution to these problems, providing greater dignity and comfort at less cost.

    D.   There is a sharp rise in suicide rate for white males when they reach their 60s.

        1.   This may indicate that white males experience aging differently than other groups.

        2.   It has been suggested that for white males aging represents a relatively greater loss of power and status than it does for other groups.

☞ KEY TERMS

After studying the chapter, review the definition for each of the following terms.

activity theory: the view that satisfaction during old age is related to a person's level and quality of activity

age cohort: people born at roughly the same time who pass through the life course together

ageism: prejudice, discrimination, and hostility directed against people because of their age; can be directed against any age group, including youth

dependency ratio: the number of workers required to support dependent persons--those 65 and older and those 15 and younger

disengagement theory: the view that society prevents disruption by having the elderly vacate (or disengage from) their positions of responsibility so that the younger generation can step into their shoes

gender age: the relative values of men's and women's ages in a particular culture

gerontocracy: a society (or some other group) run by the elderly

graying of America: a term that refers to the rising proportion of older persons as a percentage of the U.S. population

hospice: a place, or services brought into someone's home, for the purpose of bringing comfort and dignity to a dying person

life expectancy: the number of years that an average newborn can expect to live

life span: the maximum length of life of a species

☞ KEY PEOPLE

Review the major theoretical contributions or findings of these people.

Robert Butler: Butler coined the term "ageism" to refer to prejudice, discrimination and hostility directed against people because of their age.

Karen Cerulo and Janet Ruane: These sociologists have suggested that new technologies have brought on new experiences of death; they use the term "technological lifespace" to refer to an existence that is neither life nor death.

Elaine Cumming and William Henry: These two developed disengagement theory to explain how society prevents disruption when the elderly vacate their positions of responsibility.

Dorothy Jerrome: This anthropologist is critical of disengagement theory, pointing out that it contains implicit bias against old people.

Elisabeth Kübler-Ross: This psychologist found that coming face-to-face with one's own death sets in motion a five-stage process.

Meredith Minkler and Ann Robertson: These conflict sociologists investigated whether or not the government expenditures allocated for the elderly were at the expense of children and found there was no evidence of that.

Karl Pillemer and Jill Suitor: These sociologists interviewed more than 200 caregivers of Alzheimer patients and found that the precipitating cause of elder abuse is stress from caring for a person who is dependent, demanding, and even violent.

☞ "DOWN-TO-EARTH SOCIOLOGY"

This is your opportunity to apply the sociological perspective to the world around you. The questions in this section refer to material introduced in this chapter of your text. Many ask you to think about ideas and information presented in the various special "boxes" that are located throughout this chapter.

1.   What are some of the factors that are contributing to China's changing sentiments about the elderly (p. 365)? Why is it so important for the family to continue to honor its traditional obligations to its elderly members? How does the situation in China compare with that of the elderly in the U.S.? If you were given the option, which arrangement would you prefer if you were old? Which would you prefer if you were a younger person responsible for the care of an elderly family member? Why?

2.   After reading about the ways in which the mass media shape our perceptions of the elderly on page 367, can you think of some specific examples of stereotypes of the elderly that you've seen? What about ads that promote youthfulness or that portray the elderly in negative terms? Think about how you would create some positive images to replace these negative ones.

3.   "Changing Sentiment About the Elderly" on page 371 gives an example of a person who thought there was something wrong with people automatically receiving a "senior citizen discount" regardless of need. Do you think there is anything wrong with such discounts? Have you seen examples of these discounts in your community (e.g., at drug stores or restaurants)? Are the elderly entitled to special discounts? Why or why not? Should the same considerations be given to student discounts that are given to senior discounts? Why or why not?

4.   After reading about Social Security on page 372, list some of the problems with the current system. Why is the current budget surplus really not a surplus at all, but actually part of the national debt? What do you think of the proposed recommendations for solving the crisis? Would these proposals be popular? Would you support them? Why or why not?

5.   Have you ever known someone with Alzheimer's disease (p. 377)? What kind of living arrangement were they in? What are the advantages of the Swedish arrangement?

6.   What kind of life do you hope to have when you reach your senior years? Given the current conditions, do you think your view will remain accurate?

☞ SELF-TEST

After completing this self-test, check your answers against the Answer Key beginning on page 381 of this Study Guide and against the text on page(s) indicated in parentheses.

MULTIPLE CHOICE QUESTIONS

1.   The Abkhasians are an interesting example regarding age because they: (357)
        a.   live such short lives.
        b.   live such long lives.
        c.   have so many words in their language for "old people."
        d.   quit working when they are quite young.

2.   Which of the following contributes to an increase in the number of people who reach older ages? (357-358)
        a.   changing social attitudes about aging
        b.   reduction in warfare
        c.   later retirement
        d.   industrialization

3.   The process by which older persons make up an increasing proportion of the United States' population is referred to as: (359)
        a.   the aging process.
        b.   the graying of America.
        c.   the gentrification process.
        d.   None of the above.

4.   The number of years a person is likely to live is referred to as: (359)
        a.   life span.
        b.   life course.
        c.   life expectancy.
        d.   life history.

5.   The relative value that a culture places on men's and women's ages is: (363)
      a.   cultural aging.
      b.   ageism.
      c.   gender age.
      d.   relative age.

6.   Factors that may push people to apply the label of old to themselves include: (363)
      a.   personal history or biography.
      b.   cultural signals about when a person is old.
      c.   biological factors.
      d.   All of the above.

7.   A local miniature golf course bars children under the age of 16 from playing golf after 6 p.m. What does this policy reflect? (365)
      a.   sound business practices
      b.   ageism
      c.   the graying of America
      d.   misguided efforts to control juvenile customers

8.   It has been suggested that _____ will have a positive effect on U.S. social images of the elderly in the years to come, given the numbers and economic clout. (366)
      a.   Congress
      b.   the Baby Boom generation
      c.   Generation X
      d.   seniors living on Social Security

9.   The mass media: (367)
      a.   communicate messages that reflect the currently devalued status of the elderly.
      b.   tell us what people over 65 should be like.
      c.   often treat the elderly in discourteous and unflattering terms.
      d.   All of the above.

10.   Some researchers believe that the process of disengagement begins: (368)
      a.   when a person first starts a job.
      b.   during middle age.
      c.   at retirement.
      d.   about one year after retirement.

11.   _____ suggests that satisfaction in old age depends on one's level/quality of activity. (369)
      a.   Activity theory
      b.   Recreational theory
      c.   Satisfaction theory
      d.   None of the above

12. Conflict theorists believe that retirement benefits are the result of: (370)
    a.   generous hearts in Congress.
    b.   a struggle between competing interest groups.
    c.   many years of hard work by elderly Americans.
    d.   None of the above.

13. As the population of the U.S. grays, there is concern that: (372)
    a.   participation in the electoral process will decline because older citizens are less likely to vote.
    b.   the ratio of working people to retired people will become smaller, making it more difficult to support programs like Social Security.
    c.   there will be a shortage of affordable housing for widowed individuals living on a fixed income.
    d.   All of the above.

14. Isolation is a problem for many people over 65, especially for: (375)
    a.   women.
    b.   minorities.
    c.   the disabled.
    d.   immigrants.

15. Nursing homes: (376)
    a.   are very expensive.
    b.   have residents who are likely to be widowed or never married.
    c.   tend to strip away human dignity.
    d.   All of the above.

16. Researchers have found that elder abuse: (378)
    a.   occurs less frequently than one might think, given the level of abuse shown in the media.
    b.   is fairly extensive.
    c.   is most often caused by workers in nursing homes.
    d.   is easy to study because the victims are so visible.

17. The percentage of Americans aged 65 and older living below the poverty line: (379)
    a.   has declined since the 1950s.
    b.   has increased relative to the population under 65 who live below the poverty line.
    c.   has remained unchanged since the 1950s.
    d.   has become increasingly more male, as men's life expectancy has improved.

18. Karen Cerulo and Janet Ruane use the term _____ to describe a form of existence that is neither life nor death--the brain is dead but the body lives on. (380)
    a.   institutional death
    b.   technological lifespace
    c.   technological fix
    d.   living death

19. In preindustrial societies, the sick: (380)
    a. were taken care of at home.
    b. were taken care of in hospitals.
    c. were taken care of in hospices.
    d. did not live long enough to have to be taken care of by anyone.

20. In trying to explain the pattern of a sharp rise in suicide of white males when they reach their middle sixties, symbolic interactionists point out that: (383)
    a. white males may experience aging differently than other groups in our society.
    b. aging may represent a greater loss of privilege for white males than for other groups.
    c. retirement signals a decline in both power and status for them.
    d. All of the above.

TRUE-FALSE QUESTIONS

T F 1. When sociologists say that aging is socially constructed, what they mean is that attitudes about aging reflect cultural values rather than biological factors. (356)

T F 2. Industrialization is less important than cultural attitudes in influencing the growth in the number of elderly within a society. (357)

T F 3. Life expectancy and life span describe the same thing. (358-360)

T F 4. According to the symbolic interactionists, a person's perception of "old" and what it means to be old is influenced by stereotypes and societal definitions of age. (362)

T F 5. That older male news anchors are likely to be retained by news stations while female anchors who turn the same age are more likely to be transferred to a less visible position is an example of gender age. (363)

T F 6. A gerontocracy is a society run by younger people on behalf of the elderly. (364)

T F 7. In the United States today, the elderly are underrepresented on TV, in ads, and even in popular magazines. (367)

T F 8. Disengagement theory is used to explain how society prevents disruption by having the elderly vacate their positions of responsibility. (368)

T F 9. Activity theorists believe that older people who maintain a high level of activity tend to be more satisfied with life than those who do not. (369)

T F 10. According to conflict theorists, the passage of social security legislation is an example of the struggle between the young and old in society. (369)

T F 11. The dependency ratio is the number of workers required to support one person on Social Security. (372)

T F 12. The elderly are more isolated than stereotypes would lead us to believe. (375)

T F 13. Elder abuse includes financial exploitation. (378)

T F 14. America's elderly are more likely than the average American to live in poverty. (379)

T F 15. Industrialization radically altered the circumstances of dying. (380)

FILL-IN QUESTIONS

1. The process by which older persons make up an increasing proportion of the United States population is called _____. (359)

2. The _____ of an average newborn is the number years he or she can expect to live. (359)

3. While experts may disagree on the actual number, _____ refers to the maximum length of life of a species. (360)
4. The relative value that a culture places on men's and women's ages is referred to as _____. (363)
5. _____ is a society (or some other group) run by the old. (364)
6. _____ is the discrimination against the elderly because of their age. (365)
7. The _____ not only communicate messages about the devalued status of the elderly in U.S. society but also contribute to the ideas. (366)
8. An _____ is people born at roughly the same time who pass through the life course together. (367)
9. The belief that society prevents disruption by having the elderly vacate their positions of responsibility is _____. (368)
10. _____ theory asserts that satisfaction during old age is related to a person's level and quality of activity. (369)
11. The number of workers required to support the portion of the population aged 64 and older and 15 and under is the _____. (372)
12. Founded in the 1960s by Margaret Kuhn, the _____ encourages people of all ages to work for the welfare of both the old and the young. (375)
13. The organization that monitors proposed state and federal legislation and mobilizes members to act on issues affecting their welfare as senior citizens is the _____. (375)
14. Sociologists Cerulo and Ruane use the term _____ to describe a form of existence in which, due to technology, the body lives on even after brain function is gone. (380)
15. _____ is a place, or services brought into someone's home, for the purpose of bringing comfort and dignity to a dying person. (381)

MATCH THESE SOCIAL SCIENTISTS WITH THEIR CONTRIBUTIONS

___1. Robert Butler   a. *use the term "technological lifespace" for life sustained by technology*
___2. Dorothy Jerrome   b. *found no evidence that the elderly gained at children's expense*
___3. E. Kübler-Ross   c. *developed disengagement theory*
___4. Cerulo & Ruane   d. *coined "ageism" to refer to prejudice or discrimination based on age*
___5. Cumming & Henry   e. *criticized disengagement theory for its implicit bias against the old*
___6. Robertson & Minkler   f. *suggested that facing death sets in motion a five-stage process*

ESSAY QUESTIONS

1. Choose one of the three different perspectives and discuss how that perspective approaches the subject of aging. Consider both the strengths as well as the weaknesses of the perspective you chose.

2. Discuss the impact that industrialization and technology has had on aging as well as dying.

CHAPTER 14
THE ECONOMY

☞ CHAPTER SUMMARY

- The earliest hunting and gathering societies were characterized by subsistence economies; economic systems became more complex as people discovered first how to domesticate and cultivate (horticultural and pastoral societies), then to farm (agricultural societies) and finally to manufacture (industrial societies).

- In the least complex societies, people exchanged goods and services through barter. As societies and economies evolved, certain items were assigned uniform value and became the medium of exchange. Today we rely increasingly on electronic transfer of funds with credit, debit cards and e-cash.

- The two major economic systems are capitalism, in which the means of production are privately owned, and socialism, in which the means of production are state owned. There are different forms of both capitalism (laissez-faire capitalism and welfare capitalism) and socialism (democratic socialism). In recent years each system has adopted features of the other.

- Functionalists state that work is a fundamental source of social solidarity; preindustrial societies foster mechanical solidarity while industrial societies, with their more complex division of labor, are characterized by organic solidarity. This process has continued and we are now developing a global division of labor.

- Conflict theorists focus on power, noting how global capitalism affects workers and owners. Corporations dominate modern capitalism; an inner circle--a group of leaders from the major corporations--are mutually interested in making certain that corporate capitalism is protected. The sociological significance of global capitalism is that the interests of the inner circle extend beyond national boundaries. Workers lose jobs, while the inner circle maintains its power and profits.

- Most U.S. workers today are employed in white-collar jobs. A quiet revolution has occurred due to the dramatic increase in the number of married women who work for pay. The underground economy, economic activity that is not reported to the government, runs perhaps 10 to 15 percent of the regular economy. Initially, the amount of leisure decreased as the economy changed from preindustrial to industrial; with unionization workers gained back some. Because of technological changes, today there is a trend for more and more white-collar workers to work from home.

- Work will continue to be restructured as a result of downsizing, new technologies, and the expansion of global capitalism.

☞ LEARNING OBJECTIVES

As you read Chapter 14, use these learning objectives to organize your notes. After completing your reading, briefly state an answer to each of the objectives, and review the text pages in parentheses.

1. Trace the transformation of the economic systems through each of the historical stages and state the degree to which social inequality existed in each of the economies. (388-391)
2. Explain what the "medium of exchange" means and how it is vital to society. (391-393)
3. State the essential features of capitalism and socialism and explain why neither exists in its "pure" form. (393-395)

4. Identify the ideologies of capitalism and socialism. (395-396)
5. State criticisms of capitalism and socialism. (396)
6. Describe the recent changes in both capitalist and socialist economies, and explain why some theorists believe the two systems are converging. (396-399)
7. Explain the functionalist view of globalization. (399-402)
8. Outline the conflict perspective on economic life and explain the role of the inner circle, interlocking directorates, and global investing. (402-404)
9. Review recent changes in the U.S. economy, including the shift in employment, the employment of women outside the home, the growth of the underground economy, the decline in real wages, patterns of work and leisure, and the emergence of the alternative office. (405-410)
10. Consider what impact expanding global trade, new technologies, and downsizing will have on U.S. economy and society in the years to come. (412-414)

☞ CHAPTER OUTLINE

I. **The Transformation of Economic Systems**
    A. Market, or economy, is the mechanism by which values are established in order to exchange goods and services.
        1. The economy, which may be one of our most important social institutions, is the system of distribution of goods and services.
        2. The economy today, impersonal and global, is radically different from the past.
    B. As societies developed, a surplus emerged which fostered social inequality.
        1. Earliest hunting and gathering societies had subsistence economies, characterized by little trade with other groups, and a high degree of social equality.
        2. In pastoral and horticultural economies, people created more dependable food supplies. As groups settled down in one location and grew in size, a specialized division of labor developed. This led to the production of a surplus and trade between groups, all of which fostered social inequality.
        3. Agricultural economies brought even greater surpluses, magnifying prior trends in social, political and economic inequality. More people were freed from food production, a more specialized division of labor developed, and trade expanded.
    C. The surplus (and greater inequality) grew in industrial societies. As the surplus increased emphasis changed from production of goods to consumption (Thorstein Veblen coined the term conspicuous consumption).
    D. The "information explosion" and the global village are key elements of postindustrial society.
        1. According to Daniel Bell, postindustrial economies have six traits: (1) extensive trade among nations; (2) a large surplus of goods; (3) a service sector employing the majority of workers; (4) a wide variety and amount of goods available to the average person; (5) an information explosion; and (6) a global village with instantaneous, worldwide communications.
        2. Around the globe the consequences of the information explosion are uneven. Due to political and economic arrangements, some nations and individuals will prosper while others suffer.
        3. Overall, while the postindustrial economy has brought a greater availability of goods, it has not resulted in income equality.

II. **The Transformation of the Medium of Exchange**
  A. A medium of exchange is the means by which people value and exchange goods and services.
  B. One of the earliest mediums of exchange was barter, the direct exchange of one item for another.
  C. In agricultural economies, people came to use gold and silver coins. Deposit receipts, which transferred ownership of a specified amount of gold or bushels of wheat, etc. on deposit somewhere, were used. Toward the end of this period, the receipts were formalized into currency (paper money). Currency represented stored value; no more could be issued than the amount of gold or silver the currency represented.
  D. In industrial economies, bartering largely disappeared and gold was replaced by paper currency. The gold standard (a dollar represents a specified amount of gold) kept the number of dollars that could be issued to a specific limit. When "fiat money" came into existence, the currency no longer could be exchanged for gold or silver.
    1. Even without a gold standard, the amount of paper money that can be issued is limited: prices increase if a government issues currency at a rate higher than the growth of its gross national product. Issuing more produces inflation: each unit of currency will purchase fewer goods and services.
    2. Checking accounts and credit cards have become common in industrial economies, largely replacing currency.
  E. In postindustrial economies paper money is being replaced by checks, credit cards, and debit cards. The latest phase of evolution of money is e-cash, digital money stored on the user's local computer.

III. **World Economic Systems**
  A. Capitalism has three essential features: (1) the private ownership of the means of production; (2) the pursuit of profit; and (3) market competition.
    1. Pure (laissez-faire) capitalism exists only when market forces are able to operate without interference from the government.
    2. The United States today has welfare (or state) capitalism. Private citizens own the means of production and pursue profits, but do so within a vast system of laws (market restraints) that are designed to protect the public welfare.
    3. Under welfare capitalism the government supports competition but establishes its own monopoly over "common good" items, e.g. those presumed essential for the common good of the citizens.
  B. Socialism also has three essential features: (1) the public ownership of the means of production; (2) central planning; and (3) the distribution of goods without a profit motive.
    1. Under socialism, the government owns the means of production, and a central committee determines what the country needs instead of allowing market forces (supply and demand) to control production and prices. Socialism is designed to eliminate competition, to produce goods for the general welfare, and to distribute them according to people's needs, not their ability to pay.
    2. Socialism does not exist in pure form. Although the ideology of socialism calls for resources to be distributed according to need rather than position, socialist nations found it necessary to offer higher salaries for some jobs in order to entice people to take greater responsibilities.
    3. Some nations (e.g., Sweden and Denmark) have adopted democratic or welfare socialism: both the state and individuals engage in production and distribution,

although the state owns certain industries (steel, mining, forestry, telephones, television stations, and airlines) while retail stores, farms, and most service industries remain in private hands.

C. Capitalism and socialism represent distinct ideologies.
1. Capitalists believe that market forces should determine both products and prices, and that it is good for people to strive for profits.
2. Socialists believe that profit is immoral and represents excess value extracted from workers.
3. These two contrasting ideologies produce contrasting pictures of how the world should be; consequently, each sees the other ideology as not only inherently evil but also as a system of exploitation.

D. The primary criticism of capitalism is that it leads to social inequality (a top layer of wealthy, powerful people, and a bottom layer of people who are unemployed or underemployed). Socialism has been criticized for not respecting individual rights, and for not being capable of producing much wealth (thus the greater equality of socialism actually amounts to almost everyone having an equal chance of being poor).

E. In recent years, fundamental changes have taken place in these two economic systems.
1. Over the years the U.S. has adopted many socialistic practices--unemployment compensation; subsidized housing; welfare; minimum wage; and Social Security.
2. In 1989, the former Soviet Union concluded that its system of central planning had failed. It began to reinstate market forces, including private ownership of property and profits for those who produce and sell goods.
3. Despite the firm stand that Chinese leaders took in regard to Tiananmen Square, they too began to endorse capitalism, soliciting western investment, allowing the use of credit cards, and approving a stock market. The result of such measures has been an increasing standard of living.
4. As the two systems continue to adopt features of the other, convergence theory predicts that they will eventually converge, creating a hybrid economic system. Evidence for this theory is impressive. Elements of capitalist economic activity have been integrated into socialist economies like China, and citizens of the U.S. have been accustomed to certain socialist features.
5. The reality is that the two remain far from "converged" and the struggles between them continue, although they are more muted than in the past. With the pullback of socialism around the world, capitalism--in its many varieties--has a strong lead.

IV. **The Functionalist View of the Globalization of Capitalism**
A. The globalization of capitalism may be the most significant economic change in the past 100 years.
B. Work is functional for society; it binds people together.
1. Work is central to Durkheim's principles of mechanical solidarity (unity from being involved in similar occupations or activities) and organic solidarity (interdependence resulting from mutual need as each individual fulfills his job).
2. Today organic solidarity has expanded far beyond anything Durkheim envisioned, creating interdependencies that span the globe. These global interdependencies suggest a new global division of labor, although we do not yet feel a sense of unity with one another we are increasingly dependent on one another.
C. The corporation (joint ownership of a business enterprise, whose liabilities are separate from those of its owners) changed the face of capitalism.

1. One of the most significant aspects of large corporations is the separation of ownership and management, producing ownership of wealth without appreciable control, and control of wealth without appreciable ownership.

2. What makes the separation of ownership and management functional is profits. Managers are motivated to maximize profits because they will then benefit through stock options and bonuses.

3. A stockholders' revolt (stockholders of a corporation refuse to rubber stamp management decisions) is likely to occur if the profits do not meet expectations.

D. The world is divided into three primary trading blocs: North and South America dominated by the U.S., Europe dominated by Germany, and Asia dominated by Japan.

   1. If free trade is achieved within each of these trading blocs, competition will increase and prices will decrease, resulting in a higher standard of living.

   2. At the same time, there will be an enormous loss of production jobs in the most industrialized nations as production moves to where labor costs are lower.

   3. The sociological significance of global capitalism is that the multinational corporations are reshaping the globe as no political force has been able to do. Furthermore, they have loyalty to profit and market share rather than to a regional or cultural value system.

   4. On the positive side, global interconnections, which transcend national loyalties, may promote global peace. On the negative side, the world's market may come to be dominated by a handful of corporate leaders.

V. **The Conflict View of the Globalization of Capitalism**

A. The multinationals are headed by an inner circle. This group, while in competition with one another, are united by a mutual interest in preserving capitalism.

   1. Oligopolies, several large companies that dominate a single industry, dictate pricing, set the quality of their products, and protect the market. Often they use their wealth and connections for political purposes (e.g., favorable legislation giving them special tax breaks or protecting their industry from imports).

   2. Corporate capitalism refers to economic domination by giant corporations.

   3. The inner circle develops a cozy relationship with the U.S. president, such that the interests of the corporations and those of the top political leaders often converge and much of the activity of the latter is dedicated to promoting the economic interests of the country's elite.

   4. If they find hostility, some are not above plotting murder and overthrowing governments. In 1973, ITT plotted with the CIA to unseat Salvador Allende, the democratically elected president of Chile because he was a socialist, which led to his assassination.

B. Interlocking directorates occur when individuals serve as directors of several companies, concentrating power and minimizing competition.

C. As corporations have outgrown national boundaries, the result is the creation of multinational corporations, detached from the interests and values of their country of origin with no concern other than making a profit. They are becoming a primary political force in the world today.

VI. **Work in U.S. Society**

A. In our postindustrial society there are changes in the type of work that workers do.

   1. In the 1800s, most U.S. workers were farmers; today farmers represent only 2 percent of the workforce.

2. In 1940, about one-half of U.S. workers worked in blue-collar jobs; today the changing technology has reduced the market for these jobs.

3. The dominant job today is white collar.

B. A sharp increase in the number of women working outside the home has occurred in the United States.

1. How likely a woman is to work depends on several factors, such as her education and marital status; race and ethnicity have little influence.

2. Men and women have different work experiences and models for success.

3. The quiet revolution refers to the continually increasing proportions of women in the labor force. This transformation affects consumer patterns, relations at work, self-concepts, and familial relationships.

C. The underground (informal) economy involves exchange of goods and services not reported to the government, including income from work done "on the side" and from illegal activities (e.g., drug dealing). Estimates place the underground economy at 10 to 15% of the regular economy, which means it may run close to $1 trillion. As a result, the IRS loses over $100 billion a year in taxes.

D. Since 1970, increases in workers' paychecks have not kept up with inflation; consequently, workers are falling behind.

E. Different societies have had differing amounts of leisure (time not taken up by work or required activities such as eating/sleeping).

1. Early societies had a lot of time for leisure. Industrialization brought changes: bosses and machines controlled people's time.

2. It is not the activity itself that makes something leisure, but rather its purpose (e.g., driving a car for pleasure or driving it to work). Patterns of leisure change with the life course, with both the young and the old enjoying the most leisure and parents with young children having the least.

3. Compared with early industrialization, workers today have far more leisure (shorter work weeks, for example). In recent decades, the trend for more leisure has been reversed in the U.S.

F. New technologies are enabling millions of workers to work from home; they commute electronically.

VII. The Future: Facing the Consequences of Global Capitalism

A. There is every indication that global trade will continue to increase beyond anything we have ever seen, as multinational corporations continue to carve up the world into major trading blocs and push for reduction or elimination of tariffs.

B. Computer-driven production will continue to reduce the number of manufacturing jobs. While technology eliminates jobs, it also creates jobs. At the same time, those who bear the brunt of the change are low-level workers who live from paycheck to paycheck.

☞ KEY TERMS

After studying the chapter, review the definition for each of the following terms.

barter: the direct exchange of one item for another

capitalism: an economic system characterized by the private ownership of the means of production, the pursuit of profit, and market competition

conspicuous consumption: Thorstein Veblen's term for a change from the Protestant ethic to an eagerness to show off wealth by the elaborate consumption of goods

convergence theory: the view that as capitalist and socialist economic systems each adopt features of the other, a hybrid (or mixed) economic system will emerge

corporate capitalism: the domination of the economic system by giant corporations

corporation: the joint ownership of a business enterprise, whose liabilities and obligations are separate from those of the owners

credit card: a device that allows its owner to purchase goods but be billed later

currency: paper money

debit card: a device that allows its owner to charge purchases against his or her bank account

democratic socialism: a hybrid economic system in which capitalism is mixed with state ownership

deposit receipts: a receipt stating that a certain amount of goods is on deposit in a warehouse or bank; the receipt is used as a form of money

divest: to sell off

e-cash: digital money that is stored on computers

economy: a system of distribution of goods and services

fiat money: currency issued by a government that is not backed by stored value

gold standard: paper money backed by gold

gross national product (GNP): the amount of goods and services produced by a nation

inflation: an increase in prices

interlocking directorates: the same people serving on the board of directors of several companies

laissez-faire capitalism: unrestrained manufacture and trade (literally, "hands off" capitalism)

market: any process of buying and selling; on a more formal level, the mechanism that establishes values for the exchange of goods and services

market competition: the exchange of items between willing buyers and sellers

market forces: the law of supply and demand

market restraints: laws and regulations that limit the capacity to manufacture and sell products

mechanical solidarity: Durkheim's term for the unity that comes from being involved in similar occupations or activities

medium of exchange: the means by which people value goods and services in order to make an exchange, for example, currency, gold, and silver

money: any item (from sea shells to gold) that serves as a medium of exchange; today, currency is the most common form

monopoly: the control of an entire industry by a single company

oligopoly: the control of an entire industry by several large companies

organic solidarity: Durkheim's term for the interdependence that results from people's needing others to fulfill their job

private ownership of the means of production: the ownership of machines and factories by individuals, who decide what shall be produced

profession: an occupation characterized by rigorous education, a theoretical perspective, self-regulation, authority over clients, and service to society (as opposed to a job)

quiet revolution (the): the fundamental changes in society that occurred as a result of vast numbers of women entering the work force

socialism: an economic system characterized by the public ownership of the means of production, central planning, and the distribution of goods without a profit motive

stockholders' revolt: the refusal of a corporation's stockholders to rubber-stamp decisions made by its managers

stored value: the backing of a currency by goods that are stored and held in reserve

subsistence economy: the type of economy in which human groups live off the land with little or no surplus

underemployment: the condition of having to work at a job beneath one's level of training and abilities, or of being able to find only part-time work

underground economy: exchanges of goods and services that are not reported to the government and thereby escape taxation

welfare (state) capitalism: an economic system in which individuals own the means of production, but the state regulates many economic activities for the welfare of the population

☞ KEY PEOPLE

Review the major theoretical contributions or findings of these people.

Daniel Bell: Bell identified six characteristics of the postindustrial society.

Emile Durkheim: Durkheim contributed the concepts of mechanical and organic solidarity to our understanding of social cohesion.

Karl Marx: Marx was an outspoken critic of capitalism who wrote about the basis for profits under capitalism.

Michael Useem: Using a conflict perspective, Useem studied the activities of the "inner circle" of corporate executives.

Thorstein Veblen: Veblen created the term "conspicuous consumption" to refer to the eagerness to show off one's wealth through the elaborate consumption of material goods.

☞ "DOWN-TO-EARTH SOCIOLOGY"

This is your opportunity to apply the sociological perspective to the world around you. The questions in this section refer to material introduced in this chapter of your text. Many ask you to think about ideas and information presented in the various special "boxes" that are located throughout this chapter.

1. After reading "Greed is Good--Selling the American Dream" (p. 397), can you think of ways in which advertising is able to increase your desire to consume products, even when you previously felt no need for them? How does advertising affect what you wear? What you eat? What you do for recreation? How does advertising affect the way you feel about yourself?

2. What forces do you think have contributed to the emergence of bartering in the former Soviet Union (p. 398)? Have there been times when you have engaged in bartering yourself? What were the circumstances that led you to barter? What conclusions can you draw about the social--or economic --factors associated with this form of exchange?

3. What are some of the problems businessmen can run into when they move into the global marketplace (see "Doing Business in the Global Village" on page 400)? As globalization continues, do you think these kinds of problems will disappear? Why or why not?

4. Why do you think it is still necessary for women to maneuver their way through the "hidden" corporate culture (p. 408)? As the numbers of working women increase, will these kinds of strategies become less necessary?

5. When you read "Who Is Unemployed" (p. 411), were you surprised to learn that individuals who are no longer actively looking for work or who find temporary, part-time work, are <u>not</u> counted as unemployed? In what ways does this create difficulties in trying to accurately assess the level of unemployment in this country?

6. Do your concerns about technology and work mirror those voiced in "New Technology and the

Restructuring of Work" (p. 413)? What kinds of social, political, and economic conditions would have to be present for either of the future alternatives to come true?

☞ **SELF-TEST**

After completing this self-test, check your answers against the Answer Key beginning on page 384 of this Study Guide and against the text on page(s) indicated in parentheses.

MULTIPLE CHOICE QUESTIONS

1. What is a market? (389)
   a.   It is any process of buying and selling.
   b.   It is the mechanism that establishes values for the exchange of goods and services.
   c.   It means the movement of vast amounts of goods across international borders.
   d.   All of the above.

2.   Which of the following characterize hunting and gathering societies? (389)
   a.   market economy.
   b.   surplus economy.
   c.   subsistence economy.
   d.   maintenance economy.

3.   Which of the following took place in pastoral and horticultural economies? (389)
   a.   a subsistence economy existed
   b.   a more dependable food supply led to the development of a surplus
   c.   the plow was used extensively
   d.   extensive trade developed

4.   Which of the following is not a feature of industrial economies? (389-390)
   a.   Machines are powered by fuels.
   b.   A surplus unlike anything the world had seen is created.
   c.   The steam engine was invented and became the basis for the economy.
   d.   A service sector developed and employed the majority of workers.

5.   What did Veblen label the lavishly wasteful spending of goods designed to enhance social prestige? (389)
   a.   prestigious consumption
   b.   wasteful consumption
   c.   conspicuous prestige
   d.   conspicuous consumption

6.   Which of the following is not a defining characteristic of postindustrial economies? (390)
   a.   a large surplus of goods
   b.   extensive trade among nations
   c.   machines powered by fuels
   d.   a "global village"

7.   In which type of society was money first used extensively? (391)
        a.   agricultural
        b.   industrial
        c.   postindustrial
        d.   pastoral and horticultural

8.   What term is used to describe the total goods and services that a nation produces? (392)
        a.   the gross national product
        b.   the net national product
        c.   the national debt
        d.   the medium of exchange

9.   The debit card came into existence in the: (393)
        a.   agricultural economy.
        b.   industrial economy.
        c.   postindustrial economy.
        d.   None of the above.

10.   Private ownership of the means of production is an essential feature of: (393)
        a.   communism.
        b.   socialism.
        c.   democracy.
        d.   capitalism.

11.   The ownership of machines and factories by individuals, who decide what to produce, is: (393)
        a.   state socialism.
        b.   personal capitalism.
        c.   private ownership of the means of production.
        d.   public ownership of the means of production.

12.   Which system has public ownership, central planning, and no profit motive? (395)
        a.   democratic socialism.
        b.   socialism.
        c.   capitalism.
        d.   communism.

13.   For Marx, what is the amount of value created by workers' labor but withheld from them? (396)
        a.   market prices
        b.   profits
        c.   labor costs
        d.   overhead

14.   Some critics believe that underemployment is a problem caused by: (396)
        a.   socialism.
        b.   capitalism.
        c.   democratic socialism.
        d.   communism.

15. Which perspective views work as the tie which binds us together? (399)
    a. functionalist
    b. conflict
    c. symbolic interactionist
    d. ethnomethodological

16. As societies industrialize, they become based on: (400)
    a. mechanical solidarity.
    b. organic solidarity.
    c. social solidarity.
    d. None of the above.

17. Jointly owning an enterprise, with liabilities and obligations independent of its owners' is: (400)
    a. an oligopoly.
    b. a monopoly.
    c. a corporation.
    d. an interlocking directorate.

18. A stockholders' revolt occurs when: (401)
    a. major stockholders dump their holdings in the open market.
    b. stockholders lead workers in a protest against company policies.
    c. stockholders refuse to rubber-stamp the recommendations made by management.
    d. people boycott the stocks of certain companies that are socially irresponsible.

19. What is oligopoly? (401)
    a. the control of an entire industry by several large companies
    b. the control of an entire industry by a single company
    c. illegal in the United States
    d. None of the above

20. The elites who sit on the boards of directors of multiple companies are referred to as: (403)
    a. vertical integrators.
    b. interlocking trustees.
    c. interlocking directorates.
    d. oligopolies.

21. What term is used to describe the fundamental changes in society that follow the movement of vast numbers of women from the home to the work force? (406)
    a. the feminization of work
    b. the "mommy movement"
    c. the quiet revolution
    d. the backlash

22. What is the underground economy? (407)
    a.   is an exchange of goods and services that is not reported to the government.
    b.   helps many Americans avoid what they consider exorbitant taxes.
    c.   includes illegal activities such as drug dealing.
    d.   All of the above.

23. Which of the following statements about wages is <u>correct</u>? (409)
    a.   The buying power of today's wages is greater than any time in the last 30 years.
    b.   In current dollars, workers today are paid less than they were 30 years ago.
    c.   The buying power of today's wages is actually less than it was 30 years ago.
    d.   Both the buying power and current value of wages are greater today than they were 30 years ago.

24. When compared to workers in western Europe, U.S. workers have _____ leisure time. (410)
    a.   more
    b.   less
    c.   the same

25. According to conflict theory, which group bears the brunt of technological change? (412)
    a.   middle management
    b.   top-level executives
    c.   low-level workers
    d.   laborers in the least industrialized nations

<u>TRUE-FALSE QUESTIONS</u>

T F   1.   Hunting and gathering societies were the first economies to have a surplus. (389)
T F   2.   In pastoral and horticultural economies, some individuals were able for the first time in human history to develop their energies to tasks other than food production. (389)
T F   3.   The characteristics of postindustrial economies were identified by Daniel Bell. (390)
T F   4.   Industrial economies are based on information processing and providing services. (390)
T F   5.   The richest fifth of Americans earn about 47 percent of all the income in the U.S. (391)
T F   6.   The gold standard was a medium of exchange in industrial economies. (392)
T F   7.   Credit cards and debit cards are the same thing. (392-393)
T F   8.   In welfare capitalism, private citizens own the means of production and pursue profits, but do so within a vast system of laws. (393)
T F   9.   The United States government controls "common good" items. (394)
T F   10. Socialists believe that profit is immoral. (396)
T F   11. According to convergence theory, the world's nations are becoming more and more capitalistic. (398)
T F   12. Durkheim's concept of organic solidarity is an adequate concept for understanding the interdependency that exists among the nations of the world today. (400)
T F   13. The sociological significance of multinational corporations is that they owe allegiance only to profits and market share, not to any nation, not even any particular culture. (401)
T F   14. Oligopolies are formed when many different-sized companies all compete within a single industry. (402)
T F   15. The inner circle is made up of the heads of the largest multinational corporations. (402)

T F   16.   The most common work today in the United States is white-collar employment. (405)

T F   17.   Researchers have found that both men and women workers are equally concerned with maintaining a balance between their work and family lives. (406)

T F   18.   The "quiet revolution" refers to the continually increasing proportions of women who have joined the ranks of paid labor. (406)

T F   19.   In recent decades, the U.S. has followed the lead of the western nations in terms of a gradually shrinking of the work week and an increase in leisure. (410)

T F   20.   According to government records, single workers are more likely than divorced workers to experience periods of unemployment. (411)

FILL-IN QUESTIONS

1.   _____ is the term for a system of distribution of goods and services. (389)

2.   The means (for example, currency, gold, and silver) by which people value goods and services in order to make an exchange is the _____. (391)

3.   A _____ allows its owners to purchase goods but to be billed later. A _____ allows its owners to charge purchases against his or her bank account. (392-393)

4.   Digital money that is stored on a computer is called _____. (393)

5.   The control of an entire industry by a single company is a(n) _____. (394)

6.   The law of supply and demand is referred to as _____. (395)

7.   _____ is the condition of having to work at a job beneath one's level of training and abilities, or of being able to find only part-time work. (396)

8.   The view that as capitalist and socialist economic systems each adopt features of the other, a hybrid (or mixed) economic system may emerge is _____. (398)

9.   Durkheim's term for the unity that comes from being involved in similar occupations or activities is _____. (399)

10.   The refusal of a corporation's stockholders to automatically approve decisions made by managers is referred to as a _____. (401)

11.   Members of the _____ may compete with one another, but they are united by a mutual interest in preserving capitalism. (402)

12.   One way in which the wealthy use corporations to wield power is by means of _____, or serving as directors of several companies simultaneously. (403)

13.   The _____ has contributed to a transformation of consumer patterns, relations at work, self-concepts, and relationships with family and friends. (406)

14.   The _____ consists of economic activities, whether legal or illegal, that people don't report to the government. (407)

15.   _____ is time not taken up by work or required activities such as eating and sleeping. (409)

MATCH THESE SOCIAL SCIENTISTS WITH THEIR CONTRIBUTIONS

___1. Daniel Bell   a. *studied the activities of the "inner circle"*
___2. Emile Durkheim   b. *identified six characteristics of postindustrial society*
___3. Karl Marx   c. *created the term "conspicuous consumption"*
___4. Michael Useem   d. *an outspoken critic of capitalism who wrote about basis for profits*
___5. Thorstein Veblen   e. *contributed the concepts of mechanical and organic solidarity*

ESSAY QUESTIONS

1.   Discuss the advantages and disadvantages of both capitalism and socialism as ideologies and as economic systems.

2.   The author suggests that the globalization of capitalism may be the most significant economic change of the last 100 years. Discuss what the consequences of the change are for our society as well as nations around the globe.

3.   The chapter discusses several different economic trends that have been occurring in the second half of this century. Discuss the impact of each of the following: the movement of women into the economy, shrinking paychecks, changing patterns of work and leisure, and the emergence of the alternative office.

CHAPTER 15
POLITICS

☞ CHAPTER SUMMARY

- The essential nature of politics is power, the ability to carry out one's will despite resistance; every group is political. Micropolitics refers to the exercise of power in everyday life, while macropolitics refers to large-scale power, such as governing a nation.

- Authority refers to the legitimate use of power, while coercion is its illegitimate use. The state is a political entity that claims a monopoly on violence over a particular territory. Max Weber identified three types of authority, traditional, rational-legal, and charismatic, as ideal type constructs. The orderly transfer of authority at the death, resignation, or incapacitation of a leader is critical for social stability.

- Three forms of government are monarchies (power is based on hereditary rule), democracies (power is given by the citizens), and dictatorships and oligarchies (power is seized by an individual or a small group).

- In the United States, with its winner-takes-all electoral system, political parties must appeal to the center, and minority parties make little headway. In contrast, many democracies in Europe have a system of proportional representation which encourages the formation of coalitional government. Voting patterns in the United States consistently demonstrate that whites, the elderly, the rich, the employed, and the highly educated are most likely to vote. The more people are socially integrated and have a stake in the political system, the more likely they are to vote. Special interest groups, with their lobbyists and PACs, play a significant role in U.S. politics.

- Functionalists and conflict theorists have very different views on who rules the United States. According to the functionalists, no one group holds power; the outcome is that the competing interest groups balance one another (pluralism). According to conflict theorists, the United States is governed by a ruling class made up of members drawn from the elite (power elite).

- War is a common means to implement political objectives; however, dehumanization of the enemy is a particularly high cost of war.

- The global expansion of communication, transportation, and trade, the widespread adoption of capitalism and the retreat of socialism, as well as the trend toward larger political unions suggest that a new international world order may be in the process of emerging. The oppositional trend is for fierce nationalism to emerge.

☞ LEARNING OBJECTIVES

As you read Chapter 15, use these learning objectives to organize your notes. After completing your reading, briefly state an answer to each of the objectives, and review the text pages in parentheses.

1. Define the term "power," and distinguish between micropolitics and macropolitics. (418)
2. Explain the difference between authority and coercion and why the state claims a monopoly on legitimate violence. (418-419)
3. Describe the sources of authority identified by Weber, indicate why these are "ideal types," and explain how the orderly transfer of authority is achieved under each type of authority. (419-423)
4. Differentiate between monarchies, democracies, and dictatorships and oligarchies. (423-426)
5. Explain how the political system is structured in the U.S. and compare our system of democracy

with democratic systems found in Europe. (426-428)
6.   Describe U.S. voting patterns, identifying social groups likely to vote in elections. (428-430)
7.   Analyze the ways in which lobbyists and special-interest groups influence the political process. (430-431)
8.   Distinguish between the functionalist and conflict perspectives on how the U.S. political process operates, including a comparison of the power elite perspective of C. Wright Mills with William Domhoff's ruling class theory. (432-433)
9.   Discuss the uses of war. Analyze the costs and dehumanizing aspects of war. (434-438)
10.   Evaluate the possibility for global political and economic unity in the future and what impact the resurgence of fierce nationalism could have on this new world order. (438-440)

☞ CHAPTER OUTLINE

I.   **Micropolitics and Macropolitics**
      A.   Power is the ability to carry out one's will despite resistance.
      B.   Symbolic interactionists use micropolitics to refer to exercise of power in everyday life. Macropolitics is the exercise of large-scale power over a large group.
II.   **Power, Authority, and Violence**
      A.   Authority is legitimate power that people accept as right, while coercion is power that people do not accept as just.
      B.   The state is claims a monopoly on legitimate force or violence in society; violence is the ultimate foundation of political order. A government that is viewed as legitimate is more stable than one that is not; revolution (armed resistance to overthrow a government) is a rejection by the people of a government's claim to rule and of its monopoly on violence.
      C.   Traditional authority (based on custom) is prevalent in preliterate groups, where custom sets relationships. When society changes, traditional authority is undermined, but does not die. For example, parental authority is a traditional authority.
      D.   Rational-legal authority (based on written rules, also called bureaucratic authority) derives from the position an individual holds, not from the person. Everyone (no matter how high the office) is subject to the rules.
      E.   Charismatic authority (based on an individual's personal following) may pose a threat. Because this type of leader works outside the established political system and may threaten the established order, the authorities are often quick to oppose this type of leader.
      F.   Weber's three types of authority--traditional, rational-legal, and charismatic--are ideal types representing composite characteristics found in real life examples. In rare instances, traditional and rational-legal leaders possess charismatic traits, but most authority is one type or another.
      G.   Orderly transfer of authority upon death, resignation, or incapacity of a leader is critical for stability. Succession is more of a problem with charismatic authority than with traditional or rational-legal authority because there are no rules for orderly succession. Routinization of charisma refers to the transfer of authority from a charismatic leader to either traditional or rational-legal authority.
III. **Types of Government**
      A.   A monarchy is a government headed by a king or queen.
            1.   As cities developed, each city-state (an independent city whose power radiated outward, bringing adjacent areas under its rule) had its own monarchy.

2.   As city-states warred with one another, the victors would extend their rule, eventually over an entire region. As the size of these regions grew, people developed an identification with the region; over time this gave rise to the state.

B.   A democracy is a government whose authority derives from the people.

     1.   Direct democracy (eligible voters meet to discuss issues and make decisions) emerged about 2,000 years ago in Athens. Members of some Native American tribes were able to elect chiefs; in some, women also voted and even held the position of chief.

     2.   Representative democracy (voters elect representatives to govern and make decisions on their behalf) emerged as the U.S. population grew in size and spread out across the country, making direct democracy impossible. It is possible that some form of direct democracy may re-emerge, given the new interactive communications technologies which make "electronic town meetings" possible.

     3.   Today, citizenship (people have basic rights by virtue of birth or residence) is taken for granted in the U.S.; this idea is quite new to the human scene. Universal citizenship (everyone having the same basic rights) came into practice very slowly and only through fierce struggle.

C.   Dictatorship is government where power is seized and held by an individual; oligarchy results when a small group of individual seizes power. Dictators and oligarchies can be totalitarian; this is when the government exercises almost total control of a people.

IV.   The U.S. Political System

A.   The Democratic and Republican parties emerged by the time of the Civil War.

     1.   The Democrats are often associated with the poor and the working class and the Republicans with people who are financially better off.

     2.   Since each appeals to a broad membership, it is difficult to distinguish conservative Democrats from liberal Republicans; however, it is easy to discern the extremes. Those elected to Congress may cross party lines, because although office holders support their party's philosophy, they do not necessarily support all of its specific proposals.

     3.   Despite their differences, however, both parties support fundamentals of U.S. society such as freedom of religion, free public education, and capitalism.

     4.   Third parties do play a role in U.S. politics, although generally they receive little public support. Ross Perot's "United We Stand" party is one exception.

B.   Not all democracies around the world are like ours.

     1.   U.S. elections are based on a winner-takes-all electoral system; most European countries use proportional representation (legislative seats divided according to the proportion of votes each political party received).

     2.   The U.S. system discourages minority parties; the proportional representation system encourages them. The United States has centrist parties, representing the center of political opinion. Noncentrist parties (representing marginal ideas) develop in European systems with proportional representation.

     3.   Three main results follow from proportional representation: (1) minority parties can gain access to the media, which keep their issues alive; (2) minority parties can gain power beyond their numbers; and (3) the government may be unstable due to the breakdown of coalitions (a coalition occurs when a country's largest party aligns itself with one or more smaller parties to get required votes to make national decisions).

C. Voting Patterns

    1.   U.S. voting patterns are consistent: the percentage of people who vote increases with age; non-Hispanic whites are more likely to vote than African Americans, while Latinos are considerably less likely to vote than either; those with higher levels of education are more likely to vote, as are people with higher levels of income; women are slightly more likely than men to vote.

    2.   The more that people feel they have a stake in the system, the more likely they are to vote. Those who have been rewarded by the system feel more socially integrated and perceive that elections directly affect their lives and the society in which they live.

    3.   People who gain less from the system in terms of education, income, and jobs are more likely to be alienated. Those who are alienated from the system don't vote because they feel their vote won't count. Voter apathy is indifference/inaction to the political process. As a result of apathy, nearly one-half of eligible American voters do not vote for president and only one-third of eligible voters vote for members of Congress.

    4.   Voting patterns reflect life experiences, especially economic circumstances. For years there has been a large racial-ethnic gap in politics; more recently a gender gap has emerged in terms of voting for presidential candidates. Women and African Americans tend to look more favorably on government programs that redistribute income, since they are likely to earn less than men and whites.

D. Special-interest groups are people who think alike on a particular issue and can be mobilized for political action.

    1.   Lobbyists (paid to influence legislation on behalf of their clients) are employed by special interest groups and have become a major force in politics.

    2.   Political action committees (PACs) solicit and spend funds to influence legislation and bypass laws intended to limit the amount any individual, corporation, or group can give a candidate. PACs have become a powerful influence, bankrolling lobbyists and legislators, and PACs with the most clout gain the ear of Congress.

E. The cost of elections contributes to the importance of lobbyists and PACs in Washington and state capitols.

    1.   An average candidate for the Senate will spend $5 million on the campaign. Once a candidate is elected, she/he owes people who helped with financing the campaign and wants to get reelected.

    2.   The major criticism against lobbyists and PACs is that their money buys votes. Rather than representing the people who elected them, legislators support the special interests of groups able to help them stay in power.

V.   **Who Rules the United States?**

A. According to the functionalists, the state was created because it fulfilled a basic social need.

    1.   People must find a balance between having no government (anarchy) and having a government that may be too repressive, turning against its own citizens.

    2.   The functionalists say that pluralism, the diffusion of power among interest groups, prevents any one from gaining control of the government. Functionalists believe it helps keep the government from turning against its citizens.

    3.   To balance the interests of competing groups, the founders of the U.S. system of government created a system of checks and balances in which separation of

powers among the three branches of government ensures that each is able to nullify the actions of the other two, thus preventing the domination by any single branch.

4. In order to get elected and re-elected, a candidate must pay attention to groups representing special interests--ethnic groups, women, farmers, factory workers, bankers, bosses, and the retired, but to name a few. The competing activities of these groups prevents domination by any one group.

5. In this system, power is widely dispersed; as each group pursues its interests it is balanced by others pursuing theirs.

B. According to the conflict perspective, lobbyists and even Congress are not at the center of decision making; rather, the power elite makes the decisions that direct the country and shake the world.

1. As stated by C. Wright Mills, the power elite (heads of leading corporations, powerful generals and admirals in the armed forces, and certain elite politicians) rule the United States. The corporate heads are the most powerful, as all three view capitalism as essential to the welfare of the country; thus, business interests come first.

2. According to William Domhoff, the ruling class (the wealthiest and most powerful individuals in the country) run the United States. Its members control the U.S.'s top corporations and foundations; presidential cabinet members and top ambassadors to the most powerful countries are chosen from this group, which promotes the view that positions come through merit and that everyone has a chance of becoming rich.

3. The ruling class does not act in complete unity; at times the interests of one segment may conflict with those of another. At the same time the members generally see eye to eye; they have a mutual interest in solving the problems of business.

C. While the functionalist and conflict views of power in U.S. society cannot be reconciled, it is possible to employ both. The middle level of C. Wright Mills's model best reflects the functionalist view of competing interests holding each other at bay. At the top is an elite that follows its special interests, as conflict theorists suggest.

VI. **War and Terrorism: A Means to Implement Political Objectives**

A. The state uses violence to protect citizens from individuals and groups, occasionally turning violence against other nations. War (armed conflict between nations or politically distinct groups) often is part of national policy.

B. War is not characteristic of all human groups, but simply one option for settling disputes.

C. At the same time, war is a fairly common occurrence; Pitirim Sorokin counted 967 wars between 500 B.C. and A.D. 1925, for an average of one war every two to three years. Since 1850, the United States has intervened militarily around the world more than 150 times, for an average of more than once a year.

D. Nicholas Timasheff identified three essential conditions of war.

1. There is a cultural tradition of war; because they have fought wars in the past, leaders see war as an option.

2. An antagonistic situation exists, with two or more states confronting incompatible objectives.

3. A "fuel" heats the antagonistic situation to the boiling point, so that people move from thinking about war to engaging in it; Timasheff identified seven fuels.

E.   Despite the fact war is costly to society, it continues to be a common technique for pursuing political objectives.
    1.   The cost in human life grows with industrialization and technological advances.
    2.   War is costly in terms of the money spent. The United States has spent $4 trillion on nine major wars.

F.   The Most Industrialized Nations lament regional conflicts that can quickly expand into larger wars; at the same time, they relentlessly pursue profits by selling powerful weapons to the Least Industrialized Nations--the United States is the chief merchant of death to the Least Industrialized Nations.
    1.   Seeds of future wars are sown through arms deals involving conventional and nuclear weapons.
    2.   The end of the Cold War has reduced the threat of war, as the United States and Russia announced that they would no longer aim their missiles at each other's cities. At the same time, there are concerns about the stability of the current Russian government.

G.   Today terrorism directed against civilian populations is a danger.
    1.   Suicide terrorism is one of the few options available to a weaker group that wants to retaliate against a powerful country.
    2.   The real danger is from nuclear, chemical, and biological weapons which could be unleashed against civilian populations.

H.   War has an effect on morality.
    1.   Exposure to brutality and killing often causes dehumanization (reducing people to objects that do not deserve to be treated as humans).
    2.   Characteristics of dehumanization include: (1) increased emotional distance from others; (2) an emphasis on following procedures; (3) inability to resist pressures; and (4) a diminished sense of personal responsibility.
    3.   Tamotsu Shibutani stressed that dehumanization is helped along by the tendency for prolonged conflicts to be transformed into a struggle between good and evil.
    4.   Dehumanization does not always insulate the self from guilt; after the war ends, returning soldiers often find themselves disturbed by what they did during the war. Although most eventually adjust, some live with the guilt forever.

VII.   A New World Order?

A.   Today the embrace of capitalism and worldwide flow of information, capital and goods has made national boundaries less meaningful. There are many examples of nations working together to solve mutual problems -- the North American Free Trade Agreement (NAFTA), the European Union (EU), and the United Nations (UN).

B.   The resurgence of fierce nationalism represents a challenge to a new world order.

C.   If global political and economic unity does come about, it is still not clear what type of government will emerge. Under a benevolent government there is tremendous potential for human welfare. But if a totalitarian government arises, the future could be bleak.

☞ KEY TERMS

After studying the chapter, review the definition for each of the following terms.

anarchy: a condition of lawlessness or political disorder caused by the abuse or collapse of governmental authority

authority: power that people accept as rightly exercised over them; also called *legitimate power*

centrist party: a political party that represents the center of political opinion

charismatic authority: authority based on an individual's outstanding traits, which attract followers

checks and balances: the separation of powers among the three branches of U.S. government--legislative, executive and judicial--so that each is able to nullify the actions of the other two, thus preventing the domination by any single branch

citizenship: the concept that birth (and residence) in a country impart basic rights

city-state: an independent city whose power radiates outward, bringing the adjacent areas under its rule

coalition government: a government in which a country's largest party aligns itself with one or more smaller parties

coercion: power that people do not accept as rightly exercised over them; also called *illegitimate power*

dehumanization: the act or process of reducing people to objects that do not deserve the treatment accorded humans

democracy: a system of government in which authority derives from the people; the term comes from two Greek words that translate literally as "power to the people"

dictatorship: a form of government in which power is seized by an individual

direct democracy: a form of democracy in which the eligible voters meet together to discuss issues and make their decisions

lobbyists: people who influence legislation on behalf of their clients

macropolitics: the exercise of large-scale power, the government being the most common example

micropolitics: the exercise of politics in everyday life, such as deciding who is going to do the housework

monarchy: a form of government headed by a king or queen

nationalism: a strong identity with a nation, accompanied by the desire for the nation to be dominant

noncentrist party: a political party that represents marginal ideas

oligarchy: a form of government in which power is held by a small group of individuals; the rule of the many by the few

pluralism: the diffusion of power among many interest groups, preventing any single group from gaining control of the government

political action committee (PAC): an organization formed by one or more special-interest groups to solicit and spend funds for the purpose of influencing legislation

power: the ability to carry out one's will, even over the resistance of others

power elite: C. Wright Mills's term for those who rule the United States; the top people in the leading corporations, the most powerful generals and admirals of the armed forces, and certain elite politicians

proportional representation: an electoral system in which seats in a legislature are divided according to the proportion of votes each political party receives

rational-legal authority: authority based on law or written rules and regulations; also called *bureaucratic authority*

representative democracy: a form of democracy in which voters elect representatives to govern and make decisions on their behalf

revolution: armed resistance designed to overthrow a government

routinization of charisma: the transfer of authority from a charismatic figure to either a traditional or a rational-legal form of authority

ruling class: another term for the power elite

special-interest group: a group of people who have a particular issue in common who can be mobilized for political action

state: a political entity that claims a monopoly on the use of violence in some particular territory;

commonly known as a country

totalitarianism: a form of government that exerts almost total control over the people

traditional authority: authority based on custom

universal citizenship: the idea that everyone has the same basic rights by virtue of being born in a country (or by immigrating and becoming a naturalized citizen)

voter apathy: indifference and inaction on the part of individuals or groups with respect to the political process

war: armed conflict between nations or politically distinct groups

☞ KEY PEOPLE

Review the major theoretical contributions or findings of these people.

Peter Berger: Berger argued that violence is the ultimate foundation of any political order.

William Domhoff: Like Mills, Domhoff saw that power resides in the hands of an elite, which he referred to as the ruling class. He focused on the top one percent of Americans who belong to the super rich.

C. Wright Mills: Mills suggested that power resides in the hands of an elite made up of the top leaders of the largest corporations, the most powerful generals of the armed forces, and certain elite politicians.

Alejandro Portes and Ruben Rumbaut: These sociologists studied the process of assimilation of immigrants into American society, observing that the first step in this process is the group's political organization to protect their ethnic interests.

Tamotsu Shibutani: Shibutani noted that the process of dehumanization is helped along by the tendency for prolonged conflicts to be transformed into a struggle between good and evil.

Pitirim Sorokin: Sorokin studied wars from 500 B.C. to A.D. 1925 and found that war was a fairly routine experience. There had been 967 wars during this time span, for an average of a war every two or three years.

Nicholas S. Timasheff: Timasheff identified three essential conditions of war--a cultural tradition of war, an antagonistic situation in which two or more countries have incompatible objectives, and a fuel which moves the antagonisms into conflict situations.

Max Weber: Weber identified three different types of authority: traditional, rational-legal, and charismatic.

☞ "DOWN-TO-EARTH SOCIOLOGY"

This is your opportunity to apply the sociological perspective to the world around you. The questions in this section refer to material introduced in this chapter of your text. Many ask you to think about ideas and information presented in the various special "boxes" that are located throughout this chapter.

1. Do you think that the new technologies are harmful or beneficial to our democracy (p. 425)? Would you communicate directly with your elected officials, if given the chance? Why or why not? Would you vote over the Internet if you could? What are the chances that these new developments could affect voter apathy and alienation?

2. After reading "The Politics of Immigrants: Power, Ethnicity and Social Class" on page 429, think about the following questions: What role does political participation play in the process of assimilation? How do groups gain enough political power to overcome discrimination?

3. What was your reaction to the piece on biological terrorism (p. 437)? Can you understand how and why this might happen? Can you think of anything our government can do to prevent this?

4. Based on "Blockades in the Path to the new World Order: The Globalization of Capitalism versus the Resurgence of Nationalism" (p. 439), do you agree that the next twenty years may be bloody if the world cannot find a better way to answer the demands of newly emboldened nations? Why or why not? How can the needs of these new nations for national identities be balanced against the demands of an increasingly global economy?

☞ SELF-TEST

After completing this self-test, check your answers against the Answer Key beginning on page 387 of this Study Guide and against the text on page(s) indicated in parentheses.

MULTIPLE CHOICE QUESTIONS

1. Which of the following relates to power? (418)
    a. The concept was defined by Max Weber.
    b. It is the ability to carry out one's will in spite of resistance from others.
    c. It is an inevitable part of everyday life.
    d. All of the above.

2. Governments, whether dictatorships or the elected forms, are examples of: (418)
    a. coercion.
    b. macropolitics.
    c. micropolitics.
    d. None of the above.

3. What is the opposite of authority? (418)
    a. war
    b. rule of law
    c. coercion
    d. violence

4. What did Peter Berger consider to be the ultimate foundation of any political order? (419)
    a. laws
    b. elections
    c. violence
    d. leaders

5. Revolutions: (419)
    a. are most likely to occur upon the death of a charismatic leader, because there are no well-established rules regarding the orderly transfer of authority.
    b. are a people's rejection of the government's claim to rule over them.
    c. occur only when economic conditions are bleak.
    d. all of the above.

6.   Traditional authority: (419-420)
      a.   is the hallmark of preliterate groups.
      b.   is based on custom.
      c.   declines with industrialization.
      d.   All of the above.

7.   John F. Kennedy: (422)
      a.   was a rational-legal leader.
      b.   was a charismatic leader.
      c.   is an example of a leader who is difficult to classify in terms of ideal types.
      d.   All of the above.

8.   Which of the following is considered the least stable type of authority? (422)
      a.   traditional
      b.   rational-legal
      c.   charismatic
      d.   monarchy

9.   The principle that everyone has the same basic rights by virtue of being born in a country is: (424)
      a.   direct democracy.
      b.   universal citizenship.
      c.   state citizenship.
      d.   an ideal that has rarely been realized.

10.   An individual who seizes power and imposes his will onto the people is known as a: (424)
      a.   charismatic leader.
      b.   dictator.
      c.   totalitarian leader.
      d.   monarch.

11.   Which form of government exerts almost total control over the people? (425)
      a.   monarchy
      b.   dictatorship
      c.   totalitarian regime
      d.   oligarchy

12.   The United States has: (427)
      a.   centrist parties.
      b.   noncentrist parties.
      c.   proportional representation.
      d.   None of the above.

13.   Which electoral system is most likely to encourage formation of minority political parties? (427)
      a.   a winner-take-all system
      b.   a systems of proportional representation
      c.   direct democracy
      d.   representative democracy

14. What do studies of voting patterns in the United States show? (428-429)
    a. Voting patterns are too inconsistent to draw meaningful conclusions.
    b. Voting varies by age, race/ethnicity, education, employment, income, and gender.
    c. Younger people are more likely to vote than older individuals.
    d. All of the above.

15. According to Portes and Rumbaut, on what basis do immigrants initially organize politically? (429)
    a. gender
    b. age
    c. social class
    d. race-ethnicity

16. Which of the following statements regarding participation in presidential elections today is <u>correct</u>? (430)
    a. Only about 1/3rd of eligible voters actually vote.
    b. About one-half of eligible voters cast a ballot.
    c. About 3/4ths of eligible voters participate in presidential elections today.
    d. Slightly less than 2/3rds of eligible voters vote.

17. Lobbyists are: (430)
    a. people paid to influence legislation on behalf of their clients.
    b. bankrolled by political action committees.
    c. a major force in American politics.
    d. All of the above.

18. Functionalists see that _____ prevent groups from having total government control. (430)
    a. the existence of a powerful elite.
    b. the presence of checks and balances.
    c. the presence of many PACs to which politicians owe allegiance.
    d. All of the above.

19. Which perspective suggests that conflict is minimized as special-interest groups negotiate with one another and reach compromises? (432)
    a. functionalists
    b. conflict theorists
    c. symbolic interactionists
    d. political sociologists

20. Members of the power elite are drawn from: (432)
    a. the largest corporations.
    b. the armed forces.
    c. top political offices.
    d. all of the above.

21.   According to conflict theorists, the ruling class is: (433)
    a.   a group that meets together and agrees on specific matters.
    b.   a group which tends to have complete unity on issues.
    c.   made up of people whose backgrounds and orientations to life are so similar that they automatically share the same goals.
    d.   a myth.

22.   War: (434)
    a.   is armed conflict between nations or politically distinct groups.
    b.   is universal.
    c.   is chosen for dealing with disagreements by all societies at one time or another.
    d.   All of the above.

23.   Which of the following is not one of the essential conditions of war identified by Nicholas Timasheff? (434)
    a.   the existence of a strong, well-armed military force
    b.   a cultural tradition of war
    c.   an antagonistic situation in which two or more states confront incompatible objectives
    d.   the presence of a "fuel" that heats the antagonistic situation to a boiling point

24.   The process of reducing people to objects who do not deserve humane treatment is: (436)
    a.   institutionalization.
    b.   dehumanization.
    c.   regimentation.
    d.   totalitarianism.

25.   Today, national boundaries are becoming less meaningful because of: (438)
    a.   the embrace of capitalism by more and more nations.
    b.   the worldwide flow of information, capital, and goods.
    c.   the formation of large economic and political units like the European Union.
    d.   all of the above.

TRUE-FALSE QUESTIONS

T F   1.   In every group, large or small, some individuals have power over others. (418)

T F   2.   Coercion refers to legitimate power. (418)

T F   3.   The state claims a monopoly on violence within some designated territory. (419)

T F   4.   Even with industrialization some forms of traditional authority go unchallenged. (420)

T F   5.   Rational-legal authority derives from the position that an individual holds, not from the person who holds the position. (420)

T F   6.   Because the authority of charismatic leaders is based on their personal ability to attract followers, they pose no threat to the established political system. (421)

T F   7.   It is difficult to classify some leaders as having one specific type of authority. (422)

T F   8.   Routinization of charisma involves the transfer of authority from a charismatic leader to either traditional or rational-legal authority. (423)

T F   9.   Even in early societies that were small in size, there was a need for some form of political system. (423)

T F 10. Direct democracy was impossible in the United States as its population grew in number and spread out. (424)

T F 11. The concept of representative democracy based on citizenship may be the greatest gift the United States has given to the world. (424)

T F 12. The idea of universal citizenship caught on quickly in the United States. (424)

T F 13. The European system of democracy is not that different from our own. (427)

T F 14. Employment and income do not affect the probability that people will vote. (429-430)

T F 15. Most political action committees represent broad social interests such as environmental protection. (431)

T F 16. Functionalists believe that pluralism prevents any one group from gaining control of the government and using it to oppress the people. (432)

T F 17. According to C. Wright Mills, the three groups that make up the power elite share power equally. (433)

T F 18. War is universal. (434)

T F 19. Because of the massive costs in terms of lives lost and property destroyed, warfare is less common today than in previous centuries. (435)

T F 20. Terrorism is one of the few options open to a weaker political group looking for ways to retaliate against a powerful country. (436)

FILL-IN QUESTIONS

1. The exercise of power in everyday life, such as deciding who is going to do the housework, is referred to as _____. (418)

2. _____ is synonymous with government; the source of legitimate violence in society. (419)

3. A _____ is armed resistance designed to overthrow a government. (419)

4. _____ is authority based on custom. (419)

5. Bureaucratic authority is also called _____. (420)

6. An independent city whose power radiates outward, bringing the adjacent area under its rule is a _____. (423)

7. _____ is a form of democracy in which the eligible voters meet together to discuss issues and make their decisions. (424)

8. The concept that birth and residence in a country impart basic rights is known as _____. (424)

9. A form of government that exerts almost total control over the people is _____. (425)

10. An electoral system in which seats in a legislature are divided according to the proportion of votes each political party receives is called _____. (427)

11. _____ refers to indifference and inaction on the part of individuals or groups with respect to the political process. (430)

12. A state of lawlessness or political disorder caused by the absence or collapse of governmental authority is _____. (432)

13. _____ is C. Wright Mills's term for the top people in leading corporations, the most powerful generals and admirals of the armed forces, and certain elite politicians. (432)

14. The act or process of reducing people to objects that do not deserve the treatment accorded humans is _____. (436)

15. Today _____, a strong identity with a nation, accompanied by the desire for that nation to be dominant, challenges efforts to forge a new world order. (438)

MATCH THESE CONCEPTS WITH THEIR DEFINITIONS

____ 1. Peter Berger

____ 2. William Domhoff

____ 3. C. Wright Mills

____ 4. Max Weber

____ 5. Nicholas Timasheff

____ 6. Tamotsu Shibutani

____ 7. Pitirim Sorokin

____ 8. Portes & Rumbaut

a. *war as a fairly routine experience*

b. *political assimilation of immigrants*

c. *violence is the foundation of the political order*

d. *three types of authority*

e. *ruling class*

f. *the process of dehumanization*

g. *essential conditions of war*

h. *power elite*

ESSAY QUESTIONS

1.   Distinguish between macropolitics and micropolitics, explaining what each is and which perspectives are associated with each, and provide your own examples to illustrate each.

2.   Compare and contrast the systems of democracy found in the United States and Europe and discuss how some of the problems associated with our system--voter apathy, the power of political action committees, and the concentration of power--are related to our system.

3.   Discuss what you see as the future of the New World Order.

CHAPTER 16
THE FAMILY

☞ CHAPTER SUMMARY

- Because there are so many cultural variations, family structure is hard to define. Nevertheless, family is defined broadly as two or more people who consider themselves related by blood, marriage or adoption. Marriage and family patterns vary remarkably across cultures, but four universal themes in marriage are mate selection, descent, inheritance, and authority.

- According to the functionalist perspective, the family is universal because it serves six essential functions: economic production, socialization of children, care of the sick and aged, recreation, sexual control, and reproduction. Conversely, conflict theorists focus on how marriage and the family help perpetuate inequalities. Symbolic interactionists focus on the contrasting experiences and perspectives of men and women that are played out in marriage.

- The family life cycle is analyzed in terms of love and courtship, marriage, childbirth, child rearing, and the family in later life. Within the United States, marriage follows predictable patterns of age, social class, race and religion, while childbirth and childbearing vary by social class.

- Family diversity in U.S. culture is based primarily on social class rather than racial and ethnic differences. One-parent families, childless families, blended families, and gay families represent some of the different types of families today.

- Trends in American families include postponement of first marriage, cohabitation, and the emergence of the "sandwich generation" who are caught between caring for their own children and caring for their elderly parents.

- Various studies have focused on problems in measuring divorce, children of divorce, ex-spouses, and remarriage. While time seems to heal most children's wounds over the divorce of their parents, research suggests that a minority carry the scars of divorce into adulthood. Men and women experience divorce differently: for men, this event often results in a weakening of their relationships with children; for women, it means a decline in their standard of living.

- Violence and abuse--including child abuse, battering, marital rape, and incest--are the "dark side" of family life. Researchers have identified variables that help marriages last and be happy.

- The trends for the future include a continued increase in cohabitation, births to unmarried mothers, and postponement of marriage. The continuing growth in the numbers of working wives will impact on marital balance of power.

☞ LEARNING OBJECTIVES
As you read Chapter 16, use these learning objectives to organize your notes. After completing your reading, briefly state an answer to each of the objectives, and review the text pages in parentheses.

1. Explain why it is difficult to define the term "family," including the different ways in which family systems can be classified. (444-445)
2. Identify the common cultural themes that run through marriage and the family. (445-446)
3. Contrast the functionalists, conflict, and symbolic interaction perspectives regarding marriage and family. (446-451)

4.   Outline the major developments in each stage of the family life cycle and discuss the social factors that produce variations within each of these stages. (452-456)

5.   State the unique conditions experienced by African-American, Latino, Asian-American, and Native-American families. (456-459)

6.   Identify the major concerns of one-parent families, families without children, blended families, and gay and lesbian families. (459-462)

7.   Describe the current trends affecting marriage and family life in the United States. (462-464)

8.   State why it is difficult to measure divorce accurately. (465-466)

9.   Note some of the adjustment problems of children of divorce and of ex-spouses. (466-469)

10.   Explain the patterns of abuse within the family setting. (469-471)

11.   List some of the characteristics which tend to be present in marriages that work. Explain why happy and unhappy couples approach problems differently. (472)

12.   Summarize conclusions regarding the future of marriage and family in the United States. (472-473)

☞ CHAPTER OUTLINE

I.   **Marriage and Family in Global Perspective**

    A.   The term "family" is difficult to define because there are many types. A broad definition is two or more people who consider themselves related by blood, marriage, or adoption, and live together (or have lived together). A household, in contrast to a family, is all the people occupying the same housing unit.

        1.   In some societies men have more than one wife (polygyny) or women have more than one husband (polyandry).

        2.   A family is classified as a nuclear family (husband, wife, and children) or an extended family (a nuclear family plus other relatives who live together).

        3.   The family of orientation is the family in which a person grows up, while the family of procreation is the family formed when a couple's first child is born. A person who is married but has not had a child is part of a couple, not a family.

        4.   Marriage is a group's approved mating arrangements, usually marked by a ritual.

    B.   Common Cultural Themes

        1.   Each group establishes norms to govern whom you can and cannot marry. Endogamy is the practice of marrying within one's own group, while exogamy is the practice of marrying outside of one's own group. Some norms of mate selection are written into law, others are informal.

        2.   Three major patterns of descent (tracing kinship over generations) are: (a) bilateral (descent traced on both the mother's and the father's side); (b) patrilineal (descent traced only on the father's side); and matrilineal (descent traced only on the mother's side).

        3.   Mate selection and descent are regulated in all societies in order to provide an orderly way of passing property, etc., to the next generation. In a bilateral system, property passes to males and females; in a patrilineal system, property passes only to males; in a matrilineal system, property passes only to females.

        4.   Patriarchy is a social system in which men dominate women, and runs through all societies. No historical records exist of a true matriarchy. In an egalitarian social system authority is more or less equally divided between men and women.

II.   **Marriage and Family in Theoretical Perspective**

A.   The functionalist perspective stresses how the family is related to other parts of society and how it contributes to the well-being of society.

1.   The family is universal because it serves functions essential to the well-being of society: economic production, socialization of children, care of the sick and aged, recreation, sexual control, and reproduction.

2.   The incest taboo (rules specifying which people are too closely related to have sex or marry) helps the family avoid role confusion and forces people to look outside the family for marriage partners, creating a network of support.

3.   Unlike the extended family, the nuclear family has fewer people it can depend on for material and emotional support; thus, the members of a nuclear family are vulnerable to "emotional overload." The relative isolation of the nuclear family makes it easier for the "dark side" of families (incest and other types of abuse) to emerge.

B.   Central to the conflict perspective is the struggle over scarce resources; in the family this struggle centers around housework, which is actually a struggle over the scarce resources of time, energy, and leisure.

1.   Most men resist doing housework; consequently, working wives end up doing almost all of it. Wives are 8 times more likely than husbands to feel that the division of housework is unfair.

2.   Arlie Hochschild found that after an 8-hour day at work, women typically work a "second shift" at home; this means that wives work an extra month of 24-hour days each year. The result is that working wives feel deep discontent.

C.   Using the symbolic interactionist perspective, we can explore the different meaning that housework has for men and women and how each sex experiences marriage differently.

1.   When men's and women's earning are about the same, men are more likely to share in the housework; when women earn more than their husbands, the men are least likely to do housework. A wife's higher earnings tends to threaten a man's gender identity; doing "woman's work" is a further threat.

2.   Men and women perceive their marriages differently. A gulf exists because each holds down different corners of the marriage. Jessie Bernard argued that every marriage actually contains two separate marriages--his and hers.

III.   **The Family Life Cycle**

A.   Romantic love provides the ideological context in which Americans seek mates and form families. Romantic love has two components: (1) emotional, a feeling of sexual attraction; and (2) cognitive, the feeling we describe as being "in love."

B.   The social channels of love and marriage in the United States include age, education, social class, race, and religion.

1.   Homogamy is the tendency of people with similar characteristics to marry one another usually resulting from propinquity (spatial nearness).

2.   Interracial marriage, which has increased sharply, is an exception to these social patterns.

C.   Facts contradict the popular image that having a baby makes a couple deliriously happy.

1.   Marital satisfaction usually decreases with the birth of a child. Having a child usually means less time, less sleep, and heavier expenses.

2.   Lillian Rubin found that social class influences how couples adjust to children. Working-class couples are more likely to have a baby nine months after marriage and have major interpersonal and financial problems; middle-class parents are

more prepared because of more resources, postponement of the birth of the first child, and more time to adjust to one another.

D. As more mothers today are employed outside the home, child care has become an issue.

1. In comparing married couples and single mothers, child care arrangements appear to be quite similar. The main difference is the role played by the child's father while the mother is at work. For married couples, almost one of four children is cared for by the father, while for single mothers this arrangement occurs for about only one of fourteen children. Grandparents often help fill the child care gap left by absent fathers in single mother homes.

2. About one in six children is cared for in day care centers. Only a minority of U.S. day care centers offer high-quality care as measured by safety, emotional warmth and support, and stimulating learning activities.

3. Nannies have become popular among upper-middle class parents. A recurring problem is tensions between parents and nanny.

4. According to Melvin Kohn, parents socialize children into the norms of their respective work worlds. Working-class parents want their children to conform to societal expectations. Middle-class parents are more concerned that their children develop curiosity, self-expression, and self-control.

5. Birth order is significant in child rearing: first-borns tend to be disciplined more than children who follow, but also receive more attention; when the next child arrives, the first born competes to maintain attention.

E. Later stages of family life bring both pleasures and problems.

1. The empty nest is a married couple's domestic situation after the last child has left home. The empty-nest is thought to signal a difficult adjustment for women; however Lillian Rubin argues that this syndrome is largely a myth because women's satisfaction generally increases when the last child leaves home. Many couples report a renewed sense of companionship at this time.

2. With prolonged education and a growing cost of establishing households, U.S. children are leaving home much later, or are returning after having left.

3. Women are more likely than men to face the problem of adjusting to widowhood, for not only does the average woman live longer than a man but she has also married a man older than herself.

IV. **Diversity in U.S. Families**

A. As with other groups, the family life of African Americans differs by social class.

1. The upper class is concerned with maintaining family lineage and preserving their privilege and wealth; the middle-class focuses on achievement and respectability; poor African-American families face the problems that poverty brings.

2. Marriage squeeze (fewer unmarried males than unmarried females) exists among African Americans; thus women are more likely to marry men with less education, or who are unemployed or divorced, or to remain single.

B. The effects of social class on families also apply to Latinos. In addition, families differ by country of origin.

1. The Spanish language, Roman Catholic religion, and strong family ties, with a disapproval of divorce, distinguish Latino families.

2. Machismo, the emphasis on male strength and dominance, also seems to be a characteristic of Latino families. As a result, the husband-father plays a stronger role than in white or African-American families, and the wife-mother deals with

family and child-related decisions.

C. The structure of Asian-American families is almost identical to that of white families.

    1. Because Asian Americans come from 20 different countries, their family life varies considerably, reflecting these different cultures. The more recent the immigration, the closer the family life is to that of the country of origin.

    2. Bob Suzuki points out that while Chinese- and Japanese-American families have adopted the nuclear family pattern of the United States, they have retained Confucian values that provide a distinct framework to family life: humanism, collectivity, self-discipline, hierarchy, respect for the elderly, moderation, and obligation.

    3. Asian Americans tend to be more permissive than Anglos in child rearing and more likely to use shame and guilt than physical punishment to control their children's behavior.

D. For Native-American families, the issue is whether to follow traditional values or to assimilate. The structure of Native-American families is almost identical to that of Latinos; like others, these families differ by social class.

E. There has been an increase in one-parent families.

    1. This is due to the high divorce rate and the sharp increase in unwed motherhood.

    2. Most of these families are poor; the reason for the poverty is that most are headed by women who earn less than men.

    3. Children from one-parent families are more likely to drop out of school, become delinquent, be poor as adults, divorce, and have children outside of marriage.

F. Overall, about 14 percent of U.S. married couples never have children. Although somewhat influenced by race and ethnicity, in general, the more education a woman has, the more likely she is to expect to bear no children.

    1. According to Kathleen Gerson, there are a number of reasons why couples choose to be childfree--unstable marriages, lost career opportunities, and the expenses involved are among the reasons.

    2. For many families, choice is not the reason they have no children; they are infertile. Some adopt, while a few turn to new reproductive technologies.

G. A blended family is one whose members were once part of other families (two divorced persons marry, bringing children into a new family unit). Blended families are increasing in number and often experience complicated family relationships.

H. Although marriage between homosexuals is illegal in the United States, many homosexual couples live in monogamous relationships that they refer to as marriage.

    1. In 2000, Vermont became the first state to legally recognize "gay unions."

    2. Gay and lesbian couples also have the usual problems of heterosexual marriages: housework, money, careers, problems with relatives, and sexual adjustment.

V. **Trends in U.S. Families**

A. The average age of American brides is the oldest it has been since records first were kept. While many young people postpone marriage, they have not postponed the age at which they set up housekeeping with someone of the opposite sex.

B. Cohabitation is living together as an unmarried couple, and has increased about eight times in the last 25 years.

    1. Commitment is the essential difference between cohabitation and marriage: marriage assumes permanence; cohabiting assumes remaining together "as long as it works out."

2. Researchers have found that couples who cohabit before marriage are more likely to divorce than couples who do not.

C. As previously discussed there has been an increase in births to unmarried mothers.

   1. In the ten industrialized nations for which data are available, all except Japan have experienced sharp increases in births to unmarried mothers--the U.S. rate falls in the middle third of these nations.

   2. Industrialization alone is too simple an explanation for this increase. To more fully understand this trend, future research must focus on customs and values embedded within particular cultures.

D. The "sandwich generation" refers to people who find themselves sandwiched between two generations, responsible for the care of their children and for their own aging parents. Corporations have begun to offer some kind of elder care assistance to their employees, including seminars, referral services, and flexible work schedules.

VI. **Divorce and Remarriage**

A. There are problems when it comes to measuring the extent of divorce in U.S. society.

   1. Although the divorce rate is reported at 50 percent, this statistic is misleading because with rare exceptions those who divorce do not come from the group who married that year.

   2. An alternative is to compare the number of divorces in a given year to the entire group of married couples; 2.1 percent of all married couples get divorced.

   3. A third way is to calculate the percentage of all adult Americans who are divorced. The percentage for the U.S. is the highest among the most industrialized nations of the world.

   4. After rising for a century, the U.S. divorce rate leveled off and has even declined; the rate today is lower than it was in 1980.

B. Each year over one million children are in families affected by divorce. Divorce profoundly threatens a child's world.

   1. Compared with children whose parents are not divorced, children from divorced families are more likely to be hostile and anxious, have nightmares, and not do as well in school.

   2. Children whose parents divorced have been compared with children who come from homes where the parents have high levels of conflict but who remain married. Researchers found both groups of children to be anxious and depressed, but children whose parents were divorced do slightly better emotionally than children who must live with parents' constant conflict.

   3. Several factors help children adjust to divorce: both parents show understanding and affection; the child lives with the parent making a good adjustment; family routines are consistent; the family has adequate money for its needs; and, according to preliminary studies, the child lives with the parent of the same sex. Children adjust better when a second adult can be counted on for support.

   4. Grown-up children of divorce are less likely to have contact with either parent and are more likely to divorce themselves. Those whose mothers established a single, stable relationship after the divorce are more likely to be secure in their own intimate relationships.

C. A new fathering pattern, known as serial fatherhood, is beginning to emerge. Divorced fathers tend to live with, support, and play an active fathering role with children of the woman to whom they are currently married or with whom they are currently living. Over time, contact with their children from a previous marriage diminishes.

D. Women are more likely than men to feel divorce gives them a new chance at life. Divorce does not always mean the end of a relationship; some continued contact with ex-spouses occurs due to the children. Divorce likely spells economic hardship for women, especially mothers of small children; the former husband's standard of living is likely to increase.

E. Most divorced people eventually remarry, although the length of time between divorce and remarriage is longer today than in the past.

    1. Most divorced people remarry other divorced people. Men are more likely to remarry than women; women most likely to remarry are those with small children and those who have not graduated from high school.

    2. The divorce rate of remarried people without children is about the same as that of first marriages; remarriages in which children are present are more likely to end in divorce.

VII. Two Sides of Family Life

A. Spousal battering, child abuse, marital rape, and incest represent the dark side of family life.

    1. Although wives are about as likely to attack their husbands as husbands are to attack their wives, it is generally the husband who lands the last and most damaging blow. Violence against women is related to the sexist structure of society and our socialization.

    2. Each year about 3 million U.S. children are reported to the authorities as victims of abuse or neglect; about 1 million of these cases are substantiated.

    3. Marital rape is more common than previously thought. Non-battering rape is where a husband forces his wife to have sex, with no intent to hurt her physically. Battering rape adds the element of the husband intentionally inflicting physical pain to retaliate for some supposed wrongdoing on the wife's part. Husbands who commit perverted rape seem to be sexually aroused by the violent elements of rape and force their wives to submit to unusual sexual acts.

    4. Incest is sexual relations between relatives, such as brothers and sisters or parents and children. It is most likely to occur in families that are socially isolated, and is more common than it previously was thought to be. Uncles are the most common offenders; brother-sister incest is more common than father-child incest.

B. There are a number of factors that make marriages work. Variables that produce happy marriages include: spending time together, appreciating one another, having a commitment to the marriage, using good communications, being willing to confront and work through problems together, and being willing to put more into the marriage than you take out.

VIII. The Future of Marriage and the Family

A. In spite of problems, marriage will continue because it is functional. The vast proportion of Americans will continue to marry; many of those who divorce will remarry and "try again."

B. It is likely that cohabitation will increase, as will the age at first marriage, and the number of women joining the work force, with a resulting shift in marital power toward a more egalitarian norm. Finally, more families will struggle with the twin demands of raising children and caring for aging parents.

C. We will continue to deal with the conflict between the bleak picture of marriage and family painted by the media and the rosy one painted by cultural myths. Sociologists can help correct the distortions through research.

☞ KEY TERMS

After studying the chapter, review the definition for each of the following terms.

bilateral (system of descent): a system of reckoning descent that counts both the mother's and the father's side

blended family: a family whose members were once part of other families

cohabitation: an unmarried couple living together in a sexual relationship

egalitarian: authority more or less equally divided between people or groups, in this instance between husband and wife

empty nest: a married couple's domestic situation after the last child has left home

endogamy: the practice of marrying within one's own group

exogamy: the practice of marrying outside one's group

extended family: a nuclear family plus other relatives, such as grandparents, uncles and aunts, who live together

family: two or more people who consider themselves related by blood, marriage, or adoption

family of orientation: the family in which a person grows up

family of procreation: the family formed when a couple's first child is born

homogamy: the tendency of people with similar characteristics to marry one another

household: people who occupy the same housing unit

incest: sexual relations between specified relatives, such as brothers and sisters or parents and children

machismo: an emphasis on male strength and dominance

marriage: a group's approved mating arrangements, usually marked by a ritual of some sort

marriage squeeze: the difficulty   a group of men or women have in finding marriage partners, due to an imbalanced sex ratio

matriarchy: authority vested in females; female control of a society or group

matrilineal (system of descent): a system of reckoning descent that counts only the mother's side

nuclear family: a family consisting of a husband, wife, and child(ren)

patriarchy: authority vested in males; male control of a society or group

patrilineal (system of descent): a system of reckoning descent that counts only the father's side

polyandry: a marriage in which a woman has more than one husband

polygyny: a marriage in which a man has more than one wife

romantic love: feelings of erotic attraction accompanied by an idealization of the other

serial fatherhood: a pattern of parenting in which a father, after divorce, reduces contact with his own children, serves as a father to the children of the woman he marries or lives with, then ignores them after moving in with or marrying another woman; this pattern repeats

system of descent: how kinship is traced over the generations

☞ KEY PEOPLE

Review the major theoretical contributions or findings of these people.

Jessie Bernard: Bernard studied marriages and concluded that husbands and wives have different conceptions of marriage, resulting in two marriages within every union.

Philip Blumstein and Pepper Schwartz: These sociologists interviewed same sex couples and found that they face the same problems as heterosexual couples.

Urie Bronfenbrenner: This sociologist studied the impact of divorce on children and found that children adjust better if there is a second adult who can be counted on for support.

Larry Bumpass: Bumpass examined first marriages and cohabitation and discovered that, while the average age of first marriage has increased, the age at which they set up housekeeping with someone of the opposite sex has not because more young people are cohabiting before marriage.

Andrew Cherlin: Cherlin notes that our society has not yet developed adequate norms for remarriage.

Donald Dutton and Arthur Aron: These researchers compared the sexual arousal levels of men who are in dangerous situations with men in safe situations and found that the former were more sexually aroused than the latter.

David Finkelhor and Kersti Yllo: These sociologists interviewed 50 victims of marital rape and found that rape most commonly occurs during separation or during the breakup of a marriage.

Kathleen Gerson: Gerson found that there are different reasons why some couples choose not to have children--weak marriages, expenses associated with raising children, diminished career opportunities.

Alex Heckert, Thomas Nowak and Kay Snyder: These researchers did secondary analysis of data gathered on a nationally representative sample and found that divorce increases when women earn more than their husbands, the wife's health is poorer than her husband's, or the wife does less housework.

Arlie Hochschild: Hochschild conducted research on families in which both parents are employed full-time in order to find out how household tasks are divided up. She found that women do more of the housework than their husbands, resulting in women putting in a *second shift* at home after their workday has ended.

William Jankowiak and Edward Fischer: These anthropologists surveyed data on 166 societies and found that the majority of them contained the ideal of romantic love.

Susan Jekielek: This sociologist compared children whose parents had divorced with children whose parents were still married but locked in conflicted relationships. She found that the children of divorce were better off emotionally.

Melvin Kohn: Kohn studied social class differences in child-rearing.

Jeanette & Robert Lauer: These sociologists interviewed 351 couples who had been married fifteen years or longer in order to find out what makes a marriage successful.

Lillian Rubin: Rubin compared working class and middle class couples and found the key to how well the couple adjusts to the arrival of children is social class. Rubin also interviewed both career women and homemakers found that the notion of the "empty-nest" as being a difficult time for women is largely a myth and that most women's satisfaction increased when the last child left home.

Diana Russell: Russell found that incest victims who experience the most difficulty are those who have been victimized the most often, over longer periods of time, and whose incest was "more intrusive."

Nicholas Stinnett: Stinnett studied 660 families from all regions of the U.S. and parts of South America in order to find out what the characteristics of happy families are.

Murray Straus: This sociologist has studied domestic violence and found that, while husbands and wives are equally likely to attack one another, men inflict more damage on women than the reverse.

Bob Suzuki: This sociologist studied Chinese-American and Japanese-American families and identified several distinctive characteristics of this type of family.

Martin Whyte: This sociologist interviewed wives in the Detroit area and found that marital satisfaction usually decreases with the birth of a child.

☞ "DOWN-TO-EARTH SOCIOLOGY"

This is your opportunity to apply the sociological perspective to the world around you. The questions in this section refer to material introduced in this chapter of your text. Many ask you to think about ideas and information presented in the various special "boxes" that are located throughout this chapter.

1.   What was your reaction to the description of family life in Sweden (p. 447)? Do you think that such benefits should be available to new families in the United States? What consequences would this have for family life? What are some of the obstacles to implementing such a program in this country?

2.   Do you think the second shift (pp. 449-450), is a temporary problem or a long-range problem in many families? How will you resolve problems such as this in your family?

3.   Would you like to have your marriage arranged for you by your parents? Read "East is East and West is West" (p. 452). What would you gain by this? What would you lose?

4.   After reading about high-tech reproductive technologies on page 461, what are your own views on the subject? Consider both the pluses (infertile couples are able to become parents) and the minuses (the ethical considerations, the costs of the procedures) and then develop a convincing argument in favor or opposition. What new problems are created by these technologies?

5.   Did you reach the correct conclusions for the research findings reported on page 467-468? If not, were you surprised by what you read? Why?

☞ SELF-TEST

After completing this self-test, check your answers against the Answer Key beginning on page 391 of this Study Guide and against the text on page(s) indicated in parentheses.

MULTIPLE CHOICE QUESTIONS

1.   Polyandry is: (444)
    a.   a marriage in which a woman has more than one husband.
    b.   a marriage in which a man has more than one wife.
    c.   male control of a society or group.
    d.   female control of a society or group.

2.   The family of orientation: (445)
    a.   is the family formed when a couple's first child is born.
    b.   is the same thing as an extended family.
    c.   is the same as the family of procreation.
    d.   None of the above.

3.   Endogamy: (446)
    a.   is the practice of marrying outside one's group.
    b.   is the practice of marrying within one's own group.
    c.   is the practice of marrying someone within one's own family.
    d.   None of the above.

4.   In a matrilineal system: (446)
      a.   descent is figured only on the mother's side.
      b.   children are not considered related to their mother's relatives.
      c.   descent is traced on both the mother's and the father's side.
      d.   descent is figured only on the father's side.

5.   According to functionalists, the family: (447)
      a.   serves very different functions from society to society.
      b.   serves certain essential functions in all societies.
      c.   has very few functions left.
      d.   is no longer universal.

6.   The incest taboo: (447)
      a.   is rules specifying the degrees of kinship that prohibit sex or marriage.
      b.   helps families avoid role confusion.
      c.   facilitates the socialization of children.
      d.   All of the above.

7.   According to Arlie Hochschild, most men engage in strategies of resistance when it comes to doing
      housework. Which of the following is not one of the strategies she identified? (449)
      a.   *playing dumb*--By withdrawing their mental attention from the task, men get credit for
            trying and being a good sport, but in such a way that they are not chosen the next time.
      b.   *substitute labor*--By hiring someone else to do the work (a maid service, a lawn care
            company), they guarantee that the work gets done but that they're not the ones doing it.
      c.   *waiting it out*--Some men never volunteer, thereby forcing their wives to ask them to do
            household chores. Wives sometimes don't ask, because they say it feels like "begging."
      d.   *needs reduction*--The husband scales down his own housework "needs," forcing the wife to
            step in and do things herself because of her "greater need" to see them done right.

8.   According to research findings, which of the following feels most threatened by doing housework,
      and consequently does the least? (450)
      a.   men who earn significantly more money than their wives
      b.   men who earn about the same amount of money as their wives
      c.   men who earn less money than their wives
      d.   men who are employed in occupations that are highly sex-typed as masculine

9.   Why do husbands and wives disagree on an answer to such a basic question as how frequently they
      have sex? (451)
      a.   Men are embarrassed to say the real answer for fear of being viewed as inadequate.
      b.   They have different perspectives on love-making.
      c.   Women don't want to say how much sex they have because they think it is socially
            inappropriate.
      d.   They won't tell the truth because they don't trust the interviewer and don't know what the
            purpose of the research really is.

10.   The tendency of people with similar characteristics to marry one another is: (453)
        a.   propinquity.
        b.   erotic selection.
        c.   homogamy.
        d.   heterogamy.

11.   According to Lillian Rubin, what is the key to how couples adjust to the arrival of children? (453)
        a.   religion
        b.   social class
        c.   cultural background
        d.   degree of marital satisfaction

12.   In comparing child rearing styles of middle and working-class parents, Kohn concluded that: (455)
        a.   parents of all social classes socialize their children similarly.
        b.   middle-class parents are more likely to use physical punishment.
        c.   working-class parents are more likely to withdraw privileges or affection.
        d.   None of the above.

13.   The empty nest syndrome: (455-456)
        a.   is not a reality for most parents.
        b.   causes couples to feel a lack of companionship.
        c.   is easier for women who have not worked outside the home.
        d.   None of the above.

14.   According to your text, a major concern of upper class African-American families is: (457)
        a.   achievement and respectability.
        b.   problems of poverty.
        c.   maintaining family lineage.
        d.   All of the above.

15.   Machismo: (458)
        a.   distinguishes Latino families from other groups.
        b.   is an emphasis on male strength and dominance.
        c.   is seen in some Chicano families where the man has a strong role in his family.
        d.   All of the above.

16.   Since 1970, the number of one-parent families in the U.S. has: (459)
        a.   doubled.
        b.   tripled.
        c.   quadrupled.
        d.   grown only slightly.

17.   Children from single-parent families are more likely to: (460)
        a.   drop out of school.
        b.   become delinquent.
        c.   be poor as adults.
        d.   All of the above.

18. Sociologist Kathleen Gerson found that are were different reasons why couples choose not to have children. Which of the following is <u>not</u> one of the reasons identified by Gerson? (460)
    a.   unstable relationships
    b.   lost career opportunities
    c.   selfish and immature attitudes
    d.   financial considerations

19. A family whose members were once part of other families is known as a: (460)
    a.   reconstituted family.
    b.   mixed family.
    c.   blended family.
    d.   multiple nuclei family.

20. Cohabitation: (464)
    a.   is the condition of living together as an unmarried couple.
    b.   has increased eight times in the past 25 years.
    c.   has occurred before about half of all couples marry.
    d.   All of the above.

21. The "sandwich generation" refers to: (464)
    a.   stay-at-home moms who spend their days making sandwiches for their preschoolers.
    b.   people who are sandwiched between two sets of family relations because of the increase in divorce today.
    c.   young children who consume a lot of sandwiches and whose needs are often overlooked by parents whose time is stretched by work and household responsibilities.
    d.   people who find themselves caught between two generations, simultaneously responsible for the care of their children and their aging parents.

22. According to research, what percentage of children who live apart from their fathers following a divorce continue to see their dads as often as every week? (468)
    a.   one-half
    b.   one-third
    c.   one-quarter
    d.   one-sixth

23. Which statement about divorce and remarriage is <u>incorrect</u>? (469)
    a.   The divorce rate of remarried people without children is the same as that of first marriages.
    b.   Divorced people tend to marry other divorced people.
    c.   The divorce rate of remarried couples with children is higher than that of first marriages.
    d.   The presence or absence of children makes no difference in a remarried couple's chances of divorce.

24. According to research by Diana Russell, who is most likely to be the offender in incest? (471)
    a.   brothers
    b.   fathers/stepfathers
    c.   first cousins
    d.   uncles

25.   According to the author, what trend(s) are likely to continue into the next century? (473)
    a.   increase in cohabitation
    b.   increase in age at first marriage
    c.   more equality in the husband-wife relationship
    d.   All of the above

TRUE-FALSE QUESTIONS

T F   1.   Polygyny is a marriage in which a man has more than one wife. (444)
T F   2.   Families are people who live together in the same housing unit. (445)
T F   3.   Today, family authority patterns in the U.S. are becoming more egalitarian. (446)
T F   4.   Laws of endogamy in the United States prohibit interracial marriages. (446)
T F   5.   Functionalists believe that the incest taboo helps the family to avoid role confusion. (447)
T F   6.   Conflict theorists believe that one of the consequences of married women working for pay is a reshuffling of power in the home. (448)
T F   7.   Arlie Hochschild concluded that women are generally happy to work a second shift. (448)
T F   8.   According to Hochschild, it is important for a husband to express appreciation to his wife when she handles both work for wages and the second shift at home. (449)
T F   9.   Symbolic interactionists have found that husbands and wives generally share the same meanings about their marriages. (450-451)
T F   10.   Love and marriage channels include age, education, social class, race, and religion. (452)
T F   11.   Social class does not affect the ways couples adjust to the arrival of children. (453)
T F   12.   Firstborns tend to be disciplined more than children who follow. (455)
T F   13.   Researchers have found that most husbands and wives experience the empty nest when their last child leaves home. (455-456)
T F   14.   Women are about as likely as men to face the problem of adjusting to widowhood. (456)
T F   15.   The new reproductive technologies have raised ethical questions for our society. (461)
T F   16.   Two divorced people who marry and each bring their children into a new family unit become a blended family. (460)
T F   17.   Marriage between homosexuals is legal in several states, including California. (460)
T F   18.   U.S. rate of births to unmarried women is the highest among a group of ten industrialized nations for which there are accurate data. (463)
T F   19.   The usual pattern of father-child contact following a divorce is for the contact to be fairly high for several years while the child is young, but then to drop off significantly as the child moves through adolescence. (468-469)
T F   20.   According to research by Finkelhor and Yllo, one in ten women, who were part of a representative sample, reported that their husbands used physical force to compel them to have sex. (471)

FILL-IN QUESTIONS

1.   A marriage in which a man has more than one wife is _____. (444)
2.   _____ is a group who consider themselves related by blood, marriage, or adoption. (445)
3.   A(n) _____ is a family consisting of a husband, wife, and child(ren). (445)
4.   _____ is the practice of marrying outside one's group. (446)
5.   Female control of a society or group is a(n) _____. (446)
6.   Rules specifying the degrees of kinship that prohibit sex or marriage are _____. (447)

7.   Feelings of erotic attraction, accompanied by an idealization of the other, are most commonly associated with _____ . (451)

8.   _____ is the tendency of people with similar characteristics to get married. (453)

9.   A married couple's domestic situation after the last child has left home is sometimes referred to as the _____ . (455)

10.   An emphasis on male strength and dominance is _____ . (458)

11.   A _____ is one whose members were once part of another family. (462)

12.   In the U.S., _____ , living together in a sexual relationship without marriage, has increased about seven times in just over two decades. (463)

13.   The term _____ refers to people who find themselves caught between two generations and responsible for the care of both. (464)

14.   A situation in which a husband forces his wife to have sex with no intent to hurt her physically is _____ . (471)

15.   Sexual relations between specified relatives, such as brothers and sisters or parents and children is _____ . (471)

MATCH THESE CONCEPTS WITH THEIR DEFINITIONS

___1.   Jessie Bernard
___2.   Larry Bumpass
___3.   Andrew Cherlin
___4.   Finkelhor & Yllo
___5.   Kathleen Gerson
___6.   Arlie Hochschild
___7.   Melvin Kohn
___8.   Lillian Rubin
___9.   Diana Russell
__10.   Bob Suzuki

a.   *noted the existence of two marriages within one union*
b.   *studied marital rape*
c.   *found that women's satisfaction increased after last child moved out*
d.   *studied incest victims*
e.   *identified reasons why couples choose to be child-free*
f.   *studied marriage and cohabitation patterns*
g.   *identified distinctive characteristics of Asian-American families*
h.   *noted lack of norms regarding remarriage*
i.   *studied social class differences in child-rearing*
j.   *identified the second shift*

ESSAY QUESTIONS

1.   Identify the stages in the family life cycle, discussing what tasks are accomplished in each stage and what event marks the transition from one stage to the next.

2.   Identify the trends among U.S. families today and explain the social forces that have contributed to each of them.

3.   Discuss the impact that divorce has on family members--men, women, and children.

CHAPTER 17
EDUCATION

☞ CHAPTER SUMMARY

- In earlier societies, education consisted of informal learning and was synonymous with acculturation. Today, education is no longer the same as informal acculturation, for the term now refers to a group's formal system of teaching knowledge, values, and skills.

- In general, formal education reflects a nation's economy. It is more extensive in the most industrialized nations and very spotty in the least industrialized nations.

- Functionalists emphasize the functions of education, including teaching knowledge and skills, transmitting cultural values, social integration, gatekeeping, and promoting personal and social change and mainstreaming. They note that education has replaced some traditional family functions.

- Conflict theorists view education as a mechanism for maintaining social inequality and reproducing the social class system. Accordingly, they stress such matters as the way in which education reflects the social structure of society (the correspondence principle), unequal funding of schools, culturally biased IQ tests, and the hidden curriculum.

- Symbolic interactionists examine classroom interaction. They study how teacher expectations cause a self-fulfilling prophecy, producing the very behavior that the teacher is expecting.

- Problems facing the current U.S. educational system include falling SAT scores, grade inflation, social promotion, functional illiteracy, teen pregnancy and violence in schools. Suggestions for reform include implementing and maintaining a secure and safe learning environment, increasing academic standards and expectations, and implementing a school choice and site-based management program.

☞ LEARNING OBJECTIVES

As you read Chapter 17, use these learning objectives to organize your notes. After completing your reading, briefly state an answer to each of the objectives, and review the text pages in parentheses.

1. Describe education in earlier societies. (478-479)
2. Discuss the beginning of universal education in the United States. (479-480)
3. Outline the major differences in the educational systems of Japan, Russia, and Egypt. (480-484)
4. List and briefly explain the manifest and latent functions of education. (484-488)
5. Explain how education maintains social inequality using the conflict perspective. (488-493)
6. Summarize symbolic interaction research regarding teacher expectations and the self-fulfilling prophecy. (494-496)
7. Identify the problems that exist within the U.S. educational system and discuss solutions. (496-504)

☞ CHAPTER OUTLINE

I.   **The Development of Modern Education**
   A.   In earlier societies, education was synonymous with acculturation (transmission of culture from one generation to the next), not with a separate institution.

1. In societies where a sufficient surplus developed, a separate institution arose. Some individuals devoted themselves to teaching, while those who had leisure became their students. Education gradually came to refer to a group's *formal* system of teaching knowledge, values, and skills.

2. During the Dark Ages, only the monks and a handful of the wealthy nobility could read and write.

3. Industrialization created a need for the average citizen to be able to read, write, and work with figures because of the new machinery and new types of jobs.

B. In the years following the American Revolution, the founders of the republic believed formal education should be the principal means for creating a uniform national culture.

1. In the early 1800s, there was a jumble of schools administered by separate localities, with no coordination. Children of the wealthy attended private schools; children of the lower classes (and slaves) received no formal education.

2. Horace Mann, a Massachusetts educator, proposed that common schools, supported through taxes, be established throughout his state; the idea spread throughout the country.

3. Industrialization and universal education occurred at the same time. Since the economy was undergoing fundamental change, political and civic leaders recognized the need for an educated work force. They also feared the influx of foreign values and looked on public education as a way to Americanize immigrants.

4. Mandatory education laws requiring children to attend school to a specified age or a particular grade level were enacted in all U.S. states by 1918.

5. As industrialization progressed, education came to be seen as essential to the well-being of society; industrialized nations developed into credential societies.

6. Today a larger proportion of the population attends colleges and universities in the United States than in any other industrialized country in the world; 67 percent of all high school graduates now enter college.

II. **Education in Global Perspective**

A. Education in the Most Industrialized Nations: Japan

1. Japanese education reflects a group-centered ethic. Children in grade school work as a group, mastering the same skills/materials; cooperation and respect for elders (and positions of authority) are stressed.

2. College admission procedures are based on test scores; only the top scorers are admitted, regardless of social class.

3. About one-half of those who plan to go on to college attend cram schools every day after regular school as well as on weekends. Affluent parents hire tutors for their children.

B. Education in the Industrializing Nations: Russia

1. After the Revolution of 1917, the new Soviet government insisted that socialist values dominate education, seeing education as a means to undergird the new political system.

2. With the country still largely agricultural, education remained spotty; by 1950, only about half of Soviet young people were in school, and most of these came from the elite.

3. The Soviets continued to work toward universal education; education, including college, was free and math and natural sciences were stressed. The launching of

    Sputnik in the 1950s demonstrated that the Soviets had become effective in teaching mathematics, engineering, and the natural sciences.

4.   Today, Russians are in the midst of "reinventing" education. Private, religious, and even foreign-run schools are operating, teachers are allowed to develop their own curriculum, and students are encouraged to think for themselves.

5.   The primary difficulty facing the post-Soviet educational system is the rapidly changing values and world views currently underway.

C.   Education in the Least Industrialized Nations: Egypt

    1.   Several centuries before the birth of Christ, Egypt was a world-renowned center of learning. Primary areas of study during this period were physics, astronomy, geometry, geography, mathematics, philosophy, and medicine. After defeat in war, education declined, never to rise to its former prominence.

    2.   Today, the Egyptian constitution makes five years of grade school free and compulsory for all children; however, qualified teachers are few, classrooms are crowded, and education is highly limited. Those individuals that do receive a formal education attend grade school for five years, preparatory school for three years and high school for three years.

    3.   The Egyptian government specifies the manifest functions of higher education: to prepare graduates for the world of work and to develop scientific research that will serve the community and help solve economic and social problems that confront Egypt's development.

    4.   Although education is free at all levels, including college, children of the wealthy are still several times as likely to get a college education.

III.   **The Functionalist Perspective: Education's Social Benefits**

A.   Functionalists use the term *manifest function* to refer to the positive outcomes that are intended by human actions and *latent functions* to refer to positive outcomes that were not intended.

B.   Education's most obvious manifest function is to teach knowledge and skills.

    1.   Increasingly, what often counts is not the learning, but the certification of learning.

    2.   A credential society is one in which employers use diplomas and degrees to determine job eligibility. The sheer size, urbanization and consequent anonymity of U.S. society is a major reason why credentials are required. Diplomas/degrees often serve as sorting devices for employers; because they don't know the individual personally, they depend on schools to weed out the capable from the incapable.

C.   Another manifest function is cultural transmission of values. There are numerous ways in which cultural values like individualism, competition, and patriotism are transmitted-- through the curriculum, the architecture of the schools, and the structure of the school day.

D.   Schools facilitate social integration by molding students into a more cohesive unit and helping to socialize them into mainstream culture. Today, children with disabilities are increasingly being integrated in regular social activities through the policy of inclusion or mainstreaming.

E.   Gatekeeping, determining which people will enter which occupations, is another function of education. Tracking students into particular educational curricula supports gatekeeping. Schools facilitate social placement.

F.   Schools promote personal change by teaching students to "think for themselves."

G. Education contributes to social change by sponsoring research. Sociological research was used in the court case that ultimately led to school desegregation.

H. Over time, the functions of education have expanded to include many previously reserved for families.

I. Other functions include: (1) matchmaking (people finding a future spouse in school); (2) social networking; and (3) helping stabilize employment (keeping unskilled individuals out of the labor market).

V. **The Conflict Perspective: Reproducing the Social Class Structure**

A. Conflict theorists see that the educational system is a tool used by those in the controlling sector of society to maintain their dominance.

B. The hidden curriculum refers to the unwritten rules of behavior and attitude (e.g., obedience to authority, conformity to cultural norms) taught in school in addition to the formal curriculum. Such values and work habits teach the middle and lower classes to support the status quo.

C. Conflict theorists criticize IQ (intelligence quotient) testing because they not only measure intelligence but also culturally acquired knowledge.

   1. They focus only on certain components of intelligence--mathematical, spatial, symbolic, and linguistic abilities--while ignoring others.

   2. By focusing on these factors, IQ tests reflect a cultural bias that favors the middle class and discriminates against minority and lower class students.

D. Because public schools are largely financed by local property taxes, there are rich and poor school districts. Unequal funding stacks the deck against minorities and the poor.

E. The correspondence principle is how schools correspond to (or reflect) the social structure of society. The educational system reinforces the status quo, because what is taught in a nation's schools corresponds to the characteristics of that society. Thus, education perpetuates society's prevailing inequalities.

F. Schools not only reproduce social class inequalities, but also those based on race and ethnicity. Whites are more likely to complete high school, go to college, and get a degree than African Americans and Latinos. The education system helps pass privilege (or lack thereof) across generations.

VI. **The Symbolic Interaction Perspective: Teacher Expectations and the Self-Fulfilling Prophecy**

A. Symbolic interactionists study face-to-face interaction inside the classroom. They have found that expectations of teachers are especially significant in determining what students learn.

B. The Rist research (participant observation in an African-American grade school with an African-American faculty) found tracking begins with teachers' perceptions.

   1. After eight days--and without testing for ability--teachers divided the class into fast, average, and slow learners; social class was the basis for the assignments.

   2. Students from whom more was expected did the best; students in the slow group were ridiculed and disengaged themselves from classroom activities.

   3. The labels applied in kindergarten tended to follow the child through school. What occurred was a self-fulfilling prophecy (Robert Merton's term for an originally false assertion that becomes true simply because it was predicted).

C. The Rosenthal/Jacobson experiment showed that teacher expectations were based on what they had been told about their students.

   1. After testing children's abilities using standard IQ tests, researchers randomly classified 20 percent of the students as spurters. This was the basis for their report

to teachers concerning which students would probably experience a learning spurt during the school year.

    2. Those who had been labeled as "spurters" made more progress than other students simply because teachers expected them to, and encouraged them more--another example of a self-fulfilling prophecy.

D. Teachers shaped the experiences the students had within the classroom.

    1. George Farkas found students scoring the same on course matter may receive different grades: females get higher grades, as do Asian Americans.

    2. Farkas used symbolic interactionism to understand this pattern. He noticed that some students signal that they are interested in what the teacher is teaching; teachers pick up these signals and reward those students with better grades.

VIII. Problems in U.S. Education--and Their Solutions

A. A variety of factors have been identified as the major problems facing the U.S. educational system today. These problems include: falling test scores; grade inflation, and how it relates to social promotion and functional illiteracy; violence in schools; and teenage pregnancy.

B. A number of solutions have been offered to address these problems: a secure learning environment; higher academic standards and expectations; and school choice and site-based management.

☞ KEY TERMS

After studying the chapter, review the definition for each of the following terms.

acculturation: the transmission of culture from one generation to the next

correspondence principle: the sociological principle that schools correspond to (or reflect) the social structure of society

credential society: the use of diplomas and degrees to determine who is eligible for jobs, even though the diploma or degree may be irrelevant to the actual work

cultural transmission: in reference to education, the ways in which schools transmit a society's culture, especially its core values

education: a formal system of teaching knowledge, values, and skills

functional illiterate: a high school graduate who has difficulty with basic reading and math

gatekeeping: the process by which education opens and closes doors of opportunity; another term for the *social placement* function of education

grade inflation: higher grades given for the same work; a general rise in student grades without a corresponding increase in learning or test scores

hidden curriculum: the unwritten goals of schools, such as obedience to authority and conformity to cultural norms

latent functions: unintended beneficial consequences of people's actions

mainstreaming: helping people to become part of the mainstream of society

mandatory education laws: laws that require all children to attend school until a specified age or until they complete a minimum grade in school

manifest functions: intended consequences of people's actions

school choice: parents being able to choose the school their child will attend; often used in the context of expecting for-profit schools to compete for vouchers issued by the state

self-fulfilling prophecy: Robert Merton's term for an originally false assertion that becomes true simply because it was predicted

social placement: a function of education that funnels people into a society's various positions

social promotion: passing students to the next grade even though they have not mastered basic materials

tracking: the sorting of students into different educational programs on the basis of real or perceived abilities

☞ KEY PEOPLE

Review the major theoretical contributions or findings of these people.

Samuel Bowles and Herbert Gintis: Bowles and Gintis used the term correspondence principle to refer to the ways in which schools reflect the social structure of society.

James Coleman and Thomas Hoffer: A study of students in Catholic and public high schools by these two sociologists demonstrated that performance was based on setting higher standards for students rather than on individual ability.

Randall Collins: Collins studied the credential society.

Kingsley Davis and Wilbert Moore: Davis and Moore argue that a major task of society is to fill social positions with capable people and that one of the functions of schools is gatekeeping -- the funneling of people into these positions based on merit.

George Farkas: Farkas and a team of researchers investigated how teacher expectations affect student grades. They found that students signal teachers that they are good students by being eager, cooperative and working hard.

Harry Gracey: Gracey conducted a participant observation study of kindergarten and concluded that the purpose of kindergarten is to socialize students into the student role. He referred to kindergarten as a boot camp.

Donald Hayes and Loreen Wolfer: These sociologists suggest that "dummied down" textbooks are responsible for the rising mediocrity of American students.

Robert Merton: Merton coined the expression "self-fulfilling prophecy" to refer to an originally false assumption of what is going to happen that comes true simply because it is predicted.

Talcott Parsons: Another functionalist who suggested that a function of schools is to funnel people into social positions.

Ray Rist: This sociologist's classic study of an African-American grade school uncovered some of the dynamics of educational tracking.

Robert Rosenthal and Lenore Jacobson: These social psychologists conducted a study of teacher expectations and student performance and found that a self-fulfilling prophecy had taken place-- when teachers were led to believe certain students were smart, they came to expect more of them, and the students gave more in return.

☞ "DOWN-TO-EARTH SOCIOLOGY"

This is your opportunity to apply the sociological perspective to the world around you. The questions in this section refer to material introduced in this chapter of your text. Many ask you to think about ideas and information presented in the various special "boxes" that are located throughout this chapter.

1.   After reading "Kindergarten as Boot Camp" (p. 490), do you agree with Harry Gracey's ideas? Did you attend kindergarten? If so, which experiences do you remember the most vividly? Do you think it would be accurate to refer to college as a "boot camp?"

2.   Have you ever been involved in a distance learning course like the ones described on page 496? If you have, what aspects of the course did you like? What aspects did you dislike? What changes would have improved the course? In what ways might distance learning change the way in which education is organized and instruction is delivered? Thinking about the different sociological perspectives on education, analyze how each might "see" this new development in terms of addressing problems as well as creating new problems.

3.   Were you surprised to learn that the number of school shootings is not only quite low, but has actually declined over the course of the 1990s (p. 499)? Why do you think the media has exploited this issue so much?

4.   What was your reaction after reading about LEAP (p. 500)? Do you think this should serve as a model for motivating teens to stay in school and get an education? How could the program be improved even further?

5.   In his classroom, Jaime Escalante has challenged many of the assumptions about educating low-income students (p. 503-504). Is his success due to his extraordinary teaching skills or is it possible to extend his successes into classrooms across the country? If so, what changes would have to be made in education?

☞ SELF-TEST

After completing this self-test, check your answers against the Answer Key beginning on page 395 of this Study Guide and against the text on page(s) indicated in parentheses.

MULTIPLE CHOICE QUESTIONS

1.   In earlier societies: (478)
       a.   there was no separate social institution called education.
       b.   education was synonymous with acculturation.
       c.   persons who already possessed certain skills taught them to others.
       d.   All of the above.

2.   Education: (478)
       a.   is a formal system of teaching knowledge, values, and skills.
       b.   is the same as informal acculturation.
       c.   is very similar in countries throughout the world.
       d.   All of the above.

3.   "Common schools," supported through taxes, were proposed by: (479)
       a.   Thomas Jefferson.
       b.   Noah Webster.
       c.   Horace Mann.
       d.   John Dewey.

4.   Laws requiring school attendance up to a specified age or a minimum grade are: (480)
       a.   credential laws.
       b.   mandatory education laws.
       c.   compulsory education laws.
       d.   None of the above.

5. In Japan, college admission is based on: (481)
   a. the ability of parents to pay the tuition.
   b. making a high score on a national test.
   c. being known by teachers as a "hard worker."
   d. the same procedures that prevail in the United States.

6. Which of the following statements about education in Egypt is incorrect? (483-484)
   a. Because education is free at all levels, the most talented children attend, regardless of parent's economic resources.
   b. In Egyptian schools there are few qualified teachers, classrooms are crowded and educational opportunities limited.
   c. The educational system consists of five years of grade school, three years of preparatory school, and three years of high school.
   d. Only 39% of women and 64% of men are literate.

7. Using diplomas to hire employees, even when diplomas are irrelevant to the work, is: (484)
   a. a credential society.
   b. a certification mill.
   c. employer discretion in hiring.
   d. None of the above.

8. According to functionalists, all of the following are functions of education, except: (484-488)
   a. maintaining social inequality.
   b. transmitting cultural values.
   c. helping to mold students into a more or less cohesive unit.
   d. teaching patriotism.

9. Which of the following is not one of the cultural values that has been transmitted through the U.S. educational system? (485)
   a. individualism
   b. competition
   c. cooperation
   d. patriotism

10. The function of education that sorts people into various positions on the basis of merit is: (487)
    a. functional placement.
    b. social placement.
    c. railroading.
    d. social promotion.

11. The hidden curriculum refers to: (489)
    a. the extra curriculum costs that are buried in school budgets.
    b. the lessons that teachers hide from the eyes of prying school boards.
    c. the unwritten rules of behavior and attitudes that are taught in school.
    d. All of the above.

12. Public schools are largely supported by: (491)
    a. state funding.
    b. federal funding.
    c. local property taxes.
    d. None of the above.

13. The ways in which schools correspond to, or reflect, the social structure of society is: (492)
    a. the reproduction of social class.
    b. the correspondence principle.
    c. the status quo quotient.
    d. the status maintenance process.

14. From a conflict perspective, the real purpose of education is to: (493)
    a. perpetuate existing social inequalities.
    b. provide educational opportunities for students from all types of backgrounds.
    c. teach patriotism, teamwork, and cooperation.
    d. replace family functions which most families no longer fulfill.

15. Conflict theorists explain the fact that whites are more likely to complete high school, to go to college, and to get a bachelor's degree than African Americans and Latinos because: (493)
    a. the purpose of the educational system is to reproduce inequality by keeping the social class structure intact from one generation to the next.
    b. of the belief by many African Americans and Latinos that going to college will not benefit them.
    c. many African Americans and Hispanic Americans do not utilize the equal educational opportunities available in the United States.
    d. All of the above.

16. Teacher expectations and the self-fulfilling prophecy are of interest to _____ theorists. (494-495)
    a. functionalist
    b. conflict
    c. symbolic interaction
    d. educational

17. Ray Rist found that _____ was the underlying basis for assigning children to different tables in a kindergarten classroom. (494)
    a. ability
    b. maturity level
    c. social class
    d. gender

18. A self-fulfilling prophecy: (495)
    a. is an originally false assertion that becomes true simply because it was predicted.
    b. is an originally true assertion that becomes false because a person decides to prove that the label is incorrect.
    c. is a term coined by Ray Rist.
    d. All of the above.

19. The Rosenthal/Jacobson experiment tended to confirm which of these concepts? (495)
     a.   cooling out
     b.   cultural transmission
     c.   acculturation
     d.   self-fulfilling prophecy

20. Research by George Farkas focused on: (495-496)
     a.   education of elite children.
     b.   how teacher expectations affect a kindergarten class.
     c.   how teacher expectations are influenced by students' alleged IQ scores.
     d.   how teacher expectations affect students' grades.

21. When compared to scores of twenty to thirty years ago, today's student scores on tests such as the SAT: (497)
     a.   are higher.
     b.   are lower.
     c.   have remained about the same.
     d.   None of the above.

22. High school graduates who have difficulty with basic reading and math are known as: (498)
     a.   "boneheads."
     b.   functional literates.
     c.   functional illiterates.
     d.   underachievers.

23. Based on the statistics of shooting deaths that have occurred in U.S. schools, which of the following statements is <u>correct</u>? (498)
     a.   There has been a dramatic increase in the number of shooting deaths over the last decade.
     b.   The number of shooting deaths at the end of the 1990s was half what it was at the beginning of the decade.
     c.   Girls are more likely than boys to be the targets of school shootings.
     d.   Other types of homicides committed at school (stabbings, beatings, etc.) are just as common as shooting homicides.

24. Research by James Coleman and Thomas Hoffer, comparing student performance at Roman Catholic and public schools, found that: (501)
     a.   students at public schools performed better because they had more resources available to them.
     b.   students at public schools performed better because they were taught by better qualified teachers.
     c.   students at Roman Catholic schools performed better because the teachers set higher standards for them to meet.
     d.   students at Roman Catholic schools performed better because they had higher levels of faith.

25.   A concern over the use of vouchers to improve the overall quality of education is that: (502)
    a.   the jobs of public school teachers would be in jeopardy.
    b.   the resources that would otherwise go to public schools could be diverted to private schools.
    c.   the future of public education would be in question.
    d.   all of the above.

TRUE-FALSE QUESTIONS

T F   1.   In earlier societies there was a separate social institution called education. (478)
T F   2.   By 1918, all American states had mandatory education laws. (480)
T F   3.   College graduation in the United States today is still less common than high school graduation was in 1910. (480)
T F   4.   Japanese schools teach the value of competition to their students. (481)
T F   5.   Since the breakup of the Soviet Union, Russia has allowed the establishment of private, religious, and even foreign-run schools. (482)
T F   6.   Because Egyptian education is free at all levels, including college, children of the wealthy are no more likely than children of the poor to get a college education. (484)
T F   7.   The United States is a credential society. (484)
T F   8.   Education's most obvious manifest function is to teach knowledge and skills. (484)
T F   9.   American schools discourage individualism and encourage teamwork. (485)
T F   10.   Students everywhere are taught that their country is the best country in the world. (485)
T F   11.   Parental influence is strong enough to challenge the influence of peer culture when it comes to molding students' appearance, ideas, speech patterns, and interactions with the opposite sex. (486)
T F   12.   Functional theorists believe that social placement is harmful to society. (487)
T F   13.   Matchmaking is a latent function of education. (488)
T F   14.   Functionalists emphasize the hidden curriculum in their analysis of U.S. education. (489)
T F   15.   According to conflict theorists, unequal funding for education automatically stacks the deck against children from lower income families. (491)
T F   16.   The correspondence principle states that schools correspond to the social structure of society. (492)
T F   17.   Research by Ray Rist concluded that the child's journey through school was preordained by the end of the first year of kindergarten. (494)
T F   18.   George Farkas's research showed that teachers discriminate against females and some minorities because they do not fit their expectations of what a good student should be. (495)
T F   19.   Since the publication of the report *A Nation At Risk*, verbal scores on SATs have shown improvement while math scores have continued to decline. (497)
T F   20.   Research by Coleman and Hoffer demonstrated that the superior test performance of Catholic school students was due to the higher standards that teachers maintained. (501)

FILL-IN QUESTIONS

1.   _____ is the transmission of culture from one generation to the next. (478)
2.   A formal system of teaching knowledge, values, and skills is the definition for _____. (478)

3.   Using diplomas and degrees to determine eligibility for jobs occurs in a _____. (484)
4.   Transmitting cultural values is a _____ function of education. (484)
5.   A new function of education today is _____, incorporating people with disabilities into regular social activities. (486)
6.   Tracking and social placement both contribute to the _____ function of education. (487)
7.   Another term to describe the gatekeeping function of education is _____. (487)
8.   The unwritten rules of behavior and attitude, such as obedience to authority and conformity to cultural norms, is referred to as the _____. (489)
9.   _____ theorists believe that culturally biased IQ tests favor the middle classes and discriminate against minorities and students from lower-class backgrounds. (489)
10.   The idea that schools reflect the social structure of society is the _____. (492)
11.   _____ theorists found that the expectations of teachers are especially significant for determining what students learn. (494)
12.   _____ refers to the trend of giving higher grades for the same work, so that there is a general rise in student grades despite the fact that neither learning nor test scores have increased. (498)
13.   It is not uncommon today for schools to practice _____, which involves passing students to the next grade even though they have not mastered basic material. (498)
14.   Someone who has graduated from high school but still has difficulties with reading and writing is considered _____. (498)
15.   The policy of allowing parents to select the school their child will attend is referred to as _____. (502)

MATCH THESE SOCIAL SCIENTISTS WITH THEIR CONTRIBUTIONS

___1. Randall Collins
___2. Bowles and Gintis
___3. Rosenthal and Jacobson
___4. Ray Rist
___5. Coleman and Hoffer
___6. Harry Gracey
___7. Davis and Moore
___8. George Farkas

a. *gatekeeping sorts people on the basis of merit*
b. *teacher expectations and student performance*
c. *credential society*
d. *correspondence principle*
e. *tracking and expectations of kindergarten teachers*
f. *kindergarten as boot camp*
g. *student performance linked to setting higher standards*
h. *students are rewarded for signals they send teachers*

ESSAY QUESTIONS

1.   Explain the link between democracy, industrialization, and universal education.

2.   Select one of the three perspectives and design a research project to test the claims of that perspective about the nature of education.

3.   In discussing solutions to educational problems, the author suggests that one direction in which schools should go is towards setting higher educational standards. Both the research by James Coleman and Thomas Hoffer, and the success of Jaime Escalante, support this. Discuss social factors that might explain why such a proposal has not been widely adopted by public schools across the country.

CHAPTER 18
RELIGION

☞ CHAPTER SUMMARY

- The sociological study of religion involves the analysis of the relationship between society and religion to gain insight into the role of religion in people's lives. For Durkheim, the key elements of religion are beliefs separating the profane from the sacred, rituals, and a moral community.

- According to functionalists, religion meets basic human needs such as answering questions about ultimate meaning, providing emotional comfort, social solidarity, guidelines for everyday life, social control, adaptation, support for the government, and social change. Functional equivalents are groups or activities other than religion that provide these same functions. Functionalists also believe religion has two main dysfunctions: war and religious persecution.

- Symbolic interactionists focus on how religious symbols communicate meaning and how ritual and beliefs unite people into a community.

- Conflict theorists see religion as a conservative force that serves the needs of the ruling class by reflecting and reinforcing social inequality.

- Unlike Marx, who asserted that religion impedes social change by encouraging people to focus on the afterlife, Weber saw religion as a powerful force for social change. He analyzed how Protestantism gave rise to an ethic that stimulated "the spirit of capitalism." The result was capitalism, which transformed society.

- The world's major religions include Judaism, Christianity, Islam, Hinduism, Buddhism, and Confucianism. Just as different religions have distinct teachings and practices, so to within a religion different groups contrast sharply with one another.

- Sociologists have identified cults, sects, churches, and ecclesia as distinct types of religious organizations. All religions began as cults; although most ultimately fail, those that survive become sects. Both cults and sects represent belief systems that are at odds with the prevailing beliefs and values of the broader society. If a sect grows, and its members make peace with the rest of society, it changes into a church. Ecclesiac, or state religions, are rare.

- Religion in the United States is characterized by diversity, pluralism and freedom, competition, commitment, tolerance, a fundamentalist revival, and the electronic church.

- The secularization of religion, a shift from spiritual concerns to concerns of "this world," is the force behind the dynamics of religious organization. As a cult or sect evolves into a church, its teachings are adapted to reflect the changing social status of its members; dissatisfied members break away to form new cults or sects.

- Even in countries where a concerted effort was made to eliminate it, religion has continued to thrive. Religion apparently will continue to exist as long as humanity does.

☞ LEARNING OBJECTIVES

As you read Chapter 18, use these learning objectives to organize your notes. After completing your reading, briefly state an answer to each of the objectives, and review the text pages in parentheses.

1. Define religion and explain Durkheim's essential elements of religion. (508)
2. Describe the functionalist perspective on religion, including the functional equivalents of religion,

and the dysfunctions of religion. (509-511)

3.   Explain what aspects of religion are focused on by symbolic interactionists. (511-513)

4.   Identify the conflict perspective on religion and note Marx's influence. (513-514)

5.   Describe the relationship between religion and capitalism, as seen by Weber. (514-515)

6.   Outline the key characteristics of each of the world's major religions. (515-521)

7.   Define cult, sect, church, and ecclesia, and describe the process by which some groups have moved from one category to another. (521-524)

8.   Discuss why religions and cultures may conflict and describe the three major patterns of adaptations that can occur under such conditions. (524-525)

9.   State the major characteristics of religion in the U.S. (526-529)

10. Explain what secularization means in terms of religion and culture. (530-533)

11. Analyze the future of religion. State whether or not you agree with the author's assertion that science will never replace religion. (533-534)

☞ CHAPTER OUTLINE

I.   **What Is Religion?**
   A.   According to Durkheim, religion is the beliefs/practices separating the profane from the sacred, uniting adherents into a moral community.
       1.   Sacred refers to aspects of life having to do with the supernatural that inspire awe, reverence, deep respect, or deep fear.
       2.   Profane refers to the ordinary aspects of everyday life.
   B.   Durkheim defined religion by three elements: (1) beliefs that some things are sacred (forbidden, set off from the profane); (2) practices (rituals) concerning things considered sacred; (3) a moral community (a church) resulting from a group's beliefs and practices.

II. **The Functionalist Perspective**
   A.   Religion performs certain functions: (1) answering questions about ultimate meaning (the purpose of life, why people suffer); (2) providing emotional comfort; (3) uniting believers into a community that shares values and perspectives; (4) providing guidelines for life; (5) controlling behavior; (6) helping people adapt to new environments; (7) providing support for the government; and (8) spearheading social change on occasion (as in the case of the civil rights movement in the 1960s).
   B.   A functional equivalent of religion is a substitute that serves the same functions; some are difficult to distinguish from a religion. Although the substitute may perform similar functions, its activities are not directed toward God, gods, or the supernatural.
   C.   War and religious persecution are dysfunctions of religion.

III. **The Symbolic Interactionist Perspective**
   A.   Religions use symbols to provide identity and social solidarity for members. For members, these are not ordinary symbols, but sacred symbols evoking awe and reverence, which become a condensed way of communicating with others.
   B.   Rituals are ceremonies or repetitive practices helping to unite people into a moral community by creating a feeling of closeness with God and unity with one another.
   C.   Symbols, including rituals, develop from beliefs. A belief may be vague ("God is") or specific ("God wants us to prostrate ourselves and face Mecca five times each day"). Religious beliefs not only include values (what is considered good and desirable) but also a cosmology (unified picture of the world).

D. Religious experience is a sudden awareness of the supernatural or a feeling of coming in contact with God. Some Protestants use the term "born again" to describe people who have undergone a religious experience.

E. Shared meanings that come through symbols, rituals, and beliefs unite people into a moral community, which is powerful. It provides the basis for mutual identity and establishes norms that govern the behavior of members. Not only are members bound together by shared beliefs and rituals, but they are also separated from those who do not share their symbolic world.

IV. The Conflict Perspective

A. Conflict theorists are highly critical of religion. Karl Marx called religion the "opium of the people" because he believed that the workers escape into religion. He argued that religion diverts the energies of the oppressed from changing their circumstances because believers focus on the happiness they will have in the coming world rather than on their suffering in this world.

B. Religious teachings and practices reflect a society's inequalities. Gender inequalities are an example: when males completely dominated U.S. society, women's roles in churches and synagogues were limited to "feminine" activities, a condition which is beginning to change.

C. Religion legitimates social inequality; it reflects the interests of those in power by teaching that the existing social arrangements of a society represent what God desires.

V. Religion and the Spirit of Capitalism

A. Weber saw religion as a force for social change, observing that European countries industrialized under capitalism. Thus, religion held the key to modernization (transformation of traditional societies into industrial societies).

B. To explain this connection, Weber wrote *The Protestant Ethic and the Spirit of Capitalism*. In it he concluded that:

1. The spirit of capitalism (desire to accumulate capital as a duty, as an end in itself) was a radical departure from the past.

2. Religion (including a Calvinistic belief in predestination and the need for reassurance as to one's fate) is the key to why the spirit of capitalism developed in Europe.

3. A change in religion (from Catholicism to Protestantism) led to a change in thought and behavior (the Protestant ethic), which resulted in the "spirit of capitalism. "

C. Today the spirit of capitalism and the Protestant ethic are by no means limited to Protestants; they have become cultural traits that have spread throughout the world.

VI. The World's Major Religions

A. The origin of Judaism is traced to Abraham, who lived about 4,000 years ago in Mesopotamia.

1. It was the first religion based on monotheism, the belief in only one God.

2. Contemporary Judaism in the United States has three main branches: Orthodox (adheres to the laws espoused by Moses), Reform (more liberal, uses the vernacular in religious ceremonies, and has reduced much of the ritual); and Conservative (falling somewhere between).

3. The history of Judaism is marked by conflict and persecution (anti-Semitism).

4. Central to Jewish teaching is the requirement to love God and do good deeds.

B. Christianity developed out of Judaism and is based on the belief that Christ is the Messiah

God promised the Jews.

    1.   During the first 1,000 years of Christianity, there was only one church organization, directed from Rome; during the 11th century, Greek Orthodoxy was established.

    2.   In the Middle Ages, the Roman Catholic church, aligned with the political establishment, grew corrupt. The Reformation of the 16th century, led by Martin Luther, was a reaction to the Church's corruption.

    3.   The Reformation marked the beginning of a splintering of Christianity; today there are about two billion Christians, divided into hundreds of groups.

C.   Islam (whose followers are known as Muslims) began in the same part of the world as Judaism and Christianity; like the Jews, Muslims trace their ancestry to Abraham.

    1.   The founder, Muhammad, established a theocracy, a government based on God being the ruler, his laws the statutes of the land, and priests his earthly administrators.

    2.   After Muhammad's death, a struggle for control split Islam into two branches that remain today: the Shi'ites that are more conservative and inclined to fundamentalism (the belief that true religion is threatened by modernism and that faith as it was originally practiced should be restored) and the Sunni that are generally more liberal.

D.   Hinduism, the chief religion of India, goes back about 4,000 years, but has no specific founder or canonical scripture (texts thought to be inspired by God). Instead several books expound on the moral qualities people should strive to attain.

    1.   Hindus are polytheists (believe there are many gods) and believe in reincarnation, a cycle of life, death, and rebirth.

    2.   Some Hindu practices, such as child marriage and suttee (cremating a widow along with her deceased husband) have been modified as a result of protest.

E.   About 600 B.C., Siddhartha Gautama founded Buddhism, which emphasizes self-denial and compassion.

    1.   Buddhism is similar to Hinduism in that the final goal is to escape from reincarnation into nonexistence of blissful peace.

    2.   Buddhism spread rapidly into many parts of Asia.

F.   Confucius (China 551-479 B.C.) urged social reform and developed a system of morality based on peace, justice, and universal order.

    1.   The basic moral principle of Confucianism is to maintain *jen* (sympathy or concern for other humans). The basic principle was to treat those who are subordinate to you as you would like to be treated by those superior to you.

    2.   Originally, Confucianism was atheistic; however, as the centuries passed, local gods were added to the teachings, and Confucius himself was declared a god.

VII.   Types of Religious Groups

A.   A cult is a new religion with few followers, whose teachings and practices put it at odds with the dominant culture and religion.

    1.   All religions began as cults. Cults often begin with the appearance of a charismatic leader (exerting extraordinary appeal to a group of followers).

    2.   Each cult meets with rejection from society. The message given by the cult is seen as a threat to the dominant culture.

    3.   The cult demands intense commitment, and its followers confront a hostile world.

    4.   Although most cults ultimately fail because they are unable to attract a large

enough following some succeed and make history.

B. A sect is larger than a cult, but still feels substantial hostility from and toward society.

    1. At the very least, members remain uncomfortable with many of the emphases of the dominant culture; nonmembers feel uncomfortable with sect members.

    2. Sects usually are loosely organized, emphasize personal salvation (an emotional expression of one's relationship with God), and recruitment of new members (evangelism).

    3. If a sect grows, its members tend to become respectable in society, and the sect is changed into a church.

C. A church is a large, highly organized religious group with formal, sedate services and less emphasis on personal conversion. The religious group is highly bureaucratized (including national and international offices that give directions to local congregations). Most new members come from within the church, from children born to existing members, rather than from outside recruitment.

D. An ecclesia is a religious group so integrated into the dominant culture that it is difficult to tell where one begins and the other leaves off.

    1. Ecclesiae are also called state religions. The government and religion work together to try to shape the society.

    2. There is no recruitment of members, for citizenship makes everyone a member. The majority of the society belong to the religion in name only.

E. Not all religions go through all stages. Although all religions began as cults, not all varieties of a religion have done so.

    1. Some die out because they fail to attract members; some remain sects. Few become ecclesia.

    2. A denomination is a "brand name" within a major religion (e. g., Methodist).

F. Three major patterns of adaptation occur when religion and the culture in which it is embedded find themselves in conflict.

    1. Members of a religion may reject the dominant culture and withdraw from it socially, although they continue to live in the same geographic area.

    2. A cult or sect rejects only specific elements of the prevailing culture.

    3. The society rejects the religious group entirely, and may even try to destroy it. The destruction of the Branch Dividians is an example of this third pattern.

VIII. Characteristics of Religion in the United States

A. Characteristics of membership in U.S. churches:

    1. Membership is highest in the South and the Midwest, somewhat lower in the East, and much lower in the West.

    2. Each religious group draws members from all social classes, although some are more likely to draw members from the top of the social class system and others from the bottom. The most top-heavy are Episcopalians and Jews, the most bottom-heavy the Baptist and Evangelicals. People who change social class are also likely to change their denomination.

    3. All major religious groups in the United States draw from various racial and ethnic groups; however, persons of Hispanic or Irish descent are likely to be Roman Catholics, those of Greek origin to belong to the Greek Orthodox church, while African Americans are likely to be Protestants.

    4. Membership rate increases steadily with age.

B. Characteristics of religious groups in the U.S.:

1. Diversity--no state church, no ecclesia, and no single denomination dominates.
2. Pluralism and freedom--no government interference with religion.
3. Competition for believers from many religions.
4. Commitment--reflected in the high proportion who believe in God, who attend a church or synagogue, and who provide generous financial support for religion and its charities.
5. Toleration for religious beliefs other than one's own. This is reflected in the attitudes that religions have a right to exist as long as they don't brainwash or bother anyone, and no one says which religion is the true religion. While each believer may be convinced about the truth of his or her religion, trying to convert others is a violation of individual dignity.
6. Fundamentalist revival because mainstream churches fail to meet basic religious needs of large numbers of people.
7. The electronic church in which televangelists reach millions of viewers and raise millions of dollars.
8. Religious groups now maintain home pages on the Internet, and discussion groups have formed around religion.

C. Secularization is the process by which worldly affairs replace spiritual interests.
1. Secularization of religion is the replacement of a religion's other-worldly concerns with concerns about this world. It occurs when religion's influence is lessened (both on a society's institutions and on individuals). The secularization of religion explains why Christian churches have splintered into so many groups: changes in social class of the members may create different needs, thereby failing to meet the needs of those whose life situation has not changed.
2. Secularization of culture is the process whereby religion has less influence in society. Secularization is due to the spread of scientific thinking, industrialization, urbanization and mass education that reflects modernization.

IX. **The Future of Religion**
A. Marx was convinced religion would crumble when the workers threw off the chains of oppression; however, after communist countries were established (and despite persecution) people continued to be religious.
B. Others believed science would replace religion; however, science cannot answer questions about four concerns many people have: the existence of God; the purpose of life; morality; and the existence of an afterlife.
C. Neither science nor political systems can replace religion, and religion will last as long as humanity lasts.

☞ KEY TERMS

After studying the chapter, review the definition for each of the following terms.

animism: the belief that all objects in the world have spirits, some of which are dangerous and must be outwitted
anti-Semitism: prejudice, discrimination, and persecution directed against Jews
born again: a term describing Christians who have undergone a life-transforming religious experience so radical that they feel they have become new persons
charisma: literally, an extraordinary gift from God; more commonly, an outstanding, "magnetic"

personality

charismatic leader: literally, someone to whom God has given a gift; more commonly, someone who exerts extraordinary appeal to a group of followers

church: according to Durkheim, one of the three essential elements of religion--a moral community of believers; a second definition is a type of religious organization described on page 506, a large, highly organized group with formal, sedate worship services and little emphasis on personal conversion

civil religion: Robert Bellah's term for religion that is such an established feature of a country's life that its history and social institutions become sanctified by being associated with God

cosmology: teachings or ideas that provide a unified picture of the world

cult: a new religion with few followers, whose teachings and practices put it at odds with the dominant culture and religion

denomination: a "brand name" within a major religion, for example, Methodist or Baptist

ecclesia: a religious group so integrated into the dominant culture that it is difficult to tell where the one begins and the other leaves off; also called a *state religion*

evangelism: an attempt to win converts

fundamentalism: the belief that true religion is threatened by modernism and that the faith as it was originally practiced should be restored

functional equivalent: in this context, a substitute that serves the same functions (or meets the same needs) as religion, for example, psychotherapy

modernization: the transformation of traditional societies into industrial societies

monotheism: the belief that there is only one God

polytheism: the belief that there are many gods

profane: Durkheim's term for common elements of everyday life

Protestant ethic: Weber's term to describe the ideal of a self-denying, highly moral life, accompanied by hard work and frugality

reincarnation: in Hinduism and Buddhism, the return of the soul after death in a different form

religion: according to Durkheim, beliefs and practices that separate the profane from the sacred and unite its adherents into a moral community

religious experience: a sudden awareness of the supernatural or a feeling of coming in contact with God

rituals: ceremonies or repetitive practices; in this context, religious observances, or rites, often intended to evoke a sense of awe of the sacred

sacred: Durkheim's term for things set apart or forbidden, that inspire fear, awe, reverence, or deep respect

sect: a group larger than a cult that still feels substantial hostility from and toward society

secular: belonging to the world and its affairs

secularization: the process by which spiritual concerns are replaced by worldly concerns

secularization of culture: the process by which a culture becomes less influenced by religion

secularization of religion: the replacement of a religion's "otherworldly" concerns with concerns about "this world"

spirit of capitalism: Weber's term for the desire to accumulate capital as a duty -- not to spend it, but as an end in itself--and to constantly reinvest it

state religion: a government-sponsored religion

☞ KEY PEOPLE

Review the major theoretical contributions or findings of these people.

Robert Bellah: Bellah created the term "civil religion" to refer to a religion that is so firmly established within a society that social institutions become sanctified by being associated with God.

Emile Durkheim: Durkheim investigated world religions and identified elements that are common to all religions--separation of sacred from profane, beliefs about what is sacred, practices surrounding the sacred, and a moral community.

John Hostetler: Hostetler is known for his research and writings on the Amish.

Benton Johnson: Johnson analyzed types of religious groups--cults, sects, churches, and ecclesia.

William Kephart and William Zellner: These sociologists also investigated the Amish religion and way of life.

Karl Marx: Marx was critical of religion, calling it the opium of the masses.

Richard Niebuhr: This theologian suggested that the splintering of Christianity into numerous branches has more to do with social change than with religious conflict.

Liston Pope: Another sociologist who studied types of religious groups.

Ian Robertson: Robertson noted that there is a fundamental distinction between a religion and its functional equivalent--unlike the latter, the activities of a religion are directed toward God, gods, or some supernatural.

Ernst Troeltsch: Yet another sociologist who is associated with types of religious groups from cults to eccelsia.

Max Weber: Weber studied the link between Protestantism and the rise of capitalism and found that the ethic associated with Protestant denominations was compatible with the early needs of capitalism.

☞ "DOWN-TO-EARTH SOCIOLOGY"

This is your opportunity to apply the sociological perspective to the world around you. The questions in this section refer to material introduced in this chapter of your text. Many ask you to think about ideas and information presented in the various special "boxes" that are located throughout this chapter.

1. What are the main reasons why Islam is growing so rapidly in the United States (p. 519)? What does it offer to African Americans who convert? Why do the mainstream African-American Christian churches feel it necessary to launch a counterattack at the Muslim groups that are attracting members away from them?

2. After reading this chapter, and particularly the box on Heaven's Gate (p. 522), do you understand why some people are attracted to cults and willing to give their lives for them? Why do you think cults rise up at certain points in history--like the 1970s and the 1990s? What is going on in society that would make them especially attractive?

3. What evidence does the author provide to support his argument that David Koresh and the Branch Dividians were destroyed because they were considered a threat to society (pp. 525-526)? Do you feel that the government was justified in reacting the way that it did? Why or why not? Do you think there will be more Wacos in the future? Why or why not?

4. Were you aware of the Christian Motorcyclists Association before reading "Bikers and Bibles" on page 532? Do you find bikers and Bibles to be an unusual combination? Why or why not?

☞ SELF-TEST

After completing this self-test, check your answers against the Answer Key beginning on page 399 of this Study Guide and against the text on page(s) indicated in parentheses.

MULTIPLE CHOICE QUESTIONS

1. What was Durkheim's purpose in writing *The Elementary Forms of the Religious Life*? (508)
    a.   He wanted to explain the development of Protestantism.
    b.   He set out to chart the history of world religions.
    c.   He wanted to study the development of religion from sect to church.
    d.   He wanted to identify elements common to all religions.

2. According to Durkheim, a church: (508)
    a.   is a large, highly organized religious group.
    b.   has little emphasis on personal conversion.
    c.   is a group of believers with a set of beliefs and practices regarding the sacred.
    d.   All of the above.

3. All of the following are functions of religion, except: (509-510)
    a.   encouraging wars for holy causes.
    b.   support for the government.
    c.   social change.
    d.   social control.

4. War and religious persecution are: (510)
    a.   manifest functions of religion.
    b.   latent functions of religion.
    c.   dysfunctions of religion.
    d.   functional equivalents of religion.

5. What are Protestants referring to when they use the term "born again"? (512)
    a.   reincarnation
    b.   Christ's rebirth after his crucifixion
    c.   a personal life-transforming religious experience
    d.   finding salvation in the afterlife

6. Religion is the opium of the people according to some: (513)
    a.   conservatives.
    b.   functionalists.
    c.   conflict theorists.
    d.   symbolic interactionists.

7. An example of the use of religion to legitimize social inequalities is: (514)
    a.   the divine right of kings.
    b.   a declaration that the Pharaoh or Emperor is god or divine.
    c.   the defense of slavery as being God's will.
    d.   All of the above.

8.   Weber believed that religion held the key to: (514)
    a.   modernization.
    b.   bureaucratization.
    c.   institutionalization.
    d.   socialization.

9.   The spirit of capitalism is: (515)
    a.   the desire to accumulate capital so one can spend it to show how one "has it made."
    b.   Marx's term for the driving force in the exploitation of workers.
    c.   the ideal of a highly moral life, hard work, industriousness, and frugality.
    d.   None of the above.

10.   Polytheism is the belief: (516)
    a.   that God is a woman.
    b.   that there is only one God.
    c.   that there are many gods.
    d.   that God does not exist.

11.   The belief that all objects in the world have spirits is: (516)
    a.   a central belief of Islam.
    b.   referred to as animism.
    c.   no longer accepted by people around the world.
    d.   the same as monotheism.

12.   What was an unanticipated outcome of the Reformation? (517)
    a.   the splintering of Christianity
    b.   the reunification of the Catholic Church
    c.   the elimination of corruption in the Church
    d.   the downgrading of women's status in the Church hierarchy

13.   Which branch of Islam is more conservative and inclined to fundamentalism? (518)
    a.   orthodox
    b.   Sunni
    c.   Shi'ite
    d.   black Muslim

14.   The religion with no specific founder is: (519)
    a.   Islam.
    b.   Hinduism.
    c.   Buddhism.
    d.   Confucianism.

15.   Reincarnation: (520)
    a.   is found only in Buddhism.
    b.   is the return of the soul after death in the same form.
    c.   is the return of the soul after death in a different form.
    d.   None of the above.

16.   A cult: (521)
       a.   is a new religion with few followers.
       b.   has teachings and practices which put it at odds with the dominant culture.
       c.   often is at odds with other religions.
       d.   All of the above.

17.   Although larger than a cult, a _____ still feels substantial hostility from society. (523)
       a.   commune
       b.   ecclesia
       c.   sect
       d.   church

18.   Churches: (523)
       a.   are highly bureaucratized.
       b.   have more sedate worship services.
       c.   gain new members from within, from children born to existing members.
       d.   All of the above.

19.   Which type of religious organization is never engaged in the recruitment of new members? (523)
       a.   cult
       b.   sect
       c.   church
       d.   ecclesia

20.   A "brand name" within a major religion is a(n): (524)
       a.   denomination.
       b.   faction.
       c.   cult.
       d.   sect.

21.   Church membership is highest in: (527)
       a.   the South and Midwest.
       b.   the Midwest and the West.
       c.   the Northeast.
       d.   the Northwest.

22.   Which of the following is not a feature of religious groups in the United States? (528)
       a.   diversity of beliefs
       b.   competition for members
       c.   intolerance of differences
       d.   commitment to beliefs

23.   Secularization of religion occurs as a result of: (531)
       a.   industrialization.
       b.   urbanization.
       c.   mass education.
       d.   All of the above.

24.   That religion has less impact on public affairs in the U.S. today is an example of: (531)
        a.   secularization of religion.
        b.   secularization of culture.
        c.   a civil religion.
        d.   an ecclesia.

25.   Questions that science cannot answer include: (534)
        a.   Is there a God?
        b.   What is the purpose of life?
        c.   What happens when a person dies?
        d.   All of the above.

TRUE-FALSE QUESTIONS

T F   1.   The goal of the sociological study of religion is to determine which religions are most effective in peoples' lives. (508)
T F   2.   According to Durkheim, all religions separate the sacred from the profane. (508)
T F   3.   Functionalists believe that religion is universal because it meets basic human needs. (509)
T F   4.   According to Robert Bellah, state religion and civil religion are the same thing. (510)
T F   5.   The Crusades are an example of the dysfunctions of religion. (511)
T F   6.   Being born again is a term frequently used to describe reincarnation by Hindus and Buddhists. (512)
T F   7.   Karl Marx believed that religion is the opium of the people. (513)
T F   8.   Conflict theorists believe that religion mirrors and legitimates social inequalities of the larger society. (514)
T F   9.   Emile Durkheim wrote *The Protestant Ethic and the Spirit of Capitalism*. (514)
T F   10.   Contemporary Judaism in the United States comprises two main branches. (516)
T F   11.   Fundamentalism is the belief that modernism threatens religion and that the faith as it was originally practiced should be restored. (518)
T F   12.   Some Hindu practices have been modified as a consequence of social protest. (520)
T F   13.   The basic moral principle of Confucianism is to maintain sympathy or concern for other humans. (521)
T F   14.   Cults often begin with the appearance of a charismatic leader. (522)
T F   15.   Unlike cults, sects do not stress evangelism. (523)
T F   16.   Islam in Iran and Iraq is an example of ecclesia. (524)
T F   17.   The Amish never mingle with non-Amish. (525)
T F   18.   Many religions around the world are associated with race and ethnicity. (527)
T F   19.   Many local ministers are very supportive of the electronic church because they are happy to see people who do not attend church hear religious messages. (529)
T F   20.   Secularization of religion leads to a splintering of religious groups because some see it as a desertion of the group's fundamental beliefs. (531)

FILL-IN QUESTIONS

1.   Durkheim's term for common elements of everyday life was _____. (508)
2.   Answering questions about ultimate meaning, providing emotional comfort, and social solidarity are _____ of religion. (510)

3. _____ is a substitute that serves the same functions as religion. (512)
4. For Muslims, the crescent moon and star, for Jews the Star of David, and for Christians the cross, all are examples of _____. (512)
5. _____ is teachings or ideas that provide a unified picture of the world. (512)
6. According to conflict theorists, religion is the _____. (513)
7. _____ is Weber's term to describe the ideal of a highly moral life, hard work, industriousness, and frugality. (515)
8. The belief that there is only one God is _____. (516)
9. The belief that all objects in the world have spirits, many of which are dangerous and must be outwitted is _____. (516)
10. _____ is the belief that true religion is threatened by modernism and that the faith as it originally was practiced should be restored. (518)
11. A(n) _____ is someone who exerts extraordinary appeal to a group of followers. (522)
12. A group larger than a cult that still feels substantial hostility from and toward society is a(n) _____. (523)
13. A(n) _____ is a religious group so integrated into the dominant culture that it is difficult to tell where the one begins and the other leaves off. (523)
14. _____ means belonging to the world and its affairs. (530)
15. _____ is the replacement of a religion's "otherworldly" concerns with concerns about "this world." (531)

MATCH THESE SOCIAL SCIENTISTS WITH THEIR CONTRIBUTIONS

___ 1. Emile Durkheim	a.	*The Protestant Ethic and the Spirit of Capitalism*
___ 2. Robert Bellah	b.	*"religion is the opium of the people"*
___ 3. Max Weber	c.	*The Elementary Forms of Religious Life*
___ 4. John Hostetler	d.	*"civil religion"*
___ 5. Ernst Troeltsch	e.	*studied "shunning"*
___ 6. Karl Marx	f.	*cult-sect-church-ecclesia typology*

ESSAY QUESTIONS

1. Assume that you have been asked to make a presentation about religion to a group of people who have absolutely no idea what religion is. Prepare a speech in which you define religion and explain why it exists.

2. Discuss the process by which a religion matures from a cult into a church.

3. Discuss whether or not secularization is inevitable.

CHAPTER 19
MEDICINE

☞ CHAPTER SUMMARY

- Sociologists study medicine as a social institution; three of the primary characteristics of medicine as it is practiced in the U.S. are professionalization, bureaucracy, and the profit motive.

- The symbolic interactionists view health and illness as intimately related to cultural beliefs and practices; definitions of illness vary from one group to the next. The functionalists study the sick role and the ways in which the rules governing this role excuse people from normal responsibilities but obligates them to get well in order to resume those responsibilities. The conflict perspective stresses that health care is one of the scarce resources over which groups compete.

- Americans are healthier than their ancestors were; today's top ten killers did not even show up on the 1900 top ten list.

- Medicine in the United States has become a commodity, developing into the U.S.'s largest business enterprise; it is a two-tier system in which the poor receive inferior health care.

- Current issues in medical and health care include defensive medicine, depersonalization, incompetency, conflicts of interest, medical fraud, sexism, and the controversy about death, including the right to die. Health maintenance organizations (HMOs), diagnosis-related groups, and procedures instituted by insurance companies are measures taken to reduce costs. National health insurance has also been proposed.

- Major threats to health today include AIDS, smoking, alcohol abuse, disabling environments, and unethical experiments.

- Alternatives to the current health-care system include individuals taking more responsibility for their health and a fundamental shift in the medical establishment toward "wellness" and preventive medicine. Change, if it comes, is likely to be slow.

☞ LEARNING OBJECTIVES

As you read Chapter 19, use these learning objectives to organize your notes. After completing your reading, briefly state an answer to each of the objectives, and review the text pages in parentheses.

1.   Define the sociological perspective in studying medicine. (540)
2.   Discuss the symbolic interactionist perspective on the role of culture in defining health and illness, and explain the four components of health. (540-541)
3.   Identify the functionalist perspective on the purpose of the sick role and explain why everyone is not given the same right to claim this role. (541-542)
4.   Consider the conflict perspective on consequences of global stratification of health and how doctors established a medical monopoly. (542-546)
5.   Answer the question, "Were Americans healthier in the past?" (546-547)
6.   Outline and briefly explain the major issues in U.S. health and health care. (547-554)
7.   Discuss the various attempts to reduce the high cost of health care, including HMOs, national health insurance and rationing medical care. (555-556)
8.   Discuss these threats to health: AIDS, drugs, disabling environments, and misguided experiments. (557-564)

9.   Analyze the prospects for change in medicine which might be possible through preventive medicine. (564-565)
10.   Discuss the delivery of health care in other nations. (565-566)

CHAPTER OUTLINE

I.   **Sociology and the Study of Medicine**
      A.   Medicine is a society's standard way of dealing with illness and injury. U.S. medicine is a profession, a bureaucracy, and a big business.
      B.   Sociologists study how medicine is influenced by ideals of professional self-regulation, the bureaucratic structure, and the profit motive; they also are interested in how illness and health are related to cultural beliefs, lifestyle, and social class.

II.   **The Symbolic Interactionist Perspective**
      A.   Health is affected by cultural beliefs. In Western culture a person who hears voices and sees visions might be locked up; in a tribal society, such an individual might be a shaman, the healing specialist who attempts to control the spirits thought to cause a disease or injury.
      B.   Health is a human condition measured by four components: physical, mental, social, and spiritual. What makes someone healthy varies from culture to culture. Sociologists analyze the effects that people's ideas of health and illness have on their lives and even how people determine that they are sick.

III. **The Functionalist Perspective**
      A.   Functionalists point out that societies must set up ways to control sickness. They develop a system of medical care as well as make rules to keep too many people from "being sick."
      B.   The sick role is a social role that you are forced to play when you are not well.
            1.   It has four elements--you are not held responsible for being sick, you are exempt from normal responsibilities, you don't like the role, and you will get help so you can return to your usual routines. People who don't seek competent help are considered responsible for being sick and cannot claim sympathy from others.
            2.   Often there is ambiguity between the well role and the sick role because most situations are not as clear-cut as having a heart attack. A decision to claim the sick role typically is more of a social than a physical matter.
            3.   Parents and physicians are the primary gatekeepers, mediating between children's feelings of illness and the right to be released from responsibilities.
            4.   Gender is a significant factor in determining reactions to a worker's claim to the sick role. Social groups define the conditions under which people are "allowed" to be sick and legitimately excused from ordinary responsibilities.

IV.   **The Conflict Perspective**
      A.   The primary focus of conflict theorists is the struggle over scarce resources, including medical treatment.
      B.   One consequence of global domination by the Most Industrialized Nations is the international stratification of medical care.
            1.   The Least Industrialized Nations cannot afford the same lifesaving technology available in highly industrialized nations. Differences in life expectancy and infant mortality rates illustrate the consequences of global stratification.
            2.   Global stratification even changes the face of diseases. People living in the Least

Industrialized Nations located in the tropics face illness and death from four major sources: malaria, internal parasites, diarrhea, and malnutrition. People in the Most Industrialized Nations live longer, with the consequence that they face "luxury" diseases such as heart disease and cancer.

3. Many diseases that ravage populations of poor countries are controllable; the problem is having the funds to spend on public health. Generally the money is spent by members of the elite on themselves.

C. In order to understand how medicine grew into the largest business in the U.S., it is necessary to understand how medicine became professionalized.

1. In the 1700s, a person learned to be a physician by becoming an apprentice or simply hanging out a shingle to proclaim that he was a physician. During the 1800s, a few medical schools opened and there was some licensing.

2. In 1906 the American Medical Association examined the 160 medical schools in the United States and found only 82 acceptable. In 1910 the Carnegie Foundation funded Abraham Flexner to visit every medical school and make recommendations for change.

3. The Flexner Report resulted in the professionalization of medicine--the development of medicine into a field in which physicians undergo a rigorous education, claim an understanding of illness, regulate themselves, assert that they are performing a service for society, and take authority over clients.

4. Laws restricted medical licenses to graduates of approved schools; only graduates of these schools were eligible to be faculty members who trained the next generation of physicians. This select group of physicians gained control over U.S. medicine and set itself up as the medical establishment, taking control of medicine and either refusing to admit women and minorities to medical schools or placing severe enrollment limits on them.

5. U.S. medicine always had a fee-for-service approach, but now it came under the physicians' control, who set their own fees and had no competition. Although the poor received services from some physicians and hospitals, many remained without medical care.

6. The medical establishment fought all proposals for government-funded medical treatment, including Medicare (government-sponsored medical insurance for the elderly) and Medicaid (government-paid medical care for the poor), until the physicians saw how lucrative these payments could be.

7. The medical establishment consists not only of physicians, but also of nurses, hospital personnel, pharmaceutical companies, druggists, manufacturers of medical technology, and corporations that own hospitals.

V. **Historical Patterns of Health**

A. Epidemiology is the study of the distribution of medical disorders throughout a population; it provides answers about patterns of health and illness over time.

B. There are different ways of determining the current state of physical health in the United States.

1. One way is to compare leading causes of death in 1900 to the present period. Five of the top ten causes of death in 1900 aren't even on the list today. Today's top two killers -- heart disease and cancer -- ranked 4th and 8th in 1900.

2. Are Americans healthier today? If being healthier is measured by life span, then Americans are healthier than their ancestors.

C.   When it comes to mental health, no rational basis for comparisons exists. Perhaps there were fewer mental health problems in the past; however, it is also possible that there is greater mental health today than in the past.

VI.   **Issues in Health Care**

A.   A primary controversy in the U.S. is whether medical care is a right or a privilege. If it's a right, then all should have fairly equal access to it; if it's a privilege, then the rich will have access to one type of care and the poor another.

        1.   Today the average person living in the U.S. spends $4,000 a year on health care, as compared to spending $150 a year in 1960.

        2.   Factors contributing to the increase in medical costs are the growing elderly population and the new, expensive technology.

        3.   With health care considered a commodity, the result is a two-tier system of medical care--superior care for those who can afford the cost, and inferior care for those who cannot.

B.   Social class affects the incidence of illnesses and the quality of treatment.

        1.   The lower the social class, the higher the proportion of serious mental problems. As compared with middle- and upper-class Americans, the poor have less job security, lower wages, more unpaid bills and insistent bill collectors, more divorce, greater vulnerability to crime, more alcoholism, etc. Such conditions deal severe blows to their emotional well-being.

        2.   During the 1960s, a policy of deinstitutionalization was followed; patients (primarily poor) in state mental hospitals were released. The plan was to provide community-based services, but these services were never put in place.

        3.   Social inequalities also mark the treatment of mental problems. Private mental hospitals serve the wealthy (and those who have good insurance) while state hospitals are reserved for the poor. The rich are more likely to be treated with various forms of psychotherapy, the poor with medication.

        4.   In general, few poor people have a personal physician and often wait in crowded public health clinics to receive care. When hospitalized, the poor are often in understaffed/underfunded public hospitals, treated by rotation interns who do not know them and cannot follow up on their progress.

C.   Prior to this century, doctors had four main treatments (purging, bleeding, blistering, and vomiting); today, science and technology have made advances, diagnoses are more accurate, and treatments are more effective.

        1.   At the same time, the number of malpractice suits has risen; patients hold doctors to a higher standard and are quick to sue if there is a mistake.

        2.   Physicians practice defensive medicine--seeking consultations with colleagues and ordering additional lab tests--simply because a patient may sue. Defensive medicine greatly increases the cost of medicine.

D.   While medical mistakes are not everyday occurrences, they do happen.

        1.   The Institute of Medicine, a branch of the National Academy of Sciences, reports that each year between 44,000 and 98,000 Americans die at the hands of doctors.

        2.   There are various suggestions for reducing the number of needless deaths. The Institute of Medicine has recommended establishing a federal Center for Patient Safety to investigate medical injuries and deaths.

E.   Depersonalization is the practice of dealing with people as though they were cases and diseases, not individuals.

1. Many patients get the impression that they are trapped by a cash machine--the physician watches the clock and calculates dollars while talking to the patient.

2. Although students begin medical school wanting to "treat the whole person," as they progress through school, their feelings for patients are overpowered by the need to be efficient.

F. Physicians may encounter conflicts of interest in prescribing medications, referring patients to hospitals, pharmacies, or medical supply companies when they have a financial stake in the prescribed course of treatment.

G. Because of the high volume of health insurance claims that are filed on a daily basis (2 million Medicare claims daily), a large number of physicians, as well as billing companies and medical providers and suppliers, make fraudulent claims, engaging in medical fraud.

H. Medicine is not immune to sexism; there is evidence that women and men are treated differently by the medical establishment.

1. Physicians don't take women's health complaints as seriously as they do men's.

2. Women may receive unnecessary surgery, such as total hysterectomy, as some male doctors work hard to "sell" the operation in order to make money.

3. Male dominance of medicine in the United States underlies this sexism (only 25% of U.S. physicians are women). Today, women earn 41% of all U.S. medical degrees.

I. Medicalization is the transformation of something into a matter to be treated by physicians. Examples include balding, weight, wrinkles, small breasts, and insomnia--yet, there is nothing inherently medical in such conditions.

1. Symbolic interactionists stress that medicalization is based on arbitrary definitions, part of a view of life that is bound to a specific historical period.

2. Functionalists would stress how the medicalization of such issues is functional for the medical establishment, as well as for patients who have someone to listen to their problems and who are sometimes helped.

3. Conflict sociologists assert that this process is another indication of the growing power of the medical establishment, and that as physicians medicalize more aspects of life, their power and profits increase.

J. With modern technology, machines can perform most bodily functions even when the person's mind no longer works; this has created the question "Who has the right to pull the plug?"

1. Some people believe that physicians should practice euthanasia--mercy killing--and help patients die if they request death to relieve insufferable pain or to escape from an incurable disease ("assisted suicide"). Others believe that this should never occur, or that euthanasia should be allowed only in specific circumstances.

2. A living will (that people in good health sign to make clear what they wish medical personnel to do should they become dependent on artificial life-support systems) is an attempt to deal with this issue.

K. Medical costs in the U.S. have risen at about twice the rate of inflation. There are attempts today to curb costs.

1. Health maintenance organizations (HMOs) represent a recent attempt to contain medical costs. HMOs are based on paying a predetermined fee to physicians to take care of the medical needs of employees. Although this arrangement may eliminate unnecessary procedures, it also creates pressures to reduce necessary medical treatment.

2.   The federal government has classified all illnesses into 468 diagnostic-related groups and set the reimbursement amount for each. Hospitals make a profit only if they move patients through the system quickly. Although the average hospital stay has dropped, some patients are discharged before being fully ready to go home, and others are refused admittance because they might cost the hospital money instead of making it a profit.

3.   One consequence of the desire to turn a profit on patient care is the practice of dumping--sending unprofitable patients to public hospitals. With 43 million primarily poor Americans uninsured, pressure has grown for a national health insurance plan. Those in favor of national health care cite the social inequalities of medicine and the inadequacy of health care for the poor. Those opposed to national health insurance point to administrative concerns such as the vast amount of red tape that would be required.

4.   The most controversial suggestion is to ration medical care.

VI.   **Threats to Health**

A.   AIDS (Acquired Immune Deficiency Syndrome) is probably the most pressing health issue in the U.S. and around the world. Since 1981, more than 700,000 Americans have been diagnosed with AIDS; globally, 35 million have the disease.

1.   Its exact origin is unknown.

2.   It is transmitted through sexual contact as well as through transfusions of contaminated blood.

3.   AIDS is now the fourth leading cause of death among U.S. women aged 25-44 and the second leading cause of death for U.S. men in that age group. The risks vary by race and ethnicity; this is due to factors such as rates of intravenous drug use and the use of condoms, not to any genetic factors.

4.   One of the most significant sociological aspects of AIDS is the stigma, which contributes to its spreading because people are afraid to be tested and stigmatized.

5.   Drugs have been found to slow the progress of AIDS, but there is no cure.

B.   With the vast increase in global travel, diseases have become globalized. The concern today is that antibiotics are largely ineffective against many new diseases. Drug-resistant tuberculosis (TB) is an example.

C.   Alcohol and tobacco are the most frequently used drugs in the United States.

1.   Alcohol is the standard recreational drug in the United States. The average drinker in the U.S. consumes about 36 gallons of alcoholic beverages per year. Underage drinking is common, with drinking alcohol directly related to grades.

2.   Of all drugs, nicotine is the most harmful to health. Smoking increases a person's risk of heart attack and causes progressive emphysema and several types of cancer. People continue to smoke despite harmful health effects for two major reasons: addiction and advertising.

D.   A disabling environment is one that is harmful to health.

1.   Some occupations have high health risks which are evident (e.g., mining, riding bulls in a rodeo, etc.). In others, the risk becomes evident only years after people have worked at what they thought was a safe occupation (e.g., laborers who worked with asbestos).

2.   Industrialization not only increased the world's standard of living, but it has also led to the greenhouse effect--a warming of the earth that may change the globe's climate, melt its polar ice caps, and flood the earth's coastal shores. Use of

fluorocarbon gases is threatening the ozone shield (the protective layer of the earth's upper stratosphere that screens out a high proportion of the sun's ultraviolet rays). In humans, this high-intensity ultraviolet radiation causes skin cancer.

E. At times, physicians and government officials have carried out research that has jeopardized the health and welfare of the individuals they are sworn to protect.

    1. One example of such research is the Tuskegee Syphilis Experiment. In this experiment, 399 African-American men suffering from syphilis were left untreated for 40 years so that the Public Health Service could observe what happened.

    2. During the Cold War, the U.S. government conducted radiation experiments in which soldiers were ordered to march through an area just after an atomic bomb had been detonated. The purpose of this research was to determine if individuals could withstand fallout without any radiation equipment.

    3. Those in official positions, in some instances, believe that they can play God and determine who shall live and who shall die. The most expendable citizens, and therefore the ones who serve as subjects in such research, are the poor and the powerless. In order to protect ourselves against such gross abuse of professional positions, such research must be publicized and those who direct and carry out such experiments must be vigorously prosecuted.

VII. **The Search for Alternatives**

A. Values and lifestyles have a major impact on health.

    1. Within the same society, subcultural patterns and lifestyles produce specific patterns of health and illness. For example, although Nevada and Utah are adjacent states with similar levels of income, education, medical care, etc., the death rate is much higher in Nevada. This is because Utah is inhabited mostly by Mormons, who encourage conservative living and disapprove of the consumption of tobacco, alcohol, and caffeine.

    2. Many of the threats to health are preventable. Individuals can exercise regularly, eat nutritious food, maintain sexual monogamy, and avoid smoking and alcohol abuse in order to prevent disease.

    3. Instead of treatment, the U.S. medical establishment should have "wellness" as its goal. To achieve such a goal the medical establishment must make a fundamental change in its philosophy and the public must accept the benefits of "wellness".

    4. On a broader scale, there needs to be a systematic attempt to eliminate disabling environments and the use of harmful drugs.

B. The search for alternatives leads to an examination of health care in other nations.

    1. Sweden has the most comprehensive health care system in the world, with all citizens and alien residents covered by health insurance financed by contributions from the state and employers. At the same time, it is very expensive and very inefficient.

    2. In post-Soviet Russia the government owns all the health care facilities, all equipment, and determines how many students will attend the state-owned and operated medical schools. The physicians are not well trained and the overall health of the nation has been declining. Supplies and equipment are in short supply. Health care is free, but there are no choices in terms of physicians or facilities used.

    3. Most Chinese see "barefoot doctors," people with a rudimentary knowledge of

medicine. Chinese medicine relies on medicinal herbs and acupuncture. Today a system of private medical clinics is also developing. Bribery of medical personnel has become routine.

☞ KEY TERMS

After studying the chapter, review the definition for each of the following terms.

defensive medicine: medical practices done not for the patient's benefit but in order to protect a physician from malpractice suits

deinstitutionalization: the release of patients from mental hospitals into the community while receiving treatment within a network of outpatient services

depersonalization: dealing with people as though they were objects; in the case of medical care, as though patients were merely cases and diseases, not persons

disabling environment: an environment that is harmful to health

dumping: the practice of sending unprofitable patients to public hospitals

epidemiology: the study of disease and disability patterns in a population

euthanasia: mercy killing

fee for service: payment to a physician to diagnose and treat the patient's medical problems

health: a human condition measured by four components: physical, mental, social, and spiritual

health maintenance organization (HMO): a health care organization that provides medical treatment to its members for a fixed annual cost

living will: a statement people in good health sign that clearly expresses their feelings about being kept alive on artificial life support systems

medicalization: the transformation of something into a matter to be treated by physicians

medicine: one of the major social institutions that sociologists study; a society's organized ways of dealing with sickness and injury

professionalization of medicine: the development of medicine into a field in which education becomes rigorous, and in which physicians claim a theoretical understanding of illness, regulate themselves, claim to be doing a service to society (rather than just following self-interest), and take authority over clients

shaman: the healing specialist of a preliterate tribe who attempts to control the spirits thought to cause a disease or injury; commonly called a witch doctor

sick role: a social role that excuses people from normal obligations because they are sick or injured, while at the same time expecting them to seek competent help and cooperate in getting well

☞ KEY PEOPLE

Review the major theoretical contributions or findings of these people.

Sue Fisher: Fisher did participant observation in a hospital where she discovered doctors recommending total hysterectomies even when no cancer was present, because they were "potentially disease-producing" organs that were no longer needed once a woman had passed her child-bearing years.

Erich Goode: This sociologist compared the health of smokers and nonsmokers and found that smokers are three times as likely to die before reaching age 65.

Jack Haas and William Shaffir: These sociologists did a participant observation of medical students and discovered that over the course of medical school their attitudes change from wanting to "treat the whole person" to needing to be efficient in treating the specific ailment.

Elizabeth Klonoff and Hope Landrine: These researchers found that women are more willing to claim the sick role when they don't feel well; their explanation for this finding is that women experience less role conflict when they claim the sick role because they are less likely to be employed, and women had been socialized for greater dependency and self-disclosure.

Talcott Parsons: Parsons was the first sociologist to analyze the sick role, pointing out that it has four elements--not being responsible for your sickness, being exempt from normal responsibilities, not liking the role, and seeking competent help in order to return to daily routines.

Diana Scully: Scully interviewed medical residents about their attitudes towards surgical procedures involving women's reproductive organs and found that doctors try to "sell" women on the procedure, not because women need it, but because the doctors want to make money.

Leonard Stein: This physician analyzed doctor-nurse interactions in terms of a game in which the nurse (lower-status role) disguises her recommendations about patient care to the doctor (higher-status role).

☞ "DOWN-TO-EARTH SOCIOLOGY"

This is your opportunity to apply the sociological perspective to the world around you. The questions in this section refer to material introduced in this chapter of your text. Many ask you to think about ideas and information presented in the various special "boxes" that are located throughout this chapter.

1.   After reading about the elimination of midwives on page 545, why do you think the struggle is still going on between nurse-midwives and physicians about who has the right to deliver babies? Why did redefining childbirth as "men's work," make the prestige and the price go up? Do you think that the increased involvement of nurse-midwives in the labor and delivery process is seen as one way to reduce medical costs? Why or why not?

2.   Do you think "The Doctor-Nurse Game" on page 52 is an accurate description of the relationship between most doctors and nurses today? If nurses spend more time with patients, why are they not in charge of determining what care the patients should receive? What function is served by this "game" that goes on between doctors and nurses?

3.   Would you use the Internet to obtain prescription drugs (p. 553)? What are some of the advantages of this arrangement? What are some of the drawbacks? Is there any way the government could better regulate such transactions?

4.   After reading about euthanasia on page 554, what do you think about this subject? Do you agree? Do you think people have the right to decide when to die? Should doctors be able to assist them in this? Can you see a way this could be organized so that patients have rights and doctors are protected?

5.   What criteria do you think our society should use in providing access to new medical technologies (p. 557)? How would a conflict theorist answer this question? How would a functionalist?

6.   Given the descriptions of the quality of health care in other countries that is provided by "Health Care in Sweden, Russia and China," on pages 566-567, determine in which country you would like to receive medical care if you were critically ill. What are some of the advantages and disadvantages of each system?

☞ SELF-TEST

After completing this self-test, check your answers against the Answer Key beginning on page 402 of this Study Guide and against the text on page(s) indicated in parentheses.

MULTIPLE CHOICE QUESTIONS

1.   Sociologists focus on medicine as: (540)
    a.   a profession.
    b.   a bureaucracy.
    c.   a business.
    d.   All of the above.

2.   A _____ is the healing specialist of a preliterate tribe who tries to control the spirits thought to cause a disease or injury. (540)
    a.   soothsayer.
    b.   high priest.
    c.   shaman.
    d.   medicine man.

3.   Which of the following is not one of the components of health? (540-541)
    a.   physical
    b.   social
    c.   spiritual
    d.   hereditary

4.   How would a sick or injured person who can't fulfill normal role obligations be described? (541)
    a.   a hypochondriac
    b.   in the sick role
    c.   deviant
    d.   All of the above

5.   The individual's claim to the sick role is legitimized primarily by: (541)
    a.   demonstrating to others that he or she is ill.
    b.   a doctor's excuse.
    c.   employers, teachers, and sometimes parents.
    d.   other workers or students who vouch for the fact that the individual is ill.

6.   Why are women more likely than men to claim the sick role when they feel poorly? (542)
    a.   They are generally not as healthy as men.
    b.   They have more reasons to see a doctor than men, because of reproductive problems.
    c.   They are socialized for greater dependency and self-disclosure.
    d.   All of the above are true.

7. Professionalization of medicine includes: (544)
    a. rigorous education.
    b. a theoretical understanding of illness.
    c. self-regulation.
    d. All of the above.

8. Government-paid health care for the poor is: (546)
    a. Medicaid.
    b. Medicare.
    c. Medical welfare.
    d. None of the above.

9. In the United States, medicine: (547)
    a. is socialized.
    b. is a commodity.
    c. is a right.
    d. All of the above.

10. Today, the average American spends _____ a year on health care. (547)
    a. $150
    b. $1100
    c. $4000
    d. $5000

11. Which of the following statements about depersonalization is <u>incorrect</u>? (550)
    a. It is less common today because of all the reforms brought about by HMOs.
    b. It is the practice of dealing with people as though they were objects.
    c. It means treating patients as though they were merely cases and diseases.
    d. It occurs when an individual is treated as if he or she was not a person.

12. _____ is the transformation of something into a matter to be treated by physicians. (552)
    a. Sexism in medicine
    b. Medicalization of society
    c. Monopolization of medicine
    d. Holistic medicine

13. Which of these is <u>not</u> a reason why U.S. medical costs have risen dramatically? (555)
    a. Tests are performed for defensive rather than medical reasons.
    b. The size of the elderly population has increased.
    c. People want doctors to do unnecessary tests to assure themselves they are healthy.
    d. Health care is seen as a commodity.

14. Sending unprofitable patients to public hospitals is known as: (556)
    a. turfing.
    b. sidewinding.
    c. dumping.
    d. discarding.

15. AIDS is known to be transmitted by: (558)
   a.   casual contact between a carrier and a non-carrier in which bodily fluids are exchanged.
   b.   exchange of blood and/or semen.
   c.   airborne passage of the virus from carrier to non-carrier through coughing or sneezing.
   d.   All of the above.

16. Which racial and/or ethnic groups are at greater risk of contracting AIDS? (559-560)
   a.   Whites and Native Americans
   b.   African Americans and Latinos
   c.   Asian Americans and Latinos
   d.   African Americans and Asian Americans

17. A cure for AIDS: (559-560)
   a.   has been found with drugs.
   b.   can be found as soon as the one virus which causes AIDS is identified.
   c.   has not been found.
   d.   will never be found because pharmaceutical companies won't pool their research.

18. Why do diseases today have the potential of becoming truly global threats? (560)
   a.   Viruses are stronger than they used to be.
   b.   Medicine is less effective today than in the past.
   c.   There are so many more viruses today than in the past, because of gene mutation.
   d.   Contact between people of different countries has increased due to global travel.

19. Which of the following statements about smoking is incorrect? (562)
   a.   Nicotine may be as addictive as heroin.
   b.   The rate of cigarette smoking continues to climb, despite warnings about the dangers.
   c.   The tobacco industry has a huge advertising budget to encourage people to smoke.
   d.   When compared to nonsmokers, smokers are three times as likely to die before age 65.

20. An environment that is harmful to health is referred to as a(n): (563)
   a.   disabling environment.
   b.   health hazard.
   c.   harmful setting.
   d.   crippling environment.

21. Which of the following statements about the ozone shield is correct? (563)
   a.   It is the warming of the earth that may change the globe's climate.
   b.   It is destroyed by burning of vast amounts of carbon fuels.
   c.   It causes many humans to have skin cancer.
   d.   It is the protective layer of the earth's stratosphere that screens the sun's ultraviolet rays.

22. An example of physicians' and the government's callous disregard of people's health is: (563)
   a.   the delay in providing open heart surgery for women patients.
   b.   the Tuskegee syphilis experiment.
   c.   the failure to curb advertising of tobacco products.
   d.   all of the above.

23. To implement a national policy of "prevention, not intervention" would require: (565)
    a. a fundamental change in the philosophy of the medical establishment.
    b. a change in the public's attitudes towards medicine and health care.
    c. eliminating disabling environments and reducing the use of harmful drugs.
    d. all of the above.

24. Which of the following countries has the lowest infant mortality? (567)
    a. the former Soviet Union
    b. Sweden
    c. Canada
    d. the United States

25. "Barefoot doctors" provide much of the health care to the people of which nation? (566)
    a. China
    b. India
    c. Vietnam
    d. Korea

TRUE-FALSE QUESTIONS

T F 1. Health is a relative matter. (540)

T F 2. People who don't seek competent help when they are sick are just behaving as expected, according to the social definition of the sick role. (541)

T F 3. There is little ambiguity between the well role and the sick role. (541)

T F 4. Everyone is given the same right to claim the sick role. (541)

T F 5. In the Least Industrialized Nations, few people live long enough to get cancer and heart disease. (543)

T F 6. Medical schools have existed since the 1700s in the United States. (544)

T F 7. The Flexner Report had a profound impact on American medicine. (544)

T F 8. The professionalization of medicine led directly to medicine becoming a monopoly. (544)

T F 9. Professionalization of medicine includes self-regulation of physicians. (544)

T F 10. The soaring cost of medical care can be explained by the fact that Americans are sicker than they used to be. (547)

T F 11. There is a two-tier system for the treatment of mental problems that is based upon social class. (547)

T F 12. Conflicts of interest are rarely a serious problem within the medical profession because doctors are trained to put the interests of the patient above their own self-interest. (550)

T F 13. The enormous increase in the number of Medicare claims that are filed on a daily basis has contributed to the increase in medical fraud. (551)

T F 14. Medicine in the United States is male dominated. (551)

T F 15. A functionalist would argue that the medicalization of society reflects the growing power of the medical establishment because the more physicians can medicalize human affairs, the greater their profits and power. (552)

T F 16. There is a lack of consensus about the practice of euthanasia. (553)

T F 17. The most controversial suggestion for reducing medical costs is to adopt national health insurance. (556)

T F 18. Today AIDS is the leading cause of death for U.S. women aged 25 to 44. (559)

T F　19.　In general, people are very aware when they are working in a disabling environment, one that is harmful to their health. (563)

T F　20.　Nevada's overall death rate is 50 percent higher than Utah's, demonstrating the impact of lifestyle on health and illness. (565)

FILL-IN QUESTIONS

1.　The healing specialist of a preliterate tribe who attempts to control the spirits thought to cause a disease or injury is a _____. (540)

2.　_____ is a human condition measured by four components: physical, mental, social, and spiritual. (540)

3.　The _____ is a social role that excuses people from normal obligations because they are sick or injured. (541)

4.　The development of medicine into a field in which education becomes rigorous, and in which physicians claim a theoretical understanding of illness, regulate themselves, claim to be doing a service to society, and take authority over clients is the _____. (544)

5.　In general, the payment to a physician to diagnose and treat a patient's medical problems is based on _____. (546)

6.　The study of disease and disability patterns in a population is _____. (546)

7.　A major sociological characteristic of the American medical system is that medicine is viewed as a _____, not a right. (547)

8.　Seeking consultations with colleagues and ordering additional lab tests simply because a patient may sue is _____. (549)

9.　The fact that women are less likely than men to be given heart surgery, except in the more advanced stages of heart disease, is an example of _____ in medicine. (551)

10.　A(n) _____ is a statement people in good health sign that clearly expresses their feelings about being kept alive on artificial life-support systems. (553)

11.　One response to the high cost of health care is the development of _____, in which companies pay a set fee to a group of physicians to take care of the medical needs of their employees. (555)

12.　In a desire to turn a profit on patient care, some hospitals engage in the practice of _____, sending unprofitable patients to public hospitals. (556)

13.　One of the most significant sociological aspects of AIDS is its _____. (559)

14.　Lumberjacking, riding rodeo bulls, and taming lions are all examples of _____. (563)

15.　The U.S. Public Health Service was responsible for the _____, an example of a misguided and callous medical experiment. (563)

MATCH THESE SOCIAL SCIENTISTS WITH THEIR CONTRIBUTIONS

___1. Talcott Parsons

___2. Erich Goode

___3. Haas/Shaffir

___4. Klonoff/Landrine

___5. Diana Scully

___6. Leonard Stein

a. *compared health of smokers and nonsmokers*

b. *sick role*

c. *transformation of medical students*

d. *sexism in medicine*

e. *gender differences in claims to the sick role*

f. *interaction games played by doctors and nurses*

ESSAY QUESTIONS

1. Describe the elements of the sick role and identify variations in the pattern of claiming this role.

2. Explain the pattern of the worldwide AIDS epidemic and suggest reasons why this treat to the health of the world's population has not been addressed more aggressively.

3. Discuss the obstacles to developing preventive medicine and suggest ways in which these obstacles can be overcome.

CHAPTER 20
POPULATION AND URBANIZATION

☞ CHAPTER SUMMARY

- Demography is the study of the size, composition, growth, and distribution of human populations. Over 200 years ago, Thomas Malthus observed that populations grow geometrically while food supplies increase arithmetically; he argued that the population of the world would eventually outstrip its food supply. The debate between the New Malthusians and the Anti-Malthusians continues today. Starvation is due to a maldistribution of food rather than overpopulation.

- People in the Least Industrialized Nations have large families because children are viewed as gifts from God, it costs little to rear them, and they represent parents' social security. To project population trends, demographers use three demographic variables: fertility, mortality, and migration. A nation's growth rate is also affected by unanticipated variables like wars, famines, and changing economic and political conditions.

- Cities can only develop if there is an agricultural surplus; the primary impetus to the development of cities was the invention of the plow about 5 or 6 thousand years ago. For much of human history cities were small. After the Industrial Revolution cities grew quickly. Urbanization, the process by which an increasing proportion of a population lives in cities, is so extensive today that some cities have become metropolises; in some cases metropolises have merged to form a megalopolis.

- Three major models have been proposed to explain how cities expand: the concentric-zone, sector, and multiple-nuclei models. These models fail to account for medieval cities, as well as many European cities and those in the least industrialized nations.

- Some people find a sense of community in cities; others find alienation. Herbert Gans identified five types of city dwellers: cosmopolites, singles, ethnic villagers, the deprived, and the trapped. To develop community in the city, people personalize their shopping, identify with sports teams, and even become sentimental about objects in the city. An essential element in determining whether someone finds community or alienation in the city is that person's social networks. Noninvolvement is generally functional for urbanites, but it impedes giving help in emergencies.

- The decline of U.S. cities is due to forces such as disinvestment, suburbanization, and deindustrialization. Today the population of most rural counties in the U.S. is growing, as more and more people move away from cities and suburbs. Principles to guide future social policy are scale, livability, and social justice.

☞ LEARNING OBJECTIVES

As you read Chapter 20, use these learning objectives to organize your notes. After completing your reading, briefly state an answer to each of the objectives, and review the text pages in parentheses.

1. Discuss the Malthus theorem and identify key issues in the debate between New Malthusians and Anti-Malthusians regarding the specter of overpopulation. (572-576)
2. Explain why there is starvation. (576-577)
3. Explain why people in the Least Industrialized Nations have so many children and note the implications of different rates of population growth. (577-580)
4. State the three demographic variables used in estimating population growth and explain why it is

difficult to forecast population growth. (580-586)

5.   Describe urbanization and outline the history of how cities came into existence. (587-589)
6.   Identify the trends contributing to the emergence of metropolises and megalopolises. (589)
7.   Discuss urbanization in the U.S. (589-591)
8.   Review the three models of urban growth and critique each of them. (592-594)
9.   Explain why some people living in large urban areas feel a sense of alienation while others find community. (594-597)
10.   Describe the five different types of people who live in the city as identified by sociologist Herbert Gans. (597-598)
11.   Describe ways in which city people create a sense of intimacy for themselves in large urban areas. (598)
12.   Explain why the norm of noninvolvement and the diffusion of responsibility which help urban dwellers get through everyday city life may be dysfunctional in some situations. (598-599)
13.   Outline the major changes facing U.S. cities regarding suburbanization, disinvestment, and deindustrialization. (600-601)
14.   Identify "push" and "pull" factors behind the rural rebound. (601-602)
15.   State the guiding principles for developing solutions to urban problems. (602-603)

☞ CHAPTER OUTLINE

I.   **A Planet with No Space to Enjoy Life?**
        A.   Demography is the study of size, composition, growth, distribution of populations.
        B.   Thomas Malthus wrote *An Essay on the Principle of Population* (1798) stating the Malthus theorem--population grows geometrically while food supply increases arithmetically; thus, if births go unchecked, population will outstrip food supplies.
        C.   New Malthusians believe Malthus was correct. The world population is following an exponential growth curve (where numbers increase in extraordinary proportions): 1800, one billion; 1930, two billion; 1960, three billion; 1975, four billion; 1987, five billion and 1999, six billion.
        D.   Anti-Malthusians believe that the three-stage process of population growth, known as the demographic transition, provides a model for the future.
                1.   They cite the historical experiences of European countries over the last two centuries as an example.
                2.   Stage 1 is characterized by a fairly stable population (high birth rates offset by high death rates); Stage 2, by a "population explosion" (high birth rates and low death rates); and Stage 3, by population stability (low birth rates and low death rates).
                2.   They assert this transition will happen in the Least Industrialized Nations, which currently are in the second stage.
        E.   Who is correct? Only the future will prove the accuracy of either the projections of the New Malthusians or the Anti-Malthusians.
                1.   The Least Industrialized Nations are currently in stage 2 of the demographic transition--their birth rates remain high while the death rates have dropped.
                2.   The New Malthusians say that the populations in these countries will continue to climb, only at a slower rate, while the Anti-Malthusians say that the slow rate is a sign that these nations are beginning to move into stage 3.

3. Population shrinkage (a country's population is smaller because birth rate and immigration cannot replace those who die and emigrate) is now occurring in 65 nations, suggesting a fourth stage to the demographic transition.

F. Why are people starving?

1. Anti-Malthusians note that the amount of food produced for each person in the world has increased: famines are not the result of too little food production, but result from maldistribution of existing food.

2. The New Malthusians counter that the world's population continues to grow and the earth may not be able to continue to produce sufficient food.

3. The New Malthusians advocate reducing the number of people in the world, while the Anti-Malthusians would try to distribute food more equitably.

4. Recently, famines have been concentrated in Africa. However, these famines are not due to too many people living on too little land. Rather, these famines are due to drought, outmoded farming techniques and ongoing political instability that disrupt harvests and food distribution.

II. Population Growth

A. Today, the populations of the Least Industrialized Nations are growing at fifteen times the rate of the Most Industrialized Nations; at these rates, the population of the average Most Industrialized Nation will double in 583 years, while the population of the average Least Industrialized Nation will do so in just 40 years.

B. Three reasons poor nations have so many children are: (1) the status that parenthood provides; (2) the community supports this view; and (3) children are considered to be economic assets (the parents rely on the children to take care of them in their old age).

1. The symbolic interactionist perspective stresses that we need to understand these patterns within the framework of the culture and society in which the behavior occurs.

2. The conflict perspective stresses that in the Least Industrialized Nations, men dominate women in all spheres of life, including that of reproduction. There is an emphasis on male virility and dominance, including the fathering of many children, as a means of achieving status in the community.

C. Demographers use population pyramids (graphic representations of a population, divided into age and sex) to illustrate a country's population dynamics.

1. Different population growth rates have different implications. Countries with rapid growth rates have to cope with increased numbers of people among whom to share resources; this can result in a declining standard of living.

2. A declining standard of living may result in political instability followed by severe repression by the government.

D. Estimated population growth is based on three demographic variables:

1. Fertility, measured by the fertility rate (number of children an average woman bears), is sometimes confused with fecundity (number of children a woman theoretically can bear). To compute a country's fertility rate, demographers use crude birth rate (annual number of births per 1,000 people).

2. Mortality is measured by the crude death rate (number of deaths per 1,000 people).

3. Migration is measured by the net migration rate (difference between the number of immigrants moving in and emigrants moving out per 1,000 population). There are two types: movement between regions within a country and movement

between countries. "Push" factors make people want to leave where they are living (e.g., persecution, lack of economic opportunity); "pull" factors attract people (e.g., opportunities in the new locale).

4. The U.S. admits more immigrants each year than all the other nations of the world combined. There is a debate as to whether immigrants are a net contributor or a drain on our economy.

E. The growth rate equals births minus deaths, plus net migration.

1. Economic changes, government policies, famines and plagues all make it difficult to forecast population growth. The primary unknown factor that influences a country's growth rate is its rate of industrialization--in every country that industrializes, the growth rate declines.

2. Because of the difficulties in forecasting population growth, demographers formulate several predictions simultaneously, each depending on different assumptions. No one anticipates the United States will experience either population shrinkage or zero population growth.

III. The Development of Cities

A. A city is a place in which a large number of people are permanently based and do not produce their own food. Small cities with massive defensive walls existed as far back as 10,000 years ago; cities on a larger scale originated about 3500 B.C. as a result of the development of more efficient agriculture and of a surplus.

B. The Industrial Revolution drew people to cities to work. Today urbanization not only means that more people live in cities, but also that today's cities are larger; today about 300 of the world's cities contain at least one million people.

C. Urbanization is the process by which an increasing proportion of a population lives in cities. There are specific characteristics of cities, such as size and anonymity, that give them their unique urban flavor.

1. Metropolis refers to cities that grow so large that they exert influence over a region; the central city and surrounding smaller cities and suburbs are connected economically, politically, and socially.

2. Megalopolis refers to an overlapping area consisting of at least two metropolises and their suburbs, connected economically, socially, and sometimes politically.

D. In 1790, only about 5 percent of Americans lived in cities; by 1920, 50 percent of the U.S. population lived in urban areas; today, 75-80 percent of Americans live in urban areas.

1. The U.S. Census Bureau divided the country into 284 metropolitan statistical areas (MSAs)--which consist of a central city of at least 50,000 people and the urbanized areas that are linked to it. About 60 percent of the entire U.S. population lives in just 50 or so MSAs.

2. As Americans migrate in search of work and better life styles, a two-way pattern of migration between regions appears. Today ten of the twelve fastest-growing U.S. cities are in the West, the other two are in the South.

3. As Americans migrate and businesses move to serve them, edge cities have developed (a clustering of service facilities and residential areas near highway intersections).

4. Gentrification, the movement of middle-class people into rundown areas of a city, is another major U.S. urban pattern. As a consequence of gentrification, the poor are often displaced from their neighborhoods.

IV. Models of Urban Growth

    A. Robert Park coined the term "human ecology" to describe how people adapt to their environment (known as "urban ecology"); human ecologists have constructed three models that attempt to explain urban growth patterns:

    B. Ernest W. Burgess proposed the concentric-zone model.

        1. The city consists of a series of zones emanating from its center, with each characterized by a different group of people and activity: Zone 1--central business district; Zone 2--in transition with deteriorating housing and rooming houses; Zone 3--an area to which thrifty workers have moved to escape the zone in transition while maintaining access to work; Zone 4--more expensive apartments, single-family dwellings, and exclusive areas where the wealthy live; and Zone 5--commuter zone consisting of suburban areas or satellite cities that have developed around rapid transit routes.

        2. Burgess intended this model to represent the tendency for towns and cities to expand outward from the central business district.

    C. Homer Hoyt proposed the sector model, which sees urban zones as wedge-shaped sectors radiating out from the center.

        1. A zone might contain a sector of working-class housing, another sector of expensive housing, a third of businesses, and so on, all competing with one another for the same land.

        2. In an invasion-succession cycle poor immigrants move into a city, settling in the lowest-rent area available; as their numbers grow, they begin to encroach on adjacent areas. As the poor move closer to the middle class, the middle class leave, expanding the sector of lower-cost housing.

    D. The multiple-nuclei model, developed by Chauncey Harris and Edward Ullman, views the city as comprised of multiple centers or nuclei, each of which focuses on a specialized activity (e.g., retail districts, automobile dealers, etc.).

    E. Chauncey Harris later developed the peripheral model of urban development to account for more recent changes in the use of urban space. In this model, people and services move away from the central city into the periphery; highways radiating out from the center encourage this development along the edges of metropolitan areas.

    F. These models tell only a partial story of how cities are constructed. They reflect both the time frame and geographical region of the cities that were studied. They cannot explain medieval cities, nor cities in other Most Industrialized or Least Industrialized Nations.

V. City Life

    A. Cities provide opportunities but also create problems. Humans have a need for community, which some people have a hard time finding in cities.

    B. Louis Wirth argued that the city undermines kinship and neighborhood, which are the traditional bases of social control and social solidarity.

        1. Urban dwellers live in anonymity, their lives marked by segmented and superficial encounters which make them grow aloof from one another and indifferent to other people's problems.

        2. This is similar to the idea that *Gemeinschaft* (a sense of community that comes from everyone knowing everyone else) is ripped apart as a country industrializes, and *Gesellschaft* (a society characterized by secondary, impersonal relationships which result in alienation) replaces it.

    C. The city can also be viewed as containing a series of smaller worlds, within which people find a sense of community, or belonging.

D.   Herbert Gans identified five types of people who live in the city.

    1.   Cosmopolites--intellectuals and professionals, students, writers, and artists who live in the inner city to be near its conveniences and cultural benefits.

    2.   Singles--young, unmarried people who come seeking jobs and entertainment.

    3.   Ethnic villagers--live in tightly knit neighborhoods that resemble villages and small towns, united by race and social class.

    4.   The deprived--the very poor, the emotionally disturbed, and the handicapped who live in neighborhoods more like urban jungles than urban villages.

    5.   The trapped--who consist of four subtypes: those who could not afford to move when their neighborhood was invaded by another ethnic group; downwardly mobile persons who have fallen from a higher social class; elderly people who have drifted into the slums because they are not wanted elsewhere and are powerless to prevent their downward slide; and alcoholics and drug addicts.

E.   The city is divided into worlds that people come to know down to the smallest detail.

    1.   City people create a sense of intimacy for themselves by personalizing their shopping (by frequenting the same stores and restaurants, people become recognized as "regulars").

    2.   Spectator sports also engender community identification.

F.   Urban dwellers are careful to protect themselves from the unwanted intrusions of strangers.

    1.   They follow a norm of noninvolvement--such as using of a newspaper or a Walkman to indicate inaccessibility for interaction--to avoid encounters with people they do not know.

    2.   The more bystanders there are to an incident, the less likely people are to help because people's sense of responsibility becomes diffused.

    3.   The norm of noninvolvement and the diffusion of responsibility may help urban dwellers get through everyday city life, but they are dysfunctional because people do not provide assistance to others.

VI.   **Urban Problems and Social Policy**

A.   Suburbanization--the movement from the city to the suburbs--has had a profound effect on U.S. cities.

    1.   Although people have moved for over 100 years to towns next to the cities in which they worked, what is new today is the speed and extent to which people have left the city. In 1957, only 37 million Americans lived in the suburbs; today, over half do.

    2.   Central cities have lost residents, businesses, and jobs, causing the cities' tax base (which supports essential city services and schools) to shrink; people left behind are those with limited financial means.

    3.   Suburbanites, preferring that the city keep its problems to itself, fight movements to share suburbia's revenues with the city. However, the time may come when suburbanites may have to pay for their attitudes toward the city.

    4.   As suburbs age, they are becoming mirror images of the city, leading to a spiraling sense of insecurity, more middle-class flight, and a further reduction of property values.

B.   By the 1940's, the movement out of the cities to suburbs began to undermine the cities' tax base.

        1.   As the tax base eroded, services declined, buildings deteriorated, and banks began redlining (drawing a line on a map around problem areas and refusing to make loans for housing and businesses located in these areas). This disinvestment pushed these areas into further decline.

        2.   The development of a global market has led to deindustrialization. Manufacturing firms have relocated from the inner city to areas where production costs are lower. As hundreds of thousands of urban manufacturing jobs were eliminated, inner-city economies were unable to provide alternative employment for poor residents, thereby locking them out of the economy.

C.   In the 1970s, people began to move out of the cities and suburbs into rural areas.

        1.   During the 1990s, seven out of every 10 U.S. rural counties grew in population.

        2.   "Push" factors for this fundamental shift are fears of urban crime and violence. "Pull" factors are safety, lower costs of living, recreation and more space.

        3.   Making this movement possible are improvements in transportation and communications.

D.   Social policy usually takes one of two forms.

        1.   Urban renewal involves tearing down and rebuilding the buildings in an area. As a result of urban renewal, residents can no longer afford to live in the area and are displaced to adjacent areas.

        2.   Enterprise zones are economic incentives to encourage businesses to move into the area. Most businesses, however, refuse to move into high-crime areas.

        3.   If U.S. cities are to change, they must become top agenda items of the U.S. government, with adequate resources in terms of money and human talents focused on overcoming urban woes.

        4.   William Flanagan suggests three guiding principles for working out specific solutions to urban problems: (1) regional and national planning is necessary; (2) growth needs to be channeled in such a way that makes city living attractive; and (3) social policy must be evaluated by its effects on people. Finally, unless the root causes of urban problems--housing, education, and jobs--are addressed, solutions will only serve as band-aids that cover the real problems.

☞ KEY TERMS

After studying the chapter, review the definition for each of the following terms.

basic demographic equation: growth rate=births-deaths+net migration

city: a place in which a large number of people are permanently based and do not produce their own food

community: a place people identify with, where they sense that they belong and that others care what happens to them

crude birth rate: the annual number of live births per 1,000 population

crude death rate: the annual number of deaths per 1,000 population

demographic transition: a three-stage historical process of population growth; first, high birth rates and high death rates; second, high birth rates and low death rates; and third, low birth rates and low death rates; a fourth stage has begun to appear in the Most Industrialized Nations, in which population shrinks because deaths outnumber births

demographic variables: the three factors that influence population growth: fertility, mortality, and net migration

demography: the study of the size, composition, growth, and distribution of human populations

disinvestment: the withdrawal of investments by financial institutions, which seals the fate of an urban area

enterprise zone: the use of economic incentives in a designated area with the intention of encouraging investment there

edge city: a large clustering of service facilities and residential areas near highway intersections that provides a sense of place to people who live, shop, and work there

exponential growth curve: a pattern of growth in which numbers double during approximately equal intervals, thus accelerating in the latter stages

fecundity: the number of children that women are capable of bearing

fertility rate: the number of children that the average woman bears

gentrification: the displacement of the poor by the relatively affluent, who purchase and renovate the former's homes

growth rate: the net change in a population after adding births, subtracting deaths, and either adding or subtracting net migration

human ecology: Robert Park's term for the relationship between people and their environment (natural resources such as land)

invasion-succession cycle: the process of one group of people displacing a group whose racial-ethnic or social class characteristics differ from their own

Malthus theorem: an observation by Thomas Malthus that although the food supply increases only arithmetically (from 1 to 2 to 3 to 4 and so on), population grows geometrically (from 2 to 4 to 8 to 16 and so forth)

megalopolis: an urban area consisting of at least two metropolises and their many suburbs

metropolis: a central city surrounded by smaller cities and their suburbs

metropolitan statistical area (MSA): a central city and the urbanized counties adjacent to it

net migration rate: the difference between the number of immigrants and emigrants per 1,000 population

population pyramid: a graphic representation of a population, divided into age and sex

population shrinkage: the process by which a country's population becomes smaller because its birth rate and immigration are too low to replace those who die and emigrate

redlining: the officers of a financial institution deciding not to make loans in a particular area

suburb: the communities adjacent to the political boundaries of a city

suburbanization: the movement from the city to the suburbs

urban renewal: the rehabilitation of a rundown area, which usually results in the displacement of the poor who are living in that area

urbanization: the process by which an increasing proportion of a population live in cities

zero population growth: a demographic condition in which women bear only enough children to reproduce the population

☞ KEY PEOPLE

State the major theoretical contributions or findings of these people.

Ernest Burgess: Burgess developed the concentric zone model of urban development.

John Darley and Bibb Latané: These social psychologists found that people tend to remain uninvolved when they perceive there are others around who might become involved; they referred to this as the *diffusion of responsibility.*

William Flanagan: Flanagan has suggested three guiding principles for finding solutions to pressing urban problems--use of regional planning, awareness of human needs, and equalizing the benefits as well as the impact of urban change.

William Faunce: Writing about the far-reaching implications of exponential growth, this sociologist's views are consistent with the New Malthusians.

Herbert Gans: Gans studied urban neighborhoods, with the result that he documented the existence of community within cities and identified the several different types of urban dwellers that live there.

Chauncey Harris and Edward Ullman: These two geographers developed the multiple-nuclei model of urban growth. Harris later introduced the peripheral model of urban growth to account for more recent developments.

Homer Hoyt: Hoyt modified Burgess's model of urban growth with the development of the sector model.

Donald Huddle: This economist has produced figures showing that immigrants are a drain on taxpayers.

David Karp and William Yoels: These sociologists note that identification with a city's sports teams can be so intense that even after an individual moves away from the city, he continues to root for the team.

Thomas Malthus: Malthus was an economist who made dire predictions about the future of population growth.

Robert Park: Park coined the term "human ecology" to describe how people adapt to their environment.

Victor Rodriguez: This sociologist points out that many U.S. industries have abandoned local communities and moved their factories to places where labor costs are lower because of competitive pressures of a global market.

Julian Simon: Simon has argued that immigrants are a net contributor on the U.S. economy.

William Wilson: Wilson observed that the net result of shifting population and resources from central cities to suburbs was the transformation of the cities into ghettos.

Louis Wirth: Wirth wrote a classic essay, "Urbanism as a Way of Life," in which he argued that city life undermines kinship and neighborhood.

☞ "DOWN-TO-EARTH SOCIOLOGY"

This is your opportunity to apply the sociological perspective to the world around you. The questions in this section refer to material introduced in this chapter of your text. Many ask you to think about ideas and information presented in the various special "boxes" that are located throughout this chapter.

1. After reading "The Shifting U.S. Racial-Ethnic Mix" on page 582, what changes will our social institutions have to make as our population becomes more diverse? What are the chances that the U.S. government will cut off immigration? Why or why not?

2. What was your reaction after reading "Killing Little Girls" on page 585? Why is this practice common in certain cultures and not others? What social, economic or political changes would contribute to the elimination of this practice?

3. What are the factors pulling a growing number of middle class African Americans to Harlem (p. 582)? What are the consequences of this in-migration? Do you think this will become a growing trend among all racial-ethnic groups in the 21st century? Why or why not?

4. How does the picture of urban living painted on page 595 match your own "picture" of what life is like in the Least Industrialized Nations? Do the lives of people in these nations have any bearing on your life? Why or why not?

5. Would you live in a community like the ones described in "Urban Fear and the Gated Fortress" on page 599? What do you gain and lose by living in such a world?

☞ **SELF-TEST**

After completing this self-test, check your answers against the Answer Key beginning on page 406 of this Study Guide and against the text on page(s) indicated in parentheses.

MULTIPLE CHOICE QUESTIONS

1.   Who studies the size, composition, growth, and distribution of human population? (572)
     a.   Population experts
     b.   Growth specialists
     c.   Demographers
     d.   Social development professionals

2.   The proposition that the population grows geometrically while food supply increases arithmetically is known as the: (572)
     a.   food surplus equation.
     b.   Malthus theorem.
     c.   exponential growth curve.
     d.   demographic transition.

3.   Which of the following statements is consistent with beliefs of the anti-Malthusians? (574)
     a.   People will blindly reproduce until there is no room left on earth.
     b.   It is possible to project the world's current population growth into the indefinite future.
     c.   Most people do not use intelligence and rational planning when it comes to having children.
     d.   The demographic transition provides an accurate picture of what the future looks like.

4.   The three-stage historical process of population growth is known as the: (574)
     a.   demographic equation.
     b.   demographic transition.
     c.   exponential growth curve.
     d.   implosion growth curve.

5.   The process by which a country's population becomes smaller because its birth rate and immigration are too low to replace those who die and emigrate is: (575)
     a.   population transfer.
     b.   population annihilation.
     c.   population shrinkage.
     d.   population depletion.

6.   Starvation occurs because: (576)
     a.   there is not enough fertile land worldwide on which to grow food.
     b.   some parts of the world lack food while other parts of the world produce more than they can consume.
     c.   population is growing at a faster rate than the world's ability to produce food.
     d.   people don't eat a well-balanced diet.

7. Why do people in the Least Industrialized Nations have so many children? (578)
    a. parenthood provides status
    b. children are considered to be an economic asset
    c. the community encourages people to have children
    d. All of the above

8. Mexico's current population will double in _____ years. (579)
    a. 18
    b. 32
    c. 58
    d. 78

9. What are the factors that influence population growth called? (580)
    a. demographic variables
    b. demographic transitions
    c. demographic equations
    d. demographic constants

10. _____ refers to the number of children the average woman bears. (580)
    a. Fertility rate
    b. Fecundity
    c. Crude birth rate
    d. Real birth rate

11. The annual number of deaths per 1,000 population is the: (580)
    a. crude death rate.
    b. crude mortality rate.
    c. crude life expectancy rate.
    d. net death rate.

12. What factors might push someone to migrate? (582)
    a. poverty
    b. lack of religious and political freedom
    c. political persecution
    d. All of the above

13. According to your text, why is it difficult to forecast population growth? (584)
    a. Government programs may encourage or discourage women from having children.
    b. Government bureaus may be dishonest in reporting data.
    c. There is a lack of computer programs to deal with data adequately.
    d. Births, deaths, and migration are human behaviors and thus impossible to predict.

14. China's practice of female infanticide is rooted in: (585)
    a. sexism.
    b. economics.
    c. traditions that go back centuries.
    d. All of the above.

15. The process by which an increasing proportion of a population lives in cities is: (585)
    a.   suburbanization.
    b.   gentrification.
    c.   megalopolitanism.
    d.   urbanization.

16. What does today's rapid urbanization mean? (588-589)
    a.   More people live in cities.
    b.   Today's cities are larger.
    c.   About 300 of the world's cities contain at least one million people.
    d.   All of the above.

17. The area that extends from Maine along the coast to Virginia is an example of: (589)
    a.   urban sprawl.
    b.   population congestion.
    c.   megalopolis.
    d.   metropolis.

18. Edge cities: (591)
    a.   consist of a clustering of shopping malls, hotels, office parks, and residential areas near the intersection of major highways.
    b.   overlap political boundaries and include parts of several cities or towns.
    c.   provide a sense of place to those who live there.
    d.   All of the above.

19. Who first proposed the concentric-zone model? (592)
    a.   Herbert Gans.
    b.   Ernest Burgess.
    c.   Robert Park.
    d.   Homer Hoyt.

20. When a new group of immigrants enter a city, they tend to settle in low-rent areas. As their numbers increase, those already living in the area begin to move out; their departure creates more low-cost housing for the immigrants. How do sociologists refer to this process? (593)
    a.   progressive population replacement.
    b.   reverse gentrification.
    c.   cycle of assimilation.
    d.   invasion-succession cycle.

21. The model which suggests that land use in cities is based on several centers, such as a clustering of restaurants or automobile dealerships is the: (594)
    a.   sector model.
    b.   concentric-zone model.
    c.   multiple-nuclei model.
    d.   commerce model.

22.   While a sense of community is natural to *Gemeinschaft*, as a society industrializes *Gesellschaft* emerges, with relationships based on _____ . (596)
  a.   chaos
  b.   impersonality
  c.   alienation
  d.   disorientation

23.   According to Gans's typology, the trapped include: (598)
  a.   downwardly mobile persons.
  b.   elderly persons.
  c.   alcoholics and drug addicts.
  d.   All of the above.

24.   The Kitty Genovese case in an example of: (598)
  a.   ethnic villagers.
  b.   cosmopolites.
  c.   diffusion of responsibility.
  d.   community.

25.   What is suburbanization? (600)
  a.   movement from the suburbs to edge cities
  b.   movement from the city to the suburbs
  c.   movement from rural areas to suburbs
  d.   displacement of the poor by the relatively affluent, who renovate the former's homes

TRUE-FALSE QUESTIONS

T F	1.	Thomas Malthus was a sociologist at the University of Chicago in the 1920s. (572)	
T F	2.	The exponential growth curve is based on the idea that if growth doubles during approximately equal intervals of time, it accelerates in the latter stages. (573)	
T F	3.	The Anti-Malthusians believe that people breed like germs in a bucket. (573-574)	
T F	4.	There are two stages in the process of demographic transition. (574)	
T F	5.	The main reason why there is starvation is because there are too many people in the world today and too little food to feed them all. (576)	
T F	6.	The major reason why people in the Least Industrialized Nations have so many children is because they do not know how to prevent conception. (578)	
T F	7.	Population pyramids represent a population, divided into race, age, and sex. (579)	
T F	8.	Demographers study fertility, mortality, and migration to project population trends. (580)	
T F	9.	The fertility rate refers to the number of children that the average woman bears. (580)	
T F	10.	Migration rates do not affect the global population. (581)	
T F	11.	Julian Simon argues that the costs of immigrants exceed their contributions. (583)	
T F	12.	It is difficult for demographers to forecast population growth. (584)	
T F	13.	The rate and extent of urbanization in recent years is new to the world scene. (588)	
T F	14.	In recent years, U.S. cities in the West have gained population relative to cities in other regions of the country. (591)	
T F	15.	The concentric-zone model is based on the idea that cities expand radially from their central business district. (592)	
T F	16.	The multiple-nuclei model is the most accurate model of urban growth. (594)	

T F   17.   *The Urban Villagers* was written by Herbert Gans. (597)

T F   18.   Sports teams often engender community identification in urban areas. (598)

T F   19.   The norms of noninvolvement and the diffusion of responsibility can be dysfunction in some critical situations. (599)

T F   20.   Urban renewal involves tearing down deteriorated buildings and replacing them with decent, affordable housing units. (602)

FILL-IN QUESTIONS

1. _____ is the study of the size, composition, growth, and distribution of human populations. (572)

2. A pattern of growth in which numbers double during approximately equal intervals, thus accelerating in the latter stages is the _____. (573)

3. The Anti-Malthusians believe that Europe's _____, a three-stage historical process of population growth, provides an accurate picture of the future. (574)

4. When the people in a society do not produce enough children to replace the people who die, there is concern about _____ . (575)

5. A(n) _____ is a graphic representation of a population, divided into age and sex. (579)

6. The _____ refers to the number of children that the average woman bears. (580)

7. The basic demographic equation is *growth* = _____ - _____ + _____ . (584)

8. When women bear only enough children to replace the population, _____ has been achieved. (585)

9. _____ is a place in which a large number of people are permanently based and do not produce their own food. (588)

10. _____ is the process by which an increasing number of people live in cities. (589)

11. A central city, surrounded by smaller cities and their suburbs, forming an interconnected urban area is a _____. (589)

12. The displacement of the poor by the relatively affluent, who purchase and renovate the former's homes is _____. (591)

13. _____ is the relationship between people and their environment. (592)

14. _____ exists when people identify with an area and with one another. (594)

15. When officers of a financial institution decide not to make loans in a particular neighborhood or area, they are following a policy of _____ . (600)

MATCH THESE SOCIAL SCIENTISTS WITH THEIR CONTRIBUTIONS

___1. Thomas Malthus   a. *theorem on population growth*

___2. Ernest Burgess   b. *human ecology*

___3. Herbert Gans   c. *concentric-zone model*

___4. Homer Hoyt   d. *urban villagers*

___5. Robert Park   e. *sector model*

ESSAY QUESTIONS

1. State the positions of the New Malthusians and the Anti-Malthusians and discuss which view you think is more accurate, based on the information provided about each position.

2. Identify the problems that are associated with forecasting population growth.

3. Discuss whether or not cities are impersonal *Gesellschafts* or communal *Gemeinshafts*.

CHAPTER 21
COLLECTIVE BEHAVIOR AND SOCIAL MOVEMENTS

☞ CHAPTER SUMMARY

- Early theorists argued that individuals are transformed by crowds, losing all capacity for rationality. Terms such as "herd mentality," "collective mind," and "circular reaction" were developed to explain why people behaved as they did when in the midst of a crowd. According to Herbert Blumer, crowds go through five stages before they become an acting crowd: social unrest, an exciting event, milling, a common object of attention, and common impulses.

- Contemporary explanations emphasize the rationality of the crowd, the emergence of norms to govern behavior; collective behavior is seen as directed toward a goal, even if it is cruel and destructive behavior.

- Some of the major forms of collective behavior are lynchings, riots, panics, moral panics, rumors, fads, fashions, and urban legends. Conditions of discontent and uncertainty provide fertile ground for collective behavior.

- Social movements usually involve more people, are more prolonged, are more organized, and focus on social change. Depending on whether their target is individuals or society and the amount of change desired is partial or complete, social movements can be classified as alternative, redemptive, reformative, or transformative.

- Tactics are chosen on the basis of a group's levels of membership, its publics, and its relationship to authority. Because the mass media are the gatekeepers, their favorable or unfavorable coverage greatly affects a social movement's choice of tactics.

- Mass society theory, relative deprivation theory and ideological commitment theory all attempt to explain why people join social movements.

- Social movements go through distinct stages. Resource mobilization theory accounts for why some social movements never get off the ground while others enjoy great success. To succeed, social movements must focus on broad concerns, which are generally deeply embedded in society and do not lend themselves to easy solutions.

☞ LEARNING OBJECTIVES

As you read Chapter 21, use these learning objectives to organize your notes. After completing your reading, briefly state an answer to each of the objectives, and review the text pages in parentheses.

1. Discuss early explanations of collective behavior and note how these explanations focused on the transformation of the individual. (608-610)
2. Compare and contrast the minimax strategy and the emergent norm theory. (610-612)
3. Describe the forms of collective behavior, including riots, panic, moral panic, rumors, fads and fashions, and urban legends. (612-618)
4. Compare and contrast proactive and reactive social movements. (618-619)
5. List the different types of social movements, classifying them according to their target and the amount of change they seek. (619-621)
6. Describe the role that each of the following plays in influencing leadership choice of tactics: membership levels, publics, and relationships to authorities. (621-623)

7. Define propaganda and discuss the role of the mass media in social movements. (623-625)
8. Compare the different explanations of why people join social movements. (625-626)
9. Discuss the role of the agent provocateur in social movements. (626-628)
10. Identify the five stages that social movements go through as they grow and mature. (628-629)
11. State the key ingredients which contribute to the success or failure of social movements. (630)

☞ CHAPTER OUTLINE

I. **Early Explanations: The Transformation of the Individual**
   A. Collective behavior is characterized by a group of people becoming emotionally aroused and engaging in extraordinary behavior, in which the usual norms do not apply.
   B. In 1852, Charles Mackay concluded that when people were in crowds, they sometimes went "mad" and did "disgraceful and violent things"; just as a herd of cows will stampede, so too people can come under the control of a "herd mentality."
   C. Based on Mackay's idea, Gustave LeBon stressed that the individual is transformed by the crowd.
      1. In a crowd, people feel anonymous, not accountable for what they do; they develop feelings of invincibility, believing that together they can accomplish anything. A collective mind develops.
      2. They become highly suggestible; this paves the way for contagion, a kind of collective hypnosis, which releases the destructive instincts that society has so carefully repressed.
   D. To LeBon's analysis, Robert Park added the ideas of social unrest, which is transmitted from one individual to another, and circular reaction, the back-and-forth communication between the members of a crowd whereby a "collective impulse" is transmitted.
   E. Synthesizing both LeBon's and Park's ideas, Herbert Blumer identified five stages of collective behavior.
      1. A background condition of social unrest exists--when people's routine activities are thwarted or when they develop new needs that go unsatisfied.
      2. An exciting event occurs--one so startling that people are preoccupied with it.
      3. People engage in milling--the act of standing or walking around as they talk about the exciting event and circular reaction sets in.
      4. A common object of attention emerges--people's attention becomes riveted on some aspect of the event.
      5. Stimulation of the common impulses occurs--people collectively agree about what they should do. Social contagion, described as a collective excitement passed from one person to another, becomes the mechanism that stimulates these common impulses. The end result is an acting crowd--an excited group that collectively moves toward a goal, which may be constructive or destructive.

II. **The Contemporary View: The Rationality of the Crowd**
   A. Richard Berk pointed out that people use a minimax strategy (trying to minimize their costs and maximize their rewards) whether in small groups or in crowds; the fewer the costs and the greater the rewards that people anticipate, the more likely they are to carry out a particular act.
   B. Ralph Turner and Lewis Killian noted that human behavior is regulated by the normative order--socially approved ways of doing things that make up our everyday life. But when

an extraordinary event occurs and existing norms do not cover the new situation, people develop new norms to deal with the problem (emergent norms).

1. There are five kinds of crowd participants: (1) the ego-involved, who feel a high personal stake in the event; (2) the concerned, who have a personal interest in the event, but less than the ego-involved; (3) the insecure, who have little concern about the issue but have sought out the crowd because it gives them a sense of power and security; (4) the curious spectators, who are inquisitive and may cheer the crowd on even though they do not care about the issue; and (5) the exploiters, who do not care about the issue but use it for their own purposes (e.g., hawking food or T-shirts).

2. The concept of emerging norms is important because it points to a rational process as the essential component of collective behavior.

III. Forms of Collective Behavior

A. Riots, such as the one which erupted in Los Angeles after the verdict in the Rodney King trial, are usually caused by frustration and anger at deprivation.

1. Beginning with a perception of being kept out of the mainstream society--limited to a meager education and denied jobs and justice--people's frustration builds to such a boiling point that it takes only a precipitating event to erupt in collective behavior.

2. It is not only the deprived who participate in the riots; others, who are not deprived, but who still feel frustration at the underlying social conditions that place them at a disadvantage also get involved.

3. The event that precipitates a riot is much less important than the riot's general context.

B. Panic, like the one which occurred following the broadcast of H. G. Wells's "War of the Worlds," is behavior that results when people become so fearful that they cannot function normally.

1. One explanation as to why people panic is because they are anxious about some social condition.

2. It is against the law to shout "Fire!" in a public building when no such danger exists. If people fear immediate death, they will lunge toward the nearest exit in a frantic effort to escape (e. g., the Beverly Hills Supper Club fire in Kentucky in 1977, in which 165 people died trying to get out of the two exits).

3. Sociologists have found that not everyone panics in these situations, and some employees, such as some of those at the supper club, engage in role extension--the incorporation of additional activities into a role--to try to help people to safety.

C. Moral panics occur when large numbers of people become intensely concerned, even fearful, about some behavior that is perceived as a threat to morality--the threat is seen as enormous and hostility builds toward those thought responsible.

1. Like other panics, moral panics center around a sense of danger.

2. Moral panics are often fed by rumor, information for which there is no discernable source and which is usually unfounded.

3. Moral panics also thrive on uncertainty and anxiety.

D. Rumors thrive in conditions of ambiguity, functioning to fill in missing information.

1. Most rumors are short-lived and arise in a situation of ambiguity, only to dissipate when they are replaced either by another rumor or by factual information. A few rumors have a long life because they hit a responsive cord (e.g., rumors of mass

poisoning of soft drink products that spread to many countries).

2.   Three main factors in why people believe rumors are that they: (1) deal with a subject that is important to an individual; (2) replace ambiguity with some form of certainty; and (3) are attributed to a creditable source.

E.   A fad is a temporary pattern of behavior that catches people's attention, while fashion is a more enduring version of the same.

1.   John Lofland identified four types of fads: (1) object fads, such as the hula hoop or pet rocks; (2) activity fads, such as eating goldfish or playing Trivial Pursuit; (3) idea fads, such as astrology; and (4) personality fads, such as Elvis Presley, Vanna White, and Michael Jordan.

2.   Fashion is a behavior pattern that catches people's attention, lasting longer than a fad. Most often thought of in terms of clothing fashions, it can also refer to hairstyles, home decorating, design and colors of buildings, and language.

F.   Urban legends are stories with an ironic twist that sound realistic but are false. Jan Brunvand, who studied the transmission of urban legends, concluded that urban legends are passed on by people who think that the event really happened to someone, such as a "friend of a friend"; the stories have strong appeal and gain credibility from naming specific people or local places. Urban legends are "modern morality stories," with each teaching a moral lesson about life; they are related to social change; and they are calculated to instill guilt and fear.

IV.   Social Movements

A.   Social movements consist of large numbers of people, who, through deliberate and sustained efforts, organize to promote or resist social change. At the heart of social movements lie grievances and dissatisfactions.

B.   Proactive social movements promote social change because a current condition of society is intolerable. In contrast, reactive social movements resist changing conditions in society which they perceive as threatening.

C.   To further their goals, people develop social movement organizations like the National Organization of Women or the Stop-ERA. They use attention-grabbing devices to recruit members and publicize grievances.

D.   Mayer Zald suggests that a cultural crisis can give birth to a wave of social movements. According to Zald, when a society's institutions fail to keep up with social changes, many people's needs go unfulfilled, massive unrest follows, and social movements come into being to bridge the gap.

V.   Types and Tactics of Social Movements

A.   David Aberle classified social movements into four broad categories according to the type and amount of social change they seek.

1.   Two types seek to change people but differ in terms of the amount of change desired: alternative social movements seek to alter only particular aspects of people (e.g., the Women's Christian Temperance Union); while redemptive social movements seek to change people totally (e.g., a religious social movement such as fundamental Christianity that stresses conversion).

2.   Two types seek to change society but also differ in terms of the amount of change desired: reformative social movements seek to reform only one part of society (e.g., animal rights or the environment); transformative social movements seek to change the social order itself and to replace it with their own version of the ideal

society (e.g., revolutions in the American colonies, France, Russia).

    3.   One of the more interesting types of transformative social movements is the millenarian movement, which is based on prophecies of coming calamity. Cargo cults, a social movement in which South Pacific islanders destroyed their possessions in the anticipation that their ancestors would send items by ship, are an interesting example of millenarian movements.

    4.   Today some social movements, called new social movements, have a global orientation, committed to changing a specific condition throughout the world. The women's, environmental, and animal rights movements are examples.

B.   Tactics of social movements are best understood by examining levels of membership, publics they address, and their relationship to authorities.

    1.   Three levels of membership are: (1) the inner core (the leadership that sets goals, timetables, etc.); (2) people committed to the goals of the movement, but not to the same degree as members of the inner core; and (3) people who are neither as committed nor as dependable. The tactics that are chosen depend on the predispositions and backgrounds of the inner core.

    2.   Publics can be described as sympathetic (sympathize with goals of movement but have no commitment to movement), hostile (keenly aware of group's goals and want the movement stopped), and people who are unaware of or indifferent toward the movement. In selecting tactics, the leadership considers these different types of publics.

    3.   The movement's relationship to the authorities is important in determining tactics: if authorities are hostile to a social movement, aggressive or even violent tactics are likely; if authorities are sympathetic, violence is not likely. If a social movement is institutionalized, accepted by the authorities and given access to resources they control, the likelihood of violence is very low.

    4.   Other factors that can influence the choice of tactics include the nature of friendships, race, and even the size of towns.

C.   In selecting tactics, leaders of social movements are aware of their effects on the mass media. Their goal is to influence public opinion about some issue.

    1.   Propaganda is a key to understanding social movements. Propaganda simply means the presentation of information in an attempt to influence people.

    2.   The mass media play a critical role in social movements. They have become, in effect, the gatekeepers to social movements. If those who control and work in the mass media are sympathetic to a "cause," it will receive sympathetic treatment. If the social movement goes against their own biases, it will either be ignored or receive unfavorable treatment.

VI. Why People Join Social Movements

A.   In the mass society theory, William Kornhauser proposed that social movements offer a sense of belonging to people who have weak social ties.

    1.   Mass society, characterized as an industrialized, highly bureaucratized, impersonal society, makes many people feel isolated and, as a result, they are attracted to social movements because they offer a sense of belonging.

    2.   However, Doug McAdam (who studied those involved in civil rights movements) found that many who participate in social movements have strong family and community ties, and joined such movements to right wrongs and overcome injustice, not because of isolation. The most isolated (the homeless) generally do

not join anything except food lines.

B. According to deprivation theory people who are deprived of things deemed valuable in society--whether money, justice, status, or privilege--join social movements with the hope of redressing their grievances.

1. Absolute deprivation is people's actual negative condition; relative deprivation is what people think they should have relative to what others have, or even compared with their own past or perceived future.

2. While the notion of absolute deprivation provides a beginning point for looking at why people join social movements, it is even more important to look at relative deprivation in trying to understand why people join social movements.

3. Improved conditions fuel human desires for even better conditions, and thus can spark revolutions.

C. James Jasper and Dorothy Nelkin note that people join a particular social movement because of moral issues and an ideological commitment to the movement. It is the moral component, they argue, that is a primary reason for some people's involvement in social movements.

D. An agent provocateur is a special type of social movement participant.

1. An agent of the government or of a rival social movement, the agent provocateur's job is to spy on the leadership and sabotage their activities. Some are recruited from the membership itself, while others go underground and join the movement.

2. On occasion a police agent is converted to the social movement on which he or she is spying. Sociologist Gary Marx noted that this occurs because the agent, to be credible, must share at least some of the class, age, ethnic, racial, religious, or sexual characteristics of the group. This makes the agent more likely to sympathize with the movement's goals and to become disenchanted with the means being used to destroy the group.

3. Sometimes the agent provocateur will go to great lengths, even breaking the law, to push the social movement into illegal activities.

VII. **On the Success and Failure of Social Movements**

A. Social movements have a life course; that is, they go through five stages as they grow and mature.

1. Initial unrest and agitation because people are upset about some social condition; at this stage leaders emerge who verbalize people's feelings.

2. Resource mobilization by leaders of a relatively large number of people who demand that something be done about the problem; charismatic leaders emerge during this stage.

3. An organization emerges with a division of labor, a leadership who makes policy decisions, and a rank and file that actively supports the movement.

4. Institutionalization occurs as the movement becomes bureaucratized and leadership passes to career officials who may care more about their position in the organization than about the movement itself.

5. The organization declines, but there may be a possibility of resurgence. Some movements cease to exist; others become reinvigorated with new leadership from within or by coming into conflict with other social movements fighting for the opposite side of the issue--e.g., social movements relating to abortion.

B. Seldom do social movements actually solve problems. In order to mobilize sufficient resources to survive, they find it necessary to appeal to a broad constituency and, to do so, they must focus on large-scale issues which are deeply embedded in society. Such broad problems do not lend themselves to easy or quick solutions. Social movements make valuable contributions to solving problems, for they highlight areas of society to be changed.

☞ KEY TERMS

After studying the chapter, review the definition for each of the following terms.

acting crowd: Herbert Blumer's term for an excited group that collectively moves toward a goal

agent provocateur: someone who joins a group in order to spy on it and to sabotage it by *provoking* its members to commit illegal acts

alternative social movement: a social movement that seeks to alter only particular aspects of people

cargo cult: a social movement in which South Pacific islanders destroyed their possessions in the anticipation that their ancestors would send items by ship

circular reaction: Robert Park's term for a back-and-forth communication between the members of a crowd whereby a "collective impulse" is transmitted

collective behavior: extraordinary activities carried out by groups of people; includes lynchings, rumors, panics, urban legends, and fads and fashions

collective mind: Gustave LeBon's term for the tendency of people in a crowd to feel, think, and act in extraordinary ways

emergent norms: Ralph Turner and Lewis Killian's term for the development of new norms to cope with a new situation, especially among crowds

fad: a temporary pattern of behavior that catches people's attention

fashion: a pattern of behavior that catches people's attention and lasts longer than a fad

mass society: industrialized, highly bureaucratized, impersonal society

mass society theory: an explanation for participation in social movements based on the assumption that such movements offer a sense of belonging to people who have weak social ties

millenarian movement: a social movement based on the prophecy of coming social upheaval

milling: a crowd standing or walking around as they talk excitedly about some event

minimax strategy: Richard Berk's term for the effort people make to minimize their costs and maximize their rewards

moral panic: a fear that grips large numbers of people that some evil group or behavior threatens the well-being of society, followed by intense hostility, sometimes violence, toward those thought responsible

new social movement: social movements with a new emphasis on the world, instead of on a condition in a specific country

panic: the condition of being so fearful that one cannot function normally, and may even flee

proactive social movement: a social movement that promotes social change

propaganda: in its broad sense, the presentation of information in the attempt to influence people; in its narrow sense, one-sided information used to try to influence people

public: a dispersed group of people who usually have an interest in the issue on which a social movement focuses; the sympathetic and hostile publics have such an interest, but a third public is either unaware of the issue or indifferent to it

public opinion: how people think about some issue

reactive social movement: a social movement that resists social change

redemptive social movement: a social movement that seeks to change people totally

reformative social movement: a social movement that seeks to change only particular aspects of society

relative deprivation theory: in this context, the belief that people join social movements based on their evaluations of what they think they should have compared with what others have

resource mobilization: a theory that social movements succeed or fail based on their ability to mobilize resources such as time, money, and people's skills

riot: violent crowd behavior aimed against people and property

role extension: the incorporation of additional activities into a role

rumor: unfounded information spread among people

social movement: a large group of people who are organized to promote or resist social change

social movement organization: an organization developed to further the goals of a social movement

transformative social movement: a social movement that seeks to change society totally

urban legend: a story with an ironic twist that sounds realistic but is false

☞ KEY PEOPLE

Review the major theoretical contributions or findings of these people.

David Aberle: Aberle classified social movements into four types: alterative, redemptive, reformative and transformation based on the amount of intended change and the target of the change.

William Banbridge: This sociologist found that some people did become frightened following the broadcast of *War of the Worlds*, and a few even got into their cars and drove like maniacs, but most of the panic was an invention of the news media.

Richard Berk: Berk developed the minimax strategy to explain collective behavior; this is that people are more likely to act when costs are low and anticipated rewards high.

Herbert Blumer: Blumer identified five stages that precede the emergence of an active crowd (an excited group that moves towards a goal). These are: tension or unrest; an exciting event; milling; a common object of attraction; and common impulses.

Jan Brunvand: This folklorist studied urban legends and suggests that they are modern morality stories.

Hadley Cantril: This psychologist suggests that people panicked after hearing the famous *War of the Worlds* because of widespread anxiety about world conditions.

James Jasper and Dorothy Nelkin: These sociologists argue that many become involved in social movements because of moral issues and an ideological commitment.

Drue Johnston and Norris Johnson: These sociologists studied the behavior of employees during the Beverly Hills Supper Club fire and found that most continued to carry out their roles.

William Kornhauser: Kornhauser proposed mass society theory to explain why people are attracted to social movements. He suggested that these movements fill a void in some people's lives by offering them a sense of belonging.

Gustave LeBon: LeBon argued that a collective mind develops within a crowd and people are swept away by any suggestion that is made.

Alfred & Elizabeth Lee: These sociologists found that propaganda relies on seven basic techniques, which they labeled "tricks of the trade."

John Lofland: Lofland identified four different types of fads: object fads, activity fads, idea fads, and personality fads.

Charles Mackay: Mackay was the first to study collective behavior; he suggested that a "herd mentality" takes over and explains the disgraceful things people do when in crowds.

Doug McAdam: McAdam challenged the mass society theory on the basis of research findings related to people's decision to become involved in the civil rights struggle. He found they were well integrated into society rather than isolated from it, as mass society theory suggests.

John McCarthy and Mayer Zald: These sociologists investigated the resource mobilization of social movements and found that, although there may be a group of angry and agitated people, without this mobilization they will never become a social movement.

Gary Marx: This sociologist investigated the agent provocateur and found that some are converted to the movement because they share some of the same social characteristics as the movement's members.

Robert Park: Park suggested that social unrest is the result of the circular reaction of people in crowds.

Victor Rodriguez: This sociologist suggests that minorities in the middle class might participate in riots when they feel frustrated with being treated as second-class citizens even when they are employed and living stable lives.

Ellen Scott: Scott studied the movement to stop rape and found that close friendships, race, and even size of town are important in determining tactics.

Ralph Turner and Lewis Killian: These sociologists use the term "emergent norm" to explain the rules that emerge in collective behavior.

Mayer Zald: In addition to his work with John McCarthy, this sociologist explained that social movements are like a rolling sea; during one period of time a few may appear, but shortly afterward a whole wave of them role in. He suggested that cultural crises give rise to social movements.

☞ "DOWN-TO-EARTH SOCIOLOGY"

This is your opportunity to apply the sociological perspective to the world around you. The questions in this section refer to material introduced in this chapter of your text. Many ask you to think about ideas and information presented in the various special "boxes" that are located throughout this chapter.

1.   Did you, or someone you know, attend the 1995 Million Man March in Washington, D.C. (p. 619)? In what ways was this demonstration linked to past activities of the Civil Rights Movement? In what ways did it break new ground, by raising issues that had not been previously examined? How successful do you think this march was in raising awareness about racial discrimination and prejudice?

2.   After reading "Tricks of the Trade: The Fine Art of Propaganda" on page 624, listen carefully to politicians and others advocating a particular idea. Are they using some of the techniques described? If yes, which ones?

3.   Read "Which Side of the Barricades? Prochoice and Prolife as a Social Movement" on pages 629-630. Do you agree that no issue divides Americans as abortion does? How do the two sides of this issue continue to reinvigorate each other? In thinking about these two social movements, where would you place yourself in relationship to membership and/or publics? What kind of tactics does each side use in order to promote the cause without alienating sympathetic publics? How does each side try to influence public opinion by making use of some of the "tricks of the trade?"

☞ SELF-TEST

After completing this self-test, check your answers against the Answer Key beginning on page 409 of this Study Guide and against the text on page(s) indicated in parentheses.

MULTIPLE CHOICE QUESTIONS

1.   Which of the following statements about Charles MacKay is <u>incorrect</u>? (608)
    a.   He noticed that ordinary people did disgraceful things when in a crowd.
    b.   He suggested that people have a "herd mentality" when in a crowd.
    c.   He proposed that a collective mind develops once a group of people congregate.
    d.   His work marked the beginnings of the field of collective behavior.

2.   Gustave LeBon's term for the tendency of people in a crowd to feel, think, and act in extraordinary ways is: (609)
    a.   social unrest.
    b.   the "herd mentality."
    c.   collective behavior.
    d.   collective mind.

3.   According to Park, which is most conductive to the emergence of collective behavior? (609)
    a.   social alienation.
    b.   social apathy.
    c.   social unrest.
    d.   social cohesion.

4.   A crowd's back-and-forth communication whereby a collective impulse is transmitted is: (609)
    a.   a circular reaction.
    b.   milling.
    c.   an acting crowd.
    d.   a collective mind.

5.   Acting crowd: (609-610)
    a.   is a term coined by Herbert Blumer.
    b.   is an excited group that collectively moves toward a goal.
    c.   is the end result of the five stages of collective behavior.
    d.   All of the above.

6.   Richard Berk used the term "minimax strategy" to describe the tendency for: (610)
    a.   crowds to operate with a minimum of strategy.
    b.   for humans to minimize costs and maximize rewards.
    c.   those in authority to maximize the costs of an action in order to minimize rewards.
    d.   society to respond to even the most minimum of social movements.

7. The development of new norms to cope with a new situation is: (611)
   a. emergent norms.
   b. developmental norms.
   c. surfacing norms.
   d. None of the above.

8. Urban riots are usually caused by: (613)
   a. extreme poverty.
   b. social deviants who display antisocial behavior.
   c. feelings of frustration and anger at being deprived of the same opportunities as others.
   d. a population that is forced to live within a small space--overcrowded neighborhoods.

9. Failure to function normally, and even fleeing, is the result of _____. (613)
   a. disturbance.
   b. panic.
   c. fad.
   d. riot.

10. Sociologists have found that when a disaster such as a fire occurs: (614)
    a. everyone panics.
    b. some people continue to perform their roles.
    c. people leave it to the police and fire fighters to solve the problem.
    d. no one panics.

11. Which statement about moral panics is incorrect? (615)
    a. Moral panics occur when people are concerned about something viewed as immoral.
    b. Moral panics are generally based on an event that has been verified as true.
    c. Moral panics thrive on uncertainty and anxiety.
    d. Moral panics are fueled by the mass media.

12. Sociologists refer to unfounded information spread among people as: (615)
    a. hearsay.
    b. scuttlebutt.
    c. rumor.
    d. gossip.

13. A temporary pattern of behavior that catches people's attention is a: (616)
    a. panic.
    b. trend.
    c. fashion.
    d. fad.

14. Eating goldfish and bungee jumping are both examples of: (620)
    a. object fads.
    b. urban legends.
    c. activity fads.
    d. rumors.

15. Social movements that seek to change people totally are: (620)
    a.   alternative social movements.
    b.   redemptive social movements.
    c.   reformative social movements.
    d.   transformative social movements.

16. A social movement that seeks to change society totally is a(n): (620)
    a.   alternative social movement.
    b.   redemptive social movement.
    c.   reformative social movement.
    d.   transformative social movement.

17. A millenarian movement is a social movement: (620)
    a.   in which South Pacific islanders destroyed all their possessions.
    b.   that seeks to alter only particular aspects of people.
    c.   based on the prophecy of coming social upheaval.
    d.   that seeks to change individuals totally.

18. Levels of membership in social movements include: (621-622)
    a.   the inner core.
    b.   the committed.
    c.   a wider circle of members.
    d.   All of the above.

19. The public that social movements face can really be divided into: (622)
    a.   supporters and opponents.
    b.   informed supportive public, informed oppositional public, and uninformed mass.
    c.   receptive audience, hostile audience, and disinterested mass.
    d.   sympathetic public, hostile public, and disinterested people.

20. How people think about some issue is: (623)
    a.   irrelevant to most social scientists.
    b.   public opinion.
    c.   propaganda.
    d.   mass-society theory.

21. Which statement about propaganda is <u>incorrect</u>? (623)
    a.   Propaganda plays a key role in social movements.
    b.   Propaganda generally involves negative images.
    c.   Propaganda has become a regular and routine part of modern life.
    d.   Propaganda is the presentation of information in an attempt to influence people.

22. Advertising is: (624)
    a.   a type of propaganda.
    b.   an organized attempt to manipulate public opinion.
    c.   a one-sided presentation of information that distorts reality.
    d.   All of the above.

23. The mass media: (625)
   a. are the gatekeepers to social movements.
   b. engage in biased reporting, controlled by people who have an agenda to get across.
   c. are sympathetic to some social movements, while ignoring others; it all depends on their individual biases.
   d. All of the above.

24. According to mass society theory, social movements offer people: (625)
   a. a set of rules or guidelines to govern their behavior.
   b. an outlet for leisure activities.
   c. a sense of belonging.
   d. answers to basic questions concerning morality.

25. In order to turn a group of people who are upset about a social condition into a social movement, there must be: (628)
   a. agitation.
   b. resource mobilization.
   c. organization.
   d. institutionalization.

TRUE-FALSE QUESTIONS

T F 1. Collective behavior is characterized by a group of people becoming emotionally aroused and engaging in extraordinary behavior. (608)

T F 2. Gustave LeBon's central idea was that the individual is transformed by the crowd. (609)

T F 3. The term "circular reaction" refers to the process by which people become swept up in the crowd, reacting to any suggestion that is put forth. (609)

T F 4. Herbert Blumer identified five stages of collective behavior. (610)

T F 5. The term acting crowd is applied only to violent activities such as lynch mobs or people engaged in riots. (610)

T F 6. Emergent norms is the development of new norms to cope with a new situation, especially among crowds. (611)

T F 7. The event that precipitates a riot is less important than the riot's general context. (613)

T F 8. The fears that produce moral panics are generally out of proportion to any supposed danger. (615)

T F 9. People believe rumors because they replace ambiguity with some form of certainty. (616)

T F 10. Urban legends are just another kind of rumor. (617)

T F 11. To further their goals, people will sometimes form social movement organizations. Examples include the National Organization of Women and Stop-ERA. (618)

T F 12. All social movements seek to change society. (619-620)

T F 13. A social movement's relationship to authorities is significant in determining whether the tactics to be used are peaceful or violent. (622)

T F 14. Propaganda and advertising are defined quite differently from one another. (624)

T F 15. Deprivation theory and relative deprivation theory are identical perspectives. (626)

T F 16. Moral shock is of little importance in motivating people to join a social movement. (626)

T F 17. The role of the agent provocateur as a spy on the leadership of a social movement and perhaps try to sabotage their activities is generally unsuccessful. (627)

T F   18.   Before resources can be mobilized, a social movement must become organized, and in some cases even institutionalized. (628)
T F   19.   In the final stage of a social movement, decline is certain. (628)
T F   20.   Social movements seldom actually solve problems. (630)

FILL-IN QUESTIONS

1.   Gustave LeBon's term for the tendency of people in a crowd to feel, think, and act in extraordinary ways is _____. (609)
2.   A crowd standing or walking around as they talk excitedly about some event is _____. (610)
3.   Ralph Turner and Lewis Killian's term for the development of new norms to cope with a new situation, especially among crowds is _____. (611)
4.   A(n) _____ is violent crowd behavior aimed against people and property. (612)
5.   A fear that grips large numbers of people that some evil group or behavior threatens the well being of society, followed by intense hostility, and sometimes violence, towards those thought responsible is _____. (615)
6.   _____ are unfounded information spread among people. (616)
7.   A temporary pattern of behavior that catches people's attention is a(n) _____. (616)
8.   A(n) _____ is a story with an ironic twist that sounds realistic but is false. (617)
9.   Temperance, civil rights, white supremacy, and animal rights have all found expression in _____, made up of large numbers of people who organize to promote or resist social change. (618)
10.   A religious social movement that stresses conversion, which will produce a change in the entire person, is an example of _____. (620)
11.   A _____ was a social movement among South Pacific Islanders, in which they destroyed their possessions in the anticipation that their ancestors would send items by ship. (620)
12.   Social movements that span the globe, emphasizing changing conditions throughout the world rather than in just one country, are referred to as _____. (621)
13.   _____ is how people think about some issue. (623)
14.   _____ is industrialized, highly bureaucratized, impersonal society. (625)
15.   _____ states that people who are deprived of things deemed valuable in society join social movements with the hope of redressing their grievances. (625)

MATCH THESE SOCIAL SCIENTISTS WITH THEIR CONTRIBUTIONS

___1. Charles Mackay   a. *emergent norm*
___2. William Kornhauser   b. *herd mentality*
___3. Robert Park   c. *minimax strategy*
___4. Turner & Killian   d. *social movements classified by type and amount of social change*
___5. Gustave LeBon   e. *mass society theory*
___6. David Aberle   f. *social unrest and circular reaction*
___7. Herbert Blumer   g. *the acting crowd*
___8. Richard Berk   h. *collective mind*

ESSAY QUESTIONS

1.   Compare and contrast the early explanations of collective behavior, as advanced by Charles Mackay, Gustave LeBon, Robert Park, and Herbert Blumer, with more contemporary explanations developed by Richard Berk, Ralph Turner and Lewis Killian.

2.   Discuss the different theories about why people join social movements and consider how they could all be accurate.

3.   Consider why the author combined the topics of collective behavior and social movements in one chapter.

CHAPTER 22
SOCIAL CHANGE AND THE ENVIRONMENT

☞ CHAPTER SUMMARY

- Social change, the alteration of culture and society over time, is a vital part of social life. Social change has included four social revolutions--domestication, agriculture, industrialization, and information; the change from *Gemeinschaft* to *Gesellschaft* types of societies; capitalism and industrialization; modernization; and global stratification. Social movements indicate the cutting edges of social change.

- Theories of social change include: evolutionary theories (both unilinear and multilinear), cyclical theories, and conflict theories. William Ogburn identified technology as the basis cause of social change. The processes of social change are innovation, discovery, and diffusion. Cultural lag refers to the changes in the symbolic culture in response to changes in technology.

- Technology is a driving force in social change, and it can shape an entire society by changing existing technology, social organization, ideology, values, and social relationships, as is evident when the impact that both the automobile and the computer have had on American society is analyzed.

- Social change has often had a negative impact on the natural environment. Today we face problems such as acid rain, global warming, and the greenhouse effect. Environmental problems are worldwide, brought about by industrial production and urbanization, the pressures of population growth, and inadequate environmental regulation; the world today is facing a basic conflict between the lust for profits through the exploitation of the world's resources and the need to produce a sustainable environment. In response, a worldwide environmental movement has emerged, which seeks solutions in education, legislation, and political activism. If we are to survive, we must seek harmony between technology and the environment.

☞ LEARNING OBJECTIVES

As you read Chapter 22, use these learning objectives to organize your notes. After completing your reading, briefly state an answer to each of the objectives, and review the text pages in parentheses.

1. Describe the four major social revolutions which have occurred. (634-635)
2. Describe *Gemeinschaft* and *Gesellschaft* societies and outline the relationship between capitalism, industrialization and modernization. (635-636)
3. Explain why social movements often reveal the cutting edges of change in a society. (636)
4. Identify the forces behind shifts in the global map and discuss threats posed by the resurgence of ethnic conflicts. (636-638)
5. Explain the different theories of social change -- evolutionary, cyclical, and conflict -- and note the degree to which they can still be considered useful in explaining the process of change. (638-639)
6. Identify and define Ogburn's three processes of social change, explain what is meant by "cultural lag," and evaluate the utility of Ogburn's theory. (639-640)
7. Explain how technology transforms society. (641-643)

8. Discuss the impact that automobiles and computers have had on U.S. society. (643-649)
9. State the impact that computers will have on social inequality in the 21st century. (649)
10. Discuss the relationship between environmental decay and global capitalism. (649)
11. Identify the environmental problems facing the Most Industrialized Nation and contrast these with problem faced by Industrializing and the Least Industrialized Nation. (650-653)
12. Discuss the goals and activities of the environmental movement. (654)
13. List the assumptions of environmental sociology. (655)
14. Describe some of the actions which would be necessary to reach the goal of harmony between technology and the environment. (656)

☞ CHAPTER OUTLINE

I. **How Social Change Transforms Society**
   A. Social change is a shift in the characteristics of culture and societies over time.
   B. There have been four social revolutions: the domestication of plants and animals, from which pastoral and horticultural societies arose; the invention of the plow, leading to agricultural societies; the industrial revolution, which produced industrial societies; and now the information revolution, resulting in postindustrial societies.
   C. The shift from agricultural to industrial economic activity was accompanied by a change from *Gemeinschaft* (daily life centers on intimate and personal relationships) to *Gesellschaft* (people have fleeting, impersonal relationships) societies.
   D. Different sociologists have focused on different forces in order to explain the changes that took place in society at the time of the Industrial Revolution.
      1. Karl Marx identified capitalism as the basic reason behind the breakup of feudal (agricultural) societies. He focused his analysis on the means of production (factories, machinery, tools): those who owned them dictated the conditions under which workers would work and live.
      2. Max Weber saw religion as the core reason for the development of capitalism: as a result of the Reformation, Protestants no longer felt assured that they were saved by virtue of church membership and concluded that God would show visible favor to the elect. This belief encouraged Protestants to work hard and be thrifty. An economic surplus resulted, stimulating industrialization.
      3. Modernization (the change from agricultural to industrial societies) refers to the sweeping changes in societies brought about by the Industrial Revolution.
   E. Social movements highlight the cutting edges of change in a society. Large numbers of people organize to demand, or resist, changes. With globalization, these issues increasingly cut across international boundaries.
   F. A world system began to emerge in the 16th century; in the 18th and 19th centuries, capitalism and industrialization extended the economic and political ties among the world's nations.
      1. Dependency theory asserts that because those nations that were not industrialized became dependent on those that had industrialized, they were unable to develop their own resources.
      2. The world's industrial giants (the United States, Canada, Great Britain, France, Germany, Italy, and Japan -- the G7) have decided how they will share the world's markets; by regulating global economic and industrial policy they guarantee their

own dominance, including continued access to cheap raw materials from the less industrialized nations.

    3.   The recent resurgence of ethnic conflicts threatens the global map drawn by the G7.

II.   **Theories and Processes of Social Change**

    A.   Theories that focus on cultural evolution are either unilinear or multilinear.

        1.   Unilinear theories assume that all societies follow the same path, evolving from simple to complex through uniform sequences; however, these theories have been discredited, and seeing one's own society as the top of the evolutionary ladder is now considered unacceptably ethnocentric.

        2.   Multilinear theories assume that different routes can lead to a similar stage of development; thus, societies need not pass through the same sequence of stages to become industrialized.

        3.   Both unilinear and multilinear theories assume the idea that societies progress toward a higher state. However, because of the crises in Western culture today, this assumption has been cast aside and evolutionary theories have been rejected.

    B.   Theories of natural cycles examine great civilizations, not a particular society; they presume that societies are like organisms, they are born, reach adolescence, grow old, and die.

        1.   Toynbee proposed that civilization is initially able to meet challenges, yet when it becomes an empire, the ruling elite loses its capacity to keep the masses in line "by charm rather than by force," and the fabric of society is then ripped apart.

        2.   Oswald Spengler proposed that Western civilization was on the wane; some analysts think the crisis in Western civilization may indicate he was right.

    C.   Marx's conflict theory viewed social change as a dialectical process, in which a thesis (a current arrangement of power) contains its own antithesis (a contradiction or opposition), and the resulting struggle between the thesis and its antithesis leads to a synthesis (a new arrangement of power). Thus, the history of a society is a series of confrontations in which each ruling group creates the seeds of its own destruction (e.g., capitalism sets workers and capitalists on a collision course).

    D.   William Ogburn identified three processes of social change.

        1.   *Inventions* can be either material (computers) or social (capitalism); *discovery* is a new way of seeing things; and *diffusion* is the spread of an invention, discovery, or idea, from one area to another.

        2.   Ogburn coined the term "cultural lag" to describe the situation in which some elements of a culture adapt to an invention or discovery more rapidly than others. We are constantly trying to catch up with technology by adapting our customs and ways of life to meet its needs.

        3.   Ogburn has been criticized because of his view that technology controls almost all social change. People also take control over technology, developing the technology they need and selectively using existing technology. Both can happen--technology leads to social change, and social change leads to technology. In general, Ogburn stressed that the usual direction of change is for material culture (technology) to change first, and for the symbolic culture (people's ideas and ways of life) to follow.

III.   **How Technology Changes Society**

    A.   Technology refers to both the tools used to accomplish tasks and to the skills or procedures to make and use those tools.

    1.   Technology is an artificial means of extending human abilities.

    2.   Although all human groups use technology, it is the chief characteristic of postindustrial societies because it greatly extends our abilities to analyze information, to communicate, and to travel.

    3.   While all human groups make and use technology, it is the chief characteristic of postindustrial societies. The new technologies of information, communication and travel create new possibilities.

  B.   New technologies can reshape an entire society. Five ways in which technology can shape an entire society are:

    1.   Transformation of existing technologies (e.g., the computer is rendering the typewriter practically obsolete).

    2.   Changes in social organization (e.g., introduction of factories changed the nature of work: people gathered in one place to do their work, were given specialized tasks, and became responsible for only part of an item, not the entire item).

    3.   Changes in ideology (e. g., the new technology that led to the factory stimulated new ideologies such as maximizing profits).

    4.   Transformation of values (e.g., if technology is limited to clubbing animals, strength and cunning are valued; if technology requires creativity and analysis, abstract thought is valued).

    5.   Transformation of social relationships (e.g., as men went to work in the factories, family relationships changed; as more women work outside the home, family relationships again are changing).

  C.   The automobile is an example of technological change. The automobile has pushed aside old technology (the horse and buggy); it has changed the shape of cities; it has changed rural life, providing farmers a better lifestyle but drying up old villages; it has changed architecture (drive-up windows, etc.); it has changed courtship practices and sexual norms; and it has had a major effect on the lives of women, giving them the opportunity to "go shopping" and exert greater control over the family budget.

  D.   The computer is another example, changing medicine, education, and the workplace. On the negative side are increased surveillance of workers and depersonalization.

  E.   Computers shrink the world in terms of both time and space. With the information superhighway, homes and businesses are connected by a rapid flow of information. The implications of this superhighway for national and global stratification are severe.

    1.   On a national level, we may end up with information have-nots among inner-city and rural residents, thus perpetuating existing inequalities.

    2.   On a global level, the highly industrialized nations will control the information superhighway thereby destining the least industrialized nations to a perpetual pauper status.

III.   The Growth Machine versus the Earth

  A.   The globalization of capitalism underlies today's environmental decay.

    1.   The highly industrialized nations continue to push for economic growth, the industrializing nations strive to achieve faster economic growth, and the least industrialized nations, anxious to enter the race, push for even faster growth.

    2.   If our goal is a sustainable environment, we must stop turning the earth's natural resources into trash.

  B.   Industrialization led to a major assault on the environment. While it has been viewed as good for the nation's welfare, it has also contributed to today's environmental problems.

1. Many of our problems today--depletion of the ozone layer; acid rain; the greenhouse effect; and global warming--are associated with our dependence on fossil fuels.

2. There is an abundant source of natural energy that would provide low-cost power and therefore help to raise the living standards of humans across the globe. Better technology is needed to harness this energy supply. From a conflict perspective, such abundant sources of energy present a threat to the multinationals' energy monopoly. We cannot expect the practical development and widespread use of alternative sources of power until the multinationals have cornered the market on the technology that will harness them.

3. Racial minorities and the poor are disproportionately exposed to air pollution, hazardous waste, pesticides and the like. To deal with this issue a new specialty known as environmental poverty law is developing.

C. Environmental degradation is also a problem in the Industrializing and the Least Industrialized Nations, as these countries rushed into global industrial competition without the funds to purchase expensive pollution controls.

1. Pollution was treated as a state secret in the former Soviet Union. With protest stifled, no environmental protection laws to inhibit pollution, and production quotas to be met, environmental pollution was rampant. Almost one-half of Russia's arable land is unsuitable for farming, air pollution in cities is ten times higher than that which is permitted in the U.S., and half the tap water is unfit to drink.

2. The combined pressures of population growth and almost nonexistent environmental regulations destine Least Industrialized Nations to become the earth's major source of pollution. Some companies in the Most Industrialized Nations use the Least Industrialized Nations as a garbage dump for hazardous wastes and for producing chemicals no longer tolerated in their own countries.

3. As tropical rain forests are cleared for lumber, farms and pastures, the consequence may be the extinction of numerous plant and animal species. As the rain forests disappear at a rate of nearly 2,500 acres every hour, it is estimated that 10,000 species are made extinct each year.

D. Concern about the world's severe environmental problems has produced a worldwide social movement. In some countries, the environment has become a major issue in local and national elections. This movement seeks solutions in education, legislation, and political activism.

E. Environmental sociology examines the relationship between human societies and the environment. Its basic assumptions include: (1) the physical environment is a significant variable in sociological investigation; (2) humans are but one species among many that are dependent on the environment; (3) because of intricate feedbacks to nature, human actions have many unintended consequences; (4) the world is finite, so there are potential physical limits to economic growth; (5) economic expansion requires increased extraction of resources from the environment; (6) increased extraction of resources leads to ecological problems; (7) these ecological problems place restrictions on economic expansion; and (8) the state creates environmental problems by trying to create conditions for the profitable accumulation of capital.

F. If we are to have a world that is worth passing on to the coming generations, we must seek harmony between technology and the natural environment. As a parallel to development of technologies, we must develop systems to reduce technology's harm to the environment, and mechanisms to enforce rules for the production, use, and disposal of technology.

☞ KEY TERMS
After studying the chapter, review the definition of each of the following terms.

acid rain: rain containing sulfuric and nitric acid (produced by the reaction of sulfur dioxide and nitrogen oxide with moisture when released into the air with the burning of fossil fuels)

alienation: Marx's term for workers' lack of connection to the product of their labor, caused by their being assigned repetitive tasks on a small part of a product

corporate welfare: the gifts or financial incentives (tax breaks, subsidies, and even land and stadiums) given to companies in order to attract them to an area or induce them to remain

cultural lag: Ogburn's term for human behavior lagging behind technological innovation

dialectical process: each arrangement, or thesis, contains contradictions, or antitheses, which must be resolved; the new arrangement, or synthesis, contains its own contradictions, and so on

diffusion: the spread of invention or discovery from one area to another; identified by William Ogburn as the final of three processes of social change

discovery: a new way of seeing reality; identified by William Ogburn as the second of three processes of social change

ecosabotage: actions taken to sabotage the efforts of people thought to be legally harming the environment

environmental racism: the greater impact of pollution on the poor and racial-ethnic minorities

environmental sociology: a subdiscipline of sociology that examines how human activities affect the physical environment and how the physical environment affects human activities

global warming: an increase in the earth's temperature due to the greenhouse effect

greenhouse effect: the buildup of carbon dioxide in the earth's atmosphere that allows light to enter but inhibits the release of heat; believed to cause global warming

invention: the combination of existing elements and materials to form new ones; identified by William Ogburn as the first of three processes of social change

modernization: the process by which a *Gemeinschaft* society is transformed into a *Gesellschaft* society

postmodern society: another term for postindustrial society; its chief characteristic is the use of tools that extend the human abilities to gather and analyze information, to communicate, and to travel

social change: the alteration of culture and societies over time

sustainable environment: a world system that takes into account the limits of the environment, produces enough material goods for everyone's needs, and leaves a heritage of a sound environment for the next generation

technology: often defined as the applications of science, but can be conceptualized as tools, items used to accomplish tasks, along with the skills or procedures necessary to make and use those tools

☞ KEY PEOPLE
Review the major theoretical contributions or findings of these people.

Jacques Ellul: This French sociologist warned that technology is destroying traditional values and producing a monolithic world culture in which variety is mere appearance.

James Flink: Flink examined the numerous ways in which the automobile has transformed U.S. society and culture, from architecture to women's roles.

William Ogburn: Ogburn identified three processes of social change: invention, discovery, and diffusion. He also coined the term "cultural lag" to describe a situation in which some elements of culture adapt to an invention or discovery more rapidly than others.

Karl Marx: Marx developed the theory of dialectical materialism.

Lewis Henry Morgan: Morgan's theory of social development once dominated Western thought. He suggested that societies pass through three stages: savagery, barbarism, and civilization.

Oswald Spengler: Spengler wrote *The Decline of the West* in which he proposed that Western civilization was declining.

Arnold Toynbee: This historian suggested that each time a civilization successfully meets a challenge, oppositional forces are set up. Eventually, the oppositional forces are set loose, and the fabric of society is ripped apart.

Max Weber: Weber argued that capitalism grew out of the Protestant Reformation.

☞ "DOWN-TO-EARTH SOCIOLOGY"

This is your opportunity to apply the sociological perspective to the world around you. The questions in this section refer to material introduced in this chapter of your text. Many ask you to think about ideas and information presented in the various special "boxes" that are located throughout this chapter.

1. What are your views about technology's impact on our own and other societies? Do you think that technology helps or harms us? Does the Unabomber, and the Luddites before him, have a legitimate argument (p. 641)? Do you think that it is possible to control the impact of technology without having to go to such extreme measures? Why or why not?

2. Had you ever heard about corporate welfare before reading "Corporations and Big Welfare Bucks" on page 651? Should we continue to give breaks to companies even after they have an established record of polluting? How would a functionalist and a conflict theorist explain this arrangement?

3. After reading "The Rain Forest: Lost Tribes, Lost Knowledge" on page 653, why do you think there is now concern about the loss of tribal knowledge? What is the world losing as the rain forests disappear? Do you think "cultural ignorance" is a valid defense for crimes committed against such groups?

4. Do you think "Ecosabotage," (pp. 654-655), is ever justified? Do you think radical acts can do more harm than good? Do they alienate or unite supporters of the movement?

☞ SELF-TEST

After completing this self-test, check your answers against the Answer Key beginning on page 413 of this Study Guide and against the text on page(s) indicated in parentheses.

MULTIPLE CHOICE QUESTIONS

1. The alteration of culture and society over time is: (634)
   a. social transformation.
   b. social metamorphose.
   c. social alternation.
   d. social change.

2. Max Weber identified _____ as the core reason for the development of capitalism. (635)
    a. religion
    b. industrialization
    c. politics
    d. None of the above.

3. The Least Industrialized Nations become dependent on countries that have already industrialized and they are unable to develop their own resources according to: (636)
    a. dependency theory.
    b. capitalist exploitation theory.
    c. evolutionary theory.
    d. multilinear evolution theory.

4. Which of the following does the author of the text identify as a threat to the global map that was drawn up by the G7? (637)
    a. stricter environmental controls in the least industrialized nations
    b. stiffer tariff regulation world-wide
    c. resurgence of ethnic conflicts
    d. ecosabotage

5. _____ theories assume that all societies follow the same path, evolving from simple to complex through uniform sequences. (638)
    a. Cyclical
    b. Uniformity
    c. Unilinear evolution
    d. Multilinear evolution

6. Today, evolutionary theories have been: (638)
    a. accepted because history largely has proven this perspective to be correct.
    b. rejected because the assumption of progress has been cast aside.
    c. neither rejected or accepted because these theories take into account the rich diversity of traditional cultures.
    d. None of the above.

7. Which of the following attempt to account for the rise of entire civilizations, not a particular society? (638)
    a. multilinear evolutionary theory
    b. cyclical theory
    c. conflict theory
    d. epoch theory

8. According to Karl Marx, each _____ sows the seeds of its own destruction. (639)
    a. thesis
    b. ruling class
    c. epoch
    d. exploited class

9. Ogburn called the process of change that involves new ways of seeing reality as: (639)
    a. invention.
    b. discovery.
    c. diffusion.
    d. exploration.

10. The situation in which some elements of a culture adapt to an invention or discovery more rapidly than others is: (640)
    a. cultural downtime.
    b. cultural lag.
    c. cultural delay.
    d. cultural drag.

11. Ogburn's analysis has been criticized because: (640)
    a. it is too narrow in focus, not suitable for explaining the transformation of industrial into postindustrial societies.
    b. it does not recognize the importance of technology for social change.
    c. it places too great an emphasis on technology as the source for almost all social change.
    d. it predicts that material culture will change in response to symbolic culture, when in fact it is symbolic culture that changes in response to material culture.

12. Technology refers to: (641)
    a. items that people use to accomplish a wide range of tasks.
    b. skills and procedures that are employed in the development and utilization of tools.
    c. tools ranging from combs or hairbrushes to computers and the Internet.
    d. All of the above.

13. According to Karl Marx, the change-over to the factory system produced: (643)
    a. rationality.
    b. alienation.
    c. efficiency.
    d. worker satisfaction.

14. The fact that as men were drawn out of their homes to work in factories, family relationships changed is an example of: (643)
    a. changes in social organizations produced by technology.
    b. changes in social relationships produced by technology.
    c. changes in ideologies produced by technology.
    d. None of the above.

15. The automobile: (643-645)
    a. has changed the shape of cities.
    b. has stimulated mass suburbanization.
    c. has altered dating and courting rituals.
    d. All of the above.

16. A new development that allows doctors in one state or country to check the heart condition of a patient in an entirely different location is: (647)
    a. electronic imaging technology.
    b. remote heart monitoring.
    c. telemedicine.
    d. cardiac computerization.

17. Which of the following is <u>not</u> one of the ways computers transform the workplace? (648)
    a. changing the way in which we do work
    b. altering social relationships
    c. making it easier to accomplish tasks in a shorter period of time
    d. reversing the location of where work is done

18. One concern about the expansion of the information superhighway is: (649)
    a. interest in accessing it will outstrip capacity to carry so many users.
    b. social inequalities will become greater, both on a national and global basis.
    c. people will tie up the services with non-essential activities.
    d. people will become even more alienated as they relate more and more through their computers and less and less face to face.

19. The consequence of burning fossil fuels is: (651-652)
    a. acid rain.
    b. the greenhouse effect.
    c. global warming.
    d. All of the above.

20. How do conflict theorists explain the energy shortage? (652)
    a. They note that the earth has a limited supply of energy, and that multinational corporations are rapidly depleting it.
    b. There is no reliable alternative to the internal combustion engine.
    c. They argue that multinational corporations are unwilling to develop alternative energy sources, because it would threaten their monopoly over existing fossil fuels and cut into their profits.
    d. As a result of the past exploitation of natural resources by profit-hungry multinational corporations, there are no longer alternative energy resources that are reliable.

21. Which groups in U.S. society are disproportionately exposed to environmental hazards? (652)
    a. office workers and factory workers
    b. racial minorities and the poor
    c. farm workers and lumberjacks
    d. racial and ethnic groups

22. The major source of pollution in the future is likely to be: (652)
    a. the least industrialized nations.
    b. the industrializing nations.
    c. the highly industrialized nations.
    d. another planet.

23. Which of the following presents the greatest threat to the survival of numerous plant and animal species? (653)
    a. the continued burning of fossil fuels
    b. the dumping of toxic waste in the least industrialized nations
    c. the disappearance of the world's rain forests
    d. the greenhouse effect

24. Environmental sociology examines: (655-656)
    a. how the physical environment affects human activities.
    b. how human activities affect the physical environment.
    c. the unintended consequences of human actions.
    d. All of the above.

25. What is the goal of environmental sociologists? (656)
    a. to stop pollution
    b. to do research on the mutual impact that individuals and environments have on one another
    c. to empower those who are disadvantaged by environmental threats so that the quality of their lives will be improved
    d. to lobby for alternatives to fossil fuels

TRUE-FALSE QUESTIONS

T F 1. The rapid social change that the world is currently experiencing is a random event. (634)
T F 2. Our lives today are being vitally affected by a third social revolution. (634)
T F 3. Modernization is the change from agricultural to industrial societies. (636)
T F 4. Capitalism and industrialization have brought the least industrialized nations to the second stage of the demographic transition. (621-636)
T F 5. For the industrial nations, the ethnic slaughter in Africa is of significant concern. (638)
T F 6. The assumption of evolutionary theories that all societies progress from a primitive state to a highly complex state has been proven. (638)
T F 7. Cyclical theories assume that civilizations are like organisms. (639)
T F 8. Some cyclical theories predict the decline of Western civilization. (639)
T F 9. Invention, discovery, and diffusion are Ogburn's three processes of social change. (639)
T F 10. Technology usually changes first, followed by culture. (640)
T F 11. Technology is not a very powerful force for social change. (641)
T F 12. Marx believed that the change to the factory system was a source of alienation. (643)
T F 13. While technology may produce ideological changes, it has little impact on underlying social values. (643)
T F 14. Automobiles altered the architecture of American homes. (644)
T F 15. The use of computers in education will significantly reduce existing social inequalities between school districts. (648)
T F 16. Computers create the possibility for increased surveillance of workers and depersonalization. (648)
T F 17. Today's information revolution will perpetuate global stratification. (649)
T F 18. The serious assault on the environment was the result of the Industrial Revolution. (650)
T F 19. Scientists are in agreement that the problems of acid rain and the greenhouse effect must be solved quickly. (652)

T F   20.   Environmental sociology examines the relationship between human societies and the environment. (655-656)

FILL-IN QUESTIONS

1.   _____ is the alteration of culture and societies over time. (634)
2.   The process by which a *Gemeinschaft* society is transformed into a *Gesellschaft* society is _____. (636)
3.   The assumption that all societies follow the same path, evolving from the simple to the complex, is central to _____. (638)
4.   Karl Marx used the term _____ to refer to the new arrangement of power that emerges out of the struggle between the _____ (existing power arrangement) and _____ (its opposition). (639)
5.   The combination of existing elements and materials to form new ones is _____. (639)
6.   _____ is a new way of seeing reality. (639)
7.   According to Ogburn, because of travel, trade, or conquest, _____ of an invention or discovery occurs. (640)
8.   The situation in which some elements of a culture adapt to an invention or discovery more rapidly than others is _____. (640)
9.   The chief characteristic of _____ is the use of tools that extend human abilities to gather and analyze information, to communicate, and to travel. (641)
10.   _____ is Marx's term for workers' lack of connection to the product of their labor caused by their being assigned repetitive tasks on a small part of a product. (643)
11.   We use the term _____ to convey the ideas of information traveling at a high rate of speed among homes and businesses. (649)
12.   A world system that takes into account the limits of the environment, produces enough material goods for everyone's needs, and leaves a heritage of a sound environment for the next generation is the definition of _____. (649)
13.   Rain containing sulfuric and nitric acid, produced by the reaction of sulfur dioxide and nitrogen oxide with moisture when released into the air with the burning of fossil fuels is _____. (651)
14.   The greenhouse effect is believed to produce _____. (652)
15.   The destruction of _____ contributes to the extinction of numerous plant and animal species. (653)

MATCH THESE SOCIAL SCIENTISTS WITH THEIR CONTRIBUTIONS

___1. Jacques Ellul   a. *three-stage theory of social development*
___2. James Flink   b. *studied the impact of the auto on U.S. society*
___3. William Ogburn   c. *capitalism developed out of Protestantism*
___4. Karl Marx   d. *three processes of social change*
___5. Lewis Henry Morgan   e. *oppositional forces will tear society apart*
___6. Oswald Spengler   f. *technology is destroying traditional values*
___7. Arnold Toynbee   g. *theory of dialectical materialism*
___8. Max Weber   h. *proposed that Western civilization is in decline*

<u>ESSAY QUESTIONS</u>

1.   Discuss Ogburn's three processes of social change, provide examples to illustrate each and evaluate the theory.

2.   Choose a particular technology--you can use the automobile or the computer--and discuss the impact that it has had on U.S. society.

3.   Discuss the role that global stratification plays in the worldwide environmental problems.

GLOSSARY OF WORDS TO KNOW

aberration: something that is different from the expected; deviations from what is normal

abject poverty: greatest degree of most miserable poverty

ablation: surgically removing a part of the body

abuzz: filled with excitement

acquiescing: surrendering or giving in

acupuncture: piercing certain places in the body in the belief it will bring a desired result

adherents: people who believe in something

advocates: people who support a particular argument

aerodynamics: dealing with how planes, etc., fly

aghast: shocked or horrified

akin: related to

alas and alack: an expression of sorrow or regret

albeit: although

alleviate: make less painful

altruistic urge: an unselfish desire

ambivalent: uncertain, unable to make up your mind

amenable: able to be influenced

amorphous: not having a definite shape or structure

animal husbandry: growing animals such as cattle and sheep

annihilate: to eliminate completely

anonymous: the person who did it having an undisclosed identity

Antichrist: a religious belief that a great enemy of Christ is expected to fill the world with wickedness but will be conquered forever by Christ at his second coming

antonym: a word of opposite meaning

apparatus: equipment

apprenticed: learn a trade or skill by working under a master craftsman

Armageddon: the end of the world, as predicted in the Bible

armchair philosophy: to speculate about the nature things without ever doing scientific research

ascetic: a person who adheres to a strict discipline

aspirated: having been drawn out, perhaps by the use of suction

astrology: purported science of determining events by the location of planets, etc.

atonement: make up for past wrongs or sins

avengers: people who get satisfaction from punishing a wrongdoer

backlash: a strong negative reaction to a recent political or social development

bag lady: a street woman who carries her belongings in bag

bag of scum: an insulting expression, meaning someone is disgusting

ballooned: expanding rapidly

bandied about: passed along without being careful

bar codes: the lined markings printed on many products containing price information which is scanned and the information transmitted to a cash register

barrage: a massive amount of information given in a concentrated format *beer gut:* a large stomach hanging over the top of a man's belt and is associated with drinking beer

behemoth: very large corporation

bestiality: to display animal-like traits

Beavises and Butt-heads: reference to two cartoon characters who are distinguished by their crude behavior

bickering: arguing over trivial matters

bilingual: speaking at least two languages

bill of goods: a list of items to be purchased

billfold: another term of a wallet; a place to keep money (bills)

Black Maria: police wagon

blander: to become more dull

blasphemy: cursing, especially if used in connection with religion

blindfolded: having something placed over the eyes so that a person cannot see

blip: a slight irregularity

bloated: swollen, filled to capacity or overflowing

bludgeoned: to hit with heavy impact

bogus: fake

bolster: to re-enforce; to give a boost to

bondage: capturing and binding someone up; the term also refers to a form of sexual activity in which one person is put in some kind of restraints before engaging in sex

boot camp: the place where military recruits go for basic training

boozers: heavy drinkers of alcoholic beverages

bottlenecks: thin places through which large quantities need to pass, as in the opening at the top of a soda pop bottle

boycotts: protests in which individuals from a group being boycotted are not allowed to participate in activities (including sports) with others

breezeway: a covered passageway, without sides, connecting two structures

bridge the gap: to try and close the space between two phenomena

brute: cruel or savage

bull market: a condition in which traders on the stock market are engaged in trying to raise the prices of stocks that are being traded

bucolic: pastoral

buffeting: battering; striking repeatedly

burros: donkeys

burnout: condition of having become emotionally exhausted by a job, etc.

burying their heads in the sand: unwilling to recognize a situation

C

Calvinism: an early Protestant religious groups whose followers believed that their fate after death was

canonical scripture: religious teachings considered to be the final authority

cantankerous: bad-tempered

capital gains: gains from selling an asset held for investment

cardinal rule: a basic rule

carjacking: forcing a driver out of the car while it is in motion and then stealing it away from him or her

carousers: those who drank and partied

cash crops: crops that were grown exclusively for sale rather than personal consumption

catch-all: something that is intended to hold all sorts of odds and ends

cerebral cortex: the outer layer of gray matter over the brain *cesarean section:* surgery for delivering a baby by cutting through a mother's abdomen

chaos: extreme disorder

chasm: a deep or wide division

chronicle: to keep a record of

circuitry: elements through which electricity flows, as in a computer

clamored: gathered around demanding something

cling: to hold on tightly to something or someone

cliques: small, tightly-knit groups

coalesce: come together

cockeyed: slightly crazy; ridiculous

cocoon: a protective covered produced by an animal

cohesiveness: the quality of sticking together

coining: creating a new phase or expression

cold shoulder: unfriendly

collision course: a situation in which two forces are set to run headlong into one another

collusion: acting together to cause something illegal or wrong to occur

commonsense: things everyone should realize

computer conferencing: to communicate by way of computers

con artists: people who take advantage of others who are easily fooled

concrete: being solid or specific

confiscation: a taking of property by the government without payment

confrontational: opposing each other boldly

congregation: the group of people belonging to a church

conjugal rights: rights as a husband or wife

convergence: coming together; the place where that happens

coronation: ceremony proclaiming a person as king or queen

coup d'etat: the overthrow of a government

court martial: military criminal court

cramped: to be confined to a very small space

crassly: insensitively

credit histories: a written record of an individual's loans from banks and credit companies

cultural boor: someone who is rude or insensitive about the cultural norms

curfew: time of day after which a person is not allowed out of the house or into an area

curtsies: bending the knees and slightly bowing in a gesture of respect

czarist Russia: Russia during the time it was ruled by czars (monarchs)

dangled: hung loosely so as to swing freely

deaf-mute: a person who is deaf and unable to speak

death squads: military squadrons that engage in the clandestine murder of civilians

debutante balls: formal dances for young women from prominent families to be "presented" to society

decertified: the person's certification to be a member of the profession is taken away

decipher: attempt to read and understand

dedicated pacifists: people strongly opposed to any use of war

deferential behavior: very respectful behavior

defiant: bold

defrocked rabbi, priest, or nun: a person who formerly held a religious positions but no long does

deleterious: harmful

deluged: overwhelmed

delved into: studied at great length

demography: statistical study of populations

denigrate: to put down or belittle someone

deranged: crazy

derogate: lower the value or esteem of

derogatory: a degrading comment that is intended to put someone down

despicable: deserving of contempt

detriment: injury or damage

dire: desperate warning of disaster

discordant: disagreement

disequilibrium: things not being in balance

disgruntled: unhappy or discontented

disheveled: untidy, rumpled

dissertation: a lengthy paper written in connection with obtaining a doctoral degree

distended: inflated

divine providence: care or guidance coming from God

doctoral: of or relating to work towards a doctorate degree

dogmatic: putting forth ideas as being authoritative without adequate grounds

doomed: condemned

dossier: file, often used in reference to a file kept by the government on its citizens

doting: seeming overly fond of someone

drudge work: work that is considered routine and boring

drudgery: work, viewed as a chore or grind

dull: stupid, slow intellectually

dweebs, dorks, nerds: people regarded as dull

dyed-in-the-wool: holding inflexible opinions

E

earth shattering: of fundamental importance, very sensational

easel: three-legged structure to hold a chart, etc.

eclipsed: reduced in importance or repute

eerily: weirdly, disturbingly

egalitarian: characterized by people having equal rights

electrodes: terminals that conduct electricity

elicitation: a response that is called forth

elicit: to bring out, to draw forth

emblazoned: decorated

embodiment: solid example of

embryos: in humans, the period from conception to about the eighth week

encapsulate: put into condensed format

enclave: small, almost completely surrounded, areas

encompasses: contains within it

encrusted: coated over with

encumbered: burdened with something

engender: to create or produce

engulfs: surrounding something completely

enshroud: to cover or enclose something, especially by using a shroud (burial sheet or garment)

enthusiasts: people who enjoy and support something

entrenched: firmly established; protected from attacks

enveloping: enclosing one object completely with another object

epileptic seizures: type of physical and mental dysfunctions caused by nervous disorders

epoch: an extended period of time

equilibrium: balance between opposing forces

essence: the very basis

estranged: removed, detached

estrangement: separation between people who formerly were friendly

ethnic stews: a mix of ethnic groups

euphoric: extremely happy

excommunicated: expelled from the church

exploitation: taking advantage of something

extemporaneous: improvised; not formal

extol: praise

extrapolating: estimating a result based on known values

F

Fahrenheit: a scale for measuring temperature

falsification: changing something to make it appear different

far-flung: spread over a wide area

faze: disturb

feigning: pretending

felony: serious offense for which people frequently are imprisoned

feudal society: economic system where peasants (serfs) worked in the landlord's fields of the landlord, keeping a portion of what they produced and giving another portion to the lord

fiber-optic: a thin fiber of glass or plastic that transmits light throughout its length by internal refractions; capable of bending light around corners

fiefdom: a feudal estate; something over which an individual as rights or control

fine-tuning: to make adjustments in order to assure a perfect fit

flagrant: to be very obvious, conspicuous

flailing: moving his arms around wildly

flare-ups: sudden outbursts of anger

flea market: a market, usually outdoors, where items are sold cheaply

flesh this out: make this discussion more complete

floundering: acting in a clumsy or ineffective way

flunkies: servants who obediently obey their superiors

fluttered: flapped, like a bird flaps its wings

fly in the face: to act in defiance of someone; to be contrary to expectations

fly in the ointment: something that representing a sticking point in a situation

foisted: done in a way that hid the true purpose

foment: incite or promote the development of

forays: trips outside to get something or do something

freaks: people who are at odds with the norm; someone who is different

freeloaders: someone who takes advantage of another person's generosity or hospitality without sharing the costs

frequency: how often something occurs over a period of time

freshly minted: newly issued

full blown: completely developed

G

gain the ear of: get access to; are heard by

gait: a style of walking, usually involving a sequence of steps

gang turf: the neighborhood in a city that is controlled to a gang

garnered the lion's share: receiving the largest share

generic sheepskin: degree from a college not having much prestige

gleaned: collected

glee: obvious joy

glitzy: showy, pretentious

gluttons: people with a great capacity for something; overeaters

gnawing: irritating

gobbled up: eaten up quickly

graffiti: writings or drawings on walls, buses, and other public fixtures

grandstands: the stands of seating where spectators to a sport sit; usually the seats are tiered

gringo: Latin American slang for Anglo-Americans

groggy: not fully awake

grotesque: so wrong that it upsets people

grudges: deeply felt resentments

gruesome: horrible, disgusting

guesstimate: an estimate based on a guess

guilds: a medieval association of merchants or craftsmen

gunny sacks: bags such as produce is hauled to markets in

gunslinging heroes: cowboys in the Wild West who wore guns in holsters and engaged in gun fights

gynecological: relating to the female reproductive system

H

hallucinogenic: causing a person to see and hear things that don't exist

hammered that into: to repeat an idea or thought over and over until the person understands

Harley hog: slang for a motorcycle made by the Harley-Davidson Company

harried: hurried, frazzled

hassle: a troubling situation

heinous: shocking or outrageous

herald: to announce the arrival of something or someone

heretic: nonbeliever

hippy: referring to large hips

hodgepodge: loose combination

holding up: robbing

hole-in-one: an expression used in golf, meaning to get the ball in the hole in one shot

Holocaust: systematic destruction of Jews by the Nazis before and during World War II

Holsteins: a breed of cattle

home economics: a course of study in which activities associated with maintaining a home and family are stressed *hovels:* deteriorated housing units

hovered: stayed more or less in one place; very slight movement

hygiene: practices related to cleanliness

hypocrites: people who say one thing, but do another

I

immersed: absorbed or engrossed in something

impeccable: errorless, perfect

imperceptible: not easily noticed

impetus: driving force

inalienable rights: rights that may not be taken or traded away

incarcerated: jailed, confined

incongruity: inappropriate combination

indolence: laziness

infamous: having a terrible reputation, disgraceful

infrared: lying outside the visible spectrum at the red end

inherent: naturally existing

innate: existing from birth

innocuous: not harmful in any way

instantaneous: occurring immediately

internships: supervised work experiences while still a student in preparation for a particular career

interrelated: connected in various ways

interspersed: something placed between other things at intervals

intricacies: complex relationships

inveterate conformists: people who always conform to a particular way of doing things

iron-fisted: acting in both a harsh and ruthless manner

ironic: sarcastic or humorous

Islamic fundamentalism: a branch of Islam calling for a literal interpretation of religious doctrine and beliefs

J

jacuzzis: mechanisms to swirl water through a tub or hot tub

jargon: the technical terms of a special activity or group

jaywalker: person who crosses streets at improper places

jitters: being so uncomfortable about something as to want to do something, but doing nothing

jockeying: maneuvering or manipulating

Judas dollars: money that is paid to someone if they will betray others

juxtaposing: placing things side by side

K

kibbutz: a type of settlement in Israel

kinky situations: offbeat situations

Ku Klux Klan: an organization that is committed to promoting the supremacy of the white race

L

laid up: gathered and stored for later use

lap of luxury: living in grand style

lariat: a long light rope used with a loop on one end, used to catch livestock

laudable: worthy of praise

laundromats: self-service laundry establishments

leeway: a margin of freedom or tolerance that is recognized as acceptable

levy: to impose a tax

listless: lifeless, to act without any energy

liturgy: religious rite appropriate to some event

load the dice: unfairly influence the outcome

looking-glass: a mirror

lumberjacking: cutting down trees for a living

lump: not divided into parts; collecting together without making distinctions

lunged: moved suddenly

M

makeshift: crude and temporary; a substitute

maladjusted: a person who does not fit in well

malnourished: not fed enough food to be healthy

malpractice: assertion that a professional has not performed something properly

martyr: person who suffers greatly for a cause

mascot: animal or thing used by a group as a symbol

maze: a collection of many different routes through which it is hard to find the right way to go

mecca: a place sought as a goal by many people

Mecca: birthplace of Muhammad and holy city of Islam

menacing: threatening

mercenaries: paid soldiers who do not necessarily believe in the cause for which they fight

metamorphosis: process of a major change in something, as when a caterpillar turns into a butterfly

meted out: carried out the prescribed penalty

microchip: the electronic device on which information and directions are stored in a computer

milked it: getting something out of something else, as in milking a cow for her milk

mimic: to imitate closely

mind-boggling: an idea or thought that overwhelming your thinking

mired: stuck in something, such as mud

misguided do-gooders: people who get in the way while thinking they are helping

Model T: a Ford car from earlier days; it was the first automobile to be produced on an assembly line

mold: a form that is used to produce the same shape over and over

"mom & pop" stores: small, neighborhood stores that are owned and operated by a couple

monolingual: speaking only one language

monolithic: consisting of a single unit

Moonies: members of the Unification church

moonshine: liquor that is made in homemade distilleries and sold on the black market

mortgage payments: payments to a back or loan company on a home loan

mused: thought over (here, I said to myself)

mushrooming: something that is expanding rapidly

mute: make it silent

mystique: mystical quality

N

nagging: complaining

ne'er-do-wells: people who never do well or right

neck and neck: in a close race

niche: a place or activity for which a person is best suited

nightsticks: police batons, used for hitting people

nonsensitive questions: questions people feel free to answer without embarrassment

nooks and crannies: small, secluded places

nudges: gentle pushes

number crunching: the excessive analysis of numbers

O

offshoot: a branching off from the main body

onerous: particularly unpleasant or burdensome

orgies: gatherings at which everyone loses their inhibitions and does whatever they want

orphanages: institutions where children without parents are sometimes cared for

outlandish: very strange; bizarre

overarching: greater or above others

P

paleontologist: one who studies prehistoric life forms

papyrus: a written scroll made of the leaves of a papyrus plant

paranoia: a feeling that people are trying to harm you

pathogenic: diseased

pauper: someone who is very poor

pawns: people or things having little value, and tending to be used by others

pecking order: social hierarchy based on asserting rank or power

perks: benefits of a particular position or job

pertinent: particularly important or relevant

pervade: became prevalent throughout

pervasive: spread throughout

pessimists: people who have a negative view

pestilence: large-scale infectious disease

philanthropy: helping mankind, by giving gifts and doing good deeds

piercing: penetrating beyond the surface

pimping: acting as the agent for prostitutes by lining up business clients

pinpointing: locating something very specifically

piqued: to stir up an interest in something

pitch in: to offer to help out

pittance: a very small (pitiful) amount

plateau: a leveling out

plight: bad situation

plummeting: rapidly falling

plundering: pillage, to take by force

police cruiser: police car

portent: an indication that something is going to occur

precepts: rules of action or conduct

preconceived: formed in advance

prep school: school that prepares people for college

priestly benediction: a prayer said at the end of a church service by a priest or minister

profiteering: making money off of a situation

prom: a dance held in connection with graduation

promiscuous: having more than one sexual partner

propelled: driven forward by using a force

psyche: soul and intellect

psychopathology: the study of psychological or behavioral dysfunctions occurring in mental disorders

Puritans: 16th and 17th century people who belonged to a religion having strict morals and beliefs

pygmies: very short people from some African tribes

Pygmy: a member of an African tribe who are generally under five feet in height

pyramid: a solid structure with four equal sides; each side is the shape of a triangle, and the base is large, while the top is pointed

Q

quadrangle: an open area surrounded on four sides by buildings

R

racier: indecent, off-color

raised a ruckus: caused quite a bit of concern

ramifications: consequences

rampant: spreading rapidly

realms: kingdoms or domains

rear: in this case, raised from childhood to adulthood

rebut: contradict or challenge

receptive: open to new ideas or ways of doing something

reciprocal: mutual; affecting each other

red light district: a part of town where the prostitutes practice their profession

relegated: assigned to

relentless: stubborn, persistent

reminiscent: something similar from the past

remittance: payment

remnants: the small parts or portions that are left over

remunerative: providing payment that is profitable

render: to give back or to restore

repentance: to see the evil of your ways and ask forgiveness, promising not to return to your former behavior

Resurrection: the Christian belief that Christ rose from death and once again lived among mortals

reverie: a period of time spent thinking of pleasant things

rickety: not well built, thus dangerous

riveted: focused intently

Rolling Stone: a magazine whose subject matter is the youth counterculture

rotary dial telephone: a telephone where numbers were dialed by turning a wheel on the phone's face

rubber-stamp: approve almost without thinking about it

rubble heap: a place when broken and useless things are thrown away *rudimentary:* most simple

S

sabotage: deliberate actions that are intended to undermine some action

saloons: establishments in which alcoholic beverages are sold and consumed

Satanism: the worship of Satan

satellite dishes: instruments that are used to pull in television signals

scapegoating: blaming someone else for what is wrong

scribble: to write quickly or carelessly

scrimmage: practice play between two squads on a team

scrutinizing: looking closely at something

scurrying: moving along in a rapid fashion

secondhand smoke: the smoke that is breathed in by a non-smoker when a smoker exhales

seediest: very rundown, impoverished

semidarkness: almost, but not quite, dark

seminaries: schools which train people to become priests

senile: a state of forgetfulness

sexual promiscuity: engaging in sex with many persons

shadowed: followed closely

shambles: a condition of disorder or extreme confusion and mess

share-cropping: a system of farming in which the farmer is provided with credit for seed, tools, living quarters, and food in exchange for working the land. When the crop is harvested, the farmer receives an agreed upon share of the value for the crop minus the credit charges

shenanigans: dishonest tricks

shiftlessness: lazy, lacking in ambition

shoddy: poor quality

shoo off the flies: driving flies away by sounds or gestures

shop classes: classes in school where industrial and mechanical arts are taught

shoplift: steal something from a store that is open for business

shorthand: using symbols for words or thoughts

show and tell: a time in the school day when children share items or ideas with each other

shunted off: moved something out of the way

sidestepped: gotten around

sidetracked: diverted from the main issue

skewed: something that is not symmetrical

skitter: to glide of skip lightly along the surface

skittering gait: moving along quickly

skyrocketing: rising rapidly

sleight-of-hand: deceiving, as with magic tricks

smarting: embarrassing

smugness: feeling extremely correct about something; very satisfied with yourself

sniping: attacking indirectly

sniveling: falsely displaying a need for sympathy

"snotty" remarks: comments that are intended to be spiteful or unpleasant

solace: comfort

sound bites: short segments of information that are broadcast by the media

sovereign: being of the most supreme kind

spawned: produced or created

spigot: water faucet or valve

spiraling: a spreading and accelerating increase or decrease

splinter: to split into parts or factions; a group that has split off from the parent organization

split second: a really short period of time

spontaneous: occurring naturally, instead of from ritual

spurious: incorrect, artificial

Sputnik: the name given the first Russian space satellite

squandered: wasted

"squealed": informing on someone to the authorities

stampede: a group of animals rushing wildly ahead, with no sense of direction

"stand-alone": independent; in this case, the only method to be used

standoff: a counterbalancing effect; a draw

status quo: current condition

staunch: substantial, faithful

steered: pushed into following a particular course of action

stigma: a mark of shame or disgrace

stigmatize: to be branded with a stigma or mark

stooges: people who play the role of the victim of another's pranks

straitjacket: something that restrains a person

strange tongue: unaccustomed language

striptease: slowly removing clothes to excite someone

strutting: swaggering, walking with pride or to show off

stupefied: stunned, astounded

Styrofoam cup: a rigid, lightweight cup

subconscious: being aware of something without thinking about it

subjugated: brought under the control of

subpoenaed: required to be produced in connection with legal proceedings

subterranean: underground

succinct: stated clearly in a very few words

succumbed: having given in

sugarcoated: make more acceptable

superimposed: placed over something else

supposition: something that is supposed to be true

surreptitiously: secretly, furtively

surveillance: watching specific people or places, as by the police, without being seen

sutured: sewn up, as in a surgical procedure

swastikas: a symbol used by the Nazis

swerve: to abruptly change out of the path you are following

swishing: moving through a liquid with a light noise

sycophants: people who flatter others unduly for self gain

systematically: in a scientific manner

T

tailor a sentence: creating a punishment specifically to reflect individual circumstances

take potshots: attack randomly

tallied: counted

temporal: worldly; relating to time rather than space

tenacious: persistence

tendentious: argumentatively advancing a single point of view

theologians: individuals who study the works of religious bodies

thorny: particularly problematic

Thunderbird: a brand of cheap liquor

tinkering: playing around with, or trying to fix something

toast: to propose or to drink to, especially to honor someone

toddler: a very small child

toe the line: strictly follow the rules

touchdown: scoring points by crossing a goal line in football

traumatic: emotionally painful

treachery: violation of allegiance or confidence; treason

treadmill: a revolving device on which you walk without getting anywhere

tunnel vision: single-minded attention on only one thing; being extremely narrow minded

"turned ... tricks": engaged in prostitution

tweak the nose: irritate (literally, flick a finger on the nose)

unabashed: obvious, and intended to be so

underground artists: groups of artists who try not to be visible to authorities

unfettered: without any restraints

unobtrusive: not getting in people's way

uprooted: to be relocated; to be pulled out of a well-established place and moved elsewhere

usurped: taken within a right to

vagrants: people with no home or job

vanguard: the leaders at the front of something

vanquished: the people who were conquered

vegetate: engage in no activities

veneer: a thin outer layer

venerated: honored, worshipped

vested interest: a situation in which a person (or organization) has a strong personal commitment to the existing arrangements

vices: moral weaknesses or shortcoming

victimization: being made a victim

vigil: an act or a period of watching or surveillance

vignette: a brief story, a verbal sketch

virility: a characteristic in which masculinity is associated with being able to impregnate a woman

virtues: moral strengths

vocational: relating to an occupation or trade

voucher: a certificate

wait in the wings: a theatrical term, meaning for an actor to wait offstage until he or she is cued to make an appearance before the audience; in a general sense, it means to be a state of preparedness in case your involvement is required

wane: decline

wanton: lewd or sensual

warning flag: a flag that is waved as a signal of some possible danger ahead

watered down: diluted

wax eloquent: speak grandly, praising something

weeded out: removed from something more desirable

whetted: to become interested or excited about something

wholesaling: selling something in quantity

willy-nilly: randomly

window dressing: something that is done for appearance's sake

wolf down: to consume some food very quickly (like a wolf), by barely taking the time to chew it before swallowing it

womb: the uterus

wonderment: a cause or occasion for wonder

workaholic: a person addicted to work

Y

yardstick: a standard using in measuring

CHAPTER-BY-CHAPTER ANSWER KEY

☞ ANSWERS FOR CHAPTER 1

ANSWERS FOR THE MULTIPLE-CHOICE QUESTIONS

1. b   The sociological perspective is an approach to understanding human behavior by placing it within its broader social context. (4)

2. c   Generalization is one of the goals of scientific inquiry. It involves going beyond individual cases by making statements that apply to broader groups or situations. (7)

3. b   The Industrial Revolution, imperialism, and the development of the scientific method all contributed to the development of sociology. The fourth influence were the political revolutions in America and France--there was no political revolution in Britain at that time. Therefore, the correct answer is "b." (9-10)

4. d   Positivism is the application of the scientific approach to the social world. (11)

5. a   Herbert Spencer first stated the principle of "the survival of the fittest;" however, it often is attributed to Charles Darwin. (11)

6. b   The proletariat is the large group of workers who are exploited by the small group of capitalists who own the means of production, according to Karl Marx. (12)

7. a   Durkheim believed that social factors--patterns of behavior that characterize a social group-- explain many types of behavior, including suicide rates. (13)

8. b   In his research on suicide rates, Durkheim found that individuals' integration into their social groups influences the overall patterns of suicide between groups. He called this concept *social integration*. (13)

9. c   Max Weber's research on the rise of capitalism identified religious beliefs as the key. (14)

10. d   All are correct. Replication helps researchers overcome distortions that values can cause, results can be compared when a study is repeated, and replication involves the repetition of a study by other researchers. (15)

11. c   Social facts and *Verstehen* go hand-in-hand. Social facts are patterns of behavior that characterize a social group. By applying *Verstehen*--your understanding of what it means to be human and to face various situations in life--you gain an understanding of people's behavior. (16)

12. b   In the 19th century, it was unlikely that women would study sociology because sex roles were rigidly defined; women were supposed to devote themselves to the four K's--*Kirche, Küchen, Kinder, und Kleider* (church, cooking, children, and clothes). (17)

13. c   W.E.B. Du Bois was an African American sociologist who wrote extensively on race relations. In both his personal and professional life he experienced prejudice and discrimination. His commitment to racial equality led him to establish the NAACP. (18-19)

14. c   Sociologists who conduct research for government commissions or agencies investigating social problems are practicing applied sociology. (22)

15. b   Symbolic interactionism is the theoretical perspective which views society as composed of symbols that people use to establish meaning, develop their views of the world, and communicate with one another. (24)

16. c   In explaining the high U.S. divorce rate, the symbolic interaction perspective would focus on explanations such as emotional satisfaction, the meaning of children, and the meaning of parenthood. (25)

17. a   According to Robert Merton, an action intended to help maintain a system's equilibrium is a

manifest function. (27)

18. d   Industrialization and urbanization have undermined the traditional purposes of the family, according to theorists using functional analysis. (28)

19. c   The idea that conflict is inherent in all relations that have authority was first asserted by Ralph Dahrendorf. (30)

20. b   Conflict theorists might explain the high rate of divorce by looking at society's basic inequalities between males and females. (31)

21. d   Since each theoretical perspective provides a different, often sharply contrasting picture of our world, no theory or level of analysis encompasses all of reality. By putting the contributions of each perspective and level of analysis together, we gain a more comprehensive picture of social life. (32)

22. c   The first phase of sociology in the United States stretched from the founding of the first departments of sociology in the last decade of the 19th century into the 1940s. This phase was characterized by an interest in using sociological knowledge to improve social life and change society. (32)

23. a   The purpose of pure or basic sociological research is to make discoveries about life in human groups, not to make changes in those groups. On the other hand, applied and clinical sociology are more involved in suggesting or bringing about social change. (32)

24. c   In recent years more and more sociologists have sought ways in which to apply their research findings to solving social problems. This represents a return to applied sociology. (33)

25. d   The author of your text suggests that *globalization*, the breaking down of national boundaries because of communication, trade and travel, is very likely going to transform sociology in the United States. As global issues intrude more and more into U.S. society, sociologists will have to broaden the scope and focus of their research. (33)

ANSWERS FOR TRUE-FALSE QUESTIONS

1.   *True* (4)
2.   *True* (4)
3.   *True* (6)
4.   *False*. Sociologists focus on external influences (people's experiences) instead of internal mechanisms, such as instincts. (7)
5.   *True* (7)
6.   *False*. Sociology has many similarities to the other social sciences. What distinguishes sociology from other disciplines is that sociologists do not focus on single social institutions, they study industrialized societies, and they stress factors external to the individual. (7)
7.   *True* (11)
8.   *True* (11)
9.   *True* (12)
10. *True* (13)
11. *False*. Weber agreed with much of what Marx wrote, but he strongly disagreed that economics is the central force in social change. Weber saw religion as playing that role. (14)
12. *True* (16)
13. *True* (16)
14. *False*. Harriet Martineau's ground-breaking work on social life in Great Britain and the United States was largely ignored; she is remembered for her translations of Auguste Comte's work. (17)

15. *True* (22)
16. *True* (23-24)
17. *False*. Although functionalists do believe the family has lost many of its traditional purposes, they do not believe they have all been lost. Some of the existing functions are presently under assault or are being eroded. (27)
18. *False*. Some conflict theorists use this theory in a much broader sense. For example, Ralf Dahrendorf sees conflict as inherent in all relationships that have authority. (30)
19. *True* (31)
20. *False*. Many sociologists are seeking ways to apply their knowledge, and many departments of sociology now offer courses in applied sociology. (32)

ANSWERS FOR THE FILL-IN QUESTIONS

1. People's group memberships because of their location in history and society is known as SOCIAL LOCATION. (4)
2. The NATURAL SCIENCES are the intellectual and academic disciplines designed to comprehend, explain, and predict the events in our natural environment. On the other hand, the SOCIAL SCIENCES examine human relationships. (6)
3. The use of objective systematic observation to test theories is SCIENTIFIC METHOD. (11)
4. CLASS CONFLICT was Karl Marx's term for the struggle between the proletariat and the bourgeoisie. (12)
5. Durkheim used the term SOCIAL INTEGRATION to refer to the degree to which people feel a part of social groups. (13)
6. VALUE FREE is the view that a sociologist's personal values or biases should not influence social research, while OBJECTIVITY is total neutrality. (14-15)
7. The meanings that people attach to their own behavior is called SUBJECTIVE MEANINGS. (16)
8. Durkheim used the term SOCIAL FACT to refer to patterns of behavior that characterize a social group. (16)
9. A THEORY is a general statement about how some parts of the world fit together and how they work. (22)
10. The theoretical perspective in which society is viewed as composed of symbols that people use to establish meaning, develop their views of the world, and communicate with one another is SYMBOLIC INTERACTIONISM. (23)
11. FUNCTIONAL analysis is a theoretical framework in which society is viewed as composed of various parts, each with a function that contributes to society's equilibrium. (27)
12. CONFLICT THEORY stresses that women have traditionally been regarded as property and passed by one male, the father, to another, the husband. (31)
13. MACRO-LEVEL analysis examines large-scale patterns of society, while MICRO-LEVEL analysis examines small-scale patterns of society. (31)
14. PURE (OR) BASIC sociology makes discoveries about life in human groups, not to make changes in those groups; APPLIED sociology is the use of sociology to solve problems. (32-33)
15. GLOBALIZATION is the process by which national boundaries are broken down because of advances in communication, trade, and travel. (33)

ANSWERS TO MATCH THESE SOCIAL SCIENTISTS WITH THEIR CONTRIBUTIONS

1. c   Auguste Comte: *proposed the use of positivism*

2. a   Herbert Spencer: *coined the phrase "the survival of the fittest"*
3. f   Karl Marx: *believed the key to human history was class struggle*
4. g   C. Wright Mills: *encouraged the use of the sociological perspective*
5. d   Emile Durkheim: *stressed social facts*
6. h   Harriet Martineau: *published Society in America and translated Comte's work into English*
7. i   Robert K. Merton: *distinguished between functions and dysfunctions*
8. b   W.E.B. Du Bois: *was an early African American sociologist*
9. e   Max Weber: *believed religion was a central force in social change*

GUIDELINES FOR ANSWERING THE ESSAY QUESTIONS

1.   *Explain what the sociological perspective encompasses and then, using that perspective, discuss the forces that shaped the discipline of sociology.*

There are two parts to this question. First, you are asked to define the sociological perspective. As you define this, you would want to mention the idea of social location, perhaps by bringing into your essay C. Wright Mills' observations on the connection between biography and history (pp. 4-5). Another way to explain the perspective would be to contrast sociology with other disciplines, talking about what sociology is and what it isn't (pp. 6-7)

The second part of the essay involves discussing the forces that shaped sociology and its early followers. What you are being asked is to think about what was going on in the social world in the early 19th century that might have led to the birth of this new discipline. Referring back to book, you would want to identify four causes: (1) the Industrial Revolution; (2) the political revolutions of America and France; (3) imperialism; and (4) the emergence of the scientific method (pp. 9-11). You would conclude by discussing how each of the early sociologists--Auguste Comte, Herbert Spencer, Karl Marx, Emile Durkheim, and Max Weber--were influenced by these broader forces in making a contribution to sociology (pp. 11-14). You could also bring into the discussion some of the material on sexism in early sociology, noting how the ideas about the appropriate role for women in society functioned to exclude women like Harriet Martineau and Jane Addams from the discipline (p. 17), or you could talk about the emergence of sociology in North America (pp. 17-19).

2.   *The textbook notes that Verstehen and social facts go hand in hand; explain how this is so. Assume that you have been asked to carry out research to find out more about why growing numbers of women and children are homeless and what particular problems they face. Discuss how you could you use both Verstehen and social facts in your study.*

First, you would want to define what *Verstehen* and social facts are and how they are compatible in terms of arriving at a complete picture of a social pattern (pp. 16-17). Then you can argue that social facts would be most appropriate in trying to explain why growing numbers of women and children are homeless--you might suggest that you would look at the changing economic status of women in society, the increase in the number of female-headed households, and the decline in the amount of affordable housing. On the other hand, by applying *Verstehen,* you would be able to discover what particular problems they face--through face-to-face interviews at shelter sites you would be able to experience firsthand some of what they are experiencing.

3.   *Explain each of the theoretical perspectives that are used in sociology and describe how a sociologist affiliated with one of another of the perspectives might undertake a study of gangs. Discuss how all three can be used in research.*

There are three major perspectives in sociology: symbolic interactionism, functional analysis, and conflict theory. Your first step is to explain the essential nature of each perspective and then to propose a research topic that would be consistent with the perspective. Because a symbolic interactionist focuses on the symbols that people use to establish meaning, develop their views of the world, and communicate with one another, in designing a research project on gangs, he or she would want to find out what meaning gangs and gang membership have for individuals who belong to them as well as those who live in communities in which gangs operate (pp. 23-24). A functionalist, who tries to identify the functions of a particular social pattern, would choose to study what contributions gangs make within the fabric of social life as well as the dysfunctions of gangs (pp. 27). Finally, a conflict theorist would study the competition for scarce resources among gangs and between gangs and the larger society because he or she is interested in struggles over power and control within social groups (p. 30). You would conclude by noting that each perspective provides an answer to an important question about the social order and by combining them you arrive at a more complete picture. (pp. 32).

☞ ANSWERS FOR CHAPTER 2

ANSWERS FOR MULTIPLE CHOICE QUESTIONS

1. b   Sociologists would use the term "nonmaterial culture" to refer to a group's ways of thinking and doing, including language and other forms of interaction as nonmaterial culture. (38)
2. d   Material culture includes weapons and machines, eating utensils, jewelry, hairstyles, and clothing; language is part of the nonmaterial, rather than the material, culture. (38)
3. a   The one statement that is not true regarding culture is that "people generally are aware of the effects of their own culture." (39)
4. d   The disorientation that James Henslin experienced when he came into contact with the fundamentally different culture of Morocco is known as cultural shock. (39)
5. c   An American who thinks citizens of another country are barbarians if they like to attend bullfights is demonstrating ethnocentrism. (39)
6   c   Robert Edgerton cautioned against blindly accepting other cultures on the basis of their cultures and values if those customs and values threaten the quality of people's lives. He advocated rating cultures according to their quality of life. (40-41)
7. d   Gestures can lead to misunderstandings and embarrassment when their meanings are not shared. (42-43)
8. a   It is possible for human experience to be cumulative and for people to share memories because of language. (43-44)
9. c   The example of the Eskimo children and their perceptions about different types of snow illustrates the Sapir-Whorf hypothesis, which suggests that language not only reflects a culture's way of thinking and perceiving the work, but also helps to shape thought and perception. (45-46)
10. d   Moral holidays like Mardi Gras often center around drunkenness and rowdiness. They are times when people can break the norms and not be sanctioned. Therefore, the correct answer is "all of the above." (47)
11. d   You have violated a folkway, norms related to everyday behavior that are not strictly enforced. (48)
12. a   Mores are essential to our core values and require conformity. (48)
13. d   Subcultures are a world within a world; have values and related behaviors that distinguish its members from the dominant culture; and include occupational groups. Therefore, all of the above are correct. (49)
14. c   Sociologically speaking, heavy metal adherents who glorify Satanism, cruelty, and sexism are examples of countercultures. (50)

15. a   A sociologist would describe the U.S. as a pluralistic society because it is made up of many different groups. (50)
16. d   The statement that is not correct is that "They [core values] rarely create much conflict as they change." In fact, core values do not change without meeting strong resistance from traditionalists. (50-54)
17. a   Value contradictions occur when a value, such as the one that stresses group superiority, comes into direct conflict with other values, such as democracy and equality. (51)
18. c   Henslin suggests that a new value cluster, made up of the values of leisure, self-fulfillment, physical fitness, and youngness, is now emerging in the United States. (53)
19. b   Ideal culture reflects the values and norms which a people attempt to follow; it is the goals held out for them. (54-55)
20. c   George Murdock analyzed the data that anthropologists had collected on hundreds of groups around the globe and compiled a list of activities that were common to all these groups. He found that although the activities were present, the specific customs differed from one group to another. (55)
21. d   The perspective that views human behavior as the result of natural selection and considers biological characteristics to be the fundamental cause of human behavior is sociobiology. (55)
22. d   The printing press or the computer would be considered *new technologies,* because both had a significant impact on social life following their invention. (57)
23. d   Continuing to visit physicians and to rely on the judgment about diagnosis and treatment of illness, even when computer tests do a better job, is an example of cultural lag. (58)
24. c   The adoption of bagels, woks and hammocks with the United States illustrates the process of cultural diffusion. (59)
25. b   Exporting the Golden Arches of McDonald's around the globe has produced cultural leveling. (59)

ANSWERS FOR TRUE-FALSE QUESTIONS

1.   *True* (39)
2.   *False.* Culture has a great deal to do with our ideas of right and wrong. For example, folkways and mores have sanctions attached to them to encourage people to do the right thing. (39-40)
3.   *True* (40)
4.   *True* (40)
5.   *False.* The gesture of nodding the head up and down to indicate "yes" is not universal. In some societies this gesture means "no." (43)
6.   *False.* Humans could not plan future events without language to convey meanings of past, present, and future points in time. (44)
7.   *True* (47)
8.   *False.* One society's folkways may be another society's mores. (48)
9.   *False.* Motorcycle enthusiasts who emphasize personal freedom and speed, while maintaining values of success, form part of a subculture, not a counterculture. Motorcycle gangs who commit crimes and use illegal drugs are an example of a counterculture. (48)
10.   *True* (51)
11.   *True* (51)
12.   *True* (52)
13.   *False.* Concern for the environment has not always been a core value in U.S. society. It is one of the emergent values that is now increasing in importance. (53)

14. *True* (54)
15. *True* (55)
16. *True* (55-56)
17. *True* (57)
18. *False*. New technologies not only affect the material culture, but they have a profound impact on the nonmaterial culture, including the way people think and what they value. (57-58)
19. *False*. According to Ogburn, it is the *material* culture that changes first, with the *nonmaterial* culture lagging behind. (58)
20. *True*. (58-59)

ANSWERS FOR FILL-IN QUESTIONS
1. Objects such as art, buildings, weapons, utensils, machines, hairstyles, clothing, and jewelry that distinguish a group of people are known as MATERIAL CULTURE; their ways of thinking and doing are NONMATERIAL CULTURE. (38)
2. A SYMBOL is something to which people attach meaning and then use to communicate with others. (42)
3. LANGUAGE is a system of symbols that can be combined in an infinite number of ways and can represent not only objects but also abstract thought. (43)
4. VALUES are ideas of what is desirable in life. (44)
5. The expectations or rules of behavior that develop out of values are referred to as NORMS. (47)
6. A TABOO is a norm so strongly ingrained that even the thought of its violation is greeted with revulsion. (49)
7. The term that describes a world within the larger world of the dominant culture is SUBCULTURE. (49)
8. VALUE CLUSTERS are a series of interrelated values that together form a larger whole. (53)
9. Sociologists call the norms and values that people actually follow REAL CULTURE. (55)
10. CULTURAL UNIVERSALS may not exist because even though there are universal human activities, there is no universally accepted way of doing any of them. (55)
11. In its broader sense, TECHNOLOGY includes the skills or procedures necessary to make and use tools. (57)
12. Both the printing press and the computer represent NEW TECHNOLOGIES because they had a significant impact on society following their introduction. (57)
13. William Ogburn used the term CULTURAL LAG to reflect the condition in which not all parts of a culture change at the same pace. (58)
14. The spread of cultural characteristics from one group to another is CULTURAL DIFFUSION. (59)
15. When Western industrial culture is imported and diffused into developing nations, the process is called CULTURAL LEVELING. (59)

ANSWERS TO MATCH THESE SOCIAL SCIENTISTS WITH THEIR CONTRIBUTIONS
1. f   Edward Sapir and Benjamin Whorf: *stated that language shapes reality*
2. I   Robin Williams: *noted core values in U.S. society*
3. c   George Murdock: *looked for cultural universals*
4. a   Irene Pepperberg: *taught language to a parrot*
5. h   Robert Edgerton: *criticized aspects of cultural relativism*

6. g   Edward Wilson: *believed that natural selection produced human behavior*
7. j   William Sumner: *developed the concept of ethnocentrism*
8. d   Allen and Beatrice Gardner: *taught chimps a gestural language*
9. b   William Ogburn: *introduced the concept of cultural lag*
10. e   JoEllen Shively: *studied Native Americans' identification with Westerns*

GUIDELINES FOR ANSWERING THE ESSAY QUESTIONS

1.   *Explain cultural relativism and discuss both the advantages and disadvantages of practicing it.*
    You would begin your essay by defining cultural relativism and explaining that it developed in reaction to ethnocentrism. The primary advantage of this approach to looking at other cultures is that we are able to appreciate another way of life without making judgements, thereby reducing the possibilities for conflict between cultures. The primary disadvantage is that it can be used to justify any cultural practice and especially those that endanger people's health, happiness, and survival. You could conclude with a reference to Robert Edgerton's proposed "quality of life" scale. (pp. 40-41).
2.   *Consider the degree to which the real culture of the United States falls short of the ideal culture. Provide concrete examples to support your essay.*
    Your first step is to define what real and ideal culture mean (pp. 54-55). Then you would want to refer to the core values that are identified in the text as reflective of the ideal culture and discuss the ways in which Americans fall far short of upholding these values in their everyday lives (50-54). An interesting example of the difference between ideal and real culture would be the increasing value we place on leisure, and yet we are working more hours than ever before, or the value we place on physical fitness and yet we are more obese and less physically fit than ever.
3.   *Evaluate what is gained and what is lost as technology advances in society.*
    One way to frame a response to this would be to identify a specific technology that has had a significant impact on our society and then to discuss both the gains and losses. For example, the automobile provided us with new opportunities for mobility, freeing us from the constraints of public transportation. The automobile created economic opportunities, as new industries and services opened up -- car dealerships, gas stations, fast food restaurants, and malls are just a few examples. At the same time, automobiles have contributed to urban sprawl and the decline of downtown shopping areas. We have become more isolated as we travel around in our cars rather than meeting and traveling with others on public transportation. The use of automobiles has contributed to increased congestion and air pollution. Finally, you could make the argument that the automobile has contributed to cultural leveling within the U.S., as regional differences have disappeared under the spread national businesses in malls and food chains (pp. 57-59)

☞ ANSWERS FOR CHAPTER 3

ANSWERS FOR MULTIPLE CHOICE QUESTIONS

1. b   Feral children supposedly were abandoned or lost by their parents and raised by animals. (64)
2. a   From the case of Isabelle, we can conclude that humans have no natural language. (64-65)
3. c   On the basis of studies involving institutionalized children, psychologists H.M.Skeels and H.B. Dye concluded that the absence of stimulating social interaction was the basic cause of low intelligence among these children, not some biological incapacity. (66-67)
4. d   Studies of isolated rhesus monkeys demonstrated that the monkeys were not able to adjust to monkey life, did not instinctively know how to enter into "monkey interaction" with other monkeys or how to engage in sexual intercourse. (67-68)

5. b   This statement "we move beyond the looking-glass self as we mature" is incorrect. All of the other statements about the development of self are correct: the development of self is an ongoing, lifelong process; the process of the looking-glass self applies to old age; and the self is always in process. (68-69)

6. c   According to Mead's theory, children pretend to take the roles of specific people--such as the Lone Ranger, Supergirl, or Batman--during the play stage. (70)

7. a   To George Mead, the "I" is the self as subject. (70)

8. b   According to Jean Piaget, children develop the ability to use symbols during the preoperational stage. (71)

9. b   According to Lawrence Kohlberg, when a young child like Larry tries very hard to be nice to his younger sister in order to please his mother, he is in the preconventional stage of moral development. (71-72)

10. c   From her early research, Carol Gilligan concluded that women are more likely than men to evaluate morality in terms of personal relationships. On the other hand, men use abstract principles, a code of ethics that defines what is right and wrong. (72)

11. c   Freud's term for a balancing force between the inborn drives for self-gratification and the demands of society is the ego. (73)

12. b   Although people around the world may share emotions, because emotions are in part due to biology, the way they express them varies considerably, and this expression is learned through socialization. Therefore, the only statement that is correct is "How we express emotions depends on our culture and our social location." (73-74)

13. c   According to this chapter, society sets up effective controls over our behavior by socializing us into self and emotions. (74-75)

14. b   The ways in which society sets children onto different courses for life purely because they are male or female is called gender socialization. (76)

15. d   Psychologists Susan Goldberg and Michael Lewis observed mothers with their six-month-old infants in a laboratory setting and concluded that the mothers unconsciously rewarded daughters for being passive and dependent. (76)

16. a   Research by Melissa Milkie indicates that young males actively used media images to help them understand what was expected of them as males in our society. (77)

17. c   According to Melvin Kohn, middle-class parents focus on developing their children's curiosity, self-expression, and self-control. (79-80)

18. d   "All of the above" is the correct response. Participation in religious services teaches us beliefs about the hereafter; ideas about dress, and speech and manners appropriate for formal occasions. (80)

19. c   Summarizing the findings of studies on the impact that day care has on preschool children, we can say that children from poor and dysfunctional families benefit from quality day care. (80-81)

20. b   Teachers are teaching the hidden curriculum when they teach young people to think that social problems, such as poverty and homelessness, have nothing to do with economic power, oppression and exploitation. (82)

21. d   In terms of children's peer groups and academic achievement, research by Patricia and Peter Adler suggests that for boys, to do well academically is to lose popularity, while for girls, getting good grades increases social standing. (83)

22. d   Resocialization occurs when a person takes a new job, joins a cult, or goes to boot camp. (84)

23. b   The statement that is incorrect is: "They are not very effective in stripping away people's

personal freedom." In fact, total institutions are very effective in stripping away individual's personal freedom because they are isolated from the public, they suppress preexisting statuses, they suppress cultural norms, and they closely supervise the entire lives of their residents. (84-85)

24. c   Historians have concluded that childhood--as we know it--did not exist in the past; children were considered miniature adults, dressing like adults and treated like adults, expected to work from a very young age. (86-87)

25. c   For many people, the later middle years is likely to be the most comfortable period of their entire lives. (90)

ANSWERS FOR TRUE-FALSE QUESTIONS

1.   *True.* (66)
2.   *False.* Studies of institutionalized children demonstrate that some of the characteristics that we take for granted as being "human" traits result not from basic instincts but rather from early close relations with other humans. (66-67)
3.   *False.* Because humans are not monkeys, we must always be careful about extrapolating from animal studies to human behavior. (68)
4.   *True.* (69)
5.   *False.* Subsequent research found no gender differences in moral reasoning. Instead, it was demonstrated that both men and women use personal relationships and abstract principles when they make moral judgments. Consequently, Gilligan no longer supports her original position. (72)
6.   *True.* (73)
7.   *False.* Socialization has a great deal to do with how we feel. Because different individuals' socialization differs, they will actually experience different emotions. (73-74)
8.   *True.* (74-75)
9.   False. Research indicates that parents let their sons roam farther from home than their daughters and that they subtly encourage them to participate in more rough-and-tumble play. (76)
10.   *True.* (77)
11.   *False.* We do not yet have studies of how these games affect their players' ideas of gender. (77)
12.   *True.* (80-81)
13.   *False.* It is a **manifest** function of education, not a **latent** function, to transmit skills and values appropriate for earning a living. (81)
14.   *True.* (83)
15.   *False.* Resocialization does not always require learning a radically different perspective; it usually only modifies existing orientations to life. (84)
16.   *True.* (86)
17.   *True.* (88)
18.   *True.* (89)
19.   *True.* (90)
20.   *False.* Sociologists do not think of people as little robots; they recognize that the self is dynamic and that people are actively involved in the social construction of the self. (91)

ANSWERS FOR FILL-IN QUESTIONS

1.   Sociologists are interested in studying how SOCIAL ENVIRONMENT influence the development of human characteristics. (64)
2.   SOCIALIZATION is the process by which people learn the characteristics of their group--the attitudes, values, and actions thought appropriate for them. (68)
3.   Charles H. Cooley coined the term LOOKING-GLASS SELF to describe the process by which a sense of self develops. (69)
4.   SIGNIFICANT OTHER is the term used to describe someone, such as a parent and/or a sibling, who plays a major role in our social development. (69)
5.   According to George Herbert Mead, the development of the self through role-taking goes through three stages: (1) IMITATION; (2) PLAY; and (3) GAMES. (70)
6.   The idea that personality consists of the id, ego, and superego was developed by SIGMUND FREUD. (72-73)
7.   We refer to the behaviors and attitudes which are considered appropriate for females as males as GENDER ROLES. (76)
8.   Television, music, and advertising are all types of MASS MEDIA which reinforce society's expectations of gender. (76)
9.   AGENTS OF SOCIALIZATION include the family, school, religion, peers, mass media, and workplace. (79)
10. Reading, writing, and arithmetic are all part of the MANIFEST FUNCTIONS of education. (81)
11. The HIDDEN CURRICULUM refers to values that may not be taught explicitly, but nevertheless form an inherent part of a school's "message." (82)
12. PEER GROUPS are made up of individuals the same age linked by common interests. (83)
13. The mental rehearsal for some future activity, or learning to play a role before actually entering it, is referred to as ANTICIPATORY SOCIALIZATION. (84)
14. Resocialization often takes place in TOTAL INSTITUTIONS such as boot camps, prisons, and concentration camps. (84)
15. DEGRADATION CEREMONY refers to the attempt to remake the self by stripping away an individual's self-identity and stamping a new identity in its place. (84)

ANSWERS TO MATCH THESE SOCIAL SCIENTISTS WITH THEIR CONTRIBUTIONS

1. e   Melvin Kohn: *found social class differences in child rearing*
2. d   Erving Goffman: *studied total institutions*
3. c   George Herbert Mead: *coined the term "generalized other"*
4. a   Charles H. Cooley: *coined the term "looking-glass self"*
5. g   Jean Piaget: *discovered that there are four stages in cognitive development*
6. b   Harry and Margaret Harlow: *conducted studies of isolated rhesus monkeys*
7. f   Sigmund Freud: *asserted that human behavior is based on unconscious drives*
8. h   Melissa Milkie: *studied the impact of media messages on adolescent males*

GUIDELINES FOR ANSWERING THE ESSAY QUESTIONS

1.   *Explain what is necessary in order for us to develop into full human beings.*
     You might want to be begin by stating that in order for us to become full human beings we need language and intimate social connections to others. You could draw on the information presented in the previous chapter as to what language enables us to do -- grasp relationships to others, think in terms of a shared past and future, and make shared plans. Our knowledge of language, and our ability

to use it, develops out of social interaction, as the evidence of those children raised in isolation demonstrates. Furthermore, we learn how to get along with others only through close personal experiences with others. The experience of Isabelle and the children raised in institutionalized settings confirms this (pp. 64-67).

2.　　*Why do sociologists argue that socialization is a process and not a product?*

　　Sociologists would argue that socialization is a process rather than a product because there is no end to socialization. It begins at birth and continues throughout one's life, whenever you take on a new role. Cooley was the first to note that we are continually modifying our sense of self depending on our reading of others' reactions to us (p. 68-69). Mead's work on taking the role of the other in the development of the self also suggests that socialization is a process (pp. 69-71). Researchers have identified a series of stages through which we pass as we age; at each stage we are confronted by new demands and new challenges that need to be mastered (pp. 86-91).

3.　　*After reading this chapter, how would you answer the question "Are We Prisoners of Socialization?"*

　　From reading this chapter and learning more about socialization you have hopefully learned that the self is dynamic, interacting with the social environment and being affected by it and in turn affecting it. We are involved in constructing our sense of self as active players rather than passive recipients (p. 91). In answering this question, you should also refer to the work of Cooley and Mead, as well as Piaget, Kohlberg, Gilligan and Freud, which demonstrates the role we play in the development of a sense of self (pp. 68-73).

☞ ANSWERS FOR CHAPTER 4

ANSWERS FOR MULTIPLE CHOICE QUESTIONS

1. a　　Microsociology focuses on social interaction. (96)
2. c　　Sociologists who study social class and how groups are related to one another are using macrosociology. (96)
3. b　　As a budding sociologist who is interested in homeless women's parenting strategies, you would use a microsociological approach. (96)
4. d　　Income, education, and occupational prestige all define one's social class. (98)
5. b　　Social status is the term referring to the position that an individual occupies within a society or social group; social class reflects income, education and occupation, social role refers to the social expectations about the behavior appropriate to a social status, and social location refers to an individual's place in the social structure. (98)
6. d　　Being a daughter, a lawyer, a wife, and a mother represents a person's status set. (98)
7. a　　A sociologist would use the term "ascribed status" to describe race, sex, and the social class of his or her parents. (99)
8. c　　Wedding rings, military uniforms, and clerical collars are all examples of status symbols. (100)
9. c　　The incorrect statement is: "Status symbols are always positive signs or people would not wear them." Some social statuses are negative, and therefore, so are their status symbols (e.g. prison clothing issued to inmates). (100)
10. b　　A master status is one that cuts across the other statuses that a person holds. (100)
11. a　　Status inconsistency is most likely to occur when a contradiction or mismatch between statuses exists. For example, a college professor is accorded relatively high prestige while at the same time is generally not very well-paid. (100)
12. d　　The behaviors, obligations, and privileges attached to statuses are called roles. (101)

13. b   Sociologically, roles are significant because they lay out what is expected of us. (101)
14. c   Religion, politics, education, and the military are examples of social institutions. (102)
15. b   Sociologists would use the term "functional requisites" to describe such activities as replacing members and socializing new members of a society. (105)
16. b   The conflict perspective states that social institutions are controlled by an elite that uses them to its own advantage. (105-106)
17. d   All of the above is correct. Organic solidarity refers to a society with a highly specialized division of labor; whose members who are interdependent on one another; and with a high degree of impersonal relationships. (106)
18. a   *Gemeinschaft* is the type of society in which everyone knows everyone else, people conform because they are very sensitive to the opinions of others and want to avoid being gossiped about, and people draw comfort from being part of an intimate group. (107)
19. c   Personal space might be a research topic for a sociologist using symbolic interactionism. (108)
20. b   Goffman suggests that we go to **back** stages to be ourselves. (113)
21. d   Susan, both a full-time student and a full-time worker, finds herself experiencing role conflict when her boss asks her to work during the same hours that she is expected to be in class. (114)
22. a   If you have ever been in the situation described, of being torn between answering the professor's question or showing up your peers, then you have experienced role strain. (114)
23. b   The social setting, appearance, and manner are all sign-vehicles used by individuals for managing impressions. (115)
24. c   According to ethnomethodologists, people use common sense understandings to make sense out of their lives. (118)
25. c   The Thomas theorem would fall within symbolic interactionism. (119)

ANSWERS FOR TRUE-FALSE QUESTIONS

1.   *False.* Social structure has a large impact on the typical individual because it gives direction to and establishes limits on a person's behavior. (97)
2.   *True.* (98)
3.   *False.* Social class is a large number of people with similar amounts of income and education who work at jobs that are roughly comparable in prestige. Social status refers to the social position that a person occupies (mother, teacher, daughter, or wife). Thus, sociologists use the two terms quite differently. (98)
4.   *True.* (99)
5.   *True.* (100)
6.   *False.* Being male or female is considered a master status. (100)
7.   *True.* (101)
8.   *False.* The amount and nature of control that a group has over you depends on the group. Some groups, like a stamp collecting club, don't have that much control over many aspects of our behavior, while other groups, like our family or friendship group, exerts considerable control over a wide range of our behaviors. (102)
9.   *False.* Sociologists have identified at least nine basic social institutions in contemporary societies. (102)
10.   *False.* Although the author sees the mass media as another social institution, because the media influences our attitudes towards social issues, other people, and even our own self-concepts, not all sociologists would agree. (104)
11.   *False.* According to Emile Durkheim, as a society's division of labor becomes more complex,

social cohesion is achieved because people come to depend on one another. (106)

12. *False.* It is *Gesellschaft* society, not *Gemeinschaft* society, that is characterized by impersonal, short-term relationships. (107)

13. *True.* (108-110)

14. *True.* (111)

15. *False.* Researchers have found that higher-status individuals tend to touch more, because they have more social power. (112)

16. *True.* (113)

17. *False.* The same setting will often serve as both a back and a front stage. When you are alone in your car it is back stage, but when you are driving around with friends it becomes a front stage. (113)

18. *False.* Role strain, not role conflict, is defined as a conflict someone feels within a role. Role conflict is when the expectations of one role are incompatible with those of another role. (114)

19. *False.* Studied nonobservance, not impression management, is a face-saving technique in which people give the impression that they are unaware of a flaw in someone's performance. Impression management describes people's efforts to control the impressions that others receive of them. (116)

20. *False.* Symbolic interactionists do not assume that reality has an independent existence, and people must deal with it. They believe that people define their own reality and then live within those definitions. (19)

ANSWERS FOR FILL-IN QUESTIONS

1. MACROSOCIOLOGY investigates such things as social class and how groups are related to one another. (96)

2. The level of sociological analysis used by symbolic interactionists is MICROSOCIOLOGY. (96)

3. STATUS SET is all of the statuses or positions that an individual occupies. (98)

4. A social position that a person assumes voluntarily is ACHIEVED STATUS. (99)

5. STATUS SYMBOLS are signs used to identify a status. (100)

6. Groups in which people are assigned membership rather than choose to join are INVOLUNTARY MEMBERSHIPS (OR INVOLUNTARY ASSOCIATIONS). (102)

7. The FUNCTIONALIST perspective states that societies must replace their members, teach new members, produce and distribute goods and services, preserve order, and provide a sense of purpose. (105)

8. A society's basic needs, that are required in order to guarantee survival, are called FUNCTIONAL REQUISITES (105).

9. Durkheim referred to a collective consciousness that people experience due to performing the same or similar tasks as MECHANICAL SOLIDARITY. (106)

10. The assumptions we make about what people are like, based on our previous associations with them or with people who have similar characteristics are STEREOTYPES. (108)

11. Erving Goffman believed that in order to communicate information about the self, individuals use three types of SIGN-VEHICLES. (115)

12. Goffman called the sign-vehicle that refers to the attitudes that we demonstrate as we play our roles MANNER. (115)

13. BACKGROUND ASSUMPTIONS are the ideas that we have about the way life is and the way things ought to work. (118)

14.   What people define as real because of their background assumptions and life experiences is the <u>SOCIAL CONSTRUCTION OF REALITY</u>. (119)
15.   The <u>THOMAS THEOREM</u> states, "If people define situations as real, they are real in their consequences." (119)

<u>ANSWERS TO MATCH THESE SOCIAL SCIENTISTS WITH THEIR CONTRIBUTIONS</u>
1. b   Emile Durkheim: *wrote about mechanical/organic solidarity*
2. a   Ferdinand Tönnies: *described **Gemeinschaft** and **Gesellschaft** societies*
3. d   Edward Hall: *studied the concept of personal space*
4. c   Erving Goffman: *analyzed everyday life in terms of dramaturgy*
5. e   W. I. Thomas: *wrote the theorem about the nature of social reality*

<u>GUIDELINES FOR ANSWERING THE ESSAY QUESTIONS</u>
1.   *Choose a research topic and discuss how you approach this topic using both macrosociological and microsociological approaches.*

        The way to answer this question is to first think of a topic -- I've chosen the topic of labor unions. Remember that the macrosociological level focuses on the broad features of society (p. 96). So from this level, I might research the role that unions play within the economy or the political system, what types of workers are organized into unions, the level of union organization among workers, or the level of union activity. Shifting to a microsociological level of analysis (p. 96), I would want to look at what happens within unions or between unions and management in terms of social interaction. From this perspective, I might want to investigate the behavior of union members and leaders at a union meeting, or the behavior of union and management negotiators at a bargaining session. By combining both perspectives, I have achieved a much broader understanding of the role of unions within society (p. 97).

2.   *Today we can see many examples of people wanting to re-create a simpler way of life. Using Tönnies' framework, analyze this tendency.*

        You would want to begin by describing Tönnies' framework of *Gemeinshaft* and *Gesellschaft*, and discussing the characteristics of each (p. 107). Using these concepts, you would indicate that individuals' search for community reflects a rejection of the ever-increasing impersonality and formality of modern society. In their actions, people are trying to re-create a social world where everyone knows each other within the context of intimate groups. Some sociologists have used the term "pseudo-*Gemeinshaft*" to describe the attractiveness of the past -- people building colonial homes and decorating them with antiques.

3.   *Assume that you have been asked to give a presentation to your sociology class on Goffman's dramaturgy approach. Describe what information you would want to include in such a presentation.*

        You could begin by explaining how Goffman saw life as a drama that was acted out on a stage. This would lead you to making a distinction between front stage and back stage (p. 113). You might even want to provide some examples -- for instance, you are presenting on a front stage, but you practiced for this presentation in your bedroom without any audience. An important contribution of Goffman's was his insights into impression management, so you would want to explain what that is and how it involves the use of three different types of sign-vehicles -- social setting, appearance, and manner (p. 115). Finally, you could conclude with his concept of teamwork, especially as it relates to face-saving behavior (pp. 115-117). And remember to include examples of all of these concepts as you proceed.

☞ ANSWERS FOR CHAPTER 5

ANSWERS FOR MULTIPLE CHOICE QUESTIONS

1. b   A researcher interested in doing a macro level study would choose race relations as a topic. Waiting in public places, interactions between people on street corners, and meat packers at work are all topics that would interest a micro level researcher. (126)

2. d   "All of the above" is correct. Sociologists believe that research is necessary because common sense ideas may or may not be true; they want to move beyond guesswork; and researchers want to know what really is going on. (126)

3. c   Eight steps are involved in scientific research. (126-129)

4. c   Researchers review the literature in order to help them to narrow down the problem by pinpointing particular areas to examine; to get ideas about how to do their own research; and to determine whether of not the problem has been answered already. They are not concerned about whether or not the topic is controversial. (127)

5. a   A relationship between or among variables is predicted by a hypothesis. (128)

6. b   Reliability refers to the extent to which data produce consistent results. (128)

7. c   In analyzing data gathered by participant observation, a researcher is likely to choose qualitative analysis. (129)

8. c   Replication is the repetition of research in order to test its findings. (129)

9. a   Mean, median, and mode are ways to measure "average." (131)

10. a   Ethnomethodology is the study of how people use background assumptions to make sense of life and, thus, is a part of symbolic interactionism. Surveys, unobtrusive measures, and secondary analysis are research methods for gathering data. (129-139)

11. c   A sample is defined as the individuals intended to represent the population to be studied. (130)

12. c   If you had carried out the procedure described, you would have selected a stratified random sample, defined as specific subgroups of the population in which everyone in the subgroup has an equal chance of being included in the study. (131)

13. b   Given the time and cost factors, you are most likely to choose to use self-administered questionnaires, because this method allows a larger number of people to be sampled at a relatively low cost. (133)

14. b   A researcher might "load the dice" in designing a research project because of a vested interest in the outcome of the research. He or she may be hired by business firms and is thus motivated to find results that are consistent with the interests of the firm. (132)

15. b   The advantage of structured interviews is that they are faster to administer and make it easier for answers to be coded. (133-134)

16. d   Problems which must be dealt with in conducting participant observation include the researcher's personal characteristics; developing rapport with respondents; and generalizability. Therefore, "all of the above" is the correct response. (134-135)

17. c   The analysis of data already collected by other researchers is secondary analysis. (135)

18. b   Sources such as newspapers, diaries, bank records, police reports, household accounts and immigration files are documents that provide useful information for investigating social life. (135-136)

19. c   In order to study patterns of alcohol consumption in different neighborhoods, you decide to go through the recycling bins in your town and count the number of beer cans, and wine and hard liquor bottles. This study would be using unobtrusive methods because you are making observations on people without their knowledge that they are being studied. (136)

20. b The simultaneous occurrence of alcohol and abuse is known as a correlation. (137)
21. a A researcher who is trying to identify causal relationships is likely to use an experiment. (136)
22. b In an experiment, the group not exposed to the independent variable in the study is the control group. (136)
23. a The change in behavior that occurs when subjects know they are being studied is referred to as the Hawthorne effect. (138)
24. c Surveys are more likely to be used by researchers trained in quantitative techniques. (139)
25. d All of the above is correct. Research ethics require openness; that a researcher not falsify results or plagiarize someone else's work; and that research subjects should not be harmed by the research. (142-143)

ANSWERS FOR TRUE-FALSE QUESTIONS
1. *True.* (126)
2. *True.* (126-127)
3. *True.* (128)
4. *False.* Sociologists do not place one above the other. Rather, they take great care to assure that both are achieved. (128)
5. *True.* (128)
6. *True.* (129)
7. *False.* Computers are valuable to researchers not because they store information efficiently, but because they reduce large amounts of data to basic patterns, they take the drudgery out of analyzing data, they can do different statistical tests easily, and they free the researcher up to do more interpretation of the data. (129)
8. *True.* (129)
9. *False.* In survey research, it is always desirable for respondents to express their own ideas. (132)
10. *True.* (132-133)
11. *True.* (133)
12. *True.* (134)
13. *False.* Secondary analysis and use of documents are not the same thing. The data used in secondary analysis is gathered by other researchers while documents may be anything from diaries to police records. (135)
14. *False.* It is not always unethical to observe behavior in people when they do not know they are being studied. However, there are circumstances when the issue of ethics should be raised. (136)
15. *True.* (136)
16. *True.* (137)
17. *True.* (137)
18. *False.* Gender is an important factor in research, possibly contributing to interviewer bias, influencing the choice of research methods, and limiting generalizability. (142)
19. *True.* (142-143)
20. *False.* Scully and Marolla's research demonstrates that it is possible to do research that contributes to our body of sociological knowledge under less than ideal conditions. (145-146)

ANSWERS FOR FILL-IN QUESTIONS
1. A factor or concept thought to be significant for human behavior, which varies from one case

to another is a(n) <u>VARIABLE</u>. (128)
2. Hypotheses need <u>OPERATIONAL DEFINITIONS</u>, which are precise ways to measure variables. (128)
3. <u>RELIABILITY</u> is the extent to which data produce consistent results. (128)
4. The six research methods are: (1) <u>SURVEYS</u>, (2) <u>PARTICIPANT OBSERVATION</u>, (3) <u>SECONDARY ANALYSIS</u>, (4) <u>DOCUMENTS</u>, (5) <u>UNOBTRUSIVE MEASURES</u>, and (6) <u>EXPERIMENTS</u>. (129-139)
5. A(n) <u>INTERVIEW</u> is when the researcher asks the respondent questions directly, either face-to-face or by telephone. (133)
6. Closed-ended questions are used in <u>STRUCTURED INTERVIEWS</u>. Open-ended questions are used in <u>UNSTRUCTURED INTERVIEWS</u>. (134)
7. <u>RAPPORT</u> is a feeling of trust between researchers and subjects. (134)
8. Generalizability is one of the major problems in <u>PARTICIPANT OBSERVATION</u>. (135)
9. In <u>SECONDARY ANALYSIS</u> a researcher analyzes data that was originally collected by someone else. (135)
10. A research method that involves observing the behavior of people who do not know they are being studied is <u>UNOBTRUSIVE MEASURES</u>. (136)
11. To conduct an experiment, the researcher has two groups: (1) <u>EXPERIMENTAL GROUP</u> and (2) <u>CONTROL GROUP</u>. (136)
12. Research in which the emphasis is placed on precise measurement, the use of statistics and numbers is <u>QUANTITATIVE TECHNIQUES</u>. (139)
13. Research in which the emphasis is placed on describing and interpreting people's behavior is <u>QUALITATIVE TECHNIQUES</u>. (139)
14. Research <u>ETHICS</u> require openness, honesty, and truth. (142)
15. Research and <u>THEORY</u> are interdependent, and sociologists combine them in their work. (144)

ANSWERS TO THE MATCHING QUESTIONS

1. b Hawthorne effect: *behavior change due to subject's awareness of being studied*
2. f Population: *the target group to be studied*
3. h Sample: *the individuals intended to represent the population to be studied*
4. c Interview bias: *the effect that interviewers have on respondents that leads to biased answers*
5. I Coding: *the research step of categorizing data*
6. g Secondary analysis: *the analysis of data already collected by other researchers*
7. e Documents: *written sources of data*
8. j Independent variable: *a factor that causes a change in another variable*
9. d Dependent variable: *a factor that is changed by an independent variable*
10. a Unobtrusive measures: *the observation of people who do not know that they are being studied*

GUIDELINES FOR ANSWERING THE ESSAY QUESTIONS

1. *Choose a topic and explain how you would go through the different steps in the research model.*
    In order to answer this question, you must select a topic and then develop this from the beginning to the end of the research process, identifying all eight steps and explaining what tasks are carried out each step of the way. Your answer should make reference to variables, hypothesis, operational definitions, the different research methods, validity and reliability, different ways of analyzing the data, and replication (pp. 126-129).
2. *Discuss some of the things that can go wrong in the process of doing research and provide*

suggestions on how to overcome such problems.

There are a number of problems that can arise if the researcher is not careful. Included would be: (1) deriving invalid and unreliable results because of inadequate operational definitions and inaccurate sampling procedures (p. 128); (2) obtaining biased answers because biased questions were asked (p. 132); (3) failing to establish rapport with research subjects because of personal qualities or characteristics (p. 134); (4) failing to gain access to necessary documents because those who control the documents are unwilling to cooperate (p. 135-136); and (5) failing to rule out possible spurious correlations (p. 137). Each of these potential problems can be overcome if the researcher follows the steps in the research process carefully.

3.   *Explain why ethical guidelines are necessary in social science research.*

Ethical guidelines are necessary for several reasons. First and foremost, the researcher is working with human subjects; there must be guidelines to protect these subjects from any undue physical or psychological harm. Secondly, the research is only valid and reliable if the subjects have honestly and accurately provided information to the researcher. For this reason, they must have confidence in the researcher and the research process; guidelines assure subjects that their identities will remain anonymous and their information will be confidential. Finally, an essential aspect of research is that it be shared with others in the research community as well as members of the wider society. Guidelines regarding falsification and plagiarism guarantee that all research will be carefully scrutinized, thereby assuring its validity and reliability (p. 142-144).

☞ ANSWERS FOR CHAPTER 6

ANSWERS FOR MULTIPLE CHOICE QUESTIONS

1. d   People who have something in common and who believe that what they have in common is significant make up a group. (150)
2. b   The largest and most complex group that sociologists study is a society. (150)
3. c   The type of society that has been described is a hunting and gathering society. (150-151)
4. a   Of all types of societies, the most egalitarian is the hunting and gathering society. (151)
5. b   Pastoral societies are based on the pasturing of animals. (152)
6. d   "All of the above" is correct. The domestication revolution led to the human group becoming larger, the creation of a food surplus, and a more specialized division of labor. (152)
7. c   The society that emerged out of the invention of the plow was known as an agricultural society. (152)
8. d   "All of the above" is correct. Indicators of increasing equality include better housing, the abolition of slavery, and a move toward more representative political systems. (154)
9. a   Postindustrial society is based on information, services, and high technology. (154)
10. b   The United States was the first nation to have more than 50 percent of its work force employed in service industries; it was followed quickly by Japan, Australia, New Zealand, and western Europe. (154)
11. c   People who have similar characteristics are a category. (155)
12. c   Emile Durkheim believed that small groups help to prevent anomie, because, through their intimate relationships, they provide a sense of meaning and purpose to live. (155)
13. a   Cooley saw that primary groups are essential to an individual's psychological well-being. (156)
14. d   "All of the above" is correct. Secondary groups have members who are likely to interact on the basis of specific roles; are characteristic of industrial societies; and are essential to the functioning of contemporary societies. (156-157)

15. b   Groups which provide a sense of identification or belonging are referred to as in-groups. (157)

16. d   Attacks against immigrants, or a national anti-immigration policy, are examples of xenophobia, or the fear of strangers. (158)

17. c   Reference groups are important because they provide us with a standard to evaluate ourselves. Your reference group may include family and friends, with whom you engage in face-to-face interaction, or groups to which you belong and feel a sense of loyalty, but they do not have to be. They can provide you with standards even when you are not actually a member of the group. (159)

18. a   Sociologically speaking, the social ties radiating outward from the self, that link people together are social networks. (159)

19. b   While the implications for social relationships of cybercommunications are still tentative, the author of your text suggests that one development which some find disturbing is that the Internet provides easy access to people in distant lands, but can separate us from people living close by. (162)

20. d   "All of the above" is correct. Dyads are the most intense or intimate of human groups; require continuing active participation and commitment of both members. and are the most unstable of social groups. (161)

21. c   An expressive leader increases harmony and minimizes conflict in a group. (165)

22. b   Research by Lippitt and White demonstrated that authoritarian style of leader is most effective in emergency situations, and laissez-faire style is generally ineffective. The one style that is best under most circumstances was the democratic style of leader. (166)

23. d   "All of the above" is correct. According to sociologists, leaders tend to have certain characteristics which may include: they are more outgoing; they tend to be taller and are judged better-looking than others; and where they sit in a group. (166)

24. c   The Milgram experiment demonstrates how strongly people are influenced by authority. (167 168)

25. c   James Henslin suggests that the key to preventing groupthink is to guarantee that the results of social science research and the information that is gathered by media reporters is widely circulated among members of government decision-making bodies. (170)

ANSWERS FOR TRUE-FALSE QUESTIONS

1.   *True.* (150)
2.   *True.* (152)
3.   *False.* According to Elise Boulding, women's status fell rather than rose once metals were attached to plows. Plowing and the care of cows became associated with men, and their status rose even higher. (153)
4.   *False.* Industrial societies were brought about by the invention of the steam engine. (153)
5 .   True. (154)
6.   *False.* The United States was the first country to have more than 50 percent of its work force employed in service industries. (154)
7.   *True.* (154)
8.   *True.* (155)
9.   *False.* Members of secondary, not primary, groups are likely to interact on the basis of specific roles. (156-157)
10.   *True.* (158)
11.   *True.* (159)

12. *False*. A person does not have to belong to a group to use that group as a reference group. (159)
13. *True*. (159)
14. *True*. (160)
15. *False*. Dyads are more intimate than triads because there are only two members of a dyad, as opposed to three members in a triad, but their smaller size also makes them *less* stable, rather than more stable, than a triad. (161-163)
16. *True*. (163)
17. *True*. (164)
18. *False*. Sociologically speaking, a leader does not have to be officially appointed or elected to be the "leader." A leader is someone who influences the behaviors of others. (165)
19. *False*. To study conformity, the Asch experiment used cards with lines on them. To study obedience to authority, the Milgram experiment used fake electrical shocks. (167)
20. *True*. (169)

ANSWERS FOR FILL-IN QUESTIONS

1. The simplest societies are called HUNTING AND GATHERING societies. (150)
2. The AGRICULTURAL revolution was brought about by the invention of the plow. (152)
3. A society based on information, services, and high technology is called the POSTINDUSTRIAL society. (154)
4. The term AGGREGATE is used to describe individuals who temporarily share the same physical space but do not see themselves as belonging together. (155)
5. A SECONDARY group is characterized by relatively temporary, more anonymous, formal, and impersonal relationships. (156-157)
6. IN-GROUPS provide a sense of identification or belonging while producing feelings of antagonisms towards OUT-GROUPS. (157-158)
7. The groups we use as standards to evaluate ourselves are REFERENCE GROUPS. (159)
8. The social ties radiating outward from the self, that link people together are known as SOCIAL NETWORKS. (159)
9. Individuals who interact with one another on the Internet, whether on a regular basis or not, are known as a(n) ELECTRONIC COMMUNITY. (161)
10. Individuals who regularly interact on the Internet and develop close ties with one another make up a(n) "ELECTRONIC PRIMARY GROUP". (162)
11. The smallest possible group is a(n) DYAD. (161)
12. Someone who influences the behavior of others is a(n) LEADER. (165)
13. An individual who tries to keep the group moving toward its goals is a(n) INSTRUMENTAL leader. An individual who increases harmony and minimizes conflict is a(n) EXPRESSIVE leader. (165)
14. A(n) AUTHORITARIAN leader is one who gives orders; a(n) DEMOCRATIC leader is one who tries to gain consensus among group members; and a(n) LAISSEZ-FAIRE leader is one who is highly permissive. (165)
15. GROUPTHINK is a narrowing of thought by a group of people, which results in overconfidence and tunnel vision. (169)

ANSWERS TO MATCH THESE SOCIAL SCIENTISTS WITH THEIR CONTRIBUTIONS

1. f   Irving Janis: *groupthink*

2. c   Georg Simmel: *dyads*
3. e   Emile Durkheim: *small groups and anomie*
4. b   Stanley Milgram: *obedience to authority*
5. g   Solomon Asch: *conformity to peer pressure*
6. a   Charles H. Cooley: *primary group*
7. h   Robert K. Merton: *in-group prejudice leads to a double standard*
8. d   Ronald Lippitt & Ralph White: *classic study on leadership styles*

GUIDELINES FOR ANSWERING THE ESSAY QUESTIONS

1.   *After summarizing the fundamental social changes that resulted from each of the different social revolutions, evaluate the degree to which the new technology of the microchip is contributing to a similar level of fundamental change.*

You would want to begin by summarizing characteristics of the first three social revolutions. The first social revolution was the domestication of animals and plants. This created a more dependable food supply, thereby allowing groups to grow larger in size, develop a more varied division of labor and increase trade between communities; it also led to the emergence of social inequality (p. 152). The second social revolution was the agricultural revolution. The use of the plow contributed to higher crop yields using less labor, so that more people were freed to pursue other activities. Cities grew and "culture" developed. Inequality become a permanent feature of society (pp. 152-153). The third social revolution was the invention of machines powered by fuels instead of animals. Productivity was further enhanced and social inequality was initially greater than before, although over time the amount of inequality began to diminish (pp. 153-154).

Having done that, you should turn your attention to the current transformation of industrial society into a postindustrial society and the role of the microchip. You could mention the impact that computers are having on our lives, including everything from communications to the way we work (p. 154). The earlier transformations contributed to increased division of labor, changes in the level of inequality within society, and relations between social groups. Your conclusion is based on your evaluation of whether or not you think this transformation is as profound as the earlier ones.

2.   *Discuss the benefits and drawbacks to in-groups and out-groups.*

What are the benefits of such an arrangement? You could mention feelings of loyalty and a sense of belonging, and the influence that in-groups have over our behavior. Feeling a part of an in-group, set against an out-group, may also build self-esteem and contribute to social solidarity. While this is good, there are also drawbacks. Attachments to an in-group can quickly get out of hand if such feelings develop into ethnocentrism and rivalries between in-groups and out-groups. In the most extreme cases, such ethnocentrism can be the basis for very destructive actions directed against out-groups (pp. 157-158).

3.   *Explain the three different leadership styles and suggest reasons why the democratic leader is the best style of leader for most situations.*

You would want to begin by identifying the three styles of leadership and listing the characteristics of each (pp. 165-166). Then you should evaluate how characteristics of a democratic leader, like holding group discussions, outlining the steps necessary to reach the goals, suggesting alternatives, and allowing the group members to work at their own pace, all contributed to the outcomes like greater friendliness, group-mindedness, and mutual respect, and ability to work without supervision. Finally, consider why   those qualities and outcomes were judged to be the best under most circumstances.

☞ ANSWERS FOR CHAPTER 7

ANSWERS FOR MULTIPLE CHOICE QUESTIONS

1. c   Rationality is the acceptance of rules, efficiency, and practical results as the right way to approach human affairs. (174)

2. a   The idea that the past is the best guide for the present is the traditional orientation. (174)

3. b   One of the major obstacles to industrialization was a traditional orientation to life that led people to resist change. (174)

4. d   "All of the above" is correct. According to Max Weber, capitalism is the investment of capital in the hopes of producing profits. It became an outlet for the excess money of Calvinists, as well as producing success for many that was then interpreted as a sign of God's approval. (176)

5. d   Because sociologists have not been able to determine whose views are most accurate, the two views still remain side by side. (176)

6. b   A secondary group designed to achieve explicit objectives is the sociological definition of a formal organization. (177)

7. b   In a bureaucracy assignments flow downward--not upward--and accountability flows upward--not downward. (177-179)

8. a   Ideal types are composites of characteristics based on many specific examples. (179)

9. c   George Ritzer used the term "the McDonaldization of society" to refer to the increasing rationalization of daily living. (180)

10. b   The force behind "the McDonaldization of society" is the increased efficiency which contributes to lower prices. (180)

11. d   "All of the above" is correct because alienation, bureaucratic incompetence, and red tape are dysfunctions of bureaucracies. (180-182)

12. b   What Linda is feeling is referred to as alienation by sociologists. (181)

13. d   "All of the above" is correct because workers resist alienation by forming primary groups, praising each other and expressing sympathy when something goes wrong, and putting pictures and personal items in their work areas. (181-182)

14. c   According to your text, the alienated bureaucrat is not likely to do anything for the organization beyond what he or she is required to do. (182)

15. b   The Peter Principle states that each employee of a bureaucracy is promoted to his or her level of incompetence. (182)

16. c   Goal displacement occurs when an organization adopts new goals. (182)

17. d   "All of the above" is correct. Voluntary associations are groups made up of volunteers who organize on the basis of some mutual interest. They include political parties, unions, professional associations, and churches, and they have been an important part of American life. (184)

18. a   Voluntary associations exist in the United States because they meet people's basic needs. (184)

19. c   The tendency for organizations to be dominated by a small, self-perpetuating elite is called the iron law of oligarchy. (185)

20. a   According to Rosabeth Moss Kanter, in a large corporation the corporate culture determines an individual's corporate fate. (186-187)

21. d   Humanizing a work setting refers to organizing a workplace in such a way that human potential is developed rather than impeded. Among the characteristics of more humane bureaucracies are the availability of opportunities on the basis of ability and contributions, a more equal

distribution of power, and less rigid rules and more open decision making. (187)

22. d   Research on the costs and benefits of employer-financed day care demonstrates that such a benefit can save the employer money in terms of reducing employee turnover and absenteeism. (187)

23. b   The cooperative is the type of organization that attempts to provide a high level of personal satisfaction for members at the same time that they are working towards their goals. (190)

24. c   According to conflict theorists the interests of workers and owners are fundamentally opposed and, in the final analysis, workers are always exploited. (190-191)

25. d   "All of the above" is correct. Computers in the workplace have the potential of improving the quality of work life, could lead to more surveillance of workers by managers, may be the first step towards a society in which every move a citizen makes is recorded. (191)

ANSWERS FOR TRUE-FALSE QUESTIONS

1.   *True.* (174)
2.   *False.* Traditional orientation is *not* based on the idea that the present is the best guide for the future. It is based on the idea that the past is the best guide for the present. (174)
3.   *True.* (175)
4.   *False.* Max Weber did not believe that the growth of capitalism contributed to the rise of the Protestant ethic but, rather, that the rise of the Protestant ethic as a result of Calvinism contributed to the growth of capitalism. (176)
5.   *True.* (176)
6.   *False.* By definition, only secondary groups can be formal organizations. The text defines a formal organization as "a secondary group designed to achieve explicit objectives." (177)
7   *True.* (177-179)
8.   *False.* Most colleges and universities do have written systems of accountability for faculty members. As Professor Henslin notes in the text, his institution requires faculty members to fill out reports indicating how they have spent their university-related time. These materials go to committees whose task it is to evaluate the relative performance of each faculty member. Other institutions utilize such things as student evaluations of faculty as part of an accountability package. (177-178)
9.   *True.* (179)
10.   *True.* (179)
11.   *True.* (181)
12.   *False.* It is difficult for workers to resist becoming alienated because of the nature of the organizational environment in which they work. According to Marx, alienation occurs because workers are cut off from the product of their own labor, which results in estrangement not only from the products but from their whole work environment. (181-182)
13.   *False.* The Peter Principle has not been proven to be true. If it were generally true, bureaucracies would be staffed entirely be incompetents, and none of these organizations could succeed. In reality, bureaucracies are remarkably successful. (182)
14.   *True.* (184)
15.   *True.* (185)
16.   *True.* (185)
17.   *False.* Bureaucracies are not likely to disappear as our dominant form of social organization in the near future because they generally are effective in getting the job done. Most people spend their working lives in such organizational environments. (187)

18. *True.* (188-189)
19. *True.* (190)
20. *True.* (191-192)

ANSWERS FOR FILL-IN QUESTIONS

1. RATIONALITY is the acceptance of rules, efficiency, and practical results as the right way to approach human affairs. (174)
2. The idea that the past is the best guide for the present is known as TRADITIONAL ORIENTATION. (174)
3. THE PROTESTANT ETHIC AND THE SPIRIT OF CAPITALISM was written by Max Weber and emphasizes that religion holds the key to understanding the development of certain types of economic systems. (176)
4. The investment of capital in the hope of producing profits is called CAPITALISM. (176)
5. A secondary group designed to achieve explicit objectives is referred to as a(n) FORMAL ORGANIZATION. (177)
6. A type of formal organization with a hierarchy of authority and a clear division of labor is a BUREAUCRACY. (177)
7. A composite of characteristics that reflects many specific examples is an IDEAL TYPE. (179)
8. George Ritzer has coined the term "MCDONALDIZATION OF SOCIETY" to refer to the increasing rationalization of life's routine tasks. (180)
9. ALIENATION is a feeling of powerlessness and normlessness; the experience of being cut off from the product of one's labor. (181)
10. GOAL DISPLACEMENT occurs when new goals are adopted by an organization to replace previous goals which may have been fulfilled. (182)
11. A group made up of volunteers who have organized on the basis of some mutual interest is called a(n) VOLUNTARY ASSOCIATION. (184)
12. THE IRON LAW OF OLIGARCHY refers to the tendency of formal organizations to be dominated by a small, self-perpetuating elite. (185)
13. QUALITY CIRCLES consist of perhaps a dozen workers and a manager or two who meet regularly to try to improve the quality of the work setting and of the company's products. (188)
14. Humanizing a work setting is just another attempt to manipulate workers into active cooperation in their own exploitation, according to CONFLICT theorists. (190)
15. Almost total involvement, broad training, and collective decision making are characteristics of the JAPANESE CORPORATE model. (191 193)

ANSWERS TO MATCH THESE SOCIAL SCIENTISTS WITH THEIR CONTRIBUTIONS

1. e   Max Weber: *the rationalization of society*
2. a   Robert Michels: *the iron law of oligarchy*
3. f   William Ouchi: *the Japanese corporate model*
4. d   Karl Marx: *the exploitation of workers by capitalists*
5. c   Rosabeth Moss Kanter: *the hidden values in the corporate culture*
6. b   George Ritzer: *the McDonaldization of society*

GUIDELINES FOR ANSWERING THE ESSAY QUESTIONS

1. *Explain what an ideal type is and why such constructs are useful.*
   You would begin by explaining how Weber studied several different bureaucracies and used

these real entities to construct composite characteristics that he thought were typical of bureaucratic structures (p. 179). The result was a list of characteristics that a bureaucratic organization would ideally have (pp. 177-179). This constructed list of characteristics can then be used to measure the degree to which any organization is bureaucratized.

2. *Define the iron law of oligarchy and discuss why this problem occurs in voluntary associations.*

You would begin by explaining that the iron law of oligarchy is the tendency within organizations for the leadership to become self-perpetuating (pp. 185-186). Although this problem occurs in all types of organizations, it is particularly evident in voluntary associations. A major reason for this is because the membership tends to be passive, varying in its degree of commitment to and involvement in the organization. The elite keeps itself in power by passing leadership positions from one member of the clique to another. If the leadership is not responsive to the membership, it runs the risk of being removed from office by a grassroots rebellion (p. 186).

3. *Evaluate whether or not the use of computer technology to control workers is an inevitable aspect of bureaucracy.*

You would want to begin by identifying the defining characteristics of bureaucracy -- the presence of a hierarchy, a division of labor, written rules, written communications and records, and impersonality (pp. 177-179). You should then consider the ways in which computers are tied to these various characteristics. Zuboff's research noted how computers enable supervisors to monitor subordinates without ever having face-to-face contact (hierarchy), the computer's capacity to be accessed from remote sites means that managers can communicate with workers at any time and from any place and the workers input on computers enable the managers to maintain records of their productivity (written communication and records); and computers promote impersonality (p. 191). Your conclusion is to evaluate the degree to which such steps are inevitable.

☞ ANSWERS FOR CHAPTER 8

ANSWERS FOR MULTIPLE CHOICE QUESTIONS

1. b   In sociology, the term deviance refers to all violations of social rules. (198)
2. c   The function of the stigma is to define or identify the person who violates the norm as deviant. (198)
3. d   The pluralistic theory of social control takes the view that different groups mediate and balance their competing interests with the result that social stability is achieved. (200)
4. b   According to conflict theory, social control represents the interests of the wealthy and powerful. (200)
5. c   Differential association theory is based on the symbolic interactionist perspective. (202)
6. c   The idea that two control systems--inner controls and outer controls--work against our tendency toward deviance is called control theory. (205)
7. c   All of the following are ways of neutralizing deviance: appeal to higher loyalties, denial of responsibility, and denial of injury and of a victim. Denial of deviant labels is *not* one of the ways of neutralizing such behavior. (205-206)
8. a   The term for acts of deviance that have little effect on the self-concept is primary deviance. (206)
9. c   Tertiary deviance is deviant behavior that is normalized by relabeling it as nondeviant; primary deviance are the initial acts of deviance that do not become part of the individual's self-concept; secondary deviance involves self-labeling, when deviance becomes part of the self-concept.

(206)

10. b   William Chambliss's study of the Saints and the Roughnecks suggests that people often live up to the labels that a community gives them. (207-208)

11. d   "All of the above" is correct. William Chambliss states that all of these are factors which influence whether or not people will be seen as deviant: social class, the visibility of offenders, and their styles of interaction. (208)

12. a   According to the functionalist perspective, deviance promotes social unity and social change. (208-209)

13. d   Recidivism is not one of the responses to anomie identified by Merton. (210-211)

14. b   According to Merton's strain theory, people who drop out of the pursuit of success by abusing alcohol or drugs are retreatists. (211)

15. d   The illegitimate opportunity structures theory is based on the functionalist perspective. (211)

16. c   Crimes committed by people of respectable and high social status in the course of their occupations are called white-collar crime. (211)

17. d   "All of the above" is correct. The marginal working class includes people with few skills, who hold low-paying, part-time, seasonal jobs, and who are the most desperate members of the working class. (215)

18. c   Frowns, gossip, and crossing people off guest lists are examples of negative sanctions. (216)

19. a   A court martial in which the insignia of rank is publicly ripped off the uniforms of the officers found guilty is an example of degradation ceremonies. (216-217)

20. a   Halfway houses are community support facilities where ex-prisoners supervise aspects of their own lives. (220)

21. c   Rehabilitation switches the focus from punishing offenders to resocializing them so that they can become conforming citizens. (219-220)

22. b   Incapacitation is the removal of offenders from society, taking them "off the streets." (220)

23. a   As a group, African Americans are more likely than other racial/ethnic groups to be victims of hate crimes. (221)

24. b   According to official statistics working-class boys are more delinquent than middle-class boys. (222)

25. c   The medicalization of deviance refers to viewing deviance as a medical matter. (222)

ANSWERS FOR TRUE-FALSE QUESTIONS

1.   *False*. What is deviant to some is not deviant to others. This principle holds true within a society as well as across cultures. Thus, acts perfectly acceptable in one culture may be considered deviant in another culture. (198)

2.   *False*. According to your text, a college student cheating on an exam and a mugger lurking on a dark street do have something in common: they are both engaged in deviant behavior, thus making them "deviants." (198)

3.   *True*. (200)

4.   *True*. (200)

5.   *True*. (200)

6.   *True*. (202)

7.   *True*. (202)

8.   *False*. It is in the third stage (tertiary deviance), when the deviant behavior is normalized by relabeling it as nondeviant. (206)

9.   *False*. Some people and groups do embrace deviance and want to be labeled with a deviant

identity. Examples include: teenagers who make certain that their clothing, music, and hairstyles are outside adult norms; and outlaw bikers. (207)

10. *True*. (207)
11. *True*. (208)
12. *True*. (208)
13. *False*. According to strain theory, everyone does not have an equal chance to get ahead in society because of structural factors in the society (e.g. racism, sexism, and social class) which may deny them access to the approved ways of achieving cultural goals. (210)
14. *True*. (210)
15. *True*. (211)
16. *False*. White-collar crime often is more costly than street crime. Examples include the plundering of the U.S. savings and loan industry and other "crimes in the suites." (212)
17. *False*. Conflict theorists believe that the criminal justice system functions for the well-being of the capitalist class. (214-215)
18. *True*. (219)
19. *False*. The purpose of retribution is to right a wrong by making offenders suffer or pay back what they have stolen. The purpose of deterrence is to create fear so that others won't break the law. (219)
20. *False*. Official statistics are not always accurate counts of the crimes committed in our society. Both conflict theorists and symbolic interactionists believe that these statistics have bias built into them because of police discretion in arresting people, as well as many other factors. (222)

ANSWERS FOR FILL-IN QUESTIONS

1. DEVIANCE is the violation of rules or norms. (198)
2. Erving Goffman used the term STIGMA to refer to attributes that discredit people. (198)
3. Formal and informal means of enforcing norms constitute a system of SOCIAL CONTROL. (200)
4. According to the CONFLICT perspective, society is made up of competing groups, and the group that holds power uses social control to maintain its position of privilege. (200)
5. NORMS make social life possible by making behavior predictable. (200)
6. SOCIAL ORDER is a group's usual and customary social arrangements, on which its members depend and on which they base their lives. (201)
7. CONTROL theory is the idea that two control systems--inner controls and outer controls--work against our pushes and pulls toward deviance. (205)
8. Labeling theory is based on the SYMBOLIC INTERACTIONIST perspective. (205)
9. SECONDARY DEVIANCE occurs at the point when individuals incorporate a deviant identity into their self-concept. (206)
10. Strain theory is based on the idea that large number of people are socialized into desiring CULTURAL GOALS (the legitimate objects held out to everyone) but many do not have access to INSTITUTIONALIZED MEANS in order to achieve those goals. (210)
11. Robert Merton used the term ANOMIE to describe the sense of normlessness that some people are frustrated in their efforts to achieve success. (210)
12. Edwin Sutherland used the term WHITE COLLAR CRIME to refer to crimes that people of respectable and high social status commit in the course of their occupations. (211)
13. In combination the policy, courts, and prisons that deal with people who are accused of having committed crimes make up the CRIMINAL JUSTICE SYSTEM. (214)

14.   Steps to strip an individual of his or her identity as a group member occur during DEGRADATION CEREMONIES. (216)

15.   The view that deviance, including crime, is the product of mental illness is referred to as MEDICALIZATION OF DEVIANCE. (222)

ANSWERS TO MATCH THESE SOCIAL SCIENTISTS WITH THEIR CONTRIBUTIONS
1. d   Edwin Sutherland: *white collar crime*
2. a   Robert Merton: *strain theory*
3. g   Erving Goffman: *importance of stigma*
4. i   Thomas Szasz: *myth of mental illness*
5. e   Emile Durkheim: *functions of deviance*
6. f   William Chambliss: *effects of labeling*
7. h   Gresham Sykes and David Matza: *techniques of neutralization*
8. b   Walter Reckless: *control theory*
9. c   Harold Garfinkel: *degradation ceremonies*

GUIDELINES FOR ANSWERING THE ESSAY QUESTIONS
1.   *Discuss how the different sociological perspectives could be combined in order to provide a more complete picture of deviance.*
        You would begin by identifying the strengths of each perspective--symbolic interactionism focuses on group membership and interaction within and between groups (pp. 202-208), functionalism focuses on how deviance is a part of the social order (pp. 208-214), and conflict theory focuses on how social inequality impacts on definitions of and reactions to acts of deviance (pp. 214-215). An example of combining perspectives is reflected in the work of William Chambliss on the Saints and the Roughnecks; he looked at patterns of inequality and different interaction styles to explain the different treatment the two groups received (pp. 207-208). Another example would be Cloward and Ohlin's work on illegitimate opportunity structures (p. 211); they added the concept of social class inequality to the notion of the strain between institutionalized means and cultural goals to explain patterns of lower class deviance (pp. 210-211).
2.   *Explain how forms of deviance such as street gangs can be both functional and dysfunctional at the same time.*
        Jankowski studied street gangs and discovered that gangs functioned within low income neighborhoods as sources of employment (often the *only* source), recreation, and protection. In a few cases the gangs were involved in legitimate activities such as running small groceries and renovating and renting abandoned apartment buildings. All of these demonstrate the functional nature of gangs. At the same time, gangs generate most of their income through illegal activities--a dysfunctional aspect. Another dysfunctional aspect is the violence that accompanies gangs--violence that is not confined to gangs but often spills over into the neighborhood as a whole (p. 212).
3.   *In light of the different explanations for deviance, evaluate the effectiveness of the various reactions to deviance.*
        In answering this question, you would want to think about what the purpose or goal of each of the reactions is--sanctions, degradation ceremonies, and imprisonment (pp. 216-217). Then you would want to consider whether or not the goal will effectively address the deviance, given what different sociologists have said about deviance. Consider this question: Would imprisonment be effective against someone who reached the tertiary stage of deviance and has actively embraced the deviant label (pp. 206)?

☞ ANSWERS FOR CHAPTER 9

ANSWERS FOR MULTIPLE CHOICE QUESTIONS

1. b   The division of large numbers of people into layers according to their relative power, property, and prestige is social stratification. (228)
2. b   Slavery is a form of social stratification in which some people own other people. (229)
3. d   "All of the above" is correct. Slavery in the United States started as indentured service. When enough indentured servants could not be recruited, individuals were imported from Africa and turned into slaves. An ideology of racism justified these actions by asserting that the slaves were inferior, and perhaps not even fully human. Slavery became inheritable because if one's parents were slaves, the child also was considered to be a slave. (230)
4. c   India is the best example of a caste system. (231)
5. b   Caste systems practice endogamy, marriage within the group, and prohibit intermarriage. (231)
6. c   Under the estate system that existed in Europe during the Middle Ages, the clergy made up the *second estate.* (234)
7. a   Class systems are characterized by social mobility--either upward or downward. (234-235)
8. b   Marx concluded that social class depends on the means of production. (235)
9. a   According to Max Weber, social class is determined by one's property, prestige, and power. (236)
10. d   According to the functionalist view, social stratification is not dysfunctional, but is an inevitable feature of social organization. (237)
11. d   Melvin Tumin's criticisms included the measurement problems (a), the reality that family background matters (b), and the dysfunctional aspects of stratification (c). The one statement that does not reflect his criticisms is "d"--in fact, what Tumin noted was that functionalists place too great and emphasis on income and ignore the fact that some people are motivated to take jobs for reasons of status or power. (238)
12. a   A form of social stratification in which all positions are awarded on the basis of merit is called a meritocratic system. (238)
13. d   Gaetano Mosca argued that every society will be stratified by power. (238)
14. b   According to conflict theorists, the basis of social stratification is conflict over limited resources. (239)
15. d   "All of the above" is correct. The key to maintaining national stratification is having a strong police force and military to demand compliance, control of social institutions, and control of information. (240)
16. c   The British perpetuate their class system from one generation to the next by education. (242)
17. c   The system of stratification in the former Soviet Union was based on membership in the Communist Party; within the party there was also stratification, with most members at the bottom, some bureaucrats in the middle, and a small elite at the top. (242)
18. d   "All of the above" is the correct answer. (246)
19. c   The majority of the world's population lives in the Least Industrialized Nations; nearly 68 percent of the world's population lives in these nations, with the remaining 32 percent split evenly between the Most Industrialized and the Industrializing Nations. (247)
20. b   The colonialism of the United States usually involved planting corporate flags, thereby giving U.S. corporations ready access to the markets and raw materials of these colonies. (248)
21. d   According to Wallerstein these groups of interconnected nations exist: core nations which are

rich and powerful; nations on the semiperiphery which have become highly dependent on trade with core nations; nations on the periphery which sell cash crops to the core nations; and the external area--including most of Africa and Asia--which have been left out of the development of capitalism and had few, if any, economic connections with the core nations. (249)

22. b   According to dependency theory, banana republics are Central American countries that developed a single cash crop for export to the United States, thereby becoming economically dependent upon the U.S. (249)

23. c   The culture of poverty theory was used to analyze global stratification by John Kenneth Galbraith. (249)

24. b   Neocolonialism refers to the economic policies of the Most Industrialized Nations that are designed to control the markets of the Least Industrialized Nations; they are able to set the prices they will charge for their manufactured goods and control the international markets where they purchase raw materials from the Least Industrialized Nations. (250)

25. a   Multinational corporations are companies that operate across many national boundaries. According to the text, they do not always exploit the Least Industrialized Nations directly, but they do not benefit these nations as much as they do the Most Industrialized Nations. (250-251)

ANSWERS FOR TRUE-FALSE QUESTIONS

1.   *False.* Your text notes that social stratification does not simply refer to individuals but rather to a way of ranking large groups of people into a hierarchy that shows their relative privileges. (228)

2.   *False.* Historically, slavery was based on defeat in battle, a criminal act, or a debt, but not some supposedly inherently inferior status such as race. (229)

3.   *True.* (230)

4.   *True.* (231)

5.   *True.* (235)

6.   *True.* (235)

7.   *True.* (235)

8.   *True.* (237)

9.   *True.* (237)

10.   *False.* Functionalists believe that society offers greater rewards for its more responsible, demanding, and accountable positions because society works better if its most qualified people hold its most important positions. From this standpoint, unique abilities would not be more important than the type of position held by the individual. (237)

11.   *False.* In American society, most people view meritocracy positively because they like to believe that positions are awarded on the basis of merit. (e.g. "May the best person/team win!") (238)

12.   *True.* (239)

13.   *False.* Gerhard Lenski felt that the functional view of stratification was most appropriate when studying societies that did not accumulate wealth. (239)

14.   *True.* (240)

15.   *False.* In maintaining stratification, elites find that technology, especially monitoring devices, is useful. (241)

16.   *True.* (248)

17.   *False.* Beginning more than 200 years ago, most industrialized nations pursued policies of colonialism in order to expand their economic markets and gain access to cheap raw materials;

as a result of this strategy, many acquired colonies in the Middle East, Africa, Asia, and Central/South America. (248)
18. *True*. (249)
19. *False*. Most sociologists find imperialism, world systems and dependency theory preferable to an explanation based on the culture of poverty. (250)
20. *True*. (250)

ANSWERS FOR FILL-IN QUESTIONS

1. SOCIAL STRATIFICATION is a system in which people are divided into layers according to their relative power, property, and prestige. (228)
2. A form of social stratification in which some people own other people is SLAVERY. (229)
3. A CASTE system is a form of social stratification in which individual status is determined by birth and is lifelong. (231)
4. The South African practice of racial separation that existed until recently is APARTHEID. (233)
5. Sociologists refer to movement up or down the social class ladder as SOCIAL MOBILITY. (235)
6. According to Marx, the tools, factories, land, and investment capital used to produce wealth is THE MEANS OF PRODUCTION. (235)
7. According to Marx, the awareness of a common identity based on one's position in the means of production is CLASS CONSCIOUSNESS. (236)
8. Karl Marx's term for the mistaken identification of workers with the interests of capitalists was FALSE CONSCIOUSNESS. (236)
9. A MERITOCRACY is a form of social stratification in which all positions are awarded on the basis of merit. (238)
10. The DIVINE RIGHT OF KINGS is the idea that the king's authority comes directly from God. (240)
11. COLONIALISM is the process in which one nation takes over another nation, usually for the purpose of exploiting its labor and natural resources. (248)
12. GLOBALIZATION is the extensive interconnections among world nations resulting from the expansion of capitalism. (249)
13. CULTURE OF POVERTY is a way of life that perpetuates poverty from one generation to the next. (249)
14. NEOCOLONIALISM refers to the economic and political dominance of the Least Industrialized Nations by the Most Industrialized Nations. (250)
15. Companies that operate across many national boundaries are MULTINATIONAL CORPORATIONS. (250)

ANSWERS TO MATCH THESE SOCIAL SCIENTISTS WITH THEIR CONTRIBUTIONS

1. d   Karl Marx: *false consciousness*
2. e   Kingsley Davis and Wilbert Moore: *the functionalist view on stratification*
3. f   Gaetano Mosca: *forerunner of the conflict view on stratification*
4. a   Immanuel Wallerstein: *world system theory*
5. g   Michael Harrington: *neocolonialism*
6. c   John Kenneth Galbraith: *stressed the culture of poverty*
7. h   Max Weber: *class based on property, prestige and power*

8. b   Melvin Tumin: *criticism of the functionalist view on stratification*

GUIDELINES FOR ANSWERING THE ESSAY QUESTIONS

1.   *Compare and contrast Marx's theory of stratification with Weber's theory. Discuss why Weber's is more widely accepted by sociologists.*

  Your first task is to summarize these two perspectives, pointing out the similarities as well as the differences between the two (pp. 235-237) Then you would want to consider the advantages offered by Weber's theory. You could mention that Weber's concept of property (or wealth) was broadened to include *control* over decision-making as well as ownership; that prestige and power can both be based on factors other than wealth; that the three dimensions are interrelated but can, and do, operate independently. Your conclusion should be that Weber's theory offers sociologists a more complete framework for understanding and analyzing systems of stratification.

2.   *Consider why ideology is a more effective way of maintaining stratification than brute force.*

  You should begin by considering why it is even necessary to "maintain stratification." On the surface, the idea that some people get more than other people should produce widespread instability-- after all, isn't it natural for those without to want to do whatever they can to take some away from those with? However, this doesn't often happen because the elites have a number of methods for maintaining stratification, ranging from ideology to force. Without question, the most effective is ideology. Once a system of beliefs develop and people accept the idea in their minds that a particular system of stratification is right or just, then they will go along the status quo. (pp. 240-241) You could also mention Marx's notion of false consciousness -- the mistaken belief that the exploited identify their interests as identical to those of the elite (p. 236). As long as the elite is able to convince those below them that their interests are the same, there will be no revolts.

3.   *In the 1960s most former colonies around the globe won their political independence. Since that time the position of these countries has remained largely unchanged within the global system of stratification. Provide some explanation as to why political independence alone was not enough to alter their status.*

  In order to answer this question you need to review the different explanations as to the forces that led to the initial system of global stratification. Three of the four theories presented in your book focus on *economic* forces -- the only one that does not is the culture of poverty explanation (pp. 248-250). So the initial system of global stratification was most certainly based on economic relationships. Even after the Least Industrialized Nations won their political independence, they were still intimately linked together with the Most Industrialized Nations in economic terms. Therefore, the explanation as to why so little has changed continues to be economic. To explain this, you would want to refer to neocolonialism, the development of multinational corporations, and the role of technology (pp. 250-252).

☞ ANSWERS FOR CHAPTER 10

ANSWERS FOR MULTIPLE CHOICE QUESTIONS

1. c   According to your text, most sociologists agree with Max Weber that social class is best defined by employing three dimensions of social class. (256)
2. c   In fact, 68 percent of the wealth in the United States is owned by only 10 percent of the nation's families; the richest 1 percent owns more that the bottom 90 percent combined. (257)
3. c   According to economist Paul Samuelson, if an income pyramid were made out of a child's blocks, most U.S. residents would be near thc bottom of the pyramid. (257)

4. d   While it is true that the income distribution has not changed dramatically over the past 50 years, it is also true that the changes that have occurred have resulted in an increase in the percentage of income going to the top 20 percent of U.S. households and a decrease in the percentage going to the bottom 20 percent of households. (257)

5. b   Mills used the term "power elite" to refer to those at the top of society who make the important decisions. (259)

6. c   All of the following are true regarding jobs that have the most prestige--they pay more, require more education, and offer greater autonomy. They do not necessarily require special talent or skills. (260)

7. c   Gold discovered that the tenants did not like the fact that the janitors, as relatively low status workers, were earning more than themselves, so they reacted by being "snooty" to them. (262)

8. d   Wright responded to the criticism that Marx's categories were so broad that they did not accurately reflect the realities of people's lives by creating the concept of contradictory class location, which recognizes that some people can be members of more than one class simultaneously. (263)

9. b   Members of the upper middle class are the ones who owe their position to the achievement of a college and/or post-graduate degree. (265)

10. b   All of the following are characteristics of the working class: most are employed in relatively unskilled blue-collar and white-collar jobs; most hope to get ahead by achieving seniority on the job; and about thirty percent of the population belong to this class. However, most have not attended college for one or two years. (265)

11. c   According to your text, the typical mechanic in a Ford dealership would be in the working class. (266)

12. d   Differential risks of dying from accidents, nutritional differences and unequal access to medical care all help to explain the social class differences in death rates. (267)

13. b   It is actually the poor who experience higher levels of stress because they live with less job security and lower incomes; the rich have the resources to cope with life's challenges. (268)

14. c   According to Melvin Kohn lower-class parents are concerned that their children be conformists; they want them to obey conventional norms and authority figures while middle class parents encourage their children to be creative and independent. (269)

15. a   Members of the capitalist class tend to bypass public schools entirely, in favor of exclusive private schools. (269)

16. d   People in the working class are more likely to be more conservative on social issues and more liberal on economic issues. (269)

17. c   Members of the lower classes are more likely to be robbed, burglarized, or murdered. (270)

18. d   The classes which benefit from technology are the capitalist and upper middle classes. For capitalists, technology enables them to integrate production globally and to increase profits. The upper middle class benefits because they take a leading role in managing this new global economy; they also use the technology to advance in their chosen professions. (270)

19. d   A homeless person whose father was a physician has experienced downward mobility. (271)

20. a   As compared with their fathers, most U.S. men have a status higher than that of their fathers. (272)

21. c   Higgenbotham and Weber studied women professionals from working class backgrounds and found parental encouragement for postponing marriage and getting an education. (272)

22. c   The official measure of poverty, calculated to include those whose incomes equal less than three times a low-cost food budget, is the poverty line. (273)

23. c   In the United States, 11 percent of elderly population live in poverty, compared to 13 percent for the total population. (277)

24. b   In trying to explain poverty, sociologists are most likely to stress features of the social structure that contribute to poverty rather than any individual characteristics. (279)

25. d   "All of the above" is correct. The Horatio Alger myth is beneficial to society, according to the functionalists, because it shifts the blame for failure away from the social system and onto the shoulders of the individual, thereby reducing pressures on the system. It also motivates people to try harder to succeed because "anything is possible." (281)

ANSWERS FOR TRUE-FALSE QUESTIONS

1.   *False*. While there is no one definition of social class upon which all sociologists agree, most sociologists agree with Max Weber's conceptualization of social class as encompassing wealth, power and prestige. (256)

2.   *False*. Wealth and income are not the same; wealth includes both property and income. (256)

3.   *True*. (257)

4.   *True*. (257)

5.   *False*. Occupational prestige rankings are remarkably stable across countries and over time. (261)

6.   *True*. (262)

7.   *True*. (262)

8.   *True*. (264)

9.   *True*. (265)

10. *True*. (265-266)

11. *True*. (266)

12. *True*. (267)

13. *True*. (269)

14. *True*. (270)

15. *True*. (272)

16. *True*. (272)

17. *False*. The poverty rate among the rural poor is higher than the national average. This group is less likely than the non-rural poor to be on welfare and to live in single-parent households, is more likely than the non-rural poor to have low skills and less education. (274)

18. *False*. While it is true that there are more poor whites than there are poor minorities, the *rate* of poverty is much lower among the white population than minority populations. Only 11 percent of whites live below the poverty line, compared to 27 percent of Latinos and African Americans. (275)

19. *False*. Research indicates that 59 percent of families studied lived in poverty for one year or less. Only 12 percent lived in poverty for five years of more. (279)

20. *True*. (279)

ANSWERS FOR FILL-IN QUESTIONS

1.   According to Max Weber, the three dimensions of social class are: (1) WEALTH; (2) POWER; and (3) PRESTIGE. (256)

2.   Property and income together make up an individual's WEALTH. (256)

3.   According to C. Wright Mills, the POWER ELITE makes the big decisions in U.S. society. (259)

4.   A condition in which someone has a mixture of high and low ranks on the different dimensions of social class is referred to as STATUS INCONSISTENCY. (262)

5.   Erik Wright referred to a position in the class structure that generates inconsistent interests as CONTRADICTORY CLASS LOCATION. (263)

6.   According to Gilbert and Kahl, the capitalist class can be divided into two groups: (1) OLD MONEY and (2) NEW MONEY. (264)

7.   The UNDERCLASS is a small group of people for whom poverty persists year after year and across generations. (265)

8.   UPWARD MOBILITY is movement up the social class ladder. (271)

9.   Movement up or down the social class ladder that is attributed to changes in the structure of society, not to individual efforts, is STRUCTURAL MOBILITY. (272)

10.   The official measure of poverty is referred to as the POVERTY LINE; it is calculated to include those whose incomes are less than three times a low-income food budget. (273)

11.   THE FEMINIZATION OF POVERTY is a trend whereby most poor families in the U.S. are headed by women. (277)

12.   In the 1960s, social scientists like Michael Harrington and Oscar Lewis suggested that some of the poor get trapped in a CULTURE OF POVERTY. (279)

13.   The DESERVING POOR are people who, in the public mind, are poor through no fault of their own, while the UNDESERVING POOR are viewed as having brought on their own poverty. (279-280)

14.   Foregoing something in the present in hope of achieving greater gains in the future is DEFERRED GRATIFICATION. (281)

15.   The belief that anyone can get ahead if they only try hard enough is referred to as the HORATIO ALGER MYTH. (281)

ANSWERS TO MATCH THESE SOCIAL SCIENTISTS WITH THEIR CONTRIBUTIONS

1. b   Gerhard Lenski: *status inconsistency*
2. a   C. Wright Mills: *power elite*
3. e   Erik Wright: *updated Marx's model*
4. d   Gilbert & Kahl: *updated Weber's model*
5. f   Daniel Moynihan: *childhood poverty and the breakdown of the family*
6. c   Sennett & Cobb: *hidden costs of mobility*
7. b   Melvin Kohn: *social class patterns of child rearing*
8. h   Higgenbotham & Weber: *women's patterns of social mobility*

GUIDELINES FOR ANSWERING THE ESSAY QUESTIONS

1.   *Identify the three dimensions of social class and discuss some of the consequences of social class.*

        You could begin your essay by discussing how sociologists define wealth and income, power, and privilege (pp. 256-262). You might also talk about how each is unevenly distributed within American society. Finally, you should talk about the consequences of this uneven distribution in terms of physical and mental health, family life, education, religion, politics, crime and the criminal justice system, and access to new technology (pp. 267-270).

2.   *Discuss why you think women have been largely ignored in studies of mobility.*

        You would want to point out that most studies of mobility have focused on occupational mobility. Until quite recently, most women did not have continuous occupational careers because of the nature of traditional gender roles. They derived their status from their fathers and their husbands. Therefore, in studies of intergenerational mobility, they were excluded because they did not have work histories that spanned their lifetime. As women's roles have changed, so has researchers' awareness of them as research subjects. Also, because of structural changes in the economy, employment opportunities for women have opened up; this reflects structural mobility. You could point out the work by Higgenbotham and Weber as an example of research that does consider women's mobility (p. 272).

3.   *Describe which groups are at the greatest risk of poverty and then suggest ways in which poverty can be reduced by targeting these populations.*

You would want to begin by identifying those groups that are at greater risk--the rural poor, minorities, the undereducated, female heads of household, and children (pp. 274-277). You would then discuss specific ideas you have for overcoming some of the conditions that place these groups at greater risk; some possible programs would be improvements in education, including more funding for college and technical training, increases in minimum wage, increased number of jobs that pay a living wage, and more aggressive enforcement of anti-discrimination laws.

☞ ANSWERS FOR CHAPTER 11

ANSWERS FOR MULTIPLE CHOICE QUESTIONS

1. d   Gender stratification cuts across all aspects of social life and all social classes and it refers to men's and women's unequal access to power, prestige, and property on the basis of their sex. It is incorrect to think that it is not a structured feature of society. (286)

2. b   The term "sex" refers to the biological characteristics that distinguish females and males. (286)

3. c   According to sociologists, if biology were the principal factor in human behavior, around the world we would find women to be one sort of person and men another. (288)

4. d   "All of the above" is correct. Patriarchy is a society in which men dominate women, it has existed throughout history, and it is universal. (289)

5. a   The association of behaviors with one sex or the other is called sex typing. (291)

6. c   What Murdock found was that there was nothing about biology that required men and women to be assigned different work; rather it was social attitudes. (291-292)

7. c   In regard to the prestige of work, greater prestige is given to male activities. (292)

8. b   The incorrect statement is the one that claims the U.S. leads the world in the number of women who hold public office. In fact, it is Norway, where 40% of the legislators are women; U.S. percentage is 10, which is typical for most nations. (293)

9. b   Women still do not have the right to vote in Kuwait. (293)

10. d   A minority group is a group that is discriminated against on the basis of its members' physical or cultural characteristics. (295)

11. c   Historically in the United States, women could not serve on juries or hold property in their own names. They received the right to vote in the 1920, not the 1950s. They were not allowed to make legal contracts and they could not spend their own wages. (297)

12. d   All of the answers are correct. A "second wave" of protest and struggle against gender inequalities began in the 1960s when women began to compare their working conditions with those of men; it had as its goals everything from changing work roles to changing policies on violence against women. (297-298)

13. c   Gender inequality in education is perpetuated by the use of sex to sort students into different

academic disciplines. (299-300)

14. c Researchers who have studied conversation patterns between men and women conclude that even in everyday conversation, the talk between a man and a woman reflects social inequality. (302)

15. c The pay gap between men and women is found at all educational levels. (304)

16. c The glass ceiling refers to the invisible barrier that keeps women from reaching the executive suite. Men who go into fields that are traditionally associated with women often encounter a glass escalator--they advance quickly--rather than a glass ceiling. (305-306)

17. b Of the four statements, the one that says "Women do not seek out opportunities for advancement and do not spend enough time networking with powerful executives" is the only one that is not a reason why more women are not found in core corporate positions; all the rest represent valid reasons as to why women are under-represented in top corporate offices. (305-306)

18. d Felice Schwartz suggested that corporations create two parallel career paths. These are the "mommy track" and the "fast track." (307)

19. d Sexual harassment, rooted in the structure of the work place rather than individual relationships, involves a person in authority using the position to force unwanted sex on subordinates. Initially, it was seen as a women's issue, but today it is no longer exclusively a female problem. The only statement that is incorrect is that "male victims of sexual harassment receive more sympathy than female victims." (307-308)

20. d Date rape is not an isolated event; it is more likely to happen after a couple has dated for a period of time rather than on the first few dates; and it is difficult to prosecute because of the pre-existing relationship. (309)

21. a Rather than higher testosterone levels in males, feminists would point to the association of strength and virility with violence, males' frustration at their loss of power and status, and cultural traditions that are patriarchal as sources for gender violence. (310-311)

22. c Women are reluctant to get involved in politics because the demands of political life are in conflict with the demands of their roles as wives and mothers. (312)

23. b In many parts of the U.S. today, the primary concern of voters is whether the candidate can win; gender is of less concern than winning. (313)

24. d "All of the above" is correct. (313)

25. c Increased female participation in decision-making processes of social institutions is most likely going to result in breaking down the stereotypes that lock both males and females into traditional gender activities. (313)

ANSWERS FOR TRUE-FALSE QUESTIONS

1. *False*. Sex refers to biological characteristics that distinguish females and males. Gender refers to social characteristics that a society considers proper for its males and females. (286)

2. *False*. The study supports the view that biological factors play a role in structuring behavior, but that social factors are also important. Men with higher testosterone levels tend to be more aggressive and have more problems, but that there were variations by social class. (290-291)

3. *False*. Researchers have found a universal pattern of according male activities higher prestige than female activities. (292)

4. *True*. (293)

5. *False*. Female circumcision is still quite common in parts of Africa and southeast Asia. (294)

6. *True*. (295-296)

7. *True.* (297)
8. *False.* In the second wave of the U.S. women's movement, both the liberal and the conservative factions of the movement had a radical wing. (298)
9. *True.* (299)
10. *False.* While women have made gains in terms of the proportion of degrees earned, and exceed men in earning bachelor of arts degrees, they still lag behind in post-graduate and professional degrees. (299-300)
11. *True.* (301)
12. *True.* (302)
13. *False.* Men are more likely to interrupt a conversation and to control changes in topics than are women. (302)
14. *False.* Fuller and Schoenberger found that the 11 percent difference between men and women business majors in starting pay had grown to 14 percent after five years in the work place. (304-305)
15. *True.* (305-307)
16. *False.* The "glass escalator" refers to the opportunities that men have to advance quickly in traditional female occupations. (306)
17. *True.* (307)
18. *False.* In the U.S., males kill at a rate several times that of females. (309)
19. *True.* (310)
20. *False.* There are several other factors that also contribute to women not holding public office: they are under represented in law and business, traditional recruiting grounds for public office, the demands of running for and holding public office often conflict with a woman's other role responsibilities, they do not see themselves as a class in need of special representation. (312)

ANSWERS FOR FILL-IN QUESTIONS

1. Males' and females' unequal access to power, prestige, and property on the basis of sex reflects GENDER STRATIFICATION. (286)
2. SEX refers to biological characteristics that distinguish females and males, consisting of primary and secondary sex characteristics. (286)
3. The social characteristics that a society considers proper for its males and females make up an individual's GENDER. (286)
4. You inherit your SEX, but you learn your GENDER as you are socialized into specific behaviors and attitudes. (286)
5. A society in which women dominate men is called a MATRIARCHY. (289)
6. When activities become associated with one sex or the other they are said to be SEX TYPED. (291)
7. FEMALE CIRCUMCISION is a particular form of violence directed exclusively against women. (294)
8. A MINORITY is a group that is discriminated against on the basis of its members' physical characteristics. (295)
9. FEMINISM is the philosophy that men and women should be politically, economically, and socially equal. (297)
10. The GLASS CEILING prevents women from advancing to top executive positions. (305)
11. One reason why women do not reach top corporate positions is because they lack MENTORS, successful executives who take an interest in them and teach them the ropes. (306)

12.   Men who move into traditionally women's occupations are likely to climb onto a GLASS ESCALATOR, moving very quickly into more desirable work assignments, higher level positions, and larger salaries. (306)

13.   The proposed MOMMY TRACK would address the stresses that many working women experience when they attempt to combine careers and families. (307)

14.   The abuse of one's position of authority to force unwanted sexual demands on someone is referred to as SEXUAL HARASSMENT. (307)

15.   DATE RAPE most commonly occurs between couples who have known each other about a year. (309)

ANSWERS TO MATCH THESE SOCIAL SCIENTISTS WITH THEIR CONTRIBUTIONS

1. l   Janet Chafetz: *studied the second wave* of *feminism in the 1960s*
2. g   Alice Rossi: *women are better prepared biologically for "mothering" than are men*
3. e   Felice Schwartz: *associated with the notion of the Mommy track and the fast track*
4. b   Christine Williams: *men in nontraditional occupations often experience a glass escalator*
5. i   Gerda Lerner: *patriarchy may have had different origins around the globe*
6. h   Catharine McKinnon: *identified sexual harassment as a structural problem in workplaces*
7. a   George Murdock: *surveyed 324 societies and found evidence of sex-typed activities*
8. k   Samuel Stouffer: *noted the devaluation of things associated with women among soldiers*
9. c   Marvin Harris: *male dominance grew out of the greater strength that men had*
10. f   Steven Goldberg: *differences between males and females are due to inborn difference*
11. j   Frederick Engels: *male dominance developed with the origin of private property*
12. d   Douglas Foley: *study supports the view that things feminine are generally devalued*

GUIDELINES FOR ANSWERING THE ESSAY QUESTIONS

1.   Summarize the sociobiology argument concerning behavioral differences between men and women. Explain which position most closely reflects your own--biological, sociological, or sociobiological.

You would want to begin by stating how sociologists and biologists each explain the basis for differences in gendered behavior and then discuss how sociobiology tries to bridge the gulf between these two disciplines' views (p. 287-289). In discussing sociobiology you could refer to Alice Rossi's suggestion concerning the biological basis for mothering and the connection between biological predispositions and cultural norms (pp. 289). As further evidence of the relationship between biology and social forces, you could discuss the two studies cited in the text--the case of the young boy whose sex was changed and the study of Vietnam veterans (pp. 290-291). Your final task would be to state which view you think is most consistent with what you have learned about gender inequality and explain why.

2.   Compare and contrast the two waves of the feminist movement in this country by identifying the forces that contributed to both waves.

You could begin by noting that both waves of the feminist movement were committed to ending gender   stratification and both met with strong opposition from both males and females. In both cases, there were two different branches that emerged--a liberal and a conservative branch, and within these branches there were radical wings. The major difference between the two had to do with goals. The first wave was characterized by rather narrow goals--the movement focused on winning the vote for women--while the second wave was broader and wanted to address issues ranging from changing work roles to changing policies on violence against women (pp. 297-298).

3.   *Evaluate Felice's Schwartz's proposed "mommy track," stating both the strengths and weaknesses of this approach to the problem of gender inequality.*

You would want to begin by defining what Schwartz's notion of a "mommy track" is. The major strength of this proposal is that it gives working women flexibility in trying to combine work and family roles by recognizing that they often face conflicting demands. This is important for all women, but especially important for women who are single parents and need to work in order to support their families. At the same time, as the author of your text notes, this proposal has been subject to much criticism. First, it tends to confirm men's stereotypes of women executives as not seriously committed to their careers if they opt to go into this track. Second, it is not gender equitable because it assumes child care is women's job and does not provide for a parallel "daddy track." Finally, if women slow down they will never reach the top, thus maintaining a system in which men hold all the power (p. 307).

☞ ANSWERS FOR CHAPTER 12

ANSWERS FOR MULTIPLE CHOICE QUESTIONS

1. b   Race is inherited physical characteristics that distinguish one group from another. (318)
2. b   People often confuse race and ethnicity because of the cultural differences people see and the way they define race. (321)
3. a   A minority group is discriminated against because of physical or cultural differences. (321)
4. a   The dominant group in a society almost always considers its position to be due to its own innate superiority. (322)
5. d   A group's sense of ethnic identity is affected by the amount of power the group has, the size of the group, and the degree to which the group's physical appearance differs from the mainstream. Those groups with a heightened sense of ethnic identity generally have little power, are small in size, and stand out because of physical differences. (323)
6. c   Prejudice and discrimination appear to characterize every society. (324)
7. d   "All of the above" is correct. Prejudice is an attitude, it may be positive or negative, and it often is the basis for discrimination. (325)
8. d   According to research by Lawrence Bobo and James Kluegel, younger and more educated whites were more willing to have close, sustained interactions with other racial and ethnic groups than were older and less educated whites. (325)
9. a   The negative treatment of one person by another on the basis of that person's characteristics is referred to as individual discrimination. (326)
10. d   The research demonstrates that discrimination is built into the country's financial institutions; even when the credit histories were identical, African Americans and Latinos were 60 percent more likely to be rejected than whites. (327)
11. c   The functionalists see prejudice as functional because it helps to create solidarity within the group by fostering antagonisms directed against other groups; at the same time it can be dysfunctional because it has a negative impact on social relationships. (330)
12. d   "All of the above" is correct. According to conflict theorists, prejudice benefits capitalists by splitting workers along racial or ethnic lines; contributes to the exploitation of workers, thus producing a split-labor market; and is a factor in keeping workers from demanding higher wages and better working conditions. (330-331)
13. c   Symbolic interactionists stress that prejudiced people learn their prejudices in interaction with

others. (331)

14. b   From his research on racist groups, Raphael Ezekiel concluded that the leaders of these groups take advantage of the masses' anxieties concerning economic insecurity and of their tendency to see the "Establishment" as the cause of economic problems. He discovered that they are likely to see that races represent fundamental categories, with race representing the essence of the person. (332-333)

15. d   "All of the above" is correct. Genocide occurred when Hitler attempted to destroy all Jews, it is the systematic annihilation of a race or ethnic group, and it often requires the cooperation of ordinary citizens. (332)

16. b   When a minority is expelled from a country or from a particular area of a country, the process is called direct population transfer. (334)

17. c   A society's policy of exploiting a minority group, using social institutions to deny the minority access to the society's full benefits, is referred to as internal colonialism. (334)

18. b   The process of being absorbed into the mainstream culture is assimilation. (334)

19. a   WASPs, which stands for White Anglo-Saxon Protestants whose ancestors came from England, were highly ethnocentric and viewed other immigrants as inferior. Because they were the ones who settled the colonies, they were able to take power and determine the national agenda, controlling the destiny of the nation. As white Europeans from other countries arrived in America, WASPs viewed them as inferior. Rather than being embraced by WASPs, they were typically greeted with negative stereotypes. (337)

20. c   According to William Wilson, civil rights legislation created new opportunities for middle-class African Americans to move up the social class ladder. (340)

21. d   Afrocentrism is an emphasis on unique African American traditions and concerns; has encouraged the establishment of black studies courses and academic departments; and is a modified version of black nationalism. (342)

22. a   According to your text, Latinos are distinguished from other ethnic minorities in the United States by the Spanish language. (342-343)

23. c   While Asian Americans have been successful in this country, there are significant differences among Asian ethnic groups. (344-347)

24. d   Native Americans are often referred to as an "invisible minority;" because they are concentrated in a small number of states--Oklahoma, California, and Arizona--and they tend to live in rural areas, most Americans are hardly conscious of them. (348)

25. b   Most immigrants who came over to the United States during the first wave of immigration were from Europe. In the current wave of immigration, immigrants are coming from a diversity of nations. (349-350)

ANSWERS FOR TRUE-FALSE QUESTIONS

1.   *False*. There is not general agreement as to how many races there are--the range is from two to thousands. (319)

2.   *False*. Race is physical characteristics; ethnicity is cultural. (321)

3.   *True*. (321)

4.   *False*. Sociologically speaking, size is not an important defining characteristic of minority group status. Being singled out for unequal treatment and objects of collective discrimination are. (322)

5.   *True*. (322-323)

6.   *True*. (323)

7. *True* (323)
8. *False.* Although discrimination is unfair treatment, it is not based solely on racial characteristics, but can also be based many other characteristics, including age, sex, height, weight, income, education, marital status, sexual orientation, disease, disability, religion, and politics. (324)
9. *True.* (325)
10. *False.* One recent study at the University of Alabama found that members of fraternities and sororities were more likely than nonmembers to be prejudiced. (325)
11. *False.* In order to understand discrimination in the United States it is necessary to explain the patterns of institutional discrimination. (326)
12. *True.* (327)
13. *True.* (328)
14. *True.* (330)
15. *False.* Conflict theorists, not functionalists, focus on the role of the capitalist class in exploiting racism and ethnic inequalities. (330)
16. *True.* (330)
17. *True.* (332-334)
18. *True.* (334)
19. *True.* (343-344)
20. *True.* (347-349)

ANSWERS FOR FILL-IN QUESTIONS

1. The systematic annihilation or attempted annihilation of a race or ethnic group is <u>GENOCIDE</u>. (318)
2. <u>RACE</u> is inherited physical characteristics that distinguish one group from another. (318)
3. Membership in a minority group is a(n) <u>ASCRIBED</u> status; that is, it is not voluntary, but comes through birth. (322)
4. <u>RACISM</u> is discrimination on the basis of race. (324)
5. <u>INSTITUTIONAL</u> discrimination is the negative treatment of a minority group that is built into a society's institutions. (326)
6. Theodor Adorno's term for people who are prejudiced and rank high on scales of conformity, intolerance, insecurity, respect for authority, and submissiveness to superiors is <u>THE AUTHORITARIAN PERSONALITY</u>. (328)
7. <u>FUNCTIONAL</u> theorists believe that prejudice can be both functional and dysfunctional. (330)
8. Split-labor market is used by <u>CONFLICT</u> theorists to explain how the racial and ethnic strife can be used to pit workers against one another. (330)
9. The term used to describe the unemployed who can be put to work during times of high production and then discarded when no longer needed is <u>THE RESERVE LABOR FORCE</u>. (330)
10. <u>SELECTIVE PERCEPTION</u> is the ability to see certain points but remain blind to others. (331)
11. The types of population transfer are: (1) <u>DIRECT</u> and (2) <u>INDIRECT</u>. (334)
12. The policy of forced expulsion and genocide is referred to as <u>ETHNIC CLEANSING</u>. (334)
13. <u>ASSIMILATION</u> is the process of being absorbed into the mainstream culture. (334)
14. <u>MULTICULTURALISM</u> is a philosophy or political policy that permits or even encourages ethnic variation. (335)
15. Assimilation to a particular segment of a culture, rather than to the mainstream culture, is

called SEGMENTARY ASSIMILATION. (335)

ANSWERS TO MATCH THESE SOCIAL SCIENTISTS WITH THEIR CONTRIBUTIONS
1. d   Theodor Adorno: *identified the authoritarian personality type*
2. f   Ashley Doane: *identified four factors that affect an individual's sense of ethnic identity*
3. g   John Dollard: *suggested that prejudice is the result of frustration*
4. j   Raphael Ezekiel: *studied racism in neo-Nazis and the KKK organizations*
5. i   Louis Wirth: *offered a sociological definition of minority group*
6. h   Joe Feagin: *researched everyday racism*
7. a   Donald Muir: *measured racial attitudes of white students*
8. b   William Wilson: *argues that class is more important than race in explaining inequality*
9. e   Charles Willie: *argues that race is still an important criterion for discrimination*
10. c   W.I. Thomas: *observed that defining a situation as real, makes it real in its consequences*

GUIDELINES FOR ANSWERING THE ESSAY QUESTIONS
1. *Explain what the author means when he says that race is both a myth and a reality.*

You would begin by defining the concept of race (p. 318). Then you would move on to talking about the myth of race--how there is no universal agreement as to how many races there are and how a system of racial classification is more a reflection of the society in which one lives than any underlying biological bases (p. 319). At the same time, race is a reality--in terms of people's subjective feelings about race and the superiority of some, and the inferiority of other, races. You should bring Thomas's observations into the essay--if people believe something is real, then it is real in its consequences (p. 321).

2. *Using the experiences of different racial and ethnic groups in the U.S., identify and discuss the six patterns of intergroup relations.*

The book identifies six different types of intergroup relations--genocide, population transfer, internal colonialism, segregation, assimilation, and multiculturalism (pp. 332-335). You could begin by mentioning how these are arranged along a continuum from rejection and inhumanity to acceptance and humanity. Then, as you define each pattern, bring into your discussion an example, or examples, from the history of the U.S. (refer to pp. 336-349). For example, in discussing genocide you could mention the treatment of Native Americans by the U.S. military; in discussing internal colonialism you could mention the economic exploitation of Latino farmworkers. An example of assimilation would be the experiences of European immigrants.

3. *Explore how both psychological and sociological theories can be used together to gain a deeper understanding of prejudice and discrimination.*

Your essay should discuss how psychological theories provide us with a deeper understanding of individual behavior, while sociological theories provide insights into the societal framework of prejudice and discrimination. You could discuss the work of Theodor Adorno on the authoritarian personality or Dollard's work on individual frustration and the role of scapegoats (pp. 328-329). But without an understanding of the social environment, this work is incomplete. Bridging the two perspectives is symbolic interactionism and the analysis of the role of labels, selective perception, and the self-fulfilling prophecy in maintaining prejudice (p. 331). But you should also include in your essay some reference to the functionalist analysis and the work of Muzafer and Carolyn Sherif as well as the conflict theorists and how the capitalist class exploits racial and ethnic strife to retain power and control in society (pp. 330-331).

☞ ANSWERS FOR CHAPTER 13

ANSWERS FOR MULTIPLE CHOICE QUESTIONS

1. b   The Abkhasians are an interesting example regarding age because they live such long lives. (357)
2. d   It is the process of industrialization that contributes to an increase in the number of people who reach older ages. (357-358)
3. b   The process by which older persons make up an increasing proportion of the United States population is referred to as the graying of America. (359)
4. c   The number of years an individual is likely to live is referred to as his/her life expectancy. (359)
5. c   Gender age refers to the relative value that a culture places on men's and women's ages. (363)
6. d   "All of the above" is correct. Factors that may spur people to apply the label of old to themselves include personal history or biography, cultural signals about when a person is old, and biological factors. (363)
7. b   This policy reflects ageism, prejudice and discrimination based on age. (365)
8. b   It has been suggested that the Baby Boom generation will have a positive effect on U.S. social images of the elderly in the years to come, given then numbers and economic clout. (366)
9. d   "All of the above" is correct. The mass media communicate messages that reflect the currently devalued status of the elderly. It also tells us what people over sixty-five should be like and often treats the elderly in discourteous and unflattering terms. (367)
10. b   Some researchers believe that the process of disengagement begins during middle age. (368)
11. a   The belief that satisfaction during old age is related to a person's level and quality of activity is called activity theory. (369)
12. b   Conflict theorists believe that retirement benefits are the result of a struggle between competing interest groups. (370)
13. b   As the population of the U.S. grays, there is concern that the ratio of working people to retired people will become smaller, making it more difficult to support programs like Social Security. This ratio is referred to as the dependency ratio. (372)
14. a   Isolation is a problem for many people over 65, especially for women. This is because of differences in patterns of mortality between men and women. Because elderly women are more likely to live longer than their husbands, most elderly men are still living with their wives, while most elderly women are not. (375)
15. d   "All of the above" is correct. Nursing homes are very expensive; have residents who tend to be widowed or never married; and tend to strip away human dignity. (376)
16. b   Researchers have found that elder abuse is fairly extensive. (378)
17. a   Because of different government programs, the percentage of Americans 65 and over who live below the poverty line has declined since the 1950s. (379)
18. b   Karen Cerulo and Janet Ruane use the term technological lifespace to describe a form of existence that is neither life nor death--the brain is dead but the body lives on. (380)
19. a   In preindustrial societies, the sick were taken care of at home. (380)
20. d   All of the answers are correct. In trying to explain the pattern of a sharp rise in suicide of white males when they reach their middle sixties, symbolic interactionists point out that white males may experience aging differently than other groups in our society; aging may represent a greater loss of privilege for white males than for other groups; and retirement signals a decline

in both power and status for them. (383)

ANSWERS FOR TRUE-FALSE QUESTIONS
1.   *True.* (356)
2.   *False.* Industrialization is critical for the increase in the number of elderly within a society. Industrialization produces a higher standard of living, a more plentiful food supply, better public health measures, and success in fighting diseases that kill people at younger ages. (357)
3.   *False.* Life expectancy refers to the number of years an individual can expect to live, while life span refers to the maximum length of life. (358-360)
4.   *True.* (362)
5.   *True.* (363)
6.   *False.* A gerontocracy is a society (or some other group) run by the old. (364)
7.   *True.* (367)
8.   *True.* (368)
9.   *True.* (369)
10.   *True.* (369)
11.   *True.* (372)
12.   *False.* Most researchers have found that the elderly are less isolated than stereotypes would lead us to believe. (375)
13.   *True.* (378)
14.   *False.* America's elderly are <u>less</u> likely than the average American to be living in poverty. (379)
15.   *True.* (380)

ANSWERS FOR FILL-IN QUESTIONS
1.   The process by which older persons make up an increasing proportion of the United States population is called <u>THE GRAYING OF AMERICA</u>. (359)
2.   The <u>LIFE EXPECTANCY</u> of an average newborn is the number years he or she can expect to live. (359)
3.   While experts may disagree on the actual number, <u>LIFE SPAN</u> refers to the maximum length of life of a species. (360)
4.   The relative value that a culture places on men's and women's ages is referred to as <u>GENDER AGE</u>. (363)
5.   <u>GERONTOCRACY</u> is a society (or other group) run by the old. (364)
6.   <u>AGEISM</u> is the discrimination against the elderly because of their age. (365)
7.   The <u>MASS MEDIA</u> not only communicate messages about the devalued status of the elderly in American society but also contribute to the ideas. (366)
8.   An <u>AGE COHORT</u> is people born at roughly the same time who pass through the life course together. (367)
9.   The belief that society prevents disruption by having the elderly vacate their positions of responsibility is <u>DISENGAGEMENT THEORY</u>. (368)
10.   <u>ACTIVITY</u> theory asserts that satisfaction during old age is related to a person's level and quality of activity. (369)
11.   The number of workers required to support the portion of the population aged 64 and older and 15 and under is the <u>DEPENDENCY RATIO</u>. (372)
12.   Founded in the 1960s by Margaret Kuhn, the <u>GRAY PANTHERS</u> encourages people of all

ages to work for the welfare of both the old and the young. (375)

13.   The organization that monitors proposed state and federal legislation and mobilizes members to act on issues affecting their welfare as senior citizens is the <u>AMERICAN ASSOCIATION OF RETIRED PERSONS</u>. (375)

14.   Sociologists Cerulo and Ruane use the term <u>TECHNOLOGICAL LIFESPACE</u> to describe a form of existence in which, due to technology, the body lives on even after brain function is gone. (380)

15.   <u>HOSPICE</u> is a place, or services brought into someone's home, for the purpose of bringing comfort and dignity to a dying person. (381)

ANSWERS TO MATCH THESE SOCIAL SCIENTISTS WITH THEIR CONTRIBUTIONS

1. d   Robert Butler: *coined "ageism" to refer to prejudice or discrimination based on age*
2. e   Dorothy Jerrome: *criticized disengagement theory for its implicit bias against the old*
3. f   E. Kubler-Ross: *suggested that facing death sets in motion a five-stage process*
4. a   Cerulo & Ruane: *use the term "technological lifespace" for life sustained by technology*
5. c   Cumming & Henry: *developed disengagement theory*
6. b   Robertson & Minkler: *found no evidence that the elderly gained at children's expense*

GUIDELINES FOR ANSWERING THE ESSAY QUESTIONS

1.   *Choose one of the three different perspectives and discuss how that perspective approaches the subject of aging. Consider both the strengths as well as the weaknesses of the perspective you choose.*

In this question you have the option of writing about symbolic interactionism, functionalism, or conflict theory. If you choose symbolic interactionism (pp. 362-367), you would want to talk about the process of labeling--both the cultural labels and factors that affect the individual's adoption of those labels. You would also want to bring up the concept of "ageism," the role of the media in defining images, and how the labels change over time. In particular, you could discuss how these labels changed with industrialization and how they are once again changing with the advent of a postindustrial society. The strength of this perspective is that it provides us with insights into the social nature of a biological process; a weakness would be that it does not consider the conflict that may surround the labeling process.

If you choose to write about functionalism, remember that this perspective focuses on how the different parts of society work together (pp. 367-369). The two theories associated with this perspective are disengagement theory and activity theory. Strengths might be the focus on adjustment and the smooth transitioning from one generation to the next. Weaknesses are tied to the theories; disengagement theory overlooks the possibility that the elderly disengage from one set of roles (work-related) but may engage in another set of roles (friendship), while activity theory does not identify the key variables that underlie people's activities.

Finally, if you choose conflict theory, you would want to focus on the conflict that is generated between different age groups in society as they compete for scarce resources (pp. 369-375). As an example you would want to discuss the controversy over social security--from its birth to the present time. A strength of this perspective is that it provides us with an understanding of why the elderly have reduced the level of poverty over time; a weakness might be that it tends to emphasize conflict to the extent that cooperation between generations is overlooked.

2.   *Discuss the impact that industrialization and technology have had on aging as well as dying.*

You could begin the essay by talking about how technology and industrialization have brought improvements as well as new developments (pp. 357-362). You might want to refer to some of the discussion in this chapter on the cross-cultural variations in aging--the Abkhasians (pp. 356-357), the Tiwi and Eskimo (p. 364), or the Chinese (p. 365). These were all pre-industrial societies with various views on the elderly. To talk about the impact of industrialization, you should refer to the improvements in the quality of life as well as the changes in cultural views on aging (pp. 364-366). Finally, you would want to talk about how technology enables us to sustain life for longer periods of time, but that the quality of that life is often compromised (pp.380-382).

☞ ANSWERS FOR CHAPTER 14

ANSWERS FOR MULTIPLE CHOICE QUESTIONS

1. d   "All of the above" is correct. Market is any process of buying and selling. It is the mechanism that establishes values for the exchange of goods and services. It also means the movement of vast amounts of goods across international borders. (389)

2. c   Hunting and gathering societies are characterized by a subsistence economy. (389)

3. b   In pastoral and horticultural economies a more dependable food supply led to the development of a surplus. This surplus was one of the most significant events in human history because it fundamentally altered people's basic relationships. (389)

4. d   Industrial economies are based on machines powered by fuels. Industrial economies also created a surplus unlike anything the world had seen, and these economies were based on the invention of the steam engine. Therefore, the incorrect statement is "A service sector developed and employed the majority of workers"; this is actually a characteristic of a *postindustrial society.* (389-390)

5. d   Thorstein Veblen used the term conspicuous consumption to describe the lavishly wasteful spending of goods in order to enhance social prestige. (389)

6. c   Postindustrial economies are characterized by a large surplus of goods; extensive trade among nations; and a "global village." While machines may still be powered by fuel, this is not a defining characteristic of this type of economy. (390)

7. a   Money was first used extensively in agricultural societies. (391)

8. a   The gross national product is total goods and services produced by a nation. (392)

9. c   The debit card came into existence in the postindustrial economy. (393)

10. d   Private ownership of the means of production is an essential feature of capitalism. (393)

11. c   The possession of machines and factories by individuals, who decide what shall be produced, is referred to as private ownership of the means of production. (393)

12. b   An economic system characterized by the public ownership of the means of production, central planning, and the distribution of goods without a profit motive is socialism. (395)

13. b   According to Karl Marx, profits represent excess value that is extracted from workers. Because an item's value is derived from the work that goes into it, there can be no profit unless workers are paid less than the value of their labor. (396)

14. b   Some critics believe that underemployment is a problem caused by capitalism. (396)

15. a   Work binds us together, according to the functionalist perspective. (399)

16. b   As societies industrialize, they become based on organic solidarity. (400)

17. c   The joint ownership of a business enterprise, whose liabilities and obligations are separate from those of its owners, is a corporation. (400)

18. c   When stockholders are satisfied with the profits and their stock dividends, they generally just rubber-stamp whatever recommendations are made by management; a stockholders' revolt

occurs when dissatisfaction with the overall level of performance leads to their refusal to approve management's recommendations. (401)

19. a   Oligopoly is the control of an entire industry by several large companies. (402)

20. c   The elite who sit on the boards of directors of not just one but several companies are referred to as interlocking directorates. (403)

21. c   The fundamental changes in society that follow the movement of vast numbers of women from the home to the work force is referred to as the quiet revolution. (406)

22. d   "All of the above" is correct. The underground economy is an exchange of goods and services that is not reported to the government; it helps many Americans avoid what they consider exorbitant taxes; and it includes illegal activities such as drug dealing. (407)

23. c   The <u>correct</u> statement regarding wages today is "The buying power of today's wages is actually less than it was 30 years ago." Inflation has whittled away the value of the increased dollars workers are paid. (409)

24. b   When compared to workers in western Europe, U.S. workers have less leisure time. The trend toward more leisure was reversed in the 1960s. Only Japanese workers work more hours annually than workers in the U.S. (410)

25. c   According to conflict theory, low-level workers bear the brunt of technological change. (412)

ANSWERS FOR TRUE-FALSE QUESTIONS

1.   *False*. Pastoral and horticultural societies, not hunting and gathering societies, were the first economies to have a surplus. (389)

2.   *True*. (389)

3.   *True*. (390)

4.   *False*. Postindustrial economies, not industrial economies, are based on information processing and providing services. (390)

5.   *True*. (391)

6.   *True*. (392)

7.   *False*. Credit cards and debit cards are not the same thing. A credit card allows its owner to purchase goods but to be billed later. A debit card allows its owner to purchase against his or her bank account. (392-393)

8.   *True*. (393)

9.   *True*. (394)

10.   *True*. (396)

11.   *False*. According to convergence theory, socialist nations will gradually adopt features of capitalism and capitalist nations will adopt features of socialism to the point where a new, hybrid form will emerge. (398)

12.   *False*. Durkheim's concept of organic solidarity is no longer an adequate concept for understanding the interdependency that exists among the nations of the world today; the author suggests a new global division of work is now emerging. (400)

13.   *True*. (401)

14.   *False*. Oligopolies are formed when a small number of large companies operate within a single industry, dictating prices, setting the quality of their products, and protecting their markets. (402)

15.   *True*. (402)

16.   *True*. (405)

17.   *False*. Researchers have found that women workers are more likely than male workers to be

concerned with maintaining a balance between their work and family lives. (406)

18. *True.* (406)

19. *False.* In recent decades, workers in the U.S. have actually experienced an increase in work hours and a decrease in leisure, which is contrary to the pattern found in other western, industrialized nations. (410)

20. *True.* (411)

ANSWERS FOR FILL-IN QUESTIONS

1. ECONOMY is the term for a system of distribution of goods and services. (389)
2. The means (for example, currency, gold, and silver) by which people value goods and services in order to make an exchange is the MEDIUM OF EXCHANGE. (391)
3. A CREDIT CARD allows its owners to purchase goods but to be billed later. A DEBIT CARD allows its owners to charge purchases against his or her bank account. (392-393)
4. Digital money that is stored on a computer is called E-CASH. (393)
5. The control of an entire industry by a single company is a MONOPOLY. (394)
6. The law of supply and demand is referred to as MARKET FORCES. (395)
7. UNDEREMPLOYMENT is the condition of having to work at a job beneath one's level of training and abilities, or of being able to find only part-time work. (396)
8. The view that as capitalist and socialist economic systems each adopt features of the other, a hybrid (or mixed) economic system may emerge is CONVERGENCE THEORY. (398)
9. Durkheim's term for the unity that comes from being involved in similar occupations or activities is MECHANICAL SOLIDARITY. (399)
10. The refusal of a corporation's stockholders to automatically approve decisions made by managers is referred to as a STOCKHOLDERS' REVOLT. (401)
11. Members of the INNER CIRCLE may compete with one another, but they are united by a mutual interest in preserving capitalism. (402)
12. One way in which the wealthy use corporations to wield power is by means of INTERLOCKING DIRECTORSHIPS, or serving as directors of several companies simultaneously. (403)
13. The QUIET REVOLUTION has contributed to a transformation of consumer patterns, relations at work, self-concepts, and relationships with family and friends. (406)
14. The UNDERGROUND ECONOMY consists of economic activities, whether legal or illegal, that people don't report to the government. (407)
15. LEISURE is time not taken up by work or required activities such as eating and sleeping. (409)

ANSWERS TO MATCH THESE SOCIAL SCIENTISTS WITH THEIR CONTRIBUTIONS

1. b   Daniel Bell: *identified six characteristics of postindustrial society*
2. e   Emile Durkheim: *contributed the concepts of mechanical and organic solidarity*
3. d   Karl Marx: *an outspoken critic of capitalism who wrote about basis for profits*
4. a   Michael Useem: *studied the activities of the "inner circle"*
5. c   Thorstein Veblen: *created the term "conspicuous consumption"*

GUIDELINES FOR ANSWERING THE ESSAY QUESTIONS

1.   *Discuss the advantages and disadvantages of both capitalism and socialism as ideologies and as economic systems.*

This is a difficult question to answer because it is laden with social values. In this country we have been taught that capitalism is good and socialism is bad. Nevertheless, you should try to approach this from as objective a position as possible. You would want to begin by discussing the advantages and disadvantages of capitalism. For advantages you could mention the idea of private ownership and the pursuit of profits, the motivation among workers to work hard, and the vast array of goods that are available in the marketplace (pp. 393-395). Among the disadvantages you could note the possibility for monopoly, the creation of constant discontent through advertising, and the violation of certain basic human right like freedom from poverty (pp. 396-397). Turning to socialism, you could note that advantages include production for the general welfare rather than individual enrichment and the distribution of goods and services according to need rather than ability to pay (p. 395). Critics point out that socialism violates basic human rights such as individual freedom of decision and opportunity (p. 396).

2.   *The author suggests that the globalization of capitalism may be the most significant economic change of the last 100 years. Discuss what the consequences of the change are for our society as well as nations around the globe.*

        In answering this question, you will want to combine both functionalist and conflict views on globalization. You could begin by talking about the role of corporations (pp. 400, 402) in the new global marketplace and how corporations today are multinationals that are committed first and foremost to profits and market shares, not to any nation (p. 401). Another major development is the emerging global division of labor (p. 400) and the increased global trade (p. 401), which are together redefining how work is organized. Functionalists argue that these changes will lead to greater competition, increased productivity, lower prices and a higher standard of living for us all. On the other hand, conflict theorists look at the same trends and argue that some will benefit while others suffer. They see increased corporate power as well as less protection for workers from unemployment (p. 404). You could conclude by discussing the future--are we headed for utopia or a nightmare (pp. 412-414)?

3.   *The chapter discusses several different economic trends that have been occurring in the second half of this century. Discuss the impact of each of the following: the movement of women into the economy, the underground economy, shrinking paychecks, changing patterns of work and leisure, and the emergence of the alternative office.*

        The first development you will want to talk about is women's increased participation in the paid work force (p. 406). This has transformed consumption patterns, relations at work, self-concepts, and relationships with significant others. The underground economy is another major force in our society today, generating about $1 trillion. What is significant is that its presence distorts official statistics on the nation's gross national product, income, and employment. It also means that the IRS loses more than $100 billion a year in taxes (pp. 408-409). The shrinking of workers' paychecks is connected to inflation--workers are finding that their buying power is less than it was 30 years ago (p. 409). Finally, compared to a century ago, workers enjoy increased leisure, primarily because workers have organized and demanded greater leisure. At the same time, over the past 30-40 years, the trend towards greater leisure has been reversed, and workers today are working more than before (p. 410).

☞ ANSWERS FOR CHAPTER 15

ANSWERS FOR MULTIPLE CHOICE QUESTIONS

1. d   "All of the above" is correct. Power, as defined by Max Weber, is the ability to carry out one's will in spite of resistance from others; it is an inevitable part of everyday life. (418)

2. b   Governments, whether dictatorships or the elected forms, are examples of macropolitics. (418)

3. c   Authority is the power that people accept as rightly exercised or legitimate, while coercion is the power that people do not accept as rightly exercised or illegitimate. (418)

4. c   Peter Berger considered violence to be the ultimate foundation of any political order. (419)

5. b   Revolutions are people's rejection of the government's claim to rule over them. (419)

6. d   "All of the above" is correct. Traditional authority, the hallmark of preliterate groups, is based on custom. With industrialization it declines, but does not totally disappear. (419-420)

7. d   "All of the above" is correct. John F. Kennedy was a rational-legal leader; was also a charismatic leader; and is an example of a leader who is difficult to classify in terms of ideal types. (422)

8. c   The least stable type of authority is the charismatic. (422)

9. b   Universal citizenship is the principle that everyone has the same basic rights by virtue of being born in a country, or of immigrating to that country and becoming a naturalized citizen. (424)

10. b   An individual who seizes power and imposes his will onto the people is a dictator. (424)

11. c   A form of government that exerts almost total control is a totalitarian regime. (425)

12. a   The United States has centrist parties. (427)

13. b   European systems of democracy, in which seats in the national legislatures are divided according to the proportion of votes each party receives (proportional representation), encourage the formation of minority parties. (427)

14. b   Studies of voting patterns in the United States show that voting varies by age, race/ethnicity, education, employment, income, and gender. (428-429)

15. d   According to research by Portes and Rumbaut, immigrants initially organize politically along lines of race and ethnicity. Once they have achieved a certain level of political power, attaining political representation roughly equivalent to their numbers in the population, then social class becomes more significant than race and ethnicity. (429)

16. b   In recent presidential elections, only about one-half of eligible voters actually cast a ballot. (430)

17. d   "All of the above" is correct. Lobbyists are people paid to influence legislation on behalf of their clients; are employed by special-interest groups; and are a major force in American politics. (430)

18. b   Functionalists believe that any one group is prevented from gaining control of the government because of the presence of checks and balances. (432)

19. a   Functionalists suggest that political conflict is minimized as special-interest groups negotiate with one another and reach compromise. (432)

20. d   Members of the power elite are drawn from all three arenas: the largest corporations, the armed services, and political office. (432)

21. c   According to conflict theorists, the ruling class is made up of people whose backgrounds and orientations to life are so similar that they automatically share the same goals. (433)

22. a   War is armed conflict between nations or politically distinct groups. It is not necessarily universal nor is it chosen for dealing with disagreements by all societies at one time or another. (434)

23. a   A cultural tradition of war, an antagonistic situation in which two or more states confront incompatible objectives, and the presence of a "fuel" that heats the antagonistic situation to a boiling point are the three essential conditions of war identified by Nicholas Timasheff. The existence of a strong, well-armed military force was not one of the factors he identified as essential. (434)

24. b   The act or process of reducing people to objects that do not deserve the treatment accorded

humans is dehumanization. (436)

25. d   "All of the above" is correct. Today, national boundaries are becoming less meaningful because of the embrace of capitalism by more and more nations, the worldwide flow of information, capital and goods, and the formation of large economic and political units like the European Union. (438)

ANSWERS FOR TRUE-FALSE QUESTIONS

1.   *True.* (418)
2.   *False.* Authority, not coercion, refers to legitimate power. (418)
3.   *True.* (419)
4.   *True.* As societies industrialize, traditional authority is undermined; however, it never totally dies out. Parental authority provides an excellent example. (420)
5.   *True.* (420)
6.   *False.* It is because the authority of charismatic leaders is based on their personal ability to attract followers that they pose a threat to the established political system. They work outside the political structure and owe allegiance to nothing. (421)
7.   *True.* (422)
8.   *True.* (423)
9.   *False.* In early societies that were small in size there was no need for some form of political system because these societies operated more like an extended family with decisions being made as they become necessary. (423)
10. *True.* (424)
11. *True.* (424)
12. *False.* The idea of universal citizenship caught on very slowly in the United States. Initially, it was believed that certain groups--women, African Americans, Native Americans, Asian Americans and the poor--should not be given the rights of citizenship. (424)
13. *False.* The European system is based on proportional representation which encourages minority parties and the formation of noncentrist parties. (427)
14. *False.* Employment and income do affect the probability that people will vote. Those who are employed and feel their income is appropriate have a higher stake in the system and are more likely to participate, while those who are unemployed or who feel their income is inadequate are likely to feel alienated and be apathetic. (429-430)
15. *False.* Most political action committees do not represent broad social interests but, rather, stand for narrow financial concerns, such as the dairy, oil, banking, and construction industries. (431)
16. *True.* (432)
17. *False.* According to C. Wright Mills, the three groups that make up the power elite do not share power equally; the leaders of the top corporations have a greater share of the power than either of the other two groups. (433)
18. *False.* War is not universal; it is simply one option that groups may choose for dealing with disagreements. (434)
19. *False.* Despite the fact that war continues to carry massive costs in terms of lives lost and property destroyed, it remains a common technique for pursuing political objectives. (435)
20. *True.* (436)

ANSWERS FOR FILL-IN QUESTIONS

1.	The exercise of power in everyday life, such as deciding who is going to do the housework is referred to as MICROPOLITICS. (418)
2.	STATE is synonymous with government; the source of legitimate violence in society. (419)
3.	A REVOLUTION is armed resistance designed to overthrow a government. (419)
4.	TRADITIONAL AUTHORITY is authority based on custom. (419)
5.	Bureaucratic authority is also called RATIONAL-LEGAL AUTHORITY. (420)
6.	An independent city whose power radiates outward, bringing the adjacent area under its rule is a CITY-STATE. (423)
7.	DIRECT DEMOCRACY is a form of democracy in which the eligible voters meet together to discuss issues and make their decisions. (424)
8.	The concept that birth and residence in a country impart basic rights is known as CITIZENSHIP. (424)
9.	A form of government that exerts almost total control over the people is TOTALITARIANISM. (425)
10.	An electoral system in which seats in a legislature are divided according to the proportion of votes each political party receives is called PROPORTIONAL REPRESENTATION. (427)
11.	VOTER APATHY refers to indifference and inaction on the part of individuals or groups with respect to the political process. (430)
12.	A state of lawlessness or political disorder caused by the absence or collapse of governmental authority is ANARCHY. (432)
13.	POWER ELITE is C. Wright Mills's term for the top people in leading corporations, the most powerful generals and admirals of the armed forces, and certain elite politicians. (432)
14.	The act or process of reducing people to objects that do not deserve the treatment accorded humans is DEHUMANIZATION. (436)
15.	Today NATIONALISM, a strong identity with a nation, accompanied by the desire for that nation to be dominant, challenges efforts to forge a new world order. (438)

ANSWERS TO MATCH THESE SOCIAL SCIENTISTS WITH THEIR CONTRIBUTIONS
1. c	Peter Berger: *violence is the foundation of the political order*
2. e	William Domhoff: *ruling class*
3. h	C. Wright Mills: *power elite*
4. d	Max Weber: *three types of authority*
5. g	Nicholas Timasheff: *essential conditions of war*
6. f	Tamotsu Shibutani: *the process of dehumanization*
7. a	Pitirim Sorokin: *war as a fairly routine experience*
8. b	Portes & Rumbaut: *political assimilation of immigrants*

GUIDELINES FOR ANSWERING THE ESSAY QUESTIONS
1.	*Distinguish between macropolitics and micropolitics, explaining what each is and which perspectives are associated with each, and provide your own examples to illustrate each.*
	You would begin by defining what each of these is--micropolitics is the exercise of power in everyday life, while macropolitics is the exercise of large-scale power over a large group (p. 418). In general, symbolic interactionists focus more on micropolitics, because it is rooted in the social interactions that take place within social groups, although some conflict theorists could also take a micropolitical approach by focusing on the conflict that is generated by power inequalities. On the other hand, functionalists and conflict theorists are concerned with macropolitics, because they are

concerned with the large-scale structures and patterns of a society. (Note: You could refer back to pages 31-32 for a discussion of the differences between macro and micro sociology.) Finally, you would include some of your own examples of micropolitics (struggles between husbands and wives, parents and children) and macropolitics (struggles between political parties, between Congress and the President, between unions and elected officials).

2.   *Compare and contrast the systems of democracy found in the United States and Europe and discuss how some of the problems associated with our system--voter apathy, the power of political action committees, and the concentration of power--are related to our system.*

For this essay you would want to point out that both systems are democratic, which means that the ultimate power resides in the people (pp. 423-424). Both are representative rather than direct democracies, which means that citizens vote for representatives who actually make the decisions rather than the citizens themselves voting on each decision (p. 424). Despite these similarities, the two systems have differences. You would want to mention the proportional representation of the European system vs. the winner-takes-all outcomes of the American system; the encouragement of minority parties in the European system vs. their discouragement in the American system; and the centrist parties of Europe vs. the noncentrist parties of the United States (p. 427).

Finally, you would want to consider how voter apathy, the power of political action committees, and the concentration of power are related to the specific features of the U.S. system. First, you might want to talk about how the winner-takes-all arrangement encourages the development of centrist parties which are forced to appeal to the middle of the voting population in order to receive the majority of the votes; because of this, many people come to feel that the political parties are too superficial and do not really represent their ideas or interests, so they decide to sit out the elections (p. 430). The second problem--power of PACs--is also related to the particular feature of winner-takes-all systems. With so much riding on elections, candidates are pressured into spending excessive amounts of money in order to get their name and their message out to the voters. The cash requirements provide a perfect opportunity for PACs to donate and thereby influence not only the outcomes of elections but the voting behavior of the elected candidate (pp. 430-431). The final problem about the concentration of power is an outgrowth of the first two. You could go back to the discussion of the iron law of oligarchy (pp. 185-186) and make the argument that the combination of voter apathy and the financial requirements of running for office produce a small elite that becomes committed to maintaining its power (pp. 432-433).

3.   *Discuss what you see as the future of the New World Order.*

The author poses alternatives--the development of a world order that transcends national boundaries or the fracturing of the globe into warring factions based on national identities (pp. 438-440). You have your choice as to which alternative you want to support, but whichever you choose must be grounded in solid arguments. On the one hand, you could discuss how the globalization of capital, as well as recent attempts at multinational associations like NAFTA or the EU, would support the first alternative. On the other hand, the continuing tensions between national groups--Arabs and Israelis, Indians and Pakistanis, Serbs, Croatians, and Muslims in the former Yugoslavia to name a few--suggest that national identities continue to be an extremely important source of conflict and division rather than peace and unity. You should also consider which of these two trends is stronger--economic globalization or political nationalism.

☞ **ANSWERS FOR CHAPTER 16**

ANSWERS FOR MULTIPLE CHOICE QUESTIONS

1. a   Polyandry is a marriage in which a woman has more than one husband. (444)
2. d   "None of the above" is correct; family of orientation is the one in which a person grows up. (445)
3. b   Endogamy is the practice of marrying within one's own group. (446)
4. a   In a matrilineal system descent is figured only on the mother's side. (446)
5. b   According to functionalists, the family serves certain essential functions in all societies. (447)
6. d   "All of the above" is correct. The incest taboo is rules specifying the degrees of kinship that prohibit sex or marriage; helps families avoid role confusion; and facilitates the socialization of children. (447)
7. b   According to Arlie Hochschild, most men engage in the strategies of *playing dumb*, *waiting it out*, and *needs reduction*. The one that was not identified by her is *substitute labor*. (449)
8. c   According to research findings, men who earn less money than their wives feel most threatened by doing housework and consequently do the least. (450)
9. b   Researchers conclude that the reason men and women give different answers to the same question is because they have different perspectives on love-making. Jessie Bernard has concluded that in general husbands and wives see their marriage differently, resulting in two marriages within one union. (451)
10. c   The tendency of people with similar characteristics to marry one another is homogamy. (453)
11. b   According to Lillian Rubin, social class is the key to how couples adjust to the arrival of children. Among working class couples, the first baby arrives 9 months after the marriage and the couple has hardly had time to adjust to being a husband and wife before they must take on the roles of mother and father. In the middle class, the couples postponed having children until they had time to adjust to one another. (453)
12. d   "None of the above" is correct. In regard to child rearing, Melvin Kohn concluded that parents of different social classes socialize their children differently. Working-class parents are more likely to use physical punishment than middle-class parents, who are more likely to withdraw privileges or affection. (455)
13. a   The empty nest syndrome is not a reality for most parents. (455-456)
14. c   According to your text, a major concern of upper class African-American families is how to maintain family lineage. (457)
15. d   "All of the above" is correct. Machismo distinguishes Latino families from other groups; is an emphasis on male strength and dominance; and is seen in some Chicano families where the husband-father plays a strong role in his family. (458)
16. b   Since 1970, the number of one-parent families in the U.S. has tripled. (459)
17. d   "All of the above" is correct. Children from single-parent families are more likely to drop out of school; become delinquent; and be poor as adults. (460)
18. c   Sociologist Kathleen Gerson found that couples choose not to have children because of unstable relationships, lost career opportunities, and financial considerations, NOT because they had selfish and immature attitudes. (460)
19. c   A family whose members were once part of other families is known as a blended family. (460)
20. d   "All of the above" is correct. Cohabitation is the condition of living together as an unmarried couple; has increased eight times in the past 25 years; and has occurred before about half of all couples marry. (463)
21. d   The "sandwich generation" refers to people who find themselves caught between two generations, simultaneously responsible for the care of their children and their aging parents.

(464)

22. d Only about one-sixth of children who live apart from their fathers following a divorce continue to see their dads as often as every week; research demonstrates that most divorced fathers stop seeing their children altogether. This has produced a new fathering pattern known as "serial fatherhood." (468)

23. d The first three statements are all correct. The last one is incorrect; in fact, the presence of children in a second marriage significantly increases the chances of that marriage also ending in divorce. (469)

24. d According to research by Diana Russell, uncles are most likely to be the offender in instances of incest; they are followed by first cousins, fathers/stepfathers, and then brothers. (471)

25. d According to the author of the text, all of the trends--increase in cohabitation, increase in age at first marriage, and more equality in the husband-wife relationship--are likely to continue into the next century. Other trends likely to continue are more married women working for wages and more families struggling with the demands of raising children and caring for aging parents. (473)

ANSWERS FOR TRUE-FALSE QUESTIONS

1. *True.* (444)
2. *False.* Households are people who live together in the same housing unit; families consist of two or more people who consider themselves related by blood, marriage or adoption. (445)
3. *True.* (446)
4. *False.* Laws of endogamy in the U. S. which prohibit interracial marriages were repealed. (446)
5. *True.* (447)
6. *True.* (448)
7. *False.* Arlie Hochschild concluded that women who worked the second shift are generally not happy about it, but end up putting in the time because of the gendered division of labor. (448)
8. *False.* According to Arlie Hochschild, one of the strategies used by some husbands to resist doing housework is "substitute offerings"--expressing appreciation to the wife for her being so organized that she can handle both work for wages and the second shift at home--when, instead, it would be better if he actually shared the work with her. (449)
9. *False.* Symbolic interactionists have found that husbands and wives have vastly different perceptions about their marriages. For instance, when asked how much housework each does, wives and husbands give very different answers; they even disagree about whether or not they fight over doing housework! Jessie Bernard has suggested that their experiences are in such contrast that every marriage actually contains two separate marriages--his and hers. (450-451)
10. *True.* (452)
11. *False.* Social class does significantly influence the way in which couples adjust to the arrival of children. (453)
12. *True.* (455)
13. False. Researchers have found that most husbands and wives do not experience the empty nest when their last child leaves home. Often just the opposite occurs because the couple now has more time and money to use at their own discretion. (455-456)
14. *False.* Women are more likely than men to face the problem of widowhood, not only because they live longer, but also because they are likely to have married older men. (456)
15. *True.* (461)

16.   *True.* (460)
17.   *False.* Marriage between homosexuals is not legal in any state, although Vermont legally recognized "gay unions" in 2000; however, some gay churches conduct marriage ceremonies which are not recognized in the eyes of the law. (460)
18.   *False.* U.S. rate of births to unmarried women actually falls in the middle third among a group of ten industrialized nations for which there is accurate data. Sweden, Denmark, France and Great Britain are higher, while Canada, Germany, Netherlands, Italy, and Japan are lower. (463)
19.   *False.* The pattern is for contact to be high during the first 1-2 years following the divorce and then decline rapidly. (468-469)
20.   *True.* (471)

ANSWERS FOR FILL-IN QUESTIONS
1.   A marriage in which a man has more than one wife is POLYGYNY. (444)
2.   A FAMILY is a group who consider themselves related by blood, marriage, or adoption. (445)
3.   A(n) NUCLEAR FAMILY is a family consisting of a husband, wife, and child(ren). (445)
4.   EXOGAMY is the practice of marrying outside one's group. (446)
5.   Female control of a society or group is a(n) MATRIARCHY. (446)
6.   Rules specifying the degrees of kinship that prohibit sex or marriage are INCEST TABOOS. (447)
7.   Feelings of erotic attraction, accompanied by an idealization of the other, are most commonly associated with ROMANTIC LOVE. (451)
8.   HOMOGAMY is the tendency of people with similar characteristics to get married. (453)
9.   A married couple's domestic situation after the last child has left home is sometimes referred to as the EMPTY NEST. (455)
10.   An emphasis on male strength and dominance is MACHISMO. (458)
11.   A BLENDED FAMILY is one whose members were once part of another family. (462)
12.   In the U.S., COHABITATION, living together in a sexual relationship without marriage, has increased about seven times in just over two decades. (463)
13.   The term SANDWICH GENERATION refers to people who find themselves caught between two generations and responsible for the care of both. (464)
14.   A situation in which a husband forces his wife to have sex with no intent to hurt her physically is NONBATTERING MARITAL RAPE. (471)
15.   Sexual relations between specified relatives, such as brothers and sisters or parents and children is INCEST. (471)

ANSWERS TO MATCH THESE SOCIAL SCIENTISTS WITH THEIR CONTRIBUTIONS
1. a   Jessie Bernard: *noted the existence of two marriages within one union*
2. f   Larry Bumpass: *studied marriage and cohabitation patterns*
3. h   Andrew Cherlin: *noted lack of norms regarding remarriage*
4. b   Finkelhor & Yllo: *studied marital rape*
5. e   Kathleen Gerson: *identified reasons why couples choose to be child-free*
6. j   Arlie Hochschild: *identified the second shift*
7. I   Melvin Kohn: *studied social class differences in child-rearing*
8. c   Lillian Rubin: *found that women's satisfaction increased after last child moved out*
9. d   Diana Russell: *studied incest victims*

10. g   Bob Suzuki: *identified distinctive characteristics of Asian-American families*

GUIDELINES FOR ANSWERING THE ESSAY QUESTIONS

1.   *Identify the stages in the family life cycle, discussing what tasks are accomplished in each stage and what event marks that transition from one stage to the next.*

You will want to discuss each of the several stages in sequence: love and courtship, marriage, childbirth, child rearing, the empty nest, and widowhood (pp. 451-456). For each stage, you should include the work that takes place as well as the events that mark the beginning and end of that stage. For example, the first stage is love and courtship. In our culture, this involves romantic love--individuals being sexually attracted to one another and idealizing the other. There are two components--one is emotion, related to feelings of sexual attraction, and the other is cognitive, attaching labels to our feelings. The stage begins with our meeting and being attracted to another person, and ends when we decide to get engaged to be married.

2.   *Identify the trends among U. S. families today and explain the social forces that have contributed to each of them.*

This chapter identifies five trends in U.S. families: postponing marriage, cohabitation, unmarried mothers, the sandwich generation and elder care (pp. 462-464). You should take each trend in turn, identifying and explaining the pattern. For example, for the first half of the 20th century, the age at first marriage steadily declined, so that by 1950, women married at about age 20. For the next 20 years, this figure remained unchanged. Then, beginning in 1970, the average age began to climb. In 2000, women are waiting until they are almost 26 to marry (pp. 462-463). Now that you have described the pattern, you need to try and explain it. Here's where you want to apply what you have learned previously about changing norms. You can talk about how women's roles have changed tremendously since 1970 (see Chapter 11); these changes have affected women's lives and decisions on when to marry. You could also talk about attitudes about pre-marital sex which began to change in the 1960s and 1970s. More liberal attitudes about pre-marital sex and cohabitation have also affected young people's decisions about when to marry. Larry Bumpass's research on changes in marriage and cohabitation supports this (p. 463). Once you have described and analyzed this first trend, you would then go on to do the same with the other three trends.

3.   *Discuss the impact that divorce has on family members--men, women and children.*

You would want to discuss each family role separately--children, wives and husbands. In your response, be sure to talk about the research on the impact on children, both short-term and long-term. In the short-term, this includes hostility, anxiety, nightmares, and poor school performance. In the long-term, it includes a loss of connection to parents, and difficulties forming intimate relations (pp. 466-468). For spouses, there is anger, depression and anxiety following a divorce, but each also experiences unique problems related to their gender. For women, there is often a decrease in the standard of living, although the impact varies by social class. For men, there is a loss of connection to their children and the possible development of a series of families (pp. 467-468).

ANSWERS FOR CHAPTER 17

ANSWERS FOR MULTIPLE CHOICE QUESTIONS

1. d   "All of the above" is correct. In earlier societies there was no separate social institution called education; education was synonymous with acculturation; and persons who already possessed certain skills taught them to others. (478)

2. a   Education is a formal system of teaching knowledge, values, and skills. (478)

3. c   "Common schools," supported through taxes, were proposed by Horace Mann. (479)

4. b   Laws requiring all children to attend school until a specified age or until they complete a minimum grade in school are mandatory education laws. (480)

5. b   In Japan, college admission is based on making a high score on a national test. (481)

6. a   Despite the fact that education is free at all levels, including college, children of the wealthy are several times as likely as children of the non-wealthy to continue their education beyond the basics. (483-484)

7. a   The use of diplomas and degrees to determine who is eligible for jobs, even though the diploma or degree may be irrelevant to the actual work is known as a credential society. (484)

8. a   All of the following are manifest functions of education: transmitting cultural values; helping to mold students into a more or less cohesive unit; and teaching patriotism. Helping to maintain social inequality is <u>not</u> one of the functions, according to the functionalists. (484-485)

9. c   Traditionally, the educational system in the United States has taught children the value of individualism, competition, and patriotism. Cooperation is less likely to be stressed. (485)

10. b   The function of education that sorts people into a society's various positions is social placement. (487)

11. c   The hidden curriculum refers to the unwritten rules of behavior and attitudes that are taught in school. (489)

12. c   Public schools are largely supported by local property taxes. (491)

13. b   The correspondence principle is the ways in which schools correspond to, or reflect the social structure of society. (492)

14. a   From a conflict perspective, the real purpose of education is to perpetuate existing social inequalities. (493)

15. a   Conflict theorists explain the fact that whites are more likely than African Americans and Latinos to complete high school, to go to college, and to get a bachelor's degree because the purpose of the educational system is to reproduce inequality by keeping the social class structure intact from one generation to the next. (493)

16. c   Teacher expectations and the self-fulfilling prophecy are of interest to symbolic interaction theorists. (494-495)

17. c   Ray Rist found that social class was the underlying basis for assigning children to different tables in a kindergarten classroom. (494)

18. a   A self-fulfilling prophecy is an originally false assertion that becomes true simply because it was predicted. (495)

19. d   The Rosenthal/Jacobson experiment tended to confirm the concept of a self-fulfilling prophecy. (495)

20. d   Research by George Farkas focused on how teacher expectations affect students' grades. (495-496)

21. b   When compared to scores of twenty to thirty years ago, today's scores on tests such as the SAT are lower. (497)

22. c   High school graduates who have difficulty with basic reading and math are known as functional illiterates. (498)

23. b   An examination of the statistics published on page 499 of your text would lead you to conclude that the number of shooting deaths in schools at the end of the 1990s was half what it had been at the beginning of the decade. (499)

24. c   Coleman and Hoffer found that students attending Roman Catholic schools out-performed

able to move from job to job, learning new skills as the work requires. The most efficient way in which to train workers, both to have the specific skills needed for a particular job and the general skills needed to survive in a constantly changing workplace, is through universal education (p. 480). For these two reasons, universal education developed in the United States, as well as other industrialized nations.

2.   *Select one of the three perspectives and design a research project to test the claims of that perspective about the nature of education.*

In order to answer this question you must first choose one of the three perspectives. For example, you might choose the conflict perspective and decide to do a research project on the relationship between ethnicity and individual educational achievement and goals (p. 493). Your research will involve an analysis of student choices of curricula, their grades, retention rates, and graduation from a large racially/ethnically diverse high school. You have access to student records and you collect data on students in one class as this class moves through the high school. You will compare white students' records to those of African-American and Hispanic students in order to test whether the conflict theorists are correct in their assertion that the educational system reproduces the students' class background.

3.   *In discussing solutions to educational problems, the author suggests that one direction in which schools should go is towards setting higher educational standards. Both the research by James Coleman and Thomas Hoffer, and the success of Jaime Escalante, support this. Discuss social factors that might explain why such a proposal has not been widely adopted by public schools across the country.*

In answering this question you will want to focus on obstacles to implementation. You could refer to some of the research on teacher expectations and student tracking to illustrate the status quo in the majority of schools (pp. 494-496). Henslin notes that one of the biggest obstacles is bureaucracy itself, where ritual often replaces performance (p. 503). A routine becomes established and then difficult to change (refer to Chapter 7 for a complete discussion of bureaucracy). As the experience of Jaime Escalante demonstrated, it was only after he changed the system of instruction that student attitudes and performance changed (p. 503-504).

☞ ANSWERS FOR CHAPTER 18

ANSWERS FOR MULTIPLE CHOICE QUESTIONS
1. d   Durkheim wrote <u>The Elementary Forms of the Religious Life</u> in order to identify elements common to all religions. (508)
2. c   Durkheim used the word church in an unusual way to refer to a group of believers organized around a set of beliefs and practices regarding the sacred. (508)
3. a   All of the following are functions of religion: support for the government, social change, and social control. Encouraging wars for holy causes is a dysfunction of religion. (509-510)
4. c   War and religious persecution are dysfunctions of religion. (510)
5. c   When some Protestants use the term "born again" they are referring to a personal life-transforming religious experience. (512)
6. c   Religion is the opium of the people according to some conflict theorists. (513)
7. d   "All of the above" is correct. These are all examples of the use of religion to legitimize social inequalities: the divine right of kings; a declaration that the Pharaoh or Emperor is god or divine; and the defense of slavery as being God's will. (514)

8. a   Weber believed that religion held the key to modernization. (514)
9. d   None of the above is correct. The spirit of capitalism is the desire to accumulate capital as a duty--not to spend it, but as an end in itself. It is not the desire to accumulate capital in order to spend it and show others how one "has it made." Nor is it Marx's term for the driving force in the exploitation of workers or the ideal of a highly moral life, hard work, industriousness, and frugality (which is the Protestant ethic). (515)
10. c   Polytheism is the belief that there are many gods. (516)
11. b   Animism is the belief that all objects in the world have spirits. (516)
12. a   An unanticipated outcome of the Reformation was the splintering of Christianity into separate branches. (517)
13. c   The Shi'ites are the branch of Islam that are more conservative and inclined to fundamentalism. (518)
14. b   The religion with no specific founder is Hinduism. (519)
15. c   Reincarnation is the return of the soul after death in a different form. (520)
16. d   "All of the above" is correct. A cult is a new religion with few followers; has teachings and practices which put it at odds with the dominant culture; and often is at odds with other religions. (521)
17. c   Although larger than a cult, a sect still feels substantial hostility from society. (523)
18. d   "All of the above" is correct. Churches are highly bureaucratized; have more sedate worship services; and gain new members from within, from children born to existing members. (523)
19. d   The answer is "ecclesia." In an ecclesia there is no recruitment of members because all citizens are automatically members of the state religion, or ecclesia. (523)
20. a   A "brand name" within a major religion is a denomination. (524)
21. a   Church membership is highest in the South and Midwest. (527)
22. c   Rather than intolerance of differences, religion in the United States is characterized by tolerance. (528)
23. d   "All of the above" is correct. Secularization of religion occurs as a result of industrialization, urbanization, and mass education. (531)
24. b   An example of secularization of culture is that the influence of religion on public affairs has lessened today. (531)
25. d   "All of the above" is correct. Questions that science cannot answer include: Is there a God? What is the purpose of life? What happens when a person dies? (534)

ANSWERS FOR TRUE-FALSE QUESTIONS

1.   *False.* The goal of the sociological study of religion is to analyze the relationship between society and religion and to gain insight into the role that religion plays in people's lives. It is not to determine which religions are most effective in people's lives. (508)
2.   *True.* (508)
3.   *True.* (509)
4.   *False.* Bellah distinguishes between a state religion, where the government sponsors a religion, and a civil religion, where no particular religion is sponsored but religious beliefs become so firmly established in the life of the society that social institutions become sanctified by being associated with God or a supernatural. (510)
5.   *True.* (511)
6.   *False.* Being born again is a term frequently used to describe Christians who have undergone a life-transforming religious experience so radical that they feel they have become new persons.

The term does not describe reincarnation by Hindus and Buddhists. (512)

7. *True.* (513)
8. *True.* (514)
9. *False.* Max Weber wrote *The Protestant Ethic and the Spirit of Capitalism.* (514)
10. *False.* Contemporary Judaism in the United States comprises three main branches: Orthodox, Reform, and Conservative. (516)
11. *True.* (518)
12. *True.* (520)
13. *True.* (521)
14. *True.* (522)
15. *False.* Both cults and sects stress evangelism, or the active recruitment of new members. (523)
16. *True.* (524)
17. *False.* The Amish mingle with non-Amish when they go shopping and on other errands. (525)
18. *True.* (527)
19. *False.* Many local ministers view the electronic church as a competitor for the attention of their members and for money that could go to their own good causes. Thus, they are not supportive of the electronic church. (529)
20. *True.* (531)

ANSWERS FOR FILL-IN QUESTIONS

1. Durkheim's term for mundane elements of everyday life was <u>PROFANE</u>. (508)
2. Answering questions about ultimate meaning, providing emotional comfort, and social solidarity are <u>FUNCTIONS</u> of religion. (509)
3. <u>FUNCTIONAL EQUIVALENT</u> is a substitute that serves the same functions as religion. (510)
4. For Muslims, the crescent moon and star, for Jews the Star of David, and for Christians the cross, all are examples of <u>RELIGIOUS SYMBOLS</u>. (512)
5. <u>COSMOLOGY</u> is teachings or ideas that provide a unified picture of the world. (512)
6. According to conflict theorists, religion is the <u>OPIUM OF THE PEOPLE</u>. (513)
7. <u>THE PROTESTANT ETHIC</u> is Weber's term to describe the ideal of a highly moral life, hard work, industriousness, and frugality. (515)
8. The belief that there is only one God is <u>MONOTHEISM</u>. (516)
9. The belief that all objects in the world have spirits, many of which are dangerous and must be outwitted is <u>ANIMISM</u>.(516)
10. <u>FUNDAMENTALISM</u> is the belief that true religion is threatened by modernism and that the faith as it originally was practiced should be restored. (518)
11. A(n) <u>CHARISMATIC LEADER</u> is someone who exerts extraordinary appeal to a group of followers. (522)
12. A group larger than a cult that still feels substantial hostility from and toward society is a(n) <u>SECT</u>. (523)
13. A(n) <u>ECCLESIA</u> is a religious group so integrated into the dominant culture that it is difficult to tell where the one begins and the other leaves off. (523)
14. <u>SECULAR</u> means belonging to the world and its affairs. (530)
15. <u>SECULARIZATION OF RELIGION</u> is the replacement of a religion's "otherworldly" concerns with concerns about "this world." (531)

ANSWERS TO MATCH THESE SOCIAL SCIENTISTS WITH THEIR CONTRIBUTIONS

1. c   Emile Durkheim: *The Elementary Forms of the Religious Life*
2. d   Robert Bellah: *"civil religion"*
3. a   Max Weber: *The Protestant Ethic and the Spirit of Capitalism*
4. e   John Hostetler: *studied "shunning"*
5. f   Ernst Troeltsch: *cult-sect-church-ecclesia typology*
6. b   Karl Marx: *"religion is the opium of the people"*

GUIDELINES FOR ANSWERING THE ESSAY QUESTIONS

1.   *Assume that you have been asked to make a presentation about religion to a group of people who have absolutely no idea what religion is. Prepare a speech in which you define religion and explain why it exists.*

        For this question, your first task is to explain what religion is. To do this you might want to refer to Durkheim's work on the elementary forms of religious life (p. 508), talking about the differences between the sacred and profane, the presence of beliefs, practices, and a moral community. Once you've done this your next task is to discuss why religion exists. Here you could talk about either the functionalist perspective or the conflict perspective or both. If you choose to focus only on the functionalist view, you would want to talk about how religion meets basic human needs (pp. 509-511); you might also want to refer to the symbolic interactionist views on community (p. 513). If you want to focus only on conflict theory, or add that to your discussion of functionalism, you would want to talk about how, for Marx, religion is like a drug that helps the oppressed forget about their exploitation at the hands of the capitalists (pp. 513-514). Furthermore, conflict theorists point out that capitalists use religion to legitimatize social inequalities and maintain the status quo.

2.   *Discuss the process by which a religion matures from a cult into a church.*

        This is a pretty straight-forward question. All you are asked to do is to discuss the process by which a religion moves from cult to sect to church. You would want to talk about what each is, how they range along a continuum, and what events mark the shift from one type to the next (pp. 521-524).

3.   *Discuss whether or not secularization is inevitable.*

        For this answer you should explain just what secularization is (p. 530). You could distinguish between the secularization of religion and that of culture (p. 531) and what forces contribute to each. Then, in order to answer the question of whether or not secularization is inevitable, you need to consider whether the forces can be resisted. For example, the major force behind the secularization of culture is modernization (p. 530). Modernization involves industrialization, urbanization, the development of mass education, and the adoption of science and technology. Assuming that modernization is inevitable--and most would say that it is, particularly today with the increasingly global connections--then secularization of culture must also be inevitable. In your response you need to consider these types of issues.

☞ ANSWERS FOR CHAPTER 19

ANSWERS FOR MULTIPLE CHOICE QUESTIONS

1. d   Sociologists focus on medicine as a profession, a bureaucracy, and a business; therefore, "all of the above" would be the correct answer. (540)
2. c   The healing specialist of a preliterate tribe who attempts to control the spirits thought to cause a disease or injury is a shaman. (540)
3. d   The components include the physical, social, and spiritual, so the one that is not a component is

hereditary. (540-541)

4. b   When a person is unable to fulfill their normal obligations because they are sick or injured, they are said to be in the sick role. (541)

5. b   The individual's claim to the sick role is legitimized primarily by a doctor's excuse. (541)

6. c   According to research by Elizabeth Klonoff and Hope Landrine, women are more likely than men to claim the sick role when they feel poorly because they are socialized for greater dependency and self-disclosure. (541)

7. d   "All of the above" is correct. Professionalization of medicine included rigorous education, a theoretical understanding of illness, and self-regulation. (544)

8. a   Government-paid health care for the poor is Medicaid. (546)

9. b   In the United States, medicine is a commodity. (547)

10. c   Today the average American spends $4000 annually; in 1960, the average was $150. (547)

11. a   Depersonalization is the practice of dealing with people as though they were objects; means treating patients as though they were merely cases and diseases; and occurs when an individual is treated as if he or she was not a person. The one statement that is incorrect is that "It is less common today because of all the reforms brought about by HMOs." (550)

12. b   The transformation of something into a matter to be treated by physicians is referred to as medicalization. (552)

13. c   Medical costs have risen dramatically in the United States because of tests performed for defensive rather than medical reasons, an increase in the size of the elderly population, and because health care is seen as a commodity (and is operated for profit). People wanting doctors to do unnecessary tests to assure themselves they are healthy is not a factor in spiraling costs. (555)

14. c   Sending unprofitable patients to public hospitals is known as dumping. (555)

15. b   AIDS is known to be transmitted by exchange of blood and/or semen. The U.S. Centers for Disease Control say that casual contact between a carrier and a non-carrier in which bodily fluids are exchanged will not result in the transmission of the virus. (558)

16. b   African Americans and Latinos are at greater risk of contracting AIDS than are Whites, Asian Americans or Native Americans. The risk differences are related to social factors such as rates of intravenous drug use and the use of condoms. (559-560)

17. c   A cure for AIDS has not been found. (559-560)

18. d   Diseases today have the potential of becoming truly global threats because contact between people of different countries has increased due to global travel. (560)

19. b   Rather than the rate of cigarette smoking increasing, it has in fact declined. In less than two decades, cigarette smoking has been cut in half among U.S. men and by a third among U.S. women. (562)

20. a   An environment that is harmful to health is referred to as a disabling environment. (563)

21. d   The ozone shield is the protective layer of the earth's upper stratosphere that screens out a high proportion of the sun's ultraviolet rays. Use of fluorocarbon gases is threatening the ozone shield. (563)

22. b   The Tuskegee syphilis experiment is an example of the callous disregard of people's health by physicians and the U.S. government. (563)

23. d   In order to implement a national policy of "prevention, not intervention" it would be necessary for the medical establishment and the general public to eliminate disabling environments and reduce the use of harmful drugs. (565)

24. c   Among the listed countries, the lowest infant mortality is in Sweden. (567)

25. a   "Barefoot doctors" provide much of the health care to the people of China. (566)

ANSWERS FOR TRUE-FALSE QUESTIONS

1.   *True.* (540)
2.   *False.* People who don't seek competent help when they are sick are not behaving according to the expectations of the sick role; in the sick role an individual is expected to seek help in order to get better and return to his/her normal routine. Someone who doesn't do this is denied the right to claim sympathy from others; they get the cold shoulder for wrongfully claiming the sick role. (541)
3.   *False.* There is often ambiguity between the well role and the sick role because the decision to claim the sick role is often more a social than a physical matter. (541)
4.   *False.* Not everyone is given the same right to claim the sick role. The social group defines the conditions under which people are allowed to be sick and legitimately excused from ordinary responsibilities. (541)
5.   *True.* (542)
6.   *False.* Medical schools have existed since the 1800s, not the 1700s, in the United States; however, it was only after the Flexner Report in 1910 that the schools started to resemble the institutions we think of today as medical schools. (544)
7.   *True.* (544)
8.   *True.* (544)
9.   *True.* (544)
10. *False.* The soaring cost of medical care cannot be explained by the fact that Americans are sicker than they used to be. Sociological factors such as the increase in the elderly population, high tech medicine with a large price tag, and the profit orientation of American medicine have contributed to soaring costs. (547)
11. *True.* (547)
12. *False.* As physicians have acquired financial interests in hospitals, pharmaceutical companies, and medical supply companies, they are likely to prescribe drugs and order courses of treatment that benefit themselves financially, thus encountering conflicts of interest. (550)
13. *True.* (551)
14. *True.* (551)
15. *False.* It is not a functionalist but a conflict theorist who would argue that the medicalization of society reflects the growing power of the medical establishment because the more physicians can medicalize human affairs, the greater their profits and power. (552)
16. *True.* (553)
17. *False.* The most controversial suggestion for reducing medical costs today is the rationing of medical care, not the adoption of national health insurance. (556)
18. *False.* Today AIDS is the fourth leading cause of death for U.S. women between the ages of 25 and 44; it is the second leading cause of death for U.S. men in this age group. (559)
19. *False.* While the health risks of some occupations is evident -- lumberjacks, rodeo riding, lion taming -- in many occupations people do not become aware of the risks until years after they were exposed. (563)
20. *True.* (565)

ANSWERS FOR FILL-IN QUESTIONS

1.   The healing specialist of a preliterate tribe who attempts to control the spirits thought to cause a

disease or injury is a SHAMAN. (540)
2.   HEALTH is a human condition measured by four components: physical, mental, social, and spiritual. (540)
3.   The SICK ROLE is a social role that excuses people from normal obligations because they are sick or injured. (541)
4.   The development of medicine into a field in which education becomes rigorous, and in which physicians claim a theoretical understanding of illness, regulate themselves, claim to be doing a service to society, and take authority over clients is the PROFESSIONALIZATION OF MEDICINE. (544)
5.   In general, the payment to a physician to diagnose and treat a patient's medical problems is based on FEE FOR SERVICE. (546)
6.   The study of disease and disability patterns in a population is EPIDEMIOLOGY. (546)
7.   A major sociological characteristic of the American medical system is that medicine is viewed as a COMMODITY, not a right. (547)
8.   Seeking consultations with colleagues and ordering additional lab tests simply because a patient may sue is DEFENSIVE MEDICINE. (549)
9.   The fact that women are less likely than men to be given heart surgery, except in the more advanced stages of heart disease, is an example of SEXISM in medicine. (551)
10.   A LIVING WILL is a statement people in good health sign that clearly expresses their feelings about being kept alive on artificial life-support systems. (553)
11.   One response to the high cost of health care is the development of HEALTH MAINTENANCE ORGANIZATIONS (HMOs), in which companies pay a set fee to a group of physicians to take care of the medical needs of their employees. (555)
12.   In a desire to turn a profit on patient care, some hospitals engage in the practice of DUMPING, sending unprofitable patients to public hospitals. (556)
13.   One of the most significant sociological aspects of AIDS is its STIGMA. (559)
14.   Lumberjacking, riding rodeo bulls, and taming lions are all examples of DISABLING ENVIRONMENTS. (563)
15.   The U.S. Public Health Service was responsible for the TUSKEGEE SYPHILIS EXPERIMENT, an example of a misguided and callous medical experiment. (563)

ANSWERS TO MATCH THESE SOCIAL SCIENTISTS WITH THEIR CONTRIBUTIONS
1. b   Talcott Parsons: *sick role*
2. a   Erich Goode: *compared health of smokers and nonsmokers*
3. c   Haas and Shaffir: *transformation of medical students*
4. e   Klonoff and Landrine: *gender differences in claims to the sick role*
5. d   Diana Scully: *sexism in medicine*
6. f   Leonard Stein: *interaction games played by doctors and nurses*

GUIDELINES FOR ANSWERING THE ESSAY QUESTIONS
1.   *Describe the elements of the sick role and identify variations in the pattern of claiming this role.*
        In order to answer this question you will need to refer back to the discussion on page 541. You should acknowledge Talcott Parsons' contribution to our understanding of the sick role and his work in identifying the elements in that role. In terms of variations in claiming that role, the text talks about gender differences, but you could expand beyond this to talk about other variations within our society. For instance, children and old people have an easier time claiming this role than do adults because they

are seen as more vulnerable and more dependent.

2.   *Explain the pattern of the worldwide AIDS epidemic and suggest reasons why this threat to the health of the world's population has not been addressed more aggressively.*

By referring to the information found on pages 557-560, you could immediately point out that the distribution of AIDS cases is not evenly balanced around the globe, but heavily concentrated in Sub-Saharan Africa and South and Southeast Asia. Looking at AIDS globally, you would want to point out this mal-distribution and note that those countries most directly affected have the least amount of money to spend. Looking at AIDS within the U.S., you would want to point out that over half of those with AIDS are members of minorities (p. *560).* Furthermore, the most common way in which to contract the disease is through behaviors that are stigmatized in our society--homosexual sex, promiscuous heterosexual sex, and I.V. drug users. You could point out that policy makers may have been slow to respond because of the character of those most directly affected by the epidemic.

3.   *Discuss the obstacles to developing preventive medicine and suggest ways in which these obstacles can be overcome.*

To answer this question you should note the obstacles--resistance from the medical community, the public, businesses, and other nations (p. 565). In your essay remember to outline the nature of each of these obstacles. Then you should suggest ways around each of these. For example, overcoming public resistance could be accomplished through educational programs or through initiatives like lower health insurance costs for people who can demonstrate they have adopted preventive measures like regular exercise programs, altered diet, and no drug use. You would need to do this for each of the obstacles listed.

☞ ANSWERS FOR CHAPTER 20

ANSWERS FOR MULTIPLE CHOICE QUESTIONS

1. c   The specialists who study the size, composition, growth, and distribution of human population are referred to as demographers. (572)

2. b   The proposition that the population grows geometrically while food supply increases arithmetically is known as the Malthus theorem. (572)

3. d   Anti-Malthusians believe that the demographic transition, an explanation of the shift from high birth and death rates to low ones that occurred previously in Europe, is an accurate picture of what will happen in the future in the Least Industrialized Nations of the world. (574)

4. b   The three-stage historical process of population growth is the demographic transition. (574)

5. c   The process by which a country's population becomes smaller because its birth rate and immigration are too low to replace those who die and emigrate is population shrinkage. (575)

6. b   Starvation occurs not because there is not enough fertile land, or there are too many people, or that people are not eating a well-balanced diet. Rather, experts argue that it occurs because some parts of the world lack food while other parts of the world produce more than they can consume. (576)

7. d   "All of the above" is correct. People in the Least Industrialized Nations have so many children because parenthood provides status, children are considered to be an economic asset, and the community encourages people to have children. (578)

8. b   Mexico's current population will double in 34 years. (579)

9. a   Factors that influence population growth (fertility, mortality, and net migration) are demographic variables. (580)

10. a   Fertility rate is the number of children the average woman bears. (580)
11. a   Demographers use this statistic, along with crude birth rate, to compute the fertility rate of a country. (580)
12. d   "All of the above" is correct. These are considered push factors since they are things that people want to escape. (582)
13. a   According to your text, it is difficult to forecast population growth because of government programs that impact on fertility. (584)
14 d   All of the choices are correct. China's practice of female infanticide is rooted in sexism--there is a general preference for males over females, in economics--males will support parents in their old age and males are in a better position to take advantage of economic opportunities, and in traditions that go back centuries--the tradition of drowning the female newborn, the traditional expenses associated with marrying off a daughter. (585)
15. d   Urbanization is when an increasing proportion of a population lives in cities. (585)
16. d   "All of the above" is correct. Today's urbanization means that more people live in cities, today's cities are larger, and about 300 of the world's cities contain at least one million people. (585-586)
17. c   The area that extends from Maine along the coast to Virginia is an example of a megalopolis. (589)
18. d   "All of the above" is correct. Edge cities consist of a cluster of shopping malls, hotels, office parks, and residential areas near major highway intersections; overlap political boundaries and include parts of several cities or towns; and provide a sense of place to those living there. (591)
19. b   The concentric-zone model was proposed by Ernest Burgess. (592)
20. d   The pattern of a growing number of immigrants settling an area, with the consequence that those already living in the area move out because they are threatened by the immigrants' presence is referred to as an invasion-succession cycle. (593)
21. c   The model which is based on the idea that land use in cities is based on several centers, such as a clustering of restaurants or automobile dealerships is the multiple-nuclei model. (594)
22. c   While a sense of community is natural to *Gemeinschaft,* because everyone knows everyone else, alienation can result as a society industrializes and *Gesellschaft,* based on secondary, impersonal relationships, emerges. (596)
23. d   "All of the above" is correct. According to Gans' typology, the trapped includes downwardly mobile persons, elderly persons, and alcoholics and drug addicts. (598)
24. c   The Kitty Genovese case in an example of diffusion of responsibility. (598)
25. b   Suburbanization is the movement from the city to the suburbs. (600)

ANSWERS FOR TRUE-FALSE QUESTIONS
1.   *False.* Thomas Malthus was not a sociologist at the University of Chicago in the 1920s. He was an English economist who lived from 1766 to 1834. (572)
2.   *True.* (573)
3.   *False.* It is the New Malthusians, not the Anti-Malthusians, who believe that people breed like germs in a bucket. (573-574)
4.   *False.* There are three stages, not two, in the process of demographic transition, although some now recognize a fourth stage. (574)
5.   *False.* The main reason why there is starvation is because those countries that produce food surpluses have stable populations, while those with rapidly growing populations have food shortages. (576)

6.   *False.* The major reason why people in poor countries have so many children is not necessarily because they do not know how to prevent conception. The reason is more sociological in nature, including the status which is conferred on women for producing children, as well as the need for children to take care of a person when she or he is old. (578)
7.   *False.* Population pyramids represent a population, divided into age and sex--but not race. (579)
8.   *True.* (580)
9.   *True.* (580)
10.   *True.* (581)
11.   *False.* According to Julian Simon, immigrants to the United States contribute more to the country than the country expends on them. Such areas as talent and innovations cannot be measured simply in dollars. (583)
12.   *True.* (584)
13.   *True.* (588)
14.   *True.* (591)
15.   *True.* (592)
16.   *False.* No one model is considered to be the most accurate because different cities develop and grow in different ways, especially if there are certain kinds of natural barriers such as rivers or mountains. (594)
17.   *True.* (597)
18.   *True.* (598)
19.   *True.* (599)
20.   *False.* Urban renewal involves the destruction of deteriorated building and the building of stadiums, high-rise condos, luxury hotels, and expensive shops. (602)

ANSWERS FOR FILL-IN QUESTIONS
1.   DEMOGRAPHY is the study of the size, composition, growth, and distribution of human populations. (572)
2.   A pattern of growth in which numbers double during approximately equal intervals, thus accelerating in the latter stages is the EXPONENTIAL GROWTH CURVE. (573)
3.   The Anti-Malthusians believe that Europe's DEMOGRAPHIC TRANSITION, a three-stage historical process of population growth, provides an accurate picture of the future. (574)
4.   When the people in a society do not produce enough children to replace the people who die, there is concern about POPULATION SHRINKAGE. (575)
5.   A(n) POPULATION PYRAMID is a graphic representation of a population, divided into age and sex. (579)
6.   The FERTILITY RATE refers to the number of children that the average woman bears. (580)
7.   The basic demographic equation is growth = *BIRTHS-DEATHS+MIGRATION,* (584)
8.   When women bear only enough children to replace the population, ZERO POPULATION GROWTH has been achieved. (585)
9.   CITY is a place in which a large number of people are permanently based and do not produce their own food. (588)
10.   URBANIZATION is the process by which an increasing number of people live in cities. (589)
11.   A central city, surrounding smaller cities and their suburbs, forming an interconnected urban area is a METROPOLIS. (589)
12.   The displacement of the poor by the relatively affluent, who purchase and renovate the former's homes is GENTRIFICATION. (591)
13.   HUMAN ECOLOGY is the relationship between people and their environment. (592)

14.   COMMUNITY exists when people identify with an area and with one another. (594)
15.   When officers of a financial institution decide not to make loans in a particular neighborhood or area, they are following a policy of REDLINING. (600)

ANSWERS TO MATCH THESE SOCIAL SCIENTISTS WITH THEIR CONTRIBUTIONS
1. a   Thomas Malthus: *theorem on population growth*
2. c   Ernest Burgess: *concentric-zone model*
3. d   Herbert Gans: *urban villagers*
4. e   Homer Hoyt: *sector model*
5. b   Robert Park: *human ecology*

GUIDELINES FOR ANSWERING THE ESSAY QUESTIONS
1.   *State the positions of the New Malthusians and the Anti-Malthusians and discuss which view you think is more accurate, based on the information provided about each position.*
      The author outlines both positions on pages 573-575. You should begin this essay by summarizing each side's arguments. For the New Malthusians you would want to include the idea of the exponential growth curve, while for the Anti-Malthusians you would want to refer to the concepts of the demographic transition and population shrinkage. For both you would want to include some of the facts--that world population growth does seem to reflect the exponential growth curve (New Malthusians), while the Least Industrialized Nations reflect the second stage of the demographic transition and the population of European countries is shrinking (Anti-Malthusians). Finally, you need to draw conclusions about which view you think is more accurate.
2.   *Identify the problems that are associated with forecasting population growth.*
      Your first step is to define the basic demographic equation, that calculation which is used to project population growth (p. 580). Then you need to identify problems that make the demographer's job more difficult. These would include natural phenomena (famines and plagues), economic factors (short-term booms and busts as well as longer-term industrialization), political factors (wars and government policy), and social factors (educational levels). In your essay you need to not only identify these, but discuss the ways in which they make forecasting a challenge (pp. 584-585).
3.   *Discuss whether or not cities are impersonal Gesellschafts or communal Gemeinshafts.*
      For this essay you would want to refer to the work of Louis Wirth and Herbert Gans. Wirth talked about the breakup of kinship and neighborhoods with the growth of cities; the result was alienation (p. 596). On the other hand, Gans found evidence of villages embedded within urban landscapes, which provided people with a sense of community (pp. 596-598). In particular, he discusses the "ethnic villagers." If you decide to argue for the impersonality of urban life, you should also include some discussion of the norm of noninvolvement and the diffusion of responsibility (pp. 598-599). If you choose to talk about communities within cities, then you should refer to how people create intimacy by personalizing their environment, developing attachments to sports teams, objects, and even city locations (p. 598).

☞ ANSWERS FOR CHAPTER 21

ANSWERS FOR MULTIPLE CHOICE QUESTIONS
1. c   The incorrect statement is that "He proposed that a collective mind develops once a group of people congregate." It was Gustave LeBon, not Charles Mackay, who suggested that the crowd develops a collective mind. (608)
2. d   Gustave LeBon's term for the tendency of people in a crowd to feel, think, and act in extraordinary ways is collective mind. (609)
3. c   Social unrest is the condition most conducive to the emergence of collective behavior. (609)

4. a   A back-and-forth communication between the members of a crowd whereby a collective impulse is transmitted is a circular reaction. (609)

5. d   "All of the above" is correct. Acting crowd is a term coined by Herbert Blumer; is an excited group that collectively moves toward a goal; and is the end result of the five stages of collective behavior. (609-610)

6. b   Richard Berk used the term "minimax strategy" to describe the tendency for humans to minimize costs and maximize rewards. This is true whether an individual is deciding what card(s) to discard in a poker game or what store to loot in an urban riot. (610)

7. a   The development of new norms to cope with a new situation is emergent norms. (611)

8. c   Urban riots are usually caused by feelings of frustration and anger at being deprived of the same opportunities as others. (613)

9. b   A behavior that results when people become so fearful that they cannot function normally, and may even flee is a panic. (613)

10. b   Sociologists have found that when a disaster such as a fire occurs some people continue to perform their roles. (614)

11. b   Moral panics are generally fed by rumor, information for which there is no discernible source and which is usually unfounded. (615)

12. c   Sociologists refer to unfounded information spread among people as rumor. (615)

13. d   A temporary pattern of behavior that catches people's attention is a fad. (616)

14. c   Eating goldfish and bungee jumping are both examples of activity fads. Fads are novel forms of behavior that briefly catch people's attention. Other fads include object fads (pet rocks, Cabbage Patch Kids), idea fads (astrology), and personality fads (Elvis, Michael Jordan). (616)

15. b   Social movements that seek to change people totally are redemptive social movements. (620)

16. d   A social movement that seeks to change society totally is a transformative social movement. (620)

17. c   A millenarian movement is based on the prophecy of coming social upheaval. (620)

18. d   "All of the above" is correct. Levels of membership in social movements include the inner core, the committed, and a wider circle of members. (621-622)

19. d   The public that social movements face can really be divided into sympathetic public, hostile public, and disinterested people. (622)

20. b   How people think about some issue is public opinion. (623)

21. b   Although the term is often used to refer to a one-sided presentation of information that distorts reality, it is actually a neutral word. (628).

22. d   "All of the above" is correct. Advertising is a type of propaganda, an organized attempt to manipulate public opinion, and a one-sided presentation of information that distorts reality. (624)

23. d   All of the answers are correct. The mass media are the gatekeepers to social movements; they engage in biased reporting, controlled and influenced by people who have an agenda to get across; and they are sympathetic to some social movements, while ignoring others; it all depends on their individual biases. (625)

24. c   According to William Kornhauser's mass society theory, as societies become more industrialized, bureaucratized, and impersonal, members of such mass societies experience feelings of isolation. For them, social movements fill a void, because they offer them a sense of belonging. (625)

25. b   In order to turn a group of people who are upset about a social condition into a social movement, there must be resource mobilization. The resources that must be mobilized include time, money, people's skills, technologies such as direct mailings and fax machines, attention by the mass media, and even legitimacy among the public and authorities. (628)

ANSWERS FOR TRUE-FALSE QUESTIONS

1. *True.* (608)
2. *True.* (609)
3. *False.* The term "circular reaction" refers to the back-and-forth communication that goes on; it can create a "collective impulse" that comes to dominate people in the crowd. This collective impulse, similar to the collective mind described by Gustave LeBon, leads people in the crowd to act on any suggestion that is put forth. (609)
4. *True.* (610)
5. *False.* The term acting crowd is not applied just to violent activities such as lynch mobs or people engaged in riots. It includes such diverse activities as food fights! (610)
6. *True.* (611)
7. *True.* (613)
8. *True.* (615)
9. *True.* (616)
10. *False.* Urban legends are not just another kind of rumor. According to Jan Brunvand, they are passed on by people who think that the event happened to "a friend of a friend"; he sees them as modern morality stories, teaching us moral lessons about life. (617)
11. *True.* (618)
12. *False.* Not all social movements seek to change society; some seek to change people. (619-620)
13. *True.* (622)
14. *False.* Propaganda and advertising are not quite different from one another. In essence, advertising is a type of propaganda because it fits both the broad and the narrow definition of propaganda perfectly. (624)
15. *False.* Deprivation theory and relative deprivation theory are not identical perspectives. Deprivation theory is based on the idea that people who are deprived of things deemed valuable in society join social movements with the hope of redressing their grievances. Relative deprivation theory asserts that it is not people's actual negative conditions that matter but, rather, it is what people think they should have relative to what others have, or even compared with their own past or perceived future. (626)
16. *False.* For some, moral shock, a sense of outrage at finding out what is really going on, is the motivating factor in deciding to join a social movement. (626)
17. *False.* There is evidence that at times the agent provocateur has been able to push the social movement into illegal activity. (627)
18. *False.* Resources mobilization precedes the organization and institutionalization of a social movement. (628)
19. *False.* In the final stage of a social movement, decline is not always certain. Sometimes an emerging group with the same goals and new leadership will take over the "cause." (628)
20. *True.* (630)

ANSWERS FOR FILL-IN QUESTIONS

1. Gustave LeBon's term for the tendency of people in a crowd to feel, think, and act in extraordinary ways is <u>COLLECTIVE MIND</u>. (609)
2. A crowd standing or walking around as they talk excitedly about some event is <u>MILLING</u>. (610)
3. Ralph Turner and Lewis Killian's term for the development of new norms to cope with a new situation, especially among crowds is <u>EMERGENT NORMS</u>. (611)
4. A <u>RIOT</u> is violent crowd behavior aimed against people and property. (612)
5. A fear that grips large numbers of people that some evil group or behavior threatens the well

being of society, followed by intense hostility, and sometimes violence, towards those thought responsible is MORE PANIC. (615)

6.   RUMORS are unfounded information spread among people. (616)
7.   A temporary pattern of behavior that catches people's attention is a FAD. (616)
8.   An URBAN LEGEND is a story with an ironic twist that sounds realistic but is false. (617)
9.   Temperance, civil rights, white supremacy, and animal rights have all found expression in SOCIAL MOVEMENTS, made up of large numbers of people who organize to promote or resist social change. (618)
10.   A religious social movement that stresses conversion, which will produce a change in the entire person, is an example of REDEMPTIVE SOCIAL MOVEMENTS. (620)
11.   A CARGO CULT was a social movement among South Pacific Islanders, in which they destroyed their possessions in the anticipation that their ancestors would send items by ship. (620)
12.   Social movements that span the globe, emphasizing changing conditions throughout the world rather than in just one country, are referred to as NEW SOCIAL MOVEMENTS. (621)
13.   PUBLIC OPINION is how people think about some issue. (623)
14.   MASS SOCIETY is industrialized, highly bureaucratized, impersonal society. (625)
15.   DEPRIVATION THEORY states that people who are deprived of things deemed valuable in society join social movements with the hope of redressing their grievances. (625)

ANSWERS TO MATCH THESE SOCIAL SCIENTISTS WITH THEIR CONTRIBUTIONS

1. b   Charles Mackay: *herd mentality*
2. e   William Kornhauser: *mass society theory*
3. f   Robert Park: *social unrest and circular reaction*
4. a   Ralph Turner and Lewis Killian: *emergent norms*
5. h   Gustave LeBon: *collective mind*
6. d   David Aberle: *classified social movements by type and amount of social change*
7. g   Herbert Blumer: *the acting crowd*
8. c   Richard Berk: *minimax strategy*

GUIDELINES FOR ANSWERING THE ESSAY QUESTIONS

1.   *Compare and contrast the early explanations of collective behavior, as advanced by Charles Mackay, Gustave LeBon, Robert Park and Herbert Blumer, with more contemporary explanations developed by Richard Berk, Ralph Turner and Lewis Killian.*

        You must first discuss the elements that these different theories have in common and then move on to the elements that separate them. First, they are all trying to explain why people act differently when they are swept up into a crowd of people. That is probably the single point on which there is agreement. The early explanations focused on the individual and how he or she was affected by forces outside themselves. Mackay talked about the herd, LeBon the collective mind, and Park the collective impulse (pp. 608-609). While Blumer developed a more systematic explanation, also focused on events outside of the individual that impacted on his or her behavior (pp. 609-610). In contrast, the more contemporary explanations focus on the individual as a rational actor. Berk depicts humans as calculating, weighing the costs against the benefits before taking any action (p. 610). Turner and Killian also see humans as rational; in their work they argue that people develop new norms when confronted with new and unfamiliar situations. They also suggest that there are different kinds of participants, with different motives for being involved (p. 611).

2.   *Discuss the different theories about why people join social movements and consider how they could all be accurate.*

The text presents three different theories about why most people get involved in social movements--mass society theory, deprivation theory, and ideological commitment theory (pp. 625627). Each provides us with an understanding of why some people get involved, but no one theory explains why all people get involved in social movements. One theory may be more appropriate at explaining why some people get involved in some social movements but not others. By using all three, we come away with a better understanding of the process by which individuals are drawn into social movements. You might also want to tie this discussion to that of the different types of social movements (pp. 619-620) and the different types of members (pp. 621-622). For example, those people at the core of the movement may be connected for moral or ideological reasons, while those further out--the committed or less committed--may be involved because they feel isolated or alienated by modern society. Finally, a small number of people become involved in order to spy on the movement and sabotage its activities. You should mention the special case of the agent provocateur (pp. 626627).

3.   *Consider why the author combined the topics of collective behavior and social movements in one chapter.*

Different types of collective behavior--riots, panics, rumors, fads, and urban legends--that are largely unorganized and temporary seem to be incompatible with social movements, which are generally well-organized and more long-lasting. So why did the author include these two within the same chapter? One point you might want to make is that both involve large numbers of people. Both emerge out of circumstances or situations of uncertainty, change, or ambiguity. And although one is fleeting while the other hangs around for a while, neither is institutionalized and lasts across generations.

☞ ANSWERS FOR CHAPTER 22

ANSWERS FOR MULTIPLE CHOICE QUESTIONS
1. d   The shift in the characteristics of culture and society over time is social change. (634)
2. a   Max Weber identified religion as the core reason for the development of capitalism. (635)
3. a   The Least Industrialized Nations have become dependent on the Most Industrialized Nations and they are unable to develop their own resources according to dependency theory. (636)
4. c   The current resurgence of ethnic conflicts, particularly in Bosnia, threatens the global map drawn up by the G7. (637)
5. c   Unilinear evolution theories assume that all societies follow the same path, evolving from simple to complex through uniform sequences. (638)
6. b   Today, evolutionary theories have been rejected because the assumption of progress has been cast aside. (638)
7. b   Cyclical theory attempts to account for the rise of entire civilizations, rather than a particular society. (638)
8. b   According to Karl Marx, each ruling class sows the seeds of its own destruction. (639)
9. b   Ogburn called the process of change that involves new ways of seeing reality as discovery. The. other two processes he identified were invention and diffusion. (639)
10. b   The situation in which some elements of a culture adapt to an invention or discovery more rapidly than others is cultural lag. (640)
11. c   Ogburn's analysis has been criticized because it places too great an emphasis on technology as the source for almost all social change. Technology and social change actually form a two-way street: technology leads to social change and social change leads to technology. (640)
12. d   All of the choices refer to technology; it includes items that people use to accomplish a wide range of tasks; the skills and procedures that are employed in the development and utilization of tools; and tools ranging from combs or hairbrushes to computers and the Internet. (641)
13. b   According to Karl Marx, the change-over to the factory system produced alienation. (643)

14. b   The fact that as men were drawn out of their homes to work in factories, family relationships changed is an example how technology contributes to changes in social relationships. (643)

15. d   "All of the above" is correct. The automobile has changed the shape of cities; has stimulated mass suburbanization; and changes in dating and courtship rituals. (643-645)

16. c   With the latest developments in medical technology, it is now possible for a doctor at one site to check the heart condition of a patient at another site; this new arrangement is referred to as telemedicine. (647)

17. c   Computers transform the way in which we do work, they alter social relationships in the workplace, and they can even reverse the location of where work is done, but they do not necessarily make it easier to accomplish tasks in a shorter period of time. (648)

18. b   One concern about the expansion of the information superhighway is social inequalities will become greater, both on a national and global basis. (649)

19. d   Acid rain, the greenhouse effect, and global warming are all consequences of burning fossil fuels. (651-652)

20. c   Conflict theorists note that there is no energy shortage. Rather, they argue that multinational corporations are unwilling to develop alternative energy sources, because it would threaten their monopoly over existing fossil fuels and cut into their profits. (652)

21. b   Racial minorities and the poor are disproportionately exposed to environmental hazards. (652)

22. c   The major source of pollution is likely to become the Least Industrialized Nations. (638)

23. c   The disappearance of the world's rain forests presents the greatest threat to the survival of numerous plant and animal species. (653)

24. d   "All of the above" is correct. Environmental sociology examines how the physical environment affects human activities; how human activities affect the physical environment; and the unintended consequences of human actions. (655-656)

25. b   The goal of environmental sociologists is to do research on the mutual impact that individuals and environments have on one another. (656)

ANSWERS FOR TRUE-FALSE QUESTIONS

1.   *False.* The rapid social change that the world is currently experiencing is not a random event. It is the result of fundamental forms unleashed many years ago. (634)

2.   *False.* Our lives today are being vitally affected by a fourth, not a third, social revolution. This revolution has been stimulated by the invention of the microchip. (634)

3.   *True.* (636)

4.   *True.* (636)

5.   *False.* For the industrial nations, the ethnic slaughter that has erupted in Bosnia is of significant concern. If this warfare were to spread, the resulting inferno could engulf Europe and threaten the political and economic stability of the area. (638)

6.   *False.* The assumption of evolutionary theories that all societies progress from a primitive state to a highly complex state has not been proven. With Western culture in crisis, it is no longer assumed that it holds the answers to human happiness; consequently, the assumption of progress has been cast aside and evolutionary theories have been rejected. (638)

7.   *True.* (639)

8.   *True.* (639)

9.   *True.* (639) .

10.   *True.* (640)

11.   *False.* Technology is a very powerful force for social change because it alters the ways in which those tools are used. (641)

12.   *True.* (643)

13. *False.* Technology not only produces ideological changes, it can also transform social values. For example, today's emphasis on materialism depends on a certain state of technology. (643)
14. *True.* (644)
15. *False.* The use of computers in education is likely to increase, rather than decrease, the social inequality between school districts, because poor districts will not be able to afford the hardware. (648)
16. *True.* (648)
17. *True.* (649)
18. *True.* (650)
19. *False.* Scientists are not in agreement that the problems of acid rain and the greenhouse effect must be solved quickly. Some even doubt that the greenhouse effect exists. (652)
20. *True.* (655-656)

ANSWERS FOR FILL-IN QUESTIONS
1. SOCIAL CHANGE is the alteration of culture and societies over time. (634)
2. The process by which a *Gemeinschaft* society is transformed into a *Gesellschaft* society is MODERNIZATION. (636)
3. The assumption that all societies follow the same path, evolving from the simple to the complex, is central to UNILINEAR EVOLUTIONARY THEORY. (638)
4. Karl Marx used the term SYNTHESIS to refer to the new arrangement of power that emerges out of the struggle between the THESIS (existing power arrangement) and the ANTITHESIS (its opposition). (639)
5. The combination of existing elements and materials to form new ones is INVENTION. (639)
6. DISCOVERY is a new way of seeing reality. (639)
7. According to Ogburn, because of travel, trade, or conquest, DIFFUSION of an invention or discovery occurs. (640)
8. The situation in which some elements of a culture adapt to an invention or discovery more rapidly than others is CULTURAL LAG. (640)
9. The chief characteristic of POSTMODERN SOCIETY is the use of tools that extend human abilities to gather and analyze information, to communicate, and to travel. (641)
10. ALIENATION is Marx's term for workers' lack of connection to the product of their labor caused by their being assigned repetitive tasks on a small part of a product. (643)
11. We use the term INFORMATION SUPERHIGHWAY to convey the ideas of information traveling at a high rate of speed among homes and businesses. (649)
12. A world system that takes into account the limits of the environment, produces enough material goods for everyone's needs, and leaves a heritage of a sound environment for the next generation is the definition of SUSTAINABLE ENVIRONMENT. (649)
13. Rain containing sulfuric and nitric acid, produced by the reaction of sulfur dioxide and nitrogen oxide with moisture when released into the air with the burning of fossil fuels is ACID RAIN. (651)
14. The Greenhouse effect is believed to produce GLOBAL WARMING. (652)
15. The destruction of RAIN FORESTS contributes to the extinction of numerous plant and animal species. (653)

ANSWERS TO MATCH THESE SOCIAL SCIENTISTS WITH THEIR CONTRIBUTIONS
1. f   Jacques Ellul: *technology is destroying traditional values*
2. b   James Flink: *studied the impact of the auto on U. S. society*
3. d   William Ogburn: *three processes of social change*
4. g   Karl Marx: *theory of dialectical materialism*

5. a   Lewis Henry Morgan: *three stage theory of social development*
6. h   Oswald Spengler: *proposed that Western civilization is in decline*
7. e   Arnold Toynbee: *oppositional forces will tear society apart*
8. c   Max Weber: *capitalism developed out of Protestantism*

GUIDELINES FOR ANSWERING THE ESSAY QUESTIONS
1.   *Discuss Ogburn's three processes of social change, provide examples to illustrate each, and evaluate the theory.*
        This is a fairly straightforward essay question. What you need to do is to discuss each of Ogburn's processes--invention, discovery, and diffusion--and provide examples for each (pp. 639-640). Your conclusion would be an evaluation of the theory. How accurately do you think it explains the process of social change? Do you agree with the critics or do you think Ogburn is basically correct in his assumption that the material changes first and that the symbolic culture follows (p. 640)?
2.   *Choose a particular technology--you can use the automobile or the computer--and discuss the impact that it has had on U.S. society.*
        The author presents five different ways in which technology can transform society-transformation of existing technologies; changes in social organization; changes in ideology; transformation of values; and transformation of social relationships (pp. 642-643). The first part of your essay should include some discussion of these five. Then you would want to discuss how one particular technology impacts these five different aspects of social life. The book provides information on automobiles and computers (pp. 643-649), but you could choose another one--television, airplanes, the telephone but to name a few significant ones. Remember to provide examples to illustrate each aspect.
3.   *Discuss the role that global stratification plays in the worldwide environmental problems.*
        For this essay you would want to first divide the world into three camps--the Most Industrialized Nations, the Industrializing Nations, and the Least Industrialized Nations and then discuss the type of environmental problems, and the source of those problems, within each of the worlds of industrialization (pp. 650-653). You would also want to talk about how these three worlds are inter-connected when it comes to environmental problems; pollution and environmental degradation does not stop at national boundaries. It is important to bring into your discussion how the global inequalities that were first discussed in Chapter 9 play a critical role in global pollution.

Notes

Notes

Notes

Notes

Notes

Notes

Notes

Notes

Notes

Notes

Notes

Notes